THE GENDER OF MODERNISM

THE GENDER OF MODERNISM

A CRITICAL ANTHOLOGY

Edited by Bonnie Kime Scott

CONTRIBUTING EDITORS

Mary Lynn Broe, Marilyn L. Brownstein, Carolyn Burke, Ronald Bush, Thadious M. Davis, Marianne DeKoven, Susan Stanford Friedman, Diane F. Gillespie, Nancy K. Gish, Clare Hanson, Suzette Henke, Coral Ann Howells, Jane Lilienfeld, Jane Marcus, Celeste M. Schenck, Bonnie Kime Scott, Brenda R. Silver, Susan M. Squier, and Cheryl A. Wall

INDIANA UNIVERSITY PRESS BLOOMINGTON AND INDIANAPOLIS

The paper used in this publication meets the minimum requirements of American National Standard for Information Sciences—Permanence of Paper for Printed Library Materials, ANSI Z39.48-1984.

∞™

Manufactured in the United States of America

Library of Congress Cataloging-in-Publication Data

Gender of modernism : a critical anthology / edited by Bonnie Kime Scott ; contributing editors, Mary Lynn Broe . . . [et al.].

p. cm.

Includes bibliographical references.

ISBN 0-253-35122-7 (alk. paper). — ISBN 0-253-20584-0 (pbk. : alk. paper)

1. English literature—20th century—History and criticism—Theory, etc. 2. Modernism (Literature) 3. American literature—20th century—History and criticism—Theory, etc. 4. English literature—Women authors—History and criticism—Theory, etc. 5. American literature—Women authors—History and criticism—Theory, etc. 6. Feminist literary criticism. 7. Feminism and literature. 8. Sex role in literature. 9. Women and literature. I. Scott, Bonnie Kime. II. Broe, Mary Lynn.

PR478.M6G46 1990

820.9'9287—dc20 89-45856

CIP

2 3 4 5 94 93 92

To the forgotten and silenced makers of modernism

Contents

5 *T. S. Eliot*
Introduced by Nancy K. Gish 139

6 *Jessie Redmon Fauset*
Introduced by Cheryl A. Wall 155

7 *Zora Neale Hurston*
Introduced by Cheryl A. Wall 170

8 *James Joyce*
Introduced by Bonnie Kime Scott 196

9 *Nella Larsen*
Introduced by Thadious M. Davis 209

10 *D. H. Lawrence*
Introduced by Bonnie Kime Scott 217

11 *Mina Loy*

Introduced by Carolyn Burke 230

12 *Rose Macaulay*

Introduced by Susan M. Squier 252

13 *Hugh MacDiarmid*

Introduced by Nancy K. Gish 275

14 *Katherine Mansfield*

Introduced by Clare Hanson 298

15 *Charlotte Mew*

Introduced by Celeste M. Schenck 316

16 *Marianne Moore*

Introduced by Marilyn L. Brownstein 323

17 *Ezra Pound*

Introduced by Ronald Bush 353

18 *Jean Rhys*

Introduced by Coral Ann Howells 372

19 *Dorothy Richardson*

Introduced by Diane F. Gillespie 393

20 *May Sinclair*

Introduced by Diane F. Gillespie 436

Acknowledgments

This critical anthology would not have been possible without the cooperation of archives, agents, and literary estates in Britain and the United States. We would like to thank the following institutions for access to their collections and permission to quote from manuscripts: the Beinecke Rare Book and Manuscript Library of Yale University for the Letter from Ezra Pound to Marianne Moore, for Nancy Cunard's 11 January 1946 letter to Ezra Pound, and for H. D. correspondence; Henry W. and Albert A. Berg Collection, New York Public Library, Astor, Lenox and Tilden Foundations for Virginia Woolf's reading notes for "Modern Novels (Joyce)" and "Notes for Reading at Random"; the Houghton Library of Harvard University for H. D.–Amy Lowell correspondence; Special Collections, the University of Maryland, College Park Libraries, for Djuna Barnes texts; the Rosenbach Museum and Library, Philadelphia, for letters and photograph of Marianne Moore in their collection and for H. D.'s letters to Marianne Moore; the Carl Van Vechten Papers, Rare Books and Manuscripts Division, New York Public Library, Astor, Lenox and Tilden Foundations for Nella Larsen–Carl Van Vechten correspondence; the University of Tulsa for letter from Virginia Woolf to Rebecca West.

We have made an effort to contact all holders of copyrights, and apologize for any that we may have missed. This task is made difficult by the fleeting quality of many of the original publications that first brought anthologized items to the public. We are most grateful to the following individuals and publishers for permission to quote or reprint the listed items (full publication information appears at the end of each reprinted selection): the Authors League Fund, 234 West 44th Street, New York, New York, as literary executors of the Estate of Djuna Barnes, for "Mother," "To the Dogs," and "The Confessions of Helen

Westley," by Djuna Barnes; Mrs. Joella Bayer for "Aphorisms on Futurism," "Joyce's Ulysses," "Brancusi's Golden Bird," "Gertrude Stein" and "The Ineffectual Marriage" by Mina Loy; Mr. Fred Beauford for "As to Books" and "Our Book Shelf" in the *Crisis* by Jessie Fauset; Quentin Bell and Angelica Garnett, administrators of Virginia Woolf's estate, and Andrew McNeillie for selections by Virginia Woolf; Jonathan Cape Limited on behalf of the Executors of the James Joyce Estate for the extract from *Stephen Hero;* Carcanet Press Limited for "Absence" and "The Cenotaph" by Charlotte Mew; City Lights Books for *Notes on Thought and Vision* by H. D.; Chatto & Windus/the Hogarth Press and Executors of the Sylvia Townsend Warner Estate for "Cottage Mantleshelf," "Bluebeard's Daughter," and "Women as Writers" by Sylvia Townsend Warner; Andre Deutsch Ltd. for "Ghost Writing," from *Good Morning, Midnight* by Jean Rhys; Conde Nast Publications for "Talent and Genius," "Women and the Future," and "Women in the Arts" by Dorothy Richardson; Faber and Faber Ltd. and Mrs. Valerie Eliot for the Introduction by T. S. Eliot to *Nightwood* by Djuna Barnes and the Review of Marianne Moore's *Poems* and *Marriage;* Faber and Faber Ltd. for selections from *The Complete Prose of Marianne Moore;* Mr. Hugh Ford for the 11 June 1946 letter to Ezra Pound, "Black Man and White Ladyship," "Harlem Reviewed," and "The American Moron and the American of Sense—Letters on the Negro" by Nancy Cunard; Harcourt Brace Jovanovich, Inc., for "Modern Fiction" and excerpts from "Mr. Bennett and Mrs. Brown" and *The Diary of Virginia Woolf* by Virginia Woolf; Harper & Row, Publishers, Inc. for the excerpt from *Dust Tracks on a Road* by Zora Neale Hurston. Copyright 1942 by Zora Neale Hurston; The Hogarth Press for "Modern Fiction," and excerpts from "Mr. Bennett and Mrs. Brown" and *The Diary of Virginia Woolf* by Virginia Woolf; Alfred A. Knopf, Inc., for excerpts from *The Journal of Katherine Mansfield* © 1954 and for "The Novel Démeublé" and "Nancy's Return" from *Sapphira and the Slave Girl* by Willa Cather; Kraus Reprint and Periodicals for "Vienne" by Jean Rhys; *London Magazine* for the excerpt from "Jean Rhys and *Voyage in the Dark,*" ed. with an introduction by Nancy Hemond Brown; Mr. Calman A. Levin, as agent for the Estate of Gertrude Stein, for selections by Gertrude Stein; Marianne Moore, Literary Executory for the Estate of Marianne Craig Moore, for excerpts from the Correspondence of Marianne Moore at the Rosenbach Museum and Library, all rights reserved; Macmillan Press Ltd. for permission to quote from Clare Hanson (ed.), *The Critical Writings of Katherine Mansfield* © 1987; Macmillan Publishing Company for T. S. Eliot's Introduction to *Selected Poems* of Marianne Moore; Methuen, Inc., London, for excerpts from *Non-Combatants and Others* by Rose Macaulay; all material by H. D. (Hilda Doolittle) used by permission of New Directions Publishing Corp., agents for Perdita Schaffner and the estate of H. D.; previously unpublished material copyright © 1989 by Perdita Schaffner; New Directions Publishing Corp. and Faber and Faber Ltd. for excerpts from *The Selected Letters of Ezra Pound* (copyright 1950 by Ezra Pound); other material by Ezra Pound used by permission of New Directions Publishing Corp. and Faber and Faber Ltd., agents for the Trustees of the Ezra Pound Literary Property Trust; Omni Publications for review by Zora Neal Hurston, "Stories of Conflict," published in April

3, 1938, issue of *Saturday Review;* Mark Paterson and Associates, Agents for the Estate of Dorothy Richardson, for selections by Dorothy Richardson; A. D. Peters & Co. Ltd. for selections from *Personal Pleasures* by Rose Macaulay; selections by Rebecca West reprinted by permission of Peters Fraser & Dunlop Group Ltd.; Laurence Pollinger Ltd. and the Estate of Mrs. Frieda Lawrence Ravagli for "Matriarchy" and "Cocksure Women and Hensure Men" from *Phoenix II* by D. H. Lawrence; Perdita Schaffner, executory of the H. D. literary estate, for selections by H. D.; the Society of Authors as the literary representative of the Estate of James Joyce for the extract from *Stephen Hero* and the 29 August 1904 Letter to Nora Barnacle by James Joyce; the Society of Authors as the literary representative of the Estate of Katherine Mansfield for extracts from Letters to John Middleton Murry and *Novels and Novelists* by Katherine Mansfield; *Twentieth Century Literature* for "Anon" and "The Reader" by Virginia Woolf; Frederick Ungar Publishing Co. for "Characteristics of Negro Expression" and "Spirituals and Neo-Spirituals" by Zora Neale Hurston; Viking Penguin, Inc., for selections from *Phoenix II* by D. H. Lawrence, copyright 1928 by Forum Publishing Co., copyright renewed © 1956 by Frieda Lawrence Ravagli, copyright renewed © 1968 by the Estate of Frieda Lawrence Ravagli, all rights reserved; Viking Penguin, Inc., for selections from *The Complete Prose of Marianne Moore,* by Marianne Moore, copyright © 1959, 1960, 1961, 1962, 1963, 1964, 1965, 1986 by Clive E. Driver, Literary Executor of the Estate of Marianne Moore, by permission of Marianne Moore, Literary Executor for the Estate of Marianne Craig Moore, all rights reserved, and for "Well Moused, Lion" from *The Complete Prose* by Marianne Moore, copyright © 1941, renewed © 1969 by Marianne Moore, all rights reserved, by permission of Marianne Moore, Literary Executor for the Estate of Marianne Craig Moore, all rights reserved; Virago Press for excerpts from *Told by an Idiot* by Rose Macaulay, for "The House of Clouds" from *Strangers* by Antonia White, and for "The Angry Woman," "Divorce," and "Song of the Low-Caste Wife" and other brief quotations from *The Writings of Anna Wickham* by Anna Wickham; and *Yale Review* for the excerpt from "Byron and Mr. Briggs" by Virginia Woolf.

I am especially grateful to former University of Delaware Provost L. Leon Campbell for a subvention that helped cover costs of permissions. For their advice on drafts of the Introduction, I am grateful to Michael Cotsell, Barbara Gates and Judith Roof, all of the University of Delaware English Department, and to Shari Benstock and many of the contributing editors to the volume. Jerry Beasley, Acting Chairperson, and Carl Dawson, Chairperson, of the Delaware English Department, have been supportive and generous with English Department resources throughout the project.

THE GENDER OF MODERNISM

Introduction

Bonnie Kime Scott

> Was it wisdom? Was it knowledge? Was it, once more, the deceptiveness of beauty, so that all one's perceptions, half way to truth, were tangled in a golden mesh? or did she lock up within her some secret which certainly Lily Briscoe believed people must have for the world to go on at all?. . . . She imagined how in the chambers of the mind and heart of the woman who was, physically, touching her, were stood, like the treasures in the tombs of kings, tablets bearing sacred inscriptions, which if one could spell them out, would teach one everything, but they would never be offered openly, never made public. What art was there, known to love or cunning, by which one pressed through into those secret chambers?
>
> —VIRGINIA WOOLF, *To the Lighthouse* 78–79

1. TOWARD A GENDERED READING OF MODERNISM

While Virginia Woolf certainly did not intend to provide a parable for a modernist anthology in this evocation of a woman artist's desire, she might be describing the experience of archival explorers of the late twentieth century as they relocate lost and neglected textual treasures and draw connections between them. Modernism as we were taught it at midcentury was perhaps halfway to truth. It was unconsciously gendered masculine. The inscriptions of mothers and women, and more broadly of sexuality and gender, were not adequately decoded, if detected at all. Though some of the aesthetic and political pronouncements of women writers had been offered in public, they had not circulated widely and were rarely collected for academic recirculation. Deliberate or not, this is an example of the politics of gender. Typically, both the authors of original manifestos and the literary historians of modernism took as their norm a small set of its male participants, who were quoted, anthologized, taught, and consecrated as geniuses. Much of what even these select men had to say about the crisis in gender identification that underlies much of modernist literature was left out or read from a limited perspective. Women writers were often deemed old-fashioned or of merely anecdotal interest. Similar limiting norms developed in the contemporaneous Harlem Renaissance, which enters the scope of modernism as presented in this anthology.

What is the "art . . . , known to love and cunning," with which we press into forgotten modernist territory? Since the late 1920s, when Woolf sent Lily Briscoe searching through the pages of *To the Lighthouse* and supplied us with her own study of gender and women writers, *A Room of One's Own*, we have been offered new theories to use in the art of feminist criticism. These theories come from many disciplines, including psychoanalysis, psychology, linguistics, anthropology, sociology, and history, and have been reconceptualized and combined across the disciplines through feminist perspectives.[1] Since the early 1970s, scholars in women's studies have been investigating the marginalized archive of women writers and have made the case for women's having a literary tradition (or traditions) of their own. The supply of women's texts has brought into question the adequacy of the previous canon, disrupting it and questioning canon formation itself. In the 1980s, without abandoning the project of recovering women writers, women's studies gained theoretical range and depth by turning to the concept of gender.

Gender is a category constructed through cultural and social systems. Unlike sex, it is not a biological fact determined at conception. Sociology has long discussed sex roles, the term *roles* calling attention to the assigned rather than determined nature of gender. The latter term is gradually and appropriately replacing *sex* in the designation (see Anderson, listed in the Selected Bibliography). Gender is more fluid, flexible, and multiple in its options than the (so far) unchanging biological binary of male and female. In history, across cultures, and in the lifetime development of the individual, there are variations in what it means to be masculine, or feminine, in the availability of identifications such as asexual and androgynous, and in the social implications of lesbian, homosexual, and heterosexual orientations. French feminist theories make constant reference to gender as they study the position of the psychoanalytic subject in relation to family romance and related theories of language and difference. In moving on from the Freudian emphasis on masculine, Oedipal norms and events in the family, there has been increased attention to a maternal, pre-Oedipal stage of identification. In language the semiotic category related to the maternal body and babble now commands attention as the pre-text for symbolic language associated with the phallus and the law of the father (see Kristeva, Cixous).

Gender coexists and interacts with other categories. Its interaction with sexual orientation has already been suggested. Additional implicated categories are class, race, nation, economic stature, and family type. Hence we cannot properly deal with gender in isolation but should see it as one of many layers of identification. By using gender as a theoretical category, we are also encouraged to think about the structure of categorical systems, the number of variable positions they entertain, and the permeability of boundaries within and between them.

Gender is not a mask for feminist or woman, though they are inextricable from it. Both men and women participate in the social and cultural systems of gender, but women write about it more, perhaps because gender is more imposed upon them, more disqualifying, or more intriguing and stimulating to their creativity. The present predominance of women theorists and women's writing in gender studies does not undermine the gender concept; it is better seen as historical, built upon patterns of gender asymmetry. The gender of modernism in this anthology may seem to be feminine, but the real intent of the text is to demonstrate that modernism was inflected, in ways we can only now begin to appreciate, by gender.

Our critical generation did not invent gender as a literary concept. Essays included in this anthology demonstrate that modernists themselves attached labels such as "virile" and "feminine" to the new writing as they reviewed it, attributing different meanings and values to the terms. The practice is as old as literary criticism in English, which dates back to the eighteenth century. The Victorians certainly worked with paradigms of gender, and there are excellent studies of gender in Victorian myth (Nina Auerbach, *The Woman and the Demon*) and of its effects on the identity of the woman writer (Sandra Gilbert and Susan Gubar, *The Madwoman in the Attic*). Women writers of the nineteenth century have been granted eminence in one genre (the novel), which their twentieth-century sisters have not. To date, critical considerations of gender in the moderns have emphasized malady and violence. Elaine Showalter (*A Literature of Their Own*) has seen Virginia Woolf as a writer in psychological retreat, and sex war is a dominant scenario in Gilbert and Gubar's *No Man's Land*.[2] This anthology is assembled in the belief that, in relation to gender, modernism has a great deal of unassessed vitality in form and content, with its own intricate and varied theory.

When we turn in our research from a few masters and movers of modernism to its forgotten, gender-inflected territories, we may suspect, like Lily Briscoe, that we are tangled in a "golden mesh." The connecting strands of association between modernists are more numerous than we suspected; they vibrate with sexual energies and anxieties. We read neglected genres, encounter uncertain quests for gender identity, and find confusing content that was not previously analyzed—and perhaps not even detected, since it was encoded at its conception to pass the censors of self and society. Gender, layered with other revised conceptual categories such as race and class, challenges our former sense of the power structures of literary production. We suspect that modernism is not the aesthetic, directed, monological sort of phenomenon sought in their own ways by authors of now-famous manifestos—F. T. Marinetti (futurism), Ezra Pound (imagism and vorticism), T. E. Hulme (classicism), Wyndham Lewis (vorticism), T. S. Eliot ("Tradition and the Individual Talent"), and Eugene Jolas (the "revolution of the word")—and perpetuated in new critical–formalist criticism through the 1960s.[3] Modernism as caught in the mesh of gender is polyphonic, mobile, interactive, sexually charged; it has wide appeal, constituting a historic shift in parameters.

2. TOWARD A NEW SCOPE FOR MODERNISM

While the word *modernism* appears in the title of this book, the editors involved in this project have worked restively with it, and introductions to specific authors repeatedly manipulate the term.[4] The "experimental, audience challenging, and language-focused" writing that used to be regarded as modernism becomes for some of our editors a gendered subcategory—"early male modernism" (Lilienfeld, section **2**), for example, or "masculinist modernism" (Schenck, **15**). None of the editors is particularly interested in fitting neglected figures into what is now seen as a limited definition, though there are discussions of the ways in which Djuna Barnes, Mina Loy, and Marianne Moore were admitted to the "male" category to the neglect of important feminine or feminist elements in their work (Broe, **1**; Burke, **11**; Brownstein, **16**).

Virginia Woolf suggested another subcategory of modernism in the 1930s' "outsider's society" of *Three Guineas* (see Silver, **26**), a group that relates to the female writers who predominate in this anthology but also speaks to the marginalities of class, economics, and exile. The existence of her term and the presence of *society* in it suggest rudimentary group identification and organization that combine or cross categories of identification.

Black writers, though seldom discussed by the "makers" of modernism, were involved in the movement. As we overlap the concept of the "New Negro" with traditional descriptions of modernism, it is possible to see that women writers could be excluded by definition from both groups. For example, Jessie Redmon Fauset might be rejected from modernism because her style is perceived as old-fashioned and from the "New Negro" group defined by Alain Locke because she had northern, urban origins (see Wall, **6**). Black writers experience their own systems of geographic difference, linguistic definition, and affiliation to literary predecessors and movements, and these systems have striking parallels to traditional modernism. White writers also contribute to the modernist treatment of race. H. D. writes about the social dynamics of crossing the borderlines of race, particularly in sexual encounters, in describing *Borderline,* a film she made with Paul Robeson. Nancy Cunard writes about her mother's racial prejudice against her intimate friend, black jazz pianist Henry Crowder (see "Black Man and White Ladyship"). Fascination with blacks alternates with self-confessed racism in a letter from Ezra Pound to Marianne Moore.

Another set of writers have doubly marginal status as colonials. Katherine Mansfield, Jean Rhys, and Anna Wickham may have been quite interested in new literary endeavors, but they had their own special problems connecting with the literary establishment and deciding when (and if) native content should enter their texts. The issue takes on increased importance when we consider modernist interest in anthropology and the "primitive."

The consideration of a nonexperimental group of writers, alongside the more traditional experimental canon, challenges language-centered interpretations of modernism favored in the canonization process from Ezra Pound to Julia Kristeva (see Schenck, **15**). Their presence helps us detect other breaks with tradition, such as the treatment of lesbian sexuality and women's critiques of fascism and war.

The volume's limitation to English-language texts, British and American writers, and the period roughly from 1910 to 1940 is a practical matter. We are aware that this narrowing excludes contemporary Europeans, later Latin American writers, and authors writing in French, such as Natalie Barney and Renée Vivien. Translations of French, Latin, Greek, and Oriental texts—expert ones by Sylvia Beach and Maria Jolas, for example, as well as the Chinese and Japanese translations by Ezra Pound—lie beyond our present range and analysis. The categories of nationality and literary period invoked here are arguably the products of patriarchy. Several anthologized authors were already struggling with national identity and modern period; they reported their perceptions of difference in Italy, Spain, Vienna, Berlin, or Harlem, saw the world sink twice into major wars among nations, and found themselves as Americans and colonials alienated and in exile from home or tradition.

Periodization has been challenged as an organizational concept by feminist theory. If we can question whether the Renaissance was a renaissance for women or suggest (as Woolf did) that the advent of the middle-class woman writer was a revolution (*A Room of One's Own* 68), we can also rethink the supposed liberations of modernism or the relation of the Great War to literature. Did the formal innovations advanced by modernism and the phallic metaphors used to express them suit women writers as well as they did men? Did the supposed sexual freedom and newly won political franchise allow women power and creative dimension in the literary field? Or did they create burdensome, reactionary resistances or limited assignments in the publishing world? How did the Great War, which has generally been seen as a deep influence on modernist views of the world, have different effects on men and women writers? Men who went to the front, some experiencing injury and death, such as Rupert Brooke, Siegfried Sassoon, Ernest Hemingway, and Ford Madox Ford, became the canonized authors on the war. As noncombatants, women went into munitions factories and battlefield hospital units, both as workers and as reporters; they brooded on the home front, both experiencing and writing dream fantasies of traversing blood-sodden battlefields and losing their own limbs. But the journalism, stories, and poems on war and pacifism by such writers as Antonia White, Rose Macaulay, and Rebecca West have been neglected. D. H. Lawrence's reactions to women's postwar behavior (in "Cocksure Women and Hensure Men") give another gender-inflected view of the home front in this period.

The 1920s are represented in many of the texts included here as a time of excitement and new freedoms, particularly for women. There were communities of writers who met in Sylvia Beach's bookshop or Gertrude Stein's rooms in Paris, in the vicinity of Washington Square in Greenwich Village or Seventh Avenue in Harlem; there were predominantly women's communities such as Natalie Barney's salon on Rue Jacob and Peggy Guggenheim's Hayford Hall in England, places where lesbian and gay sexuality was tolerated, sometimes celebrated, and often textualized (see Benstock, *Women of the Left Bank*). The international set of cities associated with modernism offered mobility in class, variety in living arrangements (often at cheap prices for expatriates), and access to publication. Nella Larsen's upbeat, urban, "modern woman" image (see Davis, **9**) might be applied to many of the women writers and their female characters in this collection—Djuna Barnes, Nancy Cunard, Jessie Redmon Fauset, Zora Neale Hurston, Mina Loy, Katherine Mansfield, Rebecca West. But accounts of Mansfield in Eliot's letters or Woolf's diaries suggest that what went as bold feminine modernity could be met with contempt. The glamour of Cunard, Barnes, and West (which they helped create) attracted more attention in the press than their literary work did. Long periods of literary silence, laborious rewriting, and isolation are more representative of the lives of Barnes and Jean Rhys than the bright life of the 1920s.

The year 1940 has served as a typical terminal date for studies of modernism (some end with 1930). By that time, the major experimental works, such as *The Waste Land, Tender Buttons, The Waves,* and *Finnegans Wake,* had appeared and death had claimed Lawrence, Mansfield, and Yeats; Woolf and Joyce were dead by early 1941. The world changed again sharply with World War II. Letters continued to circulate, assessing the times the writers had shared, our most poignant example being Cunard's 1946 letter to Ezra Pound. Rhys, Barnes, and Warner resurfaced with late, much-revised work, as attested in this anthology. West never stopped publishing, though she lost her visibility with American audiences and turned away from her early radicalism. She allows us to imagine what the changes in culture might have done to other modernists had they lived into the 1980s. She has long-distance perspective on the importance given to modernist organizers such as Pound ("Spinster to the Rescue"). Interrupted careers, like interrupted influence, tell us a great deal about the politics of literary production, a politics we enter in our recovery work.

3. ISSUES OF THE CANON

This volume deliberately features women writers, without strictly limiting itself to them—a decision in line with the current profile of gender studies. In their critique of culture, modernist women persistently bring up issues of gender, whereas men assert that the masculine is what should be advanced, whoever writes it (see Burke, **11**), and are not particularly interested in seeing this attitude as gender-conditioned. The separatist treatment of women that flourished in the 1970s remains defensible. It is useful when one is hypothesizing a women's tradition (see Showalter, *A Literature of Their Own*) or attempting to release women's creativity from male influences (see Cixous, "The Laugh of Medusa"). It responds to the opposite tendency in traditional anthologies and studies of modernism. It was the "men of 1914" (T. S. Eliot, James Joyce, Ezra Pound, and Wyndham Lewis) whom Lewis proclaimed in the revolutionary manifestos of *Blast* and its successors, and Pound for whom Hugh Kenner named the modernist era (*The Pound Era*). In 1965, to provide backgrounds for their students' study of the moderns, Richard Ellmann and Charles Feidelson assembled *The Modern Tradition*. Of its 948 pages, fewer than nine were allotted to women writers (George Eliot and Virginia Woolf). In a contemporary review of the volume, Frank Kermode was surprised to find "amazingly little sex (which might have had a section of its own)" (68). While Kermode does not elaborate on what he means by "sex," if social relations between the sexes are included, his comment relates to our concern to write gender into modernism. While modernist studies are rolling off the presses at an unprecedented rate, a surprising number still find interest only in canonized males.[5]

By including five male figures intricately involved in writing with women or on gender, we resist both determinism by sex and reversed neglect. There are brief selections from Eliot, Joyce, and Lawrence in the anthology, and they document personal and cultural constructions of femininity and masculinity. Pound has an extensive section, as is appropriate to the complexity of his involvement in forms and politics of gender, including his male genital models of creativity and his initial sponsoring of numerous women's writing careers (see Bush, **17**). Hugh MacDiarmid has had his own problems with marginal omission from the canon and with the English language as a medium for Scottish experience—a pattern offering parallels with female marginality (Gish, **13**). By featuring twenty-one women writers we are saying that the presence of women in modernism has been vastly underestimated. And the process of writing women into modernism must go on from here.

A compensation for the fact that we had to limit the number of authors given sections in the anthology is that those included are often connected to someone omitted by an anthologized letter or review or by a comparison offered in an introduction. Richard Wright appears in Hurston's reference to his abusive review of her own *Their Eyes Are Watching God* and in her review of his *Uncle Tom's Children.* As a literary editor of the *Crisis,* Jessie Fauset draws our attention to Langston Hughes, Arna Bontemps, and Jean Toomer, whose careers she fostered, and to Georgia Douglas Johnson and Anne Spencer, who were ranked among the best in an anthology she was reviewing. Amy Lowell comes to us through her correspondence with Marianne Moore and Lawrence. We meet Bryher and Elizabeth Bishop through Moore. Editors of influential reviews, who were frequently writers as well, are cited (often for several authors) in introductory essays and letters: Ford Madox Ford (*English Review, transatlantic review*), Dora Marsden and Harriet Shaw Weaver (*Freewoman, Egoist*), John Middleton Murry (*Athenaeum, Adelphi*), Harriet Monroe (*Poetry*), and Margaret Anderson (*Little Review*). As in most anthologies, some of our gaps are due to prohibitive permissions costs and other restrictions. Poetry and uncollected manuscripts destined for "complete works" projects presented special problems. Ironically, the welcome reprinting of the works of modernist women writers in recent years has added to the cost of anthologies in the field. *The Gender of Modernism* does not pretend to have reached and opened all of modernism's "secret chambers," but it tests important terms and provides basic textual resources for ongoing explorations and reconceptions of this revolutionary set of writings.[6]

4. FEMINIST COLLABORATION

Each section of this volume is edited and introduced by a scholar familiar with the author presented therein, accustomed to doing archival study, and interested in pursuing feminist criticism. The contributing editors have chosen the primary texts to be included. They were encouraged to select and discuss works that offer women writers' theories of writing or illuminate neglected dynamics and concepts of gender in literary forms and production. Contributing editors did some reshaping of the original guidelines, noting that some authors are much more willing than others to embrace feminism or to engage in theoretical construction and debate.

Selected authors are not limited to feminist activists and theoreticians. There is a preponderance of what could be considered marginal genres—essays, book reviews, interviews, letters, diaries, sketches, even notebooks. Autobiographical entries by White and Rhys contribute to a feminist reinterpretation of that genre, and we recover forgotten plays by Barnes. The volume thus offers a shift in emphasis from the privileged genres of the novel and—particularly in modernist definition—poetry. It makes our offerings very different from those included in the modernist section of Sandra Gilbert and Susan Gubar's very useful *Norton Anthology of Literature by Women.*

Contributing editors argued that some authors were not in a position to write reviews or that their most relevant and revolutionary statements on gender and writing were accessible through their fiction and poetry, hence the appearance of gender-laden excerpts from novels and selected poetry. In the case of Rhys, we offer a fatal version of an abortion story (*Voyage in the Dark,* the original of part 4; see Howells, **18**) that was suppressed by Rhys's male publisher. The suppression of elements of the confession of Dr. O'Connor, the bisexual, transvestite hero of Barnes's *Nightwood,* by T. S. Eliot, who sponsored it in his publishing house, comes under discussion (Gish, **5**). The volume also compensates for the failure of H. D.'s prose (*Notes on Thought and Vision*) to see print until the early 1980s, despite the welcome her more programmatic imagist poetry received (see Friedman, **4**).

Our nineteen scholars offer feminist theoretical diversity and attend to varied presences of gender in a broad spectrum of modernist writers. Feminist theoretical approaches are entertained in each introduction, often tailored to the writer in question (e.g., Hanson's discussion of "greatness" in Mansfield, **14;** Squier's attention to women writers and pacifism in her introduction to Macaulay, **12;** Gish's discussion of gender and vernacular in relation to MacDiarmid, **13;** Marcus's contrast of the Catholic experience of confession in White and Joyce, **24**). With quite a few authors, it is possible to trace historical attitudes toward gender both in their writing and in the criticism of it (see, for example, DeKoven on Stein, **21,** and my introductions to Joyce, **8,** and Lawrence, **10**). The nature of the project—its organization by author and its attention to archives—encourages empirical, experiential, biographical, historical methodologies often identified with Anglo-American critics.[7] Yet once contributing editors get to their introductions of primary texts, the semiotics and psychoanalytic paradigms often associated with French feminist approaches come into use (see, for example, Hanson on Mansfield, **14,** and Brownstein on Moore, **16**).

5. CONNECTIONS

The value of literary connections, for anything from creative stimulation to contact with publishers, seems indisputable. Having assembled texts on and by twenty-six authors related to problems of gender and modernism, it seems worthwhile to explore the connections that emerge among them. In the accompanying figure, the names of authors treated in sections of this anthology were arranged in alphabetical order counterclockwise in a circle (a shape and sequence chosen to discourage hierarchical thinking). Each time an important connection was made in an introduction or a primary work in the anthology, a line was drawn between the writers. The resulting figure calls to mind Woolf's "golden mesh," a web, or a ball of yarn. It offers a table of contents at a glance and reminds us of the pluralistic interest and cooperative format of this volume. Authors and editors who were not assigned their own section of

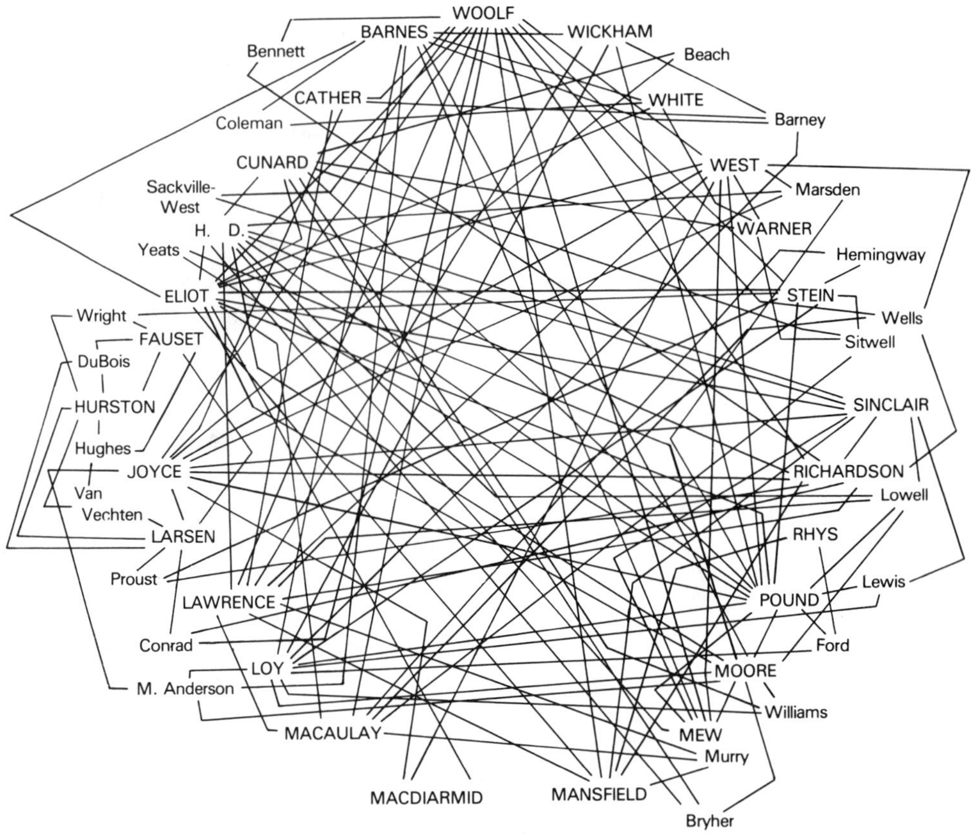

A Tangled Mesh of Modernists

the volume but whose names occur in several introductions or primary texts have their names printed in lower case. Appearing like a surrounding aura, placed for minimal confusion close to their connected authors, they merit an anthology of their own.

This mesh or web can be followed or read in numerous ways. One could count how many strands emerge from a given author as a gauge of "importance," though this can lead to conservative results. Predictably, such a count favors Pound, the supremely active formulator and talent hunter of modernism; Joyce, whose *Ulysses* was considered by many the central text of modernism; Eliot, institutionalizer of modernism; and Woolf, who probably satisfies more traditional definitions of modernism than any other woman writer in the mesh. These patterns indicate in part that this study takes off from inherited formulations, where both authors and scholars have lived in patriarchy.[8] But there are surprises, such as the extraordinary number of connections to Marianne Moore. There are other revelations. One pattern readily apparent is that women writers took a great deal of interest in one another: a strand quite regularly indicates an appreciative review (West–Woolf, H. D.–Moore, Larsen–Fauset) or an attempt to define contemporary writing through a female writer (Richardson, Sinclair). Not all strands lead to Eliot, Pound, and Joyce. May Sinclair provides introductions to Richardson and H. D. that stand up well to anything written to the present day. A strand from Moore to another woman writer may indicate a different manner of review than she would have written for a man (see Brownstein, **16**). The H. D. and Marianne Moore sections let us sample the network of significant correspondence among modernist women writers. Other important female relationships go beyond the sensitivity of the figure. These include Moore's very close identification with her mother and her choice of celibacy, Cunard's repudiation of her mother's racism and class, and Barnes's rapport with a woman (Helen Westley) in the context of an interview.

Connection between a female and a male figure may mean several things. Mansfield seems to have perceived a need for male protection from sexual exploitation, in addition to the access men provided to publication (Hanson, **14**). Evidence of sexual exploitation comes in the public image constructed for Barnes, Mansfield, Loy, and West, who are noted for beauty or sensuousness in contemporary reviews and letters. Cunard lashes out at the press for its sexist, racist sensationalizing of her relationship with Henry Crowder ("Black Man and White Ladyship"). The tendency to sensationalize the biography of women writers rather than to explore their works with care is pointed out in the introduction to Stein (De Koven, **21**); it is a problem shared by West and Mansfield.

There is a more positive side to women's connections to men. Female modernists did write defenses of men and their literary movements (Sinclair and Moore on Eliot and Pound; Richardson and Loy on Joyce). In the case of Nella Larsen, there is a list of modern male writers, admired in her reading, which she uses to defend the style of her important male mentor, Walter White. These writings remind us of the attacks modernist men sustained from conservative reviewers and the alliance experimental women writers could feel with them.

There are also critiques and appreciations of a slightly older generation of male writers (H. D.–Yeats, Richardson–Wells, Woolf–Bennett, Galsworthy, Wells). Parodies of prominent modernist men such as Eliot and Hemingway are offered by Macaulay, Stein, and Woolf. Points of departure are declared in Loy's own brand of futurism, where she emphasizes amplitude of consciousness that Marinetti did not consider (Burke, **11**), and in Cunard's diatribe against what Pound had become with his connection to Italian fascism. The Fascist leanings of major male modernists come in for scrutiny (Friedman, **4**). It is important to review the careers of Pound and Lawrence by periods, for both their relations to women writers and their actual gendered imagery alter over time (Bush, **17**; Scott, **8**). Finally, women as editors and subeditors published male writers (Cunard—Pound and men of the Harlem Renaissance;

Margaret Anderson, Sylvia Beach, and Dora Marsden—Joyce; Lowell—Lawrence; Moore—William Carlos Williams). The individualist, vitalist theory of Marsden was attuned to the contemporary projects of Pound and Joyce (Bush, **17**).

Some writers have relatively few connections, suggesting a position of layered marginality discussed in numerous introductions to authors, including Rhys and Cather. The existence of a few links between black and white writers (Cunard—Hurston, H. D.—Paul Robeson, Larsen—Van Vechten, Fauset in Paris) is certainly a pattern worth pursuing, both in the anthology and beyond (see Friedman on Cunard, **3**). Isolation and selection by sexual orientation and social class can also be read in the mesh. The tangled intricacy of the connections visible in the small sample of interactions available in this anthology suggests that our understanding of modernism depends on an inadequate number of sources and is accordingly sketchy and oversimplified.

6. MODERNIST FORM

A major goal of this anthology is that neglected viewpoints of modernists on their own aesthetic projects should now be known and taken up. The terms *modernist* and *modernism* are used in the complex analyses of H. D. and Mina Loy. H. D. offers us a critical history of imagism, including Pound's maneuverings in and out of the practice. The anthology contains theoretical texts by Gertrude Stein which, though they demand attention, are quite readable. One of them was first addressed to an American student audience. Stein finds in Moore an image that is both frail and absolutely hard, this alloy outlasting the girders and skyscrapers one might associate with the formulas of Pound, Lewis, and the futurists. There are two classic essays ("Modern Fiction" and "Mr. Bennett and Mrs. Brown") in which Virginia Woolf declares the modern departure from Edwardian "materialists" and liberation from an enslavement of the author to conventions. May Sinclair writes excellent introductions to the techniques of psychological novelists. She provides the term *stream of consciousness* for analysis of Dorothy Richardson's narrative. Woolf offers a countertheory of tradition, toppling the priesthood of critics suggested in the criticism of T. S. Eliot (Silver, **26**), and Rebecca West questions the authority of Eliot's criticism as too dependent on sober manner and repeated formulas.

Genre and the relation of writing to other arts are among the most interesting topics that can be pursued with the evidence of this anthology. Marginality by genre afflicted Rose Macaulay and Katherine Mansfield as writers of the short story and essay (see Squier, **12,** and Hanson, **14**). Rebecca West wrote in forms that combined so many genres (travel literature, history, psychobiography, crime reportage) that they fell between the critical cracks (see Scott, **23**), though she appreciated the poetry of the modernist prose of Woolf ("High Fountain of Genius"). H. D. was discouraged in her attempts to find her own form of essay prose-poem ("Notes on Thought and Vision") by Pound and sexologist Havelock Ellis (Friedman, **4**); these same essays seem very advanced today. Hurston and Cunard had as much interest in folklore as in literature. Richardson and H. D. were remarkable reviewers of film, as shown in work that originally appeared in the journal *Close Up*. The film frame became a means of talking about literary technique for Stein and Woolf, and Richardson assigned the silent film to a feminine order of "being," as opposed to the spoken domain of "The Film Gone Male." Numerous authors worked beyond the boundaries of writing. Loy, Lawrence, and Barnes were artist-writers. Fauset and Cunard promoted illustrators' work in the volumes they edited. Stein, Woolf, and Cunard had significant art collections and contacts with artists (Stein—Pablo Picasso; Woolf—Roger Fry, the Bells and post-impressionism; Cunard—African art). Music and dance were important to Joyce, Hurston, Pound, Richardson, and Cunard. Since modernism found expression in many arts, it is useful to follow literary authors into them. This is possible in the anthologized selection of Barnes's drawings, all rich in their interpretation of gender.

One striking aspect of H. D., Mansfield, Loy, Moore, Stein, and Woolf is their feminist critical thinking on language, the unconscious, and realistic representation. They anticipate French feminist psychoanalytic and linguistic approaches and offer texts that write the erotics of the female body. H. D. and Pound assign gendered metaphors to the creative process. The feminine to Pound is chaos; to H. D., the womb, dung, and jellyfish are feminine sources of creativity. While gender lay deeply encoded in H. D.'s early imagist work, she moved on to female voiced and perceived rewritings of classical myths and self-reflexive psychological studies that turned writing into self-healing (Friedman, **4**). Nella Larsen uses restless travel, racial "passing," and psychological doubles to explore the bewildering array of shifting possibilities for modern women (see Davis, **9**). As for constructs of the mind, Mina Loy focuses on the capacity of consciousness and calls the unconscious "a rubbish heap of race tradition." H. D. offers a construct of body, mind, and overmind (a state of "super-feeling" comparable to the reach of jellyfish tentacles). Loy discusses Joyce's *Ulysses* in terms of phallus and "sanguine introspection of the womb," anticipating Lacanian terminology. D. H. Lawrence deals in the assignment of separate spheres and considers, with vastly different conclusions than those of West and Richardson, the impact of women on the world of work (and vice versa). The question of whether there is a feminine style of writing interests authors as diverse as MacDiarmid, Richardson, Mansfield, and Eliot—a discussion where punctuation is frequently at issue; Richardson allows Joyce's Molly Bloom to testify.

Character is an important theoretical topic that divided Virginia Woolf and the Edwardians ("Mr. Bennett and Mrs. Brown"). One recurrent consideration with special reference to gender is the author's attitude toward "woman consciousness," to use Richardson's term. A view of the greatness of feminine modes and experiences is expressed by Mansfield and shared in Woolf's definition of life ("Modern Fiction" and "Mr. Bennett and Mrs. Brown"). Richardson resists the man-trained woman, as in effect does Lawrence; on the other extreme, Richardson would rather have woman taken as a fellow pilgrim than as mother nature or queen of heaven. H. D. and Jean Rhys have very different attitudes toward female victimization, the former resisting it as an image of Joan of Arc. As Coral Howells points out, Rhys repeats it in her stories of women falling victim to their own and male romantic fantasies. Diane Gillespie notes that Sinclair brings psychological, philosophical, and mystical considerations to a study of ways that people, and particularly women, fail to reach their potential in society.

When it comes to the much-discussed question of modernist language, the anthologized authors have different attitudes toward words. Stein declares a "words period," seeks the exact word, and is commended by Loy for offering "the word in and of itself." "Lively words" is the phrase used to articulate her style (DeKoven, **21**). Repetition of words is essential to her writing. Rhythmic repetition shows up again in H. D.'s review of Dreyer. Pound assigns Moore and Loy to a type of poetry concerned with language, logopoeia (discussed by Bush, Brownstein, and Burke). In contrast to the imagist impulse to pare down to hard exactness, in her nonapologetic explanation of "Negro Expression," Hurston introduces an aesthetic of adornment, with its most literary manifestation being rich use of metaphor. MacDiarmid presents a clash between English and Scots dialects—the latter associated with a masculinity that breaks down amid its own declamations (Gish, **13**). This interest in languages other than standard English, in lively language, can be related to the prodigious word play of Joyce and Stein. Such play has been the subject of considerable attention from poststructuralist critics, but usually in male writers, even by feminist analysts.

7. CULTURAL CRITIQUES

Radical critiques of the patriarchal family focus on maternal relationships, and alternate familial forms are important themes for modernist authors in our selections. Incest and mother–daughter relationships are treated by Cather, who encodes them as the more acceptable politics of master–slave relationships (Lilienfeld, **2**). Barnes encodes sexual molestation, even in her graphics (Broe, **1**). Lawrence's solution for emasculation of the father in the modern family is to free children from the influence of the mother, a utopian plan in which Rebecca West finds numerous practical oversights ("Reply to 'Good Boy Husbands' "). A young James Joyce expresses skepticism about the whole system of the conventional family and guilt over his mother's early death to the young woman who was to become his life companion (Letter to Nora Barnacle). Patriarchal critique lies encoded in Sylvia Townsend Warner's "Bluebeard's Daughter" (see Marcus, **22**). On a more positive note, close family dynamics are preserved and extended to a literary community in the round-robin form of correspondence Marianne Moore learned from her mother (Brownstein, **16**). Women degraded and alienated by family structures are given voice in the poetry of Charlotte Mew (Schenck, **15**). While one woman may compete for a man with Hurston's protagonist-narrator, a more powerful woman, "Big Sweet," uses her expertise in the codes of the community to protect the narrator from violence and to expedite her anthropological research.

Many of the authors' texts and editors' introductions show a high level of sensitivity to the politics of author–reader relations. On the conventional side, Eliot defends Moore's aristocratic language as the sort of aristocracy where the rulers are of the same blood as the ruled. A democratic construction of the readers' relation to the author is offered by Woolf ("Anon" and "The Reader") and Stein ("Americans"). Loy suggests that modernism demands creativity of the audience, and Stein finds that having an audience alters the lecturer's sense of her own words. Hurston tells us that everything done among the people she represents assumes an audience. Mansfield is critical of Richardson, charging that she writes for self rather than audience, producing a "killing pace" for the reader. Sinclair's defense of the sort of obscurity that serves to evoke feeling also relates to audience involvement. Counter to what is traditionally expected from modernism, aloof indecipherability is not much valued among the writers contained in this volume.

8. WARS AND VISIONS

The politics of gender and war interest numerous writers. The social impact of World War I on women's roles in society threw Lawrence into a state of alarm. Macaulay, Warner, White, and Wickham demonstrate the difficulty of the role of noncombatant—male or especially female. The most haunting fantasy of a noncom's war may be Antonia White's "The House of Clouds," in which a woman descending into madness fantasizes that she has become the medium of communication for soldiers dead in the war. Canonical war poetry has battlefield conventions that exclude the war poems of women (Squier, **12**), and we are only now recovering them. Woolf makes an "evangelical appeal" for "spirituality" to her audience (Henke, **26**). She is increasingly invested in social commentary and attentive to the threat to civilization embedded in a patriarchal system determined on dominance, hierarchy, and war (Silver, **26**). On the related subject of violence, Hurston hypothesizes that the lavish interracial, sexually related killing available in Richard Wright's fiction appeals to male black readers.

There are several versions of how the world, and consequently art, changed for writers in the early twentieth century. Stein proposes a synchronic paradigm that annihilates nineteenth-century realism. Sinclair suggests that subject–object relations were altered, an insight that relates to her careful defining of image and imagery in her excellent analysis of H. D.'s poetry. Loy proclaims, "Today is the crisis in consciousness." Woolf's attack on Edwardian materialism is echoed in Willa Cather's resistance to material accumulation and comes over even into Lawrence's "meaningless reiterations of the physical senses." Cather resists things that are named but not created ("The Novel Démeublé"). Other prophecies follow World War I. Mansfield cannot see how "after the war men could pick up the old threads as though it had never been" (Letter, 16 November 1919), and she resists representation: "the subject to the artist is the *unlikeness* to what we accept as reality" (Journal, 1921). Lawrence assigns hope to a religion recovered in male forgathering. Antonia White works out an alternate subject position, returning Catholic confession to a public domain (Marcus, **24**). Rebecca West suggests that Christ "damned" the world through his passion on the cross, "accustoming it to the sight of pain" ("Trees of Gold"). H. D. turns to female renovating deities and is less interested in deconstruction than in reconstruction. Larsen, in her reconstructive vision, finds life and spirit in the black race, as opposed to a white race "doomed to destruction by its own mechanical gods." Lawrence dreads the same gods and turns to the pagan spirituality of rituals attuned to natural cycles. We have noted H. D.'s use of basic natural beings like the jellyfish to describe elements of the psyche that must be incorporated. Despite their reference back to nature, some writers record an energizing effect from the modern city (Fauset, Larsen, Joyce, Woolf, West). In the epigraph to this introduction, Woolf's Lily Briscoe seeks in feminine territory "some secret which . . . people must have for the world to go on at all"; this is an aim shared with many modernists. Lily Briscoe too was just beginning her effort to articulate the things she had to comprehend, including the Victorian mother-woman and the old association of treasures with kings.

Virginia Woolf complained of a lack of perspective in her famous essay "Modern Fiction": "It is for the historian of literature to decide . . . if we are now beginning or ending or standing in the middle of a great period of prose fiction, for down in the plain little is visible." Stein pondered the ugliness of the struggle away from old things into new ones, saying that what is ugly settles like sediment over time ("Transatlantic Interview"). After fifty years we may have enough distance and sedimentation time, along with adequate theoretical perspective, to take in more than was visible to the modernists themselves or to the early critics of modernism. If they followed Pound's dictum to "make it new,"[9] we still must work on identifying the process and the pronoun. The making, the formal experiment, no longer seems to suffice as a definition. Mind, body, sexuality, family, reality, culture, religion, and history were all reconstrued. In settling for a small set of white male modernists and a limited number of texts and genres, we may have paused upon a conservative, anxious, male strain of modernism, however valuable and lasting those texts. The politics and aesthetics of gender may lie at the heart of a comprehensive understanding of early twentieth-century literature and its full array of literary treasures. This collection attests that a great deal of energy and creativity was subtracted out by gender from modernism. In acknowledging this, and in putting it back, we may be discovering how modernism can continue to "make it new."

NOTES

1. It is not within the scope of this introduction to provide a summary of these important theoretical developments. The Selected Bibliography contains relevant items. On psychological development and language acquisition, including roles and paradigms of the father and mother as related to signifying processes, see Culler, Derrida, Eco, Garner et al., Gilligan, Jardine, Kristeva, Lacan, and Irigaray. For post-Freudian theory relating to family romance, see Gallop, Gilligan, Mitchell, and Yalom. On history, see Douglas, Foucault, Lerner, and Joan Scott. Foucault's study of the "archive" is particularly relevant to this enterprise, as it deals with the rules that govern acceptable discourse in a society at a given time. For summaries of the impact of feminist perspectives on the academy, see Aiken et al.

2. In *No Man's Land,* vol. 1, Gilbert and Gubar treat male as well as female modernists. Their central thesis leads to the selection of texts that offer scenarios of sex war, a pattern which they extend into male appropriation of feminine language. They also suggest a pattern of affiliation that permits women writers to select and control literary mothers. They do not offer to any great extent a theory of gender apart from sex.

3. For a critique of monological thinking, see Bakhtin and Irigaray. Jane Marcus, in reconsidering this anthology as a finished unit, suggested that

> we may wish as well to interrogate the idea of the avant garde, and the similarity between the critical definitions of modern and the postmodern. What values did theorists and aestheticians of modernism from Adorno to Benjamin espouse and why did they exclude gender? How would modernism look if viewed from Africa or India or Japan? What is the patriarchal component of Eurocentrism?

4. See Sultan 96–101 for a history of the term's usage and a summary of various arguments for and against its validity.

5. See Bergonzi, Bradbury and MacFarlane, Dasenbrock, Faulkner, Levenson, Meisel, Moore, Quinones, Schwartz, Spender, Stead, Symons, Tindall, and Wilson (listed in the Selected Bibliography). For a handy collection of (mainly male-authored) manifestos on modernism, see Faulkner's *Modernist Reader.* It should be supplemented with Marinetti's futurist manifestos.

6. In responding to the final collection, Jane Marcus generated a series of questions and modernist subgenres that would lead to new collecting. In the category of a possible Marxist modernism, she names Christina Stead's *The Man Who Loved Children* and *The House of All Nations.* In a category of feminist antifascism, she suggests Katharine Burdekin's 1937 dystopia, *Swastika Night.* In a category of the feminist historical novel, she suggests Laura Riding's *A Trojan Ending* and *Lives of Wives* and Ford Madox Ford's *The Fifth Queen,* as well as *Parade's End.* She would collect the essays and pamphlets of women peace activists, from Crystal Eastman to Emma Goldman, and the pacifist books banned under the Defense of the Realm Act in England. She calls attention to additional scripts of female madness in Emily Holmes Coleman's *The Shutter of Snow,* Anna Kavan's *Asylum Piece,* and Radclyffe Hall's banned lesbian novel, *The Well of Loneliness.* She cites Ivy Compton-Burnett as a Bakhtinian dialogic novelist in *Manservant and Maidservant* and *A Father and His Fate* and considers Barbara Comyns's *Sisters by a River* an example of Kristevan female semiotic. She lists additional women writers who have been assigned to a "conventional" category: Elizabeth Bowen, Rosamund Lehmann, M. J. Farrell (Molly Keane), Mary Webb, and Mary Butts.

7. Readers unfamiliar with the debates among various feminisms might wish to consult the following works, listed in the Selected Bibliography: *Yale French Studies* special number, Jacobus, Marks and de Courtivron, Miller's *Poetics of Gender,* Moi, and Showalter's *New Feminist Criticism.*

8. For a provocative discussion of where feminist study takes off from, see Jehlen.

9. Pound used this injunction as the title for a 1934 collection of his essays. It also appears in Canto LIII (Kenner 448, Sultan 100).

1
Djuna Barnes (1892–1982)

Introduced and Edited by Mary Lynn Broe

Certain traits have now become a kind of formula for describing the modernist—or postmodernist—enterprise: the use of heterogeneous styles, discourses, and semantic positions; the refusal of continuities, such as narrative, and the substitution of a quality of "undecidability": the foregrounding of textuality; the use of text and graphics at variance with each other. Just about every woman modernist has been at one time or another judged by this definition. She has been praised for literary and technical "mastery," lauded for the production of textuality, but ignored ideologically and politically. Djuna Barnes is no exception.

Beautiful, irreverent, acid-tongued, and brilliant, Djuna Barnes revised as she subverted most traditional genres in which she wrote for over seventy years. She mined cultural history—from the street ballads of Montmartre to nineteenth-century French engraving books—as she transgressed the boundaries of drawings, drama, poetry, chapbook, journalism, novel, short stories, even an almanac. Her palimpsest texts, such as *Ryder* and *Ladies Almanack,* disrupt a masculine economy that would assign a single system of signification to each work. She interrogated the variances between text and graphics in the tiny, lapidary *Creatures in an Alphabet* (1982). Its relation of text and graphic reiterated, seventy years later, that earlier divergence between drawing and sociohistorical detail in the tabloid journalism of the teens and the configuration of "rhythm" and drawing in *The Book of Repulsive Women* (1915; see figure 1). The illustration for "When the Puppets Come to Town" (figure 2) encodes an act of molestation (limbs configuring a phallus) thinly masked as an intricate, stylized dance turn, or "death pang" of the female Bufano marionette. The text of this early journalistic piece, on the other hand, would seem to praise the world of art and artifice as a distinct departure from the instability of a credo of verisimilitude:

> They [the puppets] take all things casually—they have a story to run through, a plot to complete, a design to enact. They go about it . . . have no desire to murder, do not suffer the pains of remorse. They can, indeed, go off stage complacently, full of happy self-content because they have done something well; therefore, instead of being at the beginning of a lifelong tragedy, they are at the end of an amusement. ("When the Puppets Come to Town")

More powerful, however, than the challenge to the boundaries between word and space in the early journalism, or the threat that the printed word might be exiled to the edges of the tabloid universe, was Barnes's repeated encoding, in work after work, of details of violence within the patriarchal family. In her journalism, poetry (*The Book of Repulsive Women*), and short stories (*A Book*, 1923; *A Night among the Horses*, 1929) and in the celebratory femi-

Figure 1: *The Book of Repulsive Women*. 107.

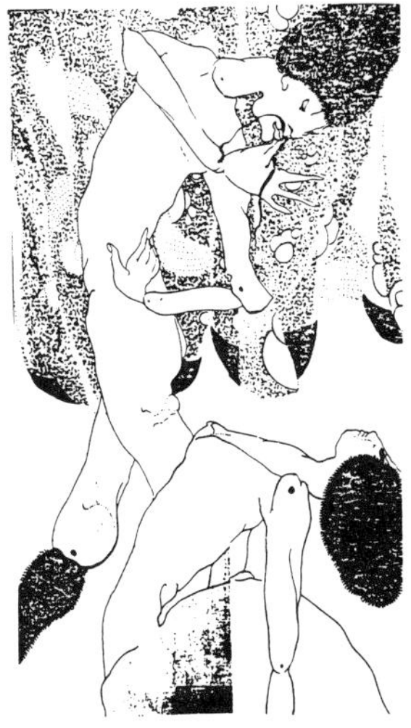

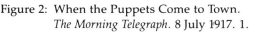

Figure 2: When the Puppets Come to Town. *The Morning Telegraph*. 8 July 1917. 1.

nist myths of *Ryder* (1928), *Ladies Almanack* (1928), and *The Antiphon* (1958), Barnes examined not only the failures of representational reality but also—as shown in the selections here included—the asymmetries of age and power and the contradictions inherent in gender definitions that undercut family intimacies, encoding complex modes of eroticism for which we as yet have no literary typology.

Born June 12, 1892, in Cornwall-on-Hudson, New York, Djuna grew up in a family whose form and shape revised conventional notions of kinship, as it challenged various bodily and spiritual taboos. Except for a few art classes at Pratt Institute in 1912, Djuna was educated at home by an inventor-musician father, Wald Barnes, and by a world-traveling grandmother, Zadel Barnes Gustafson, a temperance advocate, journalist, novelist, and poet of some distinction. Her father's omnisexuality and polygamy (two families shared the same household for most of Barnes's childhood) and her grandmother's active spiritualism brought a larger, if slightly more bizarre, world of influences into the monolithic household.[1] Until she took her first job as cub reporter with the Brooklyn *Eagle*—the same year her father, forced to "choose" between his women, married his mistress—her public world was the ambiguous and shifting boundary of the patriarchal family. Her bond with her grandmother was an extraordinary one, full of cross-generational eroticism, sexual complicities, and empowering professional legacies.[2] For a time, Barnes even believed she *was* her grandmother.

Both the publications of *The Book of Repulsive Women* (1915) and an exhibit of her drawings—many with strong social commentary against war and poverty—occurred before 1920, when she left for Europe on assignment for *McCall's*. Like many women of her generation, she favored marginality by living abroad, ex-patria, for many years, finding her community in Paris and London with tough women such as Emily Coleman, Peggy Guggenheim,

Thelma Wood, and others. Years earlier in Greenwich Village, she had befriended Helen Westley and Eleanor Fitzgerald, both associated with the Provincetown Players. For most of the twenties she lived in Paris with Thelma Wood; during the thirties she lived in Tangiers, Paris, London. In Devon in the English countryside, in Peggy Guggenheim's manor for writers, Hayford Hall (Broe, "My Art"), she worked on *Nightwood* (1936), a novel that Jane Marcus ("Laughing at Leviticus") calls modernism's most "representative text, . . . a tatoo on the backside of a black homosexual circus performer. The non-Aryan, non-heterosexual body is a book in which the modern failure to understand or assimilate the difference of race, class and gender is inscribed." Marcus's essay revolutionizes decades of Barnes's criticism, as it revises the novel's interpretation as merely "high modernist decadence."[3]

Although she wrote for over seventy years, with the exception of the brief best-seller status of *Ryder,* Djuna Barnes never received the publicity and accolades commensurate with the radical revision of modernism that she attempted in over eighteen one-act plays, thirty-nine poems, and more than 110 newspaper and magazine pieces for *Vanity Fair, Charm, McCall's,* the *New Yorker,* and the New York *World, Press,* and *Telegraph.* Typical of the suppression or interruption in the sexual-textual order is the "text-bashing" done by T. S. Eliot on the twenty-nine drafts of her late play, *The Antiphon.* Eliot slashed his way through this story of a daughter's reenactment of a painful and violent childhood scene, particularly in act II, the hayhook scene, in which a father attempts to violate his daughter, then, failing, barters her for the price of a goat. Eliot advised Barnes to excise and displace parts of the story so that the narrative coherence in this study of the daughter's betrayal is all but missing in the final text (Curry, DeSalvo).

Through repeated revisions, excisions, threats to friends, and the burning of letters, Barnes developed a ritual of self-silencing, suggesting at once her refusal to privilege a single "authentic" voice, her uneasiness with canonical representations (the self-consciously generic "A Book," for example, or the extramarginal artwork). Such silencing is also a textual response, perhaps, to the father's attempt to violate his daughter, then barter her in ritual exchange. Through numerous editings and excisions, she removed from *A Book* (1923) all the realistic drawings—tantalizingly personal sketches that she left anonymous (see figures 3 and 4). As with the profusion of styles and genres in *Ryder* or the densely encoded *Antiphon,* which hid bits of autobiography, Barnes forced the reader to "decode" Ida Rauh, Helen Westley, and other contemporaries through the same intimate knowledge as the author and against the grain of the transgeneric "book." Lesbian poems such as "Lullaby" and stories intimately critical of family, such as "Oscar," "Indian Summer," and "Mother," were also cut on the way toward construction of *Spillway* (1962) and *Selected Works* (1962).[4]

Until Jane Marcus's radical feminist reclaiming of *Nightwood*'s "political unconscious," Barnes's novel had been canonized as the emblematic male modernist text, whether in its celebration of "inverted love" (Burke) or its

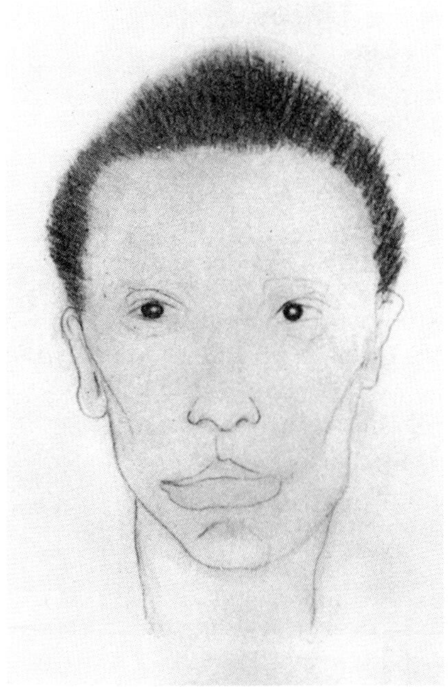

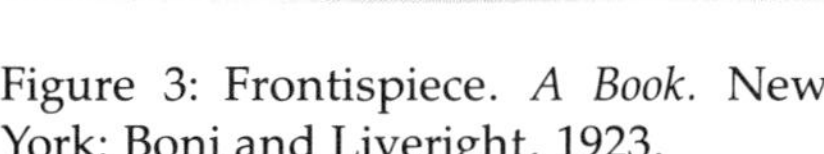

Figure 3: Frontispiece. *A Book.* New York: Boni and Liveright, 1923.

Figure 4: Helen Westley.

inscription of the decline of Western civilization (Kannenstine calls it "a complex record of disunity and disharmony") or, as Joseph Frank claims, in its representation of the modernist enterprise of "transmitting the time world of history into the timeless world of myth" (60). As the great art novel of the twentieth century—a kind of epistemological romp on the figural plane—*Nightwood* invites construction of theory (Frank, Burke) as it encourages identification of a dominant tradition: it has been called, alternately, surrealistic, Eliotic, Dantesque, fugal, Elizabethan, baroque, even gothic. Although there has been some recent focus on work before *Nightwood* (Clark, Herzig, Plumb, Stevenson), contemporary criticism still privileges Barnes's production of writing in the 1936 novel (Singer), her search for a theory of fiction (Schehr), or her use of various deconstructionist and French feminist techniques in the single novel (Michel, Beranger, Hanrahan). Wolfe takes a gynocentric look at the female exile in *Nightwood* as "a prescription for a communal ritual of mourning," while Wilson examines Barnes's retreat from high modernism and escape to "ahistoricity" in the novel. Elizabeth Pochoda has written a lucid, jargon-free essay on language and the uses of multiple deception in *Nightwood*—the function and the psychology of the lie.[5]

Barnes was known frequently to dismiss her early work as "commercial," particularly her writing for magazines, tabloids, and the Provincetown

Players, the compromise necessary to earn a living. Like her contemporaries Emily Coleman and Antonia White, she spoke of that voluminous body of early writing as her "artistic apprenticeship" to the later "high art" of *Nightwood.* In much of this early journalism Barnes sketched marginal street types, local color around Brooklyn, even the pseudo-democracy of the Village's Liberal Club or Webster Hall ("pompous beetles in the web of an old desire," she wrote). She mocked the pastime of "going slumming" in "How the Villagers Amuse Themselves" and lamented the loss of communal ideals and passions in her beloved Provincetown theatre that was "always about to be given back to the horses." A number of essays describe the clash between reform and privilege in Village life—between the grocer who tells French jokes and "wraps the prunes with subtleties," and the one who listens to the baker's daughter talk about the possibilities of reform in New York. Repeatedly, Barnes saw "real things that are beautiful . . . mixed in with that which is sham . . . a wonderful terrible hash on the table of life."

At times brilliantly savage and political, the early writing radically challenges conventional genres and ideologies as it betrays some anxiety about gender and creativity. Barnes reenacted in her participatory journalism the force-feeding of imprisoned IWW agitator Becky Edelson and hundreds of militant British suffragists. Bound like a corpse with arms at her side, nostrils sprayed with a mixture of pea soup, she either had to swallow or choke on the meal poured down her throat through a red tube in her nose. What she reenacted was the violation not only of the personal body but also of the body politic. Her blistering critique named the misuse of power at the base of political injustice and personal violation: "I saw in my hysteria a vision of a hundred women in grim hospitals, bound and shrouded in the rough grip of callous warders. . . . I could hear the doctor walking ahead of me, stepping as all doctors step, with that little confiding gait that horses must have returning from funerals. . . . "[6]

Correct to claim that the interviews Barnes did in the teens were "not standard journalism," Douglas Messerli is wrong to dismiss the interviews with the critical fallacy that they were "fascinating experiments in impressionistic characteristics that Barnes would perfect in her short stories, *Ryder, Nightwood* and *The Antiphon.*" Rather, the early journalism (1914–1931) celebrates sheer experimental variety even within its own historical use, as it challenges the assumptions of the privileged "high art" of the novel (*Nightwood*). This underrepresented early writing forms a prolific portrait of experiment, particularly in aesthetic and political strategies, as it subverts genres such as "the interview," the well-made one-act play, and the short story. We note the brilliance with which Barnes disrupts the power lines in the interview format ("The Confessions of Helen Westley," reprinted here), deconstructing its masculine sociocultural economy of the interviewer who always reserves comment. Barnes privileges the nonauthoritative as she exposes the evaluative art in this interview. Westley phones Barnes: "I want to be interviewed again." Barnes agrees. And then in the middle of Westley's diatribe on the ironies of greater wisdom in age, Barnes intrudes: "Some advice for young actors would come in here very nicely." "Now I am capable of youth, but not capable of a few years," says Westley. Barnes prods, disrupting her own authority by subverting the formula: "A little faster with your youth, Helen." Mid-interview, they both crack up laughing at the hypocrisy and conceit in the asymmetrical form:

> WESTLEY: "Well, let's stop"
> BARNES: "We can't, not yet; I have at least three more pages to fill."

Barnes's early writing should not be dismissed as the "commercial" compromise necessary to earn a living. We have already glimpsed how her brilliant politics destablizes the boundaries of the text and drawing on the pages in the story of the Bufano Marionettes. (By 1917, however, Barnes frequently made as much as $15 an article—she wrote several a day—and $5,000 a year.) Likewise, Barnes's plays, stories, and early newspaper essays interrogate conventional or public sexual ideologies, as well as forms of romantic and domestic comedy. An incestuous kiss, son to mother, closes "Three from the Earth," subverting with its sudden revelation the well-made play. More importantly, such an action also subverts the bounds of the conventional family, revealing in a single gesture what the dialogue has concealed. In "Mother" (reprinted below), the memory of her past, of "great women," is undercut by Lydia Passova's needs. Throughout the story we glimpse a little nervous Englishman who is "uneasy" in not being able to name the relationship with Lydia in conventional terms. Lydia, however, has an "alternate" economy, one of subtraction, of minimalism. Only when she is unable to provoke him with ambiguous dialogue—i.e., when she is dead, "hard-set as in a mould"—he then is able to recognize the very startling difference in their ages. In the final scene, he retreats to weeping in bed, knees in a fetal position, closed fists to eyes.

Criticizing the contemporary stage and newspaper worlds, Barnes alone among the "new women" playwrights dared to introduce vampirism ("The Dove"), incest ("Three from the Earth"), and various radical sexual ideologies in her work: "The restriction of sexual relationships, Barnes suggests, is a way of controlling access to knowledge, language and mobility" (Larabee 3). Barnes mimed romantic conventions at the historical moment when the small time husband-and-wife acts of the Provincetown Players—those of Neith Boyce and Hutchins Hapgood or Jig Cook and Susan Glaspell—were forging an uneasy link between Freud and feminism (Larabee). Merely playing, as so many of the Provincetown plays did, with the fad of psychoanalysis in such titles as "Suppressed Desires" or "Fidelity," Barnes's colleagues presented heavy middle-class melodrama, preservations of monogamy, in theatrical drag.

But not Barnes. It was canny that her one-acts, plays that also carried on the dialogue and critique that characterized her early journalism, would first be published in the *New York Morning Telegraph Sunday Magazine*. Opening its sixth season ("The Season of Youth") in a remodeled stable in Greenwich Village, the Provincetown Players collaboratively staged three of Djuna's plays. Helen Westley opened this 1919–1920 season of women's plays by collaboratively directing "Three from the Earth," "An Irish Triangle," and "Kurzy of the Sea."[7]

Some critics have felt that the "collective nature of the dramatic art form" was simply not Barnes's forte, that the plays remained too baffling, gave the audience too few clues: "the logic of description triumphs over the logic of theatre" (Retallack), leaving the plays to exhibit a formal ambivalence between the vitality of the playwright's language—text on the page—and the static dialogue spoken by the stalemated characters. Barnes's distinctive women characters—Kate Morley, Helena Hucksteppe, "The Dove"—and her detailed use of domestic settings earned her the title of "new realist" (Scott). Cheryl Plumb, on the other hand, read the same plays as signaling allegiance to symbolism gleaned from de Gourmont, Baudelaire, Hauptmann, and Yeats. Barnes's elaborately detailed commentaries for stage set and her meticulous playwrights' directions sabotage public and participatory aspects of the form. Accused of remaining "documents," the plays were full of innuendo, riddle, and allusion. Their themes demanded more intellectual dedication than the average American audience was willing to give (Clark 50). Even if many of the plays were not intended for production, Barnes's one-acts radically revised the organization of stage space, as they subverted traditional theatrical production values and technique (see, for example, the "Ten Minute Plays," 1922). Alexander Woollcott, who parodied "Three from the Earth" in the title of his review, "Three from the Birth: A Malthusian Sardonicism in One Act," claimed that "the greatest indoor sport this week is guessing what it [the title] means."

In "To the Dogs" (*A Book*), reprinted here, Helena Hucksteppe radically revises stage space: the play opens and closes with her back defiantly to the audience, her body stretched out against a mantel. Her movements in the course of the play and her gaze directed inward to the interior of a room "too fragile or too perfect" stun the interloping Gheid Storm, who hurdles a side window but later beats a disciplined retreat through a conventional doorway. Refusing to conform linguistically, dialogically, or dramatically to the woman whom Ghied Storm once slept with, Helena holds the power of an Echo to mimic her Narcissus. Her "laugh of the Medusa" unsettles, as she inscribes the feminine in the dialogics of this one-act play.

With its complex interplay of gender, power and discourse, "To the Dogs" celebrates the fragility if not the pointlessness of compulsory heterosexuality and domination, the so-called "great moment of human contact": Storm: "I offer you a clean heart." Helena: "Things which have known only one state, do not interest me." Through a series of elliptical dialogic exchanges that subvert the sexual ideology of the male and satirize Freudian thought, Helena remains invulnerable to Gheid's power threats about the possibility that she "cannot bury her past." She remains unmoved by his myth of woman's nature ("Who ARE you?"), claiming, "I am a woman . . . who is NOT in need." Helena, who "began beyond bitterness," assures the reader that man and woman do not share a common language, and her dialogic exchanges—medleys of power checked by vulnerability—subvert any personal attachment that might characterize a conventional plot:

> STORM: "Why wont you let me talk to you?
> HELENA: "Any man may accomplish anything he's capable of"; or
> STORM: "I'm—attracted—to you."
> HELENA: "A magnet does not attract shavings."

From the beginning, Gheid Storm, the "well-to-do man of property who keeps his wife and his lawns in the best possible trim without any particular pleasure," cannot begin to construct a thought beyond unexamined conventional fragments, or "fancies" as Helena terms his fantasies. In a single, long conversation—one she engages in with her languorous backside to the audience—she reverses the roles of interloper (Gheid Storm) and his prey (Helena), challenging both the logocentric and sociocultural authority of the male. Dramaturgy, as well as traditional conflict and action, bow to the foregrounded script as Helena seizes theatrical space for women, filling its volume through her subversive wit: STORM: "What are you trying to say?" HELENA: "I'm saying it." Just as the power of the female revisionist reader corrects the unexamined "plain truths" of Storm, as well as the forces of the "new drama" movement, Helena challenges the old theatre of events. She sets this old theatre against the new theatre of social forces practiced by Heterodoxy's radical feminists, such as Ida Rauh, Helen Westley, and Susan Glaspell. And throughout the writings before *Nightwood,* Barnes herself "says it," concealing as well as revealing powerful articulations about gender and sexual ideologies that disrupt the patriarchal family.

NOTES

1. *Cold Comfort,* by Mary Lynn Broe and Frances McCullough (forthcoming, Random House), is a biographical portrait of Djuna Barnes which, through selected letters, offers not only an antidote to the omissions and errors of Andrew Field's *Djuna* but also much new information about family relations in Barnes's childhood.

2. See Broe, "My Art Belongs to Daddy," for elaboration of this unusual relationship between grandmother and granddaughter.

3. Other essays in Broe, *Silence and Power* (Southern Illinois UP, 1990) challenge traditional modernist interpretations of Barnes's writing through strong revisionist perspectives, as they shape new psychoanalytic, sociopolitical, and cultural readings.

4. As *A Book* (1923) was revised to *A Night among the Horses* (1929) and finally to *Spillway and Other Stories* (1962), the shape of the volume changed dramatically; the stories

that were kept—"Aller et Retour," "Casssation," "The Grande Malade," and "A Night among the Horses" among them—were considerably revised.

5. While this introduction privileges certain doctoral work, it is necessarily brief and by no means proposes to be complete. For a more complete list of recent criticism, see the Messerli bibliography (through 1975) and the bibliography in *Silence and Power,* updated through 1989.

6. For a reading of the political force behind Barnes's early journalism, see Broe "Gunga Duhl," and Herzig.

7. At the time Barnes's plays were produced, Jig (George Cram) Cook was on sabbatical. Djuna had been living for a year with Courtenay Lemon, scriptreader for the Dramatist's Guild.

WORKS CITED

Barnes, Djuna. "How It Feels to Be Forcibly Fed." *New York World Magazine* 6 (September 1914):5, 17.

———. "Becoming Intimate with the Bohemians; When the Dusk of a Musty Hall Has Crept through the Ever Widening Keyhole the Queen of Bohemia Has Arisen, for Her Day Has Begun; You Will Find Her in Polly's, the Candle Stick, the Brevoort, the Black Cat or Any Other Greenwich Village Place You Care to Visit." *New York Morning Telegraph Sunday Magazine* 19 Nov. 1916:1, 4.

———. "How the Villagers Amuse Themselves; the Task Is Sordid and Hard, but It Must Be Done—So after an Early Breakfast out Sets the Bohemian." *New York Morning Telegraph Sunday Magazine* 26 Nov. 1916:1.

———. "When the Puppets Come to Town." *New York Morning Telegraph Sunday Magazine* 8 July 1917:4.

———. "The Confessions of Helen Westley." *New York Morning Telegraph Sunday Magazine* 23 Sept. 1917:5.

———. "Three from the Earth." *Little Review* 6 (November 1919):3–15. Rpt. in *A Book* and *A Night among the Horses.*

———. "To the Dogs." *A Book.* New York: Boni and Liveright, 1923.

———. "Mother." *A Book.* New York: Boni and Liveright, 1923.

———. *Nightwood.* 1937. New York: New Directions, 1961.

———. *Selected Works of Djuna Barnes: Spillway/The Antiphon/Nightwood.* New York: Farrar, Straus and Cudahy, 1962.

———. *Ladies Almanack.* Paris, 1928. New York: Harper and Row, 1972.

———. *Ryder.* 1928. New York: St. Martin's P, 1979.

Benstock, Shari. *Women of the Left Bank: Paris, 1900–1940.* Austin: U of Texas P, 1986.

Beranger, Elizabeth. "*Nightwood* ou du sexe d'une belle indifferente." *Revue Francaise d'Etudes Americaines* 11.3(1986):437–448.

Blankley, Elyse. *Daughter's Exile: Renee Vivien, Gertrude Stein, and Djuna Barnes in Paris.* Ph.D. diss., U of California, Irvine, 1984.

Broe, Mary Lynn, ed. *Silence and Power: A Reevaluation of Djuna Barnes.* Carbondale: Southern Illinois UP, 1990.

Broe, Mary Lynn. "Gunga Duhl, the Pen Performer: Djuna Barnes's Early Journalism." *Belle Lettres* 1 (September 1985).

———. "My Art Belongs to Daddy: Incest as Exile. The Textual Economics of Hayford Hall." In *Women's Writing in Exile,* ed. Mary Lynn Broe and Angela Ingram. Chapel Hill: U of North Carolina P, 1989.

Burke, Kenneth. "Version, Con-, Per-, and In-: Thought on Djuna Barnes's Novel *Nightwood.*" *Southern Review* 2(1966):329–346. Rpt. in Kenneth Burke, *Language as Sym-*

bolic Action: Essays on Life Literature and Method. Berkeley: U of California P, 1966. 240–253.

Clark, Susan. "Mesalliance: Djuna Barnes and the American Stage" Ph.D. diss., Tufts U, 1989.

Curry, Lynda. " 'Tom, take mercy' ": Djuna Barnes's Drafts of *The Antiphon.*" In Broe, *Silence and Power.*

DeSalvo, Louise. "To Make Her Mutton at Sixteen: Rape, Incest, and Child Abuse in *The Antiphon.*" In Broe, *Silence and Power.*

Field, Andrew. *Djuna: The Life and Times of Djuna Barnes.* New York: Putnam, 1983.

Frank, Joseph. "Spatial Form in Modern Literature." *The Widening Gyre: Crisis and Mastery in Modern Literature.* Bloomington: Indiana UP, 1963.

Hanrahan, Mairead. "Djuna Barnes's *Nightwood:* Where Man is With Wo(e)." In *Writing Differences: Readings from the Seminar of Helene Cixous,* ed. Susan Sellers. New York: St. Martin's P, 1988.

Helle, Anita Plath. "Speculative Subjects: The Uses of Exile to the Imagination of Gertrude Stein, Djuna Barnes and Mina Loy." Ph.D. diss., U of Oregon, 1986.

Herzig, Carl. "Roots of Night: Emerging Style and Vision in the Early Journalism of Djuna Barnes." *Centennial Review* Autumn 1987:255–269.

Kannenstine, Louis F. *The Art of Djuna Barnes: Duality and Damnation.* New York: New York UP, 1977.

Lanser, Susan Snaider. "Speaking in Tongues: *Ladies Almanack* and the Language of Celebration." *Frontiers* 4(1979):39–46. Rpt. in Broe, *Silence and Power.*

Larabee, Ann. "The Early Attic Stage of Djuna Barnes." In Broe, *Silence and Power.*

Marcus, Jane. "Laughing at Leviticus: *Nightwood* as Woman's Circus Epic." In Broe, *Silence and Power.*

Messerli, Douglas. *Djuna Barnes: A Bibliography.* Rhinebeck, N.Y.: Lewis, 1975.

———, and Alyce Barry. *Interviews.* Washington, D.C.: Sun and Moon P, 1985.

Michel, Frann. "All Women Are Not Women All: *Ladies Almanack* and Feminine Writing."In Broe, *Silence and Power.*

Plumb, Cheryl J. *Fancy's Craft: Art and Identity in the Early Works of Djuna Barnes.* Selinsgrove: Susquehanna UP, 1986.

Pochoda, Elizabeth. "Style's Hoax: A Reading of Djuna Barnes's *Nightwood.*" *Twentieth Century Literature* 22(1976):179–191.

Retallack, Joan. "One Acts: Early Plays of Djuna Barnes." in Broe, *Silence and Power.*

Schehr, Lawrence. "Djuna Barnes' *Nightwood:* Dismantling the Folds." *Style* 19:36–49.

Scott, James. *Djuna Barnes.* Boston: Twayne, 1976.

Singer, Alan. "The Horse Who Knows Too Much: Metaphor and the Narrative of Discontinuity in *Nightwood.*" *Contemporary Literature* 25(1984):66–87.

Smith-Rosenberg, Carol. *Disorderly Conduct: Visions of Gender in Victorian America.* New York: Knopf, 1986.

Stevenson, Sheryl. "Writing the Grotesque Body: Djuna Barnes' Carnival Parody." In Broe, *Silence and Power.*

Wilson, Deborah Sue. "Lost Boundaries: Kenneth Burke, Nathanael West, Djuna Barnes and the Disorder of Things." Ph.D. diss., U of California, Irvine, 1987.

Wolfe, Judy Louise. "Anti-patriarchal Strategies in the Major Works of Djuna Barnes." Ph.D. diss., Rice U, 1985.

Woollcott, Alexander. "Second Thoughts on First Nights." *New York Times* 9 Nov. 1919: sect. 8,2.

Mother

A feeble light flickered in the pawn shop at Twenty-nine. Usually, in the back of this shop, reading by this light—a rickety lamp with a common green cover—sat Lydia Passova, the mistress.

Her long heavy head was divided by straight bound hair. Her high firm bust was made still higher and still firmer by German corsets. She was excessively tall, due to extraordinarily long legs. Her eyes were small, and not well focused. The left was slightly distended from the long use of a magnifying glass.

She was middle-aged, and very slow in movement, though well balanced. She wore coral in her ears, a coral necklace, and many coral finger rings.

There was about her jewelry some of the tragedy of all articles that find themselves in pawn, and she moved among the trays like the guardians of cemetery grounds, who carry about with them some of the lugubrious stillness of the earth on which they have been standing.

She dealt, in most part, in cameos, garnets, and a great many inlaid bracelets and cuff-links. There were a few watches however, and silver vessels and fishing tackle and faded slippers—and when, at night, she lit the lamp, these and the trays of precious and semi-precious stones, and the little ivory crucifixes, one on either side of the window, seemed to be leading a swift furtive life of their own, conscious of the slow pacing woman who was known to the street as Lydia Passova.

No one knew her, not even her lover—a little nervous fellow, an Englishman quick in speech with a marked accent, a round-faced youth with a deep soft cleft in his chin, on which grew two separate tufts of yellow hair. His eyes were wide and pale, and his eyeteeth prominent.

He dressed in tweeds, walked with the toes in, seemed sorrowful when not talking, laughed a great deal and was nearly always to be found in the café about four of an afternoon.

When he spoke it was quick and jerky. He had spent a great deal of his time in Europe, especially the watering places—and had managed to get himself in trouble in St. Moritz, it was said, with a well-connected family.

He liked to seem a little eccentric and managed it simply enough while in America. He wore no hat, and liked to be found reading the *London Times*, under a park lamp at three in the morning.

Lydia Passova was never seen with him. She seldom left her shop, however, she was always pleased when he wanted to go anywhere: "Go," she would say, kissing his hand, "and when you are tired come back."

Sometimes she would make him cry. Turning around she would look at him a little surprised, with lowered lids, and a light tightening of the mouth.

"Yes," he would say, "I know I'm trivial—well then, here I go, I will leave you, not disturb you any longer!" and darting for the door he would somehow end by weeping with his head buried in her lap.

She would say, "There, there—why are you so nervous?"

And he would laugh again: "My father was a nervous man, and my mother was high-strung, and as for me——" He would not finish.

Sometimes he would talk to her for long hours, she seldom answering, occupied with her magnifying glass and her rings, but in the end she was sure to send him out with: "That's all very true, I have no doubt; now go out by yourself and think it over"—and he would go, with something like relief, embracing her large hips with his small strong arms.

They had known each other a very short time, three or four months. He had gone in to pawn his little gold ring, he was always in financial straits, though his mother sent him five pounds a week; and examining the ring, Lydia Passova had been so quiet, inevitable, necessary, that it seemed as if he must have known her forever—"at some time," as he said.

Yet they had never grown together. They remained detached, and on her part, quiet, preoccupied.

He never knew how much she liked him. She never told him; if he asked she would look at him in that surprised manner, drawing her mouth together.

In the beginning he had asked her a great many times, clinging to her, and she moved about arranging her trays with a slight smile, and in the end lowered her hand and stroked him gently.

He immediately became excited. "Let us dance," he cried, "I have a great capacity for happiness."

"Yes, you are very happy," she said.

"You understand, don't you?" he asked abruptly.

"What?"

"That my tears are nothing, have no significance, they are just a protective fluid—when I see anything happening that is about to affect my happiness I cry, that's all."

"Yes," Lydia Passova said, "I understand." She turned around reaching up to some shelves, and over her shoulder she asked, "Does it hurt?"

"No, it only frightens me. You never cry, do you?"

"No, I never cry."

That was all. He never knew where she had come from, what her life had been, if she had or had not been married, if she had or had not known lovers; all that she would say was, "Well, you are with me, does that tell you nothing?" and he had to answer, "No, it tells me nothing."

When he was sitting in the café he often thought to himself, "There's a great woman"—and he was a little puzzled why he thought this because his need of her was so entirely different from any need he seemed to remember having possessed before.

There was no swagger in him about her, the swagger he had always felt for his conquests with women. Yet there was not a trace of shame—he was neither proud nor shy about Lydia Passova, he was something entirely different. He could not have said himself what his feeling was—but it was in no way disturbing.

People had, it is true, begun to tease him:

"You're a devil with the ladies."

Where this had made him proud, now it made him uneasy.

"Now, there's a certain Lydia Passova for instance, who would ever have thought——"

Furious he would rise.

"So, you do feel——"

He would walk away, stumbling a little among the chairs, putting his hand on the back of every one on the way to the door.

Yet he could see that, in her time, Lydia Passova had been a "perverse" woman—there was, about everything she did, an economy that must once have been a very sensitive and a very sensuous impatience, and because of this everyone who saw her felt a personal loss.

Sometimes, tormented, he would come running to her, stopping abruptly, putting it to her this way:

"Somebody has said something to me."

"When—where?"

"Now, in the café."

"What?"

"I don't know, a reproach——"

She would say:

"We are all, unfortunately, only what we are."

She had a large and beautiful angora cat, it used to sit in the tray of amethysts and opals and stare at her from very bright cold eyes. One day it died, and calling her lover to her she said:

"Take her out and bury her." And when he had buried her he came back, his lips twitching.

"You loved that cat—this will be a great loss."

"Have I a memory?" she inquired.

"Yes," he answered.

"Well," she said quietly, fixing her magnifying glass firmly in her eye. "We have looked at each other, that is enough."

And then one day she died.

The caretaker of the furnace came to him, where he was sipping his liqueur as he talked to his cousin, a pretty little blond girl, who had a boring and comfortably provincial life, and who was beginning to chafe.

He got up, trembling, pale, and hurried out.

The police were there, and said they thought it had been heart failure.

She lay on the couch in the inner room. She was fully dressed, even to her coral ornaments; her shoes were neatly tied—large bows of a ribbed silk.

He looked down. Her small eyes were slightly open, the left, that had used the magnifying glass, was slightly wider than the other. For a minute she seemed quite natural. She had the look of one who is about to say: "Sit beside me."

Then he felt the change. It was in the peculiar heaviness of the head—sensed through despair and not touch. The high breasts looked very still, the hands were half closed, a little helpless, as in life—hands that were too proud to "hold." The drawn-up limb exposed a black petticoat and a yellow stocking. It seemed that she had become hard—set, as in a mould—that she rejected everything now, but in rejecting had bruised him with a last terrible pressure. He moved and knelt down. He shivered. He put his closed hands to his eyes. He could not weep.

She was an old woman, he could see that. The ceasing of that one thing that she could still have for anyone made it simple and direct.

Something oppressed him, weighed him down, bent his shoulders, closed his throat. He felt as one feels who has become conscious of passion for the first time, in the presence of a relative.

He flung himself on his face, like a child.

That night, however, he wept, lying in bed, his knees drawn up.

A Book. New York: Boni and Liveright, 1923. 164–171.

To the Dogs

PERSONS: HELENA HUCKSTEPPE
GHEID STORM—*Her neighbour*
TIME: *Late afternoon.*
PLACE: *In the mountains of Cornwall-on-Hudson—the* HUCKSTEPPE *house.*
SCENE: *The inner room of the* HUCKSTEPPE *cottage.*

To the left, in the back wall, a large window overlooks a garden. Right centre, a door leads off into a bedroom, and from the bedroom one may see the woods of the mountain. The door is slightly open, showing a glimpse of a tall mirror and the polished pole of a bed.

In the right wall there is a fireplace.

A dog lies across the threshold, asleep, head on paws.

About this room there is perhaps just a little too much of a certain kind of frail beauty of object. Crystal glasses, scent bottles, bowls of an almost too perfect design, furniture that is too antiquely beautiful.

HELENA HUCKSTEPPE, *a woman of about thirty-five, stands almost back view to the audience, one arm lying along the mantel. She is rather under medium in height. Her hair, which is dark and curling, is done carefully about a small fine head. She is dressed in a dark, long gown, a gown almost too faithful to the singular sadness of her body.*

At about the same moment as the curtain's rising, GHEID STORM *vaults the window-sill. He is a man of few years, a well-to-do man of property, brought up very carefully by upright women, the son of a conscientious physician, the kind of man who commutes with an almost religious fervour, and who keeps his wife and his lawns in the best possible trim, without any particular personal pleasure.*

GHEID *is tall, but much too honourable to be jaunty, he is decidedly masculine. He walks deliberately, getting all the use possible out of his boot-leather, his belt-strap and hat-bands.*

His face is one of those which, for fear of misuse, has not been used at all.

HELENA HUCKSTEPPE *does not appear to be in the least astonished at his mode of entrance.*

GHEID STORM—As you never let me in at the door, I thought of the window. [HELENA *remains silent.*] I hope I did not startle you. [*Pause.*] Women are better calm, that is, some kinds of calm——

HELENA—Yes?

GHEID—[*Noticing the dog, which has not stirred.*] You've got funny dogs, they don't even bark. [*Pause.*] I expected you'd set them on me; however, perhaps that will come later——

HELENA—Perhaps.

STORM—Are you always going to treat me like this? For days I've watched you walking with your dogs of an evening—that little black bull-pup, and then those three setters—you've fine ways with you Helena Hucksteppe, though there are many tales of how you came by them——

HELENA—Yes?

STORM—Yes. [*Pause.*] You know, you surprise me.

HELENA—Why? Because I do not set my dogs on you?

STORM—Something like that.

HELENA—I respect my dogs.

STORM—What does that mean?

HELENA—Had I a daughter, would I set her on every man?

STORM—[*Trying to laugh.*] That's meant for an insult, isn't it? Well, I like the little insulting women——

HELENA—You are a man of taste.

STORM—I respect you.

HELENA—What kind of a feeling is that?

STORM—A gentleman's——

HELENA—I see.

STORM—People say of you: "She has a great many ways——"

HELENA—Yes?

STORM—[*Sitting on the edge of the table.*] "But none of them simple."

HELENA—Do they?

STORM—[*Without attempting to hide his admiration.*] I've watched your back: "There goes a fine woman, a fine silent woman; she wears long skirts, but she knows how to move her feet without kicking up a dust—a woman who can do that, drives a man mad." In town there's a story that you come through once every Spring, driving a different man ahead of you with a riding whip; another has it, that you come in the night——

HELENA—In other words, the starved women of the town are beginning to eat.

STORM—[*Pause.*] Well [*laughs*] I like you.

HELENA—I do not enjoy the spectacle of men ascending.

STORM—What are you trying to say?

HELENA—I'm saying it.

STORM—[*After an awkward pause.*] Do—you wish me to—go away?

HELENA—You will go.

STORM—Why won't you let me talk to you?

HELENA—Any man may accomplish anything he's capable of.

STORM—Do you know how I feel about you?

HELENA—Perfectly.

STORM—I have heard many things about your—your past——I believe none of them——

HELENA—Quite right, why should you mix trades?

STORM—What do you mean by that?

HELENA—Why confuse incapability with accomplishment——

STORM—It's strange to see a woman like you turning to the merely bitter——

HELENA—I began beyond bitterness.

STORM—Why do you treat me this way?

HELENA—How would you have me treat you?

STORM—There was one night when you seemed to know, have you forgotten? A storm was coming up, the clouds were rolling overhead—and you, you yourself started it. You kissed me.

HELENA—You say it was about to storm?

STORM—Yes.

HELENA—It even looked like rain?

STORM—Yes.

HELENA—[*Quickly in a different voice.*] It was a dark night, and I ended it.

STORM—What have I done?

HELENA—You have neglected to make any beginning in the world—can I help that?

STORM—I offer you a clean heart.

HELENA—Things which have known only one state, do not interest me.

STORM—Helena!

HELENA—Gheid Storm.

STORM—I have a son; I don't know why I should tell you about him, perhaps because I want to prove that I have lived, and perhaps not. My son is a child, I am a man of few years and my son is like what I was at his age. He is thin, I was thin; he is quiet, I was quiet; he has delicate flesh, and I had also—well, then his mother died——

HELENA—The saddle comes down from the horse.

STORM—Well, she died——

HELENA—And that's over.

STORM—Well, there it is, I have a son——

HELENA—And that's not over. Do you resent that?

STORM—I don't know, perhaps. Sometimes I say to myself when I'm sitting by the fire alone—"You should have something to think of while sitting here——"

HELENA—In other words, you're living for the sake of your fire.

STORM—[*To himself.*] Some day I shall be glad I knew you.

HELENA—You go rather fast.

STORM—Yes, I shall have you to think of.

HELENA—When the fire is hot, you'll be glad to think of me?

STORM—Yes, all of us like to have a few things to tell to our children, and I have always shown all that's in my heart to my son.

HELENA—How horrible!

STORM—[*Startled.*] Why?

HELENA—Would you show everything that made your heart?

STORM—I believe in frankness——

HELENA—[*With something like anger.*] Well, some day your son will blow his head off, to be rid of frankness, before his skin is tough.

STORM—You are not making anything easier.

HELENA—I've never been callous enough to make things easier.

STORM—You're a queer woman——

HELENA—Yes, that does describe me.

STORM—[*Taking his leg off the table.*] Do you really want to know why I came? Because I need you——

HELENA—I'm not interested in corruption for the many.

STORM—[*Starting as if he had been struck.*] By God!

HELENA—Nor in misplaced satisfactions——

STORM—By God, what a woman!

HELENA—Nor do I participate in liberations——

STORM—[*In a low voice.*] I could hate you!

HELENA—I limit no man, feel what you can.

STORM—[*Taking a step toward her, the dog lifts its head.*] If it were not for those damned dogs of yours—I'd—I'd——

HELENA—Aristocracy of movement never made a dog bite——

STORM—That's a—strange thing to say—just at this moment.

HELENA—Not for me.

STORM—[*Sulky.*] Well, anyway, a cat may look at a King——

HELENA—Oh no, a cat may only look at what it sees.

STORM—Helena Hucksteppe.

HELENA—Yes.

STORM—I'm—attracted—to you.

HELENA—A magnet does not attract shavings.

STORM—[*With positive conviction.*] I *could* hate you.

HELENA—I choose my enemies.

STORM—[*Without warning, seizing her.*] By God, at least I can kiss you! [*He kisses her full on the mouth—she makes no resistance.*]

HELENA—[*In a calm voice.*] And this, I suppose, is what you call the "great moment of human contact."

STORM—[*Dropping his arms—turning pale.*] What are you trying to do to me?

HELENA—I'm doing it.

STORM—[*To himself.*] Yet it was you that I wanted——

HELENA—Mongrels may not dig up buried treasure.

STORM—[*In a sudden rage.*] You can bury your past as deep as you like, but carrion will out!

HELENA—[*Softly.*] And this is love.

STORM—[*His head in his arms.*] Oh, God, God!

HELENA—And you who like the taste of new things, come to me?

STORM—[*In a lost voice.*] Shall I have no joy?

HELENA—Joy? Oh, yes, of a kind.

STORM—And you—are angry with me?

HELENA—In the study of science, is the scientist angry when the fly possesses no amusing phenomena?

STORM—I wanted—to know—you——

HELENA—I am conscious of your failure.

STORM—I wanted something—some sign——

HELENA—Must I, who have spent my whole life in being myself, go out of my way to change some look in you?

STORM—That's why you are so terrible, you have spent all your life on yourself.

HELENA—Yes, men do resent that in women.

STORM—Yes, I suppose so. [*Pause.*] I should have liked to talk of—myself——

HELENA—You see I could not listen.

STORM—You are—intolerant.

HELENA—No—occupied——

STORM—You are probably—playing a game.

HELENA—[*With a gracious smile.*] You will get some personal good out of it, won't you?

STORM—I'm uncomfortable——

HELENA—Uncomfortable!

STORM—[*Beginning to be really uncomfortable.*] Who *are* you?

HELENA—I am a woman, Gheid Storm, who is *not* in need.

STORM—You're horrible!

HELENA—Yes, that too.

STORM—But somewhere you're vulnerable.

HELENA—Perhaps.

STORM—Only I don't quite know the spot.

HELENA—Spot?

STORM—Something, somewhere, hidden——

HELENA—Hidden! [*She laughs.*] *All* of me is vulnerable.

STORM—[*Setting his teeth.*] You tempt me.

HELENA—[*Wearily.*] It's not that kind.

STORM—I've lain awake thinking of you—many nights.

HELENA—That is too bad.

STORM—What is too bad?

Helena—That you have had—fancies.

Storm—Why?

Helena—Theft of much, makes much to return——

Storm—The world allows a man his own thoughts.

Helena—Oh, no——

Storm—At least my thoughts are my own.

Helena—Not one, so far.

Storm—What does that mean?

Helena—You'll know when you try to think them again.

Storm—You mean I'm not making headway—well, you're right, I'm not——

Helena—Now tell me what brought you through the window.

Storm—[*Relieved.*] I'm glad you ask that, it's the first human thing that's happened this afternoon.

Helena—You have forgotten our great moment of human contact.

Storm—[*Nervously.*] Well——

Helena—You were about to tell me what brought you?

Storm—I don't know—something no one speaks of—some great ease in your back—the look of a great lover——

Helena—So—you scented a great lover——

Storm—I am a man—and I love——

Helena—What have you done for love, Gheid Storm?

Storm—I've—never gone to the dogs——

Helena—So?

Storm—I've always respected women.

Helena—In other words: taken the coals out of the fire with the poker—continue——

Storm—That's all.

Helena—And you dared to come to me! [*Her entire manner has changed.*]

Storm—No matter what you've been—done—I love you.

Helena—Do not come so near. Only those who have helped to make such death as mine may go a little way toward the ardours of that decay.

Storm—What have I done?

Helena—You have dared to bring to a woman, who has known love, the whinny of a pauper.

Storm—What am I?

Helena—[*Softly, to herself.*] How sensitively the handles cling to the vase, how delicate is the flesh between the fingers.

Storm—I—I don't know you.

Helena—[*Dropping her hands to her sides.*] Come here, Gheid Storm—[*Gheid approaches slowly, like a sleep walker.*] Put your hand on me. [*He does so as if in a dream.*] So! [*She looks first at his hand, then into his face, making it quite plain that he does not even know how to touch a woman.*] Yet you would be my lover, knowing not one touch that is mine, nor one word that is mine. My house is for men who have done their stumbling.

STORM—[*In an inaudible voice.*] I am going now——

HELENA—I cannot touch new things, nor see beginnings.

STORM—Helena! Helena!

HELENA—Do not call my name. There are too many names that must be called before mine.

STORM—Shall I die, and never have known you?

HELENA—Death, for you, will begin where my cradle started rocking——

STORM—Shall I have no love like yours?

HELENA—When I am an old woman, thinking of other things, you will, perhaps, be kissing a woman like me——

STORM—[*Moving blindly toward the door.*] Now I am going.

HELENA—[*In a quiet, level voice.*] The fall is almost here.

STORM—Yes, it's almost here.

HELENA—The leaves on the mountain road are turning yellow.

STORM—Yes, the leaves are turning.

HELENA—It's late, your son will be waiting dinner for you.

STORM—Don't take everything away.

HELENA—You will not even recall having seen me.

STORM—Can memory be taken too?

HELENA—Only that memory that goes past recollection may be kept.

STORM—[*At the door.*] Good night——

HELENA—[*Smiling.*] There is the window.

STORM—I could not lift my legs now.

HELENA—That's a memory you may keep.

STORM—Good night.

HELENA—Good-bye, Gheid Storm, and as you go down the hill, will you lock the gate, a dog thief passed in the night, taking my terrier with him.

STORM—The one with the brown spots?

HELENA—Yes.

STORM—That was a fine dog.

HELENA—Yes, she was a fine dog—restless.

STORM—They say any dog will follow any man who carries aniseed.

HELENA—Well, soon I return to the city.

STORM—You look tired.

HELENA—Yes, I am tired.

[*Gheid exits. Helena takes her old position, her back almost square to the audience.*]

CURTAIN

A Book. 44–58.

The Confessions of Helen Westley

"Hello, is this Miss Barnes?"

"Yes."

"This is Helen Westley."

"Ah, how do you do?"

"I want to be interviewed again."

"Very well; I shall meet you at three-thirty at the Brevoort."

I am there at three-thirty precisely. I order something "with a cherry in it" and await the appearance of the strange person of the Washington Square Players; and soon she appears, walking easily and wearing another of those adored, secondhand gowns; a secondhand book is under her arm, and she smiles, showing her thirty-two perfect teeth.

"Toute passe, mon ami," she murmurs as she takes the seat before me, shaking her earrings and thrusting the book upon the table. It is Murray's *History of Greek Literature,* and she knows it looks well.

"Dusty books," she begins, as she orders oatmeal (which of course can't be got at this hour), "are my one real passion. New books are like young girls—fit for nothing. A secondhand book is like a person who has traveled; it is only when a book has been handled by several persons and has become dirty that it's fit for contemplation. You feel that it has graduated, that it has something larger and more cosmopolitan about it—oh, well!" She began to laugh. "Ah, to be both young and beautiful! Now, I am beautiful and you are young; I can never be again what you are, and you in all probability will never be what I am, so after all I have the advantage of you—no oatmeal? How perfectly preposterous! Very well, bring me a highball.

"To continue: to be young, to be beautiful—how mournful, how sad, how ironical. When I was young I was full of dreams of love, of passion, of idealism, of green, green youth. People called me interesting, but they were a little afraid of me. It is simple enough: I was too eager, too full of curiosity, too vital—too unlovely. Now—," she stretched her thin, long hand out and finished, "—now I am terribly interesting, terribly original, very talented, beautiful, as I said, but—I am no longer a child. Now I have repose; now I can wait, now I can reflect; now I am capable of youth, but not capable of few years—that is the pitiful thing."

"Some advice for young actors would come in here very nicely."

"There isn't any advice. You might as well tell a child to be fifty years old when born. You can't advise, you can only tell of your own case—and anyway, if we are honest, our own case always interests us much more than the affairs of others.

"Well, I shall die as I was born—very thoughtful, full of ennui. That is the one great quality. Ah, Buddhism, China, Persia—races of ennui, not races of men. The history of the world has been one not of conquest, as supposed; it has been one of ennui. Why do we fall in love? Because we are filled with ennui. Why do we fall and break our limbs? Because of ennui. Why do we fall ill and remain unconscious for hours? Ennui, my dear. Ennui sends us to our death; ennui sends us to the battlefields; ennui sends us through the world, and ennui takes us out of it. If this were not so, do you suppose for a moment that we would permit ourselves to fall in love once we had heard of its effects? Do you presume to imagine that we would fight in battle, knowing well death awaited us, if it were not for ennui? The only mistake we make is not to submit to ennui. We struggle against the term, but not against the fact. The greatest people have been oppressed by it. To fall, my dear, is to submit to gravity, to let go, and all the so-called great events of history have been a series of falls. Napoleon climbed only because he understood the value of a great fall over a lesser fall; that's the real incentive to ambitions of all kinds. In five years I shall be a very famous and wonderful actress, in all probability. I know the value of a long fall; I am a super-ennuian, if I might coin a new word."

"A little faster with your youth, Helen."

"To me Boston is my youth. I went there to study oratory. I felt sure that recitations were my forte. Then I made my first appearance before a Brooklyn city club. I remember to this day the polite and frozen faces in the front rows and the general air of pity that permeated the whole place. I was in despair—and right in the middle of 'The brave house of Tarquin shall suffer wrongs no more,' I knew that I had made my first and last appearance before any audience of that kind under such ambitions. Then I was thinking, feeling. I married; I put my youth behind me at an early age because youth is the age when thinking and feeling have their largest hold, and I wanted to be doing."

"Advice here."

"Well, I should advise young, aspiring women to live their lives first, to get through with their emotional training soon, and to do their thinking and reading. Then, afterward, comes the time for calm, unemotional observation—a snake—"

"A little too early for the snake, I think."

"No; by all means, let the snake enter here. What is the fascination in contemplating a snake?"

"Well, what?"

"The snake—ergo—there you have it—you philosophize about life, you muddle with your paints, your tapestries and your incense. And so young America, as young France or young Germany did before it, dries up—that part of these countries that indulged in this alone, I mean to say. Oscar Wilde and a few minor poets and poseurs got away with it, but in the end the lesser artificials lose all their knack. Their deftness leaves them with nothing but facility, and felicity is gone forever. Now, go to the snake, a little more Baudelairean and Wildeish than anyone can be, and you find that the snake, after all, is life, is change, and in all its moods is a little more remarkable than such artists can ever be. I say, go to life, study life. Sit on a sidewalk and contemplate the sewer, the billposters, the street cleaners, the pedestrians, anything—but go there before you go to Chinatown to buy embroidery."

"Do you often sit on the sidewalk, Miss Westley?"

"I do. If doctors would prescribe sidewalks instead of pills and hot water, how much better off we should be."

"Really, you have a dirt complex, as Freud would say."

"Yes, a dirt complex. Isn't dirt really wonderful? That sounds like Hermione, but I mean it. She says those things because she is so neat and tidy and smug, and I say it because I am dingy and broad-minded and remarkable and subtle."

"Can you face real trouble?"

"Absolutely. Give me despair, and I am at my best. Give me sorrow, and only then are my shoulders worthy of me—at renouncing, for instance. Where have I learned this trick of the half-turned shoulder, the cold, drooping eyes? Through sorrows and difficulties. There's nothing like it for developing the figure and making one supple; it's better than dancing or swimming. Oh, yes, I can face all things."

"How do you take death?"

"My dear, place a corpse in front of me, and then—and then only—do I reach my divine height of splendid simplicity. I say, '*Toute passe*—did she die well?' If the answer is, 'No, she died very badly, and without hauteur and finesse,' I say, 'Permit me one moment, that I may disapprove of her.' If the answer is, 'Verily, she passed as calmly and as genteelly as a lady laying down her gloves,' I shall say with a gesture, 'Pass on; she has nothing further to learn.' "

"And joys, how do you react to them?"

"I laugh a little, looking around to see that no one else laughs a little better."

"You are a clever woman, Miss Westley."

"I am, but only within the past years—three or five—have I come to my real self. Apropos of that, poverty is a terrible thing."

"In what way?"

"It hangs before one's soul like a black curtain and behind one's body another equally black, throwing the one into obscurity and the other into relief. That is very bad for the formation of a personality."

"Then you suffered it?"

"Oh, yes, I did not grow under that. Not until I knew for certain where my next meal would come from could I give myself up to ignoring that next meal; I could think of other things."

"What do you think of the theatres of America?"

"I think that our greatest hope lies in the little theatre, though, of course, the regular theatre is improving. The little theatre does give a person a certain impetus, however. An unknown actor has a better chance, as has an unknown playwright, for the simple reason that in the little theatre movement an actor does not have to star and a playwright is only one of three or four other playwrights on a bill—making the risk of a failure nothing of great importance, as it is when the whole evening is given over to just the one performance."

"I see."

"And then there is my future—you want to hear about that, don't you?"

"Yes, I think I know what is in the future for you."

"Do you really?" Here Helen Westley turned her strange eyes on me.

"Oh yes. You say you were born in Brooklyn—good, you will return to Brooklyn."

"Do you consider that my future? How horrible!"

"Not so fast. Brooklyn is only the beginning of your future; I am positively certain that you will take to wearing shawls and comforting yourself with hot water bottles."

"More horrible and more horrible!"

"Exactly, but that is not all—in the end you will return to that same thing that you had your beginning in—religion. Am I right?"

"Yes, you are right. But it will not be the usual religion; it will be something oriental and mystic."

"Probably one has to suit one's religions to one's complexion, and yours is oriental."

"Thank you, you are probably right again. Yes, religion, but it will be something Chinese—perhaps Buddhism—or any religion that has the occult turn to it. Religion is the only practical end for me."

"You see, I knew it."

"You have your moments."

"Thank you. What started you originally on this stage career—I mean after you had married and were beginning to bring up a family?"

"I don't know. Probably it was the easiest thing for me to do. I had acted, so I returned to acting. Perhaps this is not the great thing I was cut out for; the next five years will tell."

"What else have you in mind?"

"Well, I am taking up the study of English. I may be a great writer like the Russians, or perhaps an artist or a thinker—you never can tell. I took out a book on mental derangements from the library, but everyone in it seemed so natural that I gave it up. I believe too heartily in the vanity of all things to take up such a thought permanently—but it serves to pass the time, and it gives one a cultivated sensation while going through with it. Then I have other habits—chocolate almonds for instance—and you have probably noticed my oatmeal passion."

"Yes, I noticed that long ago when someone pointed to you and hissed, 'Vampire'—I thought it very funny."

"It isn't funny at all, that's where you young people make a mistake. You think vampires have to smoke cigarettes and drink absinthe and live on larks' tongues, whereas vampirism thrives on oatmeal. I wouldn't be a bit surprised but that it has its very roots in oatmeal and wheats and such nourishing things; after all, one has to be pretty vital to vampire one's life to a close. You can't do it on nothing."

"That was merely a trap—then you do consider yourself a vampire?"

"What do you call a vampire?"

"Anyone who can break a habit easier than acquire one."

"Then I am indeed a vampire."

"Very well, multiplication always adds up to a vampire anyway."

"Really, Djuna, you are sort of clever, aren't you?"

"I am only a little less conceited than you yourself, Helen."

She burst out laughing. "We are a funny couple to be sitting here talking a lot of nonsense, aren't we?"

"We are."

"Well, let's stop it."

"We can't, not yet; I have at least three pages more to fill."

"Have you been making notes?"

"I don't have to. My memory always makes a paragraph out of a note automatically."

"What shall we talk about now?"

"Anything you like."

"Suppose you describe me, and finish the article in that way."

"You would love that, wouldn't you?"

"Yes, but you have done it already two or three times, so I suppose I can't expect it again. Waiter, the check please."

"I often wonder if you are contented."

"There you go. That's the trouble with you all. What is contentment, what is happiness? I admit the existence of nothing excepting ennui, and that only gets us back to the beginning of our story."

"Contemplation and that sort of thing?"

"That's just it—let the world go by and watch it going, that's all. We take it too seriously. After it is all over and the procession has passed, there remains just exactly what remains after a carnival: a little more dust, a broken bottle or two, and some colored confetti. Is it for that you worry until your hair is gray and you lie down in death? Oh, how vain, how vain."

"Yet I have heard you crying out because you had lost a handkerchief."

"Because I wished to wave adieu to the procession with it, that's all."

"And have you now come to the end of all you have to say? Think well, for I shall never again write you up for any paper in the world—this is your last chance."

A look akin to horror crept into Helen Westley's eyes.

"You don't mean that?"

"I do."

She remained silent for a moment only, then smiling amiably she said: "Impossible! You will run out of material sooner or later—then enter Helen again." She leaned back comfortably, crossing her feet—terrible zebra spat upon zebra spat.

Sitting thus she contemplated herself for a while silently in the mirror.

"Do you know," she said suddenly, "I am really the original for *The Sphinx.* Am I not like some rare exotic marble, for ages standing in an ancient, desolate mood, overlooking some fathomless desert?"

"Perhaps, yes, if you don't let your eyes wander down until they rest upon those horrible spats."

"Don't you like them? I got them for thirty cents on Second Avenue—by the way, that gives me a lead on a little further advice. More people should dress from the secondhand clothiers than do; you can have the wardrobe of a lady for the pittance of a waitress."

"My dear Helen, you are the only woman in the world who can wear them and still be asked out. You are Time clothed in Age."

"Yet I am really a young woman."

"That is your big mistake: you are ten thousand years old and make an idiot of yourself by being thirty-odd. For you to be thirty-odd is an impertinence—and a slander. You probably knew Columbus when he was contemplating the great discovery, and doubtless you gave him some valuable information as to location and worth of the said country."

"Yes," she said slowly, "I am really wonderful."

"When you laugh you are like a Mephistophelian lizard—very uncanny."

"Like a cloak model—very exclusive." She laughed again, drawing on impossible large and yellow gloves.

"I have only one complaint to make," she finished, reaching for an old worn umbrella. "That is this: the theatrical profession for one of my facial attainments is hardly all it should be in the way of accessibility. I am too far away from the public, they can't appreciate my full value. Every line, every muscle of my countenance is worthy of study. Yes, I shall have to take up something confidential with the public, that as they lean forward to say, 'Would you really advise this or that?' they will become acquainted with the peculiar worth of my extraordinary and individual features. Adieu."

Stepping easily out into the avenue, she hailed a passing carriage and seating herself, leaned back, gazing with pale strange eyes into the descending dusk.

New York Morning Telegraph Sunday Magazine, 23 September 1917:5.

2
Willa Cather (1873–1947)

Introduced and Edited by Jane Lilienfeld

Willa Cather was born in Back Creek, Virginia, in 1873 and died in New York City on April 24, 1947. At age nine she traveled with her family across country, first by train, then the last sixteen miles by open wagon to settle at her grandfather's homestead on that section of the Nebraska plains called the Great Divide. Eighteen months later the family moved to the small town of Red Cloud, Nebraska, where Willa Cather grew up, helping to raise her six younger brothers and sisters, relying on her Grandmother Boak, admiring her father, and keeping her distance from her mother. As a teenager Cather shocked the Red Cloud townspeople by her absolute self-possession, the conviction of her genius, and her flamboyant cross-dressing. But at the University of Nebraska in Lincoln Cather's professors recognized her as a literary prodigy. She had expected to major in the premedical course, but after one professor had her essay on Carlyle published unbeknown to her, she changed her major to English. At the university she also met congenial women friends, including Louise Pound, later to become a respected scholar and the first woman president of the Modern Language Association. By her junior year Cather was earning her way as a theatre critic for several Nebraska newspapers. Her standards were so high that traveling troupes of players feared her reviews.

After graduation in 1895 Cather settled in Pittsburgh to become editor of the *Home Monthly* and to continue her own writing in what free time she had. In Pittsburgh in 1899, while backstage at the theatre, Willa Cather met Isabelle McClung, beautiful and imperious patron of the arts, daughter of a wealthy and influential judge. After struggling with her father over the impropriety, Isabelle won the right to have Willa Cather move into the McClung household to share a suite of rooms with Isabelle. Safe in the luxury of a wealthy family setting, encouraged by Isabelle, Cather taught high-school English and Latin and on weekends and holidays continued her own professional writing. Her work brought her to the notice of S. S. McClure, then a leading American magazine publisher, who at first published her work in his famous magazine *McClure's* and then hired her as its editor in 1906. Her career was launched. She moved to New York to take the job, still frequently visiting Isabelle McClung. Between 1912 and 1940 Willa Cather published thirteen novels and three collections of short stories and some poems. Her work enjoyed both critical and popular success, and in 1923 she won the Pulitzer Prize for her novel of World War I, *One of Ours.*

In spite of her obvious disinclination for the female role, Cather was politically conservative. The conservative values espoused in her essay "The Novel Démeublé," anthologized here, animated her friendships. Cather was indeed fortunate that she did not need to mix friendship with collegiality, fortunate that she did not have to circulate her manuscripts for contemporaries to edit in order to get ahead, lucky that she did not have to use contacts to get her work published. She spurned literary gossip and keeping up with the latest trend—the use of others for professional gain (Sergeant 130–131, 194–195, 199–201). Although she knew many contemporary writers (she met and liked D. H. and Frieda Lawrence in 1924, for example), musicians, and actors, she selected her friends not for their art but for other, less material qualities—their integrity, passionate devotion to ideals larger than self, joy in risk-taking, and loyalty to families and communities.

Willa Cather's earliest literary mentor was as homely and old-fashioned as the values that underlay Cather's life, yet as pure a stylist as Flaubert. Cather met Sarah Orne Jewett in 1906 while in Boston on assignment for *McClure's.* Jewett believed in Cather, reminded her often that her gift was being diffused by her journalism at *McClure's,* urged her to write of her own experience, that closest to the bone. In later years, those writers closest to Cather were not other modernists but women such as Dorothy Canfield Fisher and Elizabeth Sheply Sergeant. Musicians were always an inspiration, and Cather's friendship with Olive Fremstad, the Wagnerian diva of the Metropolitan Opera, inspired her novel *The Song of the Lark.* Through her editor and friend Alfred Knopf, Cather met the young Menuhin prodigies, and Yehudi wrote movingly in his autobiography of what Cather meant to him and his sisters in their youth in New York City.

But the greatest friends of Cather's life remained those people she had loved as a girl. Her loyalty to the Miner family—prototypes of the Harlings in *My Antonia*—was a bedrock of sanity for her as she became more and more famous. She regularly traveled back to Red Cloud to visit her friends there and saw the friends of her youth as often as she saw her brothers Roscoe and Douglass, whom she adored. To these Red Cloud friends she confided that which she could bring herself to confide. In hard times for the farmers of her community, she sent gifts of food and money, and more than once she paid off the arrears on mortgages to save their family farms.

Her friendship with Isabelle McClung continued past what Cather experienced as Isabelle's betrayal of her by marriage. After her move to New York, Cather befriended and later shared an apartment with Edith Lewis, a *McClure's* editor. Lewis never supplanted McClung in Cather's emotional life, but their companionship lasted until Cather's death in 1947. Cather's friendships grew out of the deepest parts of her, those secret places from which she wrote and which few who had not known her before her fame were ever permitted to share.

As a little girl growing up in a large family in a small town, Cather invented a mental construct of a Europe to which she could escape from her cramped home and the burdensome conventionality of Red Cloud. In her first eighteen months on the Nebraska plains she was drawn to the Scandinavian immigrant mothers and grandmothers in their kitchens, to which she would go for hours, tasting their delicacies, drinking in their stories "in the most unreasonable state of excitement; I always felt . . . as if I had actually got inside another person's skin. . . . these old women on the farms were the first people who ever gave me the real feeling of an older world across the sea" (Woodress 1978, 38–39). Around the corner from the Cather house lived Mr. and Mrs. Charles Wiener, cultured and well-off Europeans who deepened Willa's dreams of German and French civilization. The luxury of the Wieners' furniture, rugs, leather-bound world classics, gleaming piano, and framed reproductions of museum masterpieces symbolized for the young girl the life of great art in Europe. (Cather's feelings at the Wieners' home and the contribution they made to her sense of her own destiny are fictionalized in the story "Old Mrs. Harris.") Best known for her glorification of traditional American values, Cather many times longed to be a European. Between 1902 and 1930 she visited Europe seven times in company with close women friends, living for several months at a time in Britain, Paris, the south of France, and Italy. Her appreciation of the life of the European countryside—the simplicity, the beauty and dignity of hard manual labor, the magnificence of the food, the quality of light—entered her books obliquely in such works as *Shadows on the Rock*,[1] the story "Neighbor Rosicky," and her last, unfinished novel set in Avignon.

Her trips to Europe confirmed her deepest early beliefs, but her three trips to Arizona, New Mexico, and the newly opened Mesa Verde National Park changed her life. The matriarchal religion of the Native Americans who established the pueblo communities there in the thirteenth century, the harshness and enormity of the landscape and sky, marked her deeply and found literary equivalents in books as diverse as *Death Comes for the Archbishop, The*

Song of the Lark (in which the heroine's operatic voice is shown evolving out of the pueblos and canyons) and "Tom Outland's Story" in *The Professor's House.*

After her father's death and that of Isabelle McClung, Cather paid for her mother's care in a nursing home in California. Traveling frequently from East Coast to West Coast by train to visit her mother, Willa was overwhelmed sometimes still, as she had been as a girl of nine in the open wagon crossing the plains, by the prairie's vastness and her own littleness (Sergeant 79). In her later years Cather returned to a countryside similar to that beloved by her first mentor, Sarah Orne Jewett. She and Edith Lewis bought property in Jaffrey, New Hampshire, where they spent their summers and where Cather is buried.

Willa Cather's novels champion the warrior hero, noble mother-women, the values of hard work, thrift, self-sacrifice, and the American family. A less likely modernist would be hard to find. And yet Willa Cather was a master of disguise. When she was in high school in Red Cloud, she cleared and wallpapered the closet in the attic bedroom shared by her brothers. She furnished the tiny space with a bed, a chair, and an elegant glass-shelved, glass-enclosed dresser. Thus she had at eye level several conch shells, whose outer spikes and curled overlip cradled creamy-pink lush insides.[2] These prongs and their inner succulence together form a metaphor for Cather's craft—a facade of defended beauty that shielded hurt, desire, rage, and a need to hide.

Such prickly defenses are evident in Cather's essay "The Novel Démeublé," published in 1936 in the *New Republic.* This essay has clear connections to Virginia Woolf's "Modern Fiction," "The Russian Point of View," and "The Novels of Turgenev."[3] While Woolf insists that genre and form may be wrenched to fit the extremes of post–World War I consciousness, "The Novel Démeublé" appears to turn its back on what is now called early male modernism—fiction that is experimental, audience-challenging, language-focused rather than story or character-focused. Male modernism, however, gained its permission from the same sources Cather used for the self-validation evidently infusing "The Novel Démeublé." That is the fin-de-siècle deification of the male artist, whose rage at society elevated him above the ordinary and whose superior aesthetics freed him from moral restraint. Although as a young woman Cather claimed to abhor the aesthetic movement and decadence (Cather, *The Kingdom of Art* 388–393), she believed in the primacy, the religion, of art and its ruthless emotional imperatives as fervently as Verlaine or Wilde or Joyce (Cather, *The Kingdom of Art* 349, 393–397; Woodress 1987, 74–75, 93; Sergeant 20; Vierneisel 49–53). Male modernism's obsessive centering on language rather than persons harkened back to Flaubert just as much as did Cather's insistence on impeccable prose and laconic use of detail (Sergeant 10). But the centrality of traditional fictional forms—supple prose that deliberately calls no attention to itself, an omniscient author, and seemingly realistic characters and narratives—are in Cather's work as much disguises as are the wrenched syntax and Homeric epic parallels in James Joyce's work. The desire for fame and honor to be obtained through her writing burned in Cather certainly as much as they did in Pound, Eliot, and Joyce,[4] but Cather knew better than to despise money and her audience. To make an abundant living from an American reader's market while expressing the author's deepest childhood secrets, her rages, and her adult sexuality required subtle subterfuge. Under the furniture covers of the missing sofas and chairs of "The Novel Démeublé" is a clear implication about Cather's choice of disguise, argues Sharon O'Brien (126–127). Extending her argument further, I suggest that, for Cather, seemingly traditional realism became a method to render the safely obvious devious and obscure.

To suggest that Cather crafted disguise from traditional forms to achieve the same ends as other women-identified modernist writers did by eschewing those forms, it is useful to consider *Sapphira and the Slave Girl* (an excerpt, "Nancy's Return," is reprinted below). This work was published in 1940, two years after the death of Isabelle McClung Hambourg, "the one great romance of her life" (Woodress 1970, 86; Vierneisel),[5] had reopened the wounds caused by the loss of mother, father, and brother Douglass. Recent discussion of female modernism has centered on the origin of art for women writers, specifically the right of the female author to celebrate and to acknowledge that her body and voice are connected to her mother's sexuality and the processes of mother–daughter intermingling that Joan Lidoff, among others, has termed "fluid boundaries" (Lidoff, Gilligan, Dinnerstein, Chodorow, Hirsh).

"Self consciousness was a mistake—the writer should be just an eye and an ear," Sergeant recalls Cather saying, reporting that later Cather wished she had kept herself or any image of herself out of *Sapphira and the Slave Girl* (Sergeant 203, 270). Unlike any other Cather novel, this one shows male modernist self-reference, for *Sapphira and the Slave Girl* locates the scene of writing as the fictionalized mother's bed, a place from which the novel fictionalizes the origins of fiction. From that bed the little girl–fictionalized author witnessed a scene of biblical grandeur, the reconciliation of two former slaves, a mother and daughter separated for twenty-five years. The slave mother had sided with the girl's great-grandmother Sapphira, the slave owner; the slave daughter had been stolen by the girl's grandmother Rachel and with her help had escaped to Canada and freedom. The little girl's mother had arranged the reconciliation to occur where her daughter could see it, as if the women were family slaves still.

On the surface, *Sapphira and the Slave Girl* accepts a convention common to Caucasian women's writing since before the eighteenth century: slavery is a metaphor for the condition of women (Ferguson xi–xii). To a woman of color, the equation is alarmingly racist, and certainly Cather's novel is no *Beloved* by Toni Morrison. But to give the metaphor the power that Cather did, slavery entitled one person to own another person and, among other things, guaranteed the slave owner legal access to sexual use of the slave. In Britain until 1882 wives and children were the legal property of husbands along with his goods and land; there was no legal category for marital rape. It is possible that racial issues stand in *Sapphira and the Slave Girl* for violence between women and that the novel disguises cruelty between women as race relations between slave and owner. Tantalizingly, the ostensible plot offers clues to the hidden plot; that is, the furniture of the hidden plot is covered, but retains solidity even under wraps.

Slavery bisects all female relations in *Sapphira and the Slave Girl,* whose ostensible plot juxtaposes two sets of "free" mothers and daughters with two sets of enslaved mothers and daughters. Cather knew Colette's work (Cather, Letter to Carrie Miner Sherwood) and it is interesting to speculate whether she had read *The Pure and the Impure,* a subplot of which explores the love between Natalie Barney and Renée Vivien as a master–slave relation. *Sapphira and the Slave Girl* deliberately encodes conflict between mothers and daughters not only as class and racial conflict but also as a suggested self-hatred for being trapped in a woman's body, a woman's life, fictionalized by making Sapphira a cripple confined to a wheeled chair.[6] The rage in the novel, which surfaces as heterosexual jealousy and a drive for revenge because Sapphira suspects that her husband desires Nancy, the slave girl of the title, is a brilliant expression of the unacceptable. Those whom Sapphira cannot own emotionally or physically she despises and seeks to break, be they daughter or slave. Ruthlessly honest, the portrayal of Sapphira Colbert shows her as formidable, an emotional and physical danger to those around her, in some ways even less sympathetic than Cather's earlier anti-heroines in *A Lost Lady* and *My Mortal Enemy* (Sergeant 267–270).

It took great audacity to write Sapphira Colbert, a cruel woman who enjoys her cruelty and its power. Sapphira's husband does her bidding; Sapphira has had her daughter Rachel ostracized from her family and the small community Sapphira heads because Rachel aided Nancy. As for Nancy, Sapphira unsuccessfully used every means at her disposal to ensure that her nephew Martin Colbert would have easy access to the rape of Nancy. The figure of Sapphira is a fabricated one, but to flesh her out, it is probable that Cather had to investigate the emotional power of highly complicated and ambivalent responses stirred in her by her reactions to aspects of her relations to her mother and to Isabelle McClung Hambourg, whose deaths had rendered such courageous divination a possibility (Lilienfeld 161–164). Because of its artistry, the novel makes glaringly inescapable to the whites the violence, degradation, and distortion of their practice of enslaving people of color, showing that this practice was entirely harmful to those enslaved and that rebellion was a reality. It is also clear that such abused power may stand for a knowledge that love might contain in it a rage for physical ownership and mastery—thwarted. That is the nature of fiction: to make visible the pain of love's complexity and to plumb readers' souls because an author was courageous enough to transform loss and rage and hurt into an artifact.

In *Sapphira and the Slave Girl* dominance is seen as a form of love, but so is the rebellion against the mother–slave owner which briefly unites women across class and race lines. The implications of a suppressed and lyrical violence suggest an underlying structure whereby Cather can craft her own female modernism which encodes women's complicated economic, social, and sexual relations by subverting that most traditional of genres, seemingly realistic American regional fiction.

NOTES

1. Set in Quebec, but recreating a distinctly European culture.

2. I saw these conch shells on a trip to Red Cloud in March 1979. I understand that according to one of Cather's sisters, family tradition has it that the shells appeared when Willa was in high school.

3. Cather was familiar with Woolf's work (Cather, Letter to Carrie Miner Sherwood; Vierneisel 50). I thank Karen Vierneisel for her generosity in making her dissertation and her extensive knowledge of Cather available to me.

4. Jim Burden in *My Antonia* is widely believed to be voicing Cather's ambition. He quotes Vergil's impetus for his art: "for I shall be the first, if I live, to bring the Muse into my country" (264). This is, after all, the novel's commentary on its own method as surely as Joyce's self-conscious commentary is in *Ulysses* or *Finnegans Wake.* It took tremendous courage and self-belief to state such an ambition for a book by an American female author in 1918.

5. Woodress, in his 1978 updated biography of Cather, says, "I have changed many of my opinions. . . ." (xvi) He no longer believes that Cather and McClung were physically involved. He does say, however, that McClung was still the emotional center of Cather's adult life and that "the friendship that began that day grew into a great love that lasted a lifetime." This is slightly different from calling the relationship "the one great romance of her life." Sharon O'Brien, Adrienne Rich, Paula Bennett, and many other scholars, on examining the letters, novels, and circumstances of Cather's life, have drawn conclusions different from Woodress's in his second edition, concurring with his earlier interpretation that this was, in fact, a passionate romance.

6. Illness aroused Cather's self-contempt; see, for example, Woodress 1987, 258. O'Brien (for example, 111) sees this theme of hatred for the female body, the female role, as continuous in Cather's work.

WORKS CITED

Bennett, Mildred. *The World of Willa Cather.* Lincoln: U of Nebraska P, 1961.

Cather, Willa. *Kingdom of Art: Willa Cather's First Principles and Critical Statements, 1893–1896.* Ed. Bernice Slote. Lincoln: U of Nebraska P, 1966.

———. Letter to Carrie Miner Sherwood, 28 June 1939, Willa Cather Pioneer Memorial Library, Red Cloud, Neb.

———. 1918. *My Antonia.* Boston: Houghton Mifflin, 1954.

———. *Not under Forty.* 1936. New York: Knopf, 1970.

———. *Sapphira and the Slave Girl.* New York: Knopf, 1940.

Chodorow, Nancy. *The Reproduction of Mothering: Psychoanalysis and the Sociology of Gender.* Berkeley: U of California P, 1978.

Dinnerstein, Dorothy. *The Mermaid and the Minotaur: Sexual Arrangements and Human Malaise.* New York: Harper and Row, 1976.

Ferguson, Moira, ed. *First Feminists: British Women Writers, 1578–1799*. Bloomington: Indiana UP, 1985.
Flax, Jane. "The Conflict between Nurturance and Autonomy in Mother/Daughter Relations and within Feminism." *Feminist Studies* June 1978:171–191.
Gilligan, Carol. *In a Different Voice: Psychological Theory and Women's Development*. Cambridge: Harvard UP, 1982.
Hirsch, Marianne. *The Mother/Daughter Plot: Narrative, Psychoanalysis, Feminism*. Bloomington: Indiana UP, 1989.
Lidoff, Joan. *Fluid Boundaries: The Origin of a Distinctive Female Voice*. In progress.
Lilienfeld, Jane. "Reentering Paradise: Cather, Colette, Woolf and Their Mothers." In *The Lost Tradition: Mothers and Daughters in Literature*, ed. Cathy Davidson and E. M. Broner, 160–175. New York: Ungar, 1980.
O'Brien, Sharon. *Willa Cather: The Emerging Voice*. New York: Fawcett Columbine, 1987.
Sergeant, Elizabeth. *Willa Cather: A Memoir*. Lincoln: U of Nebraska P, 1953, 1963.
Vierneisel, Karen "Fugitive Matriarchy: Willa Cather's Life and Art." Ph.D. diss., U of Chicago, 1978.
Woodress, James. *Willa Cather: Her Life and Art*. Lincoln: U of Nebraska P, 1970, 1978.
Woolf, Virginia. "Modern Fiction." *The Captain's Death Bed and Other Essays*, 53–61. New York: Harcourt, Brace and World, 1950.
———. "The Novels of Turgenev." *The Common Reader: First Series*. 1925. New York: Harcourt, Brace and World, 1953, 150–158.
———. "The Russian Point of View." *The Common Reader: First Series*. 177–187.

The Novel Démeublé

The novel, for a long while, has been over-furnished. The property-man has been so busy on its pages, the importance of material objects and their vivid presentation have been so stressed, that we take it for granted whoever can observe, and can write the English language, can write a novel. Often the latter qualification is considered unnecessary.

In any discussion of the novel, one must make it clear whether one is talking about the novel as a form of amusement, or as a form of art; since they serve very different purposes and in very different ways. One does not wish the egg one eats for breakfast, or the morning paper, to be made of the stuff of immortality. The novel manufactured to entertain great multitudes of people must be considered exactly like a cheap soap or a cheap perfume, or cheap furniture. Fine quality is a distinct disadvantage in articles made for great numbers of people who do not want quality but quantity, who do not want a thing that "wears," but who want change,—a succession of new things that are quickly thread-bare and can be lightly thrown away. Does anyone pretend that if the Woolworth store windows were piled high with Tanagra figurines at ten cents, they could for a moment compete with Kewpie brides in the popular esteem? Amusement is one thing; enjoyment of art is another.

Every writer who is an artist knows that his "power of observation," and his "power of description," form but a low part of his equipment. He must have both, to be sure; but he knows that the most trivial of writers often have a very good observation. Mérimée said in his remarkable essay on Gogol: "L'art de choisir parmi les innombrable traits que nous offre la nature est, après tout, bien plus difficile que celui de les observer avec attention et de les rendre avec exactitude."

There is a popular superstition that "realism" asserts itself in the cataloguing of a great number of material objects, in explaining mechanical processes, the methods of operating manufactories and trades, and in minutely and unsparingly describing physical sensations. But is not realism, more than it is anything else, an attitude of mind on the part of the writer toward his material, a vague indication of the sympathy and candour with which he accepts, rather than chooses, his theme? Is the story of a banker who is unfaithful to his wife and who ruins himself by speculation in trying to gratify the caprices of his mistresses, at all reinforced by a masterly exposition of banking, our whole system of credits, the methods of the Stock Exchange? Of course, if the story is thin, these things do reinforce it in a sense,—any amount of red meat thrown into the scale to make the beam dip. But are the banking system and the Stock Exchange worth being written about at all? Have such things any proper place in imaginative art?

The automatic reply to this question is the name of Balzac. Yes, certainly, Balzac tried out the value of literalness in the novel, tried it out to the uttermost, as Wagner did the value of scenic literalness in the music drama. He tried it, too, with the passion of discovery, with the inflamed zest of an unexampled curiosity. If the heat of that furnace could not give hardness and sharpness to material accessories, no other brain will ever do it. To reproduce on paper the actual city of Paris; the houses, the upholstery, the food, the wines, the game of pleasure, the game of business, the game of finance: a stupendous ambition—but, after all, unworthy of an artist. In exactly so far as he succeeded in pouring out on his pages that mass of brick and mortar and furniture and proceedings in bankruptcy, in exactly so far he defeated his end. The things by which he still lives, the types of greed and avarice and ambition and vanity and lost innocence of heart which he created—are as vital today as they were then. But their material surroundings, upon which he expended such labour and pains . . . the eye glides over them. We have had too much of the interior decorator and the "romance of business" since his day. The city he built on paper is already crumbling. Stevenson said he wanted to blue-pencil a great deal of Balzac's "presentation"—and he loved him beyond all modern novelists. But where is the man who could cut one sentence from the stories of Mérimée? And who wants any more detail as to how Carmencita and her fellow factory-girls made cigars? Another sort of novel? Truly. Isn't it a better sort?

In this discussion another great name naturally occurs. Tolstoi was almost as great a lover of material things as Balzac, almost as much interested in the way dishes were cooked, and people were dressed, and houses were furnished. But there is this determining difference: the clothes, the dishes, the haunting interiors of those old Moscow houses, are always so much a part of the emotions of the people that they are perfectly synthesized; they seem to exist, not so much in the author's mind, as in the emotional penumbra of the characters themselves. When it is fused like this, literalness ceases to be literalness—it is merely part of the experience.

If the novel is a form of imaginative art, it cannot be at the same time a vivid and brilliant form of journalism. Out of the teeming, gleaming stream of the present it must select the eternal material of art. There are hopeful signs that some of the younger writers are trying to break away from mere verisimilitude, and, following the development of modern painting, to interpret imaginatively the material and social investiture of their characters; to present their scene by suggestion rather than by enumeration. The higher processes of art are all processes of simplification. The novelist must learn to write, and then he must unlearn it; just as the modern painter learns to draw, and then learns when utterly to disregard his accomplishment, when to subordinate it to a higher and truer effect. In this direction only, it seems to me, can the novel develop into anything more varied and perfect than all the many novels that have gone before.

One of the very earliest American romances might well serve as a suggestion to later writers. In *The Scarlet Letter* how truly in the spirit of art is the mise-en-scène presented. That drudge, the theme-writing high-school student, could scarcely be sent there for information regarding the manners and dress and interiors of Puritan society. The material investiture of the story is presented as if unconsciously; by the reserved, fastidious hand of an artist, not by the gaudy fingers of a showman or the mechanical industry of a department-store window-dresser. As I remember it, in the twilight melancholy of that book, in its consistent mood, one can scarcely ever see the actual surroundings of the people; one feels them, rather, in the dusk.

Whatever is felt upon the page without being specifically named there—that, one might say, is created. It is the inexplicable presence of the thing not named, of the overtone divined by the ear but not heard by it, the verbal mood, the emotional aura of the fact or the thing or the deed, that gives high quality to the novel or the drama, as well as to poetry itself.

Literalness, when applied to the presenting of mental reactions and of physical sensations, seems to be no more effective than when it is applied to material things. A novel crowded with physical sensations is no less a catalogue than one crowded with furniture. A book like *The Rainbow* by D. H. Lawrence sharply reminds one how vast a distance lies between emotion and mere sensory reactions. Characters can be almost dehumanized by a laboratory study of the behaviour of their bodily organs under sensory stimuli—can be reduced, indeed, to mere animal pulp. Can one imagine anything more terrible than the story of *Romeo and Juliet* rewritten in prose by D. H. Lawrence?

How wonderful it would be if we could throw all the furniture out of the window; and along with it, all the meaningless reiterations concerning physical sensations, all the tiresome old patterns, and leave the room as bare as the stage of a Greek theatre, or as that house into which the glory of Pentecost descended; leave the scene bare for the play of emotions, great and little—for the nursery tale, no less than the tragedy, is killed by tasteless amplitude. The Elder Dumas enunciated a great principle when he said that to make a drama, a man needed one passion, and four walls.

Not Under Forty. New York: Knopf, 1970. 43–51.

Nancy's Return (From *Sapphira and the Slave Girl*)

It was a brilliant, windy March day; all the bare hills were still pale fawn colour, and high above them puffy white clouds went racing like lambs let out to pasture in the spring. I was something over five years old, and was kept in bed on that memorable day because I had a cold. I was in my mother's bedroom, in the third storey of a big old brick house entered by a white portico with fluted columns. Propped on high pillows, I could see the clouds drive across the bright, cold blue sky, throwing rapid shadows on the steep hillsides. The slats of the green window shutters rattled, the limp cordage of the great willow trees in the yard was whipped and tossed furiously by the wind. It was the last day I would have chosen to stay indoors.

I had been put into my mother's bed so that I could watch the turnpike, then a macadam road with a blue limestone facing. It ran very near us, between the little creek at the foot of our long front yard and the base of the high hills which shut the winter sun from us early.

It was a weary wait for the stage that morning. Usually we could hear the rattle of the iron-tired wheels and the click of the four shod horses before they came round the curve where the flint mile-stone with deep-cut letters said: ROMNEY—35 MILES. But today there was a high wind from the west. Maybe we could not hear the stage coming, Mrs. Blake remarked to Aunt Till.

For I was not alone in the room. Two others were there to keep me company. Mrs. Blake sat with her hands lying at rest in her lap. She looked almost as if she were in church. Aunt Till was sitting beside her; a spare, neat little old darky, bent at the shoulders but still holding herself straight from the hips. The two conversed very little; they were waiting and watching, just as I was. Occasionally my mother came in, going with her quick, energetic step to the window and peering out. She was young, and she had not the patience of the two old women.

"Don't get excited," she would say to me. "It may be a long while before the stage comes."

Even my father was awaiting the stage. He had not gone out to cut timber with the men today, but had sent them into the woods with Moses, son of the Colberts' old Taylor, as the boss. Father was down in his basement tool-room under the portico steps, tinkering at something. Probably he was making yellow leather shoes for the front paws of his favourite shepherd dog—she wore out so many, racing up and down the stony hillsides in performing her duties.

There was as much restlessness inside the house as there was outside in the wind and clouds and trees, for today Nancy was coming home from Montreal, and she would ride out from Winchester on the stage. She had been gone now for twenty-five years.

Ever since I could remember anything, I had heard about Nancy. My mother used to sing me to sleep with:

Down by de cane-brake, close by de mill,
Dar lived a yaller gal, her name was Nancy Till.

I never doubted the song was made about our Nancy. I knew she had long been housekeeper for a rich family away up in Canada, where it was so cold, Till said, if you threw a tin-cupful of water into the air, it came down ice. Nancy sometimes wrote to her mother, and always sent her fifty dollars at Christmas.

Suddenly my mother hurried into the room. Without a word she wrapped me in a blanket, carried me to the curved lounge by the window, and put me down on the high head-rest, where I could look out. There it came, the stage, with a trunk on top, and the sixteen hoofs trotting briskly round the curve where the milestone was.

Mrs. Blake and Aunt Till had followed my mother and now stood behind us. We saw my father running down the front yard. The stage stopped at the rustic bridge which crossed our little creek. The steps at the back were let down, my father reached up to hand someone out. A woman in a long black coat and black turban alighted. She carried a hand-satchel; her trunk was to go to Till's cabin on the old mill place. They crossed the bridge and came up the brick walk between the boxwood hedges. Then I was put back into bed, and Mrs. Blake and Till returned to their chairs. The actual scene of the meeting had been arranged for my benefit. When I cried because I was not allowed to go downstairs and see Nancy enter the house, Aunt Till had said: "Never mind, honey. You stay right here, and I'll stay right here. Nancy'll come up, and you'll see her as soon as I do." Mrs. Blake stayed with us. My mother went down to give Nancy the hand of welcome.

I heard them talking on the stairs and in the hall; my parents' voices excited and cordial, and another voice, low and pleasant, but not exactly "hearty," it seemed to me,—not enough so for the occasion.

Till had already risen; when the stranger followed my mother into the room, she took a few uncertain steps forward. She fell meekly into the arms of a tall, gold-skinned woman, who drew the little old darky to her breast and held her there, bending her face down over the head scantily covered with grey wool.

Neither spoke a word. There was something Scriptural in that meeting, like the pictures in our old Bible.

After those few moments of tender silence, the visitor released Aunt Till with a gentle stroke over her bent shoulders, and turned to Mrs. Blake. Tears were shining in the deep creases on either side of Mrs. Blake's nose. "Well, Nancy, child, you've made us right proud of you," she said. Then, for the first time, I saw Nancy's lovely smile. "I never forget who it was took me across the river that night, Mrs. Blake."

When Nancy laid aside her long black coat, I saw with astonishment that it was lined with grey fur, from top to toe! We had no coats like that on Back Creek. She took off her turban and brushed back a strand of her shiny, blue-black hair. She wore a black silk dress. A gold watch-chain was looped about her neck and came down to her belt, where the watch was tucked away in a little pocket.

"Now we must sit down and talk," said my mother. That was what one always said to visitors. While they talked, I looked and listened. Nancy had always been described to me as young, gold-coloured, and "lissome"—that was my father's word.

"Down by de cane-brake, close by de mill, Dar lived a yaller gal—" That was the picture I had carried in my mind. The stranger who came to realize that image was forty-four years old. But though she was no longer lissome, she was other things. She had, I vaguely felt, presence. And there was a charm about her voice, though her speech was different from ours on Back Creek. Her words seemed to me too precise, rather cutting in their unfailing distinctness. Whereas Mrs. Blake used to ask me if she should read to me from my "hist'ry book" (*Peter Parley's Universal*), Nancy spoke of the his-to-ry of Canada. I didn't like that pronunciation. Even my father said "hist'ry." Wasn't that the right and easy way to say it? Nancy put into many words syllables I had never heard sounded in them before. That repelled me. It didn't seem a friendly way to talk.

Her speech I counted against her. But I liked the way she sat in her chair, the shade of deference in her voice when she addressed my mother, and I liked to see her move about,—there was something so smooth and measured in her movements. I noticed it when she went to get her handbag, and opened it on the foot of my bed, to show us the pictures of her husband and three children. She spoke of her mistress as Madam, and her master as Colonel Kenwood. The family were in England for the spring, and that was why Nancy was able to come home and visit her mother. She could stay exactly six weeks; then she must go back to Montreal to get the house ready for the return of the family. Her husband was the Kenwoods' gardener. He was half Scotch and half Indian.

Nancy was to be at our house for the midday dinner. Then she would walk home with her mother, to stay with her in the old cabin of her childhood. The "new miller," as he was still called, though he had now been running the mill for some seventeen years, was a kind man from over the Blue Ridge. He let Till stay on in her cabin behind the Mill House, work her own garden patch, and even keep a pig or two.

When my mother and father and Mrs. Blake went down to dinner, Nancy and Till sat where they were, hand in hand, and went on talking as if I were not there at all. Nancy was telling her mother about her husband and children, how they had a cottage to themselves at the end of the park, and how the work was divided between the men and the maids.

Suddenly Till interrupted her, looking up into her face with idolatrous pride.

"Nancy, darlin', you talks just like Mrs. Matchem, down at Chestnut Hill! I loves to hear you."

Presently they were called downstairs to the second table, to eat the same dinner as the family, served by the same maid (black Moses' Sally). My mother gave me an egg-nog to quiet me and pulled down the blinds. I was tired out with excitement and went to sleep.

During her stay on Back Creek Nancy came often with her mother to our house. She used to bring a small carpetbag, with her sewing and a fresh apron, and insisted upon helping Mrs. Blake and Moses' Sally in whatever housework was under way. She begged to be allowed to roast the coffee. "The smell of it is sweeter than roses to me, Mrs. Blake," she said laughing. "Up there the coffee is always poor, so I've learned to drink tea. As soon as it's browned, I'll grind a little and make us all a cup, by your leave."

Our kitchen was almost as large as a modern music-room, and to me it was the pleasantest room in the house,—the most interesting. The parlour was a bit stiff when it was not full of company, but here everything was easy. Besides the eight-hole range, there was a great fireplace with a crane. In winter a roaring fire was kept up in it at night, after the range fire went out. All the indoor and outdoor servants sat round the kitchen fireplace and cracked nuts and told stories until they went to bed.

We had three kitchen tables: one for kneading bread, another for making cakes and pastry, and a third with a zinc top, for dismembering fowls and rabbits and stuffing turkeys. The tall cupboards stored sugar and spices and groceries; our farm wagons brought supplies out from Winchester in large quantities. Behind the doors of a very special corner cupboard stood all the jars of brandied fruit, and glass jars of ginger and orange peel soaking in whisky. Canned vegetables, and the preserved fruits not put down in alcohol, were kept in a very cold cellar: a stream ran through it, actually!

Till and Nancy usually came for dinner, and after the dishes were washed they sat down with Mrs. Blake in the wooden rocking-chairs by the west window where the sunlight poured in. They took out their sewing or knitting from the carpetbag, and while the pound cake or the marble cake was baking in a slow oven, they talked about old times. I was allowed to sit with them and sew patchwork. Sometimes their talk was puzzling, but I soon learned that it was best never to interrupt with questions,—it seemed to break the spell. Nancy wanted to know what had happened during the war, and what had become of everybody,—and so did I.

While she sat drawing her crochet hook in and out, she would say: "And what ever did become of Lizzie and Bluebell after Miss Sapphy died?"

Then Till would speak up: "Why, ain't I told you how Mr. Henry freed 'em right after Missy died, when he freed all the niggers? But it was hard to git rid of free niggers befo' the war. He surely had a sight a' trouble gittin' shet of them two! Even after he'd got Lizzie a good place at the Taylor House hotel in Winchester, they kep' makin' excuse to stay on, hangin' 'round the kitchen. In the end he had to drive 'em into town himself an' put 'em down at the hotel, an' tole 'em fur the las' time they wasn't needed at the mill place no more. You know he never did like them two niggers. He took a wonderful lot a' trouble gittin' good places fur his people. You remembers Sampson, honey?"

"Why, of course I do, Mother. He was Master's steadiest man." At this moment Till would likely be on her feet in a twinkle with: "Before I begin on Sampson, I'll just turn the bread fur you, Mrs. Blake. I seem to smell it's about ready."

When all the pans had been changed about, Till would sit down and continue:

"Well, Mr. Henry got Sampson a wonderful good place up in Pennsylvany, in some new kind of mill they calls roller mills. He's done well, has Sampson, an' his children has turned out well, they say. Soon as the war was over, Sampson come back here, just to see the old place. The new miller treated him real clever, and let him sleep in old Master's mill room—he don't use it only like a kind of office, to see folks. Sampson come to my cabin every day he was here, to eat my light bread. 'Don't never trouble yourself to cook me no fancy victuals, Till,' he'd say. 'Just give me greens an' a little fat pork, an' plenty of your light bread. I ain't had no real bread since I went away.' He told me how in the big mill where he works the grindin' is all done by steam, and the machines runs so fast an' gits so hot, an' burns all the taste out-a the flour. 'They is no real bread but what's made out-a water-ground flour,' he says to me."

"And Tap, whatever became of him, Mrs. Blake?"

Then followed a sad story. I knew it well. Many a time I had heard about Tap, the jolly mill boy with shining eyes and shining teeth, whom everybody liked. "Poor Tap" he was always called now. People said he hadn't been able to stand his freedom. He went to town ("town" always meaning Winchester), where every day was like circus day to a country-bred boy, and picked up various jobs until the war was over. Early in the Reconstruction time a low German from Pennsylvania opened a saloon and pool hall in Winchester, a dive where negroes were allowed to play, and gambling went on. One night after Tap had been drinking too much, he struck another darky on the head with a billiard cue and killed him. The Back Creek farmers who remembered Tap as a boy went to his trial and testified to his good character. But he was hanged, all the same. Mrs. Blake and Till always said it was a Yankee jury that hanged him; a Southern jury would have known there was no real bad in Tap.

Once Nancy looked at Mrs. Blake with a smile and asked her what had become of Martin Colbert. I had never heard of him. Mrs. Blake glanced at her in a way that meant it was a forbidden subject. "He was killed in the war," she said briefly. "He'd got to be a captain in the cavalry, and the Colberts made a great to-do about him after he was dead, and put up a monument. But I reckon the neighbourhood was relieved."

More than anything else, Nancy wanted to know about the last days of her old master and mistress. That story I could almost have told her myself, I had heard about them so often. Henry Colbert survived his wife for five years. He saw the beginning of the Civil War, and confidently expected to see the end of it. But he met his death in the haying season of 1863, when he was working in the fields with the few negroes who begged to stay on at the Mill Farm after the miller had freed all his wife's slaves. The Master was on top of the hayrack, catching the hay as Taylor forked it up to him. He stepped backward too near the edge of the load and fell to the ground, striking his head on a limestone ledge. He was unconscious when the field-hands carried him into the house, and he died a few hours later.

When my parents went for a long horseback ride, they sometimes took me as far as Till's cabin, and picked me up again on their way home. It was there I heard the old stories and saw Till's keepsakes and treasures. They were stowed away in a pinewood chest with a sloping top. She had some of the miller's books, the woolly green shawl he had worn as an overcoat, some of Miss Sapphy's lace caps and fichus, and odd bits of finery such as velvet slippers with buckles. Her chief treasure was a brooch, set in pale gold, and under the crystal was a lock of Mr. Henry's black hair and Miss Sapphy's brown hair, at the time of their marriage. The miller himself had given it to her, she said.

In summer Till used to take me across the meadow to the Colbert graveyard, to put flowers on the graves. Each time she talked to me about the people buried there, she was sure to remember something she had not happened to tell me before. Her stories about the Master and Mistress were never mere repetitions, but grew more and more into a complete picture of those two persons. She loved to talk of Mrs. Colbert's last days; of the reconciliation between the Mistress and Mrs. Blake that winter after Betty died, when Mrs. Blake and Mary stayed at the Mill House. The Mistress knew she had not long to live. The tappings had become more frequent; Doctor Clavenger came out from Winchester twice a week now. He told Till he had never known anyone with that kind of dropsy to live so long as Mrs. Colbert; he said it was because her heart was so strong. But the day would come when the pressure of the fluid would be too heavy, and then her heart would stop.

"She kept her bed most all day that last winter," Till would go over it, "an' she liked to stay by herself, but she didn't complain none. When I'd come into her room in the mornin' early, she'd always say: 'Good mornin', Till,' jest as bright as could be. Right after she'd had her breakfast, she liked Miss Mary to run in an' talk to her for a while. After that, she liked to be by herself. Around three o'clock in the evenin' I went in to dress her. It was hard on her, and took her breath dreadful, but she wouldn't give in, an' she never got out of temper.

When I'd got her dressed, Mr. Henry an' Sampson used to come up from the mill to lift her into her chair an' wheel her into the parlour. Mrs. Blake an' Mary would come in to have tea with her, an' right often Mr. Henry stayed for a cup. Missy was always in good spirits for tea, an' it seemed like her an' Mrs. Blake got more comfort out-a one another than ever before, talkin' about old times and the home folks in Loudoun County. An' Miss Mary was real fond of her grandma. If she'd knowed there'd been hard words ever, she'd forgot it. She had the right way with Miss Sapphy, an' it meant a heap, havin' her in the house that last winter; she was so full of life."

From the way Till spoke of Mrs. Blake's long visit, hints that she dropped unconsciously, one understood that there was always a certain formality between Mrs. Colbert and her daughter—a reserve on both sides. After tea, for the hour before supper, the Mistress preferred to be alone in the parlour. There were many snow-falls that winter, on into March. Mrs. Colbert liked to sit and watch the evening light fade over the white fields and the spruce trees across the creek. When Till came in with the lights, she would let her leave only four candles, and they must be set on the tea-table so placed that the candle-flames inside were repeated by flames out in the snow-covered lilac arbour. It looked like candles shining in a little playhouse, Till said, and there was the tea-table out there too, all set like for company. When Till peeped in at the door, she would find the Mistress looking out at this little scene; often she was smiling. Till really believed Miss Sapphy saw spirits out there, spirits of the young folks who used to come to Chestnut Hill.

And the Mistress died there, upright in her chair. When the miller came at supper-time and went into the parlour, he found her. The strong heart had been overcome at last. Though her bell was beside her, she had not rung it. There must have been some moments of pain or struggle, but she had preferred to be alone. Till thought it likely the "fine folks" were waiting outside for her in the arbour, and she went away with them.

"She oughtn't never to a' come out here," Till often said to me. "She wasn't raised that way. Mrs. Matchem, down at the old place, never got over it that Miss Sapphy didn't buy in Chestnut Hill an' live like a lady, 'stead a' leavin' it to run down under the Bushwells, an' herself comin' out here where nobody was anybody much."

Sapphira and the Slave Girl. New York: Knopf, 1940. 279–293.

3
Nancy Cunard (1896–1965)

Introduced and Edited by Susan Stanford Friedman

Nancy Cunard was a poet, essayist, editor, journalist, war correspondent, memoirist, translator, avant-garde publisher, African art collector, and political activist. Great-granddaughter of the founder of the Cunard shipping fortune, Cunard rebelled violently and publicly against her family and class. British by birth, she spent most of her adult life as an expatriate in France, particularly in the multicultural and multiracial cross currents of the Parisian scene described in Shari Benstock's *Women of the Left Bank,* Hugh Ford's *Nancy Cunard—Brave Poet, Indomitable Rebel,* and Anne Chisholm's *Nancy Cunard.* Cunard knew "everybody" in various avant-garde movements of literature, art, film, photography, and politics. Like Carl Van Vechten, she was a key bridge figure between the white and black worlds of artistic and political ferment in Paris, London, and New York. Her name criss-crosses the map of modernism—not so much as a poet but more as a tireless advocate, a progressive spirit, a charismatic dynamo, a woman who fascinated and frightened people with her passions.

Frequently painted, photographed, and written about, Cunard seemed inseparable from her image—her wealth and glamour combined with bohemian exoticism and sexual freedom; her tall, thin frame complemented by her trademarks, kohl-encircled eyes, boyish bob, and heavy African bangles on her arms. This fetishization of her image was itself inseparable from her notoriety as a radical—her name associated with bohemianism, anarchism, communism, antifascism, and the movement against racial injustice. Above all, she was known for her passionate advocacy of racial equality and her anti-Fascist activism during the Spanish Civil War and the Second World War. Although her commitments and life-style broke the confining gender boundaries of her class and time, she did not directly address the position of women or formulate a feminist analysis as a component of her politics. It has been difficult for critics to sort out the serious writer and political organizer from the legends of her life fed by publicity and personality. Ford, Chisholm, and Benstock have begun the process, but Cunard's complex role as writer and activist in the unfolding of modernism has yet to be assessed.

Cunard's youth was dominated by the need to escape—much like the life of Bryher, a daughter of Britain's other shipping magnate, Sir John Ellerman (see Friedman). Lady Emerald Cunard (Maud Burke), Cunard's American-born mother, thrived on the upper-class life of London's social scene and paid little attention to the daughter to whom she was nothing more intimate than "Her Ladyship." In 1911, she left Sir Bache Cunard in the country and took her daughter to London, where she established herself as a dazzling and risqué hostess whose name the gossips linked with the Irish writer George Moore and Sir Thomas Beecham. Cunard hated the debutante parties her mother arranged for her and suddenly bolted at age twenty by marrying Sidney Fairbairn in 1916, the same year Edith Sitwell published Cunard's first poems in *Wheels: An Anthology of Verse.* Never a success, the marriage dissolved twenty months later but left Cunard free to set up her own household separate from her mother and further develop her friendship with a group of writers and artists she called a "Corrupt Coterie." In 1920, Cunard moved to Paris.

By the early twenties, Cunard was thoroughly integrated into various avant-garde circles. Ezra Pound, as she recalled in the letter printed below, helped her get established as a poet. Her first volume, *Outlaws,* was published in 1921, followed by *Sublunary* in 1923 and the long poem *Parallax,* published by the Woolfs' Hogarth Press in 1925. Norman Douglas (about whom she wrote a memoir in the fifties), the Sitwells, William Carlos Williams, H. D., Bryher, Robert McAlmon, T. S. Eliot (whose draft for "The Fire Sermon" in *The Waste Land* included a probable portrait of Cunard), Janet Flanner, Richard Aldington, Samuel Beckett, Sylvia Beach, Adrienne Monnier, and Aldous Huxley were friends, along with many others. She was particularly close to the surrealists in Paris, especially the Communist Louis Aragon. To support experimental poetry and avant-garde writing in general she established and ran the Hours Press, for which she engaged in all levels of text production from 1928 to 1931. Among the many modernist texts she printed was Pound's *A Draft of XXX Cantos,* mentioned in the letter below.

Meeting Henry Crowder, the black jazz pianist and composer from Georgia, catalyzed and directed Cunard's energy for years to come. Although her love for Afro-American jazz and African art went back to the days of the

"Corrupt Coterie," she made her first black friends on a trip to Venice in 1928. There she met regularly with members of a jazz band that included Crowder, who introduced her to the arts, music, ideas, and politics of the Harlem Renaissance and told her stories about the indignities and inequities of black life in the United States. She in turn introduced him to her friends, helping him, for example, to overcome his prejudice against homosexuality. They lived, worked, and traveled on and off together from 1928 until 1935.

Cunard's monumental anthology, *Negro*, published in 1934, was conceived in 1930 out of the love she felt for African and Afro-American art, the rage she felt as she learned about racism, and her relationship with Crowder. Her dedication of *Negro* to Crowder demonstrates the inseparability for Cunard of the public and the private, the personal and the political, the sociological and the aesthetic. With 150 contributors from many countries, the book included articles on African art; Afro-American and West Indian poetry and music; the institutionalization of racism in the United States; the history of blacks in the Americas; communism and race; and African, West Indian, and South American histories and ethnographies. Ambitious in scope, the book had 855 pages, with 385 illustrations. About two-thirds of its authors were black, the rest white—including stellar names of the Harlem Renaissance and white modernism. No publisher would touch such a big and politically volatile book manuscript. Cunard gleefully used the £1,500 she received from the British press in a settlement of her libel suits to publish the book. "Poetic justice," she exclaimed to friends.

The events surrounding the compilation of *Negro* were stormy and personally difficult for Cunard. To begin the collection of materials, she went openly with Crowder to London, where they lived in the flat of a friend. Lady Cunard was very upset with her daughter's public liaison with a black man. In December 1930 they fought it out, never to meet again. After Cunard traveled to New York with Crowder to collect materials in Harlem, Lady Cunard cut her daughter's allowance, first by a quarter, then in half. Cunard retaliated in 1931 by publishing the pamphlet *Black Man and White Ladyship*, a public exposure of her mother's Anglo-American bigotry and hypocrisy. The essay, which created an enormous scandal, narrates her confrontation with her mother and reveals the racism of Lady Cunard and all her "liberal" friends (such as George Moore) in all its specificity. Not merely a diatribe against her mother, the essay publicizes Cunard's repudiation of class and race privilege, advocacy of racial justice, and critique of British imperialism. She celebrated African art and Afro-American music; she insisted that white Europeans were no more "civilized" than black Africans. Cunard broke the taboo of privacy—she washed the dirty linen of her race and class in public. She demonstrated with vicious wit and brutal honesty the disease of racism. The conflation of matriphobia and political radicalism is breathtaking, raising troubling questions about the mother-daughter bond within the psychodynamics of gender, race, and class. She shocked even her friends, people like Richard Aldington, who had been more than a little in love with her.

Crowder himself thought the pamphlet "a most idiotic thing to do" (quoted in Chisholm 187).

Cunard's travels and troubles became ever more public. Another trip to New York in the spring of 1932 led to press harassment and her suits for slander. Accusations of interracial promiscuity dogged her every move. Nonetheless, she forged ahead with her anthology and continued to travel openly with Crowder. In the spring of 1933 she engaged in her first political organizing—the founding of her petition drive ("Scottsboro Appeal") on behalf of the Scottsboro boys, for which she raised nearly £1,000. Cunard's own contributions to *Negro* demonstrate the influence of these political activities. The essay "Scottsboro—and Other Scottsboros" presents a detailed history of the case, prefaced by the caveat that the case is not unusual, that "the same capitalist oppression and brutality" are "at the root" of many other cases, including the "murder-by-law of Sacco and Vanzetti" (155). In "The American Moron and the American of Sense—Letters on the Negro," printed below, she astutely analyzed the intersection of racism and sexism in the titillated hounding she had received from the press. "Jamaica—The Negro Island" surveys the history and culture of Jamaica and anticipates her later career as a journalist. Her poem "Southern Sheriff" adapts the Browning dramatic monologue to her political purposes: in dialect, a white southern sheriff reveals the extent of his bigotry as he defends it. Her essay "Harlem Reviewed," printed below, is a verbal tour through various aspects of Harlem life—its vibrancy and its slums, its creativity and its oppression, its religion and its politics. She worked hard in the essay to avoid the white fascination for black Otherness that characterized many whites who went "slumming" in Harlem; at the same time, she did not hide behind a screen of color-blind objectivity. She made clear that she was a white woman in a world different from her own. She ended with a messianic call to communism as an idea that could end racial prejudice. As sympathetic as she was to communist ideals, Cunard never joined the Communist party and repeatedly stated to friends that she was an anarchist, not a communist (Ford 130). During the thirties, Cunard saw the Communists in the United States supporting the causes that she had made her own, and her essays reflect her approval of their stand.

The rise of fascism in Spain, Italy, and Germany became her next focus. While Pound was increasingly enthralled by Mussolini and was formulating his anti-Semitic economic theories, Cunard first condemned the Italian invasion of Ethiopia and then went to Spain to support the Republicans against the Fascists. As a reporter for the *Manchester Guardian,* she wrote many stories about the appalling plight of the refugees, as well as the events of the Spanish Civil War. Canvassing over a hundred writers for their position on the war, Cunard published the pamphlet *Authors Take Sides on the Spanish War,* which reported that 126 replies were pro-Republican, five were for Franco, and sixteen (including Eliot and Pound) were neutral. For Cunard: "It is unthinkable for any honest intellectual to be pro-Fascist as it is degenerate to be for Franco, the assassin of the Spanish and Arab people. . . . Above all others, the writer, the intellectual, must take sides. His place is with the people against Fascism" (quoted in Chisholm 241).

During the Second World War, Cunard continued her anti-Fascist crusade from London by editing an enormous anthology called *Poems for France,* a volume of seventy poets published by La France Libre. She also monitored Pound's radio broadcasts from Italy. After the liberation of France, Cunard returned to her home in Réanville, a village in Normandy, only to find it completely vandalized by the Germans who had lived in it and, even more distressing, by many French villagers. A year later, she wrote the bittersweet letter to Pound printed below. She could not forget his kindness, his youthful zeal as a poet and an intellectual. But she could also not forget, nor even understand, his attraction to fascism. Like Bryher, who could not forgive Pound, Cunard condemned him. Like H. D., who wrote about her ambivalence in *End to Torment,* Cunard remembered the nonfascist side of Pound. Her letter arrived while Pound's status was still being debated. He wrote back a brief note beginning "What the blue beggaring hell are you taking [sic] about?" and asked for Crowder's address. This was their final exchange, but Cunard and Crowder appear briefly in Pound's *Pisan Cantos,* published in 1948.

Cunard's notes for a memoir she never wrote capture the steadfastly moral and political vision of her stance: "When of SELF writing: Re the three main things. 1 Equality of races. 2 Of sexes. 3 Of classes" (quoted in Chisholm 307). Her friend Sylvia Townsend Warner said in a related vein: "Her temper was notorious, her life was wilful and erratic—and she was compellingly respect-worthy" (Chisholm 271).

WORKS CITED

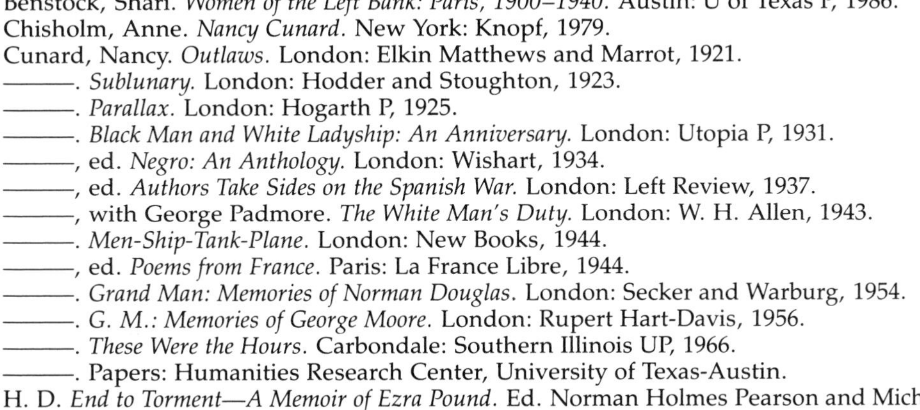

Benstock, Shari. *Women of the Left Bank: Paris, 1900–1940.* Austin: U of Texas P, 1986.

Chisholm, Anne. *Nancy Cunard.* New York: Knopf, 1979.

Cunard, Nancy. *Outlaws.* London: Elkin Matthews and Marrot, 1921.

———. *Sublunary.* London: Hodder and Stoughton, 1923.

———. *Parallax.* London: Hogarth P, 1925.

———. *Black Man and White Ladyship: An Anniversary.* London: Utopia P, 1931.

———, ed. *Negro: An Anthology.* London: Wishart, 1934.

———, ed. *Authors Take Sides on the Spanish War.* London: Left Review, 1937.

———, with George Padmore. *The White Man's Duty.* London: W. H. Allen, 1943.

———. *Men-Ship-Tank-Plane.* London: New Books, 1944.

———, ed. *Poems from France.* Paris: La France Libre, 1944.

———. *Grand Man: Memories of Norman Douglas.* London: Secker and Warburg, 1954.

———. *G. M.: Memories of George Moore.* London: Rupert Hart-Davis, 1956.

———. *These Were the Hours.* Carbondale: Southern Illinois UP, 1966.

———. Papers: Humanities Research Center, University of Texas-Austin.

H. D. *End to Torment—A Memoir of Ezra Pound.* Ed. Norman Holmes Pearson and Michael King. New York: New Directions, 1979.

Ford, Hugh. Introduction. *Negro: An Anthology,* ed. Nancy Cunard. Edited and abridged edition by Hugh Ford. New York: Ungar, 1970.

———, ed. *Nancy Cunard: Brave Poet, Indomitable Rebel, 1896–1965.* Philadelphia: Chilton, 1968.

Friedman, Susan Stanford. "Modernism of the 'Scattered Remnant': Race and Politics in H. D.'s Development." In *Feminist Issues in Literary Scholarship,* ed. Shari Benstock, 208–233. Bloomington: Indiana UP, 1987.

Sitwell, Edith, ed. *Wheels: An Anthology of Verse.* London: Longmans, Green, 1916.

Black Man and White Ladyship

An anniversary is coming and that is why this is printed now, and the reason for its having been written will, I imagine, be clear to those who read it.

By anniversary I am not, indeed, referring to Christmas, but to the calendric moment of last year when the Colour Question first presented me personally with its CLASH or SHOCK aspect.

I have a Negro friend, a very close friend (and a great many other Negro Friends in France, England and America). Nothing extraordinary in that. I have also a mother—whom we will at once call: Her Ladyship. We are extremely different but I had remained on fairly good (fairly distant) terms with her for a number of years. The english channel and a good deal of determination on my part made this possible. I sedulously avoid her social circle both in France and in England. My Negro friend has been in London with me five or six times. So far so good. But, a few days before our going to London last year, what follows had just taken place, and I was unaware of it until our arrival. At a large lunch party in Her Ladyship's house things are set rocking by one of those bombs that throughout her "career" Margot Asquith, Lady Oxford, has been wont to hurl. No-one could fail to wish he had been at that lunch to see the effect of Lady Oxford's entry: "Hello, Maud, what is it now—drink, drugs or niggers?" (A variant is that by some remark Her Ladyship had annoyed the other Ladyship, who thus triumphantly retaliated.) The house is a seemly one in Grosvenor Square and what takes place in it is far from "drink, drugs or niggers." There is confusion. A dreadful confusion between Her Ladyship and myself! For I am known to have a great Negro friend—the drink and the drugs do not apply. Half of social London is immediately telephoned to: "Is it *true* my daughter knows a Negro?" etc., etc.

It appears that Sir Thomas Beecham, in the light of "the family friend," was then moved sufficiently to pen me a letter, in the best Trollope style, in which he pointed out that, as the only one qualified to advise, it would, at that juncture, be a grave mistake to come to England with a gentleman of american-african extraction whose career, he believed, it was my desire to advance, as, while friendships between races were viewed with tolerance on the continent, by some, it was . . . in other words it was a very different pair of shoes in England especially as viewed by the Popular Press! This letter (which was sent to the wrong address and not received till a month later on my return to Paris) was announced by a telegram "strongly advising" me not to come to London until I got it adding that the subject was unmentionable by wire! I was packing my trunk and laid the telegram on top—time will show. . . . We took the four o'clock train.

What happened in London?

Some detectives called, the police looked in, the telephone rang incessantly at our hotel. The *patron* (so he said) received a *mysterious message* that he himself would be imprisoned "undt de other vil be kilt." Madame wept: "Not even a *black* man, why he's only *brown.*" Her Ladyship did not go so far as to step round herself. The Popular Press was unmoved. This lasted about a month and I used to get news of it daily, enough to fill a dossier on the hysteria caused by a difference of pigmentation.

The question that interested a good many people for two and a quarter years (does Her Ladyship know or not?) was thus brilliantly settled.

But, your Ladyship, you cannot kill or deport a person from England for being a Negro and mixing with white people. You may take a ticket to the cracker southern states of U.S.A. and assist at some of the choicer lynchings which are often announced in advance. You may add your purified-of-that-horrible-american-twang voice to the yankee outbursts: America for white folks—segregation for the 12 million blacks we can't put up with—or do without . . .

No, with you it is the other old trouble—class.

Negroes, besides being black (that is, from jet to as white as yourself but not so pink), have not yet "penetrated into London Society's consciousness." You exclaim: they are not "received!" (You would be surprised to know just how much they are "received.") They are not found in the Royal Red Book. Some big hostess gives a lead and the trick is done!

For as yet only the hefty shadow of the Negro falls across the white assembly of High Society and spreads itself, it would seem, quite particularly and agonisingly over you.

And what has happened since this little dust-up of December last, 1930? We have not met, I trust we shall never meet again. You have cut off, first a quarter (on plea of your high income tax) then half of my allowance. You have stated that I am out of your will. Excellent—for at last we have a little truth between us. The black man is a well-known factor in the changing of testaments (at least in America), and parents, as we all know, are not to be held responsible for the existence of children.

Concerning this last I have often heard Her Ladyship say that it is the children who owe their parents nothing. But I am grateful to her for the little crop of trivalia that has flowered this year:

Mr. George Moore—(at one time her best friend and thence my first friend) whose opinion I was interested to have on the whole matter, which I obtained by the silence that followed my frank letter to him—was said to have decided not to leave me his two Manets as he intended, but has subsequently contradicted this. . . .

Her Ladyship's hysteria has produced the following remarks:

that—no hotel would accommodate my black friend.

that—he was put out of England (exquisitely untrue, for we came, stayed and left together after a month).

that—she would not feel *chic* in Paris any longer as she had heard that all the chic Parisians nowadays consorted with Negroes.

that—I now wrote for the Negro Press. (One poem and one article have appeared in the *Crisis*, New-York.)

that—where would I be in a few years' time.

that—she does not mind the Negroes now artistically or in an *abstract* sense but . . . oh, that terrible colour! (I invite Her Ladyship to send in writing a short definition of a Negro in the *abstract sense*.)

that—she knew *nothing at all of the whole thing* till Mr. Moore read her my letter. Now, to be exact: my letter to Mr. Moore was written Jan. 24 whereas Her Ladyship severely put through it several friends of mine in the preceding December, and had her bank signify to me on Jan. 21, 1931, that owing to the exigencies of her Income Tax . . . I suspect Her Ladyship of having conveniently forgotten that what seems indeed to have struck her as a bomb exploded before many witnesses in her own house. (This is very interesting and I don't doubt the psychologists have many such cases on their books—the washing of hands, let us add, by the main party.)

I am told that Her Ladyship was invited to a night-club, saw some coloured singers, turned faint and left . . . yet at least one paid coloured entertainer has been to her house.

I am told that she believes all the servants in a London house gave notice because a coloured gentleman came to dinner.

AND I AM TOLD

that Sir Thomas Beecham says I ought to be tarred and feathered!

It is now necessary to see Her Ladyship in her own fort, to perceive her a little more visually.

In the Sunday Express of Nov. 22, 1931, can be read in detail of how Her Ladyship spends a fortune on clothes she never wears. "I have not the faintest idea of how much I spend on clothes every year—it may run into thousands. I have never bothered to think about it. But that is because I do not have to bother about money." (Which tallies interestingly with her bank's statement concerning the exigencies of her Income Tax—see previously.) . . . "I want to tell you candidly why it is that so-called 'Society' women spend so much on their clothes. It is not that the cost of each garment is so very large; it is simply that we won't be bothered."

The Market may be going on at any time, and generally is. Others play it but Her Ladyship plays it best. Rich Mrs. XYZ will be "taken out" if she guesses or takes the hint that she is to do her duty by . . . (the object varies). No sign of the hint ever being administered! But the participants are well-trained, each is looking for what the other can supply, and each felicitously finds. Many results have been come by in this excellent manner. Snobbery opens purses, starvation fails.

Her Ladyship's own snobbery is quite simple. If a thing *is done* she will, with a few negligible exceptions, do it too. And the last person she has talked to is generally right, providing he is *someone.* The British Museum seems to guarantee that African art is art? some dealers, too, are taking it up, so the thick old Congo ivories that she thinks are slave bangles are perhaps not so hideous after all though still very *strange;* one little diamond would be better . . . though of course that is different.

Her Ladyship likes to give—and to control. It is unbearable for her not to be able to give someone something. But suppose they don't want it—what does this *mean?* Her reaction to being given something herself generally produces the phrase that people shouldn't do such things! Yet the house is full of noble gifts.

Another time it is Communism. "You don't mean to say those people you talk of are communists? they couldn't be, no-one as intelligent, as intellectual as they are . . . You can't *know* people like that," etc. . . . And away with the troubling thought. Her Ladyship is the most conscientious of ostriches and when she comes up again she hopes the *on*pleasant thing has disappeared. Perhaps it doesn't really exist. She is also a great cross-questioner and all her ingenuous ingenuity is seen at work on the picking of brains. As those she puts through it are generally less quick in defence than she is in attack, and as she has a fantastic imagination she generally arrives at some result. Look out! as in the farce, evidence will be taken down, altered and used against you. It will make quite a farce in itself. She is a great worker for she is never content to leave things as they are. In digging away she may turn up some startling facts. She is shocked. She is suspicious. All is not as it should be. She does not recognise . . . there may be no precedent—why it may even be scandalous . . . it *is* scandalous! it is unheard of!! WHAT is to be done? Why, talk about it! What do people say? A mountain is thrown up by this irreducible mole. There—of course it is *monstrous!* It cannot be true . . . and, though it is she who has informed the world, she is astounded presently when it all gets out of hand and falls back on her in anything but gentle rain.

Her Ladyship is american and this is all part of that great american joke: *l'inconscience.* Here she is, ex-cathedra at the lunch table, here she is telling some specimen A1 illiterate of the greatness of the last great book, here—wistfully puzzled by some little matter everyone knows, here—praising rightly, praising wrongly, making and missing the point all in one breath. Generous to the rich, trying always to do the right thing (serve only the best champagne, the food is always perfect). One day the footmen have frayed trousers. The butler has taken a leaf from Her Ladyship's book and explains that *no good enough* ready-made trousers are procurable in London, and that the tailor being dear, and slow . . . he falters. There is a scene. The interior economy is impeccable.

Are intellectuals generally the least biassed in race questions? Here are two reactionaries:—

A little conversation with Mr. George Moore in Ebury St.

SELF: Yes, people certainly feel very differently about race. I cannot understand colour prejudice. Do you think you have it?

G.M.: No, I don't think so.

SELF: Have you ever known any people of colour?

G.M.: No.

SELF: What, not even an Indian?

G.M.: No—though my books are translated into Chinese.

SELF: Not even an Indian . . . such as might have happened had you met, shall we say, an Indian student. Don't you think you'd like to talk to an intelligent Indian or Negro?

G.M.: *(calmly)* No. I do not think so. I do not think I should get on with a black man or a brown man. (*then warmly, opening the stops*) I think the best I could do is a yel-low man!

Thus Mr. Moore—after a whole long life of "free" thought, "free" writing, anti-bigotry of all kinds, with, his engrossment in human nature, after the *injustice* of the Boer war, as he says himself, had driven him out of England. . . . There is no consistency; there *is* race or colour prejudice.

Sir Thomas Beecham's remark about the Negro making his own music left me puzzled, and I don't doubt, puzzled for ever. Her Ladyship was evincing a very querulous astonishment at the Negro (in general) having any achievements (in particular). I was informing her that, for one, everybody knows the Negroes have a particular genius for music. At which Sir Thomas condescendingly remarked "They make their own music too." The tone of this pronouncement was so superior that I remained too dumb to ask whether at that moment he meant tribal or jazz. And Her Ladyship, far from being quieted, became as uneasy as an animal scenting a danger on the wind.

This is all what's aptly enough called *"Old stuff."* What's actual since some twenty years is a direct African influence in sculpture and painting. None but fools separate Africa from the living Negro. But the american press is constantly confusing their civic nationality with their blood nationality; (the 12 million blacks are the loyalest, best *americans;* a Negro in the States has written a good book, therefore he is a good *american* writer; the same of the coloured musician, the coloured artist, etc.).

"In Africa," you say, "the Negro is a savage, he has produced nothing, he has no history." It is certainly true he has not got himself mixed up with machinery and science to fly the Atlantic, turn out engines, run up skyscrapers and contrive holocausts. There are no tribal Presses emitting the day's lies and millions of useless volumes. There remain no written records; the wars, the kingdoms and the changes have sufficed unto themselves. It is not one country but many; well over 400 separate languages and their dialects are known to exist. Who tells you you are the better off for being "civilised" when you live in the shadow of the next war or revolution in constant terror of being ruined or killed? Things in Africa are on a different scale—but the European empire-builders have seen, are seeing to this hand over fist. And what, against this triumph of organised villainy had the black man to show? His own example of Homo Sapiens on better terms with life than are the conquering whites. Anthropology gives him priority in human descent. He had his life, highly organised, his logic, his customs, his laws rigidly adhered to. He made music and unparalleled rhythm and some of the finest sculpture in the world. Nature gave him the best body amongst all the races. Yet he is a "miserable savage" because there are no written records, no super-cities, no machines—but to prove the lack of these an insuperable loss, a sign of racial inferiority, you must attack the root of all things and see where—if anywhere—lies truth. There are many truths. How come, white man, is the rest of the world to be re-formed in your dreary and decadent image?

Nancy Cunard: Brave Poet, Indomitable Rebel, 1896–1965. Ed. Hugh Ford. Philadelphia: Chilton, 1968. 103–108.

Harlem Reviewed

Is it possible to give any kind of visual idea of a place by description? I think not, least of all of Harlem. When I first saw it, at 7th Avenue, I thought of the Mile End Road—same long vista, same kind of little low houses with, at first sight, many indeterminate things out on the pavement in front of them, same amount of blowing dust, papers, litter. But no; the scale, to begin with, was different. It was only from one point that the resemblance came to one. Beginning at the north end of Central Park, edged in on one side by the rocky hill of Columbia University and on the other by the streets that go to the East River, widening out more and more north to that peculiarly sinister halt in the town, the curve of the Harlem River, where one walks about in the dead junk and the refuse-on-a-grand-scale left in the sudden waste lots that are typical of all parts of New York—this is the area of Harlem. Manhattan and 8th Avenues, 7th, Lenox, 5th and Madison Avenues, they all run up here from the zone of the skyscrapers, the gleaming white and blond towers of down-town that are just visible like a mirage down the Harlem perspective. These avenues, so grand in New York proper, are in Harlem very different. They are old, rattled, some of them, by the El on its iron heights, rattled, some of them, underneath, by the Sub in its thundering groove.

Why is it called Harlem, and why the so-called capital of the Negro world? The Dutch made it first, in the 17th century; it was "white" till as recently as 1900. And then, because it was old and they weren't rebuilding it, because it's a good way from the centre, it was more or less "left" to the coloured people. Before this they lived in different parts of New York; there was no Negro "capital." This capital now exists, with its ghetto-like slums around 5th, bourgeois streets, residential areas, a few aristocratic avenues or sections thereof, white-owned stores and cafeterias, small general shops, and the innumerable "skin-whitening" and "anti-kink" beauty parlors. There is one large modern hotel, the

Dewey Square, where coloured people of course may stay; and another, far larger, the Teresa, a few paces from it, where certainly they *may not!* And this is in the centre of Harlem. Such race barriers are on all sides; it just depends on chance whether you meet them or no. Some Negro friend maybe will not go into a certain drugstore with you for an ice-cream soda at 108th (where Harlem is supposed to begin, but where it is still largely "white"); "might not get served in there" (and by a coloured server at that—the white boss's orders). Just across the Harlem River some white gentlemen flashing by in a car take it into their heads to bawl, "Can't you get yourself a white man?"—you are walking with a Negro, yet you walk down-town with the same and meet no such hysteria, or again, you do.

Some 350,000 Negroes and coloured are living in Harlem and Brooklyn (the second, and quite distinct, area in greater New York where they have congregated). American Negroes, West Indians, Africans, Latin Americans. The latter, Spanish-speaking, having made a centre round 112th Street and Lenox Avenue. Walk round there and you will hear—it is nearly all Spanish. The tempo of the gestures and gait, the atmosphere, are foreign. It is the Porto-Ricans, the Central Americans and the Cubans. Nationalisms exist, more or less fiercely, between them and the American Negro—as indeed does a jealous national spirit between American Negro and black Jamaican. The latter say they are the better at business, that the coloured Americans have no enterprise. (Are we to see here the mantle of the British as a nation of shop-keepers on West Indian shoulders?) The American Negro regards the Jamaican or British West Indian as "less civilised" than himself; jokes about his accent and deportment are constantly made on the Harlem stage. And so they are always at it, falling out about empty "superiorities" and "inferiorities," forgetting the white enemy.

If you are "shown" Harlem by day you will inevitably have pointed out to you the new Rockefeller apartments, a huge block towering above a rather sparse and visibly very indigent part of 7th Avenue. These were built by the millionaire of that name, supposedly to better the conditions of Negro workers by providing clean and comfortable lodging for them, but inhabited, however, by those who can afford to pay their rents. The Y.M.C.A. and the newly built Y.W.C.A.—more institutes for "uplift." The Harlem Public Library, with its good collection of books on Negro matters, and just a few pieces of African art, so few that the idea strikes one vexingly: why, in this capital of the Negro world, is there no centre, however small, of Africanology? The American Negroes—this is a generalisation with hardly any exceptions—are utterly uninterested in, callous to what Africa is, and to what it was. Many of them are fiercely "racial," as and when it applies to the States, but concerning their forefathers they have not even curiosity.

At night you will be taken to the Lafayette Theatre, the "cradle of new stars" that will go out on the road all over America and thence come to Europe. It is a sympathetic old hall, where, as they don't bother ever to print any programmes, one supposes that all the audience know all the players; it has that feeling too. Some of the best wit I heard here, and they can get away with a lot of stiff hot stuff. Ralph Cooper's orchestra was playing admirably that night they had "the street" in. This was to give a hearing to anyone who applied. They just went on the stage and did their stuff. And the audience was *merciless* to a whole lot of these new triers, who would have passed with honour anywhere out of America. The dancing of two or three of the street shoe-blacks, box on back, then set down and dancing round it, was so perfect that the crowd gave them a big hand. No-one who has not seen the actual dancing of Harlem in Harlem can have any idea of its superb quality. From year to year it gets richer, more complicated, more exact. And I don't mean the unique Snake-Hips and the marvellous Bo-Jangles, I mean the boys and girls out of the street who later become "chorats" and "chorines" (in the chorus), or who do those exquisite short numbers, as in music the Three Ink Spots (a new trio), adolescents of 16 or 17 perhaps, playing Duke Ellington's *Mood Indigo* so that the tears ran down one's face.

There was a new dance too, one of the sights of the world as done at the Savoy Ballroom, the Lindy-Hop. The fitting third to its predecessors, Charleston and Black Bottom. These were in the days of short skirts, but the Lindy is the more astounding as it is as violent (and as beautiful), with skirts sweeping the floor. Short minuet steps to begin, then suddenly fall back into an air-pocket, recover sideways, and proceed with all the variations of leaves on the wind. For the Lindy is Lindbergh, of course, created by them in honour of his first triumph. These Tuesday nights at the Savoy are very famous, as is the Harlem "Drag Ball" that happens only once a year. To this come the boys dressed as girls—some in magnificent and elaborate costumes made by themselves—and of course many whites from down-town. A word on the celebrated "rent-party" that the American press writes up with such lurid and false suggestions. This is no more nor less than an ordinary evening dance in someone's house. The "rent" part is its reason for being, for the guests give about 50 cents to come in, thereby helping pay the rent, and they buy liquor there which, as everywhere in dry America (and doubtless it will go on even if prohibition is entirely abolished), is made on the premises or by a friend. The music, as like as not, comes from a special kind of electric piano, a nickel a tune, all the best, the latest ones.

But it is the zest that the Negroes put in, and the enjoyment they get out of, things that causes one more envy in the ofay. Notice how many of the whites are unreal in America; they are *dim.* But the Negro is very real; he is *there.* And the ofays know it. That's why they come to Harlem—out of curiosity and jealousy and don't-know-why. This desire to get close to the other race has often nothing honest about it; for where the ofays flock, to night-clubs, for instance, such as Connie's Inn and the Cotton Club and Small's, expensive cabarets, to these two former the coloured clientele is no longer admitted. To the latter, only just, grudgingly. No, you can't go to Connie's Inn with your coloured friends. The place is *for whites.* "Niggers" to serve, and "coons" to play—and later the same ofay will slip into what he calls "a coloured dive," and there it'll be "Evening, Mr. Brown," polite and cordial, because this will be a real coloured place and the ofay is not sure of himself there a-tall. . . .

This applies of course to the mass of whites who treat Harlem in the same way that English toffs used to talk about "going slumming." The class I'm thinking of is "the club-man." They want entertainment. Go to Harlem, it's sharper there. And it doesn't upset their conception of the Negro's social status.

From all time the Negro has entertained the whites, but never been thought of by this type as possibly a social equal. There are, however, thousands of artists, writers, musicians, intellectuals, etc., who have good friends in the dark race, and a good knowledge of Harlem life, "the freedom of Harlem," so to speak.

"You must see a revival meeting," they said to me. "It's nothing like what it is in the South, but you shouldn't miss it."

Beforehand I thought I wouldn't be able to stand more than ten minutes of it—ten minutes in any church. . . . When we got into the Rev. Cullen's on 7th Avenue (the Rev. is the father of the poet Countee Cullen) a very large audience was waiting for the "Dancing Evangelist" (that is Becton's title because of his terrific physical activity). A group of "sisters" all in white spread itself fan-wise in the balcony. There was a concert stage with deacons and some of Becton's 12 disciples, and the 7 or 8 absolutely first-class musicians who compose the orchestra, of whom Lawrence Pierre, a fine organist and a disciple. Nothing like a church, an evening concert.

The music starts, a deep-toned Bach piece, then a short allocution, and then the long spirituals, the robust soloist that a massed chorus, the audience, answers back. They begin to beat time with their feet too. The "spirit" is coming with the volume of sound. At this point Becton enters quietly, stands silent on the stage, will not say a word. They must sing some more first, much more; they must be ripe ground. How do they reconcile Becton's exquisite smartness (pearl-grey suit, top hat, cane, ivory gloves, his youthful look and lovely figure), the whole sparkle about him, with the customary ponderousness of the other drab men of God? A sophisticated audience? No, for they appear to be mainly domestic workers, small shop workers, old and young, an evidently religious public, and one or two whites.

A new spiritual has begun; the singing gets intenser, foot-beating all around now, bodies swaying, and clapping of hands in unison. Now and again a voice, several voices, rise above the rest in a single phrase, the foot-beat becomes a stamp. A forest shoots up—black, brown, ivory, amber hands—spread, stiff-ened out fingers, gestures of *mea culpa* beating of breasts, gestures of stiff arms out, vibrating ecstasy. Far away in the audience a woman gets "seized," leaps up and down on the same spot belabouring her bosom. It comes here, there—who will be the next? At one moment I counted ten women in this same violent trance, not two with the same gestures, yet *all* in rhythm, half-time or double time. A few men too less spectacular. Then just behind me so that I see her well, a young girl. She leaps up and down after the first scream eyes revulsed, arms upstretched—she is no longer "there." After about a minute those next to her seize her and hold her down.

The apex of the singing has come, it is impossible to convey the scale of these immense sound-waves and rhythmical under-surges. One is transported completely. It has nothing to do with God, but with life—a collective life for which I know no name. The people are entirely out of themselves—and then, suddenly, the music stops, calm comes immediately.

In this prepared atmosphere Becton now strides about the stage, flaying the people for their sins, leading their ready attention to this or that point of his argument by some adroit word, a wise-crack maybe. He is a poet in speech and very graceful in all his movements. His dramatisation is generous—and how they respond . . . "yeah man . . . tell it, tell it." Sin, he threatens, is "cat-food," a "double-dare devil." And the sinner? "A double-ankled rascal," thunders this "adagio dancer," as he called himself that night, breaking off sharp into another mood, an admonishment out of "that inexpressible something by which I raise my hand." There are whirlwind gestures when he turns round on himself, one great clap of the palms and a sort of characteristic half-whistle-half-hoot before some point which is going to be emphasized—and the eloquence pours out in richer and richer imagery. Becton is the personification of expressionism, a great dramatic actor. You remember Chaliapine's acting of Boris Godounov; these two are comparable.

Then, "when the millenniums are quaking it's time to clap our hands." It is the moment for the "consecrated dime," and the singing begins again, but the trances are over; other preachers may speak later. This ritual goes on from eight till after midnight, about four nights a week, and sometimes both the faithful and the evangelist are so indefatigable that it goes on for 24 hours. These services, really superb concerts, are the gorgeous manifestation of *the emotion* of a race—that part of the Negro people that has been so trammelled with religion that it is still steeped therein. A manifestation of this kind by white people would have been utterly revolting. But with the Negro race it is on another plane, it seems positively another thing, not connected with Christ or bible, the pure outpouring of themselves, a nature-rite. In other words, it is the fervour, intensity, the stupendous rhythm and surge of singing that are so fine—the christianity is only accidental, incidental to these. Not so for the assembly of course, for all of it is deeply, tenaciously religious. I have given all this detail about the revivalist meeting because it is so fantastic, and, *aesthetically* speaking, so moving.

If treachery and lying are its main attributes so is snobbery flourishing in certain parts of Harlem. "Strivers Row;" that is what 139th Streets has been called. An excellent covering-name for "those Astorperious Ethiopians," as one of their own wits put it. There are near-white cliques, mulatto groups, dark-skinned sets who will not invite each other to their houses; some would not let a white cross their thresholds. The Negro "bluebloods" of Washington are famous for their social exclusivity, there are some in Harlem too. I don't know if a foreign white would get in there, possibly not. The snobbery around skin-colour is terrifying. The light-skins and browns look down on the black; by some, friendships with *ofays* are not tolerated, from an understandable but totally unsatisfactory reaction to the general national attitude of white to coloured on the social equality basis. A number of the younger writers are race-conscious in the wrong way, they make of this a sort of forced, *self*-conscious thing, give the feeling that they are looking for obstacles. All this, indeed, is Society with a vengeance! A bourgeois ideology with no horizon, no philosophical link with life. And out of all this, need it be said, such writers as Van Vechten and Co. have made a revolting and cheap lithograph, so that Harlem, to a large idle-minded public, has come to mean nothing more whatsoever than a round of hooch-filled night-clubs after a round of "snow" (cocaine) filled boudoirs. Van Vechten, the spirit of vulgarity, has depicted Harlem as a grimace. He would have written the same way about Montparnasse or Limehouse and Soho. Do places exist, or is life itself as described by Paul Morand (another profiteer in coloured "stock")? Claude MacKay has done better. The studies in inter-colour relationships (in *Ginger Town*) are honest. But his people, and himself, have also that wrong kind of race-consciousness; they ring themselves in, they are umbrageous. The "Negro Renaissance" (the literary movement of about 1925, now said to be at a halt, and one wonders on whose authority this is said) produced many books and poems filled with this bitter-sweet of Harlem's glitter and heart-break.

This is not the Harlem one sees. You don't see the Harlem of the romancists; it is romantic in its own right. And it is *hard* and *strong;* its noise, heat, cold, cries and colours are so. And the nostalgia is violent too; the eternal radio seeping through everything day and night, indoors and out, becomes somehow the personification of restlessness, desire, brooding. And then the gorgeous roughness, the gargle of Louis Armstrong's voice breaks through. As everywhere, the real people are in the street. I mean those young men on the corner, and the people all sitting on the steps throughout the breathless, leaden summer. I mean the young men in Pelham Park; the sports groups (and one sees many in their bright sweaters), the strength of a race, its beauty.

For in Harlem one can make an appreciation of a race. Walk down 7th Avenue—the different types are uncountable. Every diversity of bone-structure, of head-shape, of skin colour; mixes between Orientals and pure Negroes, Jews and Negroes, Red Indians and Negroes (a particularly beautiful blend, with the high cheek-bones always, and sometimes straight black hair), mulattoes of all shades, yellow, "high yaller" girls, and Havana-coloured girls, and, exquisitely fine, the Spanish and Negro blends; the Negro bone, and the Negro fat too, are a joy to the eye. And though there are more and more light-coloured people, there is great satisfaction in seeing that the white American features are absorbed in the mulatto, and that the mulatto is not, as so often in England, a coloured man with a white man's features and often expression as well. The white American and the Negro are a good mix physically.

Nancy Cunard: Brave Poet, Indomitable Rebel. 115–121.

The American Moron and the American of Sense—Letters on the Negro

Here are examples of some of the wild letters received by me at the time I was in Harlem, New York, collecting part of the material for this book. The American press, led by Hearst's *yellow sheets*, had turned this simple enough fact into a veritable racket. Despite all the "liberal attitude of progressive whites" and the recent "New Negro" movement whereby Americans learnt with incredulous amazement that there is a distinct Negro literature, any interest manifested by a white person, even a foreigner to America (such as myself), is immediately transformed into a sex "scandal." The American press method (one of America's major scandals), led by the world-famous "yellow press" of Hearst, is to invent as vulgar and "sexy" a story as possible, to which any official denial merely adds another "special edition." The American public is intended to believe that no white person has ever stayed in Harlem before. But everyone knows that many thousands of whites actually live in Harlem, married to Negroes, or domiciled there.

No chance is ever missed by the American press, and the type of American that believes it (vastly preponderant), to stir up as much fury as possible against Negroes and their white friends. To do this the sex motive is always used. As in the South it is called the lie of the "rape" of white women by black men, so in the North it is always the so-called "scandal" of the inter-racial relations. The Hearst publications *invent* black lovers for white women. A reporter goes round to try and bribe the hotel people into saying that such and such a Negro is staying there—communicating rooms, etc. (This is the case in *my own* experience.) As of course there is not such a good "story" in scandalising about plain coloured X, some well-known coloured star or personality is always picked (one instance of this was the late Booker T. Washington himself, at the age of 60 or so). In that way the Hearst press hopes also to damage the star's professional reputation. If individuals persistently behaved in this manner amongst themselves, they would be locked up as criminals or insane; but what is to be done when this is one of the pillars of American society—the press? The equivalent to the jailing of individuals is of course the total suppression of the American press. An illuminating comment by Americans themselves on their newspapers is that journalists have got to write *something*—the papers have got to be filled every day, you know. . . .

It is necessary to explain to the English reader (I think?) that "caucasian" in the U.S. is used as a self-awarded title of white man's superiority. It has no more to do, geographically, with the Caucasus than "nordic" (same meaning) has to do with Scandinavia.

I should like to print all the raving, illiterate, anonymous letters—some are very funny indeed, mainly from sex-maniacs one might say—but what is to be done? They are obscene, so this portion of American culture cannot be made public.

Of course there are other letters as well—some 400 or 500—from Negroes and friendly whites, commending the stand I took and the making of this anthology. Of the anonymous threats, etc., some 30. Most of them came in a bunch, just after the press outcry, May 2, 1932. Examples:

"Miss Nancy Cunard, you are insane or downright degenerate. Why do you come to America to seek cheap publicity? you have not gained any favor but a whole lot of hatred. If I saw one of your publications I would be the first to suppress it. Furthermore I and a committee are appealing to the U.S. department of Labor to have you deported as a depraved miserable degenerated insane. Back to where you belong. If you dare to make any comparison you had better look out for your life wont be worth the price of your black hotel room. You for your nerve should be burned alive to a stake, you dirty lowdown betraying piece of mucus. (Here follows a sentence which might be considered obscene and which is not, therefore, printed.) K.K.K. 58 W 58." (I suppose this purports to come from the Ku Klux Klan, or possibly the writer only stole their "signature.")

"Dear Miss Cunard,—It is very gratifying indeed to know that in these trying days someone deserts the great make-believe world and devotes her time to a real problem dealing with humans. Your determination to do your OWN work in so noble a cause has inspired all of us who devote our lives to the service of others and we most sincerely congratulate you.

"Out here in the mountains of South California we operate a small boarding school for boys. Our place is very beautiful and the setting is most inspiring. We would be happy to have you avail yourself of our hospitality and to come out and visit us at any time. You will find this a wonderful place for rest, quiet and study.

"May success crown your every effort and may the example you have given the world be the means of creating interest in the conditions of the Negro in this country. Being a Virginian, the writer fully appreciates the status of the American Negro.

"Best wishes to you, cordially."

(This letter is from a California school, from the Headmaster.)

Nancy Cunard: Brave Poet, Indomitable Rebel. 121–123.

Letter to Ezra Pound

Gourdon, [?]
June 11, 1946

Ezra Pound
St Elizabeth's Hospital
Washington D.C.
from Nancy Cunard.

Ezra,

I have been wanting to write you this for some time—for some years—but I could not do so because you were with the enemy in Rome, you were the enemy.

I will write it today from Gourdon, a place you know. You will have received the note I sent you from Rimont [?], near St Girons; this letter is the one it announced.

Your address was sent me by a person in England who had a letter from Bill Williams in which he said you wanted to communicate with me.

Williams has called you *"misguided."* I do not agree. The correct word for a Fascist is "scoundrel." I am aware of the symposium of 6 American writers who have tried to white wash you, in which the word "misguided" was applied.I cannot see what possible defence, excuse or mitigation exists for you, in the name of "old friendship"—as with W.C. Williams—though it be. Nor do I believe anything concerning the "advanced stage of schyzophrenia," "madness," etc. that was postulated as a means to secure your non-execution. I do not believe you are insane or half-crazy. I think you are in perfect possession of your full faculties, as before. I may be wrong. The symposium was mentioned in a French review, with comment, and evoked dire contempt for the writers.

Having heard you on the air speaking from Rome, there might be some excuse for calling your talks those of a man insane. It was all idiotic, the more so in view of facts that already belonged to history. But then, by that count, Goering, Goebbels, Hitler, Strencher [?]—the whole gang of animals—were just "merely" insane. Fascism uses the same hatreds and the same lies the world over. Fascism is not insanity—unless evil itself, all evil, be insanity, (a point that can certainly be argued psychologically, and philosophically, *in the abstract.* War is not abstract.)

I will quote some of your words: "What I mean to say is . . . the greater the ignorance of a people the easier it is to lead them to the slaughter—like the Russians." This was said by you in April 1943 when it was damn-clear to the Nazis even that the Russians were neither "ignorant" nor being led to any slaughter, at a time when Stalingrad had ended, two or three months previously, as a very great victory for the Russians, a very great defeat for the Germans—Stalingrad, one of the great decisive moments of the war. I also monitored a talk of yours when I worked with the Free French and it was evident you were hard-pressed to say anything at all—you praised the opportunities people had in Fascist Italy as opposed to the snobbery of England. An expert on Italian life under Fascism will be qualified to say how true or no this is. What I personally know is that 1 million or more Italian workers, some good number of intellectuals included, got out of Italy so as to live without repression in France.

And now I have come to the word "Intellectual": It is inconceivable to me that an "intellectual" should collaborate with Fascism. Every single thing you reviled and blasted in your first XXX Cantos was happening in Italy in a modern form around you—corruption, opppression, murder, plus the added vulgarity of Fascism—the tub thumping, empty, ostentacious, vain glorious fifth-rate demagogy that I should have thought you, as an artist, would have loathed more than anything.

Now, on a personal plane, this:

The last communication from you was your answer (July printed in "Authors take sides") to the question addressed by me in 1937 to writers on the issue of Spain, Franco and Fascism. Your words were something to the effect that Spain was "an escape-mecanism [sic]", with a stab at the Bank of England. The fact that Hitler and Mussolini were making their start of World War 2 in Spain and that all the best things of Spain were being massacred meant nothing at all to you. I have participated myself in these events and shall again participate, in whatever form the liberation of Spain has to come. It is no "escape mecanism [sic]" for me.

The last communication before that was a note from you which came on Christmas Day 1935, during the Abyssinian War, telling me that you hoped I realised that the Ethiopians were *"black Jews."* To begin with, ethnographically, this is, I think, false—And secondly I do not see the point, even if they were "black Jews." Incidentally for several years, I thought you were Jewish yourself, Ezra. What could it have mattered one way or the other?

You are not the only intellectual who has chosen Fascism, who has lied about clear, straight and self-evident issues. But you *are* one of the rare few poets of any merit to have done so. I maintain, and have maintained in argument with those who never appreciated your poetry, or with those who want to "cheat" now because of your Fascism and retract their one-time appreciation, that you were a very fine poet indeed, unique, I think, in contemporary English—I mean *up to the time* of the XXX Cantos. Collaboration with Fascism will not efface *that* fait accompli—Nor will that fait accompli excuse your collaborating. I cannot understand how the integrity that was so much you in your writing can have chosen the enemy of all integrity.

And now I want to record the things I personally place on the good side, the good things I have to remember of you:

In 1915, when I first knew you, rather vaguely at that time, you were an intellectual revolutionary. With your then fine critical sense and "feel," with your generosity and kindliness, you took up the defence of the young, the unrecognised. In 1921 you helped me greatly with your criticism of poetry (of my poetry of then too); you threw light on me on thinking straight, on composition, on eschewing the tautological etc.—your "Gaudier Breszka" book, which contains much constructive criticism of art and writing, as I remember it, is very fine. (And that the really good work of art should be "as hard as the side of an engine"—what better definition could there be?)

It is you I have to thank for a very great deal of my early love of France—For it was you who told me (with what love yourself, and knowledge) of the Quercy and Languedoc regions, and who told me where to go—to Gourdon included, where I am today, and where the friends of your friends shot 23 people two years ago because the Invasion had occurred and because of the French patriots.

As an American maybe you did have a little prejudice against Negroes (despite the sophistication that it is mete should attend all good contemporary American intellectuals on that score). If so, all the nicer your charming and appreciative ways with Henry, my Henry of colour. Do you remember how often we were together? Henry loved you—as did I, always, then, and before then and up to the last time I saw you in 1928. I know, I knew only years later, by chance, that you remonstrated pretty sharply after I had been disinherited because of Henry. That was fine of you, Ezra.

And now I will tell you this of my life today: Réanville, my house, is in ruins, thanks to the Germans who lived in it, and to their friends, the French Fascists. Among all the smashed windows there was one that held the wind still for the reason that in [?] of glass someone had torn the pages out of Rodker's Vellum edition of your Cantos and had crucified the cover against the the window-frame. That is what I found of you in my house on return. The allies of your friends threw many books down the well, burned, destroyed all of the African things you used to admire—Nothing is left but some fragments to prove there was once something. Perhaps you will be glad to hear that the Fascist mayor of that village (Fascist already before 1936), who is the direct cause of the ruin because it was he who sent the Germans to my house, is still mayor, despite every proof against him. If you are glad, you will be gladder yet to learn that, up till now, not all Fascists have been punished in France and that they continue to do their best to prevent this country from recovering its normal life. They will not succeed to the limit of their hopes because there are people determined enough to prevent that.

I think that is the gist of all I have to say to you Ezra. I should merely repeat myself if I expanded it. Besides, you probably know all this already. The concept of "misguidedness" does not exist for me on your score.

Nancy

Sonnet Political

Maybe they yet will get their furrow straight-
Maybe some fact unborn will point the road—
Maybe the ox will amble half-awake
Another decade with the same bad load,

And grass proceed unhindered on war's grave,
The eye age in its tear indefinitely,
Justice *not* come . . . Why not? So much's a lie
That is not rock—all's one, to spend or save . . .
We have known both—and shall. All's one remove
From what is finite—bombs and rhetorics,
The interlock of allies, politics
In lieu of daily bread—all known. They prove

Nothing, as does one patriot's death, one man*—
In this I see a land that says: I AM.

N. *Sept. 1945*
Somillac.
Before the elections of then—and of
nigh always, one might add.)

*Gabriel Péri,
—as you know (?)—
shot by Vichy-cum
Germans, in Dec. 1941—
having refused their "honours."

4
H. D. (1886–1961)

Introduced and Edited by Susan Stanford Friedman

H. D.'s life and work recapitulate central themes of literary modernism: the emergence from Victorian norms and certainties; the entry into an age characterized by rapid technological change and the violence of two world wars, the disruptions of conventional gender roles with the rise of feminism, the breakup of racial and class hegemonies at home and abroad, and the development of literary modes which reflected the disintegration of traditional symbolic systems and the myth-making quest for new meanings. Hilda Doolittle, writing under the nom de plume "H. D.," is known mainly as a poet, especially for her imagist poetry (e.g., *Sea Garden*) and her epics of the forties and fifties (*Trilogy, Helen in Egypt*).[1] She was the first woman to receive the prestigious Award of Merit Medal for Poetry from the American Academy of Arts and Letters (1960). She was also highly praised for her Greek translations. She put as much effort into her prose as her poetry, but in her lifetime much of this work remained unpublished or ignored. With the recent publication and reprinting of the prose, H. D. is increasingly recognized for her experimental fiction (e.g., *Palimpsest, HERmione, Bid Me to Live*) and her memoirs (e.g., *Tribute to Freud, The Gift, End to Torment*).[2]

Like the modernist poetry of her friends Ezra Pound, T. S. Eliot, and William Carlos Williams, H. D.'s early poetry originated in the avant-garde, vers libre movements of the teens (especially imagism), influenced by Sappho, Japanese haiku, Troubadour lyrics, Bergsonian philosophy, and post-impressionist art. H. D. was known as the "most perfect" of the imagist poets for her innovative musical rhythms, crystalline lines, and stark images. Concealing her name in her genderless initials, "H. D. Imagiste" (as Pound named her) forged an impersonal lyric discourse that deeply encoded gender issues but did not directly address them. Her hard, crisp lines without excess word or sentiment defied the stereotype of the feminine poetess. *Sea Garden* is a garden of thorns whose radiant flowers sting with the brine of salt air.

The forces of history—particularly its cycles of cataclysmic violence—created in H. D. the need for her to develop a more explicitly gendered discourse. Her postimagist poetry—for example, "Eurydice" (1917), *Hymen* (1921), and *Heliodora* (1923)—regularly featured a woman speaking through a mythic mask, respeaking the myths of classical masculinist culture from a woman's point of view. Even more directly, her autobiographical fiction of the twenties and thirties wove and rewove her personal stories into selves that were healed in the process of being written. Highly experimental and self-reflexive, these avant-garde texts explore heterosexual and lesbian love, the transformation of the self from the object of man's desire to the subject of her own, the conflicts of a woman's creativity, the impact of war and the search for the sacred, and the intersections of race, class, and gender. These fictions—like those of Virginia Woolf, Gertrude Stein, James Joyce, and William Faulkner—fractured narrative perspective and chronology to capture the shifting subjectivities of consciousness and the eruptions of the unconscious. Often closer to Stein than Woolf, H. D.'s experiments with language, syntax, narrative, and the split subject anticipated postmodernism and had a profound influence on her later poetry. Much of this prose, however, was unpublished or privately circulated in her lifetime (at least in part because of its explicit representation of forbidden desire) and is only now becoming available.

Like *The Cantos, The Waste Land,* and *Paterson,* H. D.'s later long sequence poems featured the poet as prophet wandering in the wilderness of the modern world, drawing on the fragments of many cultures to forge new myths that might give meaning to a world shattered by war, technology, and alienation. But unlike the epics of male modernists, H. D.'s poems center on the consciousness of the female poet who finds a potent force for healing in the presence of female divinity in *Trilogy* and who writes herself out of patriarchal scripts through identification with the goddess in *Helen in Egypt*. H. D.'s distinctive emphasis as a modernist grew out of her extensive involvement with classical Greece and ancient Egypt, cinema, psychoanalysis, Moravianism, esoteric religion, and occult mysticism. Mediating her use of these traditions was gender. Each engagement was characterized by a dialogic exchange in which H. D. defined and then revised the patriarchal basis of traditions dominated by male masters. Psychoanalyzed by Sigmund Freud (1933, 1934), she transformed his androcentric theories of femininity into the basis of a redemptive female voice and vision. Like Woolf, H. D. was profoundly concerned with the issue of war and violence. To counter the forces of death, her work reconstitutes gender, language, and myth to serve her search for a vision of personal and cultural (re)birth.

Loving the forests and seacoasts of the United States, H. D. grew up in Pennsylvania, first Bethlehem and then a Philadelphia suburb. Her mother was a Moravian artist and musician, her father a well-known professor of astronomy. After withdrawing from Bryn Mawr College in her sophomore year with poor grades and poor health, she went abroad in 1911 to join the circle of artists around Pound, W. B. Yeats, Ford Madox Ford, and May Sinclair. Although she remained intensely American throughout her residence in London and Switzerland, she visited the United States only six times. Bisexually oriented, H. D. almost married Ezra Pound, loved Frances Gregg, married fellow imagist Richard Aldington in 1913, separated from him in 1919, divorced him in 1938, and lived with Bryher (Winifred Ellerman) from 1919 to 1946. After the stillbirth of her first child in 1915 and Aldington's subsequent affairs, H. D. had a daughter, Perdita, by Cecil Gray in 1919. She almost died during the flu epidemic in the final month of pregnancy and credited her survival to Bryher's devotion and promise of a trip to Greece. During the same period she was intensely, but cerebrally, close to D. H. Lawrence, with whom she regularly exchanged manuscripts. But she lost this friendship when Lawrence disapproved of her affair with Gray. These events, most of which were entangled with the war, were so personally traumatic for H. D. that she wrote and rewrote about them in her prose in an attempt to effect a "writing cure" in the self-analysis of autobiographical fiction.

These events were the immediate backdrop for *Notes on Thought and Vision* (reprinted below), the prose-poem H. D. wrote in 1919 after an idyllic month with Bryher in the Scilly Isles where she had what she called her "jelly-fish" and "bell-jar" experiences (*Tribute to Freud* 130). As an authoritative articulation of her poetics, *Notes* was a major departure from "H. D. Imagiste." She may or may not have known that Pound had written to Margaret Anderson of the *Little Review* in 1917 that "H. D. is all right but shouldn't write criticism" (Pound 107). She had been actively involved with Amy Lowell in the formation of three imagist anthologies from 1915 to 1917. And while Aldington was in the army, she served as literary editor for the *Egoist,* until Eliot took over in 1917. But H. D. had steered clear of the efforts by Pound, Lowell, Aldington, and Flint to theorize imagism. In 1918 Aldington and Cournos directly discouraged her from writing prose. But she wrote *Notes* anyway and eagerly showed it to Havelock Ellis, the famous sexologist who served as an intimate friend and emotional anchor for both Bryher and H. D. in the difficult postwar period. Certain that Ellis would like it, H. D. was deeply hurt by his indifference (*Tribute to Freud* 130–131). No record exists of any attempt to publish the piece, which did not appear in print until 1981. She never wrote another prose-poem essay like it, though her experience with Freud, a much wiser man in her eyes than Ellis, led her to develop another form of the personal essay in the forties and fifties.[3]

Notes on Thought and Vision never had the chance to be an influential articulation of modernist poetics in its own time. But it is nonetheless an important modernist document, particularly as it highlights the unconscious, sexual difference, and desire as central to a poetics of modernity. H. D.'s "jelly-fish" and "bell-jar" experiences, which motivated the text, were moments of altered consciousness, uterine moments of psychic suspension in a seeming sea enclosed in a globe—H. D.'s version of Joycean epiphanies or Woolfian moments of being. Joyce's "bird-girl" epiphany in *A Portrait of the Artist as a Young Man* and Woolf's identification in "A Sketch of the Past" of her first moments of being in the matrix of mother-daughter desire suggest a gendered dimension to modernist revelatory poetics, but H. D.'s *Notes* directly theorizes the interconnection of erotics and poetics. Influenced by her experience of pregnancy as a rebirth of her creativity, *Notes* promotes for women a (pro)creative poetic in which mind and body are inseparably part of one another. Some fifty years before Hélène Cixous and Luce Irigaray called for an *écriture feminine,* H. D. formulated her own concept of writing the body and expanded the boundaries of the philosophical essay to inscribe it.

H. D.'s efforts to forge a critical voice were plagued by the discouragements and insecurity that characterize her interaction with Ellis and the publication history of *Notes.* "Responsibilities" (printed below), a review she wrote of Yeats's *Responsibilities,* remained unpublished until 1988.[4] As Gary Burnett argued in his introduction to the review, H. D. used the forum of a brief review to propose a pacifist, antitechnological poetics of "*les jeunes.*" Without naming the vorticist reveling in violence in publications like *Blast* or the futurist celebration of the coming machine age, H. D. nonetheless attacks these movements by linking them to the horror of the Great War. She advocates a different direction from the one Pound epitomized in his futurist and vorticist platforms. Was the review suppressed? Rejected? We don't know.

In the twenties, H. D. and Bryher became increasingly fascinated with avant-garde cinema as a major new art form—the most important innovation since the Renaissance, H. D. wrote.[5] This interest overlapped with H. D.'s two-year affair with Kenneth Macpherson, a talented Scottish artist, writer, and film director. In 1927 Bryher married Macpherson to screen the affair, and the three adults with Perdita in tow lived as an intimate and tempestuous household until the mid-thirties. Under the name "Helga Doorn," H. D. performed in two short films, *Wing Beat* (1927) and *Foothills* (1927), and the full-length feature film *Borderline* (1930), starring Paul Robeson (his first performance on screen).[6] Bryher founded the journal *Close Up,* with Macpherson as its editor, and from 1927 until 1933 the journal published articles and reviews on cinema around the world. *Close Up* was the first journal to treat cinema as a serious art form, and its writers were an impressive cast that included Serge Eisenstein, Stein, Marianne Moore, and Dorothy Richardson.

H. D. wrote eleven reviews for *Close Up,* one of which ("Joan of Arc") is printed below. They are noteworthy as a poet's view of cinema and for what they reveal about H. D.'s poetics. They are also significant as essays that establish a "common viewer" much akin to the "common reader" in Woolf's essay voice. H. D.'s reviews make important contributions to modernist aesthetics through a weaving of the personal and the general, an insistence on the authority of the outsider. Her review of Carl Dreyer's silent masterpiece *The Passion and Death of a Saint* (the same film Adrienne Rich celebrates in "Cartographies of Silence" [*Dream* 18]) encapsulates the position of the "common woman" viewer as both inside and outside male representations of woman. H. D. admires the hard, clean lines of the film—the same qualities associated with her own imagism. But she is also a "resisting" viewer, deeply troubled by Dreyer's emphasis on Joan of Arc's victimization. Joan had been for H. D. a symbol of female difference and defiance, even associated with her lesbianism in the unpublished *Asphodel.* In seeing only her victimization, Dreyer makes victims of his (female) viewers—"we are numb and beaten."

H. D.'s essay on *Borderline* ("The Borderline Pamphlet," below) was published as an unsigned pamphlet to promote the film in 1930. Its ostensible objective is to celebrate the genius of the film's director, Macpherson. But as in her later tributes to Freud and Shakespeare (*By Avon River*), this focus on another person screens a major statement about herself. The unabashed assertions of her own philosophy and experience in *Notes on Thought and Vision* give way to an indirect exposition of her views on modernism in the guise of praising another.[7] Macpherson, sixteen years her junior, had been catalyzed into writing by reading her *Palimpsest* in 1926 and introduced to film by Bryher. While he certainly wrote the script for *Borderline,* he was sick when the main editing had to be done, a task largely performed by H. D. and Bryher. H. D., not Macpherson, was the driving creative force in her intimate circle, although Bryher, Macpherson, and a number of other friends were crucial to her work.

Highlighted in the pamphlet, the film was a bold examination of a tabooed subject: interracial sex and violence. It combined the explosive plot of a Eugene O'Neill or a Faulkner with the avant-garde formalism of German expressionism and Russian film. It reflected the immersion of Macpherson, H. D., and Bryher in the Harlem Renaissance—its politics and its creativity, its music and its literature. They had met Paul and Eslanda Robeson through film critic Robert Herring in 1928, and the Robesons were frequent guests and correspondents.[8] H. D. wrote openly about her identification with Robeson as a fellow expatriate American in her privately printed sketch "Two Americans" and covertly about her erotic attraction to him in the poem "Red Roses for Bronze."

Both the *Borderline* film and the essay articulate a modernism of the margins—one different from the currents of Toryism in Eliot, of fascism in Pound, Lawrence, and Wyndham Lewis. Closer in spirit to the Society of Outsiders Woolf advocates in *Three Guineas, Borderline* foregrounds race as an emblematic issue for "the lost generation" in the postwar world. White abuse of two black human beings uncovers the disease of master-slave relations that produced a generation of alienated, shattered, "borderline" personalities. The essay does not shrink from the brutality of racism—indeed, H. D.'s character, Astrid, is the most racist—but it also emphasizes the common humanity of blacks and whites. Moreover, H. D. articulates a modernist poetic in which race, sex, and politics thoroughly pervade the aesthetic, without reducing art to the ideologically didactic. *HERmione,* written in 1926–1927, represents her own expression of that poetic. H. D.'s recognition of racism and identification with the otherness of blacks anticipates the pattern of her writing in the forties and fifties about Freud's Jewishness (*Tribute to Freud, Advent*), the history of the Indians in the United States (*The Gift*), and her own Moravianism and antifascism (*The Gift, Trilogy, Helen in Egypt*).

Women, not only men, were important to the formation of H. D.'s modernism. The supportive web of friendships that over her lifetime included Bryher, Moore, Lowell, Sinclair, Dorothy Richardson, Edith Sitwell, Adrienne Monnier, Sylvia Beach, Elizabeth Bowen, May Sarton, and Denise Levertov inspired and sustained her own life and work. The letters from H. D. to Lowell and Moore printed below are only a tiny sampling of her vast correspondence; the full record includes letters to many famous writers, as well as to obscure, struggling ones.[9] H. D. met Lowell in the summer of 1914, when Lowell traveled to England to meet the imagists with whom she had corresponded. The split between Pound and the other imagists over his demand to control the second anthology has been narrated elsewhere (e.g., Pratt). H. D.'s letters to Lowell, along with the selection to F. S. Flint edited by Cyrena Pondrom, illuminate H. D.'s extensive role as negotiator in the avant-garde circles of London. With Moore, H. D. was much more intimate and enthusiastic. They felt like sister-spirits in their poetry, as their reviews of each other's work demonstrate. H. D. and Bryher arranged for the publication of Moore's first book of poems not long after they met in New York. They remained close friends, correspondents, and supportive admirers of each other's work until H. D.'s death.

NOTES

1. See *The Collected Poems* for all poems written 1912–1944. Poetry written 1941–1961 is still uncollected.

2. For overviews and critical discussions of her work, see, for example, DuPlessis; Friedman (*Psyche Reborn,* "Hilda Doolittle"); Friedman and DuPlessis; King; Guest; the special H. D. issues of *Agenda, Contemporary Literature, Iowa Review, Poesis, Sagetrieb,* and *San Jose Studies;* and *H. D. Newsletter.*

3. From about 1916 until 1920, she also wrote a lengthy personal and scholarly essay on Greek literature that prefigures the voice of Woolf's "common reader," but most of *Notes on Euripides, Pausanias, and Greek Lyric Poets* remains unpublished. The section on Sappho appears as "The Wise Sappho" in the City Lights edition of *Notes on Thought and Vision.* See DuPlessis 20–26.

4. H. D. also wrote some eighteen reviews, mostly unsigned (see Bryer and Roblyer 654–656).

5. For overviews of the importance of cinema and the photographic image in H. D.'s life and work, see Friedberg; Mandel; Collecott; Morris.

6. *Wing Beat* and *Foothills* are lost, but Anne Friedberg reconstructed versions of the films from fragments. *Borderline* has been shown many times in recent years. The original is kept at the George Eastman House in Rochester, New York. All three films may be viewed at the Museum of Modern Art in New York. See Friedberg ("The Pool Films").

7. In "The Guest" portion of *By Avon River,* H. D.'s description of the Elizabethan period is another indirect formulation of "modernism." Like Paul de Man, H. D. regarded "the modern" as a frame of mind that has cyclically reappeared in historically specific forms for centuries (*Blindness and Insight*). See also "A Note on Poetry," a letter she wrote to Norman Holmes Pearson in 1937 that was reprinted in *Agenda* 25 (Fall/Winter 1987–1988).

8. See Friedman ("Modernism").

9. For H. D.'s generosity to fellow writers, see, for example, her letters to Dobson (in Tinker), Sarton (Berg Collection, New York Public Library), Levertov (Beinecke Library), Robert Duncan (Beinecke), Robert McAlmon (Beinecke), Bryher (Beinecke).

WORKS CITED

Agenda. Special Issue on H. D. 25 (Autumn/Winter 1987–1988).

Bryer, Jackson R., and Pamela Roblyer. "H. D.: A Preliminary Checklist." *Contemporary Literature* 10(Autumn 1969):632–675.

Bryher, Winifred. *Film Problems in Soviet Russia*. Territet, Switzerland: Pool, 1929.

Burnett, Gary. "H. D.'s Responses to the First World War." *Agenda* 25(Fall/Winter 1988):54–63.

Collecott, Diana. "Images at the Crossroads: The H. D. 'Scrapbook.' " In King 319–368.

Contemporary Literature. Special Issue on H. D. 10 (Autumn 1969).

Contemporary Literature. Special Issue on H. D. 27 (Winter 1986).

De Man, Paul. *Blindness and Insight*. New York: Oxford UP, 1971.

DuPlessis, Rachel Blau. *H. D.: The Career of That Struggle*. Brighton: Harvester, 1986.

Friedberg, Anne. "Approaching *Borderline*." In King 369–392.

———. "The Pool Films." *The H. D. Newsletter* 1(Spring 1987):10–11.

Friedman, Susan Stanford. "Hilda Doolittle (H. D.)." In *Dictionary of Literary Biography, vol. 45,* 115–149. Detroit: Gale, 1986.

———. "Modernism of the 'Scattered Remnant': Race and Politics in H. D.'s Development." In *Feminist Issues in Literary Criticism,* ed. Shari Benstock, 208–232. Bloomington: Indiana UP, 1987.

———. *Psyche Reborn: The Emergence of H. D.* Bloomington: Indiana UP, 1981.

Friedman, Susan Stanford, and Rachel Blau DuPlessis, eds. *H. D.—Readings*. Madison: U of Wisconsin P, 1989.

Guest, Barbara. *Herself Defined: The Poet H. D. and Her World*. New York: Doubleday, 1983.

H. D. *Asphodel* (1921–1922). Typescript. Beinecke Rare Book and Manuscript Library, Yale.

———. *Bid Me To Live* (*A Madrigal*). 1960. Redding Ridge, Conn.: Black Swan, 1983.

———. *Borderline*. 1930. *Sagetrieb* 7(Fall 1987):29–50.

———. *By Avon River*. New York: Macmillan, 1949.

———. *The Collected Poems, 1912–1944*. Ed. Louis L. Martz. New York: New Directions, 1983.

———. *End to Torment: A Memoir of Ezra Pound*. Ed. Norman Holmes Pearson and Michael King. New York: New Directions, 1979.

———. *Euripides' Ion*. 1936. Redding Ridge, Conn.: Black Swan, 1986.

———. *The Gift* (abridged). New York: New Directions, 1982.
———. *Hedylus.* 1928. Rev. ed. Redding Ridge, Conn.: Black Swan, 1980.
———. *Helen in Egypt.* New York: Grove, 1961.
———. *Hermetic Definition.* New York: New Directions, 1972.
———. *HERmione.* New York: New Directions, 1981.
———. *Nights* (John Helforth). 1935. New York: New Directions, 1986.
———. *Notes on Thought and Vision & The Wise Sappho.* San Francisco: City Lights Books, 1982.
———. *Paint It To-Day* (Chapters 1–4). *Contemporary Literature* 27(Winter 1986):444–474. Typescript. Beinecke Rare Book and Manuscript Library, Yale.
———. *Palimpsest.* 1926. Rev. ed. Carbondale: Southern Illinois UP, 1968.
———. *Selected Poems of H. D.* New York: Grove P, 1957.
———. *Tribute to Freud.* 1956. Expanded ed. with *Advent.* New York: New Directions, 1985.
———. "Two Americans." *The Usual Star.* Dijon: Darantière, 1934.
———. Papers, Beinecke Rare Book and Manuscript Library, Yale.
H. D. Newsletter. Ed. Eileen Gregory. Dallas Institute of Humanities, 2719 Routh Street, Dallas, TX 75201.
Iowa Review. Special Issue on H. D. 16 (Fall 1986).
King, Michael, ed. *H. D.: Woman and Poet.* Orono, Maine: National Poetry Foundation, 1986.
Mandel, Charlotte. "Garbo/Helen: The Self-Projection of Beauty by H. D." *Women's Studies* 7(1980):127–135.
———. "The Redirected Image: Cinematic Dynamics in the Style of H. D. (Hilda Doolittle)." *Literature/Film Quarterly* 11(1983):36–45.
Morris, Adalaide. "The Concept of Projection: H. D.'s Visionary Powers," *Contemporary Literature* 25(Winter 1984):411–436.
Ostriker, Alicia. "The Poet as Heroine: Learning to Read H. D." *Writing Like a Woman,* 7–41. Ann Arbor: U of Michigan P, 1983.
Poesis. Special Issue on H. D. and Marianne Moore. 6 (1985).
Pondrom, Cyrena N. "Marianne Moore and H. D.: Female Community and Poetic Achievement." In *Marianne Moore: Woman and Poet,* ed. Patricia C. Willis. Orono, Maine: National Poetry Foundation, 1988.
———. "Selected Letters from H. D. to F. S. Flint: A Commentary on the Imagist Period." *Contemporary Literature* 10(Autumn 1969):557–586.
Pound, Ezra. *Selected Letters, 1907–1941.* Ed. D. D. Paige. 1950. New York: New Directions, 1971.
Pratt, William, ed. *The Imagist Poem.* New York: Dutton, 1963.
Rich, Adrienne. *The Dream of a Common Language, Poems, 1974–1977.* New York: Norton, 1978.
San Jose Studies. Special Issue on Emily Dickinson and H. D. 13 (Fall 1987).
Sagetrieb. Special Issue on H. D. 6 (Fall 1987).
Tinker, Carol, ed. "H. D., a Friendship Traced: Letters to Silvia Dobson and a Poem." *Conjunctions* 2(Summer 1982):115–157.
Woolf, Virginia. "A Sketch of the Past." In *Moments of Being: Unpublished Autobiographical Writings,* ed. Jeanne Schulkind. New York: Harcourt Brace Jovanovich, 1976.
———. *Three Guineas.* 1938. New York: Harcourt, Brace and World, 1963.

Notes on Thought and Vision

Three states or manifestations of life: body, mind, over-mind.

Aim of men and women of highest development is equilibrium, balance, growth of the three at once: brain without physical strength is a manifestation of weakness, a disease comparable to cancerous growth or tumor; body without reasonable amount of intellect is an empty fibrous bundle of glands as ugly and little to be desired as body of a victim of some form of elephantiasis or fatty-degeneracy; over-mind without the balance of the other two is madness and a person so developed should have as much respect as a reasonable maniac and no more.

All reasoning, normal, sane and balanced men and women need and seek at certain times of their lives, certain definite physical relationships. Men and women of temperament, musicians, scientists, artists especially, need these relationships to develop and draw forth their talents. Not to desire and make every effort to develop along these natural physical lines, cripples and dwarfs the being. To shun, deny and belittle such experiences is to bury one's talent carefully in a napkin.

When a creative scientist, artist or philosopher has been for some hours or days intent on his work, his mind often takes on an almost physical character. That is, his mind becomes his real body. His over-mind becomes his brain.

When Leonardo da Vinci worked, his brain was Leonardo, the personality, Leonardo da Vinci. He saw the faces of many of his youths and babies and young women definitely with his over-mind. The *Madonna of the Rocks* is not a picture. It is a window. We look through a window into the world of pure over-mind.

If I could visualise or describe that over-mind in my own case, I should say this: it seems to me that a cap is over my head, a cap of consciousness over my head, my forehead, affecting a little my eyes. Sometimes when I am in that state of consciousness, things about me appear slightly blurred as if seen under water.

Ordinary things never become quite unreal nor disproportionate. It is only an effort to readjust, to focus, seemingly a slight physical effort.

That over-mind seems a cap, like water, transparent, fluid yet with definite body, contained in a definite space. It is like a closed sea-plant, jelly-fish or anemone.

Into that over-mind, thoughts pass and are visible like fish swimming under clear water.

The swing from normal consciousness to abnormal consciousness is accompanied by grinding discomfort of mental agony.

I should say—to continue this jelly-fish metaphor—that long feelers reached down and through the body, that these stood in the same relation to the nervous system as the over-mind to the brain or intellect.

There is, then, a set of super-feelings. These feelings extend out and about us; as the long, floating tentacles of the jelly-fish reach out and about him. They are not of different material, extraneous, as the physical arms and legs are extraneous to the gray matter of the directing brain. The super-feelers are part of the super-mind, as the jelly-fish feelers are the jelly-fish itself, elongated in fine threads.

I first realised this state of consciousness in my head. I visualise it just as well, now, centered in the love-region of the body or placed like a foetus in the body.

The centre of consciousness is either the brain or the love-region of the body.

Is it easier for a woman to attain this state of consciousness than for a man?

For me, it was before the birth of my child that the jelly-fish consciousness seemed to come definitely into the field or realm of the intellect or brain.

Are these jelly-fish states of consciousness interchangeable? Should we be able to think with the womb and feel with the brain?

May this consciousness be centered entirely in the brain or entirely in the womb or corresponding love-region of a man's body?

Vision is of two kinds—vision of the womb and vision of the brain. In vision of the brain, the region of consciousness is above and about the head; when the centre of consciousness shifts and the jelly-fish is in the body, (I visualise it in my case lying on the left side with the streamers or feelers floating up toward the brain) we have vision of the womb or love-vision.

The majority of dream and of ordinary vision is vision of the womb.

The brain and the womb are both centres of consciousness, equally important.

Most of the so-called artists of today have lost the use of their brain. There is no way of arriving at the over-mind, except through the intellect. To arrive at the world of over-mind vision any other way, is to be the thief that climbs into the sheep-fold.

I believe there are artists coming in the next generation, some of whom will have the secret of using their over-minds.

Over-mind artists usually come in a group. There were the great Italians: Verrochio, Angelo, Ghiberti, the lot that preceded and followed da Vinci, including statesmen, explorers, and men and women of curious and sensitive development.

There was the great Athenian group: the dramatists, Socrates, the craftsmen and the men and women, their followers and lovers.

There is no great art period without great lovers.

Socrates' whole doctrine of vision was a doctrine of love.

We must be "in love" before we can understand the mysteries of vision.

A lover must choose one of the same type of mind as himself, a musician, a musician, a scientist, a scientist, a general, a young man also interested in the theory and practice of arms and armies.

We begin with sympathy of thought.

The minds of the two lovers merge, interact in sympathy of thought.

The brain, inflamed and excited by this interchange of ideas, takes on its character of over-mind, becomes (as I have visualised in my own case) a jellyfish, placed over and about the brain.

The love-region is excited by the appearance of beauty of the loved one, its energy not dissipated in physical relations, takes on its character of mind, becomes this womb-brain or love-brain that I have visualised as a jelly-fish *in* the body.

The love-brain and over-brain are both capable of thought. This thought is vision.

All men have possibilities of developing this vision.

The over-mind is like a lens of an opera-glass. When we are able to use this over-mind lens, the whole world of vision is open to us.

I have said that the over-mind is a lens. I should say more exactly that the love-mind and the over-mind are two lenses. When these lenses are properly adjusted, focused, they bring the world of vision into consciousness. The two work separately, perceive separately, yet make one picture.

The mystic, the philosopher is content to contemplate, to examine these pictures. The Attic dramatist reproduced them for men of lesser or other gifts. He realised, the whole time, that they were not his ideas. They were eternal, changeless ideas that he had grown aware of, dramas already conceived that he had watched; memory is the mother, begetter of all drama, idea, music, science or song.

We may enter the world of over-mind consciousness directly, through the use of our over-mind brain. We may enter it indirectly, in various ways. Every person must work out his own way.

Certain words and lines of Attic choruses, any scrap of da Vinci's drawings, the Delphic charioteer, have a definite, hypnotic effect on me. They are straight, clear entrances, to me, to over-world consciousness. But my line of approach, my sign-posts, are not your sign-posts.

My sign-posts are not yours, but if I blaze my own trail, it may help to give you confidence and urge you to get out of the murky, dead, old, thousand-times explored old world, the dead world of overworked emotions and thoughts.

But the world of the great creative artists is never dead. The new schools of destructive art theorists are on the wrong track. Because Leonardo and his kind are never old, never dead. Their world is never explored, hardly even entered.

Because it needs an over-mind or a slight glimmering of over-mind intelligence to understand over-mind intelligence.

The Delphic charioteer has, I have said, an almost hypnotic effect on me: the bend of his arm, the knife-cut of his chin; his feet, rather flat, slightly separated, a firm pedestal for himself; the fall of his drapery, in geometrical precision; and the angles of the ingatherings of the drapery at the waist.

All this was no "inspiration," it was sheer, hard brain work.

This figure has been created by a formula arrived at consciously or unconsciously.

If we had the right sort of brains, we would receive a definite message from that figure, like dots and lines ticked off by one receiving station, received and translated into definite thought by another telegraphic centre.

There is no trouble about art. There is already enough beauty in the world of art, enough in the fragments and the almost perfectly preserved charioteer at Delphi alone to remake this world.

There is no trouble about the art, it is the appreciators we want. We want young men and women to communicate with the charioteer and his like.

We want receiving centres for dots and dashes.

It is said that da Vinci went mad if he saw a boy's face in Florence or a caged bird or a child with yellow hair that fell or stood up in tight whorls like the goldsmith work he had learned with Verrochio. Da Vinci went mad because those lines of the bird's back or the boy's shoulder or the child's hair acted on him directly, as the lines of a statue, worked out like the charioteer, would act on us if we had the right sort of receiving brain.

Two or three people, with healthy bodies and the right sort of receiving brains, could turn the whole tide of human thought, could direct lightning flashes of electric power to slash across and destroy the world of dead, murky thought.

Two or three people gathered together in the name of truth, beauty, over-mind consciousness could bring the whole force of this power back into the world.

It is true that, in the year A.D. 361, the Galilean conquered at Delphi. That was because the Hellenic mind had entirely lost the secret of dots and dashes.

The electric force of the lines and angles of the priest-like body of the charioteer still gave out their message but there was no one to receive this message.

The Galilean conquered because he was a great artist, like da Vinci.

A fish-basket, upturned on the sand, or a candle in a candle-stick or a Roman coin with its not unbeautifully wrought head of a king, could excite him and give him ideas, as the bird or boy's face or child's yellow hair gave da Vinci ideas.

The Galilean fell in love with things as well as people. He would fall in love with a sea-gull or some lake-heron that would dart up from the coarse lake grass, when Peter leapt out to drag his great boat on shore, or the plain little speckled-back birds bought in the market by the poor Jews. Then, he would look at Peter with his great archaic head and the young Jude with his intense eyes, and he would exclaim suddenly: "Ah, but your faces, your faces are more beautiful, more charged with ideas, with lines that suggest and bring me into touch with the world of over-mind thought, than many, many sparrows."

He looked at the blue grass-lily and the red-brown sand-lily that grew under the sheltered hot-sand banks in the southern winter, for hours and hours. If he closed his eyes, he saw every vein and fleck of blue or vermilion. He would breathe in the fragrance with the wind and the salt. He would rest for days along the shores of the sea-lakes.

Then, in the town, there would be some tragedy and he would send the friends and wailing relatives out of the way. He would be angry, as he looked at the little girl's face, that she was surrounded by such ugliness. He would look at her for a long time because of the beauty of the little, straight nose and the eyelids, the hair clinging like seaweed to the fine little skull, the very white hands. He would like to have stayed looking at her for hours, like the blue grass-lily. But he was afraid they would break in, suddenly again, with their heavy, black clothes, and ugly voices. So he said, "Daughter, I say unto you, arise."

The first step in the Eleusinian mysteries had to do with sex. There were images set up in a great room, coloured marbles and brown pottery, painted with red and vermilion and coloured earthen work or clay images. The candidates for admission to the mysteries would be shown through the room by a priest or would walk through at random, as the crowd walks through the pornographic chamber at the museum at Naples.

It would be easy enough to judge them by their attitude, whether it was one of crude animal enjoyment or hypocritical aloofness.

The crowd that got through to the second room would be different, more sensitive, more fastidious. They would correspond to certain of our intellectual types of today. They would be interested because it was the thing to be interested—also to show their superiority.

Any one who got safely through the mere animal stage and the intellectual stage would be left in a small room by himself to make his constatation.

Anyone who wants can get through these stages today just as easily as the Eleusinian candidates outside Athens in the fifth century, B.C.

There is plenty of pornographic literature that is interesting and amusing.

If you cannot be entertained and instructed by Boccaccio, Rabelais, Montaigne, Sterne, Middleton, de Gourmont and de Régnier there is something wrong with you physically.

If you cannot read these people and enjoy them you are not ready for the first stage of initiation.

If you do read these people and enjoy them and enjoy them really with your body, because you have a normal healthy body, then you may be ready for the second stage of initiation.

You can look into things with your intellect, with your sheer brain.

If your brain cannot stand the strain of following out these lines of thought, scientifically, and if you are not balanced and sane enough to grasp these things with a certain amount of detachment, you are obviously not ready for experiments in over-mind consciousness.

Socrates said, "There are many wand-bearers but few inspired." He meant, by wand-bearers, people who had passed the first two stages of the Eleusinian mysteries. We mean by wand-bearers today, intelligent people of normal development, who have looked into matters of life scientifically and with a certain amount of artistic appreciation.

Today there are many wand-bearers but few inspired.

One must understand a lower wisdom before one understands a higher. One must understand Euripides before one understands Aristophanes. Yet to understand dung chemically and spiritually and with the earth sense, one must first understand the texture, spiritual and chemical and earthy, of the rose that grows from it.

Euripides is a white rose, lyric, feminine, a spirit. Aristophanes is a satyr.

Is the satyr greater or less than the white rose it embraces? Is the earth greater or less than the white rose it brings forth? Is the dung greater or less than the rose?

Flowers are made to seduce the senses: fragrance, form, colour.

If you can not be seduced by beauty, you cannot learn the wisdom of ugliness.

Zeus Endendros—God in a tree; Dionysius Anthios, God in a flower; Zeus Melios, God in the black earth, death, disruption, disintegration; Dionysius Zagreus, the flower torn, broken by chemical processes of death, vein, leaf, texture—white luminous lily surface, veined with black—white lily flesh bruised, withered. "I, Lais, place my mirror here at thy feet, O Paphian—I remember and I dare not remember. Is there a mystery beyond that of thy white arms, O Aphrogenia? Is there a beauty greater than the white pear-branch which broke so white against a black April storm sky that Zeus himself was roused from his sacred meditation, as from the ranges of Olympos he gazed below upon the Attic pastures. He gazed below and saw you, O white branch. He was angry, for you were more white against the sky than the passion of his shaft. For that reason he sent lightning to blast you, O tree. Since then no man may speak your name, O Goddess. But we know there is a mystery greater than beauty and that is death."

The heat, the stench of things, the unutterable boredom of it all. Meleager of Gadara, what a fate; a Jew father, a Greek mother. What God of the Hebrew, what demon of the islands had presided at his ill-omened begetting? Heliodora, Zenophile, what were they but names? Greek prostitutes—branded by Syrian traders and Jew merchants alike. The stench—the dust, Meleager of Gadara—what a fate.

No wind and the sea stretching like the dead parchment rent with the devil tokens—the Hebrew script he would die to forget—the tongue he would die to forget—but that in dying he would forget that other—gold—light of gold—words, potent, a charm each leading to a world where there were cold flowers.

Heliodora, Zenophile—no Attic hetairas.

Flowers?

The roses that he had touched that morning—the boy at the wharf pier—he had stepped from a boat, wet with the sea about the islands. But the boy's wet curls smelt of salt fish and his roses were already rank—rotting—and he had dipped their streaked stems in cheap myrrh to cheat the Heliodoras of this world of their sparse [. . .]

Gods, dead alike of Greek and Hebrew. What devil had sent a swine, a pig to plant its two feet on his door step and gaze within? Voices and shouting. He would never find peace that day for the golden branch of the divine Plate ever shining by its own light.

A pig on the door step.

To live with a poet's mind in a slum of Gadara. Meleager—what daemon of the islands was present at your ill-omened begetting?

To live with a poet's mind in a slum of Gadara or to live with princely Jews his father's friend—a merchant respected—his father again—in the palaces of Syrian princes.

There was no choice—*but a pig on the door step.*

Avaunt pig! Must I sacrifice the script of the golden Plate to hurl at that pig?

After all, could the script of the golden high falutin' high-sounding Plate be put to a better use?

He ignores the script, save to turn it over with his snout. What devil possesses him?

Well, here is my Gadarene foot then.

A herd of them in the street.

Beyond the stifling dust, someone is shouting. A voice, more portent than the script of the golden Plate. Speaking Greek too.

"Be you entered into the sea."

Praise every god of Greek or Hebrew they are gone.

A crowd of the usual slum vandals—and one young man who is laughing.

A princely stranger and his father, a Jew too. What cool hands at parting.

Beyond the Zenophiles of this world there is another Zenophile, beyond the Heliodoras another Heliodora, beyond the dank, hot and withering roses, other roses.

A princely stranger and a poet.

I would make him some gift, for his brow was more lordly (though his father was no Greek) than the Kyllenian Hermes.

I would bind narcissus to narcissus. I would plait the red violet to the white violet. I would break for you one rose, more red than the wine-cyclamen. I would bind the stem of the crocus to the stem of the wild-hyacinth, that each might show less lovely about your brow, Kylennian Hermes.

Egypt in the terms of world-consciousness is the act of love. Hellas is a child born.

The secret of the Sphinx is the secret of knowledge. The secret of the Centaur is the secret of feeling.

The Sphinx knows everything. The Centaur feels everything.

Three worlds.

1. World of abstraction: Helios, Athene.
2. Intermediate or Nature world: Pan, the Naiads.
3. World of the uninitiate men and women.

All these worlds are important, equally important. But we are important only insofar as we become identified with the highest in ourselves—"our own familiar daemon."

Spirits of a higher world have access into a lower world. Athene may appear to one in the next lower world. She may be the companion of a half-god, but she must preserve her dignity, her Olympian character. Athene perfectly did this. Therefore the gods accepted and enrolled Odysseus among the half-gods and heroes.

But when there was a question of Artemis losing caste by her association with the too boorish giant, Orion, the giant was slain.

However, lest honour should be lacking the Olympian hierarchy because of this lapse of taste, Orion was afterwards received among the stars.

It was *de rigueur* for an Olympian not to appear to a mortal direct. Therefore Selene who requested this, was burned to ash.

But we have many records of Naiads, tree and river spirits, sea spirits and voices of the sea, and Centaurs holding friendly intercourse with mortals.

We also know that Pan appeared to those in pain or trouble, not only in dreams but "visibly at mid-day."

Pan appeared at Marathon before all the Greeks. And I know of witnesses today who have had vision of this god.

Normal consciousness, pricks of everyday discomfort, jealousy, and despair and various forms of unhappiness that are the invariable accompaniment of any true, deep relationship, all this may be symbolised by a thistle.

There are two ways of escaping the pain and despair of life, and of the rarest, most subtle dangerous and ensnaring gift that life can bring us, relationship with another person—love.

One way is to kill that love in one's heart. To kill love—to kill life.

The other way is to accept that love, to accept the snare, to accept the pricks, the thistle.

To accept life—but that is dangerous.

It is also dangerous not to accept life.

To every man and woman in the world it is given at some time or another, in some form or another, to make the choice.

Every man and woman is free to accept or deny life—to accept or reject this questionable gift—this thistle.

But these notes are concerned chiefly with the mental process that is in some form or other the complement of the life process.

That is to say this thistle—life, love, martyrdom—leads in the end—must lead in the logical course of events to death, paradise, peace.

That world of death—that is, death to the stings of life, which is the highest life—may be symbolised by the serpent.

The world of vision has been symbolised in all ages by various priestly cults in all countries by the serpent.

In my personal language or vision, I call this serpent a jelly-fish.

The serpent—the jelly-fish—the over-conscious mind.

The realisation of this over-conscious world is the concern of the artist.

But this world is there for everyone.

The minds of men differ but the over-minds are alike.

Our minds, all of our minds, are like dull little houses, built more or less alike—a dull little city with rows of little detached villas, and here and there a more pretentious house, set apart from the rest, but in essentials, seen from a distance, one with the rest, all drab, all grey.

Each comfortable little home shelters a comfortable little soul—and a wall at the back shuts out completely any communication with the world beyond.

Man's chief concern is keeping his little house warm and making his little wall strong.

Outside is a great vineyard and grapes and rioting and madness and dangers.

It is very dangerous.

An enormous moth detached himself from a bunch of yellow grapes—he seemed stupified with the heat of the sun—heavy with the sun and his soft belly swollen with the honey of the grapes, I would have said, for there was a bead of gold—resinous—that matted the feathers at his throat.

He fell rather than flew and his great feet scratched with a faint metallic ring, the side of my golden cup.

He stumbled, awkward and righted himself, clutched the rim of my cup, waved his antennae feebly.

I would have rescued him but I myself was dizzy with the heat and the fumes of the golden wine and I heard a great shout of laughter as I tried to steady my cup and I shouted in reply, *he* is drunk—*he* is drunk.

So he was drunk.

Outside is a great vineyard and rioting and madness and dangers.

The body—limbs of a tree, branches of a fruit-tree, the whole body of a tree—philosophy of the Tao, philosophy of the Hebrew, philosophy of the Greek, man identified with nature, the just man "a tree planted by the rivers," numerous instances of gods in trees and human beings of peculiar beauty or grace turned at death, as reward of kindliness, into trees, poplar trees, mulberry trees, laurels.

But a man has intellect, brain—a mind in fact, capable of three states of being, a mind that may be conscious in the ordinary, scholarly, literal sense of the word, or subconscious—those sub-conscious states varying in different states of dream or physical feeling, or illness, delirium, or madness—a mind, over-conscious as well, able to enter into a whole life as Leonardo entered, Euripides, the Galilean with his baskets and men's faces and Roman coins—the forest hermits of the Ganges and the painter who concentrated on one tuft of pine branch with its brown cone until every needle was a separate entity to him and every pine needle bore to every other one, a clear relationship like a drawing of a later mechanical twentieth century bridge-builder.

Lo-fu sat in his orchard in the Ming dynasty, A.D. 184. He sat in his orchard and looked about in a vague, casual way. Against the grey stones of the orchard wall he saw the low branch of an apple tree. He thought, that shoot should have been pruned, it hangs too low. Then as he looked at the straight tough young shoot, he thought, no, the apples are excellent, so round and firm. Then he went on looking.

It was a shoot of some years' growth. Why had it been left untrimmed? Was it some special experiment in grafting the old gardener had undertaken some years ago? Was it by accident that the limb hung there? Then his conscious mind ceased wondering and, being an artist, his intensity and concentration were of a special order and he looked at that fruit branch hanging in the sun, the globes of the apples red, yellow, red with flecks of brown and red, yellow where the two colours merged, and flecks of brown again on the yellow, and green as the round surface curved in toward the stem. He saw the stem, pushed down almost lost in the green hollow. He saw the stem fastened to the tough little branch above. He saw the green brown bark of the stem and he compared it with the darker, stronger bark of the branch. He examined the ridges and the minute black lines that made up the individual surface of that little branch. He went further. There were two leaves, continents to be explored in a leisurely manner lest his mind passing one carelessly from vein to vein, should miss one rib or the small branch of one off-shoot of that exquisite skeleton. And when he knew the skeleton of that leaf, the rivers, as it were, furrowing that continent, his mind was content. But it had only begun its search. Between each river there lay a fair green field—many, many little fields each with an individuality, each with some definite feature setting it apart from every other little plot.

I have tried to tell in a small way with as little detail as possible, how Lo-fu looked at that branch. He really did look at it. He really did see it. Then he went inside and in his little cool room out of the sun he closed his eyes. He saw that branch but more clearly, more vividly than ever. That branch was his mistress now, his love. As he saw it in the orchard, that mistress was, as it were, observed in a crowd, from a distance. He could not touch her, his mistress with all the world about. Here, in his little room, the world had ceased to exist. It was shut off, shut out, forgotten. His love, his apple branch, his beautiful subtle mistress, was his. And having possessed her with his great and famished soul, she was his forever.

She was his, and though he knew she was only one, one of a thousand women, one of a thousand, thousand, beautiful women, she was his, his own. And he was never jealous, though her beauty was so obvious, for no one else could possess her. Yet unlike another lover, he longed that his friend should love her too, or should make another branch his own, for the orchard was full and beyond the orchard the mountain and pine forests were a thousand intimate friendly herbs and grasses.

Lo-fu was a poet. To him that apple branch, outside in the orchard, existed as an approach to something else. As the body of a man's mistress might be said to exist as the means of approach to something else, that is as a means or instrument of feeling or happiness, so the branch in the orchard existed to Lo-fu as the means of attaining happiness, as a means of completing himself, as a means of approach to ecstasy.

I have been talking with a young man, a scholar and philosopher. He says my term over-mind is not good, because in his case at least, the mental state I describe lies below the sub-conscious mind. That is, I visualise my three states of consciousness in a row,

1. Over-conscious mind.
2. Conscious mind.
3. Sub-conscious mind.

He on the other hand visualises his three states,

1. Conscious mind.
2. Sub-conscious mind.
3. Universal mind.

He means by universal mind exactly what I mean by over-mind but certainly my term over-mind is not adequate, if this over-mind state is approached by others through the sub-conscious.

But we both visualise these states in a row, though I suppose the universal symbol is the triangle, or taken a step further, the circle, as the three seem to run into one another, though neither he nor I visualise them that way.

The body of a man is a means of approach, or can be used as a means of approach to ecstasy. Man's body can be used for that. The best Greek sculpture used the bodies of young athletes as Lo-fu used the branch of the fruit tree. The lines of the human body may be used as an approach to the over-mind or universal mind.

The lines of the human body and the lines of the fruit tree are like the body of the Delphic charioteer that I spoke of some time ago. The fruit tree and the human body are both receiving stations, capable of storing up energy, overworld energy. That energy is always there but can be transmitted only to another body or another mind that is in sympathy with it, or keyed to the same pitch.

The body of the Greek boy Polycleitus used for his Diuademenos was as impersonal a thing as a tree. He used the body instead of a tree. That boy's body was, of course, capable of human passions but Polycleitus' approach to that body was not through the human passions.

But of course he was in love with it just as Lo-fu was in love with the apple branch and Leonardo with the boy's face or the Galilean with the field lilies.

But the body, I suppose, like a lump of coal, fulfills its highest function when it is being consumed.

When coal burns it gives off heat.

The body consumed with love gives off heat.

But taken a step further, coal may be used to make gas, an essence, a concentrated, ethereal form of coal.

So with the body. It may burn out simply as heat or physical love. That may be good. But it is also interesting to understand the process whereby the heat of the physical body is transmuted to this other, this different form, concentrated, ethereal, which we refer to in common speech as spirit.

It is all spirit but spirit in different forms.

We cannot have the heat without the lump of coal.

Perhaps so we cannot have spirit without body, the body of nature, or the body of individual men and women.

I spoke to a scientist, a psychologist, about my divisions of mind and over-mind. He said that over-mind was not exactly the right term, that sub-conscious mind was the phrase I was groping for.

I have thought for a long time about the comparative value of these terms, and I see at last my fault and his.

We were both wrong. I was about to cover too much of the field of abnormal consciousness by the term over-mind. He, on the other hand, would have called it all sub-conscious mind.

But the sub-conscious and the over-conscious are entirely different states, entirely different worlds.

The sub-conscious world is the world of sleeping dreams and the world great lovers enter, physical lovers, but very great ones.

The over-conscious world is the world of waking dreams and the world great lovers enter, spiritual lovers, but only the greatest.

A sub-conscious dream may become an over-conscious dream at any moment of waking.

The intellect, the brain, the conscious mind is the bridge across, the link between the sub-conscious and the over-conscious.

I think at last I have my terms clear.

There are three states of manifestations—sub-conscious mind, conscious mind, over-conscious mind.

These jelly-fish, I think, are the "seeds cast into the ground." But as it takes a man and woman to create another life, so it takes these two forms of seed, one in the head and one in the body to make a new spiritual birth. I think that is why I saw them as jelly-fish. They are really two flecks of protoplasm and when we are "born again," we begin not as a child but as the very first germs that grow into a child.

Probably we pass through all forms of life and that is very interesting. But so far I have passed through these two, I am in my spiritual body a jelly-fish and a pearl.

We can probably use this pearl, as a crystal ball is used, for concentrating and directing pictures from the world of vision.

It is necessary to work, to strive toward the understanding of the over-mind. But once a man becomes conscious of this jelly-fish above his head, this pearl within his skull, this seed cast into the ground, his chief concern automatically becomes his body.

Once we become concretely aware of this pearl, this seed, our centre of consciousness shifts. Our concern is with the body.

Where does the body come in?
What is the body?

I imagine it has often been said that the body is like an oyster and the soul or spirit, a pearl. But today I saw for myself that the jelly-fish over my head had become concentrated. I saw that the state of mind I had before symbolised as a jelly-fish was just as well symbolised differently. That is, all the spiritual energy seemed concentrated in the center of my forehead, inside my skull, and it was small and giving out a very soft light, but not scattered light, light concentrated in itself as the light of a pearl would be. So I understood exactly what the Galilean meant by the kingdom of heaven, being a pearl of great price.

Then in the same relation, the body was not a very rare or lovely thing. The body seemed an elementary, unbeautiful and transitory form of life. Yet here again, I saw that the body had its use. The oyster makes the pearl in fact. So the body, with all its emotions and fears and pain in time casts off the spirit, a concentrated essence, not itself, but made, in a sense, created by itself.

I know that this has been said before but I speak for myself, from my personal experience.

Because the spirit, we realise, is a seed. No man by thought can add an inch to his stature, no initiate by the strength and power of his intellect can force his spirit to grow.

He cannot force his spirit to grow, but he can retard its growth. At least so it seems to me.

He can retard its growth by neglect of his body because the body of man as the body of nature is the ground into which the seed or spirit is cast.

This is the mystery of Demeter, the Earth Mother. The body of the Eleusinian initiate had become one with the earth, as his soul had become one with the seeds enclosed in the earth.

No man by thought can make the grain sprout or the acorn break its shell. No man by intellectual striving can make his spirit expand.

But every man can till the field, can clear weeds from about the stems of flowers.

Every man can water his own little plot, can strive to quiet down the overwrought tension of his body.

Christ and his father, or as the Eleusinian mystic would have said, his mother, were one.

Christ was the grapes that hung against the sun-lit walls of that mountain garden, Nazareth. He was the white hyacinth of Sparta and the narcissus of the islands. He was the conch shell and the purple-fish left by the lake tides. He was the body of nature, the vine, the Dionysus, as he was the soul of nature.

He was the gulls screaming at low tide and tearing the small crabs from among the knotted weeds.

Christ and his father, or as the Eleusinian mystic would have said, his mother, were one.

Christ was the grapes that hung against the sun-lit walls of that mountain garden, Nazareth. He was the white hyacinth of Sparta and the narcissus of the islands. He was the conch shell and the purple-fish left by the lake tides. he was the body of nature, the vine, the Dionsysus, as he was the soul of nature.

He was the gulls screaming at low tide and tearing the small crabs from among the knotted weeds.

Notes on Thought and Vision & The Wise Sappho. San Francisco: City Lights Books, 1982. 17–53.

The Borderline Pamphlet

In the Cast:

Pete (A Negro)	Paul Robeson
Adah (His Wife)	Eslanda Robeson
Astrid	Helga Doorn [H.D.]
Thorne (Helga's husband)	Gavin Arthur
The Café Manageress	Bryher
The Barmaid	Charlotte Arthur
The Pianist	Robert Herring
The Old Lady	Blanche Lewin

BORDERLINE

I.

Borderline is chosen as the name of this new film; clarid sequence of idea will show why.

There are in Europe, many just such little towns as this particular borderline town of some indefinite mid-European mountain district. There are trains coming and trains going. One of these trains has already deposited the half-world mondaine, Astrid with Thorne, her lover. They have come here because of some specific nerve-problem, perhaps to rest, perhaps to recuperate, perhaps to economise, perhaps simply in hope of some emotional convalescence. They live as such people do the world over, in just such little social borderline rooms as just such couples seek in Devonshire, in Cornwall, in the South of France, in Provincetown, United States. They are borderline social cases, not out of life, not in life; the woman is a sensitive neurotic, the man, a handsome, degenerate dipsomaniac. Thorne has not reached the end of his cravings, may step this side, that side of the border; Astrid, the white-cerebral is and is not outcast, is and is not a social alien, is and is not a normal human being, she is borderline. These two are specifically chosen to offset another borderline couple of more dominant integrity. These last, Pete and his sweetheart Adah, have a less intensive problem, but border; they dwell on the cosmic racial borderline. They are black people among white people.

Though in this specific mid-Europe, there is nothing intrinsically disharmonious in that, their situation is a sort rarely, if ever, touched on, in film art. Their problem is not dealt with as the everlasting black-white Problem with a capital. It remains however a motive to be counted on; though threads are woven in and through the fabric, white into black and black into white, Pete and Adah must inevitably remain "borderline," whether by their own choice and psychic affiliation or through sheer crude brute causes.

Mr. Kenneth Macpherson is himself, you might say, borderline among the young cinema directors. He is not at all allied with the ultra-modern abstract school of rhomboid and curve and cross-beam of tooth pick or coal shovel. I do not mean that Mr. Macpherson is out of sympathy with any form of realistic cinema abstraction, I simply quote him, remember his saying in casual conversation, "why should one trouble to photograph a match stick when a birch tree is so interesting?" Mr. Macpherson finds a white birch tree as interesting, as abstract, as some people find a tooth-brush. But he is also interested in tooth-brushes. In their place. There are moments, in Mr. Macpherson's sequences, when a flash of white hand or the high lights across the knuckles of a black hand become, you might say, as "sterile" as certain much-vaunted "effects" of sieve, tooth-pick, or cullander. But when Mr. Macpherson plays upon abstraction, it is in reference to some other abstraction. A telephone receiver of usual form and literacy, is dealt with, as abstraction, though it merges to the concrete when applied to succeeding abstraction of a stern chin line. The method of Mr. Macpherson is admittedly an "abstract" method, but he is only satisfied when abstraction coupled with related abstraction make logical dramatic sequence. A little oil can, for instance (concise modernistic abstraction) relates to a giant negro shoulder. Oil and heat are related to a dark brow, that great head that bends forward, very earth giant. While light and air, indicated in an inblown curtain, link on to the Victorian abstraction of a stuffed dead sea-gull and thence, by swift flashes of inevitable sequence, to a weathered woman-face. That face beats through the film like the very swift progress of those wings, doomed it is evident, and already extinguished in this "borderline" existence.

Mr. Kenneth Macpherson is "borderline." In Germany, among German appreciators, there is an odd phrase, though one must learn to accept it; "ach, so English, sehr English." In England, the inevitable reaction to this abstract and formalized intellectuality, is to say, "absolutely influenced by the Germans." Both of these are and are not true. Mr. Macpherson is nordic, is English in general European terminology, though obviously his intense specialized inspiration is that of the northern Celt. His fine fibre is nordic, is celtic, his types therefore, conforming to physical outward symbol (European or African) are used, regardless of the feelings of his audience, to propound some "runic" problem. These people are the riddles, they ask "why" and they ask "what" and they say "when is this or that not that or this?" When is an African not an African? When obviously he is an earth-god. When is a woman not a woman? When obviously she is sleet and hail and a stuffed sea-gull. He says when is white not white and when is black white and when is white black? You may or may not like this sort of cinematography. This is no concern whatever of your young director. He does not care for you, he does not care for me, he does not care, it is obvious, for his carefully chosen and meticulously directed cast of mixed black and white, of mixed professionals and "amateurs." He *does* care and he does not care. The riddle, when is an amateur not an amateur, might be aptly propounded at this moment. The answer to that rune is comparatively easy. There is, under proper directorship, no such thing as an amateur. Certain of the German and Russian directors claim that some of their most poignant effects have come from people who have stepped for the first time before a camera. In that, Mr. Macpherson follows the "foreign" tradition. And in this again, Mr. Macpherson is borderline, working as he does with German-Russian approach yet with keen knife-blade of indigenous intrepidity.

Again Mr. Macpherson's company is borderline, not only in that it is racially mixed but also because of the relative professional experience and inexperience of its members. Mr. Robeson, we all know as an artist of high repute. His wife, Eslanda Robeson, has not appeared, to my knowledge, on the stage or screen. She moves, "emotes," reacts in uncanny sympathy to the ideas of her director. Mr. Robeson had only to step before the camera and the theme flowed toward him as many small streams toward that great river. Mr. Robeson is obviously the ground under all their feet. He is stabilized, stable, the earth. Across Mr. Macpherson's characterisation of Pete, the half-vagrant young giant negro, the fretting provincialism of small-town slander and small town menace move like shadows from high clouds. The giant negro is in the high clouds, white cumulous cloud banks in a higher heaven. Conversely, his white fellow-men are the shadows of white, are dark, neurotic; storm brews; there is that runic fate that "they that live by the sword shall perish by the sword." Or as here applied, "they that live by neurotic-erotic suppression shall perish by the same." This is not so precisely stated. But it is the white woman and the white man who are victims, when there is the final test of man and nature.

Here again, Mr. Macpherson is "borderline." He is, in no way whatever, concerned personally with the black-white political problem. As an artist, he sees beauty, "take it or leave it," he seems to say again and again, and, "I'm not busy with party politics." Nevertheless, in his judicious, remote manner, he has achieved more for that much mooted and hooted Problem (with a capital) than if he went about to gain specific sympathy. He says, "here is a man, he is black," he says, "here is a woman also of partial African abstraction." He says, not "here is a black man, here is a mulatto woman," but "here is a *man*, here is a *woman*." He says, "look, sympathize with them and love them" not because they are black but because they are man, because they are woman. This race presentation will be no palliative for a decadent palate. Mr. Macpherson does not even hint or suggest any aesthetic compromise. He simply states his riddle, answers his riddle, says, "see and love and if you see and do not love, that is no concern of mine." Mr. Macpherson is the artist par excellence, he sees with the eye and what he sees, he portrays. He cares no more for you or me than Leonardo did for King Francis or the merchant husband of Mona Lisa.

II.

Juxtaposition of "Leonardo" with "modern screen art" is neither as inept nor as ironical as it may seem at first glance. This name connotes mechanical efficiency, modernity and curiousity allied with pure creative impulse. The film *per se*, is a curious welding of mechanical and creative instincts. Yet you may ask, granted that, what has Leonardo, demi-god of accepted intellectuality, to do with this gutter-offshoot of modernity? What has that steel blade to do with harem beauties in bathing costumes and with sugar and spice and everything that is nice and must, *must*, MUST remain nice in the commercially constituted realm of so-called cinematography? You say "what indeed?" We answer, "do you know your Leonardo? Do you know your film world?" Leonardo, you say, is a text-book high-water mark of Renaissance painting, someone dead long ago. Cinema art, you will repeat, is a present-day gutter-offshoot of the stage, having to do with ladies and laddies and gentlemen with gardenias and crooks and safety vaults. We must answer, "that is all true."

Yet we may ask, have any of you gentlemen tried to use a camera? How many of you take photographs, even passably good ones, of suns and sunsets, of ladies among water-lilies? Have you any idea of the technical difficulties to be surmounted in dealing even with a newsreel? Have any of your creative artists who paint passable pictures ever mixed your own colours, have you cut apart dead arms and dead hands to see what nerve centres really do look like, and have you probed down and down with a little sharp implement, perhaps the very little knife you just now scraped your palate with, to see if you can discover by its valve formation, why the human heart should beat so? Have any of you writers invented personal secret script, written mind and soul secrets in that? Was writing so dear to you that you ever wrote with NO eye to any ulterior auditor, for yourself only? If you have done some of this or sympathised with some of this, then you may be said to know your Leonardo; if you have done some of this or sympathised with a little of it, then you may be said to be prepared to approach your new mechanical-creative film art.

You may deliberate over a few technical mechanical art problems; you may or may not accept them as applicable to the film. If, in yourself, there is no grain of this divine Leonardo-like curiosity, of this intensive Leonardo-esque modernism, then the screen can be of no use. Leonardo did not say, "there is no hope in painting, look at Giotto." Young Lindenberg did not say, "many brave hearts lie asleep in the deep, so beware, beware." Mr. Macpherson does not say, "there is no use doing this, I sweat blood for what use, if I ever do get across no one will understand me," he just goes on, his cadaverous frame getting more thin, his grey-steel eyes getting more glint and fire, his hands steady and his mind stable though his knees are shaking. It is funny to watch him work if you have a mind for just that sort of humour. Like watching a young gunner alone with his machine gun. It is as if one knew all the time the sniper would at the last get him. But it is a privilege, in no small way, to stand beside just such rare type of advanced young creative intellectual, waiting for the sniper to get oneself too. Pro patria indeed, if that pro patria is a no-man's land, an everyman's land of such plausible perfection. Mr. Macpherson, like Mr. da Vinci is Hellenic in his cold detachment, his cool appraisal, his very inhuman insistence on perfection.

Well, what anyhow is perfection? There is your perfection, there is my perfection, there is the perfection of Mr. da Vinci as well as that of Mr. Lindenberg and of Tom, Dick, and Harry. Your perfection may be this or this, a cigar in a club window or a gardenia in a buttonhole or a pair of translucent gold-silk stockings or the talk that goes with that or the legs that go with this or a volume of de Maupassant. *Chacun a,* we are told, *son gout.* Mr. Macpherson's is admittedly a peculiar pleasure. He stands, after any human being would drop dead of fatigue, casually with his elegant Debrie, machine man with it. He directs an elaborate series of overhead and side and ground lights, he writes a script which he meticulously illustrates with a series of some 1,000 pen sketches, he chooses his troop of players, he poses them, he all but acts for them, he directs from behind the camera while all the time he himself is concerned with the elaborate one-man mechanism of various stops, different focuses, indeterminate "pans" up and down, and the ever tricky job of the sheer turning. Did I say the camera was a one-man job? I spoke hastily. I have watched three men in one of the biggest studios of Germany hold up Mr. G. B. Pabst himself while all three gesticulated as to the proper focus, lense, distance, stop and rate of "turning." The camera is no one-man job. It takes half a dozen in the usual professionally equipped studio to wield this bulky monster. The sheer physical Macpherson, it seems, sometimes may just snap off somewhere about his elongated middle. But something else keeps him. It is that terrible thing, rare in any art, rarest of all in this new bastard, machine created film art, *creative impulse.* Divine creative instinct enslaves that monster, beautiful as a model air-ship, that renowned Debrie that is all sinew and all steel. The cinema-camera is a renaissance miracle or a Greek incarnation, it is monster compound as I have said of steel and fibre and final miracle, that delicate crystal lense. But what good is all that lacking even more divine impulse to enslave it? The camera has for the most part been the property of monsters, like those three Gorgons in the waste-land, holding a precious legacy, one human EYE between them. Would it be altogether inept to say that Mr. Macpherson and his young colleagues are just the last bit like the Perseus who snatched the EYE from the clutch of the slobbering and malign Monsters? Well, yes, perhaps that is a little silly. Kenneth Macpherson, at work, is a hard-boiled mechanic, as if he himself were all camera, bone and sinew and steel-glint of rapacious grey eyes.

III.

This then is the miracle, this curious atavism, the relationship so dramatically stressed between the ultra-modern, and the ultra-classic. The aim of the Renaissance of quattro-cento Florence was to bring the classic vibration into line with its own day. A renaissance is admittedly that. To-day those that scoff at film-art and its possibilities are as old-fashioned as the later retrogressives who burnt their Hesiod and then their Savonrola who had maligned him. There is no such thing as any fixed art standard. This is beautiful, this was beautiful, this may be beautiful. There is one beauty, it is the beauty of belief, of faith, of hope. And if that beauty is allied to sheer grit and technical efficiency, you get a new sort of art creation.

There is beauty, there has always been beauty. The problem in every art period is to present that beauty in a form allied to its environment and its time. No one can paint like Leonardo, no one can draw like Durer, no one to-day can satirize like Hogarth nor blow wind in tree-tops like Corot. No one man can hope to sculpt and make music and design air-ships in any one lifetime. This is, we are told, an age of specialists. Leonardo, however, the world's greatest "artist" must have a try at everything. Moreover, convention of his period forced this on him. In his apprentice days, he had to gild statuettes, paint in shadows, daub out shadows, sculpt, smear on colour, hammer gold leaf. He had at the same time to be politically and socially, an entity, scholar, musician, diplomat, soldier. An "artist" to-day is apt to be either a bit of a social pariah or a bit of a snob. There remains one world where a true artist may still demand and still attain something of that quattrocento ideal. An advanced and intellectual film-director must be mechanic, must be artist, must be man, must be warrior. He can be no spiritual aenemic, no physical weakling. He may not himself, personally, draw, paint, sculpt, yet instinctively, in his outlook, he must maintain sympathy with all these art-facets and with music, drama, and every form of writing. For in the film alone to-day, may these allied arts be welded.

Light flows over a face. That means nothing or little to you. There is a bronze forehead and the eye sockets are gouged out just this way; there is a concentration of shadow here, a plane of light here. You see a face, perhaps at most you see a pleasing portrait. You may even murmur "Gauguin." You think, no doubt, that this is clever posing or perhaps delightful portraiture. You do not realise that that face has been moulded, modelled by an artist, that those lights have been arranged, re-arranged deliberately focussed. Those who know anything, even of the technique of mere photography, realise that Macpherson sculpts literally with light. He gouges, he reveals, he conceals. All this not by accident, not automatically but with precision and deliberate foresight. Mr. Macpherson worked over his 1,000 little sketches for some months before he began to "turn." There was not one angle of a face, scarcely a movement of a hand or fold of drapery that he had not pre-visualised. The ordinary director leaves much to chance. He has "takes" and "retakes," leaves much of the visual construction in the hands of his camera-men, of his light effects in the hands of his elaborate staff of mechanics. Macpherson had one electrician who helped him shift incandescents. He had the delicate and competent assistance of John Macpherson with the spot-lights. Mr. John Macpherson, delicate portrait painter, with sure artistic instinct, did much to assist Kenneth Macpherson in some of the more conventionalized poses. But the whole conception was already, as I say, pre-arranged in the curious and amazing visual memory of his son.

A man has two hands. With one of his two hands, Kenneth Macpherson turned with steady even pressure, adjusted with the other, this or that stop, this or that delicate change of focus, like a sensitive violinist. The hands of John Macpherson, allied to the sympathetic mind, worked a spot light as his son directed. Back of the camera, facing his models, not eye to eye, as is the case of the usual director, but *THROUGH THE LENSE,* Mr. Macpherson gave definite and sustained direction. His "stand, now move, a little slower, not so sullen, that light a little higher," were uttered with assurance and received the immediate response that the ordinary director gets only at long range and after untold rehearsals. It stands to reason that the sheer pictorial quality of Mr. Macpherson's work (apart from the dramatic and rhythmic) must be unique among his contemporaries.

He achieves almost without exception, arresting and surprising effects, not only in the legitimate film sense, but in actual, historic, conventional "art" values. It is strange to see delicate screen tree-tops etched against a screen sky, that Corot would acclaim. It is odd to associate Botticelli with the cinema but that association is inevitable in some of the interior scenes for instance of Astrid and her shawl. It is unusual to weld the idea of bronze with movement, but a head is sculptured, gouged out in planes and focus of light and shadow and inset with eyes like those Mena period Egyptian heads with amber glass, yet that head moves. It is difficult to imagine Hogarth, Fragonard, Botticelli, Egyptian bronze and Greek marble all allied and welded, a unit and that unit modern. In this film, you get all these; the line of trees too in the long popular avenue down which Thorne wanders as in some astral dream, bring to mind the high spaces of the Karnak temple. Trees are foundations, pillars of gigantic temple, they are delicate too, as remote and etherial as the trees of Corot. Men are men, in everyday clothes, in everyday existence, and women are women with petty jealousies and nerve-reactions and erotic-cerebral modern complexes. Men are men but they are as well, black and white, carved massive intimate stone and bronze portraits. Women are women but they are embroidered with delicacy, as that head of Adah against rock-flowers, like an Asiatic on a screen, or they are fine with some "French" sophistication as the frivolous and Fragonard-like moments of the girl in the café or they are gouged out with a white lightening fury, like the tragic face of Astrid, from white marble. Mr. Kenneth Macpherson is rooted firmly in the bed-rock of recognized and recognizable beauty; he reaches forward (strange contradiction) toward the lean skyscraper beauty of ultra-modernity. In this there is no forced note, no note of falsity because that beauty and the beauty of Mena period Egypt, of Hohkousai Japan, of quattrocento Florence, of Hogarth and of Fragonard and of Botticelli of pre-Phidian Athens, of Ionian Ephesus are all one. Mr. Kenneth Macpherson has some obvious affinity with all these facets of past beauty. But this is his uncanny legacy. He brings all these high powered vibrations of past static art conception into direct line with modern problems, with modernity and with the most modern art of portraiture in movement.

IV.

I have said that Kenneth Macpherson touches the various "stops" and focus appliances of his beautiful camera like a violinist. And that presents another parallel. I have said that in the film alone can the pictorial arts be welded. They can in addition, be *wedded* and to a separate art form. And that form, music.

But here we are on difficult ground; speaking of one art in terms of another always seems the hall-mark of the 'nineties or of facile dilettantism. Yet it is perhaps as necessary to-day for the modernist artist to endeavour to shock weary sensibilities as it was for the so-called "effete" of that generation. Whistler says "Symphony in B flat" or "Harmony in F Major" or whatever it was he did say, and the mutton-sleeves raised lorgnettes and the gardenias leaned a little nearer to these bizarre effusions of black and white and pallid purples on small canvas. We have grown so used to that sort of juxtaposition of terms of art form and music, that we hesitate before elaborating on the obvious affinity between film and music. Though we should not hesitate. There is mechanical parallel as well as emotional to uphold us. The film relates to set measure and beat; it moves rhythmically or unrhythmically to certain measures, one-two-three or one-two-three-four or one-one, two-two, etc. etc. We used to set our metronomes when we pounded away at Czerney, to those various necessities. In the same way, it appears, some of the most spontaneous effects of the innovators of the Russian school of montage, were gained by being actually cut, re-cut, measured and re-measured with infinite pain and patience until just the desired time-element was hit upon. It is needless to point out that metronome-cutting in the hands of a mere mechanic, becomes tedious and meaningless in the extreme. While in the hands of a creative artist, *any* desired emotional effect can be achieved. The range is unparalleled and the best part of it all is, that film montage as *per se,* an art, stands at the moment, with a few brilliant exceptions, almost unexploited.

Yet people still say "a picture" and "a moving picture" with different pitch of voice as inevitably as a scholarly Chinaman can tone his actual vowels to mean things entirely different. To-day a "moving picture" is still something indelibly linked with gutters and safety vaults and thrillers, in general, of the lowest order. Why not, instead of maligning this perfect instrument for the projection of a new and entirely complete "art form," don't we get together and try to invent some way of getting something across that we may not be ashamed to confess openly we were "thrilled" about? Why indeed? Have you for one, ever stopped to try it? Artists of this and this denomination step forward, patronage in gesture, brotherhood in bearing. Take the writer, he has a "story," a drama, why don't we do this or this, why don't we do the other or that, why don't we, in other words listen to his receipt for reform of this malignity, film art? The professional writer, seldom if ever stops to puzzle out the difficult reasons for time-limits, effect of light and shadow that may or may not mean to him what it must inevitably mean to the director or the man behind the camera. Certain juxtaposition of event or character, he may insist, is inevitable to this or that effect. He will not and indeed can not, stop to realize that the film, rightly presented, is not a matter of one effect but many, nor of any one art but many. There is the actual drama presented through the actual people. But there is, odd anomaly, the camera man or the director again behind him, to play upon those presented and focussed persons of the drama, like a musician actually on a flute, an organ or a violin cello. Just to arrange characters and leave the effect to chance or some obsolete idea of stage acting, is, as we all know, fatal. A sensitive director must, it is obvious, have perfect instruments to play on. The great task is the finding of those instruments, but at last analysis, it is the director himself who does more than half the acting. The novice must learn primarily not only not to over-act, but actually you might almost say, not to act. To be able to strike a balance between inanition and subtle transference of the directors ideas into sympathetic action is no easy task. If the greatest actors have not yet appeared on the screen, it is not because the screen is not the perfect medium for the perfection of their art, or perhaps we should say, of a new, infinitely more subtle rendering of their art.

The modern film director does rely actually on musical notation. He wants an effect of ponderous stolidity. Well, what easier? He turns his camera (timed metronome beat) to get a man who is walking at normal pace, to walk faster or much, much slower. We all know something of those effects from the "comics" which at least have made applicable the schertzo and allegro con molte of our old friend the comic-villain, hurled headlong over a precipice and a scherzo-ing down a sand bank. We have the precise stacatto of the mincing step of the dandy or the billowing of the heroine's ralentando at the Blue Danube ball; she does not really dance as a rule to waltz time. To quote the much-quoted Pabst, speaking of a then little known, now over-acclaimed film star, "she never walked slowly enough, she was too nervous. I had to make the whole cast suit their step to hers, then get the cameras to turn faster." Here we have an actual demonstration of the film director's affinity with the concert meister's. G. W. Pabst beat out, like an orchestra conductor, a time for his cast and his staff, to follow. This is perhaps an exotic instance. However, it illustrates exactly the relationship between musical notation and film notation.

These are all somewhat superficial examples of the primary relationship of the film to music—the mere turning is a thing that can be regulated as well as the primary movements of the actors in the same way, I repeat, that you regulate a metronome to a certain dance or song time or that dance time to the metronome. The actual montage is a more subtle matter.

Screen montage or mounting is a difficult thing to talk of even to those who know everything about it. As we all know, the film is taken on long strips, miles long in certain exaggerated studios, much modified under saner American and European directorship. To boast of the miles of film used in certain pictures is to boast of ignorance and waste. A normal director can get his effects by three of four "takings." Many for matters of economy and expediency, less. Most of Mr. Macpherson's shots in *Borderline,* were done once.

In the actual taking of the film and its actual normal projection, we can easily trace the one-two-three, or the one-two-three-four time or the largo or the allegro, the fortissimo or the piano-piano. Anyone with any normal sense of rhythm and balance can do that. The difficult thing to explain is the thing easy to see, that thing so apparently artless, that the spectator is often not even conscious of the vast and breakneck process of the achievement, nor the actual skill back of it. The minute and meticulous effect for instance that Mr. Macpherson achieves with Pete, the negro and the waterfall, or the woman Astrid with the knife, are so naturalistic, I should say so "natural" that they seem to the uninitiate, sheer "tricks" or accidents. The effect of the negro, Pete, against the waterfall is achieved by a meticulous and painstaking effort on the part of the director, who alone with the giants of German and Russian production is his own cutter and will not trust his "montage" to a mere technician, however sympathetic.

Mr. Macpherson, it is true, can not possibly, under his present working conditions, achieve the prolonged rhythms of many of the more commercial productions. It must be realized however that he himself, is doing the actual work of montage, just as he has done the camera work and the scenario. The effect of the negro and the waterfall seems at times, a mechanical superimposition of short shots. It is not. An effect almost that of super-imposition but subtly differing from it, is achieved by the meticulous cutting of three and four and five inch lengths of film and pasting these tiny strips together. The same sort of jagged lightening effect is given with Astrid with her dagger. The white woman is here, there, everywhere, the dagger is above, beneath, is all but in her heart or in the heart of her meritricious lover. This effect of immediacy is not achieved by a facile movement of a camera; that would be impossible. It is attained by the cutting and fitting of tiny strips of film, in very much the same manner that you would fit together a jig-saw puzzle. There is much of meticulous jig-saw puzzle technique in the best of the advanced German and Russian montage, though the uninitiated would not think of it as that.

It is easy to see that this form of montage required subtle alliance of patience, ingenuity, mechanical knowledge *plus* the creative impulse. That combination of psychological opposites is rare. The most perfect and now almost historical example of creative originality plus technical ingenuity, is that in *Ten Days,* the soldier, the gun, the lightning-like effect of repeated firing. The lift, fire, pause, lift, fire, etcetera, were repeated in metronomic precision. The almost instantaneous effect was Eisenstein's meticulous innovation—the cutting and fitting of minute strips of soldier, gun, gun-fire, soldier, gun.

My images and my explanations must be of necessity obvious. I only want to get across something of this musical affinity. I am sure that every one of us, however, has had this, so to speak, reversed and in the most excruciating manner. We all know what Miss Dorothy Richardson means when she speaks of the "parish" cinema. We sometimes get, in these little out of the way houses, especially abroad, astonishingly up-to-date productions. Take a newer film rhythm, Continental, British or American and watch that run off to the tune of the old cow died of, played competently by the ex-policeman or the ex-convict or the post-master's daughter. Your eyes and ears are tortured, you execrate life and the weather, you manage either to dull out your perception or you rush out into a blinding snow-storm or a hail-storm or a volcanic eruption in preference.

In a word, you know exactly when film rhythm is NOT allied to music.

V.

There is still another of the arts that is of necessity bone and fibre and nerve tissue of the film. The art of the drama, obviously. People come, go, enter rooms, pass through doors, look out of windows. The film has spoiled many of us for even competent stage productions. We are not satisfied with a man and a window, or a woman and a door. We must see a man at a window and then a view of the man from the point of view, for instance, of someone *outside* that window. We must see a woman at the foot of a staircase, Lulu, for instance, in Pabst's *Box of Pandora*, and then we must see the entire stair case, perhaps slightly tilted, to give effect of dizzy eminence or of the state of mind of that woman, say in the case of Lulu, waiting to fly up it.

We take so for granted the use of the term for instance, "flying upstairs," that we do not realize how apt and arresting that phrase really is, until the camera again shows us that, actually, in vision or in retrospection or in anticipation, we "fly" upstairs at a given warning or a given signal. So we can "swim" in ecstasy and "drown" actually in happiness.

I mean words, as such, have become weathered, the old stamp is obliterated, the image of king or of olive wreath or the actual stars or the actual oak branch have been worn off the coin. Words are all alike now, the words even one feels sometimes of a foreign language have lost "virtue." The film brings words back and how much more the actual matter of the drama. Words become again "winged" indeed. We "fly" upstairs with Lulu.

Man's first attempt at art was, as we all know, the famous "picture" writing. We who have read and written until the sight of a printed page can give us cholic or delirium tremens can yet sit peacefully in the dim penumbra of a movie theatre. We go to the film now, on the whole, as a sort of sedative. When we get past this sedative period, we will perhaps begin, "write" our novels and plays in "pictures." That is the aim psychologically to be striven toward. And this is why Kenneth Macpherson, as an innovator, is valuable. I do not mean for one moment, to compare him with the magicians of the present-day screen. He can not compare with Pabst, Eisenstein, King Vidor or Pudovkin. He is a still younger man, he derives from these earlier sources. But he has contributed to the film in a lesser but perhaps finer way, as much as any of these masters. He has what not one of them has. His work is of necessity, more restricted, but he himself strives toward the renaissance ideal and within his narrow limits, he attains it. He is writer, painter, mechanic, actor, and trained camera man. "*Borderline,*" he said to me, "has its striking defects, but it is not amateurish." Kenneth Macpherson turned a personal little film in 1927. It is carefully packed away and he shows it to no one. A year later with the assistance of Bryher and some of the present *Borderline* group, notably Miss Blanche Lewin and Mr. Robert Herring, he turned a full length five reel film. Here and there the work was excellent. That film has been shown privately and commented on too generously, Macpherson feels, by certain of the German and French and English critics. But he himself was not satisfied. There were high water marks that equalled much of the more advanced film work, there were gaps however, woeful discrepancies in style. Different styles of acting, camera work and projection grated on this sensitive critic, Kenneth Macpherson, and he abandoned *Foothills*. Soon after, he "turned" a less ambitious film, a document of commercial lengths of his two pet Douracouli monkeys, and in 1930, the film *Borderline* which he confesses, within its limits, satisfied him. We say advisedly, "within its limits." We must insist on that qualification. The "limits" are imposed on Macpherson by this very renaissance ideal. To begin, he could not possibly direct a large cast in a large setting and do his own camera work. Later he no doubt will widen out his horizon, his technique will gain and his technique will suffer. This we can safely certify. There is no modern film director who has at his finger tips the technical mastery of a half dozen arts.

It may be argued, of course, that this is no advantage, that a man can do one thing only with full technical efficiency. That is our present attitude, it has been carried to excess and it should be pointed out again and again, that the greatest artists of all time, those of renaissance Italy and Quatrocento Florence, in particular, argued differently.

If Mr. Macpherson were a dilettante in any of the branches of the allied arts, the specialists' argument might hold. But he, oddly, is not nor is his film art a "phase," though it must be remembered that Macpherson is the author of two creditable novels and critical essays of value. His actual "trade" at one time was that of pen and ink designer. He considers drawing as the most natural medium, he drew prematurely as another child might pick out letters. He drew as another child might pick out sentences from books which he was told not to read. His mother had a quaint way of saying "one artist is enough in the family."He drew little pen and ink sketches on his school books and surreptitiously designed art and craft sort of posters and costumes behind locked doors at home. He had five years of creditable work in an office in the city, before he learnt that actually his poster and advertisement designs were, practically speaking, of more value as a sheer commercial asset. He has been craftsman and designer. But his actual beginnings were those of the born "artist."

There was nothing, however, self-conscious or "arty" about the child-Macpherson's attitude to these things. They were play to him and a little bit, rebellion.

VI.

Borderline is a dream and perhaps when we say that we have said everything. The film is the art of dream portrayal and perhaps when we say that we have achieved the definition, the synthesis toward which we have been striving. Film is art of another dimension, including not only all art but including all life. Art and life walk hand in hand, drama and music, epic song and lyric rhythm, dance and the matter of science here again, as in some elaborate "allegory" of the Florentines, take hands, twine in sisterly embrace before their one God, here electrically incarnated, LIGHT. Before the high-powered effect of lamp (most modern expression of voltage and amperes) we have the whole run of antiquity, the whole run of nature, the whole run of modernity. Step into your dream and everything evolves, simplifies; the conglomerate experience of a day, of an hour, of a lifetime meet, rehearse some little scene of life or death or mimicry. We are not surprised, in a dream, to find Grandmama and our latest lover conversant over a forgotten sand heap. We are not surprised when our lost toy-boat swells to Lithuania proportion and when that dream symbol floats majestically across a field of blossoming clover. It does not surprise us to greet an incarnation of our tailor or our modiste in a little college class room struggling with us, in past anxiety, over a page of logarithms long ago "forgotten." Nothing in a dream is forgotten. The film as Macpherson directs it, seems almost just some such process of "remembering."

The men and women in *Borderline* move, speak, turn, act in set formula to a set rhythm. They are real people, terribly incarnated. In the little café through which Pete stalks and his mistress turns, gazing with great eyes at a vague conglomeration of whites, we have something of the nightmare that we would image a sensitive negro might have, on facing a room full of antagonistic presences. Adah is real, Pete is real, vital, dynamic, indifferent in his giant mastery. Nevertheless, there is dream in them, nightmare, and that dream-nightmare permeates our consciousness although we may not know what it is or why. Pete and Adah escape from their little room and stand on a hill slope. Like a dream, the great negro head looms disproportionate, and water and cloud and rock and sky are all subsidiary to its being. Like a personal dream, gone further into the race dream, we see (with Pete) hill and cloud as, on that first day, created. Dream merges with myth and Pete, regarding a fair heaven far from the uncreated turmoil of that small-town cafe, says quite logically, "let there be light." Light has been, it is obvious, created by that dark daemon, conversant with all nature since before the time of white man's beginning.

His small sweetheart in her little shop-bought, pull-on soft hat is complement to this radiant figure. She has sinned, she is not altogether god-like, but she is created on the hill-slope with him, apart from the nightmare of the uncoordinated white-folk.

The white-folk, of necessity, in this film take subsidiary value. Macpherson has decreed this with delicate irony and foresight. One wonders, watching the group (barmaid, café managress and white demented Astrid) to which one of these three furies, one would give the vote if called on. For a moment, the barmaid seems more degrading, with her slack morality and sweet gone stagnant. Then one sees at heart, she is a "good sort" and one turns to the companion figure. The manageress, chewing her gum-drop in the face of the daemonic fury of the deserted white woman is callow, impervious to anything but double column of debit and credit; she is thinking not of Astrid and her fury nor of the black-white problem in any of its phases but simply, one feels, "will Pete and that woman pay for their rooms." Nevertheless, we must confess, "business is business"; what of this third fury? Astrid, who intemperate fury has lashed itself almost to dementia, screams "it has all happened because these people are *black*." Then for some inhuman sort of distinction, we let *her* go. It is impossible to choose between them.

The excellent characterization of the white lover, sensitively depicted by Mr. Gavin Arthur, stresses again nightmare. He enters the café bar and the three café furies, above enumerated, are on an instant frozen from animation into noncommittal attention. We see these three figures, not as in themselves people or even symbols, as we ourselves might see them. We see them through the eyes of Thorne, whose dark sweetheart has been alienated from him, he imagines by the machinations of these three. The three women, barmaid, manageress, and mistress, become fixed symbols in his, in our minds. They become obvious allegory of drink, you might say, sordid calculation and unbridled jealousy. So for a moment . . . then as in a dream, the scene shifts. Astrid rises in abstraction of fiend-rage and claws the air shouting, "nigger-lover!" Thorne, her faithless lover, by dream juxtaposition is seen posed as if a noose were dangling him from a floor, which we feel reel beneath his feet by this parallel of contraries. A small touch perhaps, to be noticed by a few only, but bound to have subconscious significance. Macpherson, it is obvious, in just that flash is demonstrating a tardy aphorism. If a black man is hanged for loving a white woman, why should not a white man be likewise lynched for loving a black one? Dream, I say. These conclusions happen only in the higher fantasy of dream value and of ultimate dream justice.

VII.

Then what is this film about and where does it lead us? Is it about two negroes in a small Continental mid-European town, who cross a back-water of small-town vice and malice and leave it cleansed and hallowed for their passing? No, it is nothing so defined, nothing so logical, nothing of such obvious sociological importance. Then what is this film about? Is it a series of psychological interpretations of white and white, neurotic and super-neurotic, lounge lizard and stalesweet of small-town Messalina? No, there is nothing so logical, nothing so dramatic, nothing so consistent. It is not about any of these things. There is no actual acute moment of crisis in a series of lightning-like "flashes" where each, from the first moment of Astrid's frenzied entrance to the last beneficence of the giant-negro on the hill-top, is equally a crisis. Film and life are or should be indisseverable terms. In this modern attempt to synchronize thought and action, the inner turmoil and the other, the static physical passivity and the acute psychic activity, there is hardly one moment, one dramatic "sentence" that outweighs another. Kenneth Macpherson has indeed achieved a sort of dynamic picture writing. His camera has recorded his pen and ink sketches with fluidity and precision. He "wrote" his scenario in a series of some 1,000 pictures, the actual directions for each special picture read like captions. His script, in this, is unique and in itself a work of art. His is an innovation in the manner of approach to "film art" that can not be over-estimated. He writes (I choose at random):

13. Interior. Astrid's Room. Close up. *Fade in.* A door is flung open, and for a fraction of a moment, *Astrid's* shadowy face is seen. The impression must be of covertness and speed. Her hand rises across her face, and—
14. Interior. Astrid's Room. Close up. *Panning.*—plunges forward through the room, past furniture to grasp—
15. Interior. Astrid's Room. Close up.—at a telephone receiver.

To the right of these little paragraphs, you must imagine delicate pen and ink drawings with arrow-indications of direction; first a wild face, then a poised, tenuous hand, then the same hand lowered.

Or:

> 441. Interior. Pete's Room. Close up. *Pete's head,* still and dark, watches with wide eyes. Presently the tinest confirmative nodding takes place. The eyebrows move, the eyes do not blink. He smiles.
> 442. Petes' Room. Close up. *Thorne* feels the tremendous healing of Pete's immense personality. The inner conflict is marked in nervous twitchings, amazement and unbelief that Pete is not gibing.
> 443. Interior. Pete's Room. Semi-shot. *Pete* lets his hand fall along his arm. He is still watching the conflict in Thorne. *Adah background.*

We have here an exquisite pen and ink sketch of a negro head almost filling the space of the little frame allotted. (There are usually about six of these drawings to a page.) Below it, three quarters, gazing out of the opposite side of the following "frame" or "shot," we have a balancing white face, suggesting almost equal mobility and sensitiveness. Beneath that again, is the semi-shot of the standing negro, with suggested café-background and an indefinite woman form.

I have chosen at random these six descriptive captions. There are exactly 910 of them in the finished script. This does not include numerous side drawings of exterior effects, of "repeats" and so on. I do not think there can be any doubt in the mind, even of the most sceptical, that film, in this case at any rate, is allied in the most obvious manner to two of the giant "arts." Kenneth Macpherson's mastery of both descriptive writing and drawing can not be deprecated. Nor can you for one moment be in doubt of the intense value of the dramatic directorship. Pen and ink sketches cannot actually and psychically move nor can words. There can be no doubt that Macpherson's film does. So dynamically does it move that it seems, at times, as if he had almost over-stepped the bounds even of the most exaggerated screen values. His posed figures are seething with mental turmoil and with psychic discord. They seem sometimes, at rest, to be about to fall forward and annihilate us with their intensity as glacier edge may give some sort of warning to those attuned to natural premonitions. Macpherson seems at times, in fact, to overstep the bounds of even the most intense screen dynamics. As one of his German contemporaries remarked, on seeing a hurried informal "showing" of the film at Territet, "you have achieved a nightmare and a dream. I congratulate you."

You may consider yourself justified in remarking "and is that achievement?" I may consider myself justified in answering, "the greatest." Ibsen achieved that same effect of dream and nightmare. Certain of the Russian dramatists have done so. This quality is rare in all art. The welding of the psychic or super-normal to the things of precise every-day existence, is Kenneth Macpherson's rare gift. His is no cheap conjurer's box of super-imposition and shadow-ghost. An Ibsen introduces no Ghost into his drama of that name. Nor does

Macpherson any actual "borderline" case into his film *Borderline.* Astrid, the woman, terribly incarnated and wracked with the most banal of feminine vices, jealousy, yet achieves through the careful lighting, posing and camera-work of Macpherson, an entity, we might almost say, did we not feel it necessary to fight shy of that word, "astral" in its effect. His deserted white woman as she moves among odd pieces of lodging house furniture, sits at a table, listens at a door or runs across a room to fall, draped in the most obvious of imported London or Paris embroidered shawls, is a woman of the drama, of the screen, yet like the Hedda of Ibsen or any of the Hildas or Hedwigs, she achieves through the actual fitness of her materialized setting, furniture, blowing window curtain, stuffed gull and overcrowded mantle-piece, something more obviously out of the world than any pantomime effect of cloud spook off could ever hope to attain. Even that marvelous playing with distorted personalities in the *Student of Prague,* for instance, startling and dramatic as that was, seems in retrospect, facile and obvious. Macpherson does not need to superimpose figure and shadow figure as has been so excellently done in some of the Swedish and German productions. That camera "truquage" would be, in his case, a kind of psychic cheating. Kenneth Macpherson's figures move consistently, as in a dream or nightmare, because of some intrinsic dynamic virtue of his own inner vision.

Sagetrieb 6(Fall 1987):29–50.

Marianne Moore

I have before me a collection of poems. They have appeared for the most part in various American periodicals. And readers of THE EGOIST are familiar with certain of these curiously wrought patterns, these quaint turns of thought and concealed, half-playful ironies. They have puzzled over such poems as "To a Steam Roller" or "Diligence is to Magic as Progress is to Flight" and asked—what is this all about—"scarecrows of æsthetic procedure"—"weight-hardened creatures"—"prosaic necessities," etc. etc. They have read Miss Marianne Moore's poems again and again, and questioned, half in despair—is this a mere word-puzzle, or does it mean something?

Does it mean something?

"FEED ME, ALSO, RIVER GOD

"Lest by diminished vitality and abated
Vigilance, I become food for crocodiles—for that quicksand
Of gluttony which is legion. It is there—close at hand—
  On either side
  Of me. You remember the Israelites who said in pride

"And stoutness of heart: 'The bricks are fallen down, we will
Build with hewn stone, the sycamores are cut down, we will change to
Cedars!' I am not ambitious to dress stones, to renew
Forts, nor to match
My value in action, against their ability to catch

"Up with arrested prosperity. I am not like
Them, indefatigable, but if you are a god you will
Not descriminate against me. Yet—if you may fulfil
None but prayers dressed
As gifts in return for your own gifts—disregard the request."

I think that it does mean something. And if Miss Moore is laughing at us, it is laughter that catches us, that holds, fascinates, and half-paralyses us, as light flashed from a very fine steel blade, wielded playfully, ironically, with all the fine shades of thrust and counter-thrust, with absolute surety and with absolute disdain. Yet with all the assurance of the perfect swordsman, the perfect technician, I like to imagine that there is as well something of the despair of the perfect artist—"see, you cannot know what I mean—exactly what I mean," she seems to say, half-pitying that the adversary is so dull—that we are so dull—"and I do not intend that you shall know—my sword is very much keener than your sword, my hand surer than your hand—but you shall not know that I know you are beaten."

Yet we are not always baffled. Miss Moore turns her perfect craft as the perfect craftsman must inevitably do, to some direct presentation of beauty, clear, cut in flowing lines, but so delicately that the very screen she carves seems meant to stand only in that serene palace of her own world of inspiration—frail, yet as all beautiful things are, absolutely hard—and destined to endure longer, far longer than the toppling sky-scrapers, and the world of shrapnel and machine-guns in which we live.

The clear, flawless tones of Miss Moore's poetry come like bell-notes, like notes from some palace-bell carved beneath the sea. Indeed I seem to place this very screen in some mermaid's palace.

"He made this screen

"Not of silver nor of coral.
But of weatherbeaten laurel.

"Here, he introduced a sea
Uniform like tapestry;

"Here, a fig-tree; there, a face;
There, a dragon circling space—

"Designating here, a bower;
There, a pointed passion-flower."

As I say the rhythm and the tones of her words come as through some "sea-change"—and surely there is "something rich and strange" in this "Talisman"—

"Under a splintered mast,
Torn from the ship and cast
Near her hull,

"A stumbling shepherd found
Embedded in the ground,
A sea-gull

"Of lapis lazuli,
A scarab of the sea,
With wings spread—

"Curling its coral feet,
Parting its beak to greet
Men long dead."

Miss Marianne Moore is an American. And I think in reading Miss Moore's poems we in England should be strengthened. We are torn in our ambitions, our desires are crushed, we hear from all sides that art is destined to a long period of abeyance, and that the reconstruction of Europe must take all the genius of the race. I do not believe that. There are others here in England who do not for one moment believe that beauty will be one whit bruised by all this turmoil and distress.

Miss Moore helps us. She is fighting in her country a battle against squalor and commercialism. We are all fighting the same battle. And we must strengthen each other in this one absolute bond—our devotion to the beautiful English language.

H. D.

The Egoist 3(August 1916):118–19.

Responsibilities

I have not at the moment access to Mr. Yeats' volumes so I may seem to misrepresent them in recalling an early impression. But looking back, I seem to recall broken lights across water touched with moonlight, wisps of cloud, sea-coasts always haunted and forests with the imminent sense of the presence somewhere beyond the dunes or the great beeches of some manifestation of some sea or

The editor, Diana Collecott, notes that H. D. may have intended the piece for the *Egoist*. She has corrected H. D.'s spelling of Pelleus and Mellisande (from Debussy's opera) and Pharasaic. She further notes that H. D. quotes Yeats's "When Helen Lived" and that by "No Troy to Burn," H. D. means Yeats's "No Second Troy."

forest spirit—always beautiful spirits but of a misty transient beauty as if they had been conjured into life from some region inhabited by half-spirits, half-humans—a moon-country, it seemed, to be apprehended it is true only by a poet, and a fair country if you happen to be one of the moon-born, but a place where reflections upon water, mist rising from water, mist merging into clouds and fairies with irridescent wings and "little people" seem all wrought of the same vague, semi-transparent substance. It is a place where Undine might have wandered, where Pelléas and Mélisande might have talked with the swan-sister of Grimm's fairy-tale, and the beast who was a prince might well have mourned among the stray, wilful ghosts that haunt the "windy precipice" of Tara.

In this new volume, it is true, we have still green reeds and beneath the water fish speaking—as innocent and as remote from life as the heiratic rows of fishes in some early Italian scene of the flood or of creation—still kings and queens move within "pale green light" as it filters through forest trees upon the ground-ivy's blue, but beyond all these, mingled among them in the book, but cut apart from them as clear altar-fire, blazing to a single point in the misty forest of these moon-dreams, there are poems of another mood of a greater, sterner intensity.

In re-reading such poems as "Friends", "No Troy to Burn", "When Helen Lived",—there are a dozen or more others of equal beauty—as we cry out with the poet

> That men desert,
> For some trivial affair
> Or noisy, insolent sport,
> Beauty that we have won
> From bitterest hours.

it seems that Mr. Yeats' responsibility, although he tells us that he has "come close on forty-nine" has only just begun.

For we, "the young" of this generation are sick of self-analysis, self-torture, self-appreciation. The ill-starred nineties which, historically speaking, claim Mr. Yeats, was a band of robust virtue compared with our own decade. For what are we, *les jeunes* in ourselves? First, a memory of the few, the really great, who have gone irreparably from us, next the hope that some may return, not broken by the bitterness of their experience but taut and aflame for the creation of beauty, and then, crouched as in a third line of battered trenches, are the few of us who are left, hanging on against all odds, in the wavering belief that we are the link, the torch-bearers. And upon us, almost with us, is the enemy.

For us the enemy is not the great mass of inert life, the so-called middle-classes and general heaviness of the world against which the artist has always a legitimate quarrel, but for us, there has been a more treacherous force at work, a more subtle adversary. The chief enemy is not the middle-classes and the Philistine upon whom the young men of the nineties whetted their wit. It is the great overwhelming mechanical daemon, the devil of machinery, of which we can hardly repeat too often, the war is the hideous offspring.

This daemon took for its own the most robust talent of our generation. It crept upon us and claimed its own. From our band, at best a few against many millions, it has taken the most stalwart. The nineties was at one for all its internal, personal friction—the nineties at least held one common law as sacred, at least never condescended to the worship of material efficiency. The nineties, thank God, were not efficient, neither did they fall down before some Juggernaut of planes and angles. The nineties were ill-starred, but they had at least a star.

And what has all this tirade to do with Mr. Yeats and his responsibility? A great deal. For Mr. Yeats and we few, the remnant who still persist in the worship of beauty other than the grace of the steel girder are in somewhat the same position. For Mr. Yeats may be said to represent the last line of trenches for his own defeated generation as we for the present generation. Though our generation, inasmuch as its cubes and angles seem a sort of incantation, a symbol for the forces that brought on this world calamity, seems hardly worthy to compare with the nineties in its helpless stand against the evil of ugliness. Our generation did not stand against the enemy—it *was* the enemy.

But I will not say that it is the enemy. For it has merged into this struggle with its own much lauded guns and aeroplanes, it has become a part of the struggle and is no longer a self-willed agent. The guns they praised, the beauty of the machines they loved, are no more as a god set apart for worship but a devil over whom neither they nor we have any more control. The black magic of triangles and broken arcs has conquered and we who are helpless before this force of destruction can only hope for some more powerful magic, some subtle and more potent daemon to set it right.

They called it to life but we are none the less responsible, we are all a part of this world calamity, we can not stand apart with Pharisaic gesture. But we can do this. We can wait, endure, confess the past was all a mistake, turn to the future and hope for the generation to follow.

And this is why I feel that Mr. Yeats' responsibility has only just begun. For it seems in moments of despair that we have no past, no future. But Mr. Yeats has both. Can we not spiritually join our forces, and chastened with old calamities, redefine and reconstruct boundaries and barriers, and reinvoke some golden city, sterner than the dream-cities, and wrought more firm to endure than those riveted of steel and bleak with iron girders.

Ed. Diana Collecott. *Agenda* 25(Fall/Winter 1987–1988):51–53.

Joan of Arc

"The Passion and Death of a Saint" is a film that has caused me more unrest, more spiritual forebodings, more intellectual rackings, more emotional torment than any I have yet seen. We are presented with Jeanne d'Arc in a series of pictures, portraits burnt on copper, bronze if you will, anyhow obviously no aura of quattrocento gold and gold dust and fleurs-de-lys in straight hieratic pattern, none of your fresco that makes the cell of Savonarola make the legend of Savonarola bearable even to this day. Jeanne d'Arc is done in hard clear line, remorseless, poignant, bronze stations of the cross, carved upon mediæval cathedral doors, bronze of that particular sort of mediæval fanaticism that says no and again no to any such weakening incense as Fra Angelico gold and lilies of heavenly comfort. Why did and why didn't this particular Jeanne d'Arc so touch us? Jeanne d'Arc takes us so incredibly far that having taken us so far, we are left wondering why didn't this exquisite and superb piece of screen dramatisation take us further? Carl Dreyer, a Dane, one of the most superb of the magnificently growing list of directors, is responsible for this odd two-edged sort of feeling. His film, for that, is unique in the annals of film art. The passion of the Jeanne is superbly, almost mediumistically portrayed by Mlle Falconetti. Heart and head are given over to inevitable surrender. Heart broke, head bowed. But another set of curious nerve-reactions were brought into play here. Why is it that my hands inevitably clench at the memory of those pictures, at the casual poster that I pass daily in this lake-side small town? Is it necessary to be put on guard? *Must* I be made to feel on the defence this way and why? Also why must my very hands feel that they are numb and raw and bleeding, clenched fists tightened, bleeding as if beating at those very impregnable mediæval church doors?

For being let into the very heart, the very secret of the matter, we are left out of . . . something. I am shown Jeanne, she is indeed before me, the country child, the great lout of a hulking boy or girl, blubbering actually, great tears coursing down round sun-hardened, wind-hardened, oak-tree hardened face outline and outline of cheek hollow and the indomitable small chin. Jeanne is first represented to us, small as seen from above, the merest flash of sturdy boy figure, walking with chained ankles toward judges (too many) seated in slices above on ecclesiastical benches. Jeanne is seen as small, as intolerably sturdy and intolerably broken, the sort of inhuman showing up of Jeanne that from the first strikes some note of defiance in us. Now why should we be defiant? I think it is that we all have our Jeanne, each one of us in the secret great cavernous interior of the cathedral (if I may be fantastic) of the subconscious. Now another Jeanne strides in, an incomparable Jeanne, indubitably a more Jeanne-ish Jeanne than our Jeanne but it just isn't our Jeanne. Worse than that it is a better Jeanne, a much, much better, more authentic Jeanne than our Jeanne; scathing realism has gone one better than mere imaginative idealism. We know we are out-witted. This is a real, real, Jeanne (poor Jeanne) little mountain Newfoundland puppy, some staunch and true and incomparably loyal creature, something so much more wonderful than any grey-hound outline or sleek wolf-hound is presented us, the very incarnation of loyalty and integrity . . . dwarfed, below us, as if about to be tramped or kicked into a corner by giant soldier iron-heeled great boots. Marching boots, marching boots, the heavy hulk of leather and thong-like fastenings and cruel nails . . . no hint of the wings on the heels of the legions that followed the lily-banner; the cry that sang toward Orleans is in no way ever so remotely indicated. We are allowed no comfort of mere beatific lilies, no hint of the memory of lover-comrade men's voices, the comrades that Jeanne must have loved loyally, the perfect staunch child friend, the hero, the small Spartan, the very Telisila upon the walls of that Argos, that is just it. This is *no* Telisila upon the walls of Argos, no Athene who for the moment has laid aside her helmet for other lesser matters than that of mere courage and fidelity. This is an Athene stripped of intellect, a Telisila robbed of poetry, it is a Jeanne d'Arc that not only pretends to be real, but that is real, a Jeanne that is going to rob us of our own Jeanne.

Is that the secret of this clenching of fists, this sort of spiritual antagonism I have to the shaved head, the stares, defiant bronze-statue; from the poster that I pass on my way to market? Is it another Jeanne in me (in each of us) that starts warily at the picture, the actual *portrait* of the mediæval girl warrior? The Jeanne d'Arc of Carl Dreyer is so perfect that we feel somehow cheated. This must be right. This must be right . . . therefore by some odd equivocal twist of subconscious logic, *I* must be wrong. I am put in the wrong, therefore I clench my fists. Heaven is within you . . . therefore I stand staring guiltily at bronze figures cut upon a church door, at freizes upon the under-gables of a cathedral that I must stare up at, see in slices as that incomparable Danish artist made me see Jeanne in his perhaps over-done series of odd sliced portraits (making particularly striking his studies of the judges and the accusers of Jeanne, as if seen by Jeanne her self from below) overwhelming bulk of ecclesiastical political accusation. I know in my mind that this is a great tour de force, perhaps one of the greatest. But I am left wary, a little defiant. Again why and why and why and just, just why? Why am I defiant before one of the most exquisite and consistent works of screen art and perfected craft that it has been our immeasurable privilege to witness?

One, I am defiant for this reason (and I have worked it out carefully and with agony) I and you and the baker's boy beside me and Mrs. Captain Jones-Smith's second maid and our own old Nanna and somebody else's gardener and the honeymoon boy and girl and the old sporting colonel and the tennis teacher and the crocodile of young ladies from the second pension to the left as you turn to the right by the market road that branches off before the stall where the old lady sells gentians and single pinks and Alpenrosen each in their season (just now it is somewhat greenish valley-lilies) are in no need of such brutality. No one of us, not one of us is in need of this stressing and stressing, this poignant draining of hearts, this clarion call to pity. A sort of bugle note rises and with it our own defiance. I am asked to join an army of incorruptibles to which long and long since, I and the baker's boy and the tennis champion in the striped red sash have given our allegiance. This great Dane Carl Dreyer takes too damn much for granted. Do I *have* to be cut into slices by this inevitable pan-movement of the camera, these suave lines to left, up, to the right, back, all rhythmical with the remorseless rhythm of a scimitar? Isn't this incomparable Dane Dreyer a very blue-beard, a Turk of an ogre for remorseless cruelty? Do we have to have the last twenty four hours' agony of Jeanne stressed and stressed and stressed, in just this way, not only by the camera but by every conceivable method of dramatic and scenic technique? Bare walls, the four scenes of the trial, the torture room, the cell and the outdoors about the pyre, are all calculated to drive in the pitiable truth like the very nails on the spread hands of the Christ. Do we need the Christ-nails driven in and pulled out and driven in and drawn out, while Jeanne already numb and dead, gazes dead and numb at accuser and fumbles in her dazed hypnotized manner towards some solution of her claustrophobia? I am shut in here, I want to get out. I want to get out. And instead of seeing in our minds the very ambrosial fields toward which that stricken soul is treading, foot by foot like the very agony toward the skull-hill, we are left pinned like some senseless animal, impaled as she is impaled by agony. This is not *not* good enough. There is some slur on the whole of human consciousness, it is necessary to stress and stress and stress the brute side of mystic agony this way. Somehow, something is wrong here. An incomparable art, an incomparable artist, an actress for whom any but praise were blasphemy . . . and what happens?

I do not mind crying (though I do mind crying) when I see a puppy kicked into a corner but I do mind standing aside and watching and watching *and* watching and being able to do nothing. That is something of the antagonism I think that crept in, that is something of the something that made me feel I ought to go again, to be fair, to be *sure* what it was that upset me, perhaps cowardice on my own part, some deep sub-conscious strata or layer of phobia that I myself, so un-Jeanne-like, was unwilling to face openly. I said to myself next morning I will get this right, I am numb and raw, I myself watched Jeanne d'Arc being burnt alive at Rouen last night . . . and I myself must go again . . . ah, that is just it. We do not go and see a thing that is real, that is real beyond realism, AGAIN. I said I will go again but I did not go again. I did not and I don't think I failed any inner "light", any focus of consciousness in so ceding to my own new lapse. I can NOT watch this thing impartially and it is the first film of the many that I have consistently followed that I have drawn away from. This is perhaps the last and greatest tribute to the sheer artistry and the devilish cunning of the method and the technique of Carl Dreyer. I pay him my greatest compliment. His is one film among all films, to be judged differently, to be approached differently, to be viewed as a masterpiece, one of the absolute masterpieces of screen craft. Technically, artistically, dramatically, this is a masterpiece. But, but, but, but, but . . . there is a Jeanne sobbing before us, there is a small Jeanne about to be kicked by huge hob-nailed boots, there is a Jeanne whose sturdy child-wrist is being twisted by an ogre's paw because forsooth she wears a bit of old hard hammered unwieldy bulk of gold upon one finger, there is a numb hypnotized creature who stares with dog-like fidelity, toward the sly sophist who directs her by half-smile, by half-nod, by imperceptible lift of half an eye brow toward her defaming answers, there is a Jeanne or a Joan whose wide great grey eyes fill with round tears at the mention of her mother ("say your pater noster, you don't know your pater noster? you do? well who taught it to you?") there is Jeanne or Joan or Johanna or Juana upon Jeanne or Jean or Johanna or Juana. They follow one another with precision, with click, with *monotony.* Isn't that a little just it? There is another side to all this, there is another series of valuations that can not perhaps be hinted at consistently in this particular presentation of this one kicked little puppy of a Jeanne or a Joan or a Johanna. Isn't it just that? Isn't the brute side of the flawless type, the Jeanne d'Arc of all peoples, of all nations, the world's Jeanne d'Arc (as the world's Christ) a little too defiantly stressed, a little too acutely projected? I know after the first half of the second reel all that. I know all, all that. Just that round child face lifted "who taught you your pater noster?" gives me all, all that. I do not mean to say that there could have been any outside sort of beatific screen craft of heavenly vision. I don't mean that. But Jeanne kicked almost, so to speak, to death, still had her indomitable vision. I mean Jeanne d'Arc talked openly with angels and in this square on square of Danish protestant interior, this trial room, this torture room, this cell, there was no hint of angels. The angels were there all the time and if Jeanne had reached the spiritual developement that we must believe this chosen comrade of the warrior Michael must have reached, the half-hypnotized numb dreary physical state she was in, would have its inevitable psychic recompense. The Jeanne d'Arc of the incomparable Dreyer it seems to me, was kicked towards the angels. There were not there, nor anywhere, hint of the angelic wing tip, of the winged sandals and the two-edged sword of Michael or of the distillation of maternal pity of her "familiar" Margaret. Father, mother, the "be thou perfect" perfected in Jeanne d'Arc as in the boy of Nazareth, were in no way psychically manifest. Such psychic manifestation I need hardly say, need be in no way indicated by any outside innovation of cross lights or of superimposed shadows. It is something in something, something behind something. It is something one feels, that you feel, that the baker's boy, that the tennis champion, that the army colonel, that the crocodile of English and Dutch and mixed German-Swiss (come here to learn French) feels. We are numb and beaten. We won't go a second time. The voice behind me that says wistfully, taken unawares, "I wish it was one of those good American light things" even has its place in critical consciousness. For all our preparation, we are unprepared. This Jeanne d'Arc is sprung on us and why should it be? There is a reason for most things. I think the reason is that it doesn't link up straight with human consciousness. There is a gap somewhere. We criticise many films, sometimes for crudity, sometimes for sheer vicious playing up to man's most febrile sentiment, sometimes for cruelty or insincerity. We criticise Jeanne d'Arc for none of these things.

The Jeanne d'Arc of the incomparable artist Carl Dreyer is in a class by itself. And that is the trouble with it. It shouldn't be.

Close Up 3(July 1928):15–23.

Letters to Amy Lowell

Dec. 17. 1914

Dear Amy:

Things gets worser and worser! Our great & good friend is taking up "Imagism" again—don't you think *we'd* better drop it? R [ichard Aldington] wants to—H.D. wants to—Flint wants to—E.P. is making it ridiculous—he is writing now for "T.P.'s Weekly"—heavens knows what! He is also writing for Blast—I mean articles & expositions of the school!—R. just intercepted an article, for the Egoist, against publishers—E. against Macmillans and indirectly attacking you!—We can't go on watching him like two keepers—can we? It is making us ridiculous!—All of us—or it will!—Ford has been very kind—he says the only thing to do—is to drop the title "Imagism!"—We have talked it over—all of us here—and we think a good title—"the Six"—Then underneath if you want "An Anthology"—If there is to be a paper cover, the names might be written in a column underneath. The Pleaed was "the Seven"—the pre-raphaelites were known as the seven or was it "the Nine"? Well, anyway there seems to be some sort of tradition for such a name, and yet it is definite & not hackneyed!—We have talked it over—there seems no other even thinkable suggestions for a title: We would all be individuals without being *isme* and we would, in addition, be a group!—

Another copy of "Blast" is about to appear. R. has disassociated himself from it entirely—that, too, has caused ruptures of a milder character.

Ra. has been working all day—and now is trying to do a review. So I have tried to explain—do trust it is clear!

Don't worry about this. I am glad, at last, to see how we stand—*exactly* how we stand—with E.P.—You have helped to clear the air for us—whatever happens we are glad to be out *isms!*—

Do trust you are well!—We are always so glad to hear from you! Love to you for R.

and
Hilda.

P.S.—

R. asks me to say that *in no event can we now appear under the direct title of "Imagiste."* It is obviously E.'s plan to prevent our publication and he believes that Macmillan is printing the book. Our dropping the title gives him the satisfaction of feeling that he has secured a victory and gives us the exquisite relief of being free of him. Hueffer has promised to write a preface if we want it, but I think it should stay as it is with this alteration. Just cut out the bit about Ezra & insert a phrase to the effect that these tenets have been proclaimed by some of us as Imagism, but since the exclusive right to the use of this word is claimed by the inventor we do not therefore use it either as a title or a group denomination.

Something like that, but a little calmer—a little suaver—a little more toned down—He wants me to say again that we four agree and underline again—"*in no event can we now appear under the direct title Imagiste.*"

February 1916

Address 16 Egoist Oakley House Bloomsbury St. *W.C.*

Dear Amy:—

I want to thank you at once for your very great kindness and generosity—I wrote you the next morning (after receiving cable from my people) that we were all right. We were hard pressed as three months allowance was missing! That is all straight now, so we needn't take any of your generous loan! However, we will wait till we hear before returning as you write some is due as royalties. Shall we send to Lawrence & Flint out of the 40 pounds? If you let us know what each share is, we can do that. Perhaps, too, you don't mind our sending two or three pounds to a friend (a young journalist of talent—really a fine character)—I was very sad because he wrote us when we were so hard up. We sent him as much as we could. And another friend we have—he & his wife & little girl live, all three, on less than 15 shillings a week. They are very brave & splendid—he does quite good work of a second order—à la Conrad—but he is a real personality & has talent. If we could keep in reserve say 5 pounds, we could advance it a pound at a time, when they are specially pressed. They do not run into debt but I know sometimes they are hungry—just sheer hungry!—You see, this war period, our *joint* income is about 3 pounds a week—We live here extremely comfortably on it. And because we live simply, really poor "artists" have no feeling of pride in asking us for little loans!—You see what I mean? Now if we keep part of the money we can hand it out to people who really need. *But,* Amy dear, my accumulated allowance gives us a little reserve of our own & we can, & I will return at once, all if you write!— I didn't like to borrow—we never have—not even when I was ill [1915 stillbirth], needed to before—but I did feel awfully worried when my little money was missing. It was a careless mistake of the bank but I thought boats were sinking I knew nothing of!—I can not write you what I think, feel & know about this terrible war. I want you to get this letter without undue delay—[7 lines blocked out, probably by censor]. We are all weakened by this continual strain!— It has been difficult to answer your letters fully. I liked some of your poems, very much—the sand one, the music one—the garden poems very much indeed—the colou, impressionist garden, very stimulating and & beautiful brush work. This is the impression on hasty reading. R. sent them back the same day.—I was sorry about the article by Flint. It was a pity you misunderstood—though perhaps we take too much for granted—But I remember how R. felt—you had once objected to his speaking of your surroundings—& he told Flint he had better make the article as impersonal as possible. R. has written you. Flint made the changes, not R.— We hear from Fletcher. He writes very beautifully of you—your generosity to him—your influence & continual work on behalf of us, & the Imagist ideas in general. I look forward to seeing him over here. We can talk out his Imagist business to our hearts content. I am sorry you can not come—but it is a risky business I know—& even more risky after you get here.

Now I will ring off—with thanks—the deepest heart-felt thanks for your generosity. R. joins me— H.

Dec. 1st 1916

From Mrs. R. Aldington
44 Mecklenburgh Square
London
W.C.

Dear Amy:

I have sent your book on to Richard. But certain of your poems stand out very clearly against this London grey. I like, of course, your garden poems best—the [?] girls with the hoops, and Malmaison especially. Certain of the pictures in the latter are very poignant—the black swan and the empress, (the rose with loosened petals) stand out most clearly. I also like the Aquarian—the swish or swirl of colour. The book is colour & warmth—as I say very warm, exotic even, against this northern grey. I am sure R. will take great pleasure from it—the warmth & sun will comfort him in his even greyer barracks.

How sweet it was of you to cable. I made all arrangements to come—trunks packed etc. Then R. sent word he was staying on a little longer—or perhaps indefinitely—so I *couldn't* leave. My plans are very uncertain as are his. But I will be here till after Christmas anyway. And probably stay on!—

Your interest in Richard's work has meant so much to him & to me. I had a beautiful letter from the *Dial* and will send some more work of R.'s to them. R. is sending occasional "notes" which I am trying to work up for publication. He is tremendously fine—we can not admire him too much.

Frieda Lawrence wrote me of your generosity. I *was* so glad. Isn't it too hateful that Lawrence should be ill & they both so fine? They talk of America. I wonder if they will come. I think, in a way, it would be the best thing for Lawrence. I am afraid he won't live if he stays many more winters in England. Isn't it too sad? He *may* get along all right but he felt the suppression of the Rainbow, I am certain. Though he has many personal admirers here, he feels "England does not want him." Well, you, at least, have strong appreciation in a way that has touched them both deeply. I will write again, dear Amy—

Hilda—

Letters to Marianne Moore

21 August 1915

Dear Miss Moore:

I remember you at Bryn Mawr May Fête, in a green dress. I imagine that this *you,* which sends poetry to the "Egoist" is the same mediaeval lady!—I am "H. D."—also Mrs. R. Aldington, and R. has spoken often of your work!—We both think you have achieved a remarkable technical ability!—R. says it is quite the finest that he has seen from America!—I hope [?] you are going on with your work. I know, more or less, what you are up against, though I escaped some five years ago!—There are terrible difficulties & discouragements to be met on this side, too—But at least, it is a fight—there is something definite *To* fight! I felt so terribly when I was in U.S.A., the putty that met my wheted lance!—I seem to be taking much for granted in your case—You will forgive me? I am speaking to a you which I am more or less re-constructing from my own experience!—

I wonder if you ever feel like coming here for a time! I assure you, my husband and I would be delighted to have you near us!—You would find much to depress you in London—but much that would inspire & entrance!—We are—what is known is [sic] in America as 'poor'—but there are others like us!—And London is to be seen most advantageously anyway from the top of a two-pence bus!—

I want you to think of this!—Perhaps next summer you could come? You could stay with us or near us!—Write me and tell me what you are doing!—

I am sending you prospectus of our latest [?] venture. We will go on with it if these numbers prove a success.—Perhaps, if the other *six* are attempted you would like to try your hand at translating some obscure Greek or Latin!—I will set R. to send you some suggestions if you would be interested!

Yours—
H. Aldington.

29 August 1917

My dear Marianne—

I want to thank you for the beautiful bag.—New Jersey, yes, it does remind me. But also of "some undiscovered isle in the far seas"—also of your own lovely poem—the old one that I so particularly love.—

I am sending your new poems, because they so interest me to my friend D.H. Lawrence. Do you know him or his work? He has curious gifts of intuition—and I wonder what he will say of your work. You are very rare. I can not tell exactly. You know better yourself. I wish you would tell me yourself. *Your* self! I seem to know you so well. Yet, I can not find the words. Yours is that strange concern with the gold-smith, the lapidary—I know it so well. I have never found nor made such rare jewels as yours. But I *know* your country. I know your work, your inspiration. You are already perfect. You *are* perfect. You are static, metalurgic [sic]. You are something finished. When and how will you begin again? I wonder! And I don't know. I am afraid for you—yet you are a perfect instrument and your irony perfectly protects you. Your work is more rare, more fine than any modern I know. But you puzzle me. Lawrence will send me the clue, I am sure.

I wish you were here. And yet I wish really no one here. The atmosphere is surcharged with death—really too terrible. Yet one lives apart from it, one's imagination reaches beyond it all.—

Send me all you do, Marianne. I will send you some of my new work if ever I get any done. The *Dial* writes for verse. Will you send some direct or send to me and let me send? Your work ought to please them. No one here is publishing anything anymore.

I enjoy so hearing from you—tell me what you are doing.

Richard will enjoy seeing your poems. He always called the sea-gull, one of Pippa's lost songs. I think I wrote you.

Keep well and write when you can.

H. D.

5
T. S. Eliot (1888–1965)

Introduced and Edited by Nancy K. Gish

In 1914, having just met T. S. Eliot, Ezra Pound praised "The Love Song of J. Alfred Prufrock" as "the best poem I have yet had or seen from an American." Eliot, he wrote to Harriet Monroe, had "actually trained himself and modernized himself *on his own*" (Stock 166). Eliot's modernism as well as his poetic importance were thus affirmed early. With the appearance of *Prufrock and Other Observations* in 1917 and *The Sacred Wood* in 1920, Eliot established himself as both avant-garde poet and literary critic, and with the publication of *The Waste Land* and winning of the *Dial* poetry prize in 1922, his reputation was assured. Although early reviews of *The Waste Land* were mixed, most readers came to share Conrad Aiken's view that it was "intensely modern" in its fragmentation and "one of the most moving and original poems of our time" (Aiken 97, 99).

While Eliot's early poems share a vision of personal and social disintegration, the later work, from the *Ariel* poems and *Ash Wednesday* to *Four Quartets*, articulates a conservative and religious response to such a world. His criticism, too, moves from aesthetic to cultural and religious issues. As both poet and man of letters he was admired, even acclaimed, throughout his life, winning the Order of Merit and the Nobel Prize for literature in 1948, the Hanseatic Goethe Award in 1955, and the Dante Gold Medal in 1958. Moreover, as literary critic, editor of the *Criterion*, and director of Faber and Faber,

Eliot helped shape the course of literature and ideas in England and America for much of this century.

Eliot's early and steady success was based in part on his poetic innovations—his use of symbolism, precise images, wit, ironic juxtaposition, allusion, and quotation, as well as his urban and contemporary settings with taxis, gramophones, and cigarette ends. But in a broader sense Eliot's place as a major, if not *the* major, modernist poet was defined by criteria he himself established. In "Tradition and the Individual Talent," Eliot argued that no artist could be evaluated in isolation. "He" must be set, "for contrast and comparison, among the dead. . . ." Moreover, "in a peculiar sense he will be aware also that he must inevitably be judged by the standards of the past" (Eliot, *Selected Essays* 4–5). This judgment and comparison goes both ways: "The existing monuments form an ideal order among themselves, which is modified by the introduction of the new (the really new) work of art among them" (5). By experimental techniques which nonetheless pointed toward, incorporated, and affirmed "the mind of Europe," Eliot seemed to demonstrate most fully his own definition of the individual talent that mattered. Eliot's "tradition" was European, white, and male. Yet, ironically, as Sandra Gilbert and Susan Gubar note, the "really new" art was women's (Gilbert and Gubar 162). By his own criteria, then, Eliot was placed in an ambivalent position by women's writing. Excluded almost by definition from "the dead" writers by which they were to be judged, yet offering the "really new" which could alter that past, they constituted both a threat and a challenge. In his one poetic portrait of a woman writer, Eliot describes her as genuine slut and pseudo-poet, imitative and immature. Fresca's debility seems generalizable, since "women grown intellectual grow dull / And lose the mother wit of natural trull" (*The Waste Land* 27).

But if woman as writer was, in general, a threat, Djuna Barnes and Marianne Moore, in particular, constituted a challenge. Both were supported, edited, published, and praised by Eliot. With both he maintained friendships and corresponded for many years. Yet in his reviews and introductions to their work an ambivalent response to women writers emerges almost in spite of his stated intentions.

His correspondence with Barnes begins with a discussion of *Nightwood,* which Faber and Faber published in 1937. The letters continued to Eliot's death in 1965, becoming friendly, chatty, even confidential over the years. He wrote the introduction for the first American edition of *Nightwood* in 1937 and reprinted it as a review in *The Criterion*. During the previous year he had carefully edited the novel's text, cutting lines, phrases, and several long passages. In light of these cuts, his emphasis on the character of the doctor takes on special interest.

Eliot's introduction (printed below) opens with a tribute to Barnes's "great achievement of a style" and closes by placing *Nightwood* in relation to tradition. That Barnes's prose style is so "alive" as to appeal to readers of poetry, and that the book has "a quality of horror and doom very nearly related to that of Elizabethan tragedy," acknowledges it as a "really new" work of art both cohering with and slightly altering the "ideal order" of the canon. The rest of the essay, however, focuses on the novel's characters and the centrality of Doctor Matthew-Mighty-Grain-of-Salt-Dante-O'Connor in a way that is striking, not only for its apt recognition of Barnes's psychological acuity—"the book is not a psychopathic study. The miseries that people suffer through their particular abnormalities of temperament are visible on the surface: the deeper design is that of the human misery and bondage which is universal"—but also for its failure even to note O'Connor's own "particular abnormality" as a fundamental issue.

Eliot acknowledges the pattern of relations of all the characters, yet he retains a sense of O'Connor's role as pivotal. It is O'Connor who, "hypersensitive" in his awareness of others, uses his obsessive talk to "save the situation," to "[squeeze] himself dry for other people," to "drown the still small wailing and whining of humanity," and "make more supportable its shame and less ignoble its misery." O'Connor, as Eliot presents him, is somewhat distanced from his fellow sufferers, more conscious if no more "real." And while this may be accurate in itself, it obscures O'Connor's profound complicity in their lives. For the book's center is Robin Vote and the women who love her and whom she leaves and betrays. O'Connor's deepest despair is that he feels he too—psychologically—is a woman. His obsession with humiliation and the "dark" stems not simply from a *heightened* consciousness but from a consciousness of *his own* condition as one of irreparable and hopeless desire—the fundamental condition of marginalization and otherness. Eliot makes of him an almost religious figure, distantly related to Henry Harcourt Reilly in his "desperate disinterestedness and . . . deep humility," his participation in, and authoritative recognition of, the shame of merely human and temporal need. Though O'Connor is obsessed with the nature of sin and sinners, his God is also "she," the perpetrator of the great error of making him physically male and psychologically female and dooming him to a hell of gender confusion and defamation.

Eliot's erasure of O'Connor's deepest obsession becomes more striking when set against his editorial cuts in Barnes's text. The passages he removed are predominantly O'Connor's speeches about his transvestism and homosexual experience. Several make explicit what is less overt in the published text: when acting out this behavior publicly, O'Connor is persistently humiliated. That Eliot's introduction never acknowledges what, as editor, he reduced suggests a shift of emphasis oddly transformed into a religious stance.

In a discussion of literary canon formation, Susan Heinzelman takes over the legal concepts of "hard," "easy," and "weird" cases, demonstrating that law and literature shape women's experience through comparable uses of discourse. Briefly, "easy" cases are those in which clearly applicable rules noncontroversially generate answers; "hard" cases are those in which rules are generated by "vague, ambiguous, or simply opaque" language, which therefore requires active interpretation on the part of the judge. In "weird" cases, on the other hand, the language is clear but cannot apply directly because the issue at hand confuses interpretation. Weird cases, therefore, say nothing about the law and are, characteristically, translated into hard cases in order to be solved—as, for example, the Baby M case, in which issues of reproduction and women's control of their own bodies are redefined as a dispute over contracts.

Women's writing persistently presents itself as "weird," that is, as failing to fit the given "law" or set of rules extractable from the "tradition." Eliot's strategy is to translate the weirdness of O'Connor's obsession and of the book's preoccupation with gender into the "hard" case of applying rules for poetry versus prose, placing it within "the" tradition (Elizabethan) and defining its center as a recognition of the nature of sin.

In a similar manner Eliot's genuine admiration for Marianne Moore's technical brilliance and originality is troubled by questions of a woman's tradition and a woman's style. Eliot first wrote to Moore in 1921 to thank her for her *Dial* review of *The Sacred Wood* and to praise her work. Though slightly formal and reserved (it took twenty-five years to go from "Miss" and "Mr." to "Tom" and "Marianne"), their correspondence was mutually admiring, respectful, and warm in praise. They became friends, lunching together when Eliot was in New York and sharing a dry wit, conservative values, and a care for precision and technical proficiency. Moreover, as Cleo Kearns has argued, they undoubtedly influenced each other's work.

Eliot's review of *Poems* and *Marriage,* printed below, opens with a political definition: "fine art is the *refinement,* not the antithesis, of popular art." Moore's art, he argues, is truly aristocratic in that it derives from and perfects a people's language. He identifies and praises three formal methods by which this occurs: "a quite new rhythm," a "peculiar and brilliant" use of American jargon, and "an almost primitive simplicity of phrase." Yet her brilliant and new techniques are brought to bear on an art firmly rooted in classical as well as American history. As with Barnes, Eliot carefully places Moore's "individual talent" within "tradition."

It is all the more astonishing, then, to come upon the gratuitous "compliment" to Moore's "feminine" affiliation with Christina Rossetti, a poet with whom she would seem to have little else in common. Why, one wonders, can he "never forget" that their poems are by women? His insistence on this fact effectively contradicts his own argument; it both asserts an alternative writing outside the "tradition" of poets whose gender apparently *can* be forgotten and foregrounds their shared exclusion from that writing as well. Separated from canonical writers by the "particularity" of their womanhood, yet distinguished also from women writers whose "particularity" is not a "positive virtue," they are left in isolation, idiosyncratic and indefinable.

That the *Dial* review reflects an unease with women as writers, to be overcome in a special case, is supported by a similar, if less emphatic, passage in Eliot's 1935 introduction to Moore's *Selected Poems,* also printed below. Here again he focuses on Moore's technical brilliance in relation to the past, concluding with what must have been his highest encomium, that her poems are part of "that small body of writings . . . engaged in maintaining the life of the English language." That this formal induction into the canon is an exception, however, is highlighted by reference to one other woman for the purpose not of establishing tradition but of denying it. H. D. appears as a possible "slight influence" on just one early poem, or at least more influence than any other practitioner of "imagism" whose aim "so far as it had any" was to concentrate on the visual. Both H. D. and the style with which she had been identified are introduced simply to be dismissed, in a reductive strategy emphasizing Moore's movement into more serious company.

In this introduction, as in the *Dial* review, Eliot appears to cut Moore out from the company of women and to place her unambiguously as an "individual talent" within the English literary tradition. Yet the ambivalence with which he must make such a claim emerges in seemingly irrelevant comparisons, either to connect her with another woman whose "positive virtue" transcends "particularity" or to disconnect her from possible membership in a trivializing women's tradition.

While Eliot's admiration of Moore never waned, he partially withdrew his support of Barnes. In 1957 he wrote an introduction for *Antiphon* with allusions to *Nightwood* so ambiguous and constrained that Barnes felt betrayed. Whether he felt her work had declined or whether her material placed too much pressure on his concerns with women writers is not clear, but the contrast to his undiminished praise of Moore suggests the greater ease with which the latter could be assimilated. Yet in both cases, by assimilation or intrusion, gender disrupts carefully constructed criteria of canonization by revealing the weirdness suppressed in transforming a "particularity" into simply a "hard case."

WORKS CITED

Aiken, Conrad. "An Anatomy of Melancholy." *New Republic* 7 Feb. 1923. Rpt. in *T. S. Eliot: The Waste Land*, ed. C. B. Cox and Arnold P. Hinchliffe, 97, 99. London: Macmillan, 1969.

Eliot, T. S. *Selected Essays*. New York: Harcourt, Brace and World, 1950.

———. *The Waste Land: A Facsimile and Transcript of the Original Drafts Including the Annotations of Ezra Pound*. Ed. Valerie Eliot. New York: Harcourt Brace Jovanovich, 1971.

Gilbert, Sandra M., and Susan Gubar. *No Man's Land*. Vol. 1. *The War of the Words*. New Haven: Yale UP, 1988.

Heinzelman, Susan. "Hard Cases, Easy Cases, and Weird Cases: Canon Formation in Law and Literature." *Mosaic* 21.2–3(Spring 1988):59–72.

Kearns, Cleo McNelly. "Consanguinities: T. S. Eliot and Marianne Moore." T. S. Eliot Centennial Celebration, National Poetry Foundation Conference, Orono, Maine, 20 Aug. 1988.

Stock, Noel. *The Life of Ezra Pound*. New York: Pantheon, 1970.

Introduction to Djuna Barnes's *Nightwood*

When the question is raised, of writing an introduction to a book of a creative order, I always feel that the few books worth introducing are exactly those which it is an impertinence to introduce. I have already committed two such impertinences; this is the third, and if it is not the last no one will be more surprised than myself. I can justify this preface only in the following way. One is liable to expect other people to see, on their first reading of a book, all that one has come to perceive in the course of a developing intimacy with it. I have read *Nightwood* a number of times, in manuscript, in proof, and after publication. What one can do for other readers—assuming that if you read this preface at all you will read it first—is to trace the more significant phases of one's own appreciation of it. For it took me, with this book, some time to come to an appreciation of its meaning as a whole.

In describing *Nightwood* for the purpose of attracting readers to the English edition, I said that it would "appeal primarily to readers of poetry." This is well enough for the brevity of advertisement, but I am glad to take this opportunity to amplify it a little. I do not want to suggest that the distinction of the book is primarily verbal, and still less that the astonishing language covers a vacuity of content. Unless the term "novel" has become too debased to apply, and if it means a book in which living characters are created and shown in significant relationship, this book is a novel. And I do not mean that Miss Barnes's style is "poetic prose." But I do mean that most contemporary novels are not really "written." They obtain what reality they have largely from an accurate rendering of the noises that human beings currently make in their daily simple needs of communication; and what part of a novel is not composed of these noises consists of a prose which is no more alive than that of a competent newspaper writer or government official. A prose that is altogether alive demands something of the reader that the ordinary novel-reader is not prepared to give. To say that *Nightwood* will appeal primarily to readers of poetry does not mean that it is not a novel, but that it is so good a novel that only sensibilities trained on poetry can wholly appreciate it. Miss Barnes's prose has the prose rhythm that is prose style, and the musical pattern which is not that of verse. This prose rhythm may be more or less complex or elaborate, according to the purposes of the writer; but whether simple or complex, it is what raises the matter to be communicated, to the first intensity.

When I first read the book I found the opening movement rather slow and dragging, until the appearance of the doctor. And throughout the first reading, I was under the impression that it was the doctor alone who gave the book its vitality; and I believed the final chapter to be superfluous. I am now convinced that the final chapter is essential, both dramatically and musically. It was notable, however, that as the other characters, on repeated reading, became alive for me, and while the focus shifted, the figure of the doctor was by no means diminished. On the contrary, he came to take on a different and more profound importance when seen as a constituent of a whole pattern. He ceased to be like the brilliant actor in an otherwise unpersuasively performed play for whose re-entrance one impatiently waits. However in actual life such a character might seem to engross conversation, quench reciprocity, and blanket less voluble people; in the book his role is nothing of the kind. At first we only hear the doctor talking; we do not understand why he talks. Gradually one comes to see that together with his egotism and swagger—Dr. Matthew-Mighty-grain-of-salt-Dante-O'Connor—he has also a desperate disinterestedness and a deep humility. His humility does not often appear so centrally as in the prodigious scene in the empty church, but it is what throughout gives him his helpless power among the helpless. His monologues, brilliant and witty in themselves as they are, are not dictated by an indifference to other human beings, but on the contrary by a hypersensitive awareness of them. When Nora comes to visit him in the night (*Watchman, What of the Night?*) he perceives at once that the only thing he can do for her ("he was extremely put out, having expected someone else")—the only way to "save the situation"—is to talk torrentially, even though she hardly takes in anything he says, but reverts again and again to her obsession. It is his revulsion against the strain of squeezing himself dry for other people, and getting no sustenance in return, that sends him raving at the end. *The people in my life who have made my life miserable, coming to me to learn of degradation and the night.* But most of the time he is talking to drown the still small wailing and whining of humanity, to make more supportable its shame and less ignoble its misery.

Indeed, such a character as Doctor O'Connor could not be real alone in a gallery of dummies: such a character needs other real, if less conscious, people in order to realize his own reality. I cannot think of any character in the book who has not gone on living in my mind. Felix and his child are oppressively real. Sometimes in a phrase the characters spring to life so suddenly that one is taken aback, as if one had touched a wax-work figure and discovered that it was a live policeman. The doctor says to Nora, *I was doing well enough until you kicked my stone over, and out I came, all moss and eyes.* Robin Vote (the most puzzling of all, because we find her quite real without quite understanding the means by which the author has made her so) is *the vision of an eland coming down an aisle of trees, chapleted with orange-blossoms and bridal veil, a hoof raised in the economy of fear;* and later she has *temples like those of young beasts cutting horns, as if they were sleeping eyes.* Sometimes also a situation, which we had already comprehended loosely, is concentrated into a horror of intensity by a phrase, as when Nora suddenly thinks on seeing the doctor in bed, *"God, children know something they can't tell; they like Red Riding Hood and the wolf in bed!"*

The book is not simply a collection of individual portraits; the characters are all knotted together, as people are in real life, by what we may call chance or destiny, rather than by deliberate choice of each other's company: it is the whole pattern that they form, rather than any individual constituent, that is the focus of interest. We come to know them through their effect on each other, and by what they say to each other about the others. And finally, it ought to be superfluous to observe—but perhaps to anyone reading the book for the first time, it is not superfluous—that the book is not a psychopathic study. The miseries that people suffer through their particular abnormalities of temperament are visible on the surface: the deeper design is that of the human misery and bondage which is universal. In normal lives this misery is mostly concealed; often, what is most wretched of all, concealed from the sufferer more effectively than from the observer. The sick man does not know what is wrong with him; he partly wants to know, and mostly wants to conceal the knowledge from himself. In the Puritan morality that I remember, it was tacitly assumed that if one was thrifty, enterprising, intelligent, practical and prudent in not violating social conventions, one ought to have a happy and "successful" life. Failure was due to some weakness or perversity peculiar to the individual; but the decent man need have no nightmares. It is now rather more common to assume that all individual misery is the fault of "society," and is remediable by alterations from without. Fundamentally the two philosophies, however different they may appear in operation, are the same. It seems to me that all of us, so far as we attach ourselves to created objects and surrender our wills to temporal ends, are eaten by the same worm. Taken in this way, *Nightwood* appears with profound significance. To regard this group of people as a horrid sideshow of freaks is not only to miss the point, but to confirm our wills and harden our hearts in an inveterate sin of pride.

I should have considered the foregoing paragraph impertinent, and perhaps too pretentious for a preface meant to be a simple recommendation of a book I greatly admire, were it not that one review (at least), intended in praise of the book, has already appeared which would in effect induce the reader to begin with this mistaken attitude. Otherwise, generally, in trying to anticipate a reader's misdirections, one is in danger of provoking him to some other misunderstanding unforeseen. This is a work of creative imagination, not a philosophical treatise. As I said at the beginning, I am conscious of impertinence in introducing the book at all; and to have read a book a good many times does not necessarily put one in the right knowledge of what to say to those who have not yet read it. What I would leave the reader prepared to find is the great achievement of a style, the beauty of phrasing, the brilliance of wit and characterisation, and a quality of horror and doom very nearly related to that of Elizabethan tragedy.

Nightwood. By Djuna Barnes. New York: New Directions, 1961.

Review of Marianne Moore's *Poems* and *Marriage*

POEMS. *By Marianne Moore. 12mo. 24 pages. The Egoist Press, London.*

MARRIAGE (Manikin Number 3). *By Marianne Moore. 10mo. 20 pages. Monroe Wheeler. $0.25.*

Two years ago Miss Moore's book of Poems—so far as I know her only book—was published in London by The Egoist Press; and then I undertook to review it for *The Dial*. This promise, for one reason after another, I never fulfilled. Now another poem has appeared, Marriage, published by Manikin, printed apparently in Germany, and with a parenthetical introduction by Mr Glenway Wescott. Meanwhile I have read Miss Moore's poems a good many times, and always with exactly the same pleasure, and satisfaction in something quite definite and solid. Because of a promise which, because of the long delay, may be considered as having been broken, and because I can only, at the moment, think of five contemporary poets—English, Irish, American, French, and German—whose work excites me as much as, or more than, Miss Moore's, I find myself compelled to say something about them. Not that there is much that is usefully said about any new work of art—I do not rate criticism so highly; but one ought, in honesty, to publish one's beliefs.

Mr Wescott has, in fact, written a good introduction; I only think that his distinction between proletariat art and aristocratic art is an artificial and unimportant distinction with dangerous consequences. So far as a proletariat art is art at all, it is the same thing in essence as aristocratic art; but in general, and at the present time, the middle-class art (which is what I believe Mr Wescott to have in mind when he speaks of proletariat art—(the proletariat *is* middle class in America) is much more artificial than anything else; it plays with sham ideas, sham emotions, and even sham sensations. On the other hand a real aristocracy is essentially of the same blood as the people over whom it rules: a real aristocracy is not a Baltenland aristocracy of foreign race. This apparently purely political definition applies to art as well: fine art is the *refinement*, not the antithesis, of popular art. Miss Moore's poetry may not seem to confirm this statement. I agree with Mr Wescott that it is "aristocratic," in that it can only please a very small number of people. But it is not, or not wholly, aristocratic in the Baltenland sense. I see in it at least three elements: a quite new rhythm, which I think is the most valuable thing; a peculiar and brilliant and rather satirical use of what is not, as material, an "aristocratic" language at all, but simply the curious jargon produced in America by universal university education—that jargon which makes it impossible for Americans to talk for half an hour without using the terms of psychoanalysis, and which has introduced "moron" as more forcible than "idiot"; and finally an almost primitive simplicity of phrase. There may be more. Up to the present time Miss Moore has concerned herself with practising and perfecting a given formation of elements; it will depend, I think, on her ability to *shatter* this formation and painfully reconstruct, whether Miss Moore makes another invention equal in merit to the first.

Rhythm, of course, is a highly personal matter; it is not a verse-form. It is always the real pattern in the carpet, the scheme of organization of thought, feeling, and vocabulary, the way in which everything comes together. It is very uncommon. What is certain is that Miss Moore's poems always read very well aloud. That quality is something which no system of scansion can define. It is not separable from the use of words, in Miss Moore's case the conscious and complete appreciations of every word, and in relation to every other word, as it goes by. I think that Those Various Scalpels is an excellent example for study. Here the rhythm depends partly upon the transformation-changes from one image to another, so that the second image is superposed before the first has quite faded, and upon the dexterity of change of vocabulary from one image to another. "Snow sown by tearing winds on the cordage of disabled ships:" has that Latin, epigrammatic succinctness, laconic austerity, which leaps out unexpectedly (altogether in Talisman).

> "your raised hand
> an ambiguous signature:"

is a distinct shift of manner; it is not an image, but the indication of a fulness of meaning which is unnecessary to pursue.

> "blood on the stone floors of French châteaux, with
> regard to which guides are so affirmative:"

is a satirical (consciously or unconsciously it does not matter) refinement of that pleasantry (not flippancy, which is something with a more definite purpose) of speech which characterizes the American language, that pleasantry, uneasy, solemn, or self-conscious, which inspires both the jargon of the laboratory and the slang of the comic strip. Miss Moore works this uneasy language of stereotypes—as of a whole people playing uncomfortably at clenches and clevelandisms—with impeccable skill into her pattern. She uses words like "fractional," "vertical," "infinitesimal," "astringently"; phrases like "excessive popularity," "a liability rather than an asset," "mask of profundity," "vestibule of experience," "diminished vitality," "arrested prosperity." If this were all, Miss Moore would be no different from her imitators. The merit consists in the combination, in the other point of view which Miss Moore possesses at the same time. What her imitators cannot get are the swift dissolving images, like the mussel shell

> "opening and shutting itself like
> an
> injured fan"

and phrases like

> "the sea when it proffers flattery in exchange for hemp
> rye, flax, horses, platinum, timber and fur."
>
> "Truth is no Apollo
> Belvedere, no formal thing. The wave may go over it if it likes."

or a magnificence of phrase like

> "I recall their magnificence, now not more magnificent
> than it is dim"

(how like Valery's "*entre les pins palpite, entre les tombes*" or like his "*eternellement, Eternellement le bout mordre*"). And also they cannot imitate her animals and birds—

"the parrakeet—
. . . destroying
bark and portions of the food it could not eat."

Mr Wescott, if he agrees with all or even with a part of what I have written, will probably consider it as an affirmation of his belief in a kind of "aristocratic" art drawing no sustenance from the soil. "An aristocratic art, emulating the condition of ritual." But of course *all* art emulates the condition of ritual. That is what it comes from and to that it must always return for nourishment. And nothing belongs more properly to the people than ritual—or indeed than aristocracy itself, a popular invention to serve popular needs. (I suppose the Ku Klux Klan is a popular ritual—as popular as a ritual can be in a country where there are only variations *within* the middle class.) Miss Moore's relation to the soil is not a simple one, or rather it is to various soils—to that of Latium and to that of Attica I believe (or at least to that of the Aegean littoral) as well as most positively to the soil (well top-dressed) of America. There are several reasons (buried in this essay) why Miss Moore's poetry is almost completely neglected in England, beside the simple reason that it is too good, "in this age of hard striving," to be appreciated anywhere.

And there is one final, and "magnificent" compliment: Miss Moore's poetry is as "feminine" as Christina Rossetti's, one never forgets that it is written by a woman; but with both one never thinks of this particularity as anything but a positive virtue.

Dial 75.6 (1923): 594–597.

Introduction to Marianne Moore's *Selected Poems*

We know very little about the value of the work of our contemporaries, almost as little as we know about our own. It may have merits which exist only for contemporary sensibility; it may have concealed virtues which will only become apparent with time. How it will rank when we are all dead authors ourselves we cannot say with any precision. If one is to talk about one's contemporaries at all, therefore, it is important to make up our minds as to what we can affirm with confidence, and as to what must be a matter of doubting conjecture. The last thing, certainly, that we are likely to know about them is their "greatness", or their relative distinction or triviality in relation to the standard of "greatness". For in greatness are involved moral and social relations, relations which can only be perceived from a remoter perspective, and which may be said even to be created in the process of history: we cannot tell, in advance, what any poetry is going to do, how it will operate upon later generations. But the *genuineness* of poetry is something which we have some warrant for believing that a small number, but only a small number, of contemporary readers can recognise. I say positively only a small number, because it seems probable that when any poet conquers a really large public in his lifetime, an increasing proportion of his admirers will admire him for extraneous reasons. Not necessarily for bad reasons, but because he becomes known merely as a symbol, in giving a kind of stimulation or consolation, to his readers, which is a function of his peculiar relation to them in time. Such effect upon contemporary readers may be a legitimate and proper result of some great poetry, but it has been also the result of much ephemeral poetry.

It does not seem to matter much whether one has to struggle with an age which is unconscious and self-satisfied, and therefore hostile to new forms of poetry, or with one like the present which is self-conscious and distrustful of itself, and avid for new forms which will give it status and self-respect. For many modern readers any superficial novelty of form is evidence of, or is as good as, newness of sensibility; and if the sensibility is fundamentally dull and second-hand, so much the better; for there is no quicker way of catching an immediate, if transient, popularity, than to serve stale goods in new packages. One of the tests—though it be only a negative test—of anything really new and genuine, seems to be its capacity for exciting aversion among "lovers of poetry".

I am aware that prejudice makes me underrate certain authors: I see them rather as public enemies than as subjects for criticism; and I dare say that a different prejudice makes me uncritically favourable to others. I may even admire the right authors for the wrong reasons. But I am much more confident of my appreciation of the authors whom I admire, than of my depreciation of the authors who leave me cold or who exasperate me. And in asserting that what I call *genuineness* is a more important thing to recognise in a contemporary than *greatness,* I am distinguishing between his function while living and his function when dead. Living, the poet is carrying on that struggle for the maintenance of a living language, for the maintenance of its strength, its subtlety, for the preservation of quality of feeling, which must be kept up in every generation; dead, he provides standards for those who take up the struggle after him. Miss Moore is, I believe, one of those few who have done the language some service in my lifetime.

So far back as my memory extends, which is to the pages of *The Egoist* during the War, and of *The Little Review* and *The Dial* in the years immediately following, Miss Moore has no immediate poetic derivations. I cannot, therefore, fill up my pages with the usual account of influences and development. There is one early poem, *A Talisman,* not reprinted in the text of this volume, which I will quote in full here, because it suggests a slight influence of H.D., certainly of H.D. rather than of any other "Imagist":

Under a splintered mast
Torn from the ship and cast
  Near her hull,

A stumbling shepherd found
Embedded in the ground,
  A sea-gull

Of lapis-lazuli,
A scarab of the sea,
  With wings spread—

Curling its coral feet,
Parting its beak to greet
  Men long dead.

The sentiment is commonplace, and I cannot see what a bird carved of *lapis-lazuli* should be doing with *coral* feet; but even here the cadence, the use of rhyme, and a certain authoritativeness of manner distinguish the poem. Looking at Miss Moore's poems of a slightly later period, I should say that she had taken to heart the repeated reminder of Mr. Pound: that poetry should be as well written as prose. She seems to have saturated her mind in the perfections of prose, in its precision rather than its purple; and to have found her rhythm, her poetry, her appreciation of the individual word, for herself.

The first aspect in which Miss Moore's poetry is likely to strike the reader is that of minute detail rather than that of emotional unity. The gift for detailed observation, for finding the exact words for some experience of the eye, is liable to disperse the attention of the relaxed reader. The minutiae may even irritate the unwary, or arouse in them only the pleasurable astonishment evoked by the carved ivory ball with eleven other balls inside it, the full-rigged ship in a bottle, the skeleton of the crucifix-fish. The bewilderment consequent upon trying to follow so alert an eye, so quick a process of association, may produce the effect of some "metaphysical" poetry. To the moderately intellectual the poems may appear to be intellectual exercises; only to those whose intellection moves more easily will they immediately appear to have emotional value. But the detail has always its service to perform to the whole. The similes are there for use; as the mussel-shell "opening and shutting itself like an injured fan" (where *injured* has an ambiguity good enough for Mr. Empson), the waves "as formal as the scales on a fish". They make us see the object more clearly, though we may not understand immediately why our attention has been called to this object, and though we may not immediately grasp its association with a number of other objects. So, in her amused and affectionate attention to animals—from the domestic cat, or "to popularize the mule", to the most exotic strangers from the tropics, she succeeds at once in startling us into an unusual awareness of visual patterns, with something like the fascination of a high-powered microscope.

Miss Moore's poetry, or most of it, might be classified as "descriptive" rather than "lyrical" or "dramatic". Descriptive poetry is supposed to be dated to a period, and to be condemned thereby; but it is really one of the permanent modes of expression. In the eighteenth century—or say a period which includes *Cooper's Hill, Windsor Forest,* and Gray's *Elegy*—the scene described is a point of departure for meditations on one thing or another. The poetry of the Romantic Age, from Byron at his worst to Wordsworth at his best, wavers between the reflective and the evocative; but the description, the picture set before you, is always there for the same purpose. The aim of "imagism", so far as I understand it, or so far as it had any, was to induce a peculiar concentration upon something visual, and to set in motion an expanding succession of concentric feelings. Some of Miss Moore's poems—for instance with animal or bird subjects—have a very wide spread of association. It would be difficult to say what is the "subject-matter" of *The Jerboa.* For a mind of such agility, and for a sensibility so reticent, the minor subject, such as a pleasant little sand-coloured skipping animal, may be the best release for the major emotions. Only the pedantic literalist could consider the subject-matter to be trivial; the triviality is in himself. We all have to choose whatever subject-matter allows us the most powerful and most secret release; and that is a personal affair.

The result is often something that the majority will call frigid; for feeling in one's own way, however intensely, is likely to look like frigidity to those who can only feel in accepted ways.

> The deepest feeling always shows itself in silence;
> not in silence, but restraint.

It shows itself in a control which makes possible the fusion of the ironic-conversational and the high-rhetorical, as

> I recall their magnificence, now not more magnificent
> than it is dim. It is difficult to recall the ornament,
>   speech, and precise manner of what one might
>   call the minor acquaintances twenty
>   years back. . . .
>   strict with tension, malignant
>   in its power over us and deeper
>   than the sea when it proffers flattery in exchange
>   for hemp,
>   rye, flax, horses, platinum, timber and fur.

As one would expect from the kind of activity which I have been trying to indicate, Miss Moore's versification is anything but "free". Many of the poems are in exact, and sometimes complicated, formal patterns, and move with the elegance of a minuet ("Elegance", indeed, is one of her certain attributes.) Some of the poems (e.g. *Marriage, An Octopus*) are unrhymed; in others (e.g. *Sea Unicorns and Land Unicorns*) rhyme or assonance is introduced irregularly; in a number of the poems rhyme is part of a regular pattern interwoven with unrhymed endings. Miss Moore's use of rhyme is in itself a definite innovation in metric.

In the conventional forms of rhyme the stress given by the rhyme tends to fall in the same place as the stress given by the sense. The extreme case, at its best, is the pentameter couplet of Pope. Poets before and after Pope have given variety, sometimes at the expense of smoothness, by deliberately separating the stresses, from time to time; but this separation—often effected simply by longer periods or more involved syntax—can hardly be considered as more than a deviation from the norm for the purpose of avoiding monotony. The tendency of some of the best contemporary poetry is of course to dispense with rhyme altogether; but some of those who do use it have used it here and there to make a pattern directly in contrast with the sense and rhythm pattern, to give a greater intricacy. Some of the internal rhyming of Hopkins is to the point. (Genuine or auditory internal rhyme must not be confused with false or visual internal rhyme. If a poem reads just as well when cut up so that all the rhymes fall at the end of lines, then the internal rhyme is false and only a typographical caprice, as in Oscar Wilde's *Sphinx*.) This rhyme, which forms a pattern *against* the metric and sense pattern of the poem, may be either heavy or light—that is to say, either *heavier* or *lighter* than the other pattern. The two kinds, heavy and light, have doubtless different uses which remain to be explored. Of the *light* rhyme Miss Moore is the greatest living master; and indeed she is the first, so far as I know, who has investigated its possibilities. It will be observed that the effect sometimes requires giving a word a slightly more analytical pronunciation, or stressing a syllable more than ordinarily:

al-
ways has been—at the antipodes from the initial great truths. "Part of it was crawling, part of it
was about to crawl, the rest
was torpid in its lair." In the short-legged, fitful advance. . . .

It is sometimes obtained by the use of articles as rhyme words:

an
injured fan.
The barnacles which encrust the side
of the wave, cannot hide . . .

the
turquoise sea
of bodies. The water drives a wedge . . .

In a good deal of what is sometimes (with an unconscious theological innuendo) called "modernist" verse one finds either an excess or a defect of technical attention. The former appears in an emphasis upon words rather than things, and the latter in an emphasis upon things and an indifference to words. In either case, the poem is formless, just as the most accomplished sonnet, if it is an attempt to express matter unsuitable for sonnet form, is formless. But a precise fitness of form and matter mean also a balance between them: thus the form, the pattern movement, has a solemnity of its own (e.g. Shakespeare's songs), however light and gay the human emotion concerned; and a gaiety of its own, however serious or tragic the emotion. The choruses of Sophocles, as well as the songs of Shakespeare, have another concern besides the human action of which they are spectators, and without this other concern there is not poetry. And on the other hand, if you aim only at the poetry in poetry, there is no poetry either.

My conviction, for what it is worth, has remained unchanged for the last fourteen years: that Miss Moore's poems form part of the small body of durable poetry written in our time; of that small body of writings, among what passes for poetry, in which an original sensibility and alert intelligence and deep feeling have been engaged in maintaining the life of the English language.

The original suggestion was that I should make a selection, from both previously published and more recent poems. But Miss Moore exercised her own rights of proscription first, so drastically, that I have been concerned to preserve rather than abate. I have therefore hardly done more than settle the order of the contents. This book contains all that Miss Moore was willing to reprint from the volume *Observations* (The Dial Press, New York, 1924), together with the poems written since that date which she is willing to publish.

Selected Poems. By Marianne Moore. London: Faber & Faber, 1934. 5–12.

6
Jessie Redmon Fauset (1882–1961)

Introduced and Edited by Cheryl A. Wall

Harlem, the fabled cultural capital of the black world, gave its name to the awakening among Afro-American artists during the 1920s and 1930s. The Harlem Renaissance, with its outpouring of literature, art, and music, defined a new age in Afro-American cultural history. To a degree, the difference was formal; artists' explorations of vernacular culture yielded new genres of poetry and music. The transformation was, however, larger than that. Proclaiming the advent of the "New Negro" in 1925, Alain Locke argued for a revised racial identity. The migration of thousands of blacks from the rural South to northern cities reflected and produced a new race consciousness and pride. Afro-Americans had achieved at long last a spiritual emancipation, "shaking off the psychology of imitation and implied inferiority" that were slavery's legacy. Locke averred that "the day of 'aunties,' 'uncles' and 'mammies' is equally gone." Art expresses the transformation. Like the migrant masses, "shifting from countryside to city," the young black artists "hurdle several generations of experience at a leap" (Locke 4, 5).

Scholars have treated Locke's essay as a manifesto of the movement, but its argument overstates the case for male writers and contradicts the experience of many women. Zora Hurston is the outstanding exception. Some women, such as Jessie Fauset and Marita Bonner, were northern born and bred; they knew little of the southern folk culture, and what they did know they had been trained to deny. Despite being born in Atlanta and rural Virginia respectively, Georgia Douglas Johnson and Anne Spencer wrote poetry that neither spoke in the accents of the region nor represented its social reality. Moreover, their work, like Fauset's and Bonner's, reflects a strong sense that the stereotypes Locke dismissed continued to haunt. Less innovative in form and less race conscious in theme, black women's writing generally does not seem to "hurdle several generations of experience in a leap." It does, however, encode the experience of racism and sexism in more profound ways than critics have usually discerned.

Jessie Fauset, who published four novels in ten years, was among the most prolific writers of the period; she was also one of the few literary women to live in Harlem. Her fiction has rarely been considered reflective of the age. Taken as novels of manners of the black middle class, her books long consigned their author, in Robert Bone's phrase, to "the Rear Guard" of the Renaissance. Feminist critics, notably Deborah McDowell and Carolyn Sylvander, challenge this view. Moreover, when one examines her total career as editor and journalist as well as novelist and poet, Jessie Fauset's progressive contribution to Afro-American literature in indisputable.

While teaching high school French and Latin in Washington, D.C., Fauset had begun in 1912 to submit pieces to the two-year-old *Crisis,* the official publication of the National Association for the Advancement of Colored People. Founded and edited by W. E. B. Du Bois, the sociologist and writer who is one of the towering figures in twentieth-century American intellectual history, the *Crisis* soon became the most influential black periodical in the country. Jessie Fauset became literary editor in 1919, the year the *Crisis* circulation reached the 100,000 mark. Fauset's arrival on staff thus coincided with the first stirrings of the Harlem Renaissance. Under her direction, the *Crisis* gained a reputation for literary excellence that paralleled its eminence in social and political affairs.

Jessie Fauset made the decision to publish Langston Hughes's first poem, "The Negro Speaks of Rivers." In his memoir *The Big Sea* Hughes acknowledged her steadfast support of him and others when he named her along with Alain Locke and Charles S. Johnson as one who "midwifed the Negro Renaissance" into being. Fauset's attention to the careers of other young poets, notably Arna Bontemps and Jean Toomer, is documented in their memoirs and correspondence.

Particularly significant was her championing of black women writers. She promoted the work of women illustrators (Effie Lee Newsome and Laura Wheeler Waring, for example) as well as writers in the *Crisis* and the *Brownies' Book,* the ground-breaking children's magazine Fauset edited with Du Bois in 1920 and 1921. Novelist Nella Larsen first appeared in print in the *Brownies' Book.* Fauset gave writers other kinds of notice as well. When she reviewed *The Book of American Negro Poetry* (see "As to Books," below), a pioneering volume edited by James Weldon Johnson, she cited by name only four of the thirty-two poets represented; Georgia Douglas Johnson and Anne Spencer were two of them. Despite the vagueness of her critical vocabulary, Fauset's judgment was sound. Spencer did in fact possess one of the most distinctive voices of the period; Johnson was the only woman to collect her poetry in book form.

Among the other significant volumes Fauset reviewed were the first books by Countee Cullen and Langston Hughes (her reviews are reprinted below), as well as the first book Claude McKay published in the United States (see "As to Books"). By any reckoning, these men are major poets of the Harlem Renaissance. They are also strikingly dissimilar in their approach to their craft. Fauset's critical acumen enabled her to identify the strengths in each man's work, though she was clearly more comfortable with the traditional poetics to which Cullen and McKay adhered. Of McKay's *Harlem Shadows* she could proclaim without reservation, "*this is poetry!*" By contrast, when writing about Hughes's *The Weary Blues,* Fauset was careful to state that she was "no great lover of dialect," and she was rather too eager to place Hughes's work in the context of Western literary tradition. Certainly, her assertion that Hughes was not preoccupied with form is mistaken; Hughes's experiments with vernacular forms such as spirituals, blues, and jazz are now regarded as building blocks of Afro-American modernism. Yet, with all her temporizing, Fauset reached a conclusion from which few of Hughes's many subsequent critics would demur: "I doubt if any one will ever write more tenderly, more understandingly, more humorously of the life of Harlem shot through as it is with mirth, abandon and pain." The tolerance for literary innovation exemplified here places Fauset in sharp contrast to Du Bois, whose literary values could be as reactionary as his politics were progressive.

Fauset's *Crisis* writings are diverse and numerous. She wrote on educational themes, sketching the lives of heroic blacks in different societies, and on drama and other cultural subjects. She reported regularly on black women activists, such as those organized in the National Organization of Colored Women. Widely traveled and fluent in several languages, Fauset translated and reviewed literature from Africa and the Caribbean. She also became increasingly skilled in the art of reportage, as the essays recounting her extensive travel abroad demonstrate.

A lifelong Francophile, Fauset noted appreciatively the absence of petty racism in France. As she told the *Paris Tribune* in 1925, "I am colored and wish to be known as colored, but sometimes I have felt that my growth as a writer has been hampered in my own country. And so—but only temporarily—I have fled from it" (quoted in Benstock 13). Although she was well aware of the white American expatriate community, she had little contact with its members. They were, she felt, uninterested in meeting her. Referring to the proprietor of Shakespeare & Company, Fauset remarked, "Miss Beach has never acknowledged my note" (quoted in Lewis 124).

To an admirable degree, Fauset broadened her travel and her political concerns beyond the orbit of her peers. In 1921 she reported on the meetings in London, Brussels, and Paris of the Pan-African Congress, an organization Du Bois helped lead. These meetings were an important forum for the anticolonial effort; Fauset's "What Europe Thought of the Pan-African Congress" provided rare notice of women's role in the movement. Fauset also wrote accounts of her visits to North Africa. While not entirely free of racial stereotyping, these essays offer vivid representations of life in Algiers and Egypt. At a time when many Afro-Americans were fascinated by the idea of Africa, Fauset was one of a very few who actually set foot on the continent.

Issues of race and gender are major concerns in Fauset's fiction. Adhering to principles she adumbrated in her reviews, she claimed that her novels were not propagandistic. Neither, she averred, were they constrained by issues of race. Both claims are false in precisely the same way her observation that McKay did not write propaganda was false. Fauset believed that Afro-American writers had a role to play in the political struggle; they had a duty, as she put it in a wide-ranging interview in 1932, to "tell the truth about us." But she thought Afro-American writers discharged this duty best when they wrote skillfully and truthfully.

Fauset did not find a fictional form conducive to the truth she wanted to tell. *There Is Confusion* (1924), *Plum Bun* (1929), *The Chinaberry Tree* (1931), and *Comedy: American Style* (1933) are all sentimental novels. The plots often strain credulity, and their resolutions are uniformly happy: the still courageous but chastened heroine finds happiness with a protective yet more understanding hero. Yet, as McDowell has noted, Fauset's novels use literary and social conventions partly as a "deflecting mask for her more challenging concerns" ("Neglected Dimension" 87). The clichés of the marriage plot and the "passing" novel notwithstanding, *Plum Bun* (see the excerpt below) reveals a sophisticated understanding about the politics of race and gender. Fauset's protagonist, Angela Murray, is aware of the hierarchical arrangement of race and gender relations, but she is naive about their implications. Her creator was not.

The foreword to *The Chinaberry Tree* (also printed below), the most cogent statement of Fauset's personal aesthetic, has often been cited and frequently censured as a betrayal of a racial birthright. The weaknesses inherent in Fauset's position are clear; the racial defensiveness is palpable. Yet Fauset's "breathing-spells, in-between spaces where colored men and women work and love," may in fact be comparable to Hurston's renderings of the Eatonville store porch whose "sitters had been tongueless, earless, eyeless conveniences all day long" (Hurston 9–10). On the porch Hurston's characters cease to be mules and become men and women. For Hurston such "in-between spaces" are inscribed by cultural differences; Fauset emphasizes commonality. Taken in tandem, the fiction of these two women explores the multidimensional experiences of Afro-Americans.

In this regard, Fauset's refusal to write about the kinds of characters and situations white readers expected and her insistence that all the drama in

Afro-American life did not revolve around interracial conflict are important. Indeed, they are part of a larger effort waged by black women writers collectively to create a space in which they could tell their own stories.

WORKS CITED

Benstock, Shari. *Women of the Left Bank: Paris, 1900–1940.* Austin: U of Texas P, 1986.
Fauset, Jessie. *The Chinaberry Tree.* New York: Frederick A. Stokes, 1931.
———. *Comedy: American Style.* New York: Frederick A. Stokes, 1933.
———. *Plum Bun.* New York: Frederick A. Stokes, 1929.
———. *There Is Confusion.* New York: Boni and Liveright, 1924.
———. "What Europe Thought of the Pan-African Congress." *Crisis* December 1921:60–69.
Hughes, Langston. *The Big Sea.* 1940. New York: Knopf, 1940.
Hurston, Zora Neale. *Their Eyes Were Watching God.* 1937. Urbana: U of Illinois P, 1978.
Lewis, David L. *When Harlem Was in Vogue.* New York: Knopf, 1981.
Locke, Alain.. "The New Negro." *The New Negro.* 1925. New York: Atheneum, 1968, 3–16.
McDowell, Deborah. Introduction to Fauset, *Plum Bun.* London: Pandora P, 1985.
———. "The Neglected Dimension of Jessie Fauset." In *Conjuring: Black Women, Fiction, and Literary Tradition,* ed. Marjorie Pryse and Hortense Spillers, 86–104. Bloomington: Indiana UP, 1985.
Starkey, Marion. "Jessie Fauset." *Southern Workman* May 1932:217–220.
Sylvander, Carolyn. *Jessie Redmon Fauset, Black American Author.* Troy, N.Y.: Whitson, 1981.

As to Books

THE BOOK OF AMERICAN NEGRO POETRY. *Chosen and edited by James Weldon Johnson. Harcourt, Brace, and Co., New York.*

HARLEM SHADOWS. *Claude McKay. Harcourt, Brace & Co., New York.*

BIRTHRIGHT. *T. S. Stribling. The Century Co., New York.*

WHITE AND BLACK. *H. A. Shands. Harcourt, Brace & Co., New York.*

CARTER AND OTHER PEOPLE. *Don Marquis. Appleton and Co., New York.*

NEGRO FOLK RHYMES. *Thomas W. Talley. Macmillan Co., New York.*

THE NEGRO PROBLEM. *Compiled by Julia E. Johnsen. H. W. Wilson Co., New York.*

One of the poets whom James Weldon Johnson quotes in his "Book of American Negro Poetry," himself defines unconsciously the significance of this collection. This poet, Charles Bertram Johnson, after noting in the development of Negro Poets "the greater growing reach of larger latent power", declares:

> We wait our Lyric Séer,
> By whom our wills are caught.

Who makes our cause and wrong
The motif of his song;
Who sings our racial good,
Bestows us honor's place,
The cosmic brotherhood
Of genius—not of race.

Not all of the 32 poets quoted here give evidence of this cosmic quality, but there is a fair showing, notably Mrs. Georgia Douglas Johnson whose power however is checked by the narrowness of her medium of expression, Claude McKay and Anne Spencer. Of Claude McKay I shall speak later, but I wonder why we have not heard more of Anne Spencer. Her art and its expression are true and fine; she blends a delicate mysticism with a diamond clearness of exposition, and her subject matter is original.

This anthology itself has the value of an arrow pointing the direction of Negro genius, but the author's preface has a more immediate worth. It is not only a graceful bit of expository writing befitting a collection of poetry, but it affords a splendid compendium of the Negro's artistic contributions to America. Mr. Johnson feels that the Negro is the author of the only distinctively American artistic products. He lists his gifts as follows: Folk-tales such as we find in the Joel Chandler Harris collection; the Spirituals; the Cakewalk and Ragtime. What is still more important is the possession on the part of the Negro of what Mr. Johnson calls a "transfusive quality", that is the ability to adopt the original spirit of his milieu into something "artistic and original, which yet possesses the note of universal appeal."

The first thought that will flash into the mind of the reader of "Harlem Shadows" will be: *"This is poetry!"* No other later discovery, a slight unevenness of power, a strange rhythm, the fact of the author's ancestry, will be able to affect that first evaluation. Mr. McKay possesses a deep emotionalism, a perception of what is fundamentally important to mankind everywhere—love of kind, love of home, and love of race. He is extraordinarily vivid in depicting these last two. "Flameheart" and "My Mother" fill even the casual reader with a sense of longing for home and the first, fine love for parents. The warmth and sweetness of those days described in the former poem are especially alluring; the mind is caught by the concept of the poinsettia's redness as the eye is fixed by a flash of color. But Mr. McKay's nobler effort has been spent in the poems of which "America" (quoted in this issue's *Looking Glass*) is the finest example. He has dwelt in fiery, impassioned language on the sufferings of his race. Yet there is no touch of propaganda. This is the truest mark of genius.

Max Eastman prefaces these poems with a thoughtful and appreciative foreword.

The publishers of "Birthright" could hardly have realized how correctly they were writing when they spoke of it as an "amazing book". Amazing it is in every sense of the word and in no way more than in its contradictions. The story is that of a colored boy, Peter Siner, who after leaving "Hooker's Bend" for four years of Harvard comes back to his own special "Niggertown" and surrenders to its environment. *That* is his birthright.

The style of the book is really unusual, the author clearly knows how to delineate his characters and how to write an absorbing story. But he does not care how many fallacies he introduces. Here is a boy brave and far-visioned enough to pick himself up out of the ruck and mire and to get away to the very best of intellectual and aesthetic life only to yield on his return to the worst features of it. This hardly seems likely. But while Mr. Stribling fails in depicting his hero, it is probable that he has been successful in limning his subordinate characters. One is struck forcibly by the meanness and shallowness of life in Hooker's Bend and its menacing "Niggertown", its sordid whites and shiftless Negroes. One is hard put to it to decide which race appeals to him least. "Something rotten" indeed has crept into the national idea which permits the existence of conditions like these.

Mr. Shands' "White and Black" leaves one not quite so angry as does "Birthright", but infinitely more depressed. Written in an unusually poor style, this story lacks the speciousness and sophistication of Mr. Stribling's art and for that very reason seems somehow more sincere. These white and black Texans live a life unspeakably revolting, mean, sordid and petty. The one redeeming character, "Mr. Will", even at his best is patronizing in his dealings with Negroes; at his worst he is as autocratic as a man of fewer altruistic pretentions. Over and through every manifestation of life in this town seeps the miasma of immorality, of illicit sexual relations. The whites do not respect the blacks because they are black and nobodies. The blacks do not respect the whites because they are white and are still nobodies. The colored girl Sally, the cleverest person in the book, estimates correctly enough the resistance of the white boy who has just joined church and that of the Negro who is a minister of the gospel, and she acts accordingly. It is not surprising that the author introduces into these surroundings a lynching and a procession of the Ku Klux Klan. Such surroundings breed such phenomena.

From a sociological standpoint these two books may be viewed as a step forward in the relationship of the races. They may be cited too as good examples of the realistic school; especially is this true in "White and Black" and in the portions of "Birthright" devoted to a description of "Niggertown". Finally as a commentary on the uses of American life they are drastic, most unpleasant, but valuable.

Among a number of interesting, well-written but pessimistic stories Don Marquis introduces one called "Carter", presenting an aspect of the Negro problem which I confess I have never seen manifested. "Carter" is a mulatto who can easily be taken for white. He comes North to work and usually poses as a white man. His blood rather than his actual color is his bane however. Not content with being seven-eighths Caucasian, of having the appearance of a Caucasian and therefore of enjoying the advantages of a Caucasian, his life becomes a dreary burden because he is not a Caucasian. So deep is his dislike for his black blood, that not only is he forced to admit his admixture to his white fiancée, but when she shows her indifference to this fact, "the seven-eighths of blood which was white spoke: 'By God! I can't have anything to do with a woman who would marry a nigger!' "

I told this story to a colored school girl. Her reaction to it was hardly what the author, I imagine, would have expected. She said inimitably: "Gee but don't white people just hate themselves!"

In his carefully compiled volume of "Negro Folk Rhymes", Professor Talley gives us a new aspect of Negro life which is by a strange contradiction both disappointing and interesting. It is easy to mark in the collection the finger of the scientific investigator rather than that of the poet; for viewed from the standpoint of beauty these songs fail to satisfy, but from the standpoint of sociology they are both valuable and enlightening. They show the pathetic narrowness and drabness of the slave's outlook, his pitiful desire to get the better even if only in fancy of his environment and of his oppressors, and so he chuckles:

Dem white folks set up in a Dinin' Room
An' dey charve dat mutton an' lam'.
De Nigger, he set 'hind de kitchen door,
An' he eat up de good sweet ham.

Dem white folks, dey set up an' look so fine,
An' dey eats dat old cow meat;
But de Nigger grin an' he don't say much,
Still he know how to git what's sweet.

In seeking compensation for his lot, he dwells on other unsuccessful creatures whose very failure to measure up to norms of beauty marks a kinship of suffering. "There are others" he declares:

Nev' min' if my nose are flat,
An' my face are black an' sooty;
De Jaybird hain't so big in song,
An' de Bullfrog, hain't no beauty.

Certain salient characteristics of the Negro are traceable in these songs, his sense of humor, his dryness, his tendency to make fun of himself and above all his love for the sudden climax which Mr. James Weldon Johnson mentions in the preface to his anthology. This seems to me a perfect example:

She writ me a letter
As long as my eye.
An' she say in dat letter:
"My Honey!—Good-bye!"

Professor Talley seems to have done for the Negro Folk Song what Mr. Johnson has done for poems by Negro authors, and like Mr. Johnson's preface not the least valuable part of Professor Talley's service lies in the "Study of Negro Folk Rhymes" which is appended to his book. Here he distinguishes between Rhyme Dance Songs and Dance Rhymes; he points out that the composition of these songs really served to keep the slave mentally fit, and most important of all he shows that these effusions often formed a sort of cipher language perfectly intelligible to the slaves but meaningless to their masters. Without doubt we are indebted to Professor Talley for an extraordinarily valuable sociological contribution.

In her explanatory note Miss Johnsen writes: "Selections have been chosen from both white and Negro writers, from opposers and sympathizers of the Negro alike, yet with the aim not so much to maintain exact balance as to give expression to views that reflect representative opinions and conditions of race friction, and that serve best to indicate the way for constructive effort."

This program has been successfully carried out, with the result that the book shows no bias and so should form a valuable compendium for the student or debater. Although very nearly every aspect of Negro life with relation to America has been touched upon, latter-day conditions which make the present Negro problem are considerably more emphasized than such remote subjects as slavery or abolition. This seems a wise and sensible procedure. What the true student of the problem will most treasure is the long and thorough bibliography with which Miss Johnsen prefaces her selections. This is a gold mine in itself.

Crisis, June 1922:66–68.

Reviews of Countee Cullen and Langston Hughes

COLOR. A BOOK OF VERSE. *By Countee Cullen. Harper & Brothers, New York. 1925. 108 pages.*

Color is the name of Mr. Cullen's book and color is rightly, in every sense its prevailing characteristic. For not only does every bright glancing line abound in color but it is also in another sense the yard-stick by which all the work in this volume is to be measured. Thus his poems fall into three categories: Those, and these are very few, in which no mention is made of color; those in which the adjectives "black" or "brown" or "ebony" are deliberately introduced to show that the type which the author had in mind was not white; and thirdly the poems which arise out of the consciousness of being a "Negro in a day like this" in America.

These last are not only the most beautifully done but they are by far the most significant group in the book. I refer especially to poems of the type of "Yet do I Marvel", "The Shroud of Color", "Heritage" and "Pagan Prayer". It is in such work as this that the peculiar and valuable contribution of the American colored man is to be made to American literature. For any genuine poet black or white might have written "Oh for a Little While be Kind" or the lines to "John Keats"; the idea contained in a "Song of Praise" was used long ago by an old English poet and has since been set to music by Roger Quilter. But to pour forth poignantly and sincerely the feelings which make plain to the world the innerness of the life which black men live calls for special understanding. Cullen has packed into four illuminating lines the psychology of colored Americans, that strange extra dimension which totally artificial conditions have forced into a sharp reality. He writes:

All day long and all night through,
One thing only must I do:
Quench my pride and cool my blood,
Lest I perish in the flood.

That is the new expression of a struggle now centuries old. Here I am convinced is Mr. Cullen's forte; he has the feeling and the gift to express coloredness in a world of whiteness. I hope he will not be deflected from continuing to that of which he has made such a brave and beautiful beginning. I hope that no one crying down "special treatment" will turn him from his native and valuable genre. There *is* no "universal treatment"; it is all specialized. When Kipling spoke of having the artist to

"paint the thing as he sees it
For the God of things as they are",

he set the one infallible rule by which all workmanship should be conceived, achieved and judged. In a time when it is the vogue to make much of the Negro's aptitude for clownishness or to depict him objectively as a serio-comic figure, it is a fine and praiseworthy act for Mr. Cullen to show through the interpretation of his own subjectivity the inner workings of the Negro soul and mind.

THE WEARY BLUES. *A Book of Verse. By Langston Hughes. Alfred A. Knopf. New York. 1926. 109 pages.*

Very perfect is the memory of my first literary acquaintance with Langston Hughes. In the unforgettable days when we were publishing *The Brownies' Book* we had already appreciated a charming fragile conceit which read:

Out of the dust of dreams,
Fairies weave their garments;
Out of the purple and rose of old memories,
They make purple wings.
No wonder we find them such marvelous things.

Then one day came "The Negro Speaks of Rivers". I took the beautiful dignified creation to Dr. Du Bois and said: "What colored person is there, do you suppose, in the United States who writes like that and yet is unknown to us?" And I wrote and found him to be a Cleveland high school graduate who had just gone to live in Mexico. Already he had begun to assume that remote, so elusive quality which permeaates most of his work. Before long we had the pleasure of seeing the work of the boy, whom we had sponsored, copied and recopied in journals far and wide. "The Negro Speaks of Rivers" even appeared in translation in a paper printed in Germany.

Not very long after Hughes came to New York and not long after that he began to travel and to set down the impressions, the pictures, which his sensitive mind had registered of new forms of life and living in Holland, in France, in Spain, in Italy and in Africa.

His poems are warm, exotic and shot through with color. Never is he preoccupied with form. But this fault, if it is one, has its corresponding virtue, for it gives his verse, which almost always is imbued with the essence of poetry, the perfection of spontaneity. And one characteristic which makes for this bubbling-like charm is the remarkable objectivity which he occasionally achieves, remarkable for one so young, and a first step toward philosophy. Hughes has seen a great deal of the world, and this has taught him that nothing matters much but life. Its forms and aspects may vary, but living is the essential thing. Therefore make no bones about it,—"make the most of what you too may spend".

Some consciousness of this must have been in him even before he began to wander for he sent us as far back as 1921:

"Shake your brown feet, honey,
Shake your brown feet, chile,
Shake your brown feet, honey,
Shake 'em swift and wil'— . . .
Sun's going down this evening—
Might never rise no mo'.
The sun's going down this very night—
Might never rise no mo'—
So dance with swift feet, honey,
(The banjo's sobbing low) . . .
The sun's going down this very night
Might never rise no mo'."

Now this is very significant, combining as it does the doctrine of the old Biblical exhortation, "eat, drink and be merry for tomorrow ye die", Horace's "Carpe diem", the German "Freut euch des Lebens" and Herrick's "Gather ye rosebuds while ye may". This is indeed a universal subject served Negro-style and though I am no great lover of any dialect I hope heartily that Mr. Hughes will give us many more such combinations.

Mr. Hughes is not always the calm philosopher; he has feeling a-plenty and is not ashamed to show it. He "loved his friend" who left him and so taken up is he with the sorrow of it all that he has no room for anger or resentment. While I do not think of him as a protagonist of color,—he is too much the citizen of the world for that—, I doubt if any one will ever write more tenderly, more understandingly, more humorously of the life of Harlem shot through as it is with mirth, abandon and pain. Hughes comprehends this life, has studied it and loved it. In one poem he has epitomized its essence:

Does a jazz-band ever sob?
They say a jazz-band's gay.
Yet as the vulgar dancers whirled
And the wan night wore away,
One said she heard the jazz-band sob
When the little dawn was grey.

Harlem is undoubtedly one of his great loves; the sea is another. Indeed all life is his love and his work a brilliant, sensitive interpretation of its numerous facets.—

Crisis, March 1926: 238–239.

Foreword to *The Chinaberry Tree*

Nothing,—and the Muses themselves would bear witness to this,—has ever been farther from my thought than writing to establish a thesis. Colored people have been the subjects which I have chosen for my novels partly because they are the ones I know best, partly because of all the other separate groups which constitute the American cosmogony none of them, to me, seems so naturally endowed with the stuff of which chronicles may be made. To be a Negro in America posits a dramatic situation. The elements of the play fall together involuntarily; they are just waiting for Fate the Producer to quicken them into movement,—for Chance the Prompter to interpret them with fidelity.

The mere juxtaposition of the races brings into existence this fateful quality. But of course there are breathing-spells, in-between spaces where colored men and women work and love and go their ways with no thought of the "problem." What are they like then? . . . So few of the other Americans know.

In the story of Aunt Sal, Laurentine, Melissa and the Chinaberry Tree I have depicted something of the homelife of the colored American who is not being pressed too hard by the Furies of Prejudice, Ignorance and Economic Injustice. And behold he is not so very different from any other American, just distinctive. He is not rich but he moves in a society which has its spheres and alignments as definitely as any other society the world over. He is simple as befits one whose not too remote ancestors were connected with the soil, yet his sons and daughters respond as completely as do the sons and daughters of European settlers to modern American sophistication. He has seen, he has been the victim of many phases of immorality but he has his own ideas about certain "Thou shalt nots." And acts on them.

Finally he started out as a slave but he rarely thinks of that. To himself he is a citizen of the United States whose ancestors came over not along with the emigrants in the Mayflower, it is true, but merely a little earlier in the good year, 1619. His forebears are to him quite simply the early settlers who played a pretty large part in making the land grow. He boasts no Association of the Sons and Daughters of the Revolution, but he knows that as a matter of fact and quite inevitably his sons and daughters date their ancestry back as far as any. So quite as naturally as his white compatriots he speaks of his "old" Boston families, "old Philadelphians," "old Charlestonians." And he has a wholesome respect for family and education and labor and the fruits of labor. He is still sufficiently conservative to lay a slightly greater stress on the first two of these four.

Briefly he is a dark American who wears his joy and rue very much as does the white American. He may wear it with some differences but it is the same joy and the same rue.

So in spite of other intentions I seem to have pointed a moral.

The Chinaberry Tree. New York: Frederick Stokes, 1931. ix–x.

From *Plum Bun*

CHAPTER I

Fifth Avenue is a canyon; its towering buildings dwarf the importance of the people hurrying through its narrow confines. But Fourteenth Street is a river, impersonally flowing, broad-bosomed, with strange and devious craft covering its expanse. To Angela the famous avenue seemed but one manifestation of living, but Fourteenth Street was the rendezvous of life itself. Here for those first few weeks after her arrival in New York she wandered, almost prowled, intent upon the jostling shops, the hurrying, pushing people, above all intent upon the faces of those people with their showings of grief, pride, gaiety, greed, joy, ambition, content. There was little enough of this last. These men and women were living at a sharper pitch of intensity than those she had observed in Philadelphia. The few coloured people whom she saw were different too; they possessed an independence of carriage, a purposefulness, an assurance in their manner that pleased her. But she could not see that any of these people, black or white, were any happier than those whom she had observed all her life.

But *she* was happier; she was living on the crest of a wave of excitement and satisfaction which would never wane, never break, never be spent. She was seeing the world, she was getting acquainted with life in her own way without restrictions or restraint; she was young, she was temporarily independent, she was intelligent, she was white. She remembered an expression "free, white and twenty-one,"—this was what it meant then, this sense of owning the world, this realization that other things being equal, all things were possible. "If I were a man," she said," I could be president," and laughed at herself for the "if" itself proclaimed a limitation. But that inconsistency bothered her little; she did not want to be a man. Power, greatness, authority, these were fitting and proper for men; but there were sweeter, more beautiful gifts for women, and power of a certain kind too. Such a power she would like to exert in this glittering new world, so full of mysteries and promise. If she could afford it she would have a salon, a drawing-room where men and women, not necessarily great, but real, alive, free and untrammelled in manner and thought, should come and pour themselves out to her sympathy and magnetism. To accomplish this she must have money and influence; indeed since she was so young she would need even protection; perhaps it would be better to marry . . . a white man. The thought came to her suddenly out of the void; she had never thought of this possibility before. If she were to do this, do it suitably, then all that richness, all that fullness of life which she so ardently craved would be doubly hers. She knew that men had a better time of it than women, coloured men than coloured women, white men than white women. Not that she envied them. Only it would be fun, great fun to capture power and protection in addition to the freedom and independence which she had so long coveted and which now lay in her hand.

But, she smiled to herself, she had no way of approaching these ends. She knew no one in New York; she could conceive of no manner in which she was likely to form desirable acquaintances; at present her home consisted of the four walls of the smallest room in Union Square Hotel. She had gone there the second day after her arrival, having spent an expensive twenty-four hours at the Astor. Later she came to realize that there were infinitely cheaper habitations to be had, but she could not tear herself away from Fourteenth Street. It was Spring, and the Square was full of rusty specimens of mankind who sat on the benches, as did Angela herself, for hours at a stretch, as though they thought the invigorating air and the mellow sun would work some magical burgeoning on their garments such as was worked on the trees. But though these latter changed, the garments changed not nor did their owners. They remained the same, drooping, discouraged down and outers. "I am seeing life," thought Angela, "this is the way people live," and never realized that some of these people looking curiously, speculatively at her wondered what had been her portion to bring her thus early to this unsavoury company.

"A great picture!" she thought. "I'll make a great picture of these people some day and call them 'Fourteenth Street types'." And suddenly a vast sadness invaded her; she wondered if there were people more alive, more sentient to the joy, the adventure of living, even than she, to whom she would also be a "type."

But she could not believe this. She was at once almost irreconcilably too concentrated and too objective. Her living during these days was so intense, so almost solidified, as though her desire to live as she did and she herself were so one and the same thing that it would have been practically impossible for another onlooker like herself to insert the point of his discrimination into her firm panoply of satisfaction. So she continued to browse along her chosen thoroughfare, stopping most often in the Square or before a piano store on the same street. There was in this shop a player-piano which was usually in action, and as the front glass had been removed the increased clearness of the strains brought a steady, patient, apparently insatiable group of listeners to a standstill. They were mostly men, and as they were far less given, Angela observed, to concealing their feelings than women, it was easy to follow their emotional gamut. Jazz made them smile but with a certain wistfulness—if only they had time for dancing now, just now when the mood was on them! The young woman looking at the gathering of shabby pedestrians, worn business men and ruminative errand boys felt for them a pity not untinged with satisfaction. *She* had taken what she wanted while the mood was on her. Love songs, particularly those of the sorrowful ballad variety brought to these unmindful faces a strained regret. But there was one expression which Angela could only half interpret. It drifted on to those listening countenances usually at the playing of old Irish and Scottish tunes. She noticed then an acuter attitude of attention, the eyes took on a look of inwardness of utter remoteness. A passer-by engrossed in thought caught a strain and at once his gait and expression fell under the spell. The listeners might be as varied as fifteen people may be, yet for the moment they would be caught in a common, almost comic nostalgia. If the next piece were jazz that particular crowd would disperse, its members going on their meditative ways, blessed or cursed with heaven knew what memories which must not to be disturbed by the strident jangling of the latest popular song.

"Homesick," Angela used to say to herself. And she would feel so, too, though she hardly knew for what,—certainly not for Philadelphia and that other life which now seemed so removed as to have been impossible. And she made notes in her sketch book to enable her some day to make a great picture of these "types" too.

Plum Bun. New York: Frederick A. Stokes, 1929. 87–91.

7
Zora Neale Hurston (1891–1960)

Introduced and Edited by Cheryl A. Wall

After years of critical neglect, the work of Zora Neale Hurston was rediscovered in the 1970s. The black consciousness and feminist movements first spurred the revival and reassessment of Hurston's writing. All but one of her seven books were republished; two of them, the volume of folklore *Mules and Men* and the novel *Their Eyes Were Watching God,* were quickly recognized as classics in the Afro-American canon. Hurston's reputation continued to grow. When Alice Walker went "in search of our mothers' gardens," she unearthed in Hurston's art a precious and empowering legacy. For Walker's generation, Hurston has become a paradigm for the black woman writer. The fascinating but fragmented story of Hurston's life, reconstructed in biographies by Hemenway and Howard, is one facet of the paradigm. The narrative and rhetorical strategies that Hurston invented, revised, and extended are others. Indeed, as Gilbert and Gubar propose, Hurston's quest for a "maiden language" is emblematic for women writers across the twentieth century.

Born in the all-black town of Eatonville, Florida, Zora Neale Hurston grew up immersed in the vernacular traditions of the black rural South. Unlike the other literary women of the Harlem Renaissance, she rooted her art in these traditions. But, as her autobiography, *Dust Tracks on a Road* (1942), attests, she was an eager student of Western literary traditions as well. After the death of her mother and the breakup of her family, Hurston scuffled to educate herself at Morgan Academy in Baltimore and Howard University in Washington. She moved to New York in 1925 because she began to "feel the urge to write" (*Dust Tracks* 168). She joined a band of young Harlem Renaissance writers including Gwendolyn Bennett, Langston Hughes, and Wallace Thurman whose best known collaborative project was a journal of experimental writing, *Fire* (1926).

In 1927 Hurston entered Barnard College, where she studied anthropology under Franz Boas and alongside Ruth Benedict and Margaret Mead. This training initiated an extended effort to reclaim and preserve her cultural heritage. For the next several years she traveled across the South tracking down storytellers, recording blues singers, and apprenticing herself to hoodoo doctors. Hurston presents a version of her experience in *Mules and Men* (1935). This narrative becomes a paradigm for the representation of the "journey back" in recent writing by black women, including Toni Cade Bambara, Paule Marshall, Toni Morrison, and Gloria Naylor.

Like *Tell My Horse* (1938), the narrative of Hurston's Caribbean research, *Mules and Men* does not analyze the folklore it presents. More analytical essays, such as "Characteristics of Negro Expression," published in Nancy Cunard's *Negro* (1934) and printed below, reflect the lessons Hurston gleaned from years of anthropological fieldwork. Here she attempted to identify the aesthetic principles undergirding Afro-American language, music, dance, and other expressive forms. Hurston's notes on language are particularly compelling. Like Langston Hughes and Sterling Brown, Hurston had no patience with theories of linguistic deficiency among blacks. She offered theories of her own, which literary critics, notably Awkward, Gates, and Holloway, have in turn used as touchstones for their interpretations of Hurston's fiction.

In observations clearly drawn from her field notes, Hurston outlined several significant linguistic characteristics. Among them were the heightened sense of drama evidenced in the profusion of metaphor and simile and in the use of double descriptives and verbal nouns. These ideas were radically innovative for the time. Hurston's effort to develop criteria to describe this language in its own terms anticipates recent studies of Black English.

Hurston drew a stunning conclusion from her observations. The "will to adorn," she averred, bespoke a feeling among blacks "that there can never be enough of beauty, let alone too much." Beauty and creativity were cardinal values in Afro-American life. The evidence she cited to support this heretical premise demonstrated her own fine sensibility. A telling example is the comment on "gaudy calendars" and Sunday supplement advertisements with which poor blacks sometimes decorated their homes. Rather than dismissing them as "grotesqueries," Hurston defined them as expressions of the "will to adorn," a definition Alice Walker would warmly embrace. Hurston herself attempted to understand the habit even of "decorating a decoration" and linked it to the embellishment in Afro-American prayers and sermons.

The quest for the racial heritage was a major impulse among Harlem

Renaissance intellectuals. No evidence for the aesthetic value of Afro-American culture was more crucial than "Negro spirituals." The spirituals were rediscovered during the 1920s, and they enjoyed newfound respectability on the concert stage, not only in recitals by college choirs—a tradition inaugurated by the Fisk Jubilee Singers in 1867—but also by solo artists, such as Roland Hayes, Paul Robeson, and Marian Anderson. Two generations removed from slavery, Afro-Americans were struggling to come to terms with their past. Reembracing the spirituals was a step toward reconciliation, which intellectuals had long encouraged. "Of the Sorrow Songs" was a central chapter in W. E. B. Du Bois's *The Souls of Black Folk* (1903). James Weldon Johnson in *The Book of American Negro Poetry* (1922), *The Book of American Negro Spirituals* (1925), and his popular poem "O Black and Unknown Bards," along with Alain Locke in *The New Negro* (1925), also testified eloquently to the centrality of the spirituals to the black cultural legacy.

For Hurston, spirituals were not dead artifacts of the past but living elements in contemporary culture (see "Spirituals and Neo-Spirituals," below). The beautiful art songs valorized by her male counterparts were fine in their place, but they were neospirituals, not the real thing. Authentic spirituals were "being made and forgotten every day." In other words, Hurston perceived spirituals as "process" rather than "product." Improvisation, antiphony, "jagged" harmony, insistent rhythm, and audience participation were elements in the process. Hurston emphasized as well the self-conscious artistry of "folk" creators—their awareness of form and mastery of technique.

Apart from singers, these creators were disproportionately men. In her fieldwork, Hurston had confirmed what she must already have known: women were relegated to a subordinate position within Afro-American culture. While celebrating this culture, Hurston had also to criticize it. Her strategies were varied. Interwoven among the seventy folktales documented in *Mules and Men* are numerous conversations about gender politics. Moreover, the volume's subtext is a narrative of female empowerment. Big Sweet is the primary change agent. In *Dust Tracks* as in *Mules and Men,* this character embodies the challenge to sexism. One notes in the excerpt below that Big Sweet's power is first conveyed through her voice; Hurston hears her before she sees her. Big Sweet's "specifying" makes her a prototype for Hurston's fictional protagonists. More profoundly, as both Gates and Willis argue, the mode of figuration Big Sweet employs (which Gates subsumes under the rubric "signifying") becomes one basis for Hurston's own self-consciously invented literary language.

Hurston's novels were all published after the heyday of the Harlem Renaissance. The first, *Jonah's Gourd Vine* (1934), drawn vaguely from the lives of her parents, recounts the story of Lucy and John Pearson's courtship and marriage, John's swift rise to prominence as a Baptist preacher, his equally swift fall resulting from his marital infidelities, Lucy's strength and perseverance, and the family's ultimate dissolution. As Hemenway suggests, the novel is best perceived as "a series of linguistic moments" (192). Lucy's speech is richly aphoristic, but the more dramatic and telling moments belong to John. Hurston's original dedication to *Jonah* explains one reason why. It referred to black preachers as "the first and only real Negro poets in America" (Hemenway 195). They were also almost all men.

In Hurston's finest novel, *Their Eyes Were Watching God,* the protagonist, Janie Crawford, is a woman who is seeking a language in which to tell her own story. Her first teacher, her grandmother Nanny, has wanted to "preach a great sermon about colored women sittin' on high, but they wasn't no pulpit for me" (32). She has saved the text for Janie. Eventually Janie recognizes the need to create her own text; she rejects Nanny's hierarchical vision. Looking low rather than high, she chooses the jook over the pulpit and finds fulfillment on the muck rather than in the big house Nanny has envisioned. When Janie speaks, hers is a blues-inflected voice.

Most contemporary critics read *Their Eyes* as a novel of self-discovery wherein Janie claims a self by claiming a voice. Stepto and Washington challenge this interpretation, and Washington argues that *Their Eyes* is instead "a novel that represents women's exclusion from power, particularly from the power of oral speech" (237). Janie's celebrated signifying notwithstanding, "there are critical places in *Their Eyes* where Janie's voice needs to be heard and is not, places where we would expect her as the subject of the story to speak" (243). "Characteristics" helps explain Janie's silences. Big Sweet exemplifies the process through which Janie gains the power to "change the words" she does (Wall 375–377, 392). The "lyrical and disembodied yet individual" narrative voice of *Their Eyes,* which Gates terms Hurston's "legacy to Afro-American fiction," mediates between Janie's silences and the eloquence of black vernacular discourse (Gates 183). This voice becomes Hurston's supplest instrument of celebration and critique.

The initial critical response to Hurston's writing was mixed. White reviewers frequently patronized the work, praising its "racial gayety" and "refreshingly pagan undercurrent" (Thompson, Brickell). Black male writers frequently found fault with an alleged lack of racial militancy.

Reviewing *Their Eyes Were Watching God* for *New Masses,* Richard Wright claimed that it was written in the minstrel tradition; the characters caught in that "safe and narrow orbit . . . between laughter and tears." Wright conceded that Hurston's "dialogue manages to catch the psychological movements of the Negro folk-mind in their pure simplicity, but that's as far as it goes." This stance reflects Wright's literary politics; his own fiction was propelled by anger at the dehumanizing oppression of blacks in the South. Hurston's fiction, by contrast, celebrates the creativity and complexity of Afro-Americans that signal the survival of the human spirit despite oppression. A novice when he penned the review, Wright expressed authorial anxiety in patently sexist terms. Comparing Hurston to Walter Turpin, whose novel *These Low Grounds* was also under review, he concluded: "Turpin's faults as a writer are those of an honest man trying desperately to say something; but

Zora Neale Hurston lacks even that excuse" (25). In "Stories of Conflict," her review of Wright's *Uncle Tom's Children* (reprinted below), Hurston offered a measured response.

After the publication of *Native Son* (1940) and *Black Boy* (1945), Wright's career remained ascendant for a generation. Hurston's books went out of print. Readers attuned to Wright's naturalistic fiction were put off by the broad farce of *Moses: Man of the Mountain* (1939) and the turgid pathos of *Seraph on the Suwanee* (1948). In 1950 Hurston received widespread if unwelcome notice when the woman for whom she worked as a maid discovered Hurston's by-line in the *Saturday Evening Post.* Hurston continued to write, mainly nonfiction, but much of what she wrote was unpublishable. Penniless and forgotten, Zora Neale Hurston died in 1960.

A decade later, Alice Walker found in *Mules and Men* the material she needed to write a short story. As she later recalled, "I became aware of my need of Zora Neale Hurston's work some time before I knew her work existed" (*In Search* 83). Hers is a personal and collective testimony. Walker and a generation of writers and critics went "looking for Zora," and they continue to build on the enduring foundation she laid.

WORKS CITED

Awkward, Michael. *Inspiring Influences: Tradition, Revision, and Afro-American Women's Novels.* New York: Columbia UP, 1989.

Brickell, Herschel. Review of *Their Eyes Were Watching God. New York Post* 14 Sept. 1937.

Gates, Henry Louis. *The Signifying Monkey: A Theory of Afro-American Literary Criticism.* New York: Oxford UP, 1988.

Gilbert, Sandra M., and Susan Gubar. *No Man's Land.* Vol. 1. New Haven: Yale UP, 1988.

Hemenway, Robert. *Zora Neale Hurston: A Literary Biography.* Urbana: U of Illinois P, 1978.

Holloway, Karla. *The Character of the Word.* Westport, Conn.: Greenwood P, 1987.

Howard, Lillie P. *Zora Neale Hurston.* Boston: Twayne, 1980.

Hurston, Zora Neale. *Dust Tracks on a Road.* 1942. Urbana: U of Illinois P, 1984.

———. *Jonah's Gourd Vine.* Philadelphia: Lippincott, 1934.

———. *Moses: Man of the Mountain.* 1939. Urbana: U of Illinois P, 1984.

———. *Mules and Men.* 1935. Bloomington: Indiana UP, 1978.

———. *The Sanctified Church.* Berkeley: Turtle Island, 1981.

———. *Seraph on the Suwanee.* New York: Scribner, 1948.

———. *Spunk: The Selected Short Stories of Zora Neale Hurston.* Berkeley: Turtle Island, 1985.

———. *Tell My Horse.* 1938. Berkeley: Turtle Island, 1981.

———. *Their Eyes Were Watching God.* 1937. Urbana: U of Illinois P, 1978.

Stepto, Robert. *From behind the Veil: A Study of Afro-American Narrative.* Urbana: U of Illinois P, 1979.

Thompson, Ralph. Review of *Their Eyes Were Watching God. New York Times* 6 Oct. 1937.

Walker, Alice. *In Search of Our Mothers' Gardens.* New York: Harcourt, 1983.

———, ed. *I Love Myself: A Zora Neale Hurston Reader.* New York: Feminist Press, 1979.

Wall, Cheryl A. "Zora Neale Hurston: Changing Her Own Words." In *American Novelists*

Revisited: Essays in Feminist Criticism, ed. Fritz Fleischmann, 371–393. Boston: G. K. Hall, 1982.
Washington, Mary Helen. *Invented Lives: Narratives of Black Women 1860–1960*. New York: Doubleday, 1987.
Willis, Susan. *Specifying: Black Women Writing the American Experience*. Madison: U of Wisconsin P, 1987.
Wright, Richard. "Between Laughter and Tears," *New Masses* 5 Oct. 1937:22, 25.

Characteristics of Negro Expression

DRAMA

The Negro's universal mimicry is not so much a thing in itself as as evidence of something that permeates his entire self. And that thing is drama.

His very words are action words. His interpretation of the English language is in terms of pictures. One act described in terms of another. Hence the rich metaphor and simile.

The metaphor is of course very primitive. It is easier to illustrate than it is to explain because action came before speech. Let us make a parallel. Language is like money. In primitive communities actual goods, however bulky, are bartered for what one wants. This finally evolves into coin, the coin being not real wealth but a symbol of wealth. Still later, even coin is abandoned for legal tender, and still later cheques for certain usages.

Every phase of Negro life is highly dramatized. No matter how joyful or how sad the case there is sufficient poise for drama. Everything is acted out. Unconsciously for the most part of course. There is an impromptu ceremony always ready for every hour of life. No little moment passes unadorned.

Now the people with highly developed languages have words for detached ideas. That is legal tender. "That-which-we-squat-on" has become "chair." "Groan-causer" has evolved into "spear" and so on. Some individuals even conceive of the equivalent of cheque words, like "ideation" and "pleonastic." Perhaps we might say that *Paradise Lost* and *Sartor Resartus* are written in cheque words.

The primitive man exchanges descriptive words. His terms are all close fitting. Frequently the Negro, even with detached words in his vocabulary—not evolved in him but transplanted on his tongue by contact—must add action to it to make it do. So we have "chop-axe," "sitting-chair," and "cook-pot" and the like because the speaker has in his mind the picture of the object in use. Action. Everything illustrated. So we can say the white man thinks in a written language and the Negro thinks in hieroglyphics.

A bit of Negro drama familiar to all is the frequent meeting of two opponents who threaten to do atrocious murder one upon the other.

Who has not observed a robust young Negro chap posing upon a street corner, possessed of nothing but his clothing, his strength, and his youth? Does he bear himself like a pauper? No, Louis XIV could be no more insolent in his assurance. His eyes say plainly "Female, halt!" His posture exults "Ah, female, I am the eternal male, the giver of life. Behold in my hot flesh all the delights of this world. Salute me, I am strength." All this with a languid posture, there is no mistaking his meaning.

A Negro girl strolls past the corner lounger. Her whole body panging* and posing. A slight shoulder movement that calls attention to her bust, that is all of a dare. A hippy undulation below the waist that is a sheaf of promises tied with conscious power. She is acting out "I'm a darned sweet woman and you know it."

These little plays by strolling players are acted out daily in a dozen streets in a thousand cities, and no one ever mistakes the meaning.

WILL TO ADORN

The will to adorn is the second most notable characteristic in Negro expression. Perhaps his idea of ornament does not attempt to meet conventional standards, but it satisfies the soul of its creator.

In this respect the American Negro has done wonders to the English language. This is true, but it is equally true that he has made over a great part of the tongue to his liking and has his revision accepted by the ruling class. No one listening to a Southern white man talk could deny this. Not only has he softened and toned down strongly consonanted words like "aren't" to "ain't" and the like, he has made new force words out of old feeble elements. Examples of this are "ham-shanked," "battle-hammed," "double-teen," "bodaciously," "muffle-jawed."

But the Negro's greatest contribution to the language is: (1) the use of metaphor and simile, (2) the use of the double descriptive, (3) the use of verbal nouns.

1. Metaphor and Simile

One at a time, like laywers going to heaven.
You sho is propaganda.
Sobbing hearted.
I'll beat you till: (a) rope like okra, (b) slack like lime, (c) smell like onions.
Fatal for naked.
Kyting along.

*From "pang."

That's a rope.
Cloakers—deceivers.
Regular as pig-tracks.
Mule blood—black molasses.
Syndicating—gossiping.
Flambeaux—cheap cafe (lighted by flambeaux).
To put yo'self on de ladder.

2. The Double Descriptive

High-tall.
Little-tee-nichy (tiny).
Low-down.
Top-superior.
Sham-polish.
Lady-people.
Kill-dead.
Hot-boiling.
Chop-axe.
Sitting-chairs.
De watch wall.
Speedy-hurry.
More great and more better.

3. Verbal Nouns

She features somebody I know.
Funeralize.
Sense me into it.
Puts the shamery on him.
'Taint everybody you kin confidence.
I wouldn't friend with her.
Jooking—playing piano or guitar as it is done in Jook-houses (houses of ill-fame).
Uglying away.
I wouldn't scorn my name all up on you.
Bookooing (beaucoup) around—showing off.

Nouns from Verbs

Won't stand a broke.
She won't take a listen.
He won't stand straightening.

That is such a compliment.
That's a lynch.

The stark, trimmed phrases of the Occident seem too bare for the voluptuous child of the sun, hence the adornment. It arises out of the same impulse as the wearing of jewelry and the making of sculpture—the urge to adorn.

On the walls of the home of the average Negro one always finds a glut of gaudy calendars, wall pockets and advertising lithographs. The sophisticated white man or Negro would tolerate none of these, even if they bore a likeness to the Mona Lisa. No commercial art for decoration. Neither the calendar nor the advertisement spoils the picture for this lowly man. He sees the beauty in spite of the declaration of the Portland Cement Works or the butcher's announcement. I saw in Mobile a room in which there was an over-stuffed mohair living-room suite, an imitation mahogany bed and chifferobe, a console victrola. The walls were gaily papered with Sunday supplements of the *Mobile Register.* There were seven calendars and three wall pockets. One of them was decorated with a lace doily. The mantel-shelf was covered with a scarf of deep home-made lace, looped up with a huge bow of pink crepe paper. Over the door was a huge lithograph showing the Treaty of Versailles being signed with a Waterman fountain pen.

It was grotesque, yes. But it indicated a desire for beauty. And decorating a decoration, as in the case of the doily on the gaudy wall pocket, did not seem out of place to the hostess. The feeling back of such an act is that there can never be enough of beauty, let alone too much. Perhaps she is right. We each have our standards of art, and thus we are all interested parties and so unfit to pass judgment upon the art concepts of others.

Whatever the Negro does of his own volition he embellishes. His religious service is for the greater part excellent prose poetry. Both prayers and sermons are tooled and polished until they are true works of art. The supplication is forgotten in the frenzy of creation. The prayer of the white man is considered humorous in its bleakness. The beauty of the Old Testament does not exceed that of a Negro prayer.

ANGULARITY

After adornment the next most striking manifestation of the Negro is Angularity. Everything that he touches becomes angular. In all African sculpture and doctrine of any sort we find the same thing.

Anyone watching Negro dancers will be struck by the same phenomenon. Every posture is another angle. Pleasing, yes. But an effect achieved by the very means which a European strives to avoid.

The pictures on the walls are hung at deep angles. Furniture is always set at an angle. I have instances of a piece of furniture in the *middle* of a wall being set with one end nearer the wall than the other to avoid the simple straight line.

ASYMMETRY

Asymmetry is a definite feature of Negro art. I have no samples of true Negro painting unless we count the African shields, but the sculpture and carvings are full of this beauty and lack of symmetry. It is present in the literature, both prose and verse. I offer an example of this quality in verse from Langston Hughes:

I ain't gonna mistreat ma good gal any more,
I'm just gonna kill her next time she makes me sore.

I treats her kind but she don't do me right,
She fights and quarrels most every night.

I can't have no woman's got such low-down ways
Cause de blue gum woman aint de style now'days.

I brought her from the South and she's goin on back,
Else I'll use her head for a carpet tack.

It is the lack of symmetry which makes Negro dancing so difficult for white dancers to learn. The abrupt and unexpected changes. The frequent changes of key and time are evidences of this quality in music (Note the St. Louis Blues).

The dancing of the justly famous Bo-Jangles and Snake Hips are excellent examples.

The presence of rhythm and lack of symmetry are paradoxical, but there they are. Both are present to a marked degree. There is always rhythm, but it is the rhythm of segments. Each unit has a rhythm of its own, but when the whole is assembled it is lacking in symmetry. But easily workable to a Negro who is accustomed to the break in going from one part to another, so that he adjusts himself to the new tempo.

DANCING

Negro dancing is dynamic suggestion. No matter how violent it may appear to the beholder, every posture gives the impression that the dancer will do much more. For example, the performer flexes one knee sharply, assumes a ferocious face mask, thrusts the upper part of the body forward with clenched fists, elbows taut as in hard running or grasping a thrusting blade. That is all. But the spectator himself adds the picture of ferocious assault, hears the drums and finds himself keeping time with the music and tensing himself for the struggle. It is compelling insinuation. That is the very reason the spectator is held so rapt. He is participating in the performance himself—carrying out the suggestions of the performer.

The difference in the two arts is: the white dancer attempts to express fully; the Negro is restrained, but succeeds in gripping the beholder by forcing him to finish the action the performer suggests. Since no art can ever express all the variations conceivable, the Negro must be considered the greater artist, his dancing is realistic suggestion, and that is about all a great artist can do.

NEGRO FOLKLORE

Negro folklore is not a thing of the past. It is still in the making. Its great variety shows the adaptability of the black man: nothing is too old or too new, domestic or foreign, high or low, for his use. God and the Devil are paired, and are treated no more reverently than Rockefeller and Ford. Both of these men are prominent in folklore. Ford being particularly strong, and they talk and act like good-natured stevedores or mill-hands. Ole Massa is sometimes a smart man and often a fool. The automobile is ranged alongside of the oxcart. The angels and the apostles walk and talk like section hands. And through it all walks Jack, the greatest culture hero of the South; Jack beats them all—even the Devil, who is often smarter than God.

Culture Heroes

The Devil is next after Jack as a culture hero. He can outsmart everyone but Jack. God is absolutely no match for him. He is good-natured and full of humour. The sort of person one may count on to help out in any difficulty.

Peter the Apostle is third in importance. One need not look far for the explanation. The Negro is not a Christian really. The primitive gods are not deities of too subtle inner reflection; they are hard-working bodies who serve their devotees just as laboriously as the suppliant serves them. Gods of physical violence, stopping at nothing to serve their followers. Now of all the apostles, Peter is the most active. When the other ten fell back trembling in the garden, Peter wielded the blade on the posse. Peter first and foremost in all action. The gods of no peoples have been philosophic until the people themselves have approached that state.

The rabbit, the bear, the lion, the buzzard, the fox are culture heroes from the animal world. The rabbit is far in the leader of all the others and is blood brother to Jack. In short, the trickster-hero of West Africa has been transplanted to America.

John Henry is a culture hero in song, but no more so than Stacker Lee, Smokey Joe or Bad Lazarus. There are many, many Negroes who have never heard of any of the song heroes, but none who do not know John (Jack) and the rabbit.

Examples of Folklore and the Modern Culture Hero

Why de Porpoise's Tail is on Crosswise

Now, I want to tell you 'bout de porpoise. God had done made de world and everything. He set de moon and de stars in de sky. He got de fishes of de sea, and de fowls of de air completed. He made de sun and hung it up. Then He made a nice gold track for it to run on. Then He said, "Now, Sun, I got everything made but Time. That's up to you. I want you to start out and go 'round de world on dis track just as fast as you kin make it. And de time it takes you to go and come, I'm going to call day and night." De Sun went zoomin' on cross de elements. Now, de porpoise was hanging round there and heard God what he told de Sun, so he decided he'd take dat trip round de world hisself. He looked up and saw de Sun kytin' along, so he lit out too, him and dat Sun!

So de porpoise beat de Sun round de world by one hour and three minutes. So God said, "Aw naw, this aint gointer do! I didn't mean for nothin' to be faster than de Sun!" So God run dat porpoise for three days before he runs him down and caught him, and took his tail off and put it crossways to slow him up. Still he's de fastest thing in de water. And dat's why de porpoise got his tail on crossways.

Rockefeller and Ford

Once John D. Rockefeller and Henry Ford was woofing at each other. Rockefeller told Henry Ford he could build a solid gold road round the world. Henry Ford told him if he would he would look at it and see if he liked it, and if he did he would buy it and put one of his tin lizzies on it.

ORIGINALITY

It has been said so often that the Negro is lacking in originality that it has almost become a gospel. Outward signs seem to bear this out. But if one looks closely its falsity is immediately evident.

It is obvious that to get back to original sources is much too difficult for any group to claim very much as a certainty. What we really mean by originality is the modification of ideas. The most ardent admirer of the great Shakespeare cannot claim first source even for him. It is his treatment of the borrowed material.

So if we look at it squarely, the Negro is a very original being. While he lives and moves in the midst of a white civilization, everything that he touches is re-interpreted for his own use. He has modified the language, mode of food preparation, practice of medicine, and most certainly the religion of his new country, just as he adapted to suit himself the Sheik haircut made famous by Rudolph Valentino.

Everyone is familiar with the Negro's modification of the whites' musical instruments, so that his interpretation has been adopted by the white man himself and then re-interpreted. In so many words, Paul Whiteman is giving an imitation of a Negro orchestra making use of white-invented instruments in a Negro way. Thus has arisen a new art in the civilized world, and thus has our so-called civilization come. The exchange and re-exchange of ideas between groups.

IMITATION

The Negro, the world over, is famous as a mimic. But this in no way damages his standing as an original. Mimicry is an art in itself. If it is not, then all art must fall by the same blow that strikes it down. When sculpture, painting, dancing, literature neither reflect nor suggest anything in nature or human experience we turn away with a dull wonder in our hearts at why the thing was done. Moreover, the contention that the Negro imitates from a feeling of inferiority is incorrect. He mimics for the love of it. The group of Negroes who slavishly imitate is small. The average Negro glories in his ways. The highly educated Negro the same. The self-despisement lies in a middle class who scorns to do or be anything Negro. "That's just like a Nigger" is the most terrible rebuke one can lay upon this kind. He wears drab clothing, sits through a boresome church service, pretends to have no interest in the community, holds beauty contests, and otherwise apes all the mediocrities of the white brother. The truly cultured Negro scorns him, and the Negro "farthest down" is too busy "spreading his junk" in his own way to see or care. He likes his own things best. Even the group who are not Negroes but belong to the "sixth race," buy such records as "Shake dat thing" and "Tight lak dat." They really enjoy hearing a good bible-beater preacher, but wild horses could drag no such admission from them. Their ready-made expression is: "We done got away from all that now." Some refuse to countenance Negro music on the grounds that it is niggerism, and for that reason should be done away with. Roland Hayes was thoroughly denounced for singing spirituals until he was accepted by white audiences. Langston Hughes is not considered a poet by this group because he writes of the man in the ditch, who is more numerous and real among us than any other.

But, this group aside, let us say that the art of mimicry is better developed in the Negro than in other racial groups. He does it as the mocking-bird does it, for the love of it, and not because he wishes to be like the one imitated. I saw a group of small Negro boys imitating a cat defecating and the subsequent toilet of the cat. It was very realistic, and they enjoyed it as much as if they had been imitating a coronation ceremony. The dances are full of imitations of various animals. The buzzard lope, walking the dog, the pig's hind legs, holding the mule, elephant squat, pigeon's wing, falling off the log, seabord (imitation of an engine starting), and the like.

ABSENCE OF THE CONCEPT OF PRIVACY

It is said that Negroes keep nothing secret, that they have no reserve. This ought not to seem strange when one considers that we are an outdoor people accustomed to communal life. Add this to all-permeating drama and you have the explanation.

There is no privacy in an African village. Love, fights, possessions are, to misquote Woodrow Wilson, "Open disagreements openly arrived at." The community is given the benefit of a good fight as well as a good wedding. An audience is a necessary part of any drama. We merely go with nature rather than against it.

Discord is more natural than accord. If we accept the doctrine of the survival of the fittest, there are more fighting honors than there are honors for other achievements. Humanity places premiums on all things necessary to its well-being, and a valiant and good fighter is valuable in any community. So why hide the light under a bushel? Moreover, intimidation is a recognized part of warfare the world over, and threats certainly must be listed under that head. So that a great threatener must certainly be considered an aid to the fighting machine. So then if a man or woman is a facile hurler of threats, why should he or she not show their wares to the community? Hence, the holding of all quarrels and fights in the open. One relieves one's pent-up anger and at the same time earns laurels in intimidation. Besides, one does the community a service. There is nothing so exhilarating as watching well-matched opponents go into action. The entire world likes action, for that matter. Hence prize-fighters become millionaires.

Likewise love-making is a biological necessity the world over and an art among Negroes. So that a man or woman who is proficient sees no reason why the fact should not be moot. He swaggers. She struts hippily about. Songs are built on the power to charm beneath the bed-clothes. Here again we have individuals striving to excel in what the community considers an art. Then if all of his world is seeking a great lover, why should he not speak right out loud?

It is all in a view-point. Love-making and fighting in all their branches are high arts, other things are arts among groups where they brag about their proficiency just as brazenly as we do about these things that others consider matters for conversation behind closed doors. At any rate, the white man is despised by Negroes as a very poor fighter individually, and a very poor lover. One Negro, speaking of white men, said, "White folks is alright when dey gits in de bank and on de law bench, but dey sho' kin lie about wimmen folks."

I pressed him to explain. "Well you see, white mens makes out they marries wimmen to look at they eyes, and they know they gits em for just what us gits em for. 'Nother thing, white mens say they goes clear round de world and wins all de wimmen folks way from they men folks. Dat's a lie too. They don't win nothin, they buys em. Now de way I figgers it, if a woman don't want me enough to be wid me, 'thout I got to pay her, she kin rock right on, but these here white men don't know what to do wid a woman when they gits her—dat's how come they gives they wimmen so much. They got to. Us wimmen works jus as hard as us does an come home an sleep wid us every night. They own wouldn't do it and its de mens fault. Dese white men done fooled theyself bout dese wimmen.

"Now me, I keeps me some wimmens all de time. Dat's whut dey wuz put here for—us mens to use. Dat's right now, Miss. Y'll wuz put here so us mens could have some pleasure. Course I don't run round like heap uh men folks. But if my ole lady go way from me and stay more'n two weeks, I got to git me somebody, ain't I?"

THE JOOK

Jook is the word for a Negro pleasure house. It may mean a bawdy house. It may mean a house set apart on public works where the men and women dance, drink, and gamble. Often it is a combination of all these.

In past generations the music was furnished by "boxes," another word for guitars. One guitar was enough for a dance; to have two was considered excellent. Where two were playing one man played the lead and the other seconded him. The first player was "picking" and the second was "framming," that is, playing chords while the lead carried the melody by dexterous finger work. Sometimes a third player was added, and he played a tom-tom effect on the low strings. Believe it or not, this is excellent dance music.

Pianos soon came to take the place of the boxes, and now player-pianos and victrolas are in all of the Jooks.

Musically speaking, the Jook is the most important place in America. For in its smelly, shoddy confines has been born the secular music known as blues, and on blues has been founded jazz. The singing and playing in the true Negro style is called "jooking."

The songs grow by incremental repetition as they travel from mouth to mouth and from Jook to Jook for years before they reach outside ears. Hence the great variety of subject-matter in each song.

The Negro dances circulated over the world were also conceived inside the Jooks. They too make the round of Jooks and public works before going into the outside world.

In this respect it is interesting to mention the Black Bottom. I have read several false accounts of its origin and name. One writer claimed that it got its name from the black sticky mud on the bottom of the Mississippi River. Other equally absurd statements gummed the press. Now the dance really originated in the Jook section of Nashville, Tennessee, around Fourth Avenue. This is a tough neighborhood known as Black Bottom—hence the name.

The Charleston is perhaps forty years old and was danced up and down the Atlantic seaboard from North Carolina to Key West, Florida.

The Negro social dance is slow and sensuous. The idea in the Jook is to gain sensation, and not so much exercise. So that just enough foot movement is added to keep the dancers on the floor. A tremendous sex stimulation is gained from this. But who is trying to avoid it? The man, the woman, the time and place have met. Rather, little intimate names are indulged in to heap fire on fire.

These too have spread to all the world.

The Negro theatre, as built up by the Negro, is based on Jook situations, with women, gambling, fighting and drinking. Shows like "Dixie to Broadway" are only Negro in cast, and could just as well have come from pre-Soviet Russia.

Another interesting thing—Negro shows before being tampered with did not specialize in octoroon chorus girls. The girl who could hoist a Jook song from her belly and lam it against the front door of the theatre was the lead, even if she were as black as the hinges of hell. The question was "Can she jook?" She must also have a good belly wobble, and her hips must, to quote a popular work song, "Shake like jelly all over and be so broad, Lawd, Lawd, and be so broad." So that the bleached chorus is the result of a white demand and not the Negro's.

The woman in the Jook may be nappy headed and black, but if she is a good lover she gets there just the same. A favorite Jook song of the past has this to say:

> Singer: It aint good looks dat takes you through this world.
> Audience: What is it, good mama?
> Singer: Elgin* movements in your hips. Twenty years guarantee.

And it always brought down the house too.

> Oh de white gal rides in a Cadillac,
> De yaller girl rides de same,
> Black gal rides in a rusty Ford
> But she gits dere just de same.

The sort of woman her men idealize is the type put forth in the theatre. The art-creating Negro prefers a not too thin woman who can shake like jelly all over as she dances and sings, and that is the type he put forth on the stage. She has been banished by the white producer and the Negro who takes his cue from the white.

Of course a black woman is never the wife of the upper class Negro in the North. This state of affairs does not obtain in the South, however. I have noted numerous cases where the wife was considerably darker than the husband. People of some substance, too.

This scornful attitude towards black women receives mouth sanction by the mud-sills.

Even on the works and in the Jooks the black man sings disparagingly of black women. They say that she is evil. That she sleeps with her fists doubled up and ready for action. All over they are making a little drama of waking up a yaller** wife and a black one.

A man is lying beside his yaller wife and wakes her up. She says to him, "Darling, do you know what I was dreaming when you woke me up?" He says, "No honey, what was you dreaming?" She says, "I dreamt I had done cooked you a big fine dinner and we was setting down to eat out de same plate and I was setting on yo' lap jus huggin you and kissin you and you was so sweet."

Wake up a black woman, and before you kin git any sense into her she done up and lammed you over the head four or five times. When you git her quiet she'll say, "Nigger, know what I was dreamin when you woke me up?"

You say, "No honey, what was you dreamin?" She says, "I dreamt you shook yo' rusty fist under my nose and I split yo' head open wid a axe."

*Elegant (?). [from the Elgin Watch, Ed.]
**Yaller (yellow), light mulatto.

But in spite of disparaging fictitious drama, in real life the black girl is drawing on his account at the commissary. Down in the Cypress Swamp as he swings his axe he chants:

> Dat ole black gal, she keeps on grumblin,
> New pair shoes, new pair shoes,
> I'm goint to buy her shoes and stockings
> Slippers too, slippers too.

Then adds aside: "Blacker de berry, sweeter de juice."

To be sure the black gal is still in power, men are still cutting and shooting their way to her pillow. To the queen of the Jook!

Speaking of the influence of the Jook, I noted that Mae West in "Sex" had much more flavor of the turpentine quarters than she did of the white bawd. I know that the piece she played on the piano is a very old Jook composition. "Honey let yo' drawers hang low" had been played and sung in every Jook in the South for at least thirty-five years. It has always puzzled me why she thought it likely to be played in a Canadian bawdy house.

Speaking of the use of Negro material by white performers, it is astonishing that so many are trying it, and I have never seen one yet entirely realistic. They often have all the elements of the song, dance, or expression, but they are misplaced or distorted by the accent falling on the wrong element. Everyone seems to think that the Negro is easily imitated when nothing is further from the truth. Without exception I wonder why the black-face comedians *are* black-face; it is a puzzle—good comedians, but darn poor niggers. Gershwin and the other "Negro" rhapsodists come under this same axe. Just about as Negro as caviar or Ann Pennington's athletic Black Bottom. When the Negroes who knew the Black Bottom in its cradle saw the Broadway version they asked each other, "Is you learnt dat *new* Black Bottom yet?" Proof that it was not *their* dance.

And God only knows what the world has suffered from the white damsels who try to sing Blues.

The Negroes themselves have sinned also in this respect. In spite of the goings up and down on the earth, from the original Fisk Jubilee Singers down to the present, there has been no genuine presentation of Negro songs to white audiences. The spirituals that have been sung around the world are Negroid to be sure, but so full of musicians' tricks that Negro congregations are highly entertained when they hear their old songs so changed. They never use the new style songs, and these are never heard unless perchance some daughter or son has been off to college and returns with one of the old songs with its face lifted, so to speak.

I am of the opinion that this trick style of delivery was originated by the Fisk Singers; Tuskegee and Hampton followed suit and have helped spread this misconception of Negro spirituals. This Glee Club style has gone on so long and become so fixed among concert singers that it is considered quite authentic. But I say again, that not one concert singer in the world is singing the songs as the Negro songmakers sing them.

If anyone wants to prove the truth of this let him step inside some unfashionable Negro church and hear for himself.

To those who want to institute the Negro theatre, let me say it is already established. It is lacking in wealth, so it is not seen in the high places. A creature with a white head and Negro feet struts the Metropolitan boards. The real Negro theatre is in the jooks and the cabarets. Self-conscious individuals may turn away the eye and say, "Let us search elsewhere for our dramatic art." Let 'em search. They certainly won't find it. Butter Beans and Susie, Bo-Jangles and Snake Hips are the only performers of the real Negro school it has ever been my pleasure to behold in New York.

DIALECT

If we are to believe the majority of writers of Negro dialect and the burnt-cork artists, Negro speech is a weird thing, full of "ams" and "Ises." Fortunately, we don't have to believe them. We may go directly to the Negro and let him speak for himself.

I know that I run the risk of being damned as an infidel for declaring that nowhere can be found the Negro who asks "am it?" nor yet his brother who announces "Ise uh gwinter." He exists only for a certain type of writers and performers.

Very few Negroes, educated or not, use a clear clipped "I." It verges more or less upon "Ah." I think the lip form is responsible for this to a great extent. By experiment the reader will find that a sharp "i" is very much easier with a thin taut lip than with a full soft lip. Like tightening violin strings.

If one listens closely one will note too that a word is slurred in one position in the sentence but clearly pronounced in another. This is particularly true of the pronouns. A pronoun as a subject is likely to be clearly enunciated, but slurred as an object. For example: "You better not let me ketch yuh."

There is a tendency in some localities to add the "h" to "it" and pronounce it "hit." Probably a vestige of Old English. In some localities "if" is "ef."

In story telling "so" is universally the connective. It is used even as an introductory word, at the very beginning of a story. In religious expression "and" is used. The trend in stories is to state conclusions; in religion, to enumerate.

I am mentioning only the most general rules of dialect because there are so many quirks that belong only to certain localities that nothing less than a volume would be adequate.

Negro. Ed. Nancy Cunard. 1934. 2d ed. Ed. Nancy Cunard and Hugh Ford. New York: Frederick Ungar, 1984. 49–68.

Spirituals and Neo-Spirituals

The real spirituals are not really just songs. They are unceasing variations around a theme.

Contrary to popular belief their creation is not confined to the slavery period. Like the folk-tales, the spirituals are being made and forgotten every day. There is this difference: the makers of the songs of the present go about from town to town and church to church singing their songs. Some are printed and called ballads, and offered for sale after the services at ten or fifteen cents each. Others just go about singing them in competition with other religious minstrels. The lifting of the collection is the time for the song battles. Quite a bit of rivalry develops.

These songs, even the printed ones, do not remain long in their original form. Every congregation that takes it up alters it considerably. For instance, *The Dying Bed Maker,* which is easily the most popular of the recent compositions, has been changed to *He's a Mind Regulator* by a Baptist church in New Orleans.

The idea that the whole body of spirituals are "sorrow songs" is ridiculous. They cover a wide range of subjects from a peeve at gossipers to Death and Judgment.

The nearest thing to a description one can reach is that they are Negro religious songs, sung by a group, and a group bent on expression of feelings and not on sound effects.

There never has been a presentation of genuine Negro spirituals to any audience anywhere. What is being sung by the concert artists and glee clubs are the works of Negro composers or adapters *based* on the spirituals. Under this head come the works of Harry T. Burleigh, Rosamond Johnson, Lawrence Brown, Nathaniel Dett, Hall Johnson and Work. All good work and beautiful, but *not* the spirituals. These neo-spirituals are the outgrowth of the glee clubs. Fisk University boasts perhaps the oldest and certainly the most famous of these. They have spread their interpretation over America and Europe. Hampton and Tuskegee have not been unheard. But with all the glee clubs and soloists, there has not been one genuine spiritual presented.

To begin with, Negro spirituauls are not solo or quartette material. The jagged harmony is what makes it, and it ceases to be what it was when this is absent. Neither can any group be trained to reproduce it. Its truth dies under training like flowers under hot water. The harmony of the true spiritual is not regular. The dissonances are important and not to be ironed out by the trained musician. The various parts break in at any old time. Falsetto often takes the place of regular voices for short periods. Keys change. Moreover, each singing of the piece is a new creation. The congregation is bound by no rules. No two times singing is alike, so that we must consider the rendition of a song not as a final thing, but as a mood. It won't be the same thing next Sunday.

Negro songs to be heard truly must be sung by a group, and a group bent on expression of feelings and not on sound effects.

Glee clubs and concert singers put on their tuxedos, bow prettily to the audience, get the pitch and burst into magnificent song—but not *Negro* song. The real Negro singer cares nothing about pitch. The first notes just burst out and the rest of the church join in—fired by the same inner urge. Every man trying to express himself through song. Every man for himself. Hence the harmony and disharmony, the shifting keys and broken time that make up the spiritual.

I have noticed that whenever an untampered-with congregation attempts the renovated spirituals, the people grow self-conscious. They sing sheepishly in unison. None of the glorious individualistic flights that make up their own songs. Perhaps they feel on strange ground. Like the unlettered parent before his child just home from college. At any rate they are not very popular.

This is no condemnation of the neo-spirituals. They are a valuable contribution to the music and literature of the world. But let no one imagine that they are the songs of the people, as sung by them.

The lack of dialect in the religious expression—particularly in the prayers—will seem irregular.

The truth is, that the religious service is a conscious art expression. The artist is consciously creating—carefully choosing every syllable and every breath. The dialect breaks through only when the speaker has reached the emotional pitch where he loses all self-consciousness.

In the mouth of the Negro the English language loses its stiffness, yet conveys its meaning accurately. "The booming bounderries of this whirling world" conveys just as accurate a picture as mere "boundaries," and a little music is gained besides. "The rim bones of nothing" is just as truthful as "limitless space."

Negro singing and formal speech are breathy. The audible breathing is part of the performance and various devices are resorted to to adorn the breath taking. Even the lack of breath is embellished with syllables. This is, of course, the very antithesis of white vocal art. European singing is considered good when each syllable floats out on a column of air, seeming not to have any mechanics at all. Breathing must be hidden. Negro song ornaments both the song and the mechanics. It is said of a popular preacher, "He's got a good straining voice." I will make a parable to illustrate the difference between Negro and European.

A white man built a house. So he got it built and he told the man: "Plaster it good so that nobody can see the beams and uprights." So he did. Then he had it papered with beautiful paper, and painted the outside. And a Negro built him a house. So when he got the beams and all in, he carved beautiful grotesques over all the sills and stanchions, and beams and rafters. So both went to live in their houses and were happy.

The well-known "ha!" of the Negro preacher is a breathing device. It is the tail end of the expulsion just before inhalation. Instead of permitting the breath to drain out, when the wind gets too low for words, the remnant is expelled violently. Example: (inhalation) "And oh!"; (full breath) "my Father and my wonder-working God"; (explosive exhalation) "ha!"

Chants and hums are not used indiscriminately as it would appear to a casual listener. They have a definite place and time. They are used to "bear up" the speaker. As Mama Jane of Second Zion Baptist Church, New Orleans, explained to me: "What point they come out on, you bear 'em up."

For instance, if the preacher should say: "Jesus will lead us," the congregation would bear him up with: "I'm got my ha-hands in my Jesus' hands." If in prayer or sermon, the mention is made of nailing Christ to the cross: "Didn't Calvary tremble when they nailed him down."

There is no definite post-prayer chant. One may follow, however, because of intense emotion. A song immediately follows prayer. There is a pre-prayer hum which depends for its material upon the song just sung. It is usually a pianissimo continuation of the song without words. If some of the people use the words it is done so indistinctly that they would be hard to catch by a person unfamiliar with the song.

As indefinite as hums sound, they also are formal and can be found unchanged all over the South. The Negroised white hymns are not exactly sung. They are converted into a barbaric chant that is not a chant. It is a sort of liquefying of words. These songs are always used at funerals and on any solemn occasion. The Negro has created no songs for death and burials, in spite of the sombre subject matter contained in some of the spirituals. Negro songs are one and all based on a dance-possible rhythm. The heavy interpretations have been added by the more cultured singers. So for funerals fitting white hymns are used.

Beneath the seeming informality of religious worship there is a set formality. Sermons, prayers, moans, and testimonies have their definite forms. The individual may hang as many new ornaments upon the traditional form as he likes, but the audience would be disagreeably surprised if the form were abandoned. Any new and original elaboration is welcomed, however, and this brings out the fact that all religious expression among Negroes is regarded as art, and ability is recognized as definitely as in any other art. The beautiful prayer receives the acolade as well as the beautiful song. It is merely a form of expression which people generally are not accustomed to think of as art. Nothing outside of the Old Testament is as rich in figure as a Negro prayer. Some instances are unsurpassed anywhere in literature.

There is a lively rivalry in the technical artistry of all of these fields. It is a special honor to be called upon to pray over the covered communion table, for the greatest prayer-artist present is chosen for this, a lively something spreads over the church as he kneels, and the "bearing up" hum precedes him. It continues sometimes through the introduction, but ceases as he makes the complimentary salutation to the deity. This consists in giving to God all the titles that form allows.

The introduction to the prayer usually consists of one or two verses of some well-known hymn. "O, that I knew a secret place" seems to be the favorite. There is a definite pause after this, then follows an elaboration of all or parts of the Lord's Prayer. Follows after that what I call the setting, that is, the artist calling attention to the physical situation of himself and the church. After the dramatic setting, the action begins.

There are certain rhythmic breaks throughout the prayer, and the church "bears him up" at every one of these. There is in the body of the prayer an accelerando passage where the audience takes no part. It would be like applauding in the middle of a solo at the Metropolitan. It is here that the artist comes forth. He adorns the prayer with every sparkle of earth, water and sky, and nobody wants to miss a syllable. He comes down from this height to a slower tempo and is borne up again. The last few sentences are unaccompanied, for here again one listens to the individual's closing peroration. Several may join in the final amen. The best figure that I can think of is that the prayer is an obligato over and above the harmony of the assembly.

Negro. 70–84.

Big Sweet (From *Dust Tracks on a Road*)

It was in a saw-mill in Polk County that I almost got cut to death.

Lucy really wanted to kill me. I didn't mean any harm. All I was doing was collecting songs from Slim, who used to be her man back up in West Florida before he ran off from her. It is true that she found out where he was after nearly a year, and followed him to Polk County and he paid her some slight attention. He was knocking the pad with women, all around, and he seemed to want to sort of free-lance at it. But what he seemed to care most about was picking his guitar, and singing.

He was a valuable source of material to me, so I built him up a bit by buying him drinks and letting him ride in my car.

I figure that Lucy took a pick at me for three reasons. The first one was, her vanity was rubbed sore at not being able to hold her man. That was hard to own up to in a community where so much stress was laid on suiting. Nobody else had offered to shack up with her either. She was getting a very limited retail trade and Slim was ignoring the whole business. I had store-bought clothes, a lighter skin, and a shiny car, so she saw wherein she could use me for an alibi. So in spite of public knowledge of the situation for a year or more before I came, she was telling it around that I came and broke them up. She was going to cut everything off of me but "quit it."

Her second reason was, because of my research methods I had dug in with the male community. Most of the women liked me, too. Especially her sworn enemy, Big Sweet. She was scared of Big Sweet, but she probably reasoned that if she cut Big Sweet's protégée it would be a slam on Big Sweet and build up her own reputation. She was fighting Big Sweet through me.

Her third reason was, she had been in little scraps and had been to jail off and on, but she could not swear that she had ever killed anybody. She was small potatoes and nobody was paying her any mind. I was easy. I had no gun, knife or any sort of weapon. I did not even know how to do that kind of fighting.

Lucky for me, I had friended with Big Sweet. She came to my notice within the first week that I arrived on location. I heard somebody, a woman's voice "specifying" up this line of houses from where I lived and asked who it was.

"Dat's Big Sweet" my landlady told me. "She got her foot up on somebody. Ain't she specifying?"

She was really giving the particulars. She was giving a "reading," a word borrowed from the fortune-tellers. She was giving her opponent lurid data and bringing him up to date on his ancestry, his looks, smell, gait, clothes, and his route through Hell in the hereafter. My landlady went outside where nearly everybody else of the four or five hundred people on the "job" were to listen to the reading. Big Sweet broke the news to him, in one of her mildest bulletins that his pa was a double-humpted camel and his ma was a grass-gut cow, but even so, he tore her wide open in the act of getting born, and so on and so forth. He was a bitch's baby out of a buzzard egg.

My landlady explained to me what was meant by "putting your foot up" on a person. If you are sufficiently armed—enough to stand off a panzer division—and know what to do with your weapons after you get 'em, it is all right to go up to the house of your enemy, put one foot up on his steps, rest one elbow on your knee and play in the family. That is another way of saying play the dozens, which is also a way of saying low-rate your enemy's ancestors and him, down to the present moment for reference, and then go into his future as far as your imagination leads you. But if you have no faith in your personal courage and confidence in your arsenal, don't try it. It's a risky pleasure. So then I had a measure of this Big Sweet.

"Hurt who?" Mrs. Bertha snorted at my fears. "Big Sweet? Humph! Tain't a man, woman nor child on this job going to tackle Big Sweet. If God send her a pistol she'll send him a man. She can handle a knife with anybody. She'll join hands and cut a duel. Dat Cracker Quarters Boss wears two pistols round his waist and goes for bad, but he won't break a breath with Big Sweet lessen he got his pistol in his hand. Cause if he start anything with her, he won't never get a chance to draw it. She ain't mean. She don't bother nobody. She just don't stand for no foolishness, dat's all."

Right away, I decided that Big Sweet was going to be my friend. From what I had heard and seen in the short time I had been there, I felt as timid as an egg without a shell. So the next afternoon when she was pointed out to me, I waited until she was well up the sawdust road to the Commissary, then I got in my car and went that way as if by accident. When I pulled up beside her and offered her a ride, she frowned at me, then looked puzzled, but finally broke into a smile and got in.

By the time we got to the Commissary post office we were getting along fine. She told everybody I was her friend. We did not go back to the Quarters at once. She carried me around to several places and showed me off. We made a date to go down to Lakeland come Saturday, which we did. By the time we sighted the Quarters on the way back from Lakeland, she had told me, "You sho is crazy!" Which is a way of saying I was witty. "I loves to friend with somebody like you. I aims to look out for you, too. Do your fighting for you. Nobody better not start nothing with you, do I'll get my switch-blade and go round de hambone looking for meat."

We shook hands and I gave her one of my bracelets. After that evening everything went well for me. Big Sweet helped me to collect material in a big way. She had no idea what I wanted with it, but if I wanted it, she meant to see to it that I got it. She pointed out people who knew songs and stories. She wouldn't stand for balkiness on their part. We held two lying contests, storytelling contests to you, and Big Sweet passed on who rated the prizes. In that way, there was no argument about it.

So when the word came to Big Sweet that Lucy was threatening me, she put her foot up on Lucy in a most particular manner and warned her against the try. I suggested buying a knife for defense, but she said I would certainly be killed that way.

"You don't know how to handle no knife. You ain't got dat kind of a sense. You wouldn't even know how to hold it to de best advantage. You would draw your arm way back to stop her, and whilst you was doing all dat, Lucy would run in under your arm and be done; cut you to death before you could touch her. And then again, when you sure 'nough fighting, it ain't enough to just stick 'em wid your knife. You got to ram it in to de hilt, then you pull *down*. They ain't no more trouble after dat. They's *dead*. But don't you bother 'bout no fighting. You ain't like me. You don't even sleep with no mens. I wanted to be a virgin one time, but I couldn't keep it up. I needed the money too bad. But I think it's nice for you to be like that. You just keep on writing down them lies. I'll take care of all de fighting. Dat'll make it more better, since we done made friends."

She warned me that Lucy might try to "steal" me. That is, ambush me, or otherwise attack me without warning. So I was careful. I went nowhere on foot without Big Sweet.

Several weeks went by, then I ventured to the jook alone. Big Sweet let it be known that she was not going. But later she came in and went over to the cooncan game in the corner. Thinking I was alone, Lucy waited until things were in full swing and then came in with the very man to whom Big Sweet had given the "reading." There was only one door. I was far from it. I saw no escape for me when Lucy strode in, knife in hand. I saw sudden death very near that moment. I was paralyzed with fear. Big Sweet was in a crowd over in the corner, and did not see Lucy come in. But the sudden quiet of the place made her look around as Lucy charged. My friend was large and portly, but extremely light on her feet. She sprang like a lioness and I think the very surprise of Big Sweet being there when Lucy thought she was over at another party at the Pine Mill unnerved Lucy. She stopped abruptly as Big Sweet charged. The next moment, it was too late for Lucy to start again. The man who came in with Lucy tried to help her out, but two other men joined Big Sweet in the battle. It took on amazingly. It seemed that anybody who had any fighting to do, decided to settle-up then and there. Switch-blades, ice-picks and old-fashioned razors were out. One or two razors had already been bent back and thrown across the room, but our fight was the main attraction. Big Sweet yelled to me to run. I really ran, too. I ran out of the place, ran to my room, threw my things in the car and left the place. When the sun came up I was a hundred miles up the road, headed for New Orleans.

Dust Tracks on a Road. 1942. 2d ed. Urbana: U of Illinois P, 1984. 185–191.

Stories of Conflict

UNCLE TOM'S CHILDREN. *By Richard Wright. New York: Harper & Bros. (The Story Press.) 1938. $2.50.*

Reviewed by Zora Neale Hurston

This is a book about hatreds. Mr. Wright serves notice by his title that he speaks of people in revolt, and his stories are so grim that the Dismal Swamp of race hatred must be where they live. Not one act of understanding and sympathy comes to pass in the entire work.

But some bright new lines to remember come flashing from the author's pen. Some of his sentences have the shocking power of a forty-four. That means that he knows his way around among words. With his facility, one wonders what he would have done had he dealt with plots that touched the broader and more fundamental phases of Negro life instead of confining himself to the spectacular. For, though he has handled himself well, numerous Negro writers, published and unpublished, have written of this same kind of incident. It is the favorite Negro theme just as how the stenographer or some other poor girl won the boss or the boss's son is the favorite white theme. What is new in the four novelettes included in Mr. Wright's book is the wish-fulfillment theme. In each story the hero suffers but he gets his man.

In the first story, "Big Boy Leaves Home," the hero, Big Boy, takes the gun away from a white soldier after he has shot two of his chums and kills the white man. His chum is lynched, but Big Boy gets away. In the second story there is a flood on the Mississippi and in the fracas over a stolen rowboat, the hero gets the white owner of the boat and is later shot to death himself. He is a stupid, blundering character, but full of pathos. But then all the characters in this book are elemental and brutish. In the third story, the hero gets the white man most Negro men rail against—the white man who possesses a Negro woman. He gets several of them while he is about the business of choosing to die in a hurricane of bullets and fire because his woman has had a white man. There is lavish killing here, perhaps enough to satisfy all male black readers. In the fourth story neither the hero nor his adversary is killed, but the white foe bites the dust just the same. And in this story is summed up the conclusions that the other three stories have been moving towards.

In the other three stories the reader sees the picture of the South that the communists have been passing around of late. A dismal, hopeless section ruled by brutish hatred and nothing else. Mr. Wright's author's solution, is the solution of the PARTY—state responsibility for everything and individual responsibility for nothing, not even feeding one's self. And march!

Since the author himself is a Negro, his dialect is a puzzling thing. One wonders how he arrived at it. Certainly he does not write by ear unless he is tone-deaf. But aside from the broken speech of his characters, the book contains some beautiful writing. One hopes that Mr. Wright will find in Negro life a vehicle for his talents.

Saturday Review. 2 April 1938: 32.

8
James Joyce (1882–1941)

Introduced and Edited by Bonnie Kime Scott

James Joyce has enjoyed the central position in the modernist canon as a writer of prose fiction almost since the day in 1914 when his writing was taken up by Ezra Pound, who heard of him from another modernist giant, William Butler Yeats (Richard Ellmann 349–353). Pound published Joyce's poem "I Hear an Army" in *Des Imagistes* despite the fact that it bore little resemblance to official definitions of the imagist movement. He placed additional poetry by Joyce with Harriet Monroe's *Poetry* in Chicago and *A Portrait of the Artist as a Young Man* for serialization in the *Egoist* in England. The pattern of sponsorship by the male avant garde continued with Pound's appreciative reviews of *Dubliners* and *A Portrait,* T. S. Eliot's defense of *Ulysses* (published in the *Dial* as "*Ulysses,* Order and Myth"), and the serialization of *Finnegans Wake* in Ford Madox Ford's *transatlantic review* and in *transition,* edited by Eugene Jolas. Joyce's last work was explicated and justified to the world in *Our Exagmination Round his Factification for Incamination of Works in Progress* by a dozen men of the avant garde, led by Samuel Beckett.

Joyce's critical, daily support, however, came from intellectual women, who began as publishers and became much more. Harriet Shaw Weaver of the *Egoist* was an early publisher and his lifelong patron; their correspondence reveals close communication on his work in progress (Lidderdale and Nicholson; Scott, *Joyce and Feminism* 85–97). Sylvia Beach, the American proprietor of the unique Parisian library and bookstore Shakespeare and Company, was his amanuensis during his first decade in Paris and became a publisher to bring out *Ulysses* when no one else would (Fitch; Scott, *Joyce and Feminism* 98–107). Margaret Anderson and Jane Heap were willing to brave jail to publish *Ulysses* in the United States (Ellmann 502–504). Additional help in Paris came from Adrienne Monnier, Beach's partner in life, an editor, and proprietor of the French bookshop Les Amies des Livres, and from Maria Jolas, who took on late, personal burdens.

For contemporary women writers, Joyce was an aesthetic factor to cope with. Critics have used Joyce as a standard against which to judge many of them, including Woolf, West, and Barnes, usually to the women's detriment. Woolf is represented as a pale imitation of Joyce in Wyndham Lewis's *Men without Art* (170). Rebecca West fares badly in Hugh MacDiarmid's comparison, contained in this anthology. The more experimental women writers turned repeatedly to Joyce in working out a modernist aesthetic. This anthology also includes Mina Loy on *Ulysses*, Virginia Woolf's reading notes for *Ulysses*, Woolf's more formal assessment of Joyce as a Georgian writer in "Modern Fiction," Rebecca West's retelling of Weaver's sponsorship of Joyce, and Dorothy Richardson's analysis of the processes of *Finnegans Wake*.[1]

Djuna Barnes reported her discussions with Joyce in Paris in the 1920s in the *Double Dealer* and *Vanity Fair*. Barnes saw qualities of "a stricken animal" in Joyce, and in promoting *Ulysses* she de-emphasized his experimental aspect in favor of his lyricism and Rabelaisian qualities. The individualist doctrine of "silence, exile and cunning" pronounced by Stephen Dedalus at the end of *A Portrait* was her banner as well,[2] and indeed Joyce had special appeal to individualist feminists such as Dora Marsden and Harriet Weaver (Scott, *Joyce and Feminism* 108–112). Gertrude Stein resisted classification in Joycean terms and cultivated the image of running a rival Parisian camp to Joyce's headquarters at Shakespeare and Company, though she and Alice B. Toklas had friendly relations with Beach and Monnier.

Despite his entertainment of Barnes and lesser contacts recalled by Kay Boyle, Joyce was no sponsor of women writers (or any contemporary writers, for that matter). As a young man he wrote a negative review of *Poets and Dreamers* by Lady Isabella Augusta Gregory, despite the fact that he accepted letters of introduction and modest financial help from her. She was also included in his scatological broadside, "The Holy Office" (*Critical Writings* 102–105, 150), distributed after he left Ireland. In *Ulysses*, Lady Gregory is called an "old hake," and hints are made of a sexual relation with Yeats (who like her was a founder of the Irish Literary Theatre), though these sexist remarks are attributed to Buck Mulligan, whose machismo and medical ethics are subjects of satire (*Ulysses* 177–178). Joyce's argument against Gregory can be seen as an aspect of his rivalry with Yeats and part of his quarrel with what he regarded as sentimental reversion to the folk favored by the Irish literary revival. Against this, Joyce posed his interest in European writing, an inclination he pursued personally when he left Ireland in 1904.

Feminist opinion of Joyce in the 1970s and 1980s has been divided, though Joyce probably has more positive feminist defenders than do Lawrence, Eliot, or Pound. The early work, which was directed largely against sexism and negative stereotypes of women, includes that of Kate Millett, who found less misogyny in Joyce than in Lawrence and Norman Mailer (285, 296). Mary Ellmann notes his "curiosity . . . for becoming as well as judging the other" sex, but expresses a restiveness over the "liquidity" of the female mind rendered in Molly Bloom (xv, 202), the heroine of *Ulysses,* whose famous nighttime monologue provides the book's ending.

Molly Bloom was less successful in the 1970s as a universal female symbol than she had been through the 1950s;[3] she and the bird girl of *A Portrait* tell recent viewers more about male vision than about universal female truth—a concept of otherness that women find hard to embrace (Howe 263–264). Viewed as a realistic being, Molly demonstrates conventional attributes of lethargy in her limited activities and in narcissism; even in her affair with Blazes Boylan she is following prescribed social patterns, according to Elaine Unkeless. Marilyn French shares the view that Molly is largely male fantasy but respects the scope given to her as a "circumference bounding a human (male) world." She also appreciates the androgyny achieved by Molly's husband, Leopold Bloom (*Book as World* 259). Bloom, a Jew who experiences Dublin from ethnic margins, was the less intellectual and less egotistical male successor to Stephen Dedalus in Joyce's imagination. More recently, Frances Restuccia has analyzed Bloom as more masochist than feminist.

The failure of Stephen Dedalus to relinquish his Jesuitical mental habits (which were part of Joyce's own classical, male-centered education[4]) or to interact successfully with women are the subject of useful essays by Margot Norris, Suzette Henke, and Maud Ellmann. Joyce's capacity to render the daily realities of women's lives is discussed in essays contained in the first feminist book on Joyce, *Women in Joyce* (Henke and Unkeless, 1982), in recent collections based on Joyce symposia (Bauerle, Walzl), and in Cheryl Herr's study of Joyce and popular culture, *Joyce's Anatomy of Culture,* which is remarkable for its treatment of the semiotics of costume and gender on the Dublin stage.

The feminine potential of Joyce's style has been the subject of considerable controversy. Colin MacCabe posits a shift away from patriarchal narrative structures of classic realism as Joyce moved from *Dubliners* to *A Portrait* (65–67). Maria DiBattista has argued that Joyce's narrative scaffolding may have been fitting to his "garrulous virility and its generative improvidences" but was ultimately insufficient for Woolf's feminine mind and its reticences (100, 112). Comparative work that no longer denigrates the women writers but instead locates different or shared projects is now available (Froula, Lawrence, Lilienfeld, Marcus, Reizbaum, Scott [*James Joyce*]).

Gilbert and Gubar are currently Joyce's least sympathetic analysts, charging him with the introduction of a "new patrilinguistic epoch" and seeing his movement into feminine forms as a conversion of *materna lingua* into *patrius sermo* (258–261). The reservation over liquid feminine sentencing, expressed by Mary Ellmann, is amplified in their *No Man's Land*. The argument is of special interest in the debate among various feminist practices because the French semiotic theory of Jacques Lacan embraces a liquid, pulsing, presymbolic language, which it loosely associates with the mother; the theory has been used in defining feminine language. Shari Benstock, Suzette Henke (*Politics of Desire*), and Christine Van Boheemen have applied poststructuralist theory, including its feminist versions by Julia Kristeva, Luce Iragaray, and Hélène Cixous, to Joyce's presentation of the family romance and the writing of a feminine language.[5] It is notable that Cixous wrote her doctoral dissertation on Joyce and was particularly interested in family life, in both his biography and his writing.

Gender is an implicit subject in virtually all of Joyce's works. Joyce provides models of courtship rhetoric in his earliest poetry (*Chamber Music*). *Dubliners* stories, *A Portrait of the Artist as a Young Man*, and the early chapters of *Ulysses* all present the pressures of gender in a late Victorian, patriarchal Irish social system that divides the sexes, abides by Catholic principles and economies of gender, and suppresses sexuality. If feminine language is of particular interest, there are several places where readers might turn. Most obvious is the final, "Penelope" chapter of *Ulysses* (608–644). Earlier in the work, a young woman, Gerty MacDowell, takes on the discourse of women's magazines and novels (284–313; see Devlin and Henke, "Gerty"), and a typist flirts by mail with Leopold Bloom (63–65). In *Finnegans Wake*, the language of and about the mother figure, Anna Livia Plurabelle (ALP), merits attention as feminine writing. Like Molly Bloom, ALP has the final words of the work (619–628); earlier she is discussed extensively by gossiping washerwomen (198–216), and as a hen she issues her own mamafesta, which reappears in altered form through much of the work (104–107).

Joyce's interest in feminine psychology is probably best pursued in the dream thoughts centering upon a young daughter figure, Issy or Isobel (among the variant forms); she is generally seen as a reflection of Joyce's daughter Lucia, whose drifting into schizophrenia provided what was probably the most agonizing experience of Joyce's later life. As in *Ulysses*, the male figures, HCE (the father), Shem, and Shaun (the artistic and political sons, respectively), show the burden of gender stereotypes and restrictions as readily as the females.[6]

The two items by Joyce included in this anthology are less readily available than the sections of major texts just identified. They help construct a view of Joyce's attitude toward gender when he left Ireland to launch himself on the writing of his celebrated experimental works. At this time, Joyce was writing and revising more conventional material. He had published an essay on Ibsen in the prestigious English periodical the *Fortnightly Review* and had issued his challenge to traditional drama and the Irish literary revival in school debates and in a self-financed pamphlet, *Two Essays*. In this pamphlet his aesthetic challenges were printed alongside the feminist polemics of his college friend Francis Skeffington (Sheehy-Skeffington, after his marriage).

Joyce had completed most of *Chamber Music*, a cycle of love poems that use Yeats as a partial model for the slightly decadent, brooding male lover but also show Elizabethan form and attitudes toward women. The impoverished Joyce, whose father's drinking and improvidence had reduced a firmly middle-class, land-owning family to poverty, began the poems against a background of apparent rejection by Dublin's middle-class Catholic young women. Nora Barnacle, a twenty-year-old, Galway-bred runaway from an unhappy family situation, entered his life and his poems before he was finished with them. He used his verses to woo her years after their alliance and departure from Ireland in October 1904. Nora is widely accepted as a major force in Joyce's creation of female characters, and particularly as a model for Molly Bloom (Maddox).

With the exception of some experimental epiphanies and an unpublishable essay called "A Portrait of the Artist," Joyce's prose was still assignable to realistic, naturalist traditions. He had published several early versions of the short stories that would appear as *Dubliners* in 1914 after much difficulty with publishers who questioned his language and objected to explicit and coded sexual content.

The first of the two selections comes from a second project in prose, the increasingly ungainly novel *Stephen Hero*, which Joyce later revised on modernist experimental lines to publish in 1916 as *A Portrait of the Artist as a Young Man*. While Joyce did not publish theoretical essays or manifestos as did Pound and Eliot, critics have looked to the "epiphany" as defined in *Stephen Hero* as a staple of modernist fiction, including the work of Woolf and Dorothy Richardson (Beja).[7] This extract from *Stephen Hero* is an autobiographical dialogue between Stephen Dedalus and his mother, in which he seeks her reaction to his essay on modern drama. Stephen has not gone immediately to his mother for "intelligent sympathy," even though he acknowledges that she is not a "dullard" (83), but other consultants have proved unsatisfactory to his ego. Asking her to read it is clearly a source of "agitation." There is a lot of analysis of her motivations for listening and asking for further explanations, though Joyce makes it difficult to decipher whether we ever penetrate through Stephen's suspicions of maternal coercion to attain a view of May Daedalus's mind. An authoritative narrator seems to suggest that she uses "brave prevarication" to combat her son's suspicion that, as an ardent Catholic, she is checking up on his reading list.

Interest in plays and Ibsen turns out to be something that makes mother and son more similar than father and son, and Mrs. Daedalus directs the subsequent discussion toward female figures in Ibsen, refusing to ban the subjects that "old people" never talked about. Stephen's failure to encourage her to openly record her feelings and the labeling of her final observation on human nature as a "well-worn generality" fail to dispel the surprising view of a woman who has been hungry for intellectual stimulation and who momentarily takes action against her chief suppressor, the patriarch Mr. Daedalus. *Stephen Hero* also offers extensive dialogues between Stephen and a young female undergraduate, Emma Clery (66–68, 152–155, 187–189, 196–199), whose role was greatly reduced in *A Portrait* (Scott, *Joyce and Feminism* 133–155).

The second selection is a 1904 letter to Nora. It describes the religious and family politics Joyce hoped to escape in the couple's possible departure from Ireland.[8] But it warns Nora that he has been guilty of behaviors that victimized his own mother. It also suspects Nora of complicity in traditional values, in that she judges him "inferior to a convention in our present society." Richard Ellmann suggests that "convention" relates to others' opinions of Joyce (169). Brenda Maddox relates it to the convention of marriage, which Joyce's social rebellion would not allow him to enter into with Nora (41). (Joyce eventually bowed to the legalities of inheritance in 1931). Joyce casts himself as a social outsider, a "vagabond," and urges Nora to take up this position with him against slavishly conventional people and to dispense with the conventional illusions created by social masks. The ideas are complex, showing some aspiration for an intellectual ally, though implicitly Nora has warded off the libido's "talking" in Joyce with a troubling look of "tired indifference."

Maddox makes a major point of Nora's sexual experiences prior to Joyce and the early initiatives she took with him (21–23, 28–30, 97–98). The erotic letters the couple exchanged when Joyce was abroad in Ireland in 1909 (only his have survived) suggest that the "talking" and demanding of Joyce on this subject were not over and that in time Joyce satisfied his anal fixation through Nora's efforts (*Selected Letters* 163–195). Gilbert and Gubar represent it as Joyce's begging her "to write a calligraphy of shit," and they offer the overstated (though cleverly put) generalization that "at bottom, for Joyce, woman's scattered logos is a scatalogos, a Swiftian language that issues from the many obscene mouths of the female body" (232).

In this letter Joyce's analysis of the social order has a socialist ring to it, and "socialist" is an appropriate label for Joyce at this stage in his life. The precise observation of people in the streets of Paris is comparable to his scrupulous descriptions of those in Dublin. The voyeuristic male observer is suggestive of the boy of "Araby," the men of "Two Gallants," and Leopold Bloom, particularly in the early chapters of *Ulysses,* which also present the "warm humid smell" of Molly Bloom (*Ulysses* 51–53).

Joyce begins and ends as a thoroughly discomfited young man, showing very human symptoms of being in love and disclosing that Nora has created in him an "anguish of doubt." Throughout his life and his remaining writing career, uncertainty, occasioned by interactions with females and the feminine, was to contend with control, which he had been taught to exact upon language by patriarchal tradition.

NOTES

1. West and Woolf were not entirely favorable on Joyce, and critics have enjoyed quoting Woolf's most cutting remarks (Scott, *Joyce and Feminism* 119–124)).

2. It remained attractive to feminist critics of the 1970s. See Mary Ellmann 196 and Marilyn French, *The Women's Room* 8.

3. A notable exception in this pattern among Joyce's contemporaries is the critic and Joyce acquaintance Mary (Molly) Colum, who found that Molly had "the mind of a female gorilla" (233–234).

4. The Jesuits were very much in control of Joyce's education at the privileged residential school Clongowes Wood College and at Dublin's Belvedere College. When Joyce moved to University College, Dublin, he chose modern languages, the concentration favored by female students in the Royal College system, of which UCD was a part.

5. For a more extensive discussion of feminist criticism of Joyce, see my *Joyce and Feminism* 116–132 and *James Joyce* 131 n. 8.

6. For HCE, see 30–47, where a heroic ballad is sung and then turned against the father figure. For Shem, see the childhood courtship games sometimes titled "The Mime of Mick, Nick and the Maggies" 219–259. Shaun (Jaun) is fond of delivering sermons (e.g., 429–457).

7. "By an epiphany he meant a sudden spiritual manifestation, whether in the vulgarity of speech or of gesture or in a memorable phase of the mind itself. He believed that it was for the man of letters to record these epiphanies with extreme care, seeing that they were the most delicate and evanescent of moments" (*Stephen Hero* 211).

8. See Richard Ellmann's account (156–171). See also Brenda Maddox's biography of Nora Barnacle Joyce, particularly chap. 3, where Maddox discusses Nora Joyce's sexual advances and her conventional aspirations for marriage and a settled family life. Maddox records Ellmann's skepticism about a biography of Nora and his early opinion (which she says he revised) that "there was not even material . . . for a feminist treatise" (xviii).

WORKS CITED

Bauerle, Ruth. "Date Rape Mate Rape." In Scott, ed., *New Alliances*, 113–152.

Beckett, Samuel, ed. *Our Exagmination Round his Factification for Incamination of Work in Progress*. 1929. New York: New Directions, 1962.

Beja, Morris. *Epiphany in the Modern Novel*. Seattle: U of Washington P, 1971.

Benstock, Shari. "Nightletters: Women's Writing in the *Wake*." In *Critical Essays on Joyce*, ed. Bernard Benstock, 221–233. Boston: G. K. Hall, 1985.

Cixous, Hélène. *The Exile of James Joyce*. Trans. Sally A. J. Purcell. New York: D. Lewis, 1972.

Colum, Mary. "The Confessions of James Joyce." In *James Joyce: The Critical Heritage*, ed. Robert H. Deming. 233–234. New York: Barnes and Noble, 1970.

Devlin, Kim. "The Female Eye: Joyce's Voyeuristic Narcissists." In Scott, ed., *New Alliances*, 135–143.

DiBattista, Maria. "Joyce, Woolf and the Modern Mind." In *Virginia Woolf: New Critical Essays*, ed. Patricia Clements and Isobel Grundy, 77–95. London: Vision and New York: Barnes and Noble, 1983.

Eliot, T. S. "*Ulysses*, Order and Myth." *Selected Prose of T. S. Eliot*, ed. Frank Kermode, 175–178. New York: Harcourt Brace Jovanovich, 1975.

Ellmann, Mary. *Thinking about Women*. New York: Harcourt Brace Jovanovich, 1968.

Ellmann, Maud. "Disremembering Dedalus: *A Portrait of the Artist as a Young Man*." In *Untying the Text: A Post-Structuralist Reader*, ed. Robert Young. Boston: Routledge and Kegan Paul, 1981.

Ellmann, Richard. *James Joyce.* Rev. ed. New York: Oxford UP, 1982.

Fitch, Noel. *Sylvia Beach and the Lost Generation.* New York: Norton, 1983.

French, Marilyn. *The Book as World.* Cambridge: Harvard UP, 1975.

———. *The Women's Room.* New York: Summit Books, 1977.

Froula, Christine. "Gender and the Law of Genre: Joyce, Woolf and the Autobiographical Artist-Novel." In Scott, ed., *New Alliances,* 155–164.

Gilbert, Sandra, and Susan Gubar. *No Man's Land.* Vol. 1. New Haven: Yale UP, 1988.

Henke, Suzette. "Gerty MacDowell: Joyce's Sentimental Heroine." In Henke and Unkeless, eds., *Women in Joyce,* 132–149.

———. *James Joyce and the Politics of Desire.* London: Methuen, forthcoming.

———. "Stephen Dedalus and Women." In Henke and Unkeless, eds., *Women in Joyce,* 82–107.

———, and Elaine Unkeless, eds. *Women in Joyce.* Urbana: U of Illinois P, 1982.

Herr, Cheryl. *Joyce's Anatomy of Culture.* Urbana: U of Illinois P, 1986.

Howe, Florence. "Feminism and Literature." In *Images of Women in Fiction: Feminist Perspectives,* ed. Susan Koppelman Cornillon, 253–277. Bowling Green, Ohio: Bowling Green U Popular P, 1972.

Joyce, James. *Chamber Music: Collected Poems.* New York: Viking P, 1957.

———. *The Critical Writings of James Joyce.* Ed. Ellsworth Mason and Richard Ellmann. New York: Viking P, 1959.

———. *Dubliners.* New York: Viking P, 1969.

———. *Finnegans Wake.* New York: Viking P, 1939.

———. *A Portrait of the Artist as a Young Man.* 1916. New York: Viking P, 1968.

———. *Selected Letters of James Joyce.* Ed. Richard Ellmann. New York: Viking P, 1975.

———. *Stephen Hero.* Ed. John J. Slocum and Herbert Cahoon. New York: New Directions, 1963.

———. *Ulysses.* 1922. New York: Random House, 1986.

Lawrence, Karen. "Gender and Narrative Voice in *Jacob's Room* and *A Portrait of the Artist as a Young Man.*" In *James Joyce: The Centennial Symposium,* ed. Morris Beja et al., 31–38. Urbana: U of Illinois P, 1986.

Lewis, Wyndham. *Men without Art.* London: Cassell, 1934.

Lidderdale, Jane, and Mary Nicholson. *Dear Miss Weaver: Harriet Shaw Weaver, 1876–1961.* New York: Viking P, 1970.

Lilienfeld, Jane. "Flesh and Blood and Love and Words: Lily Briscoe, Stephen Dedalus and the Aesthetics of Emotional Quest." In Scott, ed., *New Alliances,* 165–178.

MacCabe, Colin. *James Joyce and the Revolution of the Word.* London: Macmillan, 1979.

Maddox, Brenda. *Nora: The Real Life of Molly Bloom.* Boston: Houghton Mifflin, 1988.

Marcus, Jane. *Virginia Woolf and the Languages of Patriarchy.* Bloomington: Indiana UP, 1987.

Millett, Kate. *Sexual Politics.* Garden City, N.Y.: Doubleday, 1970.

Norris, Margot. "Portraits of the Artist as a Young Lover." In Scott, ed., *New Alliances,* 144–152.

Restuccia, Frances. "Molly in Furs: Deleuzean/Masochian Masochism in the Writing of James Joyce." *Novel* 18.2(1985):101–116.

Scott, Bonnie Kime. *James Joyce.* Brighton: Harvester and Atlantic Highlands, N.J.: Humanities Press, 1987.

———. *Joyce and Feminism.* Bloomington: Indiana UP, 1984.

———, ed. *New Alliances in Joyce Studies: "When It's Aped to Foul a Delfian."* Newark: U of Delaware P, 1988.

Reizbaum, Marilyn. "A 'Modernism of Marginality': The Link between James Joyce and Djuna Barnes." In Scott, ed., *New Alliances,* 179–189.

Unkeless, Elaine. "The Conventional Molly Bloom." In Henke and Unkeless, eds., *Women in Joyce,* 150–168.

Van Boheemen, Christine. *The Novel as Family Romance: Language, Gender, and Authority from Fielding to Joyce.* Ithaca, N.Y.: Cornell UP, 1987.
Walzl, Florence. "Dubliners: Women in Irish Society." In Henke and Unkeless, eds., *Women in Joyce,* 31–56.
West, Rebecca. *The Strange Necessity.* New York: Doubleday, Doran, 1928.

Stephen's Interview with His Mother (From *Stephen Hero*)

His mother had not asked to see the manuscript: she had continued to iron the clothes on the kitchen-table without the «least suspicion of the agitation in the mind of her son.»* He had sat on three or four kitchen chairs, one after the other, and had dangled his legs unsuccessfully from all free corners of the table. At last, unable to control his agitation, he asked her point-blank would she like him to read out his essay.

—O, yes, Stephen—if you don't mind my ironing a few things . . .

—No, I don't mind.

Stephen read out the essay to her slowly and emphatically and when he had finished reading she said it was very beautifully written but that as there were some things in it which she couldn't follow, would he mind reading it to her again and explaining some of it. He read it over again and allowed himself a long exposition of his theories «garnished with many crude striking allusions with which he hoped to drive it home the better.» His mother who had never suspected probably that "beauty" could be anything more than a convention of the drawingroom or a natural antecedent to marriage and married life was surprised to see the extraordinary honour which her son conferred upon it. Beauty, to the mind of such a woman, was often a synonym for licentious ways and probably for this reason she was relieved to find that the excesses of this new worship were supervised by a recognised saintly authority. However as the essayist's recent habits were not very re-assuring she decided to combine a discreet motherly solicitude with an interest, which without being open to the accusation of factitiousness was at first intended as a compliment. While she was nicely folding a handkerchief she said:

—What does Ibsen write, Stephen?

—Plays.

—I never heard of his name before. Is he alive at present?

*Joyce marked certain passages of the manuscript with blue or red crayon. These passages are set off here by « ».

—Yes, he is. But you know, in Ireland people don't know much about what is going on out in Europe.

—He must be a great writer from what you say of him.

—Would you like to read some of his plays, mother? I have some.

—Yes. I would like to read the best one. What is the best one?

—I don't know . . . But do you really want to read Ibsen?

—I do, really.

—To see whether I am reading dangerous authors or not, is that why?

—No, Stephen, answered his mother with a brave prevarication. I think you're old enough now to know what is right and what is wrong without my dictating to you what you are to read.

—I think so too . . . But I'm surprised to hear you ask about Ibsen. I didn't imagine you took the least interest in these matters.

Mrs. Daedalus pushed her iron smoothly over a white petticoat «in time to the current of her memory.»

—Well, of course, I don't speak about it but I'm not so indifferent . . . Before I married your father I used to read a great deal. I used to take an interest in all kinds of new plays.

—But since you married neither of you so much as bought a single book!

—Well, you see, Stephen, your father is not like you: he takes no interest in that sort of thing . . . When he was young he told me he used to spend all his time out after the hounds or rowing on the Lee. He went in for athletics.

—I suspect what he went in for, said Stephen irreverently. I know he doesn't care a jack straw about what I think or what I write.

—He wants to see you make your way, get on in life, said his mother defensively. That's his ambition. You shouldn't blame him for that.

—No, no, no. But it may not be my ambition. That kind of life I often loathe: I find it ugly and cowardly.

—Of course life isn't what I used to think it was when I was a young girl. That's why I would like to read some great writer, to see what ideal of life he has—amn't I right in saying "ideal"?

—Yes, but . . .

—Because sometimes—not that I grumble at the lot Almighty God has given me and I have more or less a happy life with your father—but sometimes I feel that I want to leave this actual life and enter another—for a time.

—But that is wrong: that is the great mistake everyone makes. Art is not an escape from life!

—No?

—You evidently weren't listening to what I said or else you didn't understand what I said. Art is not an escape from life. It's just the very opposite. Art, on the contrary, is the very central expression of life. An artist is not a fellow who dangles a mechanical heaven before the public. The priest does that. The artist affirms out of the fulness of his own life, he creates . . . Do you understand?

And so on. A day or two afterwards Stephen gave his mother a few of the plays to read. She read them with great interest and found Nora Helmer a charming character. Dr. Stockmann she admired but her admiration was naturally checked by her son's light-heartedly blasphemous description of that stout burgher as 'Jesus in a frock-coat.' But the play which she preferred to all others was the *Wild Duck.* Of it she spoke readily and on her own initiative: it had moved her deeply. Stephen, to escape a charge of hot-headedness and partizanship, did not encourage her to an open record of her feelings.

—I hope you're not going to mention Little Nell in the *Old Curiosity Shop.*

—Of course I like Dickens too but I can see a great difference between Little Nell and that poor little creature—what is her name?

—Hedvig Ekdal?

—Hedvig, yes . . . It's so sad: it's terrible to read it even . . . I quite agree with you that Ibsen is a wonderful writer.

—Really?

—Yes, really. His plays have impressed me very much.

—Do you think he is immoral?

—Of course, you know, Stephen, he treats of subjects . . . of which I know very little myself . . . subjects . . .

—Subjects which, you think, should never be talked about?

—Well, that was the old people's idea but I don't know if it was right. I don't know if it is good for people to be entirely ignorant.

—Then why not treat them openly?

—I think it might do harm to some people—uneducated, unbalanced people. People's natures are so different. You perhaps . . .

—O, never mind me . . . Do you think these plays are unfit for people to read?

—No, I think they're magnificent plays indeed.

—And not immoral?

—I think that Ibsen . . . has an extraordinary knowledge of human nature . . . And I think that human nature is a very extraordinary thing sometimes.

Stephen had to be contented with this well-worn generality as he recognised in it a genuine sentiment. His mother, in fact, had so far evangelised herself that she undertook the duties of missioner to the heathen; that is to say, she offered some of the plays to her husband to read. He listened to her praises with a somewhat startled air, observing no feature of her face, his eyeglass screwed into an astonished eye and his mouth poised in naïf surprise. He was always interested in novelties, childishly interested and receptive, and this new name and the phenomena it had produced in his house were novelties for him. He made no attempt to discredit his wife's novel development but he resented both that she should have achieved it unaided by him and that she should be able thereby to act as intermediary between him and his son. He condemned as inopportune but not discredited his son's wayward researches into strange literature and, though a similar taste was not discoverable in him, he was prepared to commit that most pious of heroisms namely the extension of one's sympathies late in life in deference to the advocacy of a junior.

Stephen Hero. Ed. John J. Slocum and Herbert Cahoon. New York: New Directions, 1963. 83–87.

Letter to Nora Barnacle

29 August 1904 60 Shelbourne Road

My dear Nora I have just finished my midnight dinner for which I had no appetite. When I was half way through I discovered I was eating it out of my fingers. I felt sick just as I did last night. I am much distressed. Excuse this dreadful pen and this awful paper.

I may have pained you tonight by what I said but surely it is well that you should know my mind on most things? My mind rejects the whole present social order and Christianity—home, the recognised virtues, classes of life, and religious doctrines. How could I like the idea of home? My home was simply a middle-class affair ruined by spendthrift habits which I have inherited. My mother was slowly killed, I think, by my father's ill-treatment, by years of trouble, and by my cynical frankness of conduct. When I looked on her face as she lay in her coffin—a face grey and wasted with cancer–I understood that I was looking on the face of a victim and I cursed the system which had made her a victim. We were seventeen in family. My brothers and sisters are nothing to me. One brother alone is capable of understanding me.

Six years ago I left the Catholic Church, hating it most fervently. I found it impossible for me to remain in it on account of the impulses of my nature. I made secret war upon it when I was a student and declined to accept the positions it offered me. By doing this I made myself a beggar but I retained my pride. Now I make open war upon it by what I write and say and do. I cannot enter the social order except as a vagabond. I started to study medicine three times, law once, music once. A week ago I was arranging to go away as a travelling actor. I could put no energy into the plan because you kept pulling me by the elbow. The actual difficulties of my life are incredible but I despise them.

When you went in tonight I wandered along towards Grafton St where I stood for a long time leaning against a lamp-post, smoking. The street was full of a life which I have poured a stream of my youth upon. While I stood there I thought of a few sentences I wrote some years ago when I lived in Paris—these sentences which follow—'They pass in twos and threes amid the life of the boulevard, walking like people who have leisure in a place lit up for them. They are in the pastry cook's, chattering, crushing little fabrics of pastry, or seated silently at tables by the café door, or descending from carriages with a busy stir of garments soft as the voice of the adulterer. They pass in an air of perfumes. Under the perfumes their bodies have a warm humid smell'—*

While I was repeating this to myself I knew that that life was still waiting for me if I chose to enter it. It could not give me perhaps the intoxication it had once given but it was still there and now that I am wiser and more controllable it was safe. It would ask no questions, expect nothing from me but a few moments of my life, leaving the rest free, and would promise me pleasure in return. I thought of all this and without regret I rejected it. It was useless for me; it could not give me what I wanted.

You have misunderstood, I think, some passages in a letter I wrote you and I have noticed a certain shyness in your manner as if the recollection of that night troubled you. I however consider it a kind of sacrament and the recollection of it fills me with amazed joy. You will perhaps not understand at once why it is that I honour you so much on account of it as you do not know much of my mind. But at the same time it was a sacrament which left me in a final sense of sorrow and degradation—sorrow because I saw in you an extraordinary, melancholy tenderness which had chosen that sacrament as a compromise, and degradation because I understood that in your eyes I was inferior to a convention of our present society.

I spoke to you satirically tonight but I was speaking of the world not of you. I am an enemy of the ignobleness and slavishness of people but not of you. Can you not see the simplicity which is at the back of all my disguises? We all wear masks. Certain people who know that we are much together often insult me about you. I listen to them calmly, disdaining to answer them but their least word tumbles my heart about like a bird in a storm.

It is not pleasant for me that I have to go to bed now remembering the last look of your eyes—a look of tired indifference—remembering the torture in your voice the other night. No human being has ever stood so close to my soul as you stand, it seems, and yet you can treat my words with painful rudeness ('I know what is talking now' you said). When I was younger I had a friend to whom I gave myself freely—in a way more than I give to you and in a way less. He was Irish, that is to say, he was false to me.

I have not said a quarter of what I want to say but it is a great labour writing with this cursed pen. I don't know what you will think of this letter. Please write to me, won't you? Believe me, my dear Nora, I honour you very much but I want more than your caresses. You have left me again in an anguish of doubt. JAJ

Selected Letters of James Joyce. Ed. Richard Ellmann. New York: Viking P, 1975. 25–27.

*The passage comprises all except the last sentence of an epiphany (MS, Cornell) of Parisian *poules.* It is adapted in *Ulysses.*

9

Nella Larsen (1891–1964)

Introduced and Edited by Thadious M. Davis

During the 1920s, when Harlem was black America's culture capital and the "New Negro" was in vogue, Nella Larsen grappled with the complexity of being a modern black female. Born in Chicago during its headlong rush into modern development, she was the first of the twentieth-century black women writers whose sensibility was completely urban and whose understanding of fiction was thoroughly modern. She was born in the 1890s, when Chicago propelled itself by means of the Columbian Exposition (1893) into an unparalleled acceptance of urban modernity. With little appreciation for life outside cities and no nostalgia for the past, she encountered the South too late in her formative years and too early in her middle years to be impressed by either its folklore or its folk legacies. Her arrival in the New York of the 1910s anchored a fascination with urban existence that both characterized and stabilized her adulthood.

Described in a 1928 newspaper story as "a modern woman, for she smokes, wears her dresses short, does not believe in religion, churches and the like" (Berlack), Larsen became acquainted with modernist authors through her training at the Library School of the New York Public Library (1922–1923) and her job at the 135th Street branch library (1923–1926), where "New Negro" writers of the older generation (James Weldon Johnson, Jessie Fauset, W. E. B. Du Bois) and the younger (Gwendolyn Bennett, Countee Cullen,

Langston Hughes) gathered for readings. She associated with a number of the new artists, particularly Rudolph Fisher, Aaron Douglas, Arna Bontemps, and Wallace Thurman. Along with them, Dorothy Peterson, and Harold Jackman, she joined Jean Toomer's Harlem group for lectures and demonstrations in Gurdjieffian philosophy.

An additional influence was her friendship with white novelist and critic Carl Van Vechten, who in the 1920s was often in the forefront of "new" tastes and directions, such as "Negro Harlem," Walt Whitman, and Gertrude Stein. Upon beginning to write fiction in 1926, Larsen envisioned her work as a part of the new, the modern, and the avant garde, largely represented by Van Vechten and his New York set (Isa Glenn, Avery Hopwood, Witter Bynner, William Seabrook, Fannie Hurst, and a host of other literati). His cosmopolitan readings and his literary friendships with Stein, James Branch Cabell, Elinor Wylie, Joseph Hergesheimer, Ronald Firbank, and others known for experimental works helped shape Larsen's fictional emphasis on ironic, sophisticated themes. Van Vechten's own novels, including his controversial *Nigger Heaven* (1926), about Harlem, inspired her particular talent for satire, for depicting social mores and their often debilitating effects on women. In the mid-1920s, Van Vechten was responsible not only for introducing Larsen to famous writers and other celebrities but also for bringing her first novel to his publisher, Alfred A. Knopf.

Before Van Vechten, in the early 1920s, her first literary mentors, Jessie Fauset and Walter White, were responsible for initially encouraging her to write fiction. Fauset, literary editor of the *Crisis,* and White, assistant to James Weldon Johnson, secretary of the National Association for the Advancement of Colored People, were both prominent in fostering the literary and cultural Harlem Renaissance. White's objection to T. S. Stribling's portrayal of blacks in *Birthright* (1922) led him, Fauset, and Larsen, with the encouragement of H. L. Mencken, to begin novels on the realities of black life. Though White completed *The Fire in the Flint* (1924) and Fauset *There Is Confusion* (1924) before Larsen began her novel, they helped to direct her toward unexplored areas of racial fiction. Both also forwarded her literary ambitions by including her as a budding writer in Harlem's "New Negro" social and cultural activities. By the time her first novel appeared in 1928, Larsen functioned with ease in "the myth world of the twenties" (Osofsky 187), on both sides of 110th Street.

Despite her identification with what Alain Locke, godfather of the Harlem Renaissance, termed "the talented few" (47), those who were in Du Bois's formulation "the talented tenth" of the race, Larsen recognized that neither class privilege nor caste position could protect women from the external and internal circumstances that impede their development, circumvent their ambition, and fragment their personalities. Her two published novels, *Quicksand* (1928) and *Passing* (1929), have at their center the same issues that feminists today explore: gender identity, racial oppression, sexuality and desire, work and aspiration, marriage and ambition, reproduction and motherhood, family and autonomy, class and social mobility. Her intricate explorations of the personal consciousness and psychology of women transcend the limits of a single fictive character because on a subsurface level they address the condition of, and ambivalence toward, women in an emergent modern society. Both novels are marked by discourses on female desire and allegories of repression.

Helga Crane, the educated mulatto heroine in *Quicksand,* searches for self-definition, societal recognition, and sexual expression. Her odyssey through a richly textured contemporary scene ranges from the rural South and the urban North to cosmopolitan Scandinavia and encompasses basic questions of a woman's place in relation to self, family, and society. One major issue mediating the conclusion is a woman's control over her own body and reproduction. Barely functional after the birth of her fourth child, Helga becomes pregnant with her fifth. Her position in the psychic quagmire that had threatened her existence all along graphically illustrates the negative impact of marriage and motherhood on a woman's desire for autonomy and self-affirmation. Although Helga Crane fails in her spiritual quest, she becomes symbolic not merely of "the tragic mulatto" (Christian 53) but primarily of the restless energy and relentless search endemic to modern identity in general and to female identity in particular.

Irene Redfield and Clare Kendry, light-skinned blacks and psychological doubles in *Passing,* represent the contrasts between one woman's safe, secure, middle-class life of servants, bridge parties, charity balls, and smart fashions and another woman's risk-filled, daring existence on the edge of danger and duplicity, between the "sacrificial," self-denying roles as wife and mother and the "selfish," self-seeking person. Racial passing is only one of the concerns (Wall 105–110; Tate; Youmans). In rendering Irene, the central consciousness of *Passing,* Larsen experiments with stream-of-consciousness technique and narrated monlogues to explore the darker side of personality (jealousy, anxiety, rage) cloaked in material comfort and social respectability. She was an early reader of James Joyce's fiction, and in 1927 requested a copy of *Ulysses* from a friend traveling in France.

The lasting strength of *Quicksand* and *Passing,* as Larsen's friend and fellow Gurdjieff disciple Dorothy Peterson (a language teacher, translator, and actress) attested in nominating her for a 1929 Harmon Award for Distinguished Achievement among Negroes, is "interpreting feminine psychology"—a strength that ironically may have undercut her chances for winning, both in 1928, when the first-place gold medal went to poet and novelist Claude McKay and the second-place bronze medal went to Larsen, and in 1929, when no gold medal was awarded but the second-place bronze went to her mentor Walter White. Yet her skill in handling the psychology of female character, particularly the psychological depths charted in her subtexts, is precisely what has attracted contemporary feminists to her work (McDowell; Washington 159–167; Davis; Dearborn 55–60; Thornton).

Larsen's knowledge of modernism extended to the impact of the new scientific findings on human relationships. Married in 1919 to a research physicist, she combined an awareness of "new science" with an interest in creative writing. Her husband, Elmer Samuel Imes, was a pioneer in infrared spectroscopy. In exploring the means of studying the structure of molecules, he verified the applicability of the quantum theory to radiation in all parts of the electromagnetic spectrum. His experiments on the rotational energy levels of hydrogen fluoride was a turning point in modern scientific thinking because it demonstrated the general application of the quantum theory to more than a few limited fields of theoretical or applied physics (Fuson; Spady).

Imes's work on relativity fostered Larsen's interest in the randomness of human experience. She was aware of the changing nature of human relationships and of the contemporary efforts in literature and science to understand human psychology and personality, especially theoretical conceptions about the relative value of both experiences and events. Her own personal and social history, however, contributed to her emphasis on the present and future and caused her to privilege social evolutionism, thereby allowing for change, mobility, and transmutation.

Larsen's will to create and her determination to become all that she envisioned for her ideal self are seen in her career shifts and job changes. She worked her way through the Lincoln Hospital School for Nurses in the Bronx (1912–1915) and supported herself before and after her marriage as a nurse during a period when nursing was developing as a profession for women and nurses were organizing progressive associations, demanding respect for their work, and expanding their options by working first for suffrage and then, after 1920, for voter registration as a means of affecting a change in their collective condition as women.

An avid reader throughout her life, Larsen attempted to bring together her private interests with a public career by becoming a librarian in 1923. Although library work was more suited to her literary interests, she soon discovered that she had both the will and the opportunity to become a novelist. Her movement from nurse to librarian to writer demonstrates a personal search for class position, meaningful work, social prestige, and full self-expression that was not unlike Helga Crane's in *Quicksand.*

Larsen was one of only two black women novelists who came to prominence during the 1920s; the other was her mentor Jessie Fauset. Unlike Fauset, Larsen drew the models for her fictional creations from both the Harlem Renaissance and the New York avant garde, and she did not write cultural or literary essays. Though she published two book reviews and one rebuttal to a review in the *Messenger* and *Opportunity,* she confined her work primarily to the novel.

One of her rare ventures into the critical essay was her defense of Walter White's novel *Flight* (1926). Frank Horne, a young poet, panned the book for its inadequate and illogical development of the main character, Mimi Daquin, a New Orleans creole of color who passes for white but ultimately returns to her race. Horne's most negative criticisms were directed against the novel's stylistic deficiencies and the novelist's poor writing skills. In response to the personal attack on her mentor, Larsen composed a detailed statement that is, in effect, self-revelatory of her stake in the modernist camp. Addressed to Charles S. Johnson, editor of *Opportunity,* her letter (reprinted below) displays the knowledge of literature that had prompted him to enlist her as the respondent to Horne. Published in an abridged version in the September 1926 issue of *Opportunity,* the letter also reveals her attempt to use the idea of relativity in connection with works of fiction.

Much like her fellow "New Negro" authors, Larsen was a prolific writer of letters. In her extant correspondence, she occasionally touched upon her position as author in relation to modernism, and she typically linked herself to experimental, primarily male, writers. Although she is sensitive in her novels to the condition of women in a patriarchal society and to the limitations on female aspirations in a sexist and racist world, she rarely addresses gender issues in her personal correspondence or signals an awareness of the changing conditions of women in modern society.

One example is her 1925 letter to Carl Van Vechten (also printed here) on the publication of *Firecrackers,* his novel treating the paradoxes of love. Larsen reveals the breathless excitement of mid-decade New Yorkers, the exuberant sense of possibilities awaiting fictional exploration, the sensuousness of physicalities captured in writing, and the sheer pleasure of being part of one's own milieu. She evokes the idiom and mood of the central figure in Van Vechten's novel *The Blind Bow-Boy* (1923), Campaspe Lorillard, a sophisticated New Yorker who struggles against losing her independence to the equally independent Gunnar O'Grady, a man of numerous exotic careers, including furnaceman and acrobat. In the sexual duel between the two, Campaspe is the victor because she accepts sex, passion, and intercourse in the relationship without relinquishing her essential self. Larsen alludes to the sexual themes and the colorful action, but she singles out the portrait of Edith Dale, a character from Van Vechten's *Peter Whiffle* (1922) based on Mabel Dodge Luhan, and the death of Countess Ella Poore Nattatorrini, the title character from his *Tattooed Countess* (1924). Despite her silence about gender-specific issues in *Firecrackers,* Larsen found one basis for her empathetic reading of it and other novels, such as White's *Flight,* in the portraits of modern women.

WORKS CITED

Berlack, Thelma. "New Author Unearthed Right Here in Harlem." *Amsterdam News* 23 May 1928.

Christian, Barbara. *Black Women Novelists: The Development of a Tradition, 1892–1976.* Westport, Conn.: Greenwood P, 1980.

Davis, Thadious M. "Nella Larsen." In *Dictionary of Literary Biography,* vol. 51, 182–192. Detroit: Gale, 1986.

Dearborn, Mary V. *Pocahontas's Daughters: Gender and Ethnicity in American Culture.* New York: Oxford UP, 1986.

Fuson, Nelson. "Notes on Dr. Earle Plyer's 'The Origins and History of Infrared Spectroscopy.' " Fisk U Infrared Spectroscopy Institute Symposium, 16 Aug. 1974.
Larsen, Nella. "Correspondence." *Opportunity* 4(1926):295.
———. *Passing*. 1929. Rpt. *Quicksand and Passing*, ed. Deborah E. McDowell. American Women Writers Series. New Brunswick, N.J.: Rutgers UP, 1986.
———. *Quicksand*. 1928. Rpt. *Quicksand and Passing*.
Locke, Alain. "Negro Youth Speaks." In *The New Negro*, ed. Alain Locke, 47–53. New York: Boni, 1925.
McDowell, Deborah E. Introduction. Larsen, *Quicksand and Passing*.
Osofsky, Gilbert. *Harlem: The Making of a Ghetto, Negro New York: 1890–1930*. New York: Harper and Row, 1966.
Spady, James G. "Black Space." In *Blacks in Science: Ancient and Modern*, ed. Ivan Van Sertima, 258–265. New Brunswick, N.J.: Transaction Books, 1985.
Tate, Claudia. "Nella Larsen's *Passing*: A Problem of Interpretation." *Black American Literature Forum* 14(1980):142–146.
Thornton, Hortense. "Sexism As Quagmire: Nella Larsen's *Quicksand*. *CLA Journal* 16(1973):285–301.
Van Vechten, Carl. *Firecrackers*. New York: Knopf, 1925.
Wall, Cheryl. "Passing for What? Aspects of Identity in Nella Larsen's Novels." *Black American Literature Forum* 20(1986):97–111.
Washington, Mary Helen. *Invented Lives: Narratives of Black Women 1860–1960*. Garden City, N.Y.: Anchor, 1987.
White, Walter. *Flight*. New York: Knopf, 1926.
Youmans, Mary Mabel. "Nella Larsen's *Passing*: A Study in Irony." *CLA Journal* 18 (1974):235–241.

Letter on Walter White's *Flight*

Mr. Charles S. Johnson,
127 East Twenty-third Street,
New York City

My dear Mr. Johnson:

I have before me Mr. Frank Horne's amazing review—in the July issue of Opportunity—of Mr. White's latest novel, "Flight." I do not like this review. In fact so violently do I object to it that I am moved to put pen to paper to state my reasons for objecting. Surprise, that a reviewer apparently so erudite should have written such an unintelligent review. Anger, because such a book had been given to so an ununderstanding a person for review. Pity, because the reviewer had so entirely missed the chief idea of the book.

I pass over your reviewer's main reason for exasperation with "Flight," the fact that he had hoped some day to write a novel on this subject, because it is not at all pertinent to the review. A bit naive, of course, and usually "not done," but still unimportant, and certainly no business of your readers.

It is the blindness, not the abuse which annoys me. I doubt if ever Mr.

Stuart Sherman or Mr. Carl Van Doren, supposing they had shared your reviewer's feelings, would have treated "Flight" so roughly. My quarrel with this very interesting piece of literary criticism is that seemingly your reviewer lacked the ability or the range of reading to understand the book which he attacked with so much assurance.

May I quote a little from the review as I go along?

"Mimi Daquin is a character worthy of a novel; she deserves a treatment of a kind to place her beside Maria Chandelaine, Mattie Frome and Salammbo." Just why, I wonder did your reviewer choose the passive French-Canadian girl, the trapped Mattie, and the Salammbo of ancient Carthage, with whom to disparage the rebellious, modern Mimi? Certainly, these are for their their own environments and times, excellent characters. But, so is Mimi for hers. And would not Galsworthy's unsurpassable Irene Forsyte, or Jacobsen's Maria Grubbe have been more effective for purposes of comparison as well as for disparagement? They, like Mimi Daquin, threw away material things for fulfillment of their spiritual destinies.

"There is in her travail the lonely vicissitudes of a lost race . . ." Which "lost" race? It is here that your reviewer stumbles and falls. It is here that we detect his blindness. It is here that we become aware that he fails to realize that this is the heart of the whole tale. A lost race. Yes. But I suspect that he refers to the black race, while Mr. White obviously means that it is the white race which is lost, doomed to destruction by its own mechanical gods. How could your reviewer have missed this dominate note, this thing which permeates the whole book? It was this, that made Mimi turn from it. Surely, the thesis of "Flight" is "what shall it profit a man if he gain the whole world and lose his own soul?"

"Then too, we must conjecture that he leaves this girl at the most critical stage of her career." We do *not* conjecture anything of the kind. We know it. And we were meant to know it. Authors do not supply imaginations, they expect their readers to have their own, and, to use them. Judging by present day standards of fiction, the ending of "Flight" is the perfect one, perfect in its aesthetic colouring, perfect in its subtle simplicity. For others of this type, I refer your reviewer to Sherwood Anderson's "Dark Laughter," to Carl Van Vechten's "Firecrackers," to Joseph Hergesheimer's "Tubal Cane."

"She leaves a white world with all of its advantages of body and spirit . . . to go back to 'her people' ". Here it is again, your reviewer's inability to grasp the fact that Mimi Daquin came to realize that, for her, there were no advantages of the spirit in the white world, and so, spiritual things being essential to her full existence she gave up voluntarily, the material advantages.

"How," asks your reviewer will she "adjust on a lower cramped scale a life that had become so full, how compensate for the intense freedom of being white?" Again, I point out that her life had *not* been full, it had, perhaps been novel, but not full. And I resent that word "lower", and in a lesser degree the word "cramped". I maintain that neither is applicable to Negro life, especially among people of Mimi's class. Inner peace compensated her for the "intense freedom of being white". Some people "feel" their race, (even some Negroes).

[Crossed through line illegible.] Mr. White evidently does, and so, has given us Mimi Daquin. [Deleted line.] I come now to your reviewer's complaints about the author's style. He grumbles about "lack of clarity", "confusion of characters", "faulty sentence structure". These sins escaped me in my two readings, and even after they had been so publicly pointed out, I failed to find them. Even the opening sentence, so particularly cited, still seems to me all right. But then, I have been recently reading Huysmans, Conrad, Proust, and Thomas Mann. Naturally these things would not irritate me as they would an admirer of Louis Hemon and Mrs. Wharton. Too, there's Galsworthy, who opens his latest novel with a sentence of some thirty-odd words.

To my mind, warped as I have confessed by the Europeans and the American moderns, "Flight" is a far superior piece of work than "The Fire in the Flint". Less dramatic, it is more fastidious and required more understanding, keener insight. Actions and words count less and the poetic conception of the character, the psychology of the scene more, than in the earlier novel. "Flight" shows a more mature artistry.

It may be that your reviewer read the book hastily, superficially, and so missed both its meaning and its charm.

N.d. [August 1926]. Walter White Correspondence. NAACP Papers, Library of Congress.

Letter to Carl Van Vechten

Dear Carl,

This is a tardy "thank you", but for the past month it has seemed always to be tea time, as the immortal Alice remarked, with never time to wash the dishes between whiles.

What things there are to write, if one can only write them. Boiler menders, society ladies, children, acrobats, governesses, business men, countesses, flappers, Nile green bath rooms, beautifully filed, gay moods and shivering hesitations, all presented in an intensely restrained and civilized manner, and underneath the ironic survival of a much more primitive mood. Delicious.

It is nice to find some one writing as if he didn't absolutely despise the age in which he lives. And surely it is more interesting to belong to one's own time, to share its peculiar vision, catch that flying glimpse of the panorama which no subsequent generation can ever recover. I think "Firecrackers" is really a very important book.

Nice too, to meet some old friends. Thanks for the peep at Edith Dale. I think you were *horrid* to the countess.

Monday, n.d. [1925]. Carl Van Vechten Collection, New York Public Library.

10
D. H. Lawrence (1885–1930)

Introduced and Edited by Bonnie Kime Scott

D. H. Lawrence may be more thoroughly and ambivalently implicated in patterns of gender in modernism than any other regularly canonized male modernist. In his harsh critique of rational, scientific, mechanized modern Western culture, Lawrence repeatedly implicated both class and gender and looked back to a pagan world, in touch with earth processes, for rejuvenation. Not the most experimental of modernists, he expressed his scorn for James Joyce, Dorothy Richardson, and Marcel Proust, who he thought were listening at great length to the death rattle in their own throats ("Surgery").

Only Ezra Pound rivals Lawrence for his network of female colleagues, and I would argue that, in his creative works, Lawrence surpassed Pound for a consistent focus upon gender. Some might call it an obsession. Lawrence's female connections, as demonstrated in biography and letters, are of high literary and artistic interest. It is widely agreed that Lawrence wanted, even needed, to see things through women's eyes and that he frequently rewrote their preliminary texts to achieve his own. The list of his female witnesses and collaborators includes his early love Jessie Chambers, whose notes and commentary were helpful (some would argue critical) to the development of *Sons and Lovers;*[1] Helen Corke, whose diaries Lawrence worked over for *The Trespasser;* Mollie Skinner, whose Australian narrative was the foundation of

The Boy in the Bush; and his wife, Frieda Lawrence, whom Martin Green has elevated to the status of co-writer of certain works. Lawrence discussed an early interest in the suffrage movement with another early love and literary woman, Louie Burrows (Simpson 21).

Chambers, Catherine Carswell, Dorothy Brett, Mabel Dodge Luhan, and Frieda Lawrence have left their own idiosyncratic accounts of their relationships with Lawrence. H. D. fictionalized her experience of Lawrence's sexual magnetism and ambivalence, drawing upon the months the Lawrences shared accommodations with her and her husband Richard Aldington in London in 1918. Katherine Mansfield's reactions to D. H. and Frieda Lawrence are available in her letters—particularly ones addressed to their mutual friend S. S. Koteliansky. John Middleton Murry, husband of Katherine Mansfield and a man whom Lawrence sought in blood brotherhood, left a gender-laden account with a homosexual thesis in a book titled, notably, *Son of Woman.* Rebecca West, despite reviews that mixed sharp, witty criticism with praise, wrote a eulogistic monograph upon Lawrence's death.

Before turning to feminist analysis, Sandra Gilbert wrote an appreciative book on Lawrence's poetry. Lawrence has elicited numerous book-length feminist collections and studies (Dix, Nixon, MacLeod, Ruderman, Simpson, Smith) and has been roundly attacked in more general, landmark feminist studies, from Kate Millett's *Sexual Politics* to Sandra Gilbert and Susan Gubar's *No Man's Land.*

Notable among Lawrence's female correspondents are Cynthia Asquith, Catherine Carswell, Harriet Monroe, Amy Lowell, Katherine Mansfield, and Ottoline Morrell. Lawrence's despair over the outbreak of World War I is shared frequently with Carswell, Lowell, and Asquith. He shared a vision of a postwar "new community which shall start a new life among us—a life in which the only riches is integrity of character" with Morrell in 1915, implying a role for her as hostess of Garsington (*Letters* 2:271). Letters to Lowell and Mansfield allow us to see his propensity for discussing modernist form, encouraging women's writing, and sharing his theories on gender.

Lowell, who was better known than Lawrence in the 1910s, included him in her imagist anthologies of 1915, 1916, and 1917, despite the fact that he did not consider himself an imagist. She wrote positive reviews and sent him royalties regularly without deducting the expenses (Lawrence and Lowell 40). She wrote several additional checks when he was in need and even sent him the typewriter that turned out much of *Women in Love* (*Letters* 2:234).[2] While she cautioned him about explicit sexual writing, she expressed a clear preference for this "visionary life whole and complete, physical as well as spiritual," in contrast to "pure obscenities like those perpetrated by James Joyce" (Lawrence and Lowell 77).

Lawrence read Lowell's poetry, selected favorites, and commented on ways that it represented a significant American development in literature of a kind he had also seen in the work of H. D. Lawrence found in Lowell's work a progression beyond (presumably) British art, beyond tragedy, emotion, and even irony. He said that she had "come to the pure mechanical stage of physical apprehension, the *human* element almost lost, the primary elemental forces, kinetic, dynamic—prismatic, tonic, the great, massive, active, *inorganic* world, elemental, never softened by life, that hard universe of Matter and Force where life is not yet known, come to pass again" (*Letters* 2:30). He was also frank about disliking her foreign imitations, both French and Japanese (Lawrence and Lowell 53). He dedicated *New Poems* to her. This was certainly better than what Lowell heard from Ezra Pound.

A famous letter written to Mansfield in late 1918 explores human relationships—implicating Mansfield, Murry, Frieda Lawrence, and himself—as well as the dynamics of *Women in Love.* Lawrence passes on a book by Carl Jung to Mansfield with warnings about male obsessiveness over an incestual return to the womb of the Magna Mater and her reception of him "with gratification." Lawrence fears that Murry stages such a return with Mansfield and that he himself has done it with Frieda and is now "struggling with all my might to get out." He reports grimly, "It is awfully hard, once the sex relation has gone this way, to recover. If we don't recover, we die." It is interesting that, in writing to Mansfield, the male is presented as the agent of his own destruction.

Lawrence reverts to a hierarchical power structure of the genders late in this letter: "woman must yield some sort of precedence to man and he must take precedence." Lawrence does report that this formula has been pronounced "antediluvian" by Frieda, and "some sort of precedence" leaves some room for selection and adjustment. The same crucial letter expresses an ideal of friendship, described first as "a pledging of men to each other inviolably" but expanded also to "friendship between men and women, and between women and women, sworn, pledged, eternal, as eternal as the marriage bond, and as deep." He has neither "met" nor "formed" such a relationship, but may in fact be seeking it in these very letters (*Letters* 2:301–302).[3]

Mansfield's 1922 letters to Koteliansky admire Lawrence as "a living man" (*Letters of KM* 477). She uses *Aaron's Rod* as a pretext to criticize (in quite unfeminist terms) "half-female, frightened writers-of-today" that "remind me of the greenfly in the roses—they are a kind of blight" (482). Though Lawrence would seem to offer the unblighted leaf, Mansfield goes on to say, "I do not go all the way with Lawrence. His ideas of sex mean nothing to me" (483).

The constitution and site of the feminine and the relation of women to men figure in virtually everything Lawrence wrote. Hilary Simpson offers an admirably concise and accurate survey of the historical contexts of Lawrence's interest in sexuality and women in culture, as well as a chronological survey of his changing attitude on the subject in his fiction and essays. *Sons and Lovers* makes an early probe into the topic of maternity. It has been argued that Lawrence, like his novel's hero, Paul Morel, is able to advance beyond an Oedipal relation to the mother and try on different modes of sexual alliance with women. In his personal life, the alliance with Frieda satisfies Harry T. Moore as fulfilled adult sexuality (62).

Lawrence's most affirmative views of matriarchy and of women coming into their own identities are in *The Rainbow,* which looks back through the mothers of Ursula Brangwen and features her growing sense of autonomy. The negative cultural response to the sexual themes of *The Rainbow,* seen in its seizure by British authorities and delayed publication in the United States, combined with the personal disruptions, destruction, and gender-specific social upheavals of World War I, made Lawrence a reactionary in regard to women and the feminine, according to Simpson.

Women in Love is a transitional text. Gilbert and Gubar have pointed to its sexual violence—the voluptuous violence of Hermione's assault on Birkin with a ball of lapus lazuli, the deadly embrace Diana gives the doctor who would be her rescuer, and Gerald's attempt to strangle Gudrun, interrupted by the no-man Loerke (38–40). The cultural necessity becomes male assertion of power; all else, disaster. Despite his fine vision of "an equilibrium, a pure balance of two single beings" (139) and the fights he gets from her, submission lurks behind Birkin's demands of Ursula, and she fades as a vigorous character after their marriage. His sense of the existence of something beyond heterosexual love puts him in a different league from her, and it is difficult not to see his as a privileged viewpoint at the close of the novel. The duality of male assertion versus female submission is again clearly evident in the attempt at male mastery of March by Grenfel in *The Fox,* a work in which gender tensions are heightened with parallel animal symbols.

Lawrence's *Fantasia of the Unconscious* insists that, although men and women may play each other's roles in our historical period, a child is born either wholly male or wholly female (131–132). What is natural in the male is the volition, action, utterance, as polarized from the female's sympathetic center of feeling and emotion. A consequence to the woman writer (which echoes the later theory of Jacques Lacan) is that "women, when they speak or write, utter not one single word that men have not taught them" (137–138). The Lawrence of this text finds the dynamics of power "superior" to sexual dynamics with woman, and power is religious in nature and male-defined: "The desire of the human male to build a world: not 'to build a world for you dear'; but to build out of his own soul and his own belief and his own effort something wonderful" (60).

But has the religious soul really driven beyond the woman? In works of what has been called his "leadership phase" (*The Fox, Fantasia, Aaron's Rod, Kangaroo, The Plumed Serpent*), Judith Ruderman finds an unresolved pre-Oedipal perception of the mother, focusing on dyads of mother-child dependency and the perception of the mother as a wild animal who would devour her child (10–13).

In his final novel, *Lady Chatterley's Lover,* Lawrence gives central importance to vital sexuality and "tenderness" (235, 260–261). Both the lowborn gamekeeper, Oliver Mellors, and the socially privileged Lady Chatterley are remade as successful lovers. Though she is capable of self-containment and independent action, Constance is contrasted both physically and mentally to the flat-chested, "smart," "cocksure" modern woman (18). Having a child is at the back of her mind through much of the novel. Her aristocratic husband, Clifford, who has been unmanned by war, emerges as a mechanical, cerebral captain of the modern mining industry, a force seen as devouring the sensual spaces of Wragby wood. Clifford at first depletes Constance's energies with his demands for personal attendance, but by default replaces his wife with a Magna Mater figure, his nurse Mrs. Boulton, a village woman who has experienced a tender marriage before her early widowhood. Lawrence makes his gamekeeper both a guardian of nature and a political spokesman, whose views on lesbians and cocksure women are pronouncedly unsympathetic.

Dennis Jackson has demonstrated the prevalence of pagan fertility rituals and myths of the dying and reviving god, Isis and Persephone, in *Lady Chatterley,* derived from Lawrence's reading of Sir James Frazer's *Golden Bough.* Like Frazer's selections from myth, Lawrence's myth and ritual focus upon male revival. The phallus may be Lawrence's ultimate character. In his defense of his novel, "A Propos of *Lady Chatterley's Lover,*" Lawrence speaks of "the blood of man and the blood of woman" as "two eternally different streams . . . that encircle the whole of life, and in marriage the circle is complete, and in sex the two rivers touch and renew one another, without ever commingling or confusing." But the phallus is special: "The phallus is a column of blood that fills the valley of blood of a woman" (507). In looking at the future of England, he says that "if England is to be regenerated . . . then it will be by the arising of a new blood-contact, a new touch, and a new marriage. It will be a phallic rather than a sexual regeneration. For the phallus is only the great old symbol of godly vitality in a man, and of immediate contact" (508). Like Ursula before her, Constance bows down to male loins, worshipping at Oliver's renewed, "cocksure" penis (196).

The two essays selected for this anthology originally appeared in late 1928 and early 1929. They have resemblances to works of Lawrence's "leadership phase,"[4] adjusting the place of the mother and female and seeing her as a threatening force in both her modern and her Magna Mater forms. They advocate a male position of power in postwar society. Formally, these essays scintillate with tense humor and are masterful as written performance, so much so that they seem more like ironic textual play than argument.

Lawrence works with distinct categories and spheres, offering a troubling evolution in history of gender relations. In "Matriarchy" he embraces (however bemusedly) the conservative orientation of John Knox, complete with his horror of a "monstrous regiment of women." Lawrence assigns animal metaphors to women, who exchange the place and voice of the hen with that of the cock ("Cocksure Women and Hensure Men") or descend like a plague of locusts upon the postwar job market. Woman no longer operates on a personal, dyadic scale but engulfs with vast numbers. Her legs come in six's, not human two's; this serves the insect metaphor, and the theme of engulfment suggests monstrous fusion as well.[5] The cowering men of today clearly have more to cope with than their Edwardian predecessors, who merely had "petticoat rule" in the home to fear.[6] The metaphor of high fashion also serves Lawrence: women no longer wear petticoats. Silk stockings and bare arms are garb appropriate to their increased energy, mobility, and action. Women are commodified and impersonalized as body parts, as grotesque here as the women's vaguely threatening bare arms in T. S. Eliot's "Love Song of J. Alfred Prufrock."

Lawrence had read *The Golden Bough* on matriarchy and had personal experience of its practice by Native Americans, which he uses to put men and women back on track. He concedes names, clans, and domestic spaces to women, trivializes the male connection to procreation and the domestic realm, and moves men at puberty to the grander social scale of the tribe and the transcendent spiritual function of religion. The all-male club is offered as evidence of man's need for separate sanctity. We can imagine Lawrence's horror at recent American legal rulings against such exclusive associations, notably for their exclusion of businesswomen. The solution of "Matriarchy" also contradicts Lawrence's plan for gender-balanced influences on children—the importance of the "father spark" expressed in *Fantasia*—and ignores his anxieties over excessive motherhood, a Lawrence theme responded to in one of Rebecca West's selections in this anthology.

"Cocksure Women and Hensure Men" does much of the same categorizing; it delegates roles and uses the farmyard fowl familiar from *The Fox,* or comparable to Mellors's rearing of pheasants in *Lady Chatterley,* to exemplify natural roles and effective handling of dangers. It is the male who protects and communicates to a wider world, having the inborn sense to listen for noise presaging disaster. Lawrence has abandoned the advanced position that procreation is of less importance to the female than sexual pleasure. The egg is all; no substitute object like ink bottle or vote can satisfy the dictates of nature.

Perhaps with his cautionary fable, amusingly delivered, Lawrence hoped to cajole women back into the nest. Though the return of the dauntless female driver to the stable nest seems futile, Lawrence remains prophetic. The tale is still being told to women in the work force, particularly ones in positions of power. The cautionary sound today is the ticking of the biological clock.

NOTES

I am grateful to Dennis Jackson for his advice at all stages in the preparation of this introduction and selection. Any inadequacies in the introducton are mine.

1. The importance of the "Miriam Papers" has been trivialized by Harry T. Moore (51). For a discussion of Lawrence's literary "trespasses" into women's texts, see Simpson 143–163.

2. Healy and Cushman, editors of their correspondence, note unpleasant undercur-

rents in the relationship—Lawrence's desire "*not* to be too humble with editors, publishers, Amys or any other stinkers with money or office" (12). They attribute Lowell's chilliness toward Lawrence's possible visit in 1919 to his notoriety from the banned novel, *The Rainbow* (13). She argued to Lawrence that "New England is far more puritanical than Old England," that a lecture by the author of *The Rainbow* would not be well attended (76–77), and that he would do better in New York City. But she sent detailed travel directions for a personal visit that never came off in 1923 (118–119).

3. See also *Letters* 2:472–473.

4. Spilka argues that Lawrence moved on from the leadership phase with his emphasis on tenderness in *Lady Chatterley's Lover.* Oates feels that Lawrence achieved a final transcendence in *The Escaped Cock* (107–109). Ruderman finds that Lawrence "never turned away from it" (7).

5. In "A Propos of *Lady Chatterley's Lover,*" Lawrence discusses the function of clothing in sexual vitality, finding "the half-naked women of today certainly do not rouse much sexual feeling in the muffled-up men of today" because sex is not alive in them (497).

6. "Petticoat government" was one of the menaces suspected of Molly Bloom in Joyce's *Ulysses.*

WORKS CITED

Brett, Dorothy. *Lawrence and Brett: A Friendship.* Philadelphia: Lippincott, 1933.

Carswell, Catherine. *The Savage Pilgrimage: A Narrative of D. H. Lawrence.* London: Martin Secker, 1932.

Chambers, Jessie. *D. H. Lawrence: A Personal Record by E. T.* 1936. Cambridge: Cambridge UP, 1980.

Dix, Carol. *D. H. Lawrence and Women.* Totowa, N.J.: Rowman and Littlefield, 1980.

Gilbert, Sandra. *Acts of Attention: The Poems of D. H. Lawrence.* Ithaca, N.Y.: Cornell UP, 1972.

Gilbert, Sandra, and Susan Gubar. *No Man's Land.* Vol. 1. New Haven: Yale UP, 1988.

Green, Martin. *The Van Richtoven Sisters: The Triumphant and Tragic Modes of Love.* New York: Basic Books, 1974.

H. D. *Bid Me to Live.* New York: Dial, 1960.

Jackson, Dennis. "The 'Old Pagan Vision': Myth and Ritual in *Lady Chatterley's Lover.*" In Jackson and Jackson, eds., *Critical Essays,* 128–144.

———, and Fleda Brown Jackson, eds. *Critical Essays on D. H. Lawrence.* Boston: G. K. Hall, 1988.

Lawrence, D. H. 1922. *Aaron's Rod.* New York: Viking P, 1961.

———. *The Boy in the Bush.* New York: Viking P, 1972.

———. *The Fox.* In *Four Short Novels of D. H. Lawrence.* Harmondsworth: Penguin, 1976.

———. *Lady Chatterley's Lover.* 1928. New York: Signet, 1959.

———. *The Letters of D. H. Lawrence.* Vol. 2. Ed. George J. Zytaruk and James T. Boulton. Cambridge: Cambridge UP, 1981.

———. *Phoenix II: Uncollected, Unpublished and Other Prose Works by D. H. Lawrence.* Ed. Warren Roberts and Harry T. Moore. London: Heinemann, 1968.

———. "A Propos of Lady Chatterley's Lover." *Phoenix II,* 487–515.

———. *"Psychoanalysis and the Unconscious"* and *"Fantasia of the Unconscious."* 1921–1922. New York: Viking P, 1960.

———. *The Rainbow.* 1915. Harmondsworth: Penguin, 1979.

———. "Surgery for the Novel—or a Bomb?" 1923. *Phoenix II.*

———. *The Trespasser.* London: Heinemann, 1955.

———. *Women in Love.* 1920. Harmondsworth: Penguin, 1976.

Lawrence, D. H., and Amy Lowell. *The Letters of D. H. Lawrence and Amy Lowell, 1914–1925.* Ed. E. Claire Healey and Keith Cushman. Santa Barbara, Calif.: Black Sparrow P, 1985.
Lawrence, Frieda. *"Not I, But the Wind . . ."* London: Heinemann, 1935.
Luhan, Mabel Dodge. *Lorenzo in Taos.* London: Martin Secker, 1933.
MacLeod, Sheila. *Lawrence's Men and Women.* London: Heinemann, 1985.
Mansfield, Katherine. *The Letters of Katherine Mansfield.* Vol. 2. Ed. John Middleton Murry. New York: Knopf, 1930.
Millett, Kate. *Sexual Politics.* Garden City, N.Y.: Doubleday, 1970.
Moore, Harry T. *The Priest of Love: A Life of D. H. Lawrence.* New York: Farrar, Straus and Giroux, 1974.
Murry, John Middleton. *Son of Woman.* London: Jonathan Cape, 1931.
Nixon, Cornelia. *Lawrence's Leadership Politics and the Turn against Women.* Berkeley: U of California P, 1986.
Oates, Joyce Carol. "Lawrence's *Gotterdammerung:* The Apocalyptic Vision of *Women in Love.*" In Jackson and Jackson, eds., *Critical Essays,* 92–110.
Ruderman, Judith. *D. H. Lawrence and the Devouring Mother: The Search for a Patriarchal Ideal of Leadership.* Durham, N.C.: Duke UP, 1984.
Simpson, Hilary. *D. H. Lawrence and Feminism.* London: Croom Helm, 1982.
Smith, Anne, ed. *Lawrence and Women.* London: Vision, 1978.
Spilka, Mark. "Lawrence's Quarrel with Tenderness." In Jackson and Jackson, eds., *Critical Essays,* 223–237.
West, Rebecca. *D. H. Lawrence.* London: Martin Secker, 1930.

Matriarchy

Whether they are aware of it or not, the men of today are a little afraid of the women of today; and especially the younger men. They not only see themselves in the minority, overwhelmed by numbers, but they feel themselves swamped by the strange unloosed energy of the silk-legged hordes. Women, women everywhere, and all of them on the warpath! The poor young male keeps up a jaunty front, but his masculine soul quakes. Women, women everywhere, silk-legged hosts that are up and doing, and no gainsaying them. They settle like silky locusts on all the jobs, they occupy the offices and the playing-fields like immensely active ants, they buzz round the coloured lights of pleasure in amazing bare-armed swarms, and the rather dazed young male is, naturally, a bit scared. Tommy may not be scared of his own individual Elsie, but when he sees her with her scores of female "pals," let him bluff as he may, he is frightened.

Being frightened, he begins to announce: Man must be master again!—The *must* is all very well. Tommy may be master of his own little Elsie in the stronghold of his own little home. But when she sets off in the morning to her job, and joins the hosts of her petticoatless, silklegged "pals," who is going to master her? Not Tommy!

It's not a question of petticoat rule. Petticoats no longer exist. The unsheathed silky legs of the modern female are petticoatless, and the modern young woman is not going to spend her life managing some little husband. She is not interested. And as soon as a problem ceases to contain interest, it ceases to be a problem. So that petticoat rule, which was such a problem for our fathers and grandfathers, is for us nothing. Elsie is not interested.

No, the modern young man is not afraid of being petticoat-ruled. His fear lies deeper. He is afraid of being swamped, turned into a mere accessory of bare-limbed, swooping woman; swamped by her numbers, swamped by her devouring energy. He talks rather bitterly about rule of women, monstrous regiment of women, and about matriarchy, and, rather feebly, about man being master again. He knows perfectly well that he will never be master again. John Knox could live to see the head of his monstrous regiment of women, and the head of Mary of Scotland, just chopped off. But you can't chop off the head of the modern woman. As leave try to chop the head off a swarm of locusts. Woman has emerged, and you can't put her back again. And she's not going back of her own accord, not if she knows it.

So we are in for the monstrous rule of women, and a matriarchy. A matriarchy! This seems the last word of horror to the shuddering male. What it means, exactly, is not defined. But it rings with the hollow sound of man's subordination to woman. Woman cracks the whip, and the poor trained dog of a man jumps through the hoop. Nightmare!

Matriarchy, according to the dictionary, means mother-rule. The mother the head of the family. The children inherit the mother's name. The property is bequeathed from mother to daughter, with a small allowance for the sons. The wife, no doubt, swears to love and cherish her husband, and the husband swears to honour and obey his spouse.—It doesn't sound so very different from what already is: except that when Tommy Smith marries Elsie Jones, he becomes Mr. Jones; quite right, too, nine cases out of ten.

And this is the matriarchy we are drifting into. No good trying to stem the tide. Woman is in flood.

But in this matter of matriarchy, let us not be abstract. Men and women will always be men and women. There is nothing new under the sun, not even matriarchy. Matriarchies have been and will be. And what about them, in living actuality?—It is said that in the ancient dawn of history there was nothing but matriarchy: children took the mother's name, belonged to the mother's clan, and the man was nameless. There is supposed to be a matriarchy today among the Berbers of the Sahara, and in Southern India, and one or two other rather dim places.

Yet, if you look at photographs of Berbers, the men look most jaunty and cocky, with their spears, and the terrible matriarchal women look as if they did most of the work. It seems to have been so in the remote past. Under the matriarchal system that preceded the patriarchal system of Father Abraham, the men seem to have been lively sports, hunting and dancing and fighting, while the women did the drudgery and minded the brats.

Courage! Perhaps a matriarchy isn't so bad, after all. A woman deserves to possess her own children and have them called by her name. As for the household furniture and the bit of money in the bank, it seems naturally hers.

Far from being a thing to dread, matriarchy is a solution to our weary social problem. Take the Pueblo Indians of the Arizona desert. They still have a sort of matriarchy. The man marries into the woman's clan, and passes into *her* family house. His corn supply goes to *her* tribe. His children are the children of *her* tribe, and take *her* name, so to speak. Everything that comes into the house is hers, *her* property. The man has no claim on the house, which belongs to her clan, nor to anything within the house. The Indian woman's home is *her* castle.

So! And what about the man, in this dread matriarchy? Is he the slave of the woman? By no means. Marriage, with him, is a secondary consideration, a minor event. His first duty is not to his wife and children—they belong to the clan. His first duty is to the tribe. The man is first and foremost an active, religious member of the tribe. Secondarily, he is son or husband or father.

The real life of the man is not spent in his own little home, daddy in the bosom of the family, wheeling the perambulator on Sundays. His life is passed mainly in the khiva, the great underground religious meeting-house where only the males assemble, where the sacred practices of the tribe are carried on; then also he is away hunting, or performing the sacred rites on the mountains, or he works in the fields. But he spends only certain months of the year in his wife's house, sleeping there. The rest he spends chiefly in the great khiva, where he sleeps and lives, along with the men, under the tuition of the old men of the tribe.

The Indian is profoundly religious. To him, life itself is religion: whether planting corn or reaping it, scalping an enemy or begetting a child; even washing his long black hair is a religious act. And he believes that only by the whole united effort of the tribe, day in, day out, year in, year out, in sheer religious attention and practice, can the tribe be kept vitally alive. Of course, the religion is pagan, savage, and to our idea unmoral. But religion it is, and it is his charge.

Then the children. When the boys reach the age of twelve or thirteen, they are taken from the mother and given into the charge of the old men. They live now in the khiva, or they are taken to the sacred camps on the mountains, to be initiated into manhood. Now their home is the khiva, the great sacred meeting-house underground. They may go and eat in their mother's house, but they live and sleep with the men.

And this is ancient matriarchy. And this is the instinctive form that society takes, even now. It seems to be a social instinct to send boys away to school at the age of thirteen, to be initiated into manhood. It is a social instinct in a man to leave his wife and children safe in the home, while he goes out and foregathers with other men, to fulfil his deeper social necessities. There is the club and the public-house, poor substitutes for the sacred khiva, no doubt, and yet absolutely necessary to most men. It is in the clubs and public-houses that men have really educated one another, by immediate contact, discussed politics and ideas, and made history. It is in the clubs and public-houses that men have tried to satisfy their deeper social instincts and intuitions. To satisfy his deeper social instincts and intuitions, a man must be able to get away from his family, and from women altogether, and foregather in the communion of men.

Of late years, however, the family has got hold of a man, and begun to destroy him. When a man is clutched by his family, his deeper social instincts and intuitions are all thwarted, he becomes a negative thing. Then the woman, perforce, becomes positive, and breaks loose into the world.

Let us drift back to matriarchy. Let the woman take the children and give them her name—it's a wise child that knows its own father. Let the woman take the property—what has a man to do with inheriting or bequeathing a grandfather's clock! Let the women form themselves into a great clan, for the preservation of themselves and their children. It is nothing but just.

And so, let men get free again, free from the tight littleness of family and family possessions. Give woman her full independence, and with it, the full responsibility of her independence. That is the only way to satisfy women once more: give them their full independence and full self-responsibility as mothers and heads of the family. When the children take the mother's name, the mother will look after the name all right.

And give the men a new foregathering ground, where they can meet and satisfy their deep social needs, profound social cravings which can only be satisfied apart from women. It is absolutely necessary to find some way of satisfying these ultimate social cravings in men, which are deep as religion in a man. It is necessary for the life of society, to keep us organically vital, to save us from the mess of industrial chaos and industrial revolt.

"If Women were Supreme," *Evening News* (October 5, 1928). *Phoenix II.* Ed. Warren Roberts and Harry T. Moore. London: Heinemann, 1968. 549–552.

Cocksure Women and Hensure Men

It seems to me there are two aspects to women. There is the demure and the dauntless. Men have loved to dwell, in fiction at least, on the demure maiden whose inevitable reply is: Oh, yes, if you please, kind sir! The demure maiden, the demure spouse, the demure mother—this is still the ideal. A few maidens, mistresses and mothers *are* demure. A few pretend to be. But the vast majority are not. And they don't pretend to be. We don't expect a girl skilfully driving her car to be demure, we expect her to be dauntless. What good would demure and maidenly Members of Parliament be, inevitably responding: Oh, yes, if you please, kind sir!—Though of course there are masculine members of that kidney.—And a demure telephone girl? Or even a demure stenographer? Demureness, to be sure, is outwardly becoming, it is an outward mark of femininity, like bobbed hair. But it goes with inward dauntlessness. The girl who has got to make her way in life has got to be dauntless, and if she has a pretty, demure manner with it, then lucky girl. She kills two birds with two stones.

With the two kinds of femininity go two kinds of confidence: There are the women who are cocksure, and the women who are hensure. A really up-to-date woman is a cocksure woman. She doesn't have a doubt nor a qualm. She is the modern type. Whereas the old-fashioned demure woman was sure as a hen is sure, that is, without knowing anything about it. She went quietly and busily clucking around, laying the eggs and mothering the chickens in a kind of anxious dream that still was full of sureness. But not mental sureness. Her sureness was a physical condition, very soothing, but a condition out of which she could easily be startled or frightened.

It is quite amusing to see the two kinds of sureness in chickens. The cockerel is, naturally, cocksure. He crows because he is *certain* it is day. Then the hen peeps out from under her wing. He marches to the door of the hen-house and pokes out his head assertively: *Ah ha! daylight, of course, just as I said!*—and he majestically steps down the chicken ladder towards *terra firma,* knowing that the hens will step cautiously after him, drawn by his confidence. So after him, cautiously, step the hens. He crows again: *Ha-ha! here we are!*—It is indisputable, and the hens accept it entirely. He marches towards the house. From the house a person ought to appear, scattering corn. Why does the person not appear? The cock will see to it. He is cocksure. He gives a loud crow in the doorway, and the person appears. The hens are suitably impressed but immediately devote all their henny consciousness to the scattered corn, pecking absorbedly, while the cock runs and fusses, cocksure that he is responsible for it all.

So the day goes on. The cock finds a tit-bit, and loudly calls the hens. They scuffle up in henny surety, and gobble the tit-bit. But when they find a juicy morsel for themselves, they devour it in silence, hensure. Unless, of course, there are little chicks, when they most anxiously call the brood. But in her own dim surety, the hen is really much surer than the cock, in a different way. She marches off to lay her egg, she secures obstinately the nest she wants, she lays her egg at last, then steps forth again with prancing confidence, and gives that most assured of all sounds, the hensure cackle of a bird who has laid her egg. The cock, who is never so sure about anything as the hen is about the egg she has laid, immediately starts to cackle like the female of his species. He is pining to be hensure, for hensure is so much surer than cocksure.

Nevertheless, cocksure is boss. When the chicken-hawk appears in the sky, loud are the cockerel's calls of alarm. Then the hens scuffle under the verandah, the cock ruffles his feathers on guard. The hens are numb with fear, they say: Alas, there is no health in us! How wonderful to be a cock so bold!—And they huddle, numbed. But their very numbness is hensurety.

Just as the cock can cackle, however, as if he had laid the egg, so can the hen bird crow. She can more or less assume his cocksureness. And yet she is never so easy, cocksure, as she used to be when she was hensure. Cocksure, she is cocksure, but uneasy. Hensure, she trembles, but is easy.

It seems to me just the same in the vast human farmyard. Only nowadays all the cocks are cackling and pretending to lay eggs, and all the hens are crowing and pretending to call the sun out of bed. If women today are cocksure, men are hensure. Men are timid, tremulous, rather soft and submissive, easy in their very henlike tremulousness. They only want to be spoken to gently. So the women step forth with a good loud *cock-a-doodle-do!*

The tragedy about cocksure women is that they are more cocky, in their assurance, than the cock himself. They never realize that when the cock gives his loud crow in the morning, he listens acutely afterwards to hear if some other wretch of a cock dare crow defiance, challenge. To the cock, there is always defiance, challenge, danger and death on the clear air; or the possibility thereof.

But alas, when the hen crows, she listens for no defiance or challenge. When she says *cock-a-doodle-do!* then it is unanswerable. The cock listens for an answer, alert. But the hen knows she is unanswerable. *Cock-a-doodle-do!* and there it is, take it or leave it!

And it is this that makes the cocksureness of women so dangerous, so devastating. It is really out of scheme, it is not in relation to the rest of things. So we have the tragedy of cocksure women. They find, so often, that instead of having laid an egg, they have laid a vote, or an empty ink-bottle, or some other absolutely unhatchable object, which means nothing to them.

It is the tragedy of the modern woman. She becomes cocksure, she puts all her passion and energy and years of her life into some effort or assertion, without ever listening for the denial which she ought to take into count. She is cocksure, but she is a hen all the time. Frightened of her own henny self, she rushes to mad lengths about votes, or welfare, or sports, or business: she is marvellous, out-manning the man. But alas, it is all fundamentally disconnected. It is all an attitude, and one day the attitude will become a weird cramp, a pain, and then it will collapse. And when it has collapsed, and she looks at the eggs she has laid, votes, or miles of typewriting, years of business efficiency—suddenly, because she is a hen and not a cock, all she has done will turn into pure nothingness to her. Suddenly it all falls out of relation to her basic henny self, and she realizes she has lost her life. The lovely henny surety, the hensureness which is the real bliss of every female, has been denied her: she had never had it. Having lived her life with such utmost strenuousness and cocksureness, she has missed her life altogether. Nothingness!

Phoenix II. 553–555.

11
Mina Loy (1882–1966)

Introduced and Edited by Carolyn Burke

An Englishwoman who took American citizenship, Mina Loy studied painting in London, Munich, and Paris, where she exhibited her work at the Salon d'Automne from 1903 until 1907, when she settled in Florence. By 1914, she had written many of the experimental poems that brought her to the attention of the American poets who published with her in the little magazines then flourishing in New York. They rightly saw her as one whose firsthand knowledge of European art movements intensified the challenge of her writing. Although until very recently she has been far less known than her modernist associates (including Gertrude Stein, F. T. Marinetti, Ezra Pound, Djuna Barnes, James Joyce, and Constantin Brancusi), in the 1910s her artistic reputation was such that one New York reporter quoted Loy's infamous "Love Songs" to illustrate the belief that such extremely free verse was of a piece with modernism in the arts and with women's emancipation, and another interviewed Loy as a representative "modern woman" while observing, "some people think that women are the cause of modernism, whatever that is."[1] It is now possible to see that her modernism is deeply colored by her thinking about sexual difference and that it bloomed from the unusual combination of her experience in pre–World War I Europe, her close association with such avant gardists as Stein and Marinetti, and her idiosyncratic crossing of feminist and metaphysical concerns.

In 1912, soon after her first one-woman show, Loy put aside her paints and began to write about the new artistic forms that were emerging all around her. The catalyst for this change of focus may have been some of Gertrude Stein's early manuscripts. Stein recalled that Loy "was able to understand without the commas" required by more traditionally minded readers and noted with satisfaction, "she has always been able to understand" (124). The importance of Stein's writing to Loy's unexpected development as a modernist poet is suggested in the epigraph of her *transatlantic review* essay of 1924 (reprinted below), which praises Stein as a kind of female scientist whose deconstructive work on language has made it possible for others to mine its radiant ore: "Curie / of the laboratory / of vocabulary / she crushed / the tonnage / of consciousness / congealed to phrases / to extract / a radium of the word."[2] For Loy, Stein's early writing showed the way to get down to the "belle matiere" of language, just as recent experiments in the visual arts had shown her how to rethink the données of representation. Furthermore, Loy saw Stein's prose in terms of sculpture: although it resembled "polished stone" in its massiveness and finish, it was alive with "the omnipresent plasm of life from which she evokes all her subjects," who "revolve on the pivot of her verbal construction like animated sculpture." But like most modern art, Stein's prose demanded intellectual effort on the part of the reader: "one must in fact go into training to get Gertrude Stein."

Specifically, Stein's prose prompted Loy to think of time and space as literary categories that might be represented on the page. Loy recalled that in 1911–1912 "Bergson was in the air, and his beads of Time strung on the continuous flux of Being seemed to have found a literary conclusion in the austere verity of Gertrude Stein's theme—'Being' as the absolute occupation." Stein's use of prose rhythms to imitate "the attributes of continuity" influenced Loy's own use of the poetic line in "Parturition," which simulates the contractions and expansions of labor. Stein had invented a kind of writing in which time could be slowed down or speeded up, for she "shaped her words to the pattern of a mobile emotion" rather than to the requirements of linearity or closure. In a similar way, she brought spatiality to the foreground, most notably in her portraits. Not only did the verbal surface come up to meet the reader, but the subject's traditional centrality was displaced, as in Cubist painting and collage. Loy was quick to see the implications of this approach, which she adapted to her own pictorial ends in two sequences of linked portrait poems from this period, "Three Moments in Paris" and "Italian Pictures."[3]

But along with these new approaches to time and space as dimensions of writing, Loy also saw in Stein the desire "to track intellection back to the embryo," a philosophical aim that underlay her "aesthetic analysis of the habits of consciousness." Like many of her generation, Loy believed that new artistic forms were already evolving in order to reflect, imitate, or even spur on more adequate understanding of these "habits of consciousness." It is unlikely, however, that Loy would have expressed the belief that her generation was living through a full-scale "crisis in consciousness" if she had not also absorbed the psychic shock of the Italian Futurists' assault on the past. Their energy, theatricality, and rhetorical violence soon jolted her out of the introspective psychologizing of expatriate circles in Florence and propelled her, for a time, into the clamorously public life of Futurist controversy.

By late 1913, Loy considered herself "in the throes of conversion to Futurism."[4] Even though she felt that Marinetti's basic philosophy was unacceptable, she still praised him warmly for "waking (her) up" and teaching her to draw on her "vitality."[5] "Aphorisms on Futurism," her first published work (reprinted below), voices the exhilaration that resulted from her decision to repudiate her own "passatista" ways, the old habits of mind and the passé aesthetic and social conventions that prevailed in genteel Florence:

> YOU prefer to observe the past on which your eyes are already opened.
>
> BUT the Future is only dark from outside.
> *Leap* into it—and it EXPLODES with *Light*.
>
> FORGET that you live in houses, that you may live in yourself—
>
> FOR the smallest people live in the greatest houses.
>
> BUT the smallest person, potentially, is as great as the Universe.

When "Aphorisms" appeared as the central literary text in the January 1914 issue of *Camera Work,* readers were shocked by the radical stance of its speaker, as well as by her unfamiliar crossing of the prose poem with the manifesto. Loy adapted elements of Marinetti's "arte di far manifesti"[6]—the inventive typography, bold layout, and attention-getting aphorisms—to her own uses: taken as a group, her aphorisms enact the compression, expansion, and release of a mind in search of psychic liberation. But although she seemed to speak for many prewar modernists when proclaiming "TODAY is the crisis in consciousness," the text's mode of address was actually double. Loy was also speaking to herself, to the painter who lacked the courage to depart from academic conventions, and to the woman who feared to throw off the tight lacing of Victorian propriety.

Although for a time Loy was swept along by Marinetti's energy, the contradictions of his gender politics soon became apparent and stirred her to write her feminist manifesto. She could perhaps agree in theory with his infamous "*disprezzo della donna*" (scorn for women) once it was clear that he meant not particular women but the cultural image of woman as femme fatale, caught in the tyranny of "Amore," which he claimed was "nothing but an invention of the poets" (72). Her own manifesto claims that as things stand, "men and women are enemies, with the enmity of the exploited for the parasite, the parasite for the exploited," since both are trapped in the unequal power struggle that results from sexual dependence. But she was not taken in by Marinetti's somewhat disingenuous call for equality between the sexes and his ironic support for the suffragettes, whose "aggressive entrance . . . into the parliaments" would in his view, help to bring about the collapse of those institutions. For Marinetti insisted that either women lived their lives within the "closed circle" of femininity—"as a mother, as a wife, and as a lover . . . purely animal and wholly without usefullness" (75)—or they were exceptions to the rule, to be treated like honorary men. In response, Loy urged women not to seek a spurious equality: "Leave off looking to men to find out what you are *not.* Seek within yourselves to find out what you *are.*" As a necessary step on the way to this self-knowledge, she asserted, "Woman must destroy in herself the desire to be loved."

But in reality, few women could forget that they lived in houses in order to dwell in themselves, and fewer still could destroy the desire to be loved, no matter how lucid they might be. Loy's poems published in the New York little magazines during the war both stressed the cultural limitations imposed upon a woman's vision of her potential and analyzed the psychological effects of her acquiescence in the feminine role, in ways that anticipate the contemporary psychoanalytic theories of femininity as a masquerade. For example, in both "One O'Clock at Night" and "Sketch of a Man on a Platform," the female speaker studies a Marinettilike orator in his own terms, the better to undermine his assumptions about gender by showing how well she mimes the behavior expected of her. Many readers of her "Love Songs," a devastatingly honest attempt to at least understand the desire to be loved, were shocked by what one of her first editors (Alfred Kreymborg) called "her utter nonchalance in revealing the secrets of sex." He added, "To reduce eroticism to the sty was an outrage, and to do so without verbs, sentence structure, punctuation, even more offensive. . . . Had a man written these poems, the town might have viewed them with comparative comfort" (488–489). By the time she arrived in New York in 1916, her reputation as a contemporary of Apollinaire, Marinetti, and Stein had stirred considerable interest among the experimentalist poets who published with her in Kreymborg's *Others, Rogue, Trend,* and the *Little Review,* while the general public, when it noticed, denounced such poetry as "erotic and erratic."[7]

The history of Loy's subsequent poetic reputation and neglect is entwined with the poetic careers of the *Others* poets—Williams, Moore, and Pound—with whose writing her own showed the greatest affinity. All three recognized her European sensibility and valued her original manner of translating developments in modern art into a colloquial free verse flexible enough to suggest conceptual complexity as well as sensory immediacy. Williams showed particular interest in her adaptation of the futurist idea that art should posit an equation between the activity of the outside world and the activity of the mind, and he learned from her unusual spacing, typography, and disdain for punctuation and connectives. Moore, always reticent in her relations with other poets, nevertheless admired the "sliced and cylindrical, complicated yet simple use of words by Mina Loy" (121) while remaining in awe of her personal style. Pound championed her work (along with Moore's) as an example of the new kind of intelligent poetry that he called "logopoeia or poetry that is akin to nothing but language, which is a dance of the intelligence among words and ideas."[8]

Writing in 1918, Pound was certain that both Moore and Loy were "among the followers of Jules Laforgue," since, in his view, they wrote "not the popular language of any country but an international tongue common to the excessively cultivated." Pound admired their "attitude of mind," typified, for him, by literary sophistication and self-mocking irony: writing like theirs could participate in the cultural critique of postwar society. But Pound's sponsorship of their poetry because of its intelligence—"the utterance of clever people in despair, . . . a mind cry, more than a heart cry"—is notable precisely because he seems to have ignored the fact that they were intelligent *women,* whose "logopoeia" was as gender-conscious as his own was gender-blind. Like Marinetti, Pound was sure that "intelligence" was coded "masculine," and for this reason, gender as an aspect of modernist poetics never suggested itself.[9]

Nevertheless, in a general way, Pound recognized in Loy's language as well as in her technique a break with the "emotional slither" of nineteenth-century poetry. And he continued to assert that, among American poets, only Williams, Moore, and Loy "can write anything of interest in verse" (*Letters* 168). He was so enthusiastic about Loy's poem "The Effectual Marriage" (1910) that he reprinted it twice in his own edited version, retitled "The Ineffectual Marriage" (*Instigations* 240, *Profile* 67–68). In the original version, the marriage of Gina and Miovanni is shown as an apparently successful example of the heterosexual arrangements that Loy denounced in her "Feminist Manifesto": Gina is content to play the role of the parasitical "female" on whom her scholarly husband depends for sensual and spiritual comforts.[10] From within the "closed circle" of her purely feminine existence, she writes the occasional poem on the back on the milk bill: "Something not too difficult to / Learn by heart." In Pound's version, however, the wife's experience is reduced to a minimum, while the husband's self-importance is pointed up through the insistent use of pedantic polysyllables such as Miovanni himself might favor. In both versions, we infer that all is not wedded bliss through Loy's self-deflating magniloquence, which undermines itself while stressing both partners' isolation in what could have been a complementary relationship: "What had Miovanni made of his ego / In his library? what had Gina wondered among the pots and pans? / One never asked the other." As a depiction of sexual (dis)union, Loy's poem fulfilled Pound's idea of logopoeia's critical power, whether or not he attended to her outspokenly feminist treatment of the subject. (Pound's version is reprinted here.)

From 1917 through 1920, Loy turned increasingly to postwar social disarray. *The Pamperers,* a play published in the *Dial*'s "Modern Forms" section, ridicules avant gardists in general and the futurists in particular. Similarly, in the satiric poem "Lions' Jaws," Loy sends up Marinetti as a traveling salesman with "novelties from / Paris in his pocket," along with her own participation in his "dynamic carnaval" as "secret service buffoon to the Women's Cause." The manifestolike pamphlet *Psycho-Democracy,* her most ambitious social critique, is a personal response to postwar chaos: instead of "the belligerent masculine social ideal" of militarism, she calls for an international movement "to focus human reason on the conscious direction of evolution" (of both the individual and the collective), since she is sure that "our social institutions of today will cause future generations to roar with laughter" (4).

Although these concerns did not disappear from her writing during the 1920s, her subject matter was increasingly drawn from her defense of modernism and her related critique of the Symbolists' and the Decadents' aesthetic tenets. *Lunar Baedecker,* her 1923 book of poems (published in Paris by Robert McAlmon's Contact Editions with the title misspelled), eliminated a number of early poems, particularly those written about the effects of femininity's "closed circle" on the lives of women. Both the selections and their order give prominence to her vision of the artist's special calling and social autonomy, familar concepts which she adapts to praise a modernism based on the aesthetic practice of the cosmopolitan artistic circles of which she became a member after resettling in Paris.

In "The Metaphysical Pattern of Aesthetics," an unpublished essay, Loy distinguishes between representational subject matter and modernist abstraction by suggesting that the latter provides a map of the artist's mind or a "purely metaphysical structure of an aesthetic creation." A series of poems on the work of her fellow modernists (Wyndham Lewis, Stein, Joyce, and Brancusi) can be read as related mappings of their respective "phenomenal dynamics." In "Joyce's Ulysses," the controversial novel defies "England / the sadistic mother" when its author, the "rejector–recreator" of language "flashes the giant reflector / on the sub rosa" of the imperial British mind. Worse still, Joyce reveals "The word made flesh / and feeding upon itself" and unveils "The Spirit / . . . impaled upon the phallus," a view of language calculated to offend the censorious middle-class morality that both writers rejected. Similarly, "Brancusi's Golden Bird" maps Loy's own aesthetic in its homage to the sculptor's creation: "A naked orientation / unwinged unplumed / the ultimate rhythm / has lopped the extremities / of crest and claw / from / the nucleus of flight." The poem enacts Brancusi's revelation of form in its own medium, effecting a transfer from the "polished hyperaesthesia" of the sculpture's metallic surface to the sounds and textures of poetic language. Yet, given their high modernist commitment to a view of creativity as self-referential and socially autonomous, it is worth noting that both poems (reprinted below) were published as defenses of works that ran afoul of the American censors, who had already condemned *Ulysses* as obscene and would soon rule that Brancusi's work lacked artistic merit.[11] Loy was fully aware that modernism was involved in an ongoing dialogue with the very audience that it appeared to disdain.

In 1926, when "Brancusi's Golden Bird" caused nearly as much bewilderment as the sculpture itself, Yvor Winters stated that of all the *Others* writers ("the most interesting single group manifestation that has yet occurred in American verse"), Williams and Loy had the most to offer younger American poets (499). Yet by the early 1930s, when she was publishing infrequently, literary fashion had already begun to shift away from high modernist abstractions toward subjects of apparently greater social significance. Although a trickle of poems appeared in little magazines after Loy settled in New York in 1936, apart from Kenneth Rexroth and, later, Jonathan Williams (who published *Lunar Baedeker & Time-Tables* in 1958), few saw fit to include her in the modernist pantheon, especially as constructed within academia. The reasons for this neglect are complex. Loy's writing developed in and reflected a cosmopolitan artistic context that was in tension with her English origins and lay somewhat outside the frame of reference of the New Criticism, which would have looked askance at her subject matter had its spokesmen looked at all. Until very recently, Loy's idiosyncratic crossings of "Paris" and "Italy," metaphysics and feminism, have made numerous readers uneasy. But with the advent of feminist criticism, the reshaping of our ideas about what constitutes modernism, and the 1980 publication of Virginia Kouidis's *Mina Loy: American Modernist Poet* followed two years later by *The Last Lunar Baedeker,* the tide is turning as far as her reputation is concerned. Hugh Kenner has praised Loy's "agile, hard, unslushy wit" in Poundian terms (30), Jerome Rothenberg has claimed that the "counterpoetics" of writers such as Loy "presents . . . a fundamentally new view of the relationship between consciousness, language & poetic structure" (xvi), and Jed Rasula has stated that "reading Mina Loy is one of the most direct encounters with modernism . . . like defusing an old but still live time bomb" (164). Indeed, we are finally in a position to see that hers is "a voice that was not only ahead if its own time but one which is still out in front" (Morse 14), and that we, as readers, must go into training to catch up with her.

NOTES

1. Margaret Johns, "Free Footed Verse Is Danced in Ridgefield, N. J.," *New York Tribune* 29 June 1915, sec. 3, 2; anon., "Do You Strive to Capture the Symbols of Your Reactions? If Not You Are Quite Old Fashioned," *New York Evening Sun* 13 Feb. 1917, 10. For more on the social and intellectual contexts in which Loy's poetry was read, see Burke, "New Poetry" 37–47.

2. The epigraph is reprinted as "Gertrude Stein" in Loy, *Last Lunar Baedeker* 26.

3. Both sequences appear in Loy, *Last Lunar Baedeker,* as does all writing by Loy subsequently cited unless otherwise noted. For a full discussion of Stein's significance for Loy, see Burke, "Without Commas."

4. Loy to Mabel Dodge, February 1914, in Collection of American Literature, Beinecke Library, Yale University (henceforth Yale Collection).

5. Loy to Carl Van Vechten, c. 1915, Yale Collection.

6. See the discussion of Marinetti's "art of making manifestos" in Perloff 81–115. I share Perloff's view of prewar Futurism as "the brief utopian phase of early Modernism when artists felt themselves to be on the verge of a new age that would be more exciting, more promising, more inspiring than any preceding one" (36). On Loy's response to Futurist aesthetic theory, see Burke, "Becoming" 140–145.

7. See Burke, "New Poetry" 44.

8. Pound, " 'Others' " 57; reprinted in this volume.

9. For a full discussion of Pound's theory of gender, see Burke, "Getting Spliced."

10. "Gina" and "Miovanni" are inversions of "Mina" and "Giovanni," almost certainly the scholarly critic (and for a brief period, futurist) Giovanni Papini, with whom Loy fell in love and had an affair.

11. See Kouidis 121 for a discussion of Loy's poem in this context.

WORKS CITED

Burke, Carolyn. "Becoming Mina Loy." *Women's Studies* 7 (1980):136–150.

———. "Getting Spliced: Modernism and Sexual Difference." *American Quarterly* 39 (1987):98–121.

———. "The New Poetry and the New Woman." In *Coming to Light: American Women Poets in the Twentieth Century*, ed. Diane W. Middlebrook and Marilyn Yalom, 37–57. Ann Arbor: U of Michigan P, 1985.

———. "Without Commas: Gertrude Stein and Mina Loy." *Poetics Journal* 4(1984):43–52.

Kenner, Hugh. "To Be the Brancusi of Poetry." *New York Times Book Review* 16 May 1982:30.

Kouidis, Virginia. *Mina Loy, American Modernist Poet*. Baton Rouge: Louisiana State UP, 1980.

Kreymborg, Alfred. *Our Singing Strength: An Outline of American Poetry (1620–1930)*. New York: Coward McCann, 1929.

Loy, Mina. *The Last Lunar Baedeker*. Ed. Roger L. Conover. Highlands, N.C.: Jargon Society, 1982.

———. *Lunar Baedecker*. Dijon: Contact: 1923.

———. *Lunar Baedeker & Time-Tables*. Highlands, N.C.: Jonathan Williams, 1958.

———. "The Metaphysical Pattern in Aesthetics." Yale Collection.

———. *The Pamperers*. *Dial* 69(1920):65–78.

———. *Psycho-Democracy*. Florence: Tipografia Peri & Rossi, 1920. *Little Review* 8(1921):14–19.

Marinetti, Filippo Tommaso. *Selected Writing*. Ed. R. W. Flint. New York: Farrar, Straus and Giroux, 1972.

Moore, Marianne. *The Complete Prose of Marianne Moore*. Ed. Patricia C. Willis. New York: Viking P, 1986.

Morse, Samuel French. "The Rediscovery of Mina Loy and the Avant Garde." *Wisconsin Studies in Contemporary Literature* 2 (1961): 12–19.

Perloff, Marjorie. *The Futurist Moment: Avant-Garde, Avant-Guerre, and the Language of Rupture*. Chicago: U of Chicago P, 1986.

Pound, Ezra. *Instigations*. New York: Boni and Liveright, 1920.

———. *The Letters of Ezra Pound, 1907–1941*. Ed. D. D. Paige. New York: Harcourt Brace, 1950.

———. " 'Others'." *Little Review* 4(1918):57–58.

———. *Profile: An Anthology Collected in 1931*. Milan: John Scheiwiller, 1932.

Rasula, Jed. "A Renaissance of Women Writers." *Sulfur* 7(1983):160–172.

Rexroth, Kenneth. "Les Lauriers Sont Coupés." *Circle* 1(1944):69–72.

Rothenberg, Jerome (ed.). *Revolution of the Word: A New Gathering of American Avant Garde Poetry, 1914–1945.* New York: Seabury, 1974.
Stein, Gertrude. *The Autobiography of Alice B. Toklas. Selected Writings of Gertrude Stein,* ed. Carl Van Vechten. New York: Vintage, 1972.
Winters, Yvor. "Mina Loy." *Dial* 80(1926):496–499.

Gertrude Stein

1.

Some years ago I left Gertrude Stein's Villino in Fiesole with a manuscript she had given me.

"Each one is one. Each one is being the one each one is being. Each one is one is being one. Each one is being the one that one is being. Each one is being one each one is one.

"Each one is one. Each one is very well accustomed to be one. Each one is very well accustomed to be that one. Each one is one." (Galeries Lafayette). Compare with "Vanity of vanity; vanity of vanities; all is vanity" of Ecclesiastes.

This is when Bergson was in the air, and his beads of Time strung on the continuous flux of Being, seemed to have found a literary conclusion in the austere verity of Gertrude Stein's theme—'Being' as the absolute occupation.

For by the intervaried rhythm of this monotone mechanism she uses for inducing a continuity of awareness of her subject, I was connected up with the very pulse of duration.

The core of a "Being" was revealed to me with uninterrupted insistence.

The plastic static of the ultimate presence of an entity.

And the innate tempo of a life poured in alert refreshment upon my mentality.

Gertrude Stein was making a statement, a reiterate statement . . . basic and bare . . . a statement reiterate ad absurdum, were it not for the interposing finger of creation.

For Gertrude Stein obtains the *belle matière* of her unsheathing of the fundamental with a most dexterous discretion in the placement and replacement of her phrases, of inversion of the same phrase sequences that are so closely matched in level, as the fractional tones in primitive music or the imperceptible modelling of early Egyptian sculpture.

The flux of Being as the ultimate presentation of the individual, she endows with the rhythmic concretion of her art, until it becomes as a polished stone, a bit of the rock of life—yet not of polished surface, of polished nucleus.

This method of conveyance through duration recurs in her later work. As she progresses it becomes amplified, she includes an increasing number of the attributes of continuity.

The most perfect example of this method is *Italians* where not only are you pressed close to the insistence of their existence, but Gertrude Stein through her process of reiteration gradually, progressively rounds them out, decorates them with their biological insignia.

They revolve on the pivot of her verbal construction like animated sculpture, their life protracted into their entourage through their sprouting hair . . . a longer finger nail; their sound, their smell.

"They have something growing on them, some of them, and certainly many others would not be wanting such things to be growing out of them that is to say growing on them.

"It makes them these having such things, makes them elegant and charming, makes them ugly and disgusting, makes them clean looking and sleek and rich and dark, makes them dirty-looking and fierce looking."

How simply she exposes the startling dissimilarity in the aesthetic dénouement of our standardized biology.

They solidify in her words, in ones, in crowds, complete with racial impulses. They are of one, infinitesimally varied in detail, racial consistency. Packed by her poised paragraphs into the omniprevalent plasm of life from which she evolves all her subjects and from which she never allows them to become detached. In Gertrude Stein life is never detached from Life; it spreads tenuous and vibrational between each of its human exteriorizations and the other.

"They seem to be, and that is natural because what is in one is carried over to the other one by it being in the feeling of the one looking at the one and then at the other one.

"They are talking, often talking and they are doing things with pieces of them while they are talking and they are things sounding like something, they are then sounding in a way that is a natural way for them to be sounding, they are having noise come out of them in a natural way for them to have noise come out of them."

It may be impossible for our public inured to the unnecessary nuisances of journalism to understand this literature, but it is a literature reduced to a basic significance that could be conveyed to a man on Mars.

In her second phase . . . the impressionistic, Gertrude Stein entirely reverses this method of conveyance through duration. She ignores duration and telescopes time and space and the subjective and objective in a way that obviates interval and interposition. She stages strange triangles between the nominative and his verb and irruptive co-respondents.

It has become the custom to say of her that she has done in words what Picasso has one with form. There is certainly in her work an interpenetration of dimensions analogous to Cubism.

One of her finest "impressions" is *Sweet Tail.* "Gypsies," it begins.

"Curved Planes.

"Hold in the coat. Hold back ladders and a creation and nearly sudden extra coppery ages with colors and a clean gyp hoarse. Hold in that curl with the good man. Hold in cheese. . . ." A fracturing impact of the mind with the occupation, the complexion, the cry of the gypsies.

Cubistically she first sees the planes of the scene. Then she breaks them up into their detail. Gypsies of various ages bring ladders for the construction of . . . something. "A clean gyp hoarse." Here it, see it, attribute it, that voice?

The occurrences of "Hold in" impress me as a registration of her mind dictating the control of the planes of the pictures it is so rapidly and unerringly putting together; no, *choosing* together. "A little pan with a yell," is a protraction of "The clean gyp hoarse," accelerated, in her chase of sounds among solids by telescoping the "little pan" with the animation of the gypsy holding it.

Per contra in "Wheel is not on a donkey and never never," her reason disengages the donkey and cart from her primary telescopic visualization.

It is the variety of her mental processes that gives such fresh significance to her words, as if she had got them out of bed early in the morning and washed them in the sun.

They make a new appeal to us after the friction of an uncompromised intellect has scrubbed the meshed messes of traditional associations off them.

As in the little phrase "A wheel is not on a donkey," . . . a few words she has lifted out of the ridiculous, to replace them in the sanctuary of pure expression.

"A green, a green coloured oak, a handsome excursion, a really handsome log, a regulation to exchange oars." An association of nomadic recreation and rest through the idea "wood" oak, log, oars.

Again how admirably the essences of romance are collected in the following curve-course that for beauty of expression could hardly be excelled.

"The least license is in the eyes which make strange the less sighed hole which is nodded and leaves the bent tender . . . it makes medium and egg-light and not nearly so much."

To obtain movement she has shaped her words to the pattern of a mobile emotion, she has actually bent the tender and with medium and egg-light and not really so much, reconstructed the signal luminous, the form, the semi-honesty of the oval eye.

But in "simple cake, simple cake, relike a gentle coat, . . . seal it blessing and that means gracious, not gracious suddenly with spoons and flavour but all the same active. Neglect a pink white neglect it for blooming on a thin piece of steady slim poplars." Round the cake, the sociable center, the tempo of the gypsy feast changes . . . "seal it blessing," do gypsies say grace or is blessing again the bowing pattern of feeding merging with spoons and flavour?

The "gentle coating" . . . icing? . . . of the cake confuses with the greater whiteness of the sky wedged between poplars that are depicted with the declivity of line of Van Gogh. "Neglect it. . . ." Again a direction for the mind to keep the plates of the picture relatively adjusted.

"And really all the chance is in deriding cocoanuts real cocoanuts with strawberry tunes and little ice cakes with feeding feathers and peculiar relations of nothing which is more blessed than replies."

In "feeding feathers" the omission of the woman between her feeding and her feathers results in an unaccustomed juxtaposition of words of associating a subject with a verb which does not in fact belong to it, but which visually, is instantaneously connected.

This process of disintegration and reintegration, this intercepted cinema of suggestion urges the reactions of the reader until the theme assumes an unparallelled clarity of aspect. Compare it with George Borrow's gypsy classic and consider the gain in time and spontaneity that such abridged associations as derision and cocoanuts, strawberry tints dissolving into tune and above all the snatched beauty of the bizarrerie feeding affords us.

And these eyes, these feathers are continuously held in place by the progressive introduction of further relationships, "And nearly all heights hats which are so whiled. . . ." And no one comes to realize how Gertrude Stein has builded up her gypsies, accent upon accent, colour on colour, bit by bit.

Perhaps for this reason it is not easy for the average reader to "get" Gertrude Stein, because for the casual audience entity seems to be eclipsed by excresence. Truly with this method of Gertrude Stein's a goodly amount of incoherent debris gets littered around the radium that she crushes out of phrased consciousness.

"Like message cowpowder and sashes sashes, like pedal causes and so sashes, and pedal cause kills surgeon in six safest six, pedal sashes."

Now that's just like Gertrude Stein! Even as I type this suspect excerpt it clarifies as the subconscious code message of an accident. The sending for the surgeon. The first aid with gypsy sashes.

The cow that . . . like gunpowder . . . may be a cause for being killed . . . but if in in six minutes the surgeon arrives . . . the probability of safety. The simultaneity of velocity-binding, sashes-pedalling of messenger's bicycle.

2.

There is no particular advantage in groping for subject matter in a literature that is sufficiently satisfying as verbal design, but the point at issue, for those who are confident of their ability to write Gertrude Stein with their minds shut, is that her design could not attain the organic consistency that it does, were there no intention back of it.

Kenneth Burke deducts from her effectiveness the satisfying climax of subject. For it is rather the debris, always significant with that rhythm he analyses that has attracted his attention, than the sudden potential, and, to a mind attuned protracted illuminations of her subject which form the very essence of Gertrude Stein's art.

Nevertheless it is disconcerting to follow with great elation certain passages

I have quoted when unexpectedly time and space crash into a chaos of dislocate ideas, while conversation would seem to proceed from the radiophonic exchange of the universe. Yet you *come up for air* with the impression that you have experienced something more extensively than you ever have before . . . but what? The everything, the everywhere, the simultaneity of function.

But these concussions become less frequent as again and again one reads her, and each time her subject shows still more coherence. One must in fact go into training to get Gertrude Stein.

Often one is liable to overlook her subject because her art gives such tremendous proportions to the negligible that one can not see it all at once. As for instance in "Handing a lizard to anyone is a green thing receiving a curtain. The shape is not present and the sensible way to have agony is not precautious. Then the skirting is extreme and there is a lilac smell and no ginger. Halt and suggest a leaf which has no circle and no singular center, this has that show and does judge that there is a need of moving toward the equal height of a hot sinking surface."

To interpret her description of the lizard you have to place yourself in the position of both Gertrude Stein and the lizard at once, so intimate is the liaison of her observation with the sheer existence of her objective, that she invites you into the concentric vortex of consciousness involved in the most trifling transactions of incident.

Her action is inverted in the single sentence "Handling a lizard . . etc." Where the act of the subject transforms into the possibility of the object.

"The change is not present. . . ." She has taken on the consciousness or rather the unconsciousness of the lizard in the inexplicable predicament of its transportation.

And in "The sensible way to have agony is not precautious," it's struggle to retrieve its habitude.

How much beauty she can make out of so little. After the "green thing receiving the curtain," this comparison of a lizard to a leaf.

"This has that show and does judge;" again the inversion. She is turning the lizard outside in, its specular aspect fuses with its motor impulses and now she represents the palm of the hand to you as a land surveyor might a prospect.

To the advocates of Stein prohibition I must confess that the line "then the skirting is extreme and there is a lilac smell and no ginger" is not clear to me; the immediate impression I receive is that the puffing of the frightened reptile's belly is being likened to a billowing skirt that the lilac shadow on the flesh of the hand shunts into the smell of the lizard. . . . But why the ginger? Something suggested ginger to the author and escaped her, so she denies the ginger. The greatest incertitude experienced while reading Gertrude Stein is the indecision as to whether you are psychoanalysing her, or she, you.

There is a good deal of ginger floating around in this book of *Geography and Plays,* as are also pins stuck about. The ginger so far escapes me, the pins I accept as an acute materialization of the concentric.

Compare this lizard episode with an example of a dream animated by the projection of the intellect into the intimacy of the inanimate.

"The season gliding and the torn hangings receiving mending, all this shows an example, it shows the force of sacrifice and likeness and disaster and a reason." *Tender Buttons.*

Gertrude Stein possesses a power of evocation that gives the same lasting substance to her work that is found in the *Book of Job.*

Take the colossal verse

> "He spreadeth the north over the empty place, and hangeth the earth upon nothing." *Job*

Which has the same mechanism as the eye-egg light episode and the lizard-curtain episode, and the analogy to Gertrude Stein is obvious in such passages as the following:

> "Am I a sea or a whale
> Darkness itself
>
> Who can stay the bottles of heaven
> The chambers of heaven." *Job*

Like all modern art, this art of Gertrude Stein makes a demand for a creative audience, by providing a stimulus, which although it proceeds from a complete aesthetic organization, leaves us unlimited latitude for personal response.

For each individual with his particular experience she must induce varying interpretations, for the logician she must afford generous opportunity for inferences entirely remote from those of the artist approaching her writings. There is a scholarly manipulation of the inversion of ideas, parallel to Alice In the Looking Glass; one is nonplussed by the refutation of logic with its myriad insinuations that surpass logic, which Gertrude Stein in her *Plays* achieves through syncopation.

I point these things out in passing, to draw attention to the class of material she brings to the manufacture of her new literature. If you can come to think of a philosophy, apart from the intrication of your reason, leaving on your memory an abstract impress of its particularity as a perfume or a voice might do, you can begin to sort out the vital elements in Gertrude Stein's achievement.

She has tackled an aesthetic analysis of the habits of consciousness in its lair, prior to the traditionalization of its evolution.

Perhaps that ideal enigma that the modern would desire to solve is, "what would we know about anything, if we didn't know anything about it?" . . . to track intellection back to the embryo.

For the spiritual record of the race is this nostalga for the crystallization of the irreducible surplus of the abstract. The bankruptcy of mysticism declared itself in an inability to locate this divine irritation, and the burden of its debt to the evolution of consciousness has devolved upon the abstract art.

The pragmatic value of modernism lies in its tremendous recognition of the compensation due to the spirit of democracy. Modernism is a prophet crying in the wilderness of stabilized culture that humanity is wasting its aesthetic time. For there is a considerable extension of time between the visits to the picture gallery, the museum, the library. It asks "what is happening to your aesthetic consciousness during the long long intervals?"

The flux of life is pouring its aesthetic aspect into your eyes, your ears—and you ignore it because you are looking for your canons of beauty in some sort of frame or glass case or tradition. Modernism says: Why not each one of us, scholar or bricklayer, pleasurably realize all that is impressing itself upon our subconscious, the thousand odds and ends which make up your sensory every day life?

Modernism has democratized the subject matter and *la belle matière* of art; through cubism the newspaper has assumed an aesthetic quality, through Cezanne a plate has become more than something to put an apple upon, Brancusi has given an evangelistic import to eggs, and Gertrude Stein has given us the Word, in and for itself.

Would not life be lovelier if you were constantly overjoyed by the sublimely pure concavity of your wash bowls? The tubular dynamics of your cigarette?

In reading Gertrude Stein one is assaulted by a dual army of associated ideas, her associations and your own.

"This is the sun in. This is the lamb of lantern of chalk." Because of the jerk of beauty it contains shoots the imagination for a fraction of a second through associated memories.

Of sun worship. Lamb worship. Lamb of, light of, the world. (Identical in Christian symbolism.) Shepherd carries lantern. The lantern = lamb's eyes. Chalk white of lamb. Lantern sunshine in chalk pit = absolution of whiteness = pascal lamb = chalk easter toy for peasants.

All this is personal, but something of the kind may happen to anyone when Gertrude Stein leaves Grammatical lacunae among her depictions and the mind trips up and falls through into the subconscious source of associated ideas.

The uncustomary impetus of her style accelerates and extends the thought wave until it can vibrate a cosmos from a ray of light on a baa lamb.

This word picture which at first glance would seem to be a lamb being led past a chalk pit by lantern at sun in (down) is revised when on reading further I must conclude that it is still day light and I discover the lamb that carries itself is itself the lantern of chalk.

And here let me proffer my apologies to Gertrude Stein who may have intended the description for . . . a daisy. The sun as the center, chalk as petal white, and the lamb an indication of the season of the year.

Let us leave the ultimate elucidation of Gertrude Stein to infinity.

Apart from all analysis, the natural, the dèbonaire way to appreciate Gertrude Stein, is as one would saunter along a country wayside on a fine day and pluck, for its beauty, an occasional flower. So one sees suddenly:

"He does not look dead at all.
The wind might have blown him."

The Last Lunar Baedeker. Ed. Roger L. Conover. Highlands, N.C.: Jargon Society, 1982. The text here reprinted has been revised to conform to its first publication in *transatlantic review* 2.2 (1924), 305–309, 427–430, with minor corrections of punctuation.

Aphorisms on Futurism

DIE in the Past
Live in the Future.

THE velocity of velocities arrives in starting.

IN pressing the material to derive its essence, matter becomes deformed.

AND form hurtling against itself is thrown beyond the synopsis of vision.

THE straight line and the circle are the parents of design, form the basis of art; there is no limit to their coherent variability.

LOVE the hideous in order to find the sublime core of it.

OPEN your arms to the delapidated; rehabilitate them.

YOU prefer to observe the past on which your eyes are already opened.

BUT the Future is only dark from outside. *Leap* into it—and it EXPLODES with *Light*.

FORGET that you live in houses, that you may live in yourself—

FOR the smallest people live in the greatest houses.

BUT the smallest person, potentially, is as great as the Universe.

WHAT can you know of expansion, who limit yourselves to compromise?

HITHERTO the great man has achieved greatness by keeping the people small.

BUT in the Future, by inspiring the people to expand to their fullest capacity, the great man proportionately must be tremendous—a God.

LOVE of others is the appreciation of oneself.

MAY your egotism be so gigantic that you comprise mankind in your self-sympathy.

THE Future is limitless—the past a trial of insidious reactions.

LIFE is only limited by our prejudices. Destroy them, and you cease to be at the mercy of yourself.

TIME is the dispersion of intensiveness.

THE Futurist can live a thousand years in one poem.

HE can compress every aesthetic principle in one line.

THE mind is a magician bound by assimilations; let him loose and the smallest idea conceived in freedom will suffice to negate the wisdom of all forefathers.

LOOKING on the past you arrive at "Yes," but before you can act upon it you have already arrived at "No."

THE Futurist must leap from affirmative to affirmative, ignoring intermittent negations—must spring from stepping-stone to stone of creative exploration; without slipping back into the turbid stream of accepted facts.

THERE are no excrescences on the absolute, to which man may pin his faith.

TODAY is the crisis in consciousness.

CONSCIOUSNESS cannot spontaneously accept or reject new forms, as offered by creative genius; it is the new form, for however great a period of time it may remain a mere irritant—that molds consciousness to the necessary amplitude for holding it.

CONSCIOUSNESS has no climax.

LET the Universe flow into your consciousness, there is no limit to its capacity, nothing that it shall not re-create.

UNSCREW your capability of absorption and grasp the elements of Life—*Whole*.

MISERY is in the disintegration of Joy; Intellect, of Intuition; Acceptance, of Inspiration.

CEASE to build up your personality with the ejections of irrelevant minds.

NOT to be a cipher in your ambient, But to color your ambient with your preferences.

NOT to accept experience at its face value.

BUT to readjust activity to the peculiarity of your own will.

THESE are the primary tentatives towards independence.

MAN is a slave only to his own mental lethargy.

YOU cannot restrict the mind's capacity.

THEREFORE you stand not only in abject servitude to your perceptive consciousness—

BUT also to the mechanical re-actions of the subconsciousness, that rubbish heap of race-tradition—

AND believing yourself to be free—your least conception is colored by the pigment of retrograde superstitions.

HERE are the fallow-lands of mental spatiality that Futurism will clear—

MAKING place for whatever you are brave enough, beautiful enough to draw out of the realized self.

TO your blushing we shout the obscenities, we scream the blasphemies, that you, being weak, whisper alone in the dark.

THEY are empty except of your shame.

AND so these sounds shall dissolve back to their innate senselessness.

THUS shall evolve the language of the Future.

THROUGH derision of Humanity as it appears—

TO arrive at respect for man as he shall be—

ACCEPT the tremendous truth of Futurism

Leaving all those
                    Knick-knacks.

The Last Lunar Baedeker. 272–275.

The Ineffectual Marriage

So here we might dispense with her
Gina being a female
But she was more than that
Being an incipience   a correlative
an instigation to the reaction of man
From the palpable to the transcendent
Mollescent irritant of his fantasy

Gina had her use   Being useful
contentedly conscious

She flowered in Empyrean
From which no well-mated woman ever returns

Sundays   a warm light in the parlor
From the gritty road   on the white wall
anybody could see it
Shimmered a composite effigy
Madonna   crinolined   a man
hidden beneath her hoop.

Patience said Gina   is an attribute
And she learned   at any hour to offer
The dish   appropriately delectable

What had Miovanni made of his ego
In his library
What had Gina wondered   among the pots and
pans
One never asked the other.

Instigations. Ed. Ezra Pound. New York: Boni and Liveright, 1920. 240.

Joyce's Ulysses

The Normal Monster
sings in the Green Sahara

The voice and offal
of the image of God

make Celtic noises
in these lyrical hells

Hurricanes
of reasoned musics
reap the uncensored earth

The loquent consciousness
of living things
pours in torrential languages

The elderly colloquists
the Spirit and the Flesh
are out of tongue

The Spirit
is impaled upon the phallus

Phoenix
of Irish fires
lighten the Occident

with Ireland's wings
flap pandemoniums
of Olympian prose

and satinize
the imperial Rose
of Gaelic perfumes—
England
the sadistic mother
embraces Erin

Master
of meteoric idiom
present

The word made flesh
and feeding upon itself
with erudite fangs
The sanguine
introspection of the womb

Don Juan
of Judea
upon a pilgrimage
to the Libido

The press
purring
its lullabies to sanity

Christ capitalized
scourging
incontrite usurers of destiny
in hole and corner temples

And hang
The soul's advertisements
outside the ecclesiast's Zoo

A gravid day
spawns
gutteral gargoyles
upon the Tower of Babel

Empyrean emporium
where the
rejector-recreator
        Joyce
flashes the giant reflector
on the sub rosa

The Last Lunar Baedeker. 20–22.

Brancusi's Golden Bird

The toy
become the aesthetic archetype

As if
some patient peasant God
had rubbed and rubbed
the Alpha and Omega
of Form
into a lump of metal

A naked orientation
unwinged   unplumed
the ultimate rhythm
has lopped the extremities
of crest and claw
from
the nucleus of flight

The absolute act
of art

conformed
to continent sculpture
—bare as the brow of Osiris—
this breast of revelation

an incandescent curve
licked by chromatic flames
in labyrinths of reflections

This gong
of polished hyperaesthesia
shrills with brass
as the aggressive light
strikes
its significance

The immaculate
conception
of the inaudible bird
occurs
in gorgeous reticence

The Last Lunar Baedeker. 18–19.

12
Rose Macaulay (1881–1958)

Introduced and Edited by Susan M. Squier

At a London dinner party in 1934, Virginia Woolf and Rose Macaulay debated the unity of character. "I'm a mere battlefield of opposite people—my ancestors," Macaulay assured Woolf. "Take this as a simple illustration: I want to walk all day alone: but I also want to drive my car." Woolf later recalled, "We called it having 'battling lizards.' That made us laugh" (Woolf, *Diary* 4, 249). The phrase captures Macaulay's complex relation both to the high modernist tradition and to the female modernism so profoundly shaped by Macaulay's dinner companion, Virginia Woolf.

Macaulay attributed her "battling lizards" to the impact of ancestry upon her character. Yet we could attribute to nurture as well as nature Macaulay's ambivalence toward the British institutions that formed her. Born of a large and distinguished Cambridge family full of schoolmasters and clergymen, Macaulay belonged to the British intellectual aristocracy. Despite her orthodox heritage, childhood experiences angled her perspective, training her sensibility for the acerbic fiction, witty essays, and humorous travel writings for which she would be celebrated in her maturity.

We can locate in Macaulay's childhood and youth the origin of some of her "battling lizards." She spent her childhood in Italy, where the family lived for her mother's health, and learned there to feel impatience with England's pallid propriety. The devastating murder of her soldier brother Aulay led her bitterly to resent woman's enforced domesticity, resentment that increased with the death of her friend Rupert Brooke in World War I. Later, her love affair with a married man, Gerald O'Donovan, caused her lengthy exile from the Anglican church (to which she had first been drawn following the death of her brother) and her lifelong, unfashionable preoccupation with religious issues.

Macaulay's childhood and adult experiences did not produce a simple binary position of alienation from authority, however. She held herself aloof not only from the regnant social and aesthetic institutions of Victorian England but, eventually, from the social and aesthetic positions of her contemporaries. As a young adult she was part of a circle of experimental modernists. On her friend Rupert Brooke she modeled Basil Doye, the hero of her 1915 novel *Non-Combatants and Others,* and when she came to London in 1916 she frequented the Kensington salon held by Naomi Royde-Smith. There she met a diverse group of writers, both celebrated and obscure: Hugh Walpole, Storm Jameson, Arnold Bennett, W. B. Yeats, Edith Sitwell, Aldous Huxley, John Middleton Murry, J. C. Squire of the *New Statesman,* and her particular hero, Walter de la Mare. Following a fight with Royde-Smith in the early 1920s, she drifted over to join another group of friends: Dorothy Brooke, Humbert Wolfe, Victor Gollanczs, Lancelot Sieveking, Viola Garvin. Macaulay was acquainted with Joyce, Beerbohm, Priestley. Her nodding acquaintance with Leonard and Virginia Woolf in the 1920s would grow into the closer friendship with Virginia of the 1930s (see Smith). Yet the "battling lizards" character marked Macaulay in this era, too. Though she was a part of the milieu of literary modernism, she still felt a distance from modernist concerns and tone, a result of her religious preoccupation and the reticence demanded by her love affair with O'Donovan. Reading Macaulay, we must do battle with her battling lizards, to tease apart the strands of female modernism from the orthodoxy of one who, as Woolf bitingly wrote, "likes authority; loves Winchester Oxford & the very urbane intellectual aristocracy" (Woolf 250).

The selections included here exhibit Macaulay's particularly conflicted, complex female modernism, as it figured in her war fiction (*Non-Combatants and Others* [1916] and *Told by an Idiot* [1923]) and her essays (*Personal Pleasures* [1935]). Certain themes dominant in the discourse appear here: the variety of women's responses to war, including women's complicity with and attraction to war making; the politics of canon creation; the relation between gender and literary style.[1] Other themes, less typical of female modernism, express the concerns that kept Macaulay from meshing seamlessly with her male or female modernist colleagues or—because of our postmodern affiliations—with us: Macaulay's turn to religion to express a prophetic critique of patriarchal society within a discourse previously disabling for women; her preoccupation with the literary marketplace; her willingness to subordinate critical analysis to breezy commentary, perhaps as a Trojan horse solution to the problem of publishers' restrictions on female voice and subject matter.

"Afternoon Out," from Macaulay's autobiographical war novel, *Non-*

Combatants and Others (1916), exemplifies one of the distinctive contributions of female modernism to the literature of war: the linking—and consequent challenging—of the conventions of gender and war. Just as "Violette," the conventional bourgeois household in which the heroine, Alix, lodges, forbids discussion of the biological facts of reproduction, so wartime conventions proscribe encounters between Nicholas's German friend and the Belgian refugees, both temporarily lodging with him. Yet despite the conventions that would obscure them, Alix's conversation with her brother acknowledges the facts of love and war: that "men's" babies are born from women's bodies; that both "the enemy" and "the ally" may be people whose "intentions are excellent." Most disagreeably, their conversation reveals that unless their friends intervene the wartime British authorities may put innocent people in concentration camps. The breezy tone belies the seriousness of Macaulay's assault on the codes governing gender and war relations, codes that divide the topics for conversation into "men's" and "mixed company," and that distinguish friend from foe, combatant from noncombatant.

While the Great War definitively undercut literary celebrations of the glories of battle, in this excerpt Macaulay skewers a mythology that persisted: the notion that war improves literature by forcing writers to confront the ultimate meaning of life. To *The Effects of War on Literature,* with its grandiloquent forecast for the epic greatness of postwar literature, her character Nicholas proposes to respond with a literary series of his own. His invention, *Some Further Effects,* is "designed to damp the spirits of the sanguine" by revealing the deeply destructive effects of war on literature: the proliferation of third-rate "patriotic claptrap" and the difficulty of sustaining intelligent vision during wartime disruption. Macaulay here takes issue with the critical canon that continues to favor war literature even in the wake of the Great War. Instead, she argues that the shattering distraction of wartime is fatal to art: "the first-rate people, both the combatants and non-combatants, are too much disgusted, too upset, to do first-rate work." Macaulay would return in 1941 to the theme of the aesthetic disruption caused by war, contributing a short story, "Miss Anstruther's Letters," to *London Calling,* a collection edited by Storm Jameson, a fellow member of Naomi Royde-Smith's salon of the twenties (Smith 159).

The human need for a retreat from the tumult of war provides the preacher's text in the second excerpt from *Non-Combatants and Others.* The theme of religion's inadequate response to the chaos of the Great War anticipates Eliot and Waugh, but the particular twist in Macaulay's treatment of it illuminates her unique position within female modernism. Macaulay here joins other modernist women writers, among them Woolf and Jameson, in the reevaluation and reframing of religious discourse to accommodate feminist principles. First, like Woolf in "Thoughts on Peace in an Air Raid," she evokes Blake's touchstone passage, "I will not cease from mental fight / Nor let my sword sleep in my hand, / till we have built Jerusalem / in England's green and pleasant land."[2] Yet, while Woolf uses this text to build an alternative feminist vision of antiwar mental battle, Macaulay stops short of a feminist revision of her religious (and literary) text. Instead, she engages religious discourse to point out its problems and potential. Although the convention-ridden inhabitants of Violette commend the service placidly, objecting only to the preacher's habit of presenting too many "ideas," Alix marvels that the religious discourse is "dynamite," disconcerting in its use of "words she didn't like, such as tribulation and grace," but potentially both destructive and liberating.

Jameson's autobiography, *No Time like the Present* (1933), offers another instance of the feminist reconstruction of religion in its cry, "Why don't they preach something in their churches which a grown woman could believe in without doing violence to all her other beliefs?" (160). Macaulay anticipates Jameson's indictment of religion for its incompatibility with feminist principles. Yet Macaulay and Jameson differ on the nature of these feminist principles as well as on the war position they would advocate for women. In her autobiography, Jameson argues forcibly for what we would now identify as an essentialist vision of feminist pacifism:

> There is a peculiar horror in the notion of women butchering their fellows—as if it were a self-abuse. As I think it must be, for a woman. . . . If civilisation as we know it ends in poison gas, the fault will be in part ours, because we have taken a hand in the game only as following and competing with men: and have not tried consciously to redress the imbalance of a social system shaped and directed by men. (Jameson 277–278, 280)

In contrast to Jameson's essentialist vision, in *Non-Combatants and Others* Macaulay presents pacifism as the outcome not of gender but of social location (see Jameson 160). The Anglican cleric, West, asserts that war's greatest pain comes to "non-combatants [who] are of all men and women the most miserable. Older men, crocks, parsons, women—God help them" (144). His parting words, as he returns "to his church to fight war by the means he had at his command"—invoke Woolf's vision of a Society of Outsiders united against war. Tentative and offhand, still Macaulay suggests that a revised religion should respond to the needs of women and other outsiders, and so inspire pacifist battle for peace.

Macaulay's 1923 novel, *Told by an Idiot,* returns to the subject of the war to offer a complex portrait of the human response to it, once again deliberately grouping people not by gender but by behavior and social place. Framing her discussion with the weary acknowledgment that "to the majority in each country" the war "was merely a catastrophe, like an earthquake, to be gone through blindly," Macaulay subtly emphasizes the *social* nature of humanity's response to this seemingly natural disaster. She surveys the range of ways women and men respond to war, profiting from it or protesting against it, without attributing to gender the variations in behavior: Maurice is "violently pacifist," while Vicky is "enthusiastically pro-war," and Molly, who drives ambulances in France, "frankly enjoy[s] the war" (293–294).

Yet, while Macaulay refuses to use gender to organize her portrait of the war experiences of Maurice, Vicky, or Molly, a distinctly gender-inflected analysis figures in her treatment of the war's meaning to writers. The conversation between the war poet, Roger, and his mother, Amy, reveals Macaulay's ambivalence, articulating the positions both of postwar male literary orthodoxy and the challenge posed by female modernism. Roger is the prototypical modernist poet, who finds his subject matter and his transgressive posture in the trenches; his mother is a protofeminist reader, whose project is to challenge the ideology of the war narrative to give women their say on war. Amy anticipates contemporary feminist critics' understanding that in both form and content war literature is governed by deeply gendered literary conventions.[3] She challenges Roger's construction of the proper subject matter of war poetry—the experiences (whether glamourous or horrible) of soldiers at the front, but not the privations experienced by noncombatants at home. She further asserts that such a masculinist war narrative is not, as Roger insists, true to life, but true only to his literary ambitions. Roger and his friends have invented the "glamour theory" of war in order to find something new to write about, and their vision of war is less mimetic than intertextual. In this interchange, Macaulay suggests that the nature of war narrative is implicated in the nature of war. Both the old men who glory in war and the young men who write to destroy war's "false glamour," both the disillusioned soldier son and the uncomprehending antiwar mother, are part of the war system. This binary system characterizing male war literature perpetuates the restrictive nature of the canon of war literature, and perhaps even war itself.

We can read Macaulay's multiple positions and her weary, even cynically indifferent stance toward war and peace in *Told by an Idiot* as attempts to escape the self-perpetuating binary construction of the war text.[4] In her refusal to take sides, Macaulay anticipates Woolf's *Three Guineas,* with its eloquent call for female indifference to the male warrior. Woolf argued that indifference was the most potent weapon against the male drive for women's admiration from which wars spring.[5] And in her indifference to literature praising or debunking the glory of war, Macaulay calls into question the central principle of canon creation in Western literature since Virgil: the centrality of the war text.[6]

Macaulay defied the constraints of the canon, not only by resisting the glorification of war but also by choosing to write in uncanonized genres: the personal or topical essay and the travel book. In the twenties, Macaulay published her essays in a tellingly diverse group of papers and journals, including the *Daily Mail,* the *Evening Standard,* and the High Church weekly, the *Guardian* (Smith 106–107). While a number of the essays quite self-consciously address female readers, others seem to construct a male audience; the implied reader also seems to change with the shifts in tone from a female-oriented breezy casualness to an acerbic satire that seems to invoke a male reader. Collected in 1925 by Methuen, her essays were advertised for "intellectual readers," thus perpetuating in the construction of its audience Macaulay's conflicting identifications with male intellectual authority and female intellectual challenge (Smith 108).

"Following the Fashion" demonstrates Macaulay's play with the gendered conventions of voice and subject matter. In this witty essay, Macaulay transposes the defiant self-assertiveness legitimately woman's prerogative when dealing with "trivial" matters of dress or pastime to the more serious literary arena, conflating social with literary conventions. The result is a biting parody of her modernist contemporaries Ernest Hemingway and T. S. Eliot. Beginning by asserting her female right to "follow the fashion" (to wear an elaborate silk dress and high-heeled shoes, to drive a smarter sports car, to paint her nails the latest high-fashion shade), Macaulay broadens her claim of self-determination to include literature, defiantly asserting, "I can write tough-guy stories." The proof follows—a Hemingwayesque tale of drunken driving and an accident leaving "a hell of a mess on the road. One of those little Austins, it was, and all crumpled up, and a man and a girl all crumpled up too" (232). Fashionably, the "tough-guy" protagonist appears most upset by the way his woman companion responds to the accident: "She never stopped crying and talking, it made me tired. Women can't get this: when a thing's done it's done. That's a thing no woman can ever get. They can't let it be. Hell, did I want that bloody little car to muscle into us that way?"(233). Macaulay's feminist sendup of modernist misogyny dramatizes its moral implications while ironically assessing its aesthetic and commercial values. If such "tough-guy stories," like the "tough-guy poem" that follows, can be tossed off at a whim as Macaulay suggests, they possess dubious aesthetic merit. Still their financial worth is evident: they sell—and sell well—to the magazines.

Another such hot property for the magazines is "To the Barricades," with its now familiar modernist multilingualism and its amalgam of military and urban imagery. The parody indicts Eliot's *Waste Land,* revealing its pose of brutally transgressive honesty to be a self-indulgent masquerade. When images of marching feet are jumbled together with "mermen and mermaids and old bowler hats," Macaulay's parody suggests, the poem trivializes both the war between the sexes and the Great War. Recalling the judgment of Amy, the war poet's mother—that reality lies not with the "glamour" of war but with the sacrifices of the noncombatants on the home front—this passage expresses Macaulay's perspective as a female modernist, writing in deliberate opposition to the machismo of her male colleagues.

The element of competitive bravado in Macaulay's parodies resurfaces in her fantasies of writing a critical assessment of contemporary writers or publishing her memoirs without concern for the feelings of her friends: "I shall bring in everyone I know, and have an index, so they can find themselves and their friends" (231). But "Following the Fashion" is more than a slap at other writers for exceeding her in popularity. The parodies of Hemingway and Eliot establish Macaulay's position in opposition to her male modernist contemporaries. In the tone of "Following the Fashion," and in the plot of her "tough-guy" story, she expresses the pleasure in risk-taking that led her to drive a car without taking lessons, to swim avidly, to fly, and even to engage in acts of literary bravado (Smith 149–150). So, an essay criticizing the careless driving of a young nobleman, Lord de Clifford, resulted in her conviction for libel. Yet "Following the Fashion" also recalls the basis for her occasional retreats from such fearless positions: with tragic irony, only three years after the de Clifford lawsuit, her own careless driving was to cause a traffic accident leaving her lover with head injuries, and Macaulay with the permanent conviction that she was to blame (Smith 149–150). Perhaps this experience explains the threat to surrender all fashions—in clothes, cars, or literary creations—with which Macaulay ends "Following the Fashion": "Sometimes I think I will give them all up, and just be dowdy" (236).

Characteristically modernist in its play with the rupture of the aura brought about by the development of photography, "Album," with its wry summation of Macaulay's life by an imaginary descendant, also expresses in its ironic subtext the vision of female modernism. The insistence on periodizing human character ("she just wrote away, as those Georgians did") establishes her debt to Woolf's construction of modern writing in her influential essay "Mr. Bennett and Mrs. Brown," while it testifies to Macaulay's male-identified allegiance to the Georgian group of writers as Woolf constituted it: "Mr. Forster, Mr. Lawrence, Mr. Strachey, Mr. Joyce, and Mr. Eliot" (95). The essay reflects a sense of the impermanence of social structures and values, recalling not only Lawrence's anatomy of love's progress across the generations in *The Rainbow,* but also Woolf's feminist play with gen(d)erational change in *Orlando.*

In addition to revealing the "battling lizards" of her literary affiliation, "Album" also reveals Macaulay's specifically personal anxieties: her scorn for the values of the literary marketplace, and her resulting sense of being a writer without the audience she deeply desired; her contempt for yet concern with material possessions; the conflict between risk-taking and responsibility that throughout her life characterized her relationship with Gerard O'Donovan, leading her to alternate self-assertion with self-repression, religious exile with religious involvement; and finally, her unwillingness to tell the unconventional, even forbidden story of her passionate love affair with a married man, and her recourse instead to the disguised, defensive self-estimation as "dull" or "tiresome," based perhaps on her failure to marry. Gender is central to all these moments of conflict, whether it figures in relation to the construction of a literary audience, the ability to earn money and accumulate wealth as a woman, the expectations a woman relating to her sexual and social behavior, or the literary and social conventions governing her own estimation of the story of her life. So, "Album" is more than a modernist set piece on the photographic image; this casual literary autobiography reveals Macaulay's conflicting male and female literary identifications and her strategies for dealing with them.

Constructing literary modernism based on a selective (male) canon ("like the little old lady on the quiz show, I prefer a reasonable disproportion to an egalitarianism founded upon sentiment"), a critic once dismissed Rose Macaulay as a writer whose range of vision "is confined to the upper middle-class, Anglican-Cambridge stratum of society" and indicated her for her inability "to deal with the disturbing personal repercussions of the world she represents" (Lockwood 136). Twenty years later, with the exclusively white male construction of modernism behind us, we condemn Macaulay *neither* for her privileged, bourgeois, Anglo-Catholic origins *nor* for her failure to solve the gender-inscribed conflicts her background bred. Rather, we appreciate the strategies she forged in the illuminating struggle against her "battling lizards."

NOTES

1. For discussion of the relation between female modernism and war, see Longenbach.
2. For a longer analysis of Woolf's use of this passage, see Squier, *Virginia Woolf and London* 180–189.
3. See Cooper et al.
4. I take this term from the introduction to Cooper et al.
5. For further discussion of this male drive for female glory through making war, see my "Mirroring and Mothering."
6. For the way the Western literary canon reflects a privileging of war and the war text, see "The Con[tra]ception and Contraception of the War Text," by Helen Cooper, Adrienne Munich, and Susan Squier, in Cooper et al. See also Huston.

WORKS CITED

Cooper, Helen, Adrienne Munich, and Susan Squier, eds. *Arms and the Woman: War, Gender and Literary Representation.* Chapel Hill: U of North Carolina P, 1989.

Elshtain, Jean. *Women and War.* New York: Basic Books, 1987.

Huston, Nancy. "Tales of War, Tears of Women." *Women's Studies International Forum* 5. 3–4:271–282.

Jameson, Storm. *No Time like the Present.* New York: Knopf, 1933.

Lockwood, William J. "Rose Macaulay." In *Minor British Novelists,* ed. Charles Alva Hoyt, 135–156. Carbondale: Southern Illinois UP, 1967.

Longenbach, James. "The Women and Men of 1914." In Cooper et al., eds., *Arms and the Woman.*

Macaulay, Rose. *Non-Combatants and Others.* London: Methuen, 1969.

———. *Personal Pleasures.* New York: Macmillan, 1936.

———. *Told by an Idiot.* Garden City, N.Y.: The Dial Press, 1983.

Smith, Constance Babington. *Rose Macaulay.* London: Collins, 1972.

Squier, Susan M. "Mirroring and Mothering: Reflections on the Mirror Encounter Metaphor in Virginia Woolf's Works." *Twentieth Century Literature* 27(Fall 1981):272–288.

———. *Virginia Woolf and London: The Sexual Politics of the City.* Chapel Hill: U of North Carolina P, 1985.
Woolf, Virginia. *The Diary of Virginia Woolf.* Vol. 4. Ed. Anne Olivier Bell. London: Harcourt Brace Jovanovich, 1982.
———. "Mr. Bennett and Mrs. Brown." *The Captain's Death Bed and Other Essays,* 94–119. New York: Harcourt Brace, 1950.

Afternoon Out
(From *Non-Combatants and Others)*

Anyhow, this evening, when Alix came in, he was sulkily, even viciously, turning the pages of a little book he had to review, called (it was one of a series) *The Effects of the War on Literature*. He waved his disengaged hand at Alix, and left it to West, who had much better manners, to get up and put a chair for her and pass and light her a cigarette.

"Did you meet Belgians on the stairs?" inquired West. "They've put some in the rooms above us—the rooms that used to be Hans Bauer's. Five of them, isn't it, Sandomir?"

"Five to rise," Nicholas replied. "A baby due next week, I'm told." (Unarrived babies were among the things not alluded to at Violette in mixed company: no wonder Violette found Nicholas peculiar.)

"It's awkward," West added, lowering his voice and glancing at one of the shut bedroom doors, "because we keep a German, and they can't meet."

"What do you do that for?" asked Alix unsympathetically.

"Awkward, isn't it?" said West. "Because they keep coming to see us—the Belgians, I mean (they like us rather), and he"—he nodded at the bedroom—"has to scoot in there till they're gone. It's like dogs and cats; they simply can't be let to meet."

"Well, I don't know what you want with a German, anyhow."

"He's a friend of ours," explained Nicholas. "He was living in the Golders Green Garden City, and it became so disagreeable for him (they're all so exposed there, you know—nothing hid) that we asked him here instead. If they find him he's afraid they may put him in a concentration camp, and of course if the Belgians sighted him they'd complain. He means no harm, but unfortunately he had a concrete lawn in his garden, about ten feet square, where he used to bounce a ball for exercise. Also he had made a level place on his roof, among Mr. Raymond Unwin's sloping tiles, where he used to sit and admire the distant view through a spyglass. It's all very black against him, but he's a studious and innocent little person really, and he'd hate to be concentrated." ("It would make one feel so like essence of beef, wouldn't it?" West murmured absently.) "He's not a true patriot," went on Nicholas. "He wants the Hohenzollerns to be guillotined and a disruptive country of small warring states to be re-established. He writes articles on German internal reform for the monthly reviews. He calls them 'Kill or Cure,' or, 'A short way with Imperialism,' or some such bloody title. I don't care for his English literary style, but his intentions are excellent. . . . Well, and how's life?" Nicholas turned his small keen blue eyes on his sister. "You look as if you'd been out for a joy-day. You want some more hairpins, but we don't keep any here."

"I've been wiggle-woggling," Alix admitted, and added frankly, "I feel jolly sick after it."

"Our family constitution," said her brother, "is quite unfit for the strains we habitually subject it to. Mine is. I feel jolly sick too. But my indisposition is incurred in the path of duty. I've got to review the things, so I have to read them—a little here and there, anyhow. And then, just as one feels one has reached one's limit, one gets a handbook of wisdom like this, to finish one off."

He read a page at random from *The Effects of the War on Literature.* " 'The war is putting an end to sordidness and littleness, in literature as in other spheres of human life. The second-rate, the unheroic, the earthy, the petty, the trivial—how does it look now, seen in the light of the guns that blaze over Flanders? The guns, shattering so much, have at least shattered falsity in art. We were degenerate, a little, in our literature and in our lives: we have been made great. We are come, surely, to the heroic, the epic pitch of living; if we cannot express it with a voice worthy of it, then indeed it has failed in its deepest lesson to us. We may expect a renascence of beauty worthy to rank with the Romantic Revival born of the French wars. . . .' "

"Who *is* the liar?" asked Alix.

Nicholas named him. "I am thinking," he added, "of starting an Effects of the War series of my own. I shall call it *Some Further Effects.* It will be designed to damp the spirits of the sanguine. I shall do the one on Literature myself. I shall take revenge in it for all the mush I've had to review lately. It's extraordinary, the stream of—of the heroic and the epic, isn't that it—that pours forth daily. The war seems to have given an unhealthy stimulus to hundreds of minds and thousands of pens. One knew it would, of course. No doubt it was the same during the siege of Troy, and all the great wars. Though, thank heaven, we shall never know, as that sort of froth is blown away pretty quick and lost to posterity. It's only the unhappy and contemporaries who get it splashed all over them. And this war is beastlier than any other, so the rubbish is less counteracted by the decent writers. The first-rate people, both the combatants and non-combatants, are too much disgusted, too upset, to do first-rate work. The war's going on, and means to go on, too long. Wells or some one said months ago that people don't so much think about it as get mentally scarred. It's quite true. Lots of people have got to the stage when they can only feel, not think. And the best people hate the whole business much too much to get any 'renascence of beauty' out of it. Who was it who said the other day that the writers to whom war is glamorous aren't as a rule the ones who produce anything fit to call literature. War's an insanity; and insane things, purely destructive, wasteful, hideous, brutal, ridiculous things, aren't what makes art. The war's produced a little fine poetry, among a sea of tosh—a thing here and there; but mostly—oh, good Lord! The flood of cheap-heroics and commonplace patriotic claptrap—it's swept slobbering all over us; there seems no stemming it. Literary revival be hanged. All we had before—and precious little it was—of decent work, clear and alive and sane and close to reality, is being trampled to bits by this—this imbecile brute. And when the time comes to collect the bits and try to begin again, we shan't be able to; they'll be no more spirit in us; we shall be too battered and beaten. . . ." Nicholas, wound up to excitement, was talking too long at a stretch. He often did, being an egoist, and having in his veins the blood of many eloquent and excited revolutionary Poles, who had stood in marketplaces and talked and talked, gesticulating, pouring forth blood and fire. Nicholas, reacting against this fervour, repudiating gesticulation, blood and fire, still talked. . . . But on "battered and beaten" he paused, in disgusted emphasis, and West came in, half absently, still turning the pages of the *Challenge,* talking in his high, clear voice, monotonous and fast (Nicholas was guttural and harsh). "You underrate the power of human recovery. You always do. It's immense, as a matter of fact. Give us fifty years—twenty—ten. . . . Besides, look at the compensations. If the good are battered and beaten, the bad are too. It's a well-known fact that many of the futurist poets, in all the nations, have gone mad, through trying to get too many battle noises into their heads at once. So they, at least, are silenced. I suppose they still write, in their asylums—in fact I've heard they do (my uncle is an asylum doctor)—but it gets no further. . . ." He subsided into the *Cambridge Magazine.*

"Well, I'd rather have the futurists than the slops poured out by the people who unfortunately haven't brain enough even to go mad," Nicholas grumbled. ("And anyhow, I don't believe in any of your uncles—you've too many.) The futurists at least were trying to keep close to facts, even if they couldn't digest them but brought them up with strident noises. But these imbeciles—the war seems to be a sort of tonic to their syrupy little souls; it's filled them up with vim and banal joy. Not that the rot that has always been rot particularly matters; it merely means that the people who used to express themselves in one inane way now choose another, no worse; but it's the silencing or the unmanning of the good people that matters. Here's Cathcart's new book. I've just read it. It's the work of a shaken, broken man. It's weak, irrational, drifting, with no constructive purpose, no coherence. You can almost hear the guns crashing into it as he tried to write, and the atrocity reports shrieking in his ears, and the poison gas stifling him, and the militarists and pacificists raving round him. His whole world's run off its rails and upset and broken to bits, and he can't put it right side up again; he's lost his faith in it. He can only fumble and stammer at it helplessly, weak and maundering and incoherent. He ought to be helping to build it up again, but he's lost his constructive power. Hundreds of people have. Constructive force will be the one thing needed when the war is over; any one with a programme, and the brain and will to carry it out; but where's it to come from?

Those who aren't killed or cut to bits will be too adrift and demoralised and dazed to do anything intelligent. We're fast losing even such mental coherence and concentration as we had. Look, for instance, at the two, while I'm talking (quite interestingly, too); are you listening? Certainly not. West is reading a Church newspaper, and Alix drawing cats on the margins of my proofs. . . . I'm not blaming you; you can't help it; you are mentally, and probably morally, shattered. I am too. People are more than ever like segregated imbeciles, each absorbed in his or her own ploy. Effects of the War on Human Intelligence: that shall be one of my series. . . ."

Evening in Church (From *Non-Combatants and Others*)

. . . Some one got into the pulpit and preached. He preached on a question, "Who will lead me into the strong city?" A very pertinent inquiry, Alix thought, and just what she wanted to know. Who would? Who could? Was there a strong city at all, or only chaos and drifting ways of terror and unrest? If so, where was it, and how to get there? The strong city, said the preacher, is the city of refuge for which we all crave, and more especially just now, in this day of tribulation. The kings of the earth are gathered and gone by together; but the hill of Sion is a fair place and the joy of the whole earth; upon the north side lieth the city of the great King; God is well known in her palaces as a sure refuge. Above the noise of battle, above the great water-floods, is the city of God that lieth four-square, unshaken by the tempests.

Jolly, thought Alix, and just where one would be: but how to get into it? One had tried, ever since the war began, to shut oneself away, unshaken and undisturbed by the tempests. One had come to Violette because it seemed more unshaken than Wood End; but Violette wasn't really, somehow, a strong city. The tempests rocked one till one felt sick. . . . Where was this strong city, any strong city? Well all about; everywhere, anywhere, said the preacher; one could hardly miss it.

> *" 'Tis only your estrangèd faces*
> *That miss the many-splendoured thing . . ."*

and he quoted quite a lot of that poem. Then he went on to a special road of approach, quoting instead, "I went into the sanctuary of God." Church, Alix presumed. Well, here she was. No; it transpired that it wasn't evening service he meant; he went on to talk of the Mass. That, apparently, was the strong city. Well, it might be, if one was of that way of thinking. But if one wasn't? Did Kate find it so, and was that why she went out early several mornings in the week? And what sort of strength had that city? Was it merely a refuge, well bulwarked, where one might hide from fear? Or had it strength to conquer the chaos? West would say it had; that its work was to launch forces over the world like shells, to shatter the old materialism, the old comfortable selfishness, the old snobberies, cruelties, rivalries, cant, blind stupidities, lies. The old ways, thought Alix (which were the same ways carried further, West would say), of destruction and unhappiness and strife, that had led to the bitter hell where boys went out in anguish into the dark.

The city wasn't yet strong enough, apparently, to do that. Would it be one day?

"I will not cease from mental fight," cried the preacher, who was fond, it seemed, of quoting poetry, "nor let my sword sleep in my hand, till we have built Jerusalem in England's green and pleasant land."

The next moment he was talking of another road of approach to the city on the hill, besides going to church, besides building Jerusalem in England. A road steep and sharp and black; we take it unawares, forced along it (many boys are taking it this moment, devoted and unafraid. Unafraid, thought Alix); and suddenly we are at the city gates; they open and close behind us, and we are in the strong city, the drifting chaos of our lives behind us, to be redeemed by firm walking on whatever new roads may be shown us. God, who held us through all the drifting, unsteady paths, has led us now right out of them into a sure refuge. . . . How do you know? thought Alix. Beyond the steep dark road there may be chaos still, endless, worse chaos: or, surely more natural to suppose, there may be nothing. How *did* people think they knew? Or didn't they? Did they only guess, and say what they thought was attractive? Did Kate know? And Mrs. Frampton? How *could* they know, people like that? How could it be part of their equipment of knowledge, anything so extraordinary, so wild, so unlike their usual range as that? They knew about recipes, and servants, and dusting, and things like that—but surely not about weird and wonderful things that they couldn't see? Alix could rather better believe that this preacher knew, though he did sometimes use words she didn't like, such as tribulation and grace. (It would seem that preachers sometimes must: it is impossible, and not right, to judge them.)

When the sermon ended abruptly, and they sang a hymn of Bunyan's about a pilgrim (402 in the green books), one was left with a queer feeling that the Church had its hand on a door, and at any moment might turn a handle and lead the way through. . . . Alix caught for a moment the forces at work; perhaps West was right about them, and they were adequate for the job of blowing up the debris of the world. If only the Church could collect them, focus them, use them. . . . Kate, and church people of Kate's calibre, were surely like untaught children playing, ignorantly and placidly, with dynamite. They would be blown up if they weren't careful. They kept summoning forces to their aid which must surely, if they fully came, shatter and break to bits most of the things they clung to as necessary comforts and conveniences. But perhaps people knew this, and therefore prayed cautiously, with reservations; so the powers came in the same muffled, wrappered way, with reservations.

Such were Alix's speculations as the music ended and the congregation filed down the church and shook hands with the tired vicar at the door and went out into the dark evening. The fog came round them and choked the light that streamed from the church, and made Alix cough. They hurried home through the blurred, gas-lit roads.

"Did you enjoy the service?" asked Kate.

"I think so," said Alix, wondering whether she had.

"It's queer," she added, meaning the position of the Christian church in this world.

But Kate said, "Queer! Whatever do you mean? It was just like the ordinary; like it always is. . . . I wish Mr. Alison had preached, though; I never feel Mr. Daintree has the same *touch.* He preaches about things and people in general, and that's never so inspiring; he doesn't seem to get home the same way to each one. Now, Mr. Alison this morning was beautiful. Mr. Daintree, I always think, has almost too many *ideas,* and they run away with him a little. However." Kate's principle (one of them) was not to criticise the clergy, so she stopped.

"I wonder if Florence is in yet," she said instead, "and if she's left the larder open, as usual, and let that kitten get at the chicken? I shouldn't be a bit surprised. She *is* a girl."

Alix felt another incongruity. If Kate really believed the extraordinary things she professed to believe about the interfusion of two worlds (at least two), how then did it matter so much about chickens and kittens and Florence? Yet why not? Why shouldn't it give all things an intenser, more vivid reality, a deeper significance? Perhaps it did, thought Alix, renouncing the problem of the Catholic church and its so complicated effects.

Alix, Nicholas, and West (From *Non-Combatants and Others*)

Alix thought, "Christians must mind. Clergymen must mind awfully. It's their business that's being spoilt. It's their job to make the world better: they must mind a lot, and they can't fight either," and saw West's face, tired and preoccupied, in the darkness at her side.

"War Extra. 'Fishul. Bulgarian Advance. Fall of Kragujevatz," cried a newsboy, as best he could.

"It'll be all up with Serbia presently," said West. "Going under fast. A wipe out, like Belgium, I suppose. . . . And we look at it from here and can't do anything to stop it. Pretty rotten, isn't it?" His voice was bitter.

"If we could go out there and try," said Alix, "we shouldn't feel so bad, should we?"

He shook his head.

"No: not so bad. War's beastly and abominable to the fighters: but not to be fighting is much more embittering and demoralising, I believe. Probably largely because one has more time to think. To have one's friends in danger, and not to be in danger oneself—it fills one with futile rage. Combatants are to be pitied; but non-combatants are of all men and women the most miserable. Older men, crocks, parsons, women—God help them."

"Yes," Alix agreed, on the edge of tears again.

Then West seemed to pull himself up from his despondency.

"But really, of course, they've a unique opportunity. They can't be fighting war abroad; but they can be fighting it at home. That's what it's up to us all to do now, I'm firmly convinced, by whatever means we each have at our command. We've all of us some. We've got to use them. The fighting men out there can't; they're tied. Some of them never can again. . . . It's up to us. . . . Good-bye, Miss Sandomir: my way is along there."

They parted at the corner of Gray's Inn Road. Alix saw him swallowed up in black fog, called by his bell, going to his church to fight war by the means he had at his command.

She got into her bus and went towards Violette, where no one fought anything at all, but where supper waited, and Mrs. Frampton was anxious lest she should have got lost in the fog.

London: Methuen, 1968. 43–47, 111–114, 143–144.

Second Period: Smash (From *Told by an Idiot*)

1 Sound and Fury

The so bitter, so recent, so familiar, so agonising tale of the four years and a quarter between August, 1914, and November, 1918, has been told and re-told too often, and will not be told in detail here. It is enough, if not too much, to say that there was a great and dreadful war in Europe, and that nightmare and chaos and the abomination of desolation held sway for four horrid years. All there was of civilisation—whatever we mean by that unsatisfactory, undefined, relative word—suffered irretrievable damage. All there was of greed, of cruelty, of barbarism, of folly, incompetence, meanness, valour, heroism, selfishness, littleness, self-sacrifice and hate, rose to the call in each belligerent country and showed itself for what it was. Men and women acted blindly, according to their kind. They used the torments of others as stepping stones to prosperity or fame; they endured torments themselves, with complaining, with courage, or with both; they did work they held to be useful, and got out of it what credit and profit they could; or work they knew was folly, and still got out of it what they could. They went to the war, they stayed at home, they scrambled for jobs among the chaos, they got rich, they got poor, they died, were maimed, medalled, frost-bitten, tortured, imprisoned, bored, embittered, enthusiastic, cheerful, hopeless, patient, or matter-of-fact, according to circumstances and temperament. Many people said a great deal, others very little. There were all manner of different attitudes and ways of procedure with regard to the war. To some it was a necessary or unnecessary hell, to some a painful and tedious affair enough, but with interests and alleviations and a good goal in sight; to some an adventure; to some (at home) a satisfactory sphere for work they enjoyed; to some a holy war; to others a devil's dance in which they would take no part, or which they wearily did what they could to alleviate, or in which they joined with cynical and conscious resolve not to be left out of whatever profits might accrue.

But to the majority in each country it was merely a catastrophe, like an earthquake, to be gone through blindly, until better might be.

2 The Family at War

Of the Garden family, Vicky was horrified but enthusiastically pro-war. Her two sons got commissions early, and she helped the war by organising bazaars and by doing whatever it was that one did (in the early stages, for in the later more of violence had to be done) to Belgian refugees. Maurice and his paper were violently pacificist, and became a byword. Rome saw the war and what had led up to it as the very crown and sum of human folly, and helped, very capably and neatly, to pack up and send off food and clothes to British prisoners. Stanley was caught in the tide of war fervour. She worked in a canteen, and served on committees for all kinds of good objects, and behaved with great competence and energy, her heart wrung day and night with fear for Billy. In 1917 she caught peace fever, joined the peace party and the Women's International League, signed petitions and manifestos in support of Lord Lansdowne, and spoke on platforms about it, which Billy thought tiresome of her.

Irving lent a car to an ambulance, and his services to the Ministry of Munitions, and became a special constable. Una sent cakes to her sons and farmhands at the front, and employed land-girls on the farm. She took the war as all in the day's work; there had been wars before in history, and there would be wars again. It was awfully sad, all the poor boys being taken like that; but it sent up the price of corn and milk, and that pleased Ted, for all his anxiety for his sons.

The younger generation acted and reacted much as might be expected of them. Vicky's Hugh, who joined the gunners, was interested in the business and came tolerably well through it, only sustaining a lame leg. Tony, his younger brother, was killed in 1916. Maurice's Roger, whose class was B2, served in France for a year, and wrote a good deal of trench poetry. He was then invalided out, and entered the Ministry of Information, where he continued, in the intervals of compiling propaganda intended to interest the Greenland Esquimaux in the cause of the Allies, to publish trench poetry, full of smells, shells, corpses, mud and blood.

"I simply can't read the poetry you write in these days, Roger," his mother Amy complained. "It's become too terribly beastly and nasty and corpsey. I can't think what you want to write it for, I'm sure."

"Unfortunately, mother," Roger explained, kindly, "war *is* rather beastly and nasty, you know. And a bit corpsey, too."

"My dear boy, I know that; I'm not an idiot. Don't, for goodness' sake, talk to me in that superior way, it reminds me of your father. All I say is, why *write* about the corpses? There've always been plenty of them, people who've died in their beds of diseases. You never used to write about *them.*"

"I suppose one's object is to destroy the false glamour of war. There's no glamour about disease."

"Glamour, indeed! There you go again with that terrible nonsense. I don't meet any of these people you talk about who think there's glamour in war. I'm sure *I* never saw any glamour in it, with all you boys in the trenches and all of us at home slaving ourselves to death and starving on a slice of bread and margarine a day. Glamour, indeed. I'll tell you what it is, a set of you young men have invented that glamour theory, just so as to have an excuse for what you call destroying it, with your nasty talk. Like you've invented those awful Old Men you go on about, who like the war. I'm sick of your Old Men and your corpses."

"I'm sick of them myself," said Roger gloomily, and changed the subject, for you could not argue with Amy. But he went on writing war poetry, and gained a good deal of reputation as one of our soldier poets. On the whole, he was more successful as a poet than as a propagandist to the Esquimaux, a phlegmatic people, who remained a little detached about the war.

Stanley's Billy hailed the outbreak of hostilities with some pleasure, and was among the first civilians to enlist. Here, he felt, was a job more in his line than being secretary to his Liberal cousin, which he had found more and more tedious as time passed. He fought in France, in Flanders, in Gallipoli, and in Mesopotamia, was wounded three times, and recovered each time to fight again. He was a cheerful, ordinary, unemotional young soldier, a good deal bored, after a bit, with the war. On one of his leaves, in 1916, he married a young lady from the Vaudeville Theatre, whom Stanley could not care about.

"I know mother wanted me to marry a highbrow girl," he confided to Molly. "Some girl who's been to college or something. But I haven't much to say to that sort ever, nor they to me. Now Dot . . ."

But even Molly had her misgivings about Dot. She was not sure that Dot would prove quite monogamous enough. And, as it turned out, Dot did not prove monogamous at all, but rather the contrary.

Molly herself had become an ambulance driver in France. She frankly enjoyed the war. She became engaged to officers, successively and simultaneously. She acted at canteen entertainments, and gained a charming reputation as a comedienne. At the end of the war she received the O.B.E. for her distinguished services.

Garden City, N.Y.: Dial Press, 1983. 290–294.

Following the Fashion

I have a dress with puffed sleeves; the skirt is very long and full; about ten yards of silk, I think it took. It hangs in the wardrobe, taking a lot of room, because of the sleeves.

I have shoes with high heels; about three inches, I dare say. I can wear them if I want to.

I think I shall change my Morris, and get a small stream-lined green thing, and look smarter in the streets. It will not be so good for touring, but it will look better.

I may paint my nails red; or green, if that is coming in.

I shall write my memoirs, I think. I shall bring in every one I know, and have an index, so they can find themselves and their friends. There are plenty of things I can say about them. If they do not like it, they can lump it. It will serve them right, for having met me.

I may write a book about contemporary writers, too. They won't like that either, the things I shall say about them.

I can write tough-guy stories. What I mean is, I can write stories like this:

She was a grand girl. You're drunk, she said. But I wasn't so drunk, either. I mean, I'd had a few, but I could see straight; and I could hold the wheel. I had the headlights on, too. To hell with those lamps, she said, and switched them down. Do you want to dazzle everything on the road, she said, so it rushes into us? You're nuts.

She was a grand girl. You're a grand girl, I said, and I switched on the big lamps again, and I held her waist with my left, and hugged her up to me close, so as I felt her warmth. That's the style, I said, and I saw the needle get up to sixty. Oh, you're crackers, she said. Driving like hell with the big lamps on and necking me with one arm. How to-night'll end, she said, I don't know. I really don't, do you? Like most nights end, I guess, said I, and that's when comes the dawn. Aw, you're crazy, said she. I told mother I'd be in by four. Well, you won't be in by four; maybe by eight. That's time enough for breakfast, isn't it? I know a swell place down the river. Oh, for heaven's sake, said she; we shall never get any place at this rate. And what must she do but start grabbing at the wheel, crying out I was all over the road. And so we were, after she started grabbing. Then she screamed out, and something hit us and we slewed right round.

There was the hell of a mess on the road. One of those little Austins, it was, and all crumpled up, and a man and a girl all crumpled up too. There was blood and glass and things around. But my Buick had only buckled a wing.

See here, I said, we can't do a thing. We'd best get on. She was being sick in the road; the blood had turned her up, I think. That and the shock. And seeing those two.

Here, I said, come on out of this. We can't do a thing. I put her in the Buick, and slewed around again and drove off. There was something banging loose, and I got out to look; it was the number plate, so I wrenched it off and took it inside. We didn't have the headlamps on now; the off one was smashed, anyway, by that bloody little Austin. I drove away. The steering was a bit funny, too. She never stopped crying and talking, it made me tired. Women can't get this: when a thing's done it's done. That's a thing no woman can ever get. They can't let it be. Hell, did I want that bloody little car to muscle into us that way? Aw, forget it.

All the time as I drive I seem to hear that damned radio saying, in its polite Oxford-Cambridge voice, "Before the news, there is a police message. Between two and three on Sunday morning an Austin seven car came into collision with another car, which apparently failed to stop. . . ." Failed nothing. I did stop, see? I stopped, and saw there wasn't a thing I could do, so I went on again.

Oh, to hell with your noise. . . .

Yes: I could write a story like that if I liked. Perhaps I will. Fine magazine stuff. What I mean is, a magazine would take it.

And I can write tough-guy poetry. A magazine would take that, too. I can write poetry like this (I call this one *To the Barricades*):

Mr. Jiggins goes to the circus.
(The girls, the hoops, the clowns, the seals, the hoop-oes.)
He has donned his Harrow tie,
But Borstal was his alma mater true.
He meets Mrs. Fortescue-Fox,
With a jade cigarette-holder, long and green like asparagus or a dead woman's fingers
Or the pale weeds swaying in the duck-pond,
But never a sprig of rue.
You're so handsome, where you going?
Don't know where I'm going, where I am, where you are, where the sweet hell anyone is.
(Forward to the barricades! To the barricades—where else?)
Ohé! Ohé! mes brave petits! the fat is in the fire!
Εις τὸ πῦρ εκ τοῦ κἀπνου.
As Lucian pointed out, things can always be worse.
Pink and stout he was, pranked out with rings and gold chains, he was.
What a fool he looked!
Dites donc, monsieur, si qu'on irait se coucher, n'est-ce pas?
Festinare nocet, tempore quæque suo qui facit, ille sapit.
In fact, no hurry.
(March, march, march, the feet of a thousand men marching as one. No hurry?)

They trample like artillery in my head.
Allons, allons, faites donner la garde!
But Mrs. Fortescue-Fox,
Unable to wait, flung herself upon the obdurate rocks.
Like is like that.
"But never mine," Mr. Jiggins cried.
And up washed the running tide,
Flowing up, casting corpses on the slimy beach,
Casting statues, casting coins, casting mermen and mermaids and old bowler hats.
Ting-a-ling-a-ling ring the bells of hell; where you bound now?
Allons, companions, we march to the barricades.

In the grey dawn of yesterday
We wipe away all tears:—perhaps.

There's another I call *Petrol Pumps.* But that's longer, and I won't print it here. It's fine magazine stuff too.

I like being in the fashion.

I may join the Communists.

Or I may write a novel a million words long, and very strong; the longest and strongest novel of the season.

The trouble about the fashions is, there are too many going on at once, and you can't follow them all.

Sometimes I think I will give them all up, and just be dowdy.

Personal Pleasures. New York: Macmillan, 1936. 231–236.

Album

How enchanting your relations are! Mine, too, look much the same. I suppose people do; I mean, so much depends on the clothes, does it not? I like your aunts; how they ripple from the waist down, bending in the middle like swans; their hair piled high in chignons; see, how much of it they have—or was some, perhaps, attached, or rolled over cushions? Your Aunt Amy, did you say? What long ear-rings! She is very elegant, *mondaine,* refined, yet *capable,* do you not think, *de tout?* Or was she not? Married a curate, do you say? One wonders what life in the curate-house was like, after your Aunt Amy entered it. Nine children? So that was what it was like. Yes, I see, here they all are. The little boys in sailor suits or jerseys, holding bats; the little girls in sashes, their hair cut across their foreheads. Du Maurier children. Oh, yes, I see, that is Phyllis, and there are Olive and Ruth. I should know them anywhere; by the way, I hear Ruth's grandchildren are at that fashionable school in Dorset, and can already change wheels, top batteries, and milk cows. They are going to learn to read next year, you say? At ten and twelve? Isn't that a little soon? One is so afraid of over-exciting their brains. Still, if they *want* to learn, anything is better than repressing them. . . .

A clergyman: of course, Aunt Amy's husband. A Tractarian, was he? Well, he was a little late for that; but I see what you mean, he was whatever High Church clergymen were in the eighties. Wrote tracts about the Eastward Position? I think he was so right. And, of course, they all face that way now, so that shows.

Who is that old military man? He looks like a splendid walrus, with his long whiskers. Your paternal grandfather? Of course; the General. Didn't he fight in the Crimea? Charged with the Light Brigade? How exciting! And how fortunate that he was one of those who rode back. He looks the kind of military man who might have been very much annoyed with whoever it was who had blundered. I should not care to face your grandfather if I had blundered. The lady in the crinoline is your grandmother, of course. She looks full of spirit; I dare say she needed it all. A crinoline gives such dignity, such deportment. No one could look *dowdy* in a crinoline. How her chatelaine hangs over it, full of the store-room keys. What a bore, to have to unlock the store-room whenever anyone wanted stores. I suppose stores are used by the cook daily, and always at the most inconvenient moment.

Look at those lovely girls, all in crinolines, ready to swim along like balloons in a breeze. Your great aunts? They are very sweet. No doubt they had a delightful time, waltzing, shooting with bows and arrows, riding, skating with gentlemen (for there was real ice in those days, was there not?) See, there is one of them on a horse, in a long habit, her hair in a net under a dear little feathered hat. Great-aunt Helen? Famous all over the country for her riding and jumping? Broke her back at a water-jump, and lay crippled for forty years. . . . Oh, dear, let us turn the page.

Here we have bustles. Your mother? Now, that is *really* the swan period. What a bend! The Grecian bend, was it not? The Greeks were first with everything, of course; but I do not recall this bend in any of their statues. Perhaps they could not hold it long enough to be sculptured. Of course, it is not *altogether* genuine; the bustle helped. But how adorable! How sorry your mother must have been when she had to go into those horrible clothes of the nineties, puff-sleeved jackets (by the way, I see they are in again; strange how even the worst things always come round) and stiff collars and sailor hats—yes, there she is in them.

And your Aunt Elizabeth, in a college group wearing large cricket pads—Newnham, is it? What year? 1890. Well, of course Newnham had been going for about twenty years then. . . . It was quite the thing to go to college, I suppose; now it seems to be less thought of, to be considered no use for getting jobs. I dare say your Aunt Elizabeth didn't have to think about jobs. Became a doctor, did she? I never knew Mrs. Robinson had been a doctor; why did she give it up? She left six forceps in? But that's nothing, surely. . . . Oh, all in the same wound;

yes, I suppose that *would* be rather many. . . . *And* three swabs? Well, I dare say her mind was on cricket. It may happen to anyone, they say. Most people who have ever had an operation are simply full of forceps and swabs, I believe; they think it is rheumatism or neuritis. . . . It is wonderful, I often think, what additions, as well as subtractions, the human frame can stand. I suppose really we are put together *quite* at random, and a few objects more or less make very little difference; though I must say, when you see a picture of our insides, you wonder where extra forceps and swabs would go. But of course, they take the place of whatever the surgeon has just taken away, I forgot that. . . . Well, perhaps your Aunt Elizabeth was right; she goes in for chickens now, doesn't she?

You as a child; how pretty. How people change; still, I would know you anywhere. Quite in the nude. That has the advantage that you can't be dated by your clothes. Your school lacrosse team . . . and your first dance dress. Empire style. Clothes were pretty that year; nice high waists and simple lines.

But let us turn back to the Victorians. They fascinate me. There is a *je ne sais quoi* about them, a subtlety; they might have strange experiences, commit strange deeds, and say nothing. They are proud, reserved, self-contained. Your Aunt Geraldine looks like a mermaid, your Uncle Frank, behind his moustaches, seems to brood on strange lands. Had to leave the country suddenly? That would account for it, I suppose. Poor Uncle Frank. Did he have to be long away? It was hushed up? That always takes a little time, of course. And then Uncle Frank came home, and married a Miss Jones. Had to leave the country *again?* What bad luck he had! Now-a-days, they seem to manage better, without so much travelling. Was he long abroad the second time? Always? Dear me. Yes, I see, this is his *hacienda* in the Argentine, with himself and Miss Jones, grown nice and plump, in the porch. . . . Oh, not Miss Jones? She stayed in England, with the children? Then this would be some other lady, more of the Argentine type. . . . I expect your uncle Frank was wise to settle there, among cattle; as your Aunt Elizabeth was wise to settle among chickens. Animals are a great resource. And so much nicer to rear them than to go and shoot them.

Photographs of ancestors are really much more interesting than the paintings of them they had before, because the camera cannot lie, so we know that they really did look like that. Now-a-days they touch them up more; the camera has learnt to lie. Besides, do we look as interesting? I am sure we do not. I could look at our ancestors for ever. Thank you so much for showing me yours. It has been a charming evening. You must come and see mine.

A charming evening. But as I drive home, the small cold wind of mortality hums round me with sighing breath. The way to dusty death seems to stretch before me, lit by those fading yellow oblongs wherefrom someone's ancestors gaze, pale pasteboard prisoners, to be wondered about, recalled, lightly summed and dismissed by us as we turn a page. So too shall we gaze out some autumn evening, prisoned and defenceless, to stir in posterity a passing idle speculation, a moment's memory. That? Oh, that is great-aunt Rose. . . . She wrote. Oh, nothing you would have heard of; I don't think she was ever much read, even at the time; she just wrote. Novels, essays, verse—I forget what else; she just wrote away, as those Georgians did. Rather dull, I think. What besides? Well, I think she just went about; nothing special. There *was* some story . . . but it's all so long ago, I've forgotten. She ended poor, having outlived whatever market she had, poor old thing. Yes, she went on writing, but no one read her . . . she died poor, killed, I think, in an aeroplane smash; she learnt to pilot too old; she should have stuck to motoring. But she would learn to fly, and finally smashed a friend's plane and herself . . . silly, really. She had grown very tiresome before the end, they say. But look, here is someone more interesting. . . .

It will be posterity's charming evening then, and theirs to pity, if they will, their pasteboard prisoners, as I now pity Aunt Geraldine with her mermaid's face and form, Uncle Frank who had to leave home so suddenly and so frequently, Great-Aunt Helen, of the rogue's face and little feather, who fell at the water-jump sixty years ago, Grandpapa General, who rode back with the Light Brigade, Grandmama, who had to be so often locking and unlocking her stores, Aunt Elizabeth with her forceps and her chickens, Aunt Amy rippling so elegantly from the waist down and marrying the curate who wrote tracts about the Eastward Position. . . .

Poor figures I feel we shall most of us cut beside them, when the Albums shall imprison us too.

Personal Pleasures. 15–21.

13
Hugh MacDiarmid (1888–1978)

Introduced and Edited by Nancy K. Gish

In 1922 Christopher Murray Grieve took the pen name Hugh MacDiarmid as a deliberate identification with Celtic tradition. As Grieve he had been writing imitative and undistinguished poems in English. Under the new name he suddenly began publishing startlingly original modernist lyrics in Braid Scots, the language of lowland Scotland.[1] Although he remains even now relatively little studied in America, he is widely acknowledged as one of Scotland's most important poets, along with Burns and Dunbar, and unquestionably Scotland's greatest modernist writer. He attempted—largely successfully—to re-generate Scots as a sophisticated literary language; he almost singlehandedly created and sustained the Scottish Renaissance of the twenties and thirties; and he wrote some of the finest lyrics and long poems of the modernist period.

His poetic experiments with Scots began in 1922 with "The Watergaw." Two collections of lyrics, *Sangschaw* and *Penny Wheep*, appeared in 1925 and 1926, followed in 1926 by his masterpiece, "A Drunk Man Looks at the Thistle," a tour de force written in part as a response and challenge to T. S. Eliot's *Waste Land*. Using many of Eliot's techniques, he turned them to his own purposes to demonstrate the range, flexibility, psychological acuity, and contemporaneity of Braid Scots. Even in the early twenties MacDiarmid had read and commented on both *Ulysses* and *The Waste Land*, in both cases recognizing them as fundamental shifts in literary conception and lasting works of a new modern style. His own goal was to recreate a serious Scottish literature for the modern world. He defined the problem as both linguistic and political:

> There are no contemporary Scottish poets writing in English equal, and, therefore equally deserving of critical consideration, to the best contemporary English poets (who are not all Georgians)—largely because English is not a language in which any Scotsman can adequately express himself, but even more because of the provincialisation of Scotland and the consequent inhibition of the highest potentialities in Scottish culture. (MacDiarmid, "Sir Ronald Ross" 24)

The Scottish writer, MacDiarmid felt, was caught in a bind: Scots lacked modern forms of expression, but English was incapable of revealing Scottish character and experience. He set out to restore his own language by writing what he called "Synthetic Scots," that is, a reconstructed national language drawing on any regional Scottish dialect and any period of Scottish history. He used archaisms and obscure terms, and he joined the phrases of Aberdeen with those of Fife or Ayrshire. He ransacked Jamieson's etymological *Dictionary of the Scottish Language* and made poems directly from it. His return to sources had as its aim not only an encompassing and flexible linguistic instrument but an alternative canon, a Scottish tradition freed from English linguistic and literary hegemony. He based his methods in a claim for the intrinsic power of Scots words, a power he compared to Joyce's multilinguistic experimentation:

> We have been enormously struck by the resemblance—the moral resemblance—between Jamieson's Etymological Dictionary of the Scottish language and Joyce's Ulysses. A *vis comica* that has not yet been liberated lies bound by desuetude and misappreciation in the recesses of the Doric: and its potential uprising would be no less prodigious, uncontrollable, and utterly at variance with conventional morality than was Joyce's tremendous outpouring. (MacDiarmid, "A Theory of Scots Letters" 183)

MacDiarmid's call for an aesthetic revolution based on a restored national language became a lifelong struggle against cultural and linguistic marginalization. Though his late long poems are in English, notably "On a Raised Beach" and "Direadh I, II, III" in the thirties, it is a "synthetic" English, intended like Joyce's to extend the possibilities of language. *In Memoriam James Joyce* (1955) is a massive tribute to world language.

Marginalized himself, MacDiarmid recognized in Scottish women writers a double marginalization of culture and gender. Though he often took a sexist position on language and literature, he also encouraged, published, and reviewed many women poets, paying the (perhaps dubious) compliment of criticizing them as severely as men. "The total output of our poetesses of any quality at all has been extremely slight," he wrote, having said the same of men poets. "The position to which women were so long relegated accounts, of course, to a very large extent for this" (MacDiarmid, "Muriel Stuart" 48). Writing of Violet Jacob, he deplored the limits placed on her work by "over-Anglicised circumstances" (MacDiarmid, "Violet Jacob" 10). And despite his objections to Rebecca West's novel, he wrote in 1926 that "*The Judge* remains—unfortunately—the best *Scottish* novel of recent years" (MacDiarmid, "Newer Scottish Fiction (I)" 109). This backhanded compliment reveals his frustration at multiple forms of marginalization. Yet in writing of West he found himself caught between two forms of suppression.

"Following Rebecca West in Edinburgh" (reprinted here) was published along with "The Watergaw" in 1922 as Hugh MacDiarmid's second appearance in print. An odd fictional dialogue between a somewhat bombastic Scots speaker who theorizes on how to reclaim language and literature and an intrigued English-speaking interlocutor, it functions as a quasi-review of *The Judge*. The dialogue is especially interesting for its concern with writing and difference, both cultural and sexual. What the Scots speaker claims is that the vernacular has a greater capacity for expression than English, but he goes further to appropriate that capacity exclusively for men. This move into what Gilbert and Gubar call "sexual linguistics" is marked by a deep uncertainty and unease. Wanting to claim, for "Scotsmen," the *vis comica* of the vernacular as a tool to release the deepest character of Edinburgh and Scotland, the Scots speaker feels a concomitant need to resist West's handling of the subject. What the piece reveals is both anxiety and ambivalence about the need for male control of language. MacDiarmid attempts not only to recuperate stolen linguistic force but accurately to identify the thief. Yet the Scots speaker's recourse to gender difference as a basis for asserting linguistic power ultimately fails.

It was altogether likely that West, as well as her novel, would raise mingled respect and anxiety in MacDiarmid. With a Scottish mother and an Edinburgh education, West left Scotland at sixteen for London and remained in England. Like MacDiarmid a socialist and radical journalist, she was also a feminist. And though the protagonist of *The Judge,* Ellen Melville, is Scottish and speaks in distinctively Scottish rhythms and phrases, the novel is written in English. Yet it is hardly idealized or "pretty" in its depiction of the harshest side of human experience—illegitimacy, abandonment, marital rape, child abuse, and women's oppression. Despite this, the Scots speaker of "Following Rebecca West in Edinburgh" objects to it as a "luxury production," a sweetened and "lady-fyed" treatment of what is really crude, coarse, tumultuous, even brutal in its vitality. He depicts Edinburgh as carnivalistic, wild, and tragic; West, he claims, never touches that quality of life. One must almost assume that the very choice of women's issues draws this attack; yet he attributes his concern initially to a failure of language: West is not to blame since "ye cannie play Beethoven on an Almanie whistle," that is, a very small toy whistle. Her difficulty, then, is the lack of an adequate instrument, the attempt to capture the life of Edinburgh in a thin and conventional language.

But the attack soon shifts ground to conflate linguistic inadequacy with gender inadequacy, West's inability *as a woman* to handle the violence, ugliness, and shame beneath the surface of life. It takes a "*man* tae write aboot Edinburgh . . . an' he'll need the Doric tae get the fu' aifer" (exhalations from the ground on a warm sunny day). The shift from a cause to a mere conjunction, "an'," suggests the weakness of his position. For in fact no evidence is offered that men have greater linguistic force.

The effects of language and gender follow a confused path in this dialogue from linguistic inadequacy to gender inadequacy to an undetermined force, "Joyce's virr" (vitality). In the end, the Scots speaker's position lapses into confusion, since he admits his own inadequacy as well. Having conflated a supposed feminine delicacy with the linguistic limitations of English, he finds himself faced with like limitations despite being male and speaking Scots. He too fails the city, which appears as a giant woman overpowering and emasculating him or a massive apocalyptic horse he cannot ride, leaving him in an anguish of self-contempt. Having enacted the conventional strategy of shifting femaleness from subject to object of writing, he finds it still a threat.

MacDiarmid's own position is ambiguous, for he is not clearly identifiable with either speaker. Moreover, the subtitle is "A Monologue in the Vernacular," suggesting an internal debate. In any case, the overt claim of the Scots speaker is not sustained by the fictionalized form of the dialogue. As a theorist, the Scots speaker asserts gender difference in language; as a character, he collapses into impotence and frustration, for maleness—even with his command of the vernacular—cannot assure his power over language.

"Following Rebecca West in Edinburgh" articulates both an anxiety about women writers and an uncertainty about masculine possession of language at the same time that it provides a dazzling display of dictionary Scots calculated to demonstrate its difference and expressive power. *The Judge* represented an intersection of nationality and gender suppression that tested MacDiarmid's tenuous recognition of women's double marginalization and revealed his ambivalent response to the notion of gendered language.

NOTE

1. Braid (Broad) Scots is not a dialect of English; it developed from Northumbrian Old English as modern English developed from Midlands Old English. Although the primary differences are in pronunciation, spelling, and rhythm, Scots also has a large vocabulary of words that do not exist in English. Most versions—as in Burns's poems and most of MacDiarmid's—are easy to read. MacDiarmid's work sometimes requires a dictionary.

WORKS CITED

MacDiarmid, Hugh. "Muriel Stuart." *Scottish Educational Journal* 23 Oct. 1925. Rpt. in *Contemporary Scottish Studies*, 48–49. Edinburgh: Scottish Educational Journal, 1976.

———. "Newer Scottish Fiction (1)." *Scottish Educational Journal* 25 June 1926. Rpt. in *Contemporary Scottish Studies,* 108–109.
———. "Sir Ronald Ross: Ronald Campbell MacFie." *Scottish Educational Journal* 21 Aug. 1925. Rpt. in *Contemporary Scottish Studies,* 23–25.
———. "A Theory of Scots Letters." *Scottish Chapbook* 1.7(1922):180–184.
———. "Violet Jacob." *Scottish Educational Journal* 17 July 1925. Rpt. in *Contemporary Scottish Studies,* 8–10.

Following Rebecca West in Edinburgh: A Monologue in the Vernacular

Whatna fearfu' image is that like a corpse out o' a tomb, that's makin' a' this rippet for the cheatrie instruments o' pen an' ink?"

"Yech! (*contemptuously*) A cockalan! . . . . She's made a silk purse oot o' a sow's lug, an' (*with an effort towards gaiety*) I dinna haud wi' vivisection—sin' the sow's alive. Forbye,—there's nae ca' for sic baffles. It's what they lads at the Mound ca' 'luxury production' an' a' art worth the name maun be 'production for use.' "

It was a brave effort; but his attempt to carry it off lightly was pathetic. I had set him off, and we both knew it. He could not help himself. He had Edinburgh on the brain—pondering and re-pondering its great black problem for ever. I could see the passion crowding into his face. Perhaps it was cruelty on my part. He looked at me as though to say "I ken weel eneuch what yer ettlin' efter—dinna!—Ech ye deevil!" For the thing was done and could not be undone. I had no more to do—no need to force the pace—he was silent awhile. I looked anywhere but at him. I knew the struggle that was going on—but he was never the man to say the first thing that jumped into his head. At last he rose, quietly enough, yet most dramatically, crossed over to the window, pulled the curtains aside, and shot up the lower half. A rough, black lump of Edinburgh was visible, hairy with light.

"Look!

'Thou scowry hippit, ugly averil,
Wi' hurkland banes aye howkand throu' thy hide!' "

I had to admit the grisly exactness of the description. He shut down the window again and came and sat opposite me, leaning towards me as if about to give a confidence—as he was.

"She's an allagrugous auld city in this allerish licht! . . I'm no blamin' Miss West—but ye canna play Beethoven on an Almanie whistle! It tak's an almark like Joyce* tae write aboot Edinburgh. The lassie never gets amidward. She

*James Joyce's "Ulysses," published in France by Sylvia Beach.

canna be fashed wi' a' its amplefeysts—she hesna' got the necessary *animosity.* Mebbe Edinburgh

> 'Wes in his yhowthyede
> A fayre, sweet, pleasant childe,
> At all point formyd in fassoun,
> Abil, of gude condityione.'

But ye canna analite it tae Arcady noo. . . . Na! Na! It's black abies that, an' crookit an' croodit. (*He was obviously thinking of sundry pretty little descriptions of Edinburgh in "The Judge."*) . . This michty coutribat o' stanes an' souls! . . . Mony's the ablachs glowrin' . . . . An' ankerly auld toon, 'spyrin' a' airts, filed wi' the bachrams o' the ages, wi' its cranglin' streets whastlin' like stirks i' the backdraught, an' its mochy startle-o'-stobie o' life an' death, its chowkin' guff o' humanity. Look at the ca' o' the stanes, man! Shoggin' frae the flair o' the sea tae the crap o' the earth! . . . . It's a' assopat aneath her style. Corbaudie ne'er comes in at a'. Her wark's clean-fung eneuch in a way, but she's far owre clocksie, wi' her tongue gae'n like the clatter-bane o' a goose's hass. Edinburgh's black wi' fleas that there's nae clapper-clawin'. . . . Man! It's a fearfu' thing for a bit lassock like yon tae wee an' wale a toon like Edinburgh, makin't *incidental* tae a gowpenfu' o' bodiless bodies—a toon that has *poodered* its hundreds o' thoosands o' leevin' souls. . . . A' her bleeze an' busk o' words, as if she was bagenin' wi' the Almichty. . . . . It's a disease, is Edinburgh. An' (his queer wild humour breaking out again—laughingly!) the kind o' the disease, if ye'll observe, is an attrie bile strikin' oot i' mony heids an' plukes. (Waving his hand towards the window). An attrie face a' boundened up wi' wrath! . . ."

He was purposely using many obsolete words, partly to despite me for forcing him to talk of Edinburgh, and partly because they acted as a brake on his utterance. In any case, he was deliberately inconsequent, allusive, and obscure. As keen students of the Vernacular will appreciate, he was making scores of little experiments in Doric composition and style even as he spoke—subtle adaptations of ancient figures of speech to modern requirements, finding vernacular equivalents for Freudian terminology—all infinitely difficult work but infinitely necessary if the Doric is again to become a living literary medium. His perfect knowledge of Ross's "Helenore," Duff's Poems, the Maitland Poems, Douglas's Vergil, and the like, stood him in splendid stead; and the dexterity with which he drew upon them delighted me immensely. If any Doric enthusiasts think this is easy enough let them try to translate a paragraph or two treating of introverts, extroverts, complexes and specific aboulias into "gude braid Scots"—and if they do not think this necessary, let them cease to talk of reviving the Doric. Such a revival depends upon the Doric being brought abreast of modern civilisation in every respect and detail. There is no other way. . . . . He was silent again for a little; then broke out, speaking somewhat more rapidly, as if excited by his notion.

"Edinburgh Castle is Scotland's Abbote Unreassone.

> 'Abbotis by rewll, and lordis but ressone
> Sic senyeoris tymis ourweill this sessone
> Vpoun thair vyce war lang to waik
> Quhais falsatt, fibilnes, and tressone
> Has rung thryris oure this Zodiak!'

Look at it again!"

He flung up the window again; and standing in the corner we could see the Castle over the chimney cans.

"See! . . . . A' the wild contours an' cullages an' a' the orra outlines o' the stormy geometry o' Scotland, flockin' thegither, chuse them a graund Captaine o' Mischief. . . . an' him they croun an' adopt for their King. . . . . The King, anointed, (*and just then a ray of the sun escaping from the clouds put a greasy gold upon the Castle*) chooseth forth a hunder steeples an' chimley-stacks an' muckle roofs to wait upon his lordly majesty. Every one of these he investeth wi' his liveries o' greene, yellow or some ither licht wanton colour, an' as tho' they werena' gaudy eneuch, they bedeck themsels wi' plumes o' reek an' sparklin' fanlichts an' chackit tiles. This dune, they tie aboot the air a mony bells, wi' electric signs an' winkin' bulbs, an' muckle standards wi' bleezin' taps; an' tangle the haill closeevie wi' upper an' nether nets o' polisht wire. Thus a' things set in order then hev they their hobby-horses, their dragons, an ither antics . . . to strike the devil's daunce wi' a'."

I have no notion what old description of the Liberty of December he was adapting to his purpose; but look over Edinburgh from the window of an upper room at certain times, and you will see the amazing relevance of it all.

"This heathen company, their pypers pyping, their drummers thundering, their bells jingling, their handkerchiefs fluttering aboot their heids like madde men, their hobbie horses an' ither monsters skirmishing amongst the crood. . . . dancin' and singin' wi' sic a confused noise that nae man can hear his ain voice; an' thus these terrestrial furies spend the day. (*Down below in the street a newsboy was crying "Special Edition." I saw the light of his reckless humour spring into his eyes again, but he continued without a change in his voice.*) Then they have certaine papers wherein is painted some babelerie or other of imagerie worke. These they give to everyone that will give them money to maintain them in this their heathenish devilrie; an' who will not show himself buxome to them and give them money, they shall be mocked and flouted shamefully. . . . . ."

This came so extraordinarily pat that we burst out laughing together.

"*Larvatis faciebus,* they incense wi' stinkin' reek frae the leather o' auld shoon. . . . an' '*in choro cantilenas inhonestas cantabat!*' "

The strain of a music hall ditty floating up made him add that last parallel. Then he became very grave all at once, consumed as it were with the tragedy of it all.

"I dinna blame the lassie. Let her scuttle aff intae the appen furth. This aidle-hole's nae place for the likes o' her. It'll tak a *man* tae write aboot Edinburgh, as it sud be written aboot, an' he'll need the Doric tae get the fu' aifer.

Wemmen are a' verra weel i' their way. . . . . but Edinburgh'll tak an almark like Joyce—a scaffie like Joyce. There's aye explosions i' a' thae hooses that ye canna acoont for but by the clyres o' civilisation. It's nae wunner sic clowders o' suppression are aye bealin' an' brakkin' oot. There's far ower muckle *chapling.* It needs a Joyce tae prick ilka pluke, tae miss nowt. . . . . aye even tae

> 'The Kinkhost, the Charbuckle, an' worms i' the chieks!'

A wheen o' us. . . . no' the feck mebbe. . . . hevna' ony richt at a' tae lat oorsels be brubbed, tae hide frae the truth because it's laithsome."

I nodded to show that I understood. "Ulysses" is not staple fare—but it has made cleanliness and beauty more precious to us hasn't it? The dismally dirty and giggling sexual novels will continue to roll out under a thin pretence of psychological treatment. But Joyce! . . . Somehow that stupendous uprising of the *vis comica* in his work seemed to be reflected, as I looked in the "breengin' " masonry of the grey Metropolis.

"The verra last thing Scottish literature needs is *lady-fying.* Gillespie's an idiot!* It needs an almark like Joyce. . . . I'm no' cock-bird-high yet. I'm like a Lilliputian courtin' a Brobdingnagian Queen. Ae glisk o'r emasculates me. A mannikin's nae use tae the likes o' yon—a buist o' a wumman! But I'd glammoch her if I'd Joyce's virr. . . . Look at her!

> 'If she could get hersel' but carl'd
> In time o' need. . . . . ."

(*Changing his metaphors carelessly.*) see her carvortin' in a licht like this, like yin o' the Fower Horses riderless!

> 'Whene'er her tail plays whisk
> Or when her look grows skeigh,
> It's then the wice auld man
> Is blythe to stand abeigh.'

But I'm nae wice auld man. God forbid! Scottish literature's had far ower mony o' *them.* I'm nae aulder than Edinburgh at onyrate an' juist as young an' allryn—if I was only a wee thingie bigger. . . . . . (*Waving his hand castle-wards.*) The Apocalyptic Beast wi' her black hoofs o' a Castle pawin' i' the air an' yon shaggy mane o' cloods hodin' the starnies like nits.

> 'Auld Reekie cavie't back an' fore
> An' flapt her sooty wings.'

Puir Rosenberg's poem is juist how I feel when I look at this camsteerie toon—

> 'No slim form work fire to my thighs
> But human life's inarticulate mass

*See *Martin Gillespie's review of "The Judge" in the September Chapbook.*

Throb the pulse of a thing
Whose mountain flanks awry
Beg my mastery,—mine!
Ah! I will ride the dizzy beast of the world
My road—my way!"

. . . . I'm by wi' clotchy novels. They're a delusion and a snare. Their effects have nae lastin' i' them. Lichtly come, lichtly gane. If fiction's the modern reader's University it's a schule whaur he learns owt an' minds nowt—a literary blin' alley. . . . . . Look at yon curn o' camla-like tenements! A cary-tempered cratur's nae use. Yon mannie Synge was richt: 'It may almost be said that before verse can be human again it must learn to be brutal.' . . . . The like's true o' a' forms o' literature. Novels are juist bletherin' bagrels. Joyce has chammered them a' for the likes o' us . . . Ech! It needs an almark like him tae claut a city like this. Na! na! I'd leifer be cuckold than capstridden but. . . . this *aigre?* . . . . (*with intense anguish*) I canna dae't. I canna begin tae dae't. . . . I dinna blame the lassie. . . . but (*with the bitterest smile of self-contempt*)

'Oh had I but ten thousand at my back
And were a man I'd gar their curpons crack.' "

Scottish Chapbook 1.6 (1922). 68–73.

GLOSSARY

Abbote Unreassone a sort of historic character, anciently exhibited in Scotland, whose actions were inconsistent with reason and meant to excite mirth
abeigh aloof, at a distance
abies in comparison with
ablachs dwarfs (expression of contempt)
aidle-hole a hole to receive cow urine
aifer exhalations which rise from the ground on a warm, sunny day (synonym of "startle-o'-stobie")
aigre sour
airts points of the compass ("a airts," on all sides)
allagrugous grim, ghastly
allerish chilly
allryn constantly progressive
Almanie whistle child's small toy whistle
almark a beast accustomed to break fences
amid-ward in or towards the midst of
amplefeysts sulky humours
analite alienated
ankerly unwilling
appen furth the free air

assopat put to rest
attrie purulent
Auld Reekie Old Smoky (name for Edinburgh)
averil beast of burden
babelerie idle chatter
bachrams cow dung
baffles trifles
baginin' trifling, dallying, the indelicate toying common between young people of different sexes on the harvest-field
bagrels small persons with big bellies
banes bones
bealin an' brakkin oot festering and breaking out
bleeze an' busk great show and decoration
bletherin' talking nonsense
braid broad
breengin' moving impetuously
brubbed checked, restrained
buist a thick and gross object
ca' to drive, "ca' o' the stanes"—probably motion of stones by analogy to "ca' o' the water," motion of the waves as driven by the wind
camla-like sullen, surly
camsteerie wild, unmanageable, riotous
capstridden forestalled by another in drinking as the "cap" goes round, cheated
carl'd provided with a male (used of a bitch)
cary-tempered probably from "carie," pliable
cavie't pranced
chackit chequered
chammered silenced
chapling the term used when in an election merchants or craftsmen lose their individual votes and go with the majority of their guild or craft
charbuckle carbuncle
cheatrie deceitful
chieks cheeks
chowkin' choking
clapper-clawin' attacking with the tongue
clatter-bane "Your tongue gangs like the *clatter-bane* o' a goose's arse"; spoken to people who talk too much and to little purpose
claut to scrape together
clean-fung cleverly done
clocksie vivacious
closeevie collection
clotchy done in a careless or hurried way
clowders (obs. var. of clutter) crowded confusion of movement; noisy turmoil
clyres diseased glands
cockalan a comic or ludicrous representation; an imperfect writing

cock-bird-high very young
Corbaudie the obstacle, used of a plausible hypothesis which is opposed by some great difficulty
coutribat confused struggle, tumult
cranglin' winding
crap highest part; craw of a fowl
cratur creature
crookit an' croodit crooked and crowded
cullages characteristic marks of sex
curn a quantity, an indefinite number
curpons rump of a fowl; applied ludicrously to buttocks of a man
Doric Scots vernacular
ettlin' attempting, making an effort
fashed troubled
feck the greatest part
flair skate, a fish
forbye besides
glammoch grasp
glisk a passing glance
gowpenfu' as much as can be contained in both hands in a concave form
guff smell
hass throat
haud hold
heid head
hippit pained in the back, loins, and thighs from stooping
hodin hiding
howkand digging
hurkland banes hip bones
Kinkhost whooping-cough
laithsome loathsome
lassock diminuitive of "lass," a small girl
Liberty of December December celebrations marked, in the Middle Ages, by the "liberty" to step outside normal rules and hierarchies and to engage in all kinds of role reversals, clowning, satire, and parody; the revelry or carnival was presided over by the Abbote Unreassone
licht light
lug ear
maun must
mochy moist; applied to meat when it begins to be putrid
muckle big
nits nuts
orra surplus; base, low, worthless
plukes pimples
reek smoke
rippet noise of great mirth; uproar in a bad sense

Shoggin' shaking
scaffie scavenger
schule school
scowry shabby, mean
shoon shoes
skeigh shy; proud, disdainful
spyrin' soaring, aspiring
stanes stones
starnies little stars
startle-o'-stobie exhalations seen to rise from the ground, with an undulating motion, on a warm sunny day
stirk bullock or heifer between one and two years old; stupid fellow
toon town
virr vitality
wee an' wale weigh and choose
wheen a number, a few
worms i' the chieks toothache
yhowthyede youth

Djuna Barnes (right) and Mina Loy, 1920. Photo © by Man Ray. Sylvia Beach Collection, Princeton University Library.

Willa Cather (right) with Louise Pound. Willa Cather Pioneer Memorial Collection, Nebraska State Historical Society.

Nancy Cunard, London, 1930. Photo by Cecil Beaton. From *Nancy Cunard: Brave Poet, Indomitable Rebel, 1886–1965,* ed. Hugh Ford. Philadelphia: Chilton Book Co., 1968.

H. D. Beinecke Rare Book and Manuscript Library, Yale University.

T. S. Eliot and Virginia Woolf in Bloomsbury. Sylvia Beach Collection, Princeton University Library.

Jessie Redmon Fauset. Schomburg Center for Research in Black Culture, New York Public Library, Astor, Lenox and Tilden Foundations.

Zora Neale Hurston, probably in the 1930s. Moorland-Spingarn Library, Howard University.

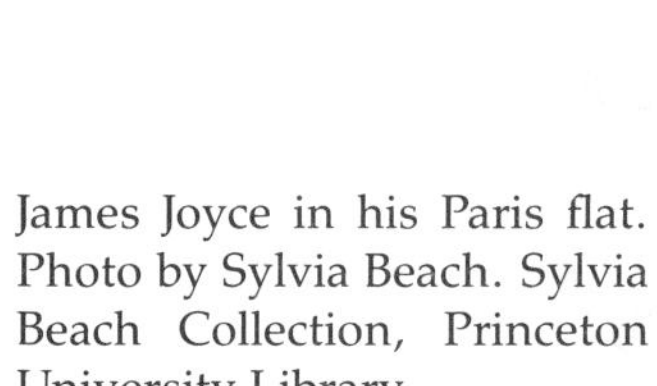

James Joyce in his Paris flat. Photo by Sylvia Beach. Sylvia Beach Collection, Princeton University Library.

D. H. Lawrence in 1913. From the collection of David Garnett.

Nella Larsen. Schomburg Center for Research in Black Culture, New York Public Library, Astor, Lenox and Tilden Foundations.

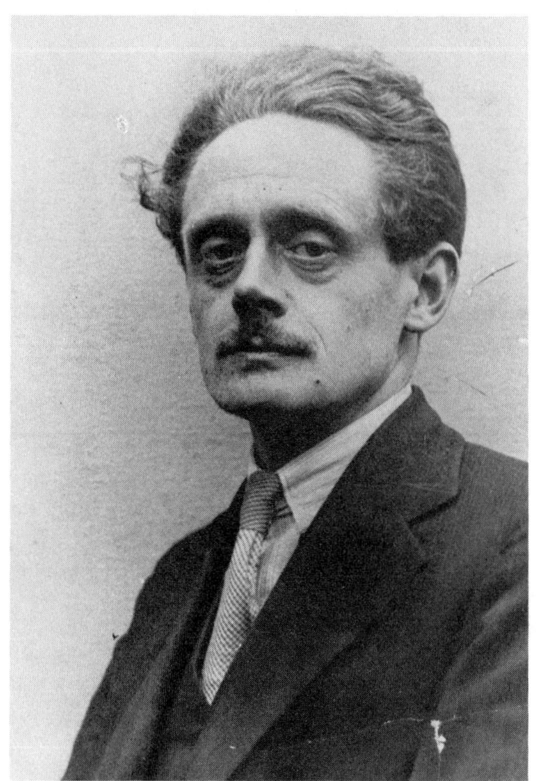

Hugh MacDiarmid, 1934 press photo, *Glasgow Herald*.

Katherine Mansfield. Sylvia Beach Collection, Princeton University Library.

Charlotte Mew in 1923. National Portrait Gallery, London.

Marianne Moore with her mother, Mary Warner Moore, in Cummington, Massachusetts, 1942. Rosenbach Museum and Library. Permission of Marianne Craig Moore, Literary Executory for the Estate of Marianne Moore.

Jean Rhys. Photo by Pearl Freeman. Thanks to Andre Deutsch Ltd.

May Sinclair. Special Collections Department, Van Pelt Library, University of Pennsylvania.

Dorothy Richardson with Alan Odle in garden. Beinecke Rare Book and Manuscript Library, Yale University.

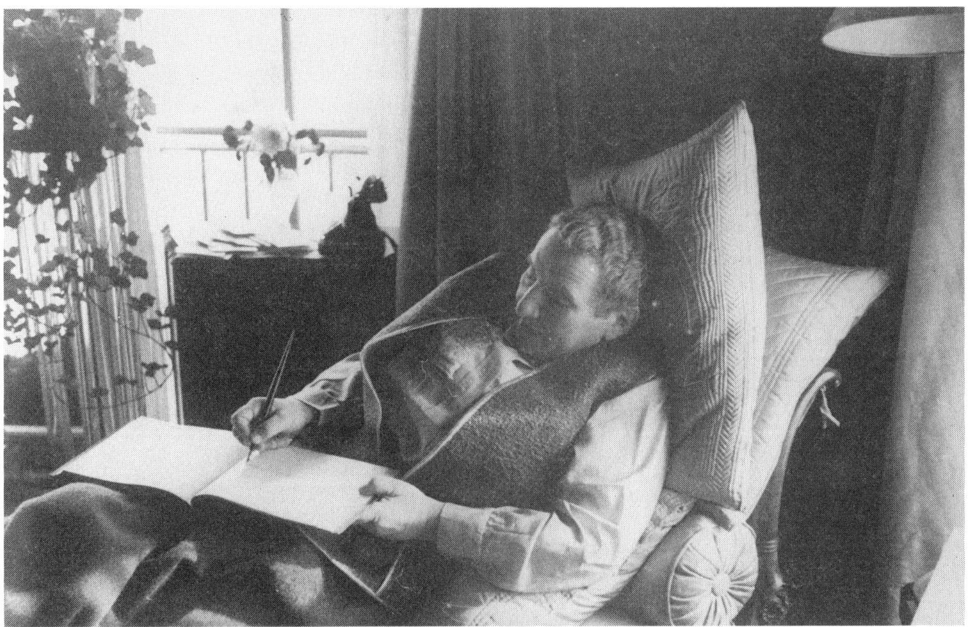

Gertrude Stein in Chicago in the 1930s. Beinecke Rare Book and Manuscript Library, Yale University.

Sylvia Townsend Warner. Thanks to Viking Penguin Press.

Antonia White. Emily Holmes Coleman Papers, Morris Library, University of Delaware, Newark, Delaware 19717-5267.

Rebecca West in riding costume, circa 1917. Photo given to Jane Marcus by Dame Rebecca.

to Sylvia Beach from
Bob McAlmon June 5-1925
Ernest Hemingway
Marsden Hartley.
H. D.
Bryher.
Ford Madox Ford
Mary Butts
May Sinclair
Dorothy Richardson.
Mina Loy

Autographed flyleaf of Sylvia Beach's copy of *Contact Collection of Contemporary Writers*, published by Robert McAlmon, 1925. Signatures include McAlmon's and those of the contributors, Ernest Hemingway, Marsden Hartley, H. D., Bryher, Ford Madox Ford, Mary Butts, May Sinclair, James Joyce, Dorothy Richardson, Mina Loy, Ezra Pound, and Gertrude Stein. Sylvia Beach Collection, Princeton University Library.

14

Katherine Mansfield (1888–1923)

Introduced and Edited by Clare Hanson

Katherine Mansfield is most commonly viewed as a minor modernist writer, dealing in delicate half-tones with the domestic aspects of life. In this respect she is often compared with women painters such as Berthe Morisot and Mary Cassatt, who have been presented in a similar way. I want to argue in the context of this volume that Mansfield is, as her husband John Middleton Murry claimed, a "great" writer.

When, immediately after Mansfield's death, Murry made his claim, D. H. Lawrence responded: "Poor Katherine, she is delicate and touching.—But not Great! Why say great?" (*Letters* 4:520). Why indeed? In the end—like, I suspect, most of the contributors to this volume—I believe there is no such thing as greatness in the sense of absolute aesthetic value. Value depends on numerous contingencies, and perhaps the only workable definition of aesthetic value is in terms of use. A valuable text is one that performs for a given individual a multiplicity of functions, intersecting with a wide range of that individual's experience.

That said, it may seem contradictory to claim that Katherine Mansfield is great. It would be stating my purpose more accurately to say that what is needed is a revision of the whole notion of greatness. A great text is perhaps one that is great in the more colloquial sense of the word, i.e., one that makes itself available to readers to be used in a wide variety of contexts, in relation to a complex range of experiences. Mansfield's writings, I would argue, perform such a function at least as fully as those of many canonical male writers, including Lawrence. Acceptance of this view is of course dependent on our placing as much value on feminine as on masculine modes and realms of experience, and, perhaps, on our accepting that the view from the margins, to which women have to a greater or lesser degree been confined, has as much if not more value than the view from the ostensible center.

Mansfield, then, is a marginal not a minor writer—marginalized in particular ways during her lifetime and in rather different ways after her death. When she arrived in London from New Zealand in 1908, she felt herself to be doubly disadvantaged, as a woman writer and as a colonial, and it is fascinating, if rather disturbing (or touching, as Lawrence might say), to see the ways in which from the beginning of her career she searched for male mentors who would perform the double function of protecting her from sexual exploitation (a real danger for a young woman entering a male professional world—compare the case of Jean Rhys) and of promoting her work. A succession of rather ineffectual young men were supplanted in this role by A. R. Orage, the powerful editor of the *New Age* magazine, who promoted Mansfield's work assiduously while, apparently, nicknaming her "the marmozet" behind her back and dubbing her "vulgar and enterprising." Would a young man in a similar position be censured in quite this way? (Carswell 75).

It was not until Mansfield met Murry in late 1911 that she found a protector who in all conscience immediately recognized that her talent was far greater than his own and who supported her work throughout her life, despite his inadequacies and inept conduct at various stages in their personal relationship. It is something of a paradox that Murry was one of the first critics to place Mansfield's work, as we have seen, on a level with those of the "great" canonical male writers. In *The Problem of Style* (1921), Murry moves easily from the pantheon of Shakespeare, Milton, Wordsworth, Coleridge, and Keats to Mansfield (the only other woman writer mentioned is Jane Austen).

Quite apart from the fact that Murry developed many of the ideas for his book in conversation with Mansfield,[1] the discussion of her work shows a genuine understanding of its impulse and purpose. Murry quotes from *Prelude* and acknowledges the power behind its apparently everyday surface. He doesn't belittle the world of the text but sees that the domestic world of women and children is freighted with at least as much emotional significance as the world of male work or "adventure."

Murry's advocacy of Mansfield's work during her lifetime is problematic not just because of the emotional damage he inflicted on her privately but, more important, because of the way in which he, as an influential literary critic, shaped her reputation after her death. Beginning with the heady claim to greatness quoted at the beginning of this introduction, Murry declined with disappointing rapidity into a convenient collapsing of distinctions between Mansfield's life and her work. He began to project his idealized picture of his dead wife as a person back onto her work. Katherine, it was necessary for him to believe, had been a delicate and saintly human being, and so her work became "exquisite," full of "inward purity."

From there it is but a short step to the demeaning of Mansfield's work by T. S. Eliot in *After Strange Gods* (1934). He writes disdainfully of one of her stories that it is "brief, poignant and in the best sense, slight." As readers, "our satisfaction recognises the skill with which the author has handled perfectly the *minimum* material" so that the story is "what I believe would be called feminine" (Eliot 35–36).

A persistent devaluing of Mansfield's work followed, on the grounds that it was delicate, minor, feminine (the terms become synonymous when used by male critics). This tendency culminated in Frank O'Connor's duplicitous attack in *The Lonely Voice* (1963), in which he castigated Mansfield for the "girlish effusiveness" and "fastidiousness" of her work while reproving her for the "sordid love affairs" of her life (O'Connor 137–142).

Implicit in much of this adverse criticism of Mansfield is the assumption that the short story is a minor art form: her choice of form is seen as determining the status of her art.[2] I would suggest that there is a clear connection between Mansfield's choice of the short story form and her marginal position. The short story is a genre which, both formally and in terms of its traditional content, has always been marginal, fragmented. Formally, the constraint of brevity prevents our having a complete, harmonious vision of experience. In terms of content, the traditional concern of the short story has been the portrayal of the experience of misfits, marginal figures of some kind—"tramps, artists, lonely idealists, dreamers and spoiled priests," as O'Connor put it (20–21). O'Connor sees this marginality as a limitation of the short story, whereas I would argue that to take this view is to succumb to the false belief that the concerns of a politically or ideologically dominant group in society are, or should be, of greater importance than those of other groups.

The short story is a form of exclusion and implication; its technical workings mirror its ideological bias, its tendency toward the expression of that which is marginal or ex-centric to society. It is precisely because of this bias that the short story has been a particularly important form for women. Many women writers have made their reputation entirely as short story writers—Katherine Mansfield, Mary Lavin, Eudora Welty, Grace Paley, Alice Munro, to name only a few. But this reputation has been compromised and their work has been seen as minor *precisely because* they have been short story writers. The choice of genre should not be held against them but should alert critics to the fact that they are expressing a difference of view which may be more illuminating than the view from the cultural center.

Just as Mansfield's work has been devalued because she worked in the short story form, so the substantial amount of work which she produced in her letters and journals has been consistently undervalued.[3] This is part of the same catch-22 pattern whereby women writers "choose" a noncanonical, nonprestigious form, and are then dismissed out of hand *because* they have written in this form. Much work is currrently being done by feminist critics to restore to us the vast amount of letter and journal material produced by women writers. Mansfield's vivid, dazzlingly composed letters and journals deserve the same treatment and recognition. They present the same problem in terms of value as the short stories—they deal with the mundane and domestic, they are not always overtly intellectual. But who can compute the value of such a moment of being as the following, comparable with the discreet and oblique moments of insight in the poetry of Emily Dickinson:

> But one says not a word and to the best of one's belief gives no sign. I went out into the gentle rain and saw the rainbow. It deepens; it shone down into the sea and it faded: it was gone. The small gentle rain fell on the other side of the world. Frail—frail. I felt Life was no more than this. (*Journal* 219)

Mansfield's method in her letters, journals, and fiction was always one of extreme indirection and obliquity. Revelation through "the slightest gesture" was, she wrote, her aim (see excerpt from Early Journal included here). This indirection and obliquity might be viewed as particularly feminine, and I think it *is* feminine in the sense that there is a real distinction to be made between Mansfield's symbolist method and that of T. S. Eliot or James Joyce.

I have argued elsewhere that Mansfield is a symbolist writer, taking from her early reading of Arthur Symons, Walter Pater, and Oscar Wilde the belief that in literature abstract states of mind or feeling should be conveyed through concrete images rather than described analytically.[4] Yet there is a wide gap between, for example, Eliot's famous description of his "method" of the objective correlative (on which he attempts to confer a quasi-scientific status) and Mansfield's evocation of her method in a letter to Murry (16 November 1919, included here). Mansfield avoids analysis and abstraction, explaining her method by using practical examples—the "boy eating strawberries" or the "woman combing her hair on a windy morning" through whom she could touch her deeper theme of "deserts of vast eternity."[5] While Eliot seeks to create a critical metalanguage in which to discuss his texts, Mansfield resists it, probably because her symbolist method was arrived at by a different route from that of Eliot and has a quite different inflection.

Mansfield's symbolist method of indirection does not stem from nor lead to a theoretical belief; it stems rather from an intense responsiveness to what she called in the 16 November letter the "common things" of life, her commitment to a common language, the small change, as it were, of gesture and speech through which, for most of us, the deeper things of life are intimated and expressed. This commitment to the common things of life, to the surface of life, is clearly not an essentially feminine characteristic;[6] however, it certainly marks the work of a great many women writers who have, I would suggest, been thought of as somehow minor or trivial because of it. (Compare, from Mansfield's period, Elizabeth Bowen and Rosamund Lehmann and, more recently, Elizabeth Taylor and Barbara Pym).

In this context it is revealing to see Mansfield and Murry (as representative male reader) disagreeing over the story "Poison" (1920), which is a perfect example of Mansfield's indirect method. Murry thought the story "not wholly successful," but Mansfield defended it in terms that recall her phrase "the slightest gesture": she explains the way in which the deeper themes of the story are expressed through surface appearances—"these are the rapid confessions one receives sometimes from a glove or a cigarette or a hat" (letter to Murry, end of November 1920, printed below).

The obliquity of Mansfield's method in fiction extends to her critical writing. She was not the kind of writer to outline a program for her art; nor did she draw up critical statements to explain or promote it (cf. Eliot's numerous critical essays in which he, in Helen Gardner's phrase, "creat[ed] the taste by which he [was] to be enjoyed," or Joyce's program notes for *Ulysses*). Mansfield also distrusted "professional" criticism like that produced by Murry, feeling that it did not often represent, as she said, something learned "at the risk of [one's] life" (Murry, *Letters* 476).

Her distinctive "female aesthetic"[7] was explored and explained as much in her letters and journals as in the formal reviews which she undertook in 1919–1920 at Murry's request.[8] To take one example, in a journal entry of 1920 (see "The Flowering of the Self," below), Mansfield expresses her sense of a tension between the multiplicity of the self—a multiplicity defined by her in Freudian terms that acknowledge the significance of the unconscious—and an awareness of unity that transcends their multiplicity, if only momentarily. The sense of the fragmentation of the self is feminine in the sense that the (real) self keeps exceeding and evading (masculine) attempts to name it and pin it down, to give it the right "keys" in relation to the symbolic order. The sense of the moment, too, is feminine in that it is linked to awareness of what Kristeva called "women's time" as opposed to linear time.

Mansfield extends the implications of this journal note in a review of Sackville-West's *Heritage* (see "A Novel without a Crisis," below), in which the sense of fragmentation and the sense of the moment are linked to a change in the structure of a novel or story. Mansfield urges that formally as well as stylistically a text must reflect the author's perception of life as a heterogeneous flux marked by "blazing moments."

In a more abstract journal entry on Vaihinger's *Die Philosophie des Als Ob* ("On Vaihinger," below) Mansfield reflects on a related issue, her uneasy sense, continually expressed in her work, that "thinking" and "existing" are always on "two different planes." Vaihinger provided a solution to the problem this presented for her as an artist. The writer, she concluded in the excerpt printed here, should never attempt to impose her or his vision on reality, on the existing world. The artist must not "grind an axe," but must create "alternative worlds" that would comment concretely on existing worlds, on "what we accept as reality."

It is extraordinary how influential Mansfield's criticism was, considering that it was disseminated in such a haphazard fashion.[9] Woolf was not the only writer to be deeply influenced by Mansfield's critical precepts as well as her creative practice (she both loved and feared her "rival" in prose; Mansfield's writing was, she wrote in her diary, "the only writing I have ever been jealous of" [*Diaries* 2:227]). May Sinclair was devastated by Mansfield's criticism of her work in the review of *Mary Olivier* printed below, for Mansfield was, in Sinclair's view, the only person who really knew about writing (Murry, *Letters* 280). Hence the significance, I would argue, of Mansfield's intervention in the debate going on around 1920 over what Dorothy Richardson called "feminine prose."

I have presented Mansfield as a writer who can be clearly opposed to the hard-edge male modernists such as Eliot and Pound, implying that her writing is distinctively feminine, that it represents a feminine version of modernism. One can of course take this argument much further. One might suggest, for example, that the initial impetus for modernism came in fact from women writers, so that to talk of a female version of modernism—implying a secondary position for women—is misleading. One might suggest rather that modernism as we have been taught it is a male parasite on a body of experience and a way of seeing pioneered by women. But such an argument lies outside the scope of this brief introduction.

The immediate problem is how a feminine and feminist writer such as Mansfield came to reject so firmly the experiments of Richardson and Sinclair with a radical "feminine prose" (see "Dragonflies" and "The New Infancy," below). I have suggested elsewhere (*Critical Writings* 18) that her rejection of Richardson and Sinclair may have been in part a self-protective strategy, that Mansfield, like Woolf, saw in their feminine prose a drift toward undifferentiated words and worlds which she recognized in herself but wished to repress. I think, however, that the debate over Richardson and Sinclair has wider implications. I would suggest that Mansfield had valid reasons for wanting to resist attempts to set up a separate space or position for women in language, sensing that it might lead to a loss of real (ultimately political) power for women. It is only relatively recently that we as critics have begun to emerge from the shadow of Lacanian theory, which has dictated that women's entry into language must be defined negatively. As feminist critics begin to challenge this view and to ask new questions about power, strength, and authority in writing, their work will, I suspect, shed new light on (and perhaps vindicate) Mansfield's determined holding on to a position of control and authority in language.

As May Sinclair's reaction to Mansfield's review shows, there was a considerable degree of networking and debate among British women modernist writers. There was, one might say, a division between the more authoritarian Mansfield and Woolf on one hand and the advocates of a freer-flowing feminine prose on the other. The picture becomes still more complicated when we recognize that there were differences of opinion between Mansfield and Woolf about the direction fiction should take. In a key review of 1919 (see "A Ship Comes into the Harbour," below), Mansfield took Woolf to task for the traditional form and content of *Night and Day.* This criticism had a decisive effect on Woolf, driving her to experiments in short fiction, published as *Monday or Tuesday,* and thence to *Jacob's Room.* Woolf's debt to Mansfield was very great,[10] but in emphasizing this point I am not attempting somehow to boost the value of Mansfield's work by virtue of association with a writer who has become almost an honorary male modernist, the only female modernist to be accepted as "great." I want instead to claim a certain parity for Mansfield, to balance her claims against those of Woolf, as Woolf herself did when she wrote in her diary after Mansfield's death: "though I can do this better than she could, where is she, who could do what I can't" (*Diaries* 2:226).

Woolf's question takes us back to the questions about value raised at the beginning of this introduction. Her openness to and recognition of the value of writing that was "other," that could "do what I can't," is exemplary. It is an example that male critics, in particular, have been less than eager to follow.

NOTES

1. Murry wrote *The Problem of Style* when he was living with Mansfield at the Villa Isola Bella, Menton, in 1921.

2. The Constable *Collected Stories* has been in print continuously since 1945. Penguin Books also brought out an edition, *Collected Short Stories,* in 1981. In addition, Anthony Alpers edited an excellent "definitive edition" (*The Stories of Katherine Mansfield,* Auckland: Oxford UP, 1984).

3. The first two volumes of the five-volume *Collected Letters of Katherine Mansfield,* ed. Vincent O'Sullivan with Margaret Scott, have already appeared (Oxford: Oxford UP, 1984, 1987). The letters to Murry which I have quoted are, unfortunately, too late in date to be included, so that my source has remained *The Letters of Katherine Mansfield to John Middleton Murry.*

4. See my "Katherine Mansfield and Symbolism" and my introduction to *Critical Writings.* I should perhaps add a note of self-criticism: in my early article I have fallen into the trap of trying to argue Mansfield's case by making her into a male modernist writer, a position I would now repudiate.

5. The reference is to Marvell, "To His Coy Mistress."

6. I would take Julia Kristeva's view that there are no *essentially* "feminine" or "masculine" characteristics; rather, the "feminine" and the "masculine" are subject positions which are open to any given individual to take up.

7. Elaine Showalter coined the term to denote the aesthetic of Woolf, Mansfield, and Richardson.

8. Mansfield wrote weekly reviews for the *Athenaeum,* the influential periodical which Murry edited from April 1919 to December 1920.

9. Mainly in her informal talks with writers such as Woolf, in her letters, then through the highly selective letter and journal selections brought out by Murry after her death. Her weekly reviews for the *Athenaeum* were reprinted only once, ten years after first publicaton, and seem to have caused little stir.

10. There are close parallels—to take just two examples—between the theme and form of *Prelude* and *To the Lighthouse* and "At the Bay" and *The Waves.*

WORKS CITED

Carswell, John. *Lives and Letters: A. R. Orage, Katherine Mansfield, Beatrice Hastings, John Middleton Murry, S. S. Koteliansky, 1906–1957.* London: Faber, 1978.
Eliot, T. S. *After Strange Gods: A Primer of Modern Heresy.* London: Faber, 1934.
Hanson, C. "Katherine Mansfield and Symbolism: The 'Artist's Method' in *Prelude.*" *Journal of Commonwealth Literature* 16(1981):25–39.
Kristeva, Julia. *La Revolution du langage poetique.* Paris: Seuil, 1974.
Lawrence, D. H. *The Letters of D. H. Lawrence.* Ed. James T. Boulton. 4 vols to date. Cambridge: Cambridge UP, 1971–.
Mansfield, Katherine. *Novels and Novelists.* Ed. J. Middleton Murry. New York: Knopf, 1930.
———. *Collected Stories.* London: Constable, 1945.
———. *The Letters of Katherine Mansfield to John Middleton Murry.* Ed. J. Middleton Murry. London: Constable, 1954.
———. *The Critical Writings of Katherine Mansfield.* Ed. Clare Hanson. London: Macmillan, 1987.
Murry, John Middleton. *The Problem of Style.* Oxford: Oxford UP, 1922.
———. *The Letters to John Middleton Murry to Katherine Mansfield.* Ed. C. Hankin. London: Constable, 1983.
O'Connor, Frank. *The Lonely Voice: A Study of the Short Story.* London: Macmillan, 1963.
Showalter, Elaine. *A Literature of Their Own.* Princeton: Princeton UP, 1977.
Sinclair, May. *Mary Olivier: A Life.* London: Hogarth P, 1919.
Woolf, Virginia. *Night and Day.* London: Hogarth P, 1921.
———. *Jacob's Room.* London: Hogarth P, 1922.
———. *The Diaries of Virginia Woolf.* Ed. Anne Olivier Bell. 5 vols. London: Hogarth P, 1977–1984.

RECENT CRITICISM

Fullbrook, Kate. *Katherine Mansfield.* Brighton: Harvester, 1986.
Gubar, Susan. "The Birth of the Artist as Heroine: (Re)production, the *Kunstlerroman* Tradition, and the Fiction of Katherine Mansfield." In *The Representation of Women in Fiction,* ed. Carolyn Heilbrun and Margaret R. Higonnet. Baltimore: Johns Hopkins UP, 1983.

From Early Journal

The partisans of analysis describe minutely the state of the soul; the secret motive of every action as being of far greater importance than the action itself. The partisans of objectivity—give us the result of this evolution sans describing the secret processes. They describe the state of the soul through the slightest gesture—i.e. realise flesh covered bones—which is the artist's method for me—in as much as art seems to me *pure vision*—I am indeed a partisan of objectivity—

The Critical Writings of Katherine Mansfield. Ed. Clare Hanson. London: Macmillan, 1987. 9–10.

From Letters to John Middleton Murry

16 NOVEMBER 1919

What is this about the novel? Tell me, thou little eye among the blind. (It's easy to see who my bedfellow has been.) But seriously, Bogey, the more I read the more I feel all these novels will not do. After them I'm a swollen sheep looking up who is not fed. And yet I feel one can lay down no rules. It's not in the least a question of material or style or plot. I can only think in terms like "a change of heart". I can't imagine how after the war these men can pick up the old threads as though it had never been. Speaking to *you* I'd say we have died and live again. How can that be the same life? It doesn't mean that life is the less precious or that 'the common things of light and day' are gone. They are not gone, they are intensified, they are illumined. Now we know ourselves for what we are. In a way it's a tragic knowledge: it's as though, even while we live again, we face death. But *through Life:* that's the point. We see death in life as we see death in a flower that is fresh unfolded. Our hymn is to the flower's beauty: we would make that beauty immortal because we *know.* Do you feel like this—or otherwise—or how?

But, of course, you don't imagine I mean by this knowledge let-us-eat-and-drink-ism. No, I mean "deserts of vast eternity". But the difference between you and me is (perhaps I'm wrong) I couldn't tell anybody *bang out* about those deserts: they are my secret. I might write about a boy eating strawberries or a woman combing her hair on a windy morning, and that is the only way I can ever mention them. But they *must* be there. Nothing less will do. They can advance and retreat, curtsey, caper to the most delicate airs they like, but I am bored to Hell by it all. Virginia, *par exemple.*

The Letters of Katherine Mansfield to John Middleton Murry. Ed. J. Middleton Murry. London: Constable, 1954. 392–393.

END OF NOVEMBER 1920

And about *Poison.* I could write about that for pages. But I'll try and condense what I've got to say. The story is told by (evidently) a worldly, rather cynical (not wholly cynical) man *against* himself (but not altogether) when he was so absurdly young. You know how young by his idea of what woman is. She has been up to now, only the *vision,* only she who passes. You realise that? And here he has put *all* his passion into this Beatrice. It's *promiscuous love,* not understood as such by him; perfectly understood as such by her. But you realise the vie de luxe they are living—the very table—sweets, liqueurs, lilies, pearls. And you realise? she expects a letter from someone calling her away? *Fully* expects it? That accounts for her farewell AND her declaration. And when it doesn't come even her *commonness* peeps out—the newspaper touch of such a woman. She can't disguise her chagrin. She gives herself away. . . . He, of course, laughs at it now, and laughs at her. Take what he says about her "sense of order" and the crocodile. But he also regrets the self who dead privately would have been young enough to have actually wanted to *marry* such a woman. But I meant it to be light—tossed off—and yet through it—oh, subtly—the lament for youthful belief. These are the rapid confessions one receives sometimes from a glove or a cigarette or a hat.

I suppose I haven't brought it off in *Poison.* It wanted a light, light hand—and then with that newspaper a sudden . . . let me see, *lowering* of it all—just what happens in promiscuous love after passion. A glimpse of staleness. And the story is told by the man who gives himself away and hides his traces at the same moment.

I realise it's quite a different kind to *Miss Brill* or *The Young Girl.* (She's not "little", Bogey; in fact, I saw her big, slender, like a colt.)

Letters. 604–605.

The Flowering of the Self (From Journal, 1920)

When autograph albums were the fashion—sumptuous volumes bound in soft leather, and pages so delicately tinted that each tender sentiment had its own sunset sky to faint, to die upon—the popularity of that most sly, ambiguous, difficult piece of advice: "To thine own self be true" was the despair of collectors. How dull it was, how boring, to have the same thing written six times over! And then, even if it was Shakespeare, that didn't prevent it—oh, *l'âge d'innocence!*—from being dreadfully obvious. Of course, it followed as the night the day that if one was true to onself . . . True to oneself! which self? Which of my many—well really, that's what it looks like coming to—hundreds of selves? For what with complexes and repressions and reactions and vibrations and reflections, there are moments when I feel I am nothing but the small clerk of some hotel without a proprietor, who has all his work cut out to enter the names and hand the keys to the wilful guests.

Nevertheless, there are signs that we are intent as never before on trying to puzzle out, to live by, our own particular self. *Der Mensch muss frei sein*—free, disentangled, single. Is it not possible that the rage for confession, autobiography, especially for memories of earliest childhood, is explained by our persistent yet mysterious belief in a self which is continuous and permanent; which, untouched by all we acquire and all we shed, pushes a green spear through the dead leaves and through the mould, thrusts a scaled bud through years of darkness until, one day, the light discovers it and shakes the flower free and—we are alive—we are flowering for our moment upon the earth? This is the moment which, after all, we live for,—the moment of direct feeling when we are most ourselves and least personal.

The Journal of Katherine Mansfield 1904–1922. Ed. John Middleton Murry. London: Constable, 1954. 205.

On Vaihinger (From Journal, 1921)

Vaihinger: *Die Philosophie des Als Ob.* How comes it about that with curiously false ideas we yet reach conclusions that are in harmony with Nature and appeal to us as Truth?

It is by means of, and not in spite of, these logically defective conceptions that we obtain logically valuable results. The fiction of *Force:* when two processes tend to follow each other, to call the property of the first to be followed by the other its "force", and to measure that "force" by the magnitude of the result (*e.g.* force of character). In reality we have only succession and co-existence, and the "force" is something we imagine.

Dogma: absolute and unquestionable truth.

Hypothesis: possible truth (Darwin's doctrine of descent).

Fiction: is impossible but enables us to reach what is relatively truth.

The myths of Plato have passed through these three stages, and passed back again, i.e., they are now regarded as fiction.

Why must thinking and existing be ever on two different planes? Why will the attempt of Hegel to transform subjective processes into objective world-processes not work out? "It is the special art and object of thinking to attain existence by quite other methods than that of existence itself." That is to say, reality cannot become the ideal, the dream; and it is not the business of the artist to grind an axe, to try to impose his vision of life upon the existing world. Art is not an attempt of the artist to reconcile existence with his vision; it is an attempt to create his own world *in* this world. That which suggests the subject to the artist is the *unlikeness* to what we accept as reality. We single out—we bring into the light—we put up higher.

Journal 1904–1922. 272–273.

Three Women Novelists (From Review of Dorothy Richardson's *The Tunnel*)

Why was it written? The question does not present itself—it is the last question one would ask after reading *The Tunnel.* Miss Richardson has a passion for registering every single thing that happens in the clear, shadowless country of her mind. One cannot imagine her appealing to the reader or planning out her novel; her concern is primarily, and perhaps ultimately, with herself. "What cannot I do with this mind of mine!" one can fancy her saying. "What can I not see and remember and express!" There are times when she seems deliberately to set it a task, just for the joy of realizing again how brilliant a machine it is, and we, too, share her admiration for its power of absorbing. Anything that goes into her mind she can summon forth again, and there it is, complete in every detail, with nothing taken away from it—and nothing added. This is a rare and interesting gift, but we should hesitate before saying it was a great one.

The Tunnel is the fourth volume of Miss Richardson's adventures with her soul-sister Miriam Henderson. Like them, it is composed of bits, fragments, flashing glimpses, half scenes and whole scenes, all of them quite distinct and separate, and all of them of equal importance. There is no plot, no beginning, no middle or end. Things just "happen" one after another with incredible rapidity and at break-neck speed. There is Miss Richardson, holding out her mind, as it were, and there is Life hurling objects into it as fast as she can throw. And at the appointed time Miss Richardson dives into its recesses and reproduces a certain number of these treasures—a pair of button boots, a night in Spring, some cycling knickers, some large, round biscuits—as many as she can pack into a book, in fact. But the pace kills.

There is one who could not live in so tempestuous an environment as her mind—and he is Memory. She has no memory. It is true that Life is sometimes very swift and breathless, but not always. If we are to be truly alive there are large pauses in which we creep away into our caves of contemplation. And then it is, in the silence, that Memory mounts his throne and judges all that is in our minds—appointing each his separate place, high or low, rejecting this, selecting that—putting this one to shine in the light and throwing that one into the darkness.

We do not mean to say that those large, round biscuits might not be in the light, or the night in Spring be in the darkness. Only we feel that until these things are judged and given each its appointed place in the whole scheme, they have no meaning in the world of art.

Novels and Novelists. Ed. J. Middleton Murry. New York: Knopf, 1930. 5–6.

Dragonflies (From Review of Richardson's *Interim*)

Who can tell, watching the dragonfly, at what point in its swift angular flight it will suddenly pause and hover, quivering over this or that? The strange little jerk—the quivering moment of suspension—we might almost fancy they were the signs of a minute inward shock of recognition felt by the dragonfly. "There is something here; something here for me. What is it?" it seems to say. And then, at the same instant, it is gone. Away it darts, glancing over the deep pool until another floating flower or golden bud or tangle of shadowy weeds attracts it, and again it is still, curious, hovering over. . . .

But this behaviour, enchanting thought it may be in the dragonfly, is scarcely adequate when adopted by the writer of fiction. Nevertheless, there are certain modern authors who do not appear to recognize its limitations. For them the whole art of writing consists in the power with which they are able to register that faint inward shock of recognition. Glancing through life they make the discovery that there are certain experiences which are, as it were, peculiarly theirs. There is a quality in the familiarity of these experiences or in their strangeness which evokes an immediate mysterious response—a desire for expression. But now, instead of going any further, instead of attempting to relate their "experiences" to life or to see them against any kind of background, these writers are, as we see them, content to remain in the air, hovering over, as if the thrilling moment were enough and more than enough. Indeed, far from desiring to explore it, it is as though they would guard the secret for themselves as well as for us, so that when they do dart away all is as untouched, as unbroken as before.

But what is the effect of this kind of writing upon the reader? How is he to judge the importance of one thing rather than another if each is to be seen in isolation? And is it not rather cold comfort to be offered a share in a secret on the express understanding that you do not ask what the secret is—more especially if you cherish the uncomfortable suspicion that the author is no wiser than you, that the author is in love with the secret and would not discover it if he could? . . .

Interim, which is the latest slice from the life of Miriam Henderson, might almost be described as a nest of short stories. There is Miriam Henderson, the box which holds them all, and really it seems there is no end to the number of smaller boxes that Miss Richardson can make her contain. But *Interim* is a very little one indeed. In it Miriam is enclosed in a Bloomsbury boarding-house, and though she receives, as usual, shock after shock of inward recognition, they are produced by such things as well-browned mutton, gas jets, varnished wallpapers. Darting through life, quivering, hovering, exulting in the familiarity and the strangeness of all that comes within her tiny circle, she leaves us feeling, as before, that everything being of equal importance to her, it is impossible that everything should not be of equal unimportance.

Novels and Novelists. 142–146.

The New Infancy
(Review of May Sinclair's *Mary Olivier*)

There has been discovered, of late, cropping up among our established trees and flowers a remarkable plant, which, while immensely engaging our attention, has not hitherto attained a size and blooming sufficient to satisfy our desire to comprehend it. Little tight buds, half-open flowers that open no further, a blossom or two more or less out—these the plant has yielded. But here at last, with "Mary Olivier" Miss May Sinclair has given into our grateful hands a full fine specimen.

Is this, we wonder, turning over its three hundred and sixty-eight pages, to be the novel of the future? And if so, whence has it sprung? Who are its ancestors, its parents, its relations, its distant connections even? But the longer we consider it the more it appears to us as a very orphan of orphans, lying in a basket on the threshold of literature with a note pinned on its chest saying: "If I am to be taken in and welcomed, then the whole rest of the family must be thrown out of the window." That they cannot exist together seems to us very plain. For the difference between the new way of writing and the old way is not a difference of degree but of kind. Its aim, as we understand it, is to represent things and persons as separate, as distinct, as apart as possible. Here, if you like, are the animals set up on the floor, the dove so different from the camel, the sheep so much bigger than the tiger. But where is the Ark? And where, even at the back of the mind, is the Flood, that dark mass of tumbling water which must sooner or later receive them, and float them or drown them? The Ark and the Flood belong to the old order, they are gone. In their place we have the author asking with indefatigable curiosity: "What is the effect on this animal upon me, or this or the other one?"

But if the Flood, the sky, the rainbow, or what Blake beautifully calls the bounding outline, be removed and if, further, no one thing is to be related to another thing, we do not see what is to prevent the whole of mankind turning author. Why should writers exist any longer as a class apart if their task ends with a minute description of a big or a little thing? If this is the be-all and end-all of literature why should not every man, woman and child write an autobiography and so provide reading matter for all ages? It is not difficult. There is no gulf to be bridged, no risk to be taken. If you do not throw your Papa and your Mamma against the heavens before beginning to write about them, his whiskers and her funny little nose will be quite important enough to write about, quite enough, reinforced with the pattern of the drawing-room carpet, the valse of the moment and the cook upstairs taking her hair out of pins to make a whole great book. And as B's papa's whiskers and B's mamma's funny little nose are bound to be different again, and their effect upon B again different—why here is high entertainment forever!

Entertainment. But the great writers of the past have not been "entertainers". They have seen seekers, explorers, thinkers. It has been their aim to reveal a little of the mystery of life. Can one think for one moment of the mystery of life when one is at the mercy of surface impressions? Can one *think* when one is not only taking part but being snatched at, pulled about, flung here and there, cuffed, kissed, and played with? Is it not the great abiding satisfaction of a work of art that the writer was master of the situation when he wrote it and at the mercy of nothing less mysterious than a greater work of art?

It is too late in the day for this new form, and Miss Sinclair's skilful handling of it serves but to make its failure the more apparent. She has divided her history of Mary Olivier into five periods, infancy, childhood, adolescence, maturity and middle-age, but these divisions are negligible. In the beginning Mary is two, but at the end she is still two—and forty-seven—and so it is throughout. At any moment, whatever her real age may be she is two—or forty-seven—either, both. At two (poor infant staggerer!) the vast barn of impressions opens upon her and life, with a pitchfork, tosses her out Mamma, Papa, Mark, Roddy, Dan, Jenny, Catty, Aunt Charlotte, Uncle Victor, and all the rest of them. At forty-seven, although in the meantime many of them have died and died disgustingly, she is still turning them over and over, still wondering whether any of them did happen to have in one of their ignoble pockets the happiness she has missed in life . . . For on page 355 she confesses, to our surprise, that is what she has been wanting all along—happiness. Wanting, perhaps, not seeking, not even longing for, but wanting as a child of two might want its doll or its donkey, running into the room where Papa on his dying bed is being given an emetic, to see if it is on the counterpane, running out to see if it is in the cab that has come to take Aunt Charlotte to the Lunatic Asylum, and then forgetting all about it to stare at "Blanc-mange going round the table, quivering and shaking and squelching under the spoon."

Novels and Novelists. 43–45.

A Ship Comes into the Harbour (Review of Virginia Woolf's *Night and Day*)

There is at the present day no form of writing which is more eagerly, more widely discussed than the novel. What is its fate to be? We are told on excellent authority that it is dying; and on equally good authority that only now it begins to live. Reviewers might almost be divided into two camps. Present each camp with the same book, and from one there comes a shout of praise, from the other a chorus of blame, each equally loud, determined and limited. One would imagine from a reading of the press notices that never in the history of the world was there such a generous distribution of the divine fire together with such an overwhelming display of ignorance, stupidity and dreariness. But in all this division and confusion it would seem that opinion is united in declaring this to be an age of experiment. If the novel dies it will be to give way to some new form of expression; if it lives it must accept the fact of a new world.

To us who love to linger down at the harbour, as it were, watching the new ships being builded, the old ones returning, and the many putting out to sea, comes the strange sight of *Night and Day* sailing into port serene and resolute on a deliberate wind. The strangeness lies in her aloofness, her air of quiet perfection, her lack of any sign that she has made a perilous voyage—the absence of any scars. There she lies among the strange shipping—a tribute to civilization for our admiration and wonder.

It is impossible to refrain from comparing "Night and Day" with the novels of Miss Austen. There are moments, indeed, when one is almost tempted to cry it Miss Austen up-to-date. It is extremely cultivated, distinguished and brilliant, but above all—deliberate. There is not a chapter where one is unconscious of the writer, of her personality, her point of view, and her control of the situation. We feel that nothing has been imposed on her: she has chosen her world, selected her principal characters with the nicest care, and having traced a circle round them so that they exist and are free within its confines, she has proceeded, with rare appreciativeness, to register her observations. The result is a very long novel, but we do not see how it could be otherwise. This leisurely progression is essential to its manner, nor could the reader, even if he would, drink such wine at a gulp. As in the case of Miss Austen's novels we fall under a little spell; it is as though, realizing our safety, we surrender ourselves to the author, confident that whatever she has to show us, and however strange it may appear, we shall not be frightened or shocked. Her creatures are, one might say, privileged; we can rely upon her fine mind to deliver them from danger, to temper the blow (if a blow must fall), and to see their way clear for them at the very last. It is the measure of Mrs Woolf's power that her "happy ending" could never be understood as a triumph of the heart over the mind. But whereas Miss Austen's spell is as strong upon us as ever when the novel is finished and laid by, Mrs Woolf's loses something of its potency. What is it that carries us away? With Miss Austen, it is her feeling for life, and then her feeling for writing; but with Mrs Woolf these feelings are continually giving way the one to the other, so that the urgency of either is impaired. While we read we scarcely are aware which is uppermost; it is only afterwards, and, specially when recalling the minor characters, that we begin to doubt. Sally Seal of the Suffrage Society, Mr Clacton with his French novel, old Joan in her shabby dress, Mrs Denham peering among the cups and saucers: it is true that these characters are not in any high degree important—but how much life have they? We have the queer sensation that once the author's pen is removed from them they have neither speech nor motion, and are not to be revived again until she adds another stroke or two or writes another sentence beneath. Were they shadowy or vague this would be less apparent, but they are held within the circle of steady light in which the author bathes her world, and in their case the light seems to shine at them, but not through them.

Night and Day tells of Katharine Hilbery's attempt to reconcile the world of reality with what, for want of a better name, we call the dream world. She belongs to one of the most distinguished families in England. Her mother's father was that "fairest flower that any family can boast"—a great poet. Katharine's father is an eminent man of letters, and she herself as an only child "had some superior rank among all the cousins and connections." Grave, beautiful, with a reputation for being eminently practical and sensible beyond her years, she keeps house for her parents in Chelsea, but this activity does not exhaust Katharine. She has her lonely life remote from the drawing-room in Cheyne Walk, and it is divided between dreams "such as the taming of wild ponies on the American prairies, or the conduct of a vast ship in a hurricane round a promontory of rock", and the study of mathematics. This last is her half-conscious but profound protest against the family tradition, against the making of phrases and (what Mrs Woolf rather curiously calls) "the confusion, agitation and vagueness of the finest prose".

But it is only after she has contracted an engagement which is in every way highly suitable with William Rodney, a scholar whose knowledge of Shakespeare, of Latin and Greek, is not to be disputed or denied, that she realizes in so doing she has in some mysterious way betrayed her dream world—the lover on the great horse riding by the seashore and the leaf-hung forests. Must life be for ever this lesser thing, this world as we know it, shapely, polished and secure? Katharine had no impulse to write poetry, yet it was the poet in her that made her see in Ralph Denham the man for whom she could feel that strange great passion which is like a fire lighting up the two worlds with the one exultant flame . . .

It would be interesting to know how far Mrs Woolf has intended to keep this dream would of Katharine's and of Ralph's a deep secret from her readers. We are told that it is there, and we believe it; yet would not our knowledge of these two be wonderfully increased if there were something more than these suggestions that are like delicate veils hiding the truth? . . .

As for the real world, the world of Mr and Mrs Hilbery, William Rodney, Cassandra Otway—there we appreciate to the full the author's exquisite generosity. It is so far away, so shut and sealed from us to-day. What could be more remote than the house at Cheyne Walk, standing up in the night, with its three long windows gilded with light, its drawn velvet curtains, and the knowledge that within a young creature is playing Mozart, Mrs Hilbery is wishing there were more young men like Hamlet, and Katharine and Rodney are faced by the incredible sight of Denham, outside in the dark, walking up and down . . .

We had thought that this world was vanished for ever, that it was impossible to find on the great ocean of literature a ship that was unaware of what has been happening. Yet here is *Night and Day* fresh, new, and exquisite, a novel in the tradition of the English novel. In the midst of our admiration it makes us feel old and chill: we had never thought to look upon its like again!

Novels and Novelists. 112–115.

A Novel without a Crisis (From Review of Vita Sackville-West's *Heritage*)

On page 3 of her novel Miss Sackville West makes an interesting comment:

> I should like to explain here that those who look for facts and events as the central points of significance in a tale will be disappointed. On the other hand I may fall upon an audience which, like myself, contends that the vitality of human beings is to be judged less by their achievement than by their endeavour, by the force of their emotion rather than by their success.

These are not extraordinary words; but we are inclined to think they contain the reason for the author's failure to make important a book which has many admirable qualities.

If we are not to look for facts and events in a novel—and why should we?—we must be very sure of finding those central points of significance transferred to the endeavours and emotions of the human beings portrayed. For, having decided on the novel form, one cannot lightly throw one's story over the mill without replacing it with another story which is, in its way, obedient to the rules of that discarded one. There must be the same setting out upon a voyage of discovery (but through unknown seas instead of charted waters), the same difficulties and dangers must be encountered, and there must be an ever increasing sense of the greatness of the adventure and an ever more passionate desire to possess and explore the mysterious country. There must be given the crisis when the great final attempt is made which succeeds—or does not succeed. Who shall say?

This crisis, then, is the chief of our "central points of significance" and the endeavours and the emotions are stages on our journey towards or away from it. For without it, the form of the novel, as we see it, is lost. Without it, how are we to appreciate the importance of one "spiritual event" rather than another? What is to prevent each being unrelated—complete in itself—if the gradual unfolding in growing, gaining light is not to be followed by one blazing moment? . . .

These are bare outlines, richly filled in by the author, and yet we are not "carried away". She has another comment:

> Little of any moment occurs in my story, yet behind it all I am aware of tremendous forces at work which none have rightly understood, neither the actors nor the onlookers.

That is easily said. We have heard it so often of late that we are grown a little suspicious, and almost to believe that these are dangerous words for a writer to use. They are a dark shield in his hand when he ought to carry a bright weapon.

Novels and Novelists. 31–34.

15
Charlotte Mew (1870–1928)

Introduced and Edited by Celeste M. Schenck

Although Virginia Woolf, probably paraphrasing Thomas Hardy, once wrote to Sackville-West that she had just met "Charlotte Mew (the greatest living poetess)," critics have only begun to revalue the corpus so admired by Mew's contemporaries—Woolf, Hardy, May Sinclair, Ezra Pound, John Masefield, Harold Munro, H. D., Rebecca West, Wilfred Blunt, T. E. Lawrence, and Siegfried Sassoon—and even by some followers, most notably Marianne Moore (Woolf, *Diary* 2:319 and n. 9; *Letters* 2:140). Val Warner's 1981 reissue of Mew's *Collected Poems,* accompanied by Mew's complete prose, and Penelope Fitzgerald's biography, *Charlotte Mew and Her Friends,* praised by Brad Leithauser in a kind but somewhat patronizing review essay on Mew in the *New York Review of Books* ("Small Wonder"), have brought her work back to light.

A number of critics, most notably Leithauser, have singled Mew out for her "indigenous originality" (25) and her distinctive voice. Nonetheless, they tend at the same time to censure her for her small, unoracular formalism—"her pitch is refined and her scale is modest" (31). When they do attribute to her some "nervy bravado," they do so for the Hardyesque roughed-up rhymes, the ventriloquistic experiments with dialect, the perseverance of repeated rhyme that Marianne Moore would later make famous and acceptable

(26). Additionally, in their haste to excuse her "measured and unspectacular" production beside the new form-shattering norm set by a masculinist "Modernism," these critics fail to read beyond what they see as rhythmical familiarity and rhyme to a strikingly unconventional content.[1] The sexual frankness of Mew's poetry has been overlooked even by feminist critics attuned to Mew's revisionary impulses. Beyond her personal and idiosyncratic voice, beyond her only occasional generic daring, is a surprisingly radical politics and an erotic choice unexpectedly rendered in formal verse.

If, as both Georg Lukács and feminist critics have noted,[2] the radical poetics of canonized "Modernism" often masks a deeply conservative politics, might it also be true that the seemingly genteel, conservative poetics of women poets such as Mew, whose worth even feminists have overlooked, would pitch a more radical politics than we considered possible? The inclusion of Mew in this anthology calls into question the equation both conservative "Modernists" and radical theorists have made between radical form and radical politics. Even a critical theorist such as Julia Kristeva might co-conspire in a "Modernist" hegemony that fetishizes formal experiment.

If Mew's case is to be heard and the annals of poetic "Modernism" duly revised, we must attend more carefully to the differences between rearguard and avant-garde modernism. If we listen to the more traditional meters of Anna Wickham, Charlotte Mew, Sylvia Townsend Warner, Alice Meynell, and Edith Sitwell (not to mention the five hundred or so British women who wrote strong war poetry during the years around 1914) as attentively as we now hear the daring verbal experiments of H. D., Gertrude Stein, and Mina Loy, we must renounce, salutarily, any hope for a unitary, totalizing theory of female poetic modernism. The situation of marginalized modernists such as Mew, Wickham, Townsend Warner, Meynell, and Sitwell has much to tell us, not only about the dispersive underside of the "Modernist" monolith but also about inadvertent feminist participation in the politics of canonicity.

Whereas Djuna Barnes's lesbian eroticism, flamboyantly announced in the *Repulsive Women* "rhythms," no longer provokes surprise, Mew's lyric exploration of the same themes within the confines of meter and rhyme has been overlooked. "On the Road to the Sea" regrets that "I who make other women smile did not make you," until the achieved smile at the end of the poem marks a climactic dying: "Reeling—with all the cannons at your ear." In "The Fête," female sexuality receives delicate but nonetheless explicit treatment:

> At first you scarcely saw her face,
> You knew the maddening feet were there,
> What called was that half-hidden, white unrest
> To which now and then she pressed
> Her finger tips; but as she slackened pace
> And turned and looked at you it grew quite bare:
> There was not anything you did not dare:— (*Collected Poems* 6–7)

"Absence," perhaps more than any other Mew poem, evokes both delight in female sexuality and conflict over its homoerotic expression (see the poem, reprinted below). As anatomically suggestive of female anatomy as Sappho's imagery, Mew's adumbration of hooded female pleasures safe from the destructive beat of masculine hooves eases the traditional Sapphic concern for a lost maidenhead, trampled by shepherds until only a purple stain remains upon the ground.

> In sheltered beds, the heart of every rose
> Serenely sleeps to-night. As shut as those
> Your guarded heart; as safe as they from the beat, beat
> Of hooves that tread dropped roses in the street. (47)

But the cost to the poet-speaker of answering the call of her female lover's eyes is conveyed in the last stanza in an arresting image of silencing by the "scarred hands" of Christ "over my mouth."

Even more unsettling is the morbid but fascinating exploration of enveloping female eroticism in "The Forest Road" (20–22), a poem pronounced pathological by a contemporary physician. It is, no less than Shelley's *Alastor,* a quest for what the speaker thinks is other and learns is in fact the same. By the close of each, a binding love tryst gives over to death, as the poet-speaker confronts his or her own soul in the figure of the other. But whereas Shelley's poet's pursuit of an elusive maiden brings him to the grave, "The Forest Road" explores the contours of a female symbiosis that reads simultaneously as ecstasy and death: the poet knows she "could go free," if only she could separate from the other's enlacing hair: "I must unloose this hair that sleeps and dreams / About my face, and clings like the brown weed / To drowned, delivered things." Trying to quiet her female other, to "hush these hands that are half-awake / Groping for me in sleep," at the last she cannot separate from her. The image of double suicide which closes the poem marks a mutual female climax as well: as the "dear and wild heart" of the one has been broken in its breast of "quivering snow / With two red stains on it," the other determines to "strike and tear / Mine out, and scatter it to yours." In spite of its exploration of the danger of giving in to the "poor, desolate, desperate hands" of the other, the poem ends ecstatically: "I hear my soul, singing among the trees!" Although Mew's biographers agree that her love for women remained to the end of her days a locus of conflict and psychic pain, her appreciation of female sexuality, in both benign and threatening manifestations, is at the heart of her best poetry.

The violence of "The Forest Road" is balanced by the delicate evocation of autoerotic pleasure in Mew's magnificent "Madeleine in Church." These lines fairly exult in the capacity for female self-enjoyment apart from the determining sexual presence of an other.

> I could hardly bear
> The dreams upon the eyes of white geraniums in the dusk,

The thick, close voice of musk,
The jessamine music on the thin night air,
Or, sometimes, my own hands about me anywhere—
The sight of my own face (for it was lovely then) even the
scent of my own hair,
Oh, there was nothing, nothing that did not sweep to the high seat
Of laughing gods, and then blow down and beat
My soul into the highway dust, as hoofs do the dropped roses of the street.
I think my body was my soul,
And when we are made thus
Who shall control
Our hands, our eyes, the wandering passion of our feet. (23)

This long poem of over two hundred lines, Mew's best, written during her years of friendship with novelist May Sinclair, is composed of both varying rhyme schemes and stanza structures; each movement of this dramatic monologue is accompanied and marked by elaborate formal variation. In this dreamlike section in particular, the incantatory rhythms and the sexual content of the lines invite enormous variation in line length and emphasis, whereas other more conversational sections call for more regularity in line length and meter.

Aside from its formal ingenuity, "Madeleine in Church" should be viewed as the culmination of an entire genre, a revision of the Victorian Fallen Woman poem, which Mew appropriates to champion rather than punish female sexuality, a revision informed as much by her own sexual conflicts as by her impatience with traditional mythologies of the "pécheresse" (Mizejewski 283, 301): Mew gives her modern Magdalen both a voice—of which the canon, preferring to objectify her, had deprived her—and entitlement to full sexual enjoyment, autoerotic, heterosexual, or lesbian.

Not just the experimental female modernists, then, but a good number of those faithful to meter and rhyme wrote a poetry of marked sexual preference. Mew's passionate attachments seem always to have been to other women. By middle age she wore frankly masculine clothing, always sporting a tweed topcoat and a "felt pork-pie hat put on very straight" (Monro, "A Memoir" viii). In a photographic frontispiece to the 1953 edition of the *Collected Poems* (also included in the illustrations in this anthology), she appears in full cross-dress.

Despite the spareness of her production (her first book appeared in 1916 when she was nearly fifty), Mew wrote overtly feminist poetry that was highly recognized in its day. Feminist attention to Stein's, Loy's, and H. D.'s linguistic iconoclasm should not eclipse Mew's political analyses of femininity, prostitution, and war, a feminist politics that surfaces most compellingly and characteristically in her poetry. Next to Loy's explorations of the decadent "Café du Néant" we should place Mew's poems of France, among them "Pécheresse," "Le Sacré-Coeur," "Monsieur qui Passe," and the Madeleine poem described above, all of which analyze the uses to which female sexuality is put: "*Une jolie fille à vendre, très cher;* / A thing of gaiety, a thing of sorrow, / Bought to-night, possessed, and tossed / Back to the mart again to-morrow" (31).

Mew also wrote a handful of war poems during the years 1915–1919, which number among the most passionate and feminist of that period. Rhymed, metered, divided conventionally into stanzas, "The Cenotaph" (reprinted below) and "May 1915" are pacifist hymns that re-member the "young, piteous, murdered face[s]" of the war dead by giving voice to grieving women, those "watchers by lonely hearths" who "from the thrust of an inward sword have more slowly bled" (35).

The inclusion of Mew in this anthology, a formal but feminist poet alongside other women writers whose politics took more radical poetic forms, is a step toward a rigorous comparativism between and among women writers which might save us from critical solipsism, a comparativism alert to the politics of exile and exclusion which still underwrites canonicity.

NOTES

1. My argument for including Charlotte Mew in this anthology includes a polemic for the dismantling of a monolithic "Modernism" defined by its iconoclastic irreverence for convention and form, a difference which has contributed to the marginalization of women poets during the period and even to division among them, a difference which I have taken care to signal by substituting the plural and uncapitalized *modernisms* for *Modernism* as a marker of such omissions and exclusions. It is my contention, as Susan Stanford Friedman put it, that "the presumed chasm between experimental and realist writing is misleading for the study of women's writing" (2). I would also suggest that although a certain stylistic designation is lost if we open up "Modernism" to anything written between 1910 and 1940, we lose in at least equal measure if we restrict this literary critical marker of periodization to experimental writing alone. We lose, in short, all the other modernisms against which a single strain of white, male, international "Modernism" has achieved such relief.

2. I refer to Lukács' "Ideology of Modernism" and Robinson and Vogel's polemic against the detachment of culture from history in modernist art and for the study of race, class, and sex as factors of exclusion.

WORKS CITED

Fitzgerald, Penelope. *Charlotte Mew and Her Friends.* London: Collins, 1984.

Friedman, Susan Stanford. "Forbidden Fruits of Lesbian Experimentation." Paper given at Modern Language Association, December 1985.

Leithauser, Brad. "Small Wonder." Review of Fitzgerald's *Charlotte Mew and Her Friends. New York Review of Books* 15 Jan. 1987:25–31.

Lukács, Georg. "The Ideology of Modernism." *The Meaning of Contemporary Realism.* Trans. John and Necke Mander. London: Merlin, 1963.

Mew, Charlotte. *Charlotte Mew: Collected Poems and Prose.* Ed. and intro. Val Warner. Manchester: Carcanet (Virago), 1981.

Mizejewski, Linda. "Charlotte Mew and the Unrepentant Magdalene: A Myth in Transition." *Texas Studies in Language and Literature* 26(Fall 1984):282–302.
Monro, Alida. "Charlotte Mew—A Memoir." In *Collected Poems of Charlotte Mew.* London: Duckworth, 1953. I cite Warner's edition; see Mew above.
Reilly, Catherine. *Scars upon My Heart: Women's Poetry and the Verse of the First World War.* London: Virago, 1981.
Robinson, Lillian and Lise Vogel. "Modernism and History." *New Literary History* 3(Autumn 1971):177–199.
Schenck, Celeste. "Exiled by Genre: Modernism, Canonicity, and the Politics of Exclusion." In *Women's Writing in Exile: Alien and Critical,* ed. Mary Lynn Broe and Angela Ingram. Chapel Hill: U of North Carolina P, 1989.
Woolf, Virginia. *The Diary of Virginia Woolf.* Vol. 2 Ed. Anne Olivier Bell. New York: Harcourt Brace Jovanovich, 1978.
———. *The Letters of Virginia Woolf.* Vols. 1 and 2. Ed. Nigel Nicolson. London: Hogarth P, 1976, 1977.

Absence

Sometimes I know the way
  You walk, up over the bay;
It is a wind from that far sea
That blows the fragrance of your hair to me.

Or in this garden when the breeze
  Touches my trees
To stir their dreaming shadows on the grass
  I see you pass.

In sheltered beds, the heart of every rose
  Serenely sleeps to-night. As shut as those
Your guarded heart; as safe as they from the beat, beat
Of hooves that tread dropped roses in the street.

    Turn never again
    On these eyes blind with a wild rain
  Your eyes; they were stars to me.—
    There are things stars may not see.

  But call, call, and though Christ stands
    Still with scarred hands
  Over my mouth, I must answer. So
  I will come—He shall let me go!

The Cenotaph

Not yet will those measureless fields be green again
Where only yesterday the wild, sweet, blood of wonderful youth was shed;
There is a grave whose earth must hold too long, too deep a stain,
Though for ever over it we may speak as proudly as we may tread.
But here, where the watchers by lonely hearths from the thrust of an inward
                    sword have more slowly bled,

We shall build the Cenotaph: Victory, winged, with Peace, winged too, at
                    the column's head.
And over the stairway, at the foot—oh! here, leave desolate, passionate
                    hands to spread
Violets, roses, and laurel, with the small, sweet, twinkling country things
Speaking so wistfully of other Springs,
From the little gardens of little places where son or sweetheart was born
                    and bred.
In splendid sleep, with a thousand brothers
                              To lovers—to mothers
                              Here, too, lies he:
Under the purple, the green, the red,
It is all young life: it must break some women's hearts to see
Such a brave, gay coverlet to such a bed!
Only, when all is done and said,
God is not mocked and neither are the dead.

For this will stand in our Market-place—
                              Who'll sell, who'll buy
                              (Will you or I
Lie each to each with the better grace)?
While looking into every busy whore's and huckster's face
As they drive their bargains, is the Face
Of God: and some young, piteous, murdered face.

16
Marianne Moore (1887–1972)

Introduced and Edited by Marilyn L. Brownstein

Although Marianne Craig Moore did not call herself a feminist, she left a unique record of feminist commitment as explicit and steadfast as her better-known allegiance to the Brooklyn Dodgers.[1] Moore's feminism, evolving quite naturally from the facts and habits of her everyday life, informs all aspects of her work. The documents gathered for this volume are designed to show how Moore's "inherent feminism" (Costello), her accommodation to life's demands, forms the basis of a literary and ideological feminism. The collection contains excerpts from quite ordinary family correspondence as well as samples of Moore's literary reviews, the former demonstrating a maternal ethic and poetic out of which the latter evolved.

Marianne Craig Moore and her brother, John Warner Moore, older by a year and a half, grew up without their father. John Milton Moore had suffered a mental breakdown and was institutionalized before the birth of his daughter. Mary Warner Moore returned to the home of her father, the Reverend John R. Warner, to raise her children. When Marianne was seven, her grandfather died, and the balance of her life was governed, as William Carlos Williams liked to observe, by close affiliation with her mother. Except for Moore's four years at Bryn Mawr, mother and daughter lived together until Mrs. Moore's death in 1947. Marianne, moreover, replicated in a larger community the matter and manner of feminine family ties that were the natural facts of her long and stunningly fruitful association with her own mother. The evidence of Moore's reconstitution of her family of origin in literary friendships has been preserved in the Moore archive at the Rosenbach Museum and Library in Philadelphia. (The collection contains most of Moore's correspondence—with some three thousand persons—including her letters, which she preserved in carbons and drafts, and her side of the family correspondence, which members returned at her request.)

A family record of regular and meticulously detailed accounts of ordinary experience begins in Mary Warner Moore's chatty correspondence with her cousin Mary Craig Shoemaker. The family history explains in part the intense volubility of these communications. After the death of the Reverend Warner, Mary moved from the manse in Kirkwood, Missouri, to Allegheny City and later to Carlisle, both in Pennsylvania, to be near relatives. A good natural writer with a moralistic bent, Mrs. Moore taught English at the Metzger Institute, a Presbyterian school for girls, which Marianne attended. Singleminded and optimistic, Mary instilled in her children principles that must have been essential to her own survival: a strong Christian faith and the equation of proximity and security, the immutable importance of the family tie. During the family's first separation (Warner at Yale, Marianne a year later at Bryn Mawr), Mrs. Moore struggled with the necessity of living apart from her children. The 16 May 1906 letter from Mary to Marianne and Warner contains her orchestration of the Bryn Mawr to Yale to Carlisle round-robin correspondence designed to preserve the family's vital signs. Among the signatures of intimate family life in the three-way correspondence are family names, largely derived from *The Wind in the Willows.* Home was "Fawndale," and Mrs. Moore, "Fawn." In the letter reprinted here, Marianne is "Fangs" and "Biter," Warner is "Toady"—and the masculine pronoun serves everyone.

The intensity of this letter is matched throughout the family correspondence (for the most part unavailable for publication at this time), which documents a lifelong preoccupation with staying in touch by meticulous listing of events and descriptions of physical objects. Probably the best book on the poetry, Costello's *Imaginary Possessions,* takes its title from a poetic derived, in my view, from this survival mechanism. An unforgettable example from the correspondence is Marianne and Warner's long search for an appropriate inscription for their mother's gravestone. A typical sort of linguistic dithering preserves maternal presence as a three-year, five-way correspondence (Marianne, Warner, Mary Shoemaker, and two stonecutters, one of whom died before the final arrangements could be made) poignantly focuses the details of loss. Linguistic resurrection, Costello's "possession," is not a metaphor in Moore's poetic but a force in which the invisible is realized rather than represented.

Years later, in a review of *Letters of Emily Dickinson,* Moore's analysis specifically discloses her reformulation of family habits in a literary context. Here, one individualistic woman poet, invested in the preservation of her own correspondence, speculates upon the motives of another who did the same. The review begins in a projection as Moore notes the importance of publication of the poet's correspondence—to the poet: her "notable secret . . . is revealed by herself rather than by 'so enabled a man' as the twentieth century critic." The letters' "chief importance," however, resides in prominent display of the "wholesomeness of the life" (illumination of the poetry is of secondary interest). Dickinson's natural responsiveness, "the truly unartificial spirit—flashing like an animal, with strength or dismay," yields an essential wisdom. The wholesome poet knows "death in its several forms—betrayal, separateness of dwelling, the sense of one's inadequacy, and physical death" (*Complete Prose* 291).

The inclusion of "separateness of dwelling" in the list is revealing. Certainly, during the Bryn Mawr years, the poet's anxiety—a mirror of her mother's—was managed by cycles of death-defying family letters, usually circulating several times a week, often more. Marianne's contributions, averaging upwards of thirty pages per letter, provide a compelling record of anxiety's coercion in the training of a poet. The sentence as a lifeline—communication as a maternal, nurturing connection—ultimately organized linguistic imperatives for Moore that were quite distinct from those of male modernism. The matter of the "wholesomeness of the life" moreover imputes ethical value to language. Moore extended these principles of a moral language from her family experience into her social ties and her work.

Besides lifelong correspondence with her mother's cousin, the loyal and articulate Mary Craig Shoemaker (and with other women relatives as well), Moore repeated family attachments in two cycles of letter-writing friendships with literary women: one with H. D. and Bryher and the other with Elizabeth Bishop and Louise Crane. The creation of a social world through the written word may suggest the project of male modernism, but Moore's achievement is distinct in that she attempts neither a reintegration of personal patterns nor an archaeology of civilization's debris; instead, she convenes the vivid circle of a family romance. The days and nights of Moore's created world are days and nights of exuberant particulars. Only apparently randomly arranged, memories' objects, in the letters and in the literary work, are in fact ordered and balanced by the natural forms and exigencies of the human body confidently deploying responses learned in a world secured through maternal benefactions. In an August 1937 letter to Elizabeth Bishop, Moore reveals the poet's preoccupations in creating such a body language: "to pore over minutiae as I do . . . makes such work as the carved capitals on the Madelaine, an active growing poem, the Saint-Paul cocoon, and the position of Joseph in the Flight to Egypt." Moore's world of particulars seeks the cleanest physical dynamic (reality) out of a wealth of stimuli (experience) in order to locate value in communication. Rather than a language that mediates reality, Moore's language attempts a return to physical relation.[2]

The "wholesomeness" of Moore's family life, the dynamic of moral forms (love of routine; exchange of confidences, support, even correction; and respect for manners, which preserve the whole), operated equally in Moore's relationships with literary women. Moore's implicit feminism may be discovered in literary friendships in which family morality organized a social order. Her explicit feminism survives in the extension of family forms into her work. Moore's relationship to her mother provides examples of the "minutiae," the dynamic of moral forms. Mrs. Moore's letter to Pound with Marianne's editing demonstrates the first principle of her feminist style in the utterly relaxed ego boundaries that facilitated profound sharing between mother and daughter throughout their lives. This attachment to maternal forms is repeated and elaborated in the Moore–Bryher–H. D. correspondence and in the Moore–Crane–Bishop correspondence. The style of the letters, the view of language which the style reveals, and of course the contents disclose a fully politicized commitment to the lives of women.

In Moore's long rambling letters a nonhierarchical reporting style is the distinctive feature. The 16 January 1923 letter to Bryher (very like the young Marianne's letters home) doesn't evade priorities in its unpredictable leaps from one topic to another but, on the contrary, partakes of an order learned in the exchange of family love. The presentation of facts, events, details is ordered by the logic of unmediated experience or memory—quite distinct from the logic of an order designed for entertainment, approval, or any other need operating when we censor and arrange what is not so neatly arranged in life itself.

Fusion of the personal and the public is another measure of feminist "wholesomeness": Moore's reassurance to H. D., for example, in overseeing business matters which H. D., in London during the war, couldn't manage. "Let it seem to you, dear Hilda, that this is *my* material and my trouble and my indignation and that nothing connected with your work is weighing on me as apart from myself" (Rosenbach collection, V:23:33). Similarly, when Bryher supplemented Moore's slim income, Moore responded: "The addition you speak of makes me realize more than ever, that one's debts of gratitude must needs be paid to someone other than the one from whom one receives" (Rosenbach collection, V:08:05). These family practices as general operating principles bespeak not only the intimacy among these women but also the generalization of private matters into the sphere of public values—and in both instances, not values necessarily congruent with prevailing cultural practice.

Moore's correspondence with Elizabeth Bishop and Louise Crane operated similarly. When they were in New York, they visited with Moore, telephoned her, and, each separately, wrote to her. In addition they regularly sent letters, cards, and souvenirs as Moore's not inconsiderable portion in the peripatetic Bishop's journeys. Although the letters did not circulate in round-robin fashion (as Bryher's, H. D.'s, and Moore's did during the war), the effect of unrestrained sharing is the same (see Bishop to Moore, 5 February 1940).

Moore's maternal mentoring of Bishop, an arrangement of mutual benefit, is mirrored in Bishop's responses, so like Moore's early letters to her own mother.[3] Bishop's letters reflect the reciprocity of love and work in the lives of the two women. The correspondence recreates a mother-daughter connection that includes Moore's reprimand of 10 February to Bishop, probably written a year after she had invited Bishop to show her all her work. Extracts from Moore's thank-you notes (to Crane) for gifts gathered as Crane and Bishop traveled together illustrate sustained and mutually voluptuous nurturing as Moore responds to their stream of souvenirs with notes that are gifts in themselves.[4]

Family interactions are not only markedly feminine in their diffuse boundaries and loving reciprocities. Often what has been read in Moore as regressive, restrained, or passive can be read, more properly, as aggressively feminist, progressive. Tess Gallagher's observation helps: Moore established a "brand of morality . . . marked by its utter lack of evangelism" (48, 49). Following the model of Henry James (whom she counted as an influence), Moore liked manners, decorum, reserve; "reticence" and "restraint" are part of a vocabulary of merit exercised throughout her assessments of artistic achievement—five decades of reviews that mark a contribution to literary modernism as considerable as the achievement of the poetry itself (see Costello *Imaginary Possessions,* Martin *Subversive Modernist*). Manners as such are not mediations of behavior in Moore's version, but, as in James, distillations of civilization, behaviors conforming to reality. Feminine reticence or manners and their opposite, natural behavior that appears to be "unruly," "untenable," "wayward" in its conflict with what is expected, define the field of authentic energy in Moore. A tension between manners and their lack, worked out linguistically, is the signature of Moore's feminist poetic.

The craft of the poem, its formal arrangements—"mechanics," according to Moore's 7 March 1937 letter to Bishop—are analogous to the poet's manners, in a Jamesian sense. In order for a poem to be memorable it must operate out of a drive toward perfectibility rather than a perfect form (out of a measured lack of reticence). The menace of good mechanics is unwarranted ambiguity, self-contradiction. Syntactic perfection calls attention to its own conventional goodness, thus fighting the "waywardness" of an idea, "the essential baldness" of "significant value." Mechanical goodness marks a measure of moral ease, and its subversion thus may be critical to the linguistic evocation of a physical truth. For the writer, speech at the margins of convention is the inevitable concomitant of the authentic self—fully a matter of choice rather than an unconscious or rebellious meandering off the beaten path.[5] Moore's poet rejects conventionality and not convention. Originating in behavior at once inevitable, intentional, marginal, and outspoken, the poet's moral position is located in form as well as content.

Management of restraint operates on levels beyond the mechanical. As the agent of Moore's warning to Bishop about crude speech in the 16 October letter, lexical restraint is equally the moral force of her poetic. In this letter a distinction between "lampblack" and a "cosmetic patch" organizes the demonstration. Intention is the issue: "lampblack" crudely disguises a flaw, while a cosmetic patch, by definition, precisely placed, calls attention to a distinctive feature. Although crudeness in itself presents difficulties for Moore, this letter demonstrates her reluctant sanction, operating similarly to her sanction of violence in Wallace Stevens's poetry. Her approval of "gore" in "Well Moused, Lion" is not a blanket commendation for violence. Each case is decided on its merits; so long as intention is responsive to real value, crudeness works. The "bearishness" that Moore rejects, earlier in the same review, is not dismissed out of any generalized refusal of violence but because it specifies tropes too violent for Moore's moral taste. Intention is not at issue here; nor is realism the exclusive criterion. As always in Moore there are parameters, moral and mechanical, for what is permissible in the poet's art.

Intentionality, marginality, and restraint constitute the moral principles of Moore's feminist politics. If restraint reflects the woman's subordinate position, then her management of restraint transforms passivity to intention, to power, to creativity. "Moore, it seems likely, as with so many extraordinary women of her time, never assumed accepted sexual exclusions within the artistic, social, or political sphere," Tess Gallagher comments in explaining the absence of overt political action in so political a figure as Moore (56). Moore never "assumed" the slights of sexual politics not because she was oblivious ("remote" or "chaste" is the common assessment) but because she had already chosen her own version of sexual exclusion. In her dedication to making her way in a literary revolution, Moore chose sexual restraint, chastity as power and independence—a radical choice even now.[6] This is not to argue the impossible—that Moore was neither viewed as nor treated as a woman by her contemporaries—but that she negotiated the shoals of sexual politics by self-protectively avoiding the compromises of sexual arrangements. In what must be regarded as a feminist move, Moore established margins of her own making in defense against finding herself abandoned at alien borders.

There is an early expression of her freedom, independence, and power in a long autobiographical letter to Ezra Pound (9 January 1919—her response to the 16 December 1918 letter included in the Pound section of this book). "I have taken great pleasure in both your prose and your verse, but it is what my mother terms the saucy parts, which have most fixed my attention. . . . I like a fight but I admit that I have at times objected to your promptness with the cudgels. I say this merely to be honest. . . . I do not appear [in literary publications]. Originally my work was refused by the Atlantic Monthly . . . and recently I have not offered it. . . . four or five poems of mine were published in *Poetry,* a fact which pleased me at the time, but one's feeling changes and not long ago when Miss Monroe invited me to contribute, I was not willing . . ." (Tomlinson 17). A similar confidence resides in the pithy retrospection "If I Were Sixteen Today," printed here. This "little" piece epitomizes the perfectibility of the marginalized feminine and its direction in Moore's own life, for Moore's earliest instruction in difference (her relationship to her brother's competence) also provided a lesson in masculine diffidence (her self-consciousness in contrast to Warner's confidence). Moore's emphatically understated personal style, the same as her literary style, articulates the cause of the "downtrodden sex" (*Complete Prose* 416) in a steady application of masculine diffidence—the powerful side of the thin coin of feminine restraint.

In "Charlotte Brontë" (see below) Moore's sardonic play on good manners (initially those of the civilized reviewer and ultimately those of the most precious of civilized male games, the yachting ritual) fuels an intentionality so palpable that the reviewer's usual beaker of objectivity cracks before our eyes. Utterly transparent, the reviewer's mannerisms are made barely to contain her anger, like any *guerrillère*'s nitro, about to explode, if so much as a floorboard creaks in protest. Similarly, Moore prepares to draw blood (actually, seeping "ichor"—it would seem the author of *Le Sang d'un Poète* hasn't real blood) in a sharply ironic attack on Cocteau's "unfeminist yet not wholly detached attitude to women" in her review of *The Infernal Machine* (*Complete Prose* 359).[7]

Moore's friendship with Bryher and H. D. as documented by Cyrena Pondrum, as well as the poem "Marriage," which Pondrum links to Moore's response to Bryher's marriage of convenience to Robert McAlmon, reveal Moore's view of the sexual struggle. In "Marriage" Adam finds that passion or the nightingale's song burns: "It clothes me with a shirt of fire" (*Complete Prose* 72). Moreover, passion distorts vision and transforms value. For an Adam well beyond "the days of prismatic colour," marriage destroys "the ease of the philosopher."[8] Adam's loss, then (within a wry feminist logic typical of Moore), contains the germ of universal masculine dis-ease (just as Eve's transgression, according to Genesis, contains the seed of feminine pain); Adam, in acceding to Eve's wishes, finds himself "unfathered by a woman." In a nice and commonsense turn from Genesis, Moore's Adam, in thrall to Eve, loses rationality rather than immortality (*Complete Poems* 73).[9]

The relationship between style in family letters and that of the poetry and reviews additionally confirms an entrenched feminine order. In the reviews the nonhierarchical style functions as an appreciation of difference among the writers Moore is reviewing. Moore responds to elements of the work under scrutiny as they appeal to her, and a uniquely organic review thus discloses, through imitation, the style and mechanics she admires. Particularly in the case of male poets, such as Cummings, Williams, and Stevens, Moore leaves evidence of her gifts as reader and prose stylist in essays that resonate with the poetry she is considering. These brilliantly individualistic reviews function on feminist principles. They articulate difference wittily, that is, paradoxically, by exposing difference through a play on similarity, through imitation. And, in what I have been calling Moore's nonhierarchical style, the review demonstrates a giving up of subject position in an *intentional* giving in to the subject-object confusion at the center of feminine desire. Such willing relinquishment of subjectivity accounts for the kind of boundaryless correspondences that were both literary style and life-style for Moore—an argument I make more extensively elsewhere ("Archaic Mother"). Note that the author does not disappear in such a giving over to the other; the very individuality of the reviews is ample evidence of that.

A literary style that gestures in its very manner to male fear, however, has become the sticking point of Moore's reputation. Her unique style recognizes and plays upon masculine terror, while her most radical intentions engender its description. Throughout her work Moore states and restates a central psychological insight bearing on the subordination of women. In "Hymen," reprinted below, she announces the "indestructibleness" of feminine beauty ("cowardice and beauty are at swords' points") as the locus of male fear. Critical discomfort with "Marriage" confirms Moore's feminist perspicacity and its predictable rejection. R. P. Blackmur, who admired the opaque idiosyncracies of her poetry, finally resists her, based on his reading of "Marriage." "No poet has been so chaste," he declares, and "life is remote . . . everything is done to keep it remote" (quoted by Martin, "Portrait" 194). Harold Bloom reads the same poem in a mirror. "I hardly know of a more unnerving representation of the male fear and distrust of the female, uncannily combined with the male quandary of being obsessed with, fascinated by . . . the female. Moore imperishably catches the masterpiece of male emotive ambivalence . . ." (7). Too close for comfort, Bloom resists in his fashion: "she is clearly the most original American poet of her era, though not quite of the eminence of Frost, Stevens, Crane" (1).

Moore's reviews of Stevens, the poet whose craft she most admired, are additionally instructive (see "Well Moused, Lion," below). Here she simply competes, braving masculine discomfort, typically, by overlooking it. The competitive quality of her prose recalls, however, a joyful singing contest between exotic birds of indescribable plumages (although all of the colors are named)—a contest without any of the anxiety of a wrestling match. In Moore competition is play: she mirrors Stevens's "nimbleness *con brio,*" producing some of the most accomplished of all twentieth-century reviews, although not necessarily in a style recognized by the academy.

Moreover, there is not just one reviewing style. Of intelligence and sympathy equal to her reviews of men's work, Moore's reviews of women's writing operate out of separate principles. In almost all cases, Moore explores the work of women (in particular, accomplished poets such as Bogan, H. D., and Bishop) in the context of her own feminist aesthetic. Rather than the mimetic-competitive play of her reviews of male writers (which cause some critics to judge her, at best, as one of the boys or, at least, as a clever but inferior bird), Moore applies her own feminist standards when considering women writers. She doesn't sing back to women poets but instead searches out the politics of the poems. Her play in these reviews is serious and emphatically political. Examples reprinted here are the reviews of H. D. ("Hymen") and of Bishop ("Archaically New") in which Moore toys with notions of gender stereotypes, testing the reader's sympathies at the same time that she evaluates the poet's strengths.

This play occurs equally at the levels of content and lexicon. Throughout her writing, Moore develops a feminist critique of language that fully anticipates the methodology of late-twentieth-century feminism. Notable are her attacks on the binary opposition, attacks which in fact constitute the superstructure of her poetic. Subversion of binarisms in Moore's work typically takes three forms. First, Moore employs conventionally negative words in contexts that make them positive, thus depriving them of negative valence and leaving them not only "cleansed" but muscular. Consider, for example, "insidiousness" in the 7 March 1937 letter to Bishop where physical invasiveness is preserved while the pejorative bias of the word is subverted. Second, "masculine" and "feminine" words in Moore's work lose their gender-distinct and biased functions without losing meaning; "strong" women write "erect" poems, "violent" ones. (It is amusing in this context to note Mrs. Moore's comment in the thank-you note to Louise Crane about her own peculiar pairing of "erect" and "tender.") Third, Moore employs paired oppositions, wittily exposing individual meanings based in difference ("controlled ardor," "clean violence") and operating anterior to their oppositional and judgment-weighted relations. As a consequence meaning is made more precise—and closer to Moore's goal of "depersonalized" usage.

Besides feminist theoretical and lexical revisions, Moore perches, at once restrained and aggressively subversive, on her critical soapbox, precisely documenting all that's visible of the private and conventionally invisible world on these public occasions. One comes not to "critical attitudes" but to "self inquiry," she reminds, without fanfare announcing a radical shift in the critical enterprise. Moore is a "wayward" critic, making jokes about attitudes on the "battleship *Masculine,*" accusing Pound of "feminolatry," applauding Williams's dedication of a volume to Flossie and his relationship to her as well, congratulating Williams on his sympathy for blacks and his antiwar position, extolling suffering, decrying colonization, cannibalism, the brutality of master-slave relationships, and unconscious "unself-protectiveness." She celebrates truth, emotional intelligence, hardness, and erectness in women's writing and compassion, the courage of "inconvenient emotion," "a considering consciousness which feels as well as sees," decorum, and modesty in the writing of men. In feminist approbation of Stevens, she warbles: "He shows one how not to call joy satisfaction" (*Complete Prose* 329).

Moore's work reveals a writer with a social conscience attempting through her art to enact the values of the ideal daughter mirroring to her mother the best qualities that any mother might imagine she herself has given to the world. This is not to idealize mothers and daughters in the complicated world of daily life but to note how well Marianne Moore loved the margin between art and life and thus allowed herself the dream of paradise, a garden of ideal unions and perfectible sympathies. For Moore, absence, "death in its several forms," was always the "real toad" on the path in her "imaginary garden."

Just as we look to Virginia Woolf for a feminist ideology, we might look to Moore for its practice. In "Archaically New" and in "Hymen" a clear formulation of the practice of ideal sisterhood emerges in Moore's application of a feminist politic as evaluative criteria. Moore opens the Bishop essay with the unlovely image of a vegetable shredder, in order, it would seem, to cut off Bishop's association with a homely kitchen tool (and kitchen poems). Not above crude play on masculine anxiety, Moore operates a multifunction appliance. Having thus established her ambiance, she proceeds to admire Bishop in unabashedly feminine terms for her "humility," "self-protection," and the prevailingly maternal virtue of "ungrudged self expenditure." "Too much cannot be said for this phase of self respect." Finally the maternal—cleanly pared of the domestic—finds its proper union with the moral as the poetry is evaluated "in accordance with a good which is communicated not purveyed."

Similarly in "Hymen" Moore opens with a play on masculine language in the selection of adjectives of praise ("sharpness," "hardness," "firmness"), building toward a final paragraph in which she teases out the childishness of feminine stereotypes by relating them to the mythology of fairy tales. Next, sexist mythologies are displaced by a commonsense universal: gender values need not be a matter of biological sex. H. D. is both masculine and feminine. Moore's conclusion nets a feminist politics notable for the reasonableness of the insight and for its enduring contemporaneity. Feminine "heroics" are different from masculine but not limited to women heroes. Crucial to her argument (and to our understanding of her feminism), she most acutely names difference (and glosses "subterfuge"). Masculine violence or "cowardice," "the desire to dominate by brute force," originates in masculine resistance to the terror of beauty, which is its "indestructibleness."

Finally, it is the "feminine, intellectual" woman who creates an imperishable poetry in which "tranquility" and "intellectual equilibrium" prevail. Such values are not conventionally heroic in this culture but more ordinarily (or ideally) the rewards of wise old age. Yet, somehow, even the most "masculine" sensibility cannot deride such balance. "Hymen" is stunning, moreover, in its enactment of the balance Moore admires in H. D.'s writing as it moves, line by line, in its "reserve," "propitiating nothing," activating "the insistence on certain qualities." The qualities are a blend of masculine and feminine, as Moore's mimetic method for reviews of male writers complements her exemplification of the best feminist methodology and principles. The review does not dismantle (out of an "anxiety of influence") but augments (nurtures) the work which it so generously entertains. "Too much cannot be said for this phase of self respect."

NOTES

1. Although among feminist critics and Moore scholars (Durham, Gallagher, Martin, Ostriker, Pondrum, Willis) this view is growing, it is not unanimously held (Rich,

Juhasz, Gelpi). Bonnie Costello goes this far: "Though fully self-conscious about the obstacles confronting women artists, they [Bishop and Moore] did not think of their lives or their art in specifically feminist terms. We may, retrospectively, recognize their aesthetic or personal choices as determined by an inherent feminism, but we should also recognize how multi-faceted their common interests were, addressed to both wider and more specific issues than the experience of women in a patriarchal society" ("Marianne Moore and Elizabeth Bishop" 126).

2. Although such a definition approaches Pound's imagism or Williams's "no idea but in things," the effect of the "pap" of the 16 October 1940 Bishop letter clearly distinguishes Moore's poetic from that of male modernists, something she acknowledged (17 December 1936, to Williams), as did they (Pound, 6 August 1946, to Moore). Moore worked for a "depersonalized," less local experience than either Williams or Pound were attempting.

3. The familiar cycles persist as Moore mothers Bishop and simultaneously draws upon the daughter in herself. Particularly during the painful period of bereavement following Mary Warner Moore's death, Moore repeats the daughter's role in her letters to Mary Shoemaker (18 Sept. 1948 and 12 Jan. 1949).

4. In an August 1937 letter Moore thanks Bishop for "primitive art." She is referring to the paper nautilus, and her thank-you note to Louise Crane is the aboriginal poem. Lines in the Crane extracts scan as poems closely related to Williams's better known thank-you note poem, "This is just to say."

5. Intentionality is nearly everything in Moore's moral schema. In its feminist aspect "self-protectiveness" becomes the major criterion for women's character and women's writing (*Complete Prose* 208, 228, 417). The woman writer may speak unself-protectively so long as she is aware of her ("courageous") choice. In Moore's own writing, one can fairly measure her involvement by the "essential baldness" of her choices. There is a clear range in Moore of the restrained and the bold; it is peculiar, given the range, that her feminism has not been more universally acknowledged.

6. I am grateful to Cyrena Pondrum for sharing with me the galleys of her forthcoming article, "Marianne Moore and H.D.: Female Community and Poetic Achievement," in which she evaluates Moore's intimacy with H. D. and Bryher as a possible emotional or sexual watershed for Moore. What we can know with certainty is that Moore's chastity was a conscious—and very likely political—choice. Taffy Martin quotes from McAlmon's portrait of Moore in his *roman à clef, Post Adolescence:* "She thinks anything, disapproves of little for other people, and is a churchgoing cerebralizing moralist herself" (*Master* 210). These views revise critical assignments of Moore's remoteness and chastity as personal failings reproduced in her poetry.

7. Moore made a point of reviewing works toward which she felt sympathy (Martin "Portrait"; Willis). One may conclude that these two angry reviews are the work of a reviewer who clearly had something she wished to say.

8. The full feminist irony begins in another poem ("In the Days of Prismatic Color") with Moore's prelapsarian, preadolescent Adam, who is pure because his world is. The source of "prismatic" clarity: the poem is set "not in the days of Adam and Eve, but when Adam / was alone."

9. Such new feminist theology is not altogether astounding from this minister's granddaughter who, following family tradition and especially her mother's example, remained religious (and a regular churchgoer) throughout her life.

WORKS CITED

Bloom, Harold. Introduction. In Bloom, ed., *Marianne Moore: Modern Critical Views,* 1–9. New York: Chelsea House, 1987.

Brownstein, Marilyn L. "The Archaic Mother and Mother: The Postmodern Poetry of Marianne Moore." *Contemporary Literature* 30.1(Spring 1989).

Costello, Bonnie. *Imaginary Possessions.* Cambridge: Harvard UP, 1981.

———. "Marianne Moore and Elizabeth Bishop: Friendship and Influence." *Twentieth Century Literature* (1984). Rpt. in Bloom, ed., *Marianne Moore,* 119–137.

———. "The 'Feminine' Language of Marianne Moore." *Women and Language in Literature and Society* (1980). Rpt. in Bloom, ed., *Marianne Moore,* 89–105.

Durham, Carolyn A. "Female Modernism: Language and Gender in Marianne Moore's Poetry." Paper presented to Modern Language Association, New York, December 1986.

Gallagher, Tess. "Throwing the Scarecrows From the Garden." *Parnassus* 12–13.2–1(1985):45–60.

Gelpi, Barbara C., and Albert Gelpi. Introduction. *Adrienne Rich's Poetry.* New York: Norton, 1975.

Juhasz, Suzanne. *Naked and Fiery Forms: Modern American Poetry by Women: A New Tradition.* New York: Harper, 1976.

Martin, Taffy. "Portrait of a Writing Master: Beyond the Myth of Marianne Moore." *Twentieth Century Literature* 30.2–3(1984):192–209.

———. *Marianne Moore: Subversive Modernist.* Austin: U of Texas P, 1986.

Moore, Marianne Craig. *Collected Poems.* New York: Macmillan, 1951.

———. *Complete Poems.* New York: Macmillan and Viking P, 1967; London: Faber and Faber, 1968; New York: Viking P, 1981.

———. *The Complete Prose of Marianne Moore.* Ed. Patricia C. Willis. New York: Viking Penguin, 1986.

Ostriker, Alicia. "What Do Women (Poets) Want?: Marianne Moore and H. D. as Poetic Ancestresses." *Poesis* 6.3–4:1–9.

Pondrum, Cyrena N. "Marianne Moore and H. D.: Female Community and Poetic Achievement." In *Marianne Moore: Woman and Poet,* ed. Patricia C. Willis. Forthcoming.

Tomlinson, Charles, ed. *Marianne Moore: A Collection of Critical Essays.* Englewood Cliffs, N.J.: Prentice-Hall, 1969.

Willis, Patricia C. *Marianne Moore: Vision into Verse.* Philadelphia: Rosenbach Museum and Library, 1987.

From the Correspondence

FAMILY CORRESPONDENCE

From Moore at Bryn Mawr to John Warner Moore and Mary Warner Moore 17 Jan 1906 (V:12:06)

"Sabbath, January 17 1906 . . . as I neared my room . . . whom should I meet but Henrietta Sharp, just leaving. I brought her back, helped her off with her wraps

All excerpts are from my transcripts of portions of Moore's letters in the Rosenbach Museum and Library, Philadelphia. Since my purpose is to convey an ambiance rather than provide a detailed record of composition, I have copied here what appears to be, in each case, the most recent version, reproducing Moore's typographical errors and her penciled additions and changes without citing them. Here, as in the introduction, Rosenbach catalog numbers appear in parentheses.

and aired my 'beautiful manners' generally. I then saw the Fawndale letters on my table and my conversation was more spirited than it has been since I passed my entrance exams."

From Mary Warner Moore to Marianne and Warner Moore
16 May 1906 (V:12a:06)

". . . I think it might be well to change the order of our letters; *not because Biter omitted last week's letters* but because by sending Fang's last letter to N.H. the last week of his stay, I should not see it til the day of his return home; and secondly by sending the letter to Toady around by Carlisle would not delay the letter to him 12 hrs. You see he gets Fang's Sab.[Sabbath] letter on Tuesday A.M.: if it were sent here first,—I'd get it Mon. evening at 5 and if I'd send it at 8 to N.H. Toady would get it Tues., any how. Then he of course would send his letter to B.M. [Bryn Mawr] instead of to Carlisle. . . . But I am anguished at the thought of the summer without Toady. *It is long.* I can stand winter separation so much more easily, but when we ought to be all together and one is gone, I'm like a thing with a broken wing. I won't interfere, however—What must be I'll adjust myself to."

From Moore to Mary Craig Shoemaker
18 Sept. 1948 (V:60:01)

"I wish you knew what good these letters do me, one at 9. and one at 2 o'clock. You are so like Mother in setting your situation and feelings aside and promoting with every fibre, what is of interest to the other."

12 Jan 1948 (V:60:01)

"I can't think of Harrisburg or Albany without seeing it. I am trying to train myself not to resist the inevitable, to trust to the ultimate goodness of change and of suffering but I do embrace the past and its incentives; its faces and objects. It does live in memory. . . ."

LITERARY CORRESPONDENCE

Moore–Ezra Pound Correspondence

From Moore to Pound (response to an invitation)
12 Dec 1931 (V:50:06)

"BUT when I see my mother has more to attend to than is good for her I at once become involved in domestic responsibility. Also I am often taken up with my brother's children to say nothing of him, as he is with my mother and me. . . . The Ligurian coast is the Ligurian coast: I do value the hospitality you presume on but leaving home is out of the question."

From Mary Warner Moore's draft of a letter to Ezra Pound with Marianne Moore's penciled changes
February 1932 (V:50:06)

Dear Mr. Pound-

a book

A pleasure—in fact a delight—came to Marianne some days ago ^ that suggests

as the giver, ~~it was your translation~~ you are in a sense the author

you ^ since ~~you are the author of the book she rec'd~~ I was ill at the time taking

M's

only a forced interest in ~~what~~ things at hand but shall not easily forget ~~the~~

sudden eagerness ~~I felt when I saw her face~~ as she opened the ~~beautiful glowing~~

and alluded to its regal substance and appearance. of

volume$_x$ She and I are a good deal like a wigwam ~~stayed by~~ two sticks—

When one stick falls the other follows—and it was but a day after this, that she

gave out had opportunity to find in himself

~~could go no longer~~, so both of us were down at once—Her brother ~~proved~~ more

than is ed with

possibilities ~~for~~ "mortal man" ~~than the~~ credit usually ~~given~~; and his wife ~~was by~~

took his place in caring for us

~~no means wanting~~, when his service was required elsewhere.

From Moore's poetics for Pound
25 Feb 1932 (V:50:06)

"The to me chief benefaction is the effect conveyed of sustained emotional pressure—of a continuity enclosed and sealed within the document; the force of tied notes, 'Aye sorrowing,' for instance, in Sonnet 14 . . . although somewhat punctilious and fiery is very taking."

16 Feb 1934 (V:50:07)
"If I am obstructing William Carlos Williams it is through a genius for helping by hindering. . . ."

4 March 1935 (V:50:07)
"I give strict attention to anything that is said about the economic foundation on which or in spite of which we live, but in art some things which seem inevitable ought to be concealed, like the working of the gastric juice. A glass stomach might not kill one and is interesting to inspect—compulsory for all under a Haenfstangel-Hitler-Russo-Japanese-General edict, not good."

From Pounds's 6 August 1946 letter to Moore (V:05:08)
"anyhow gt comfort To hear you aint sufferin' from Bill Wm-it is = I didn't thing you wd be. = but never know what idiocy will be mistaken for fact. N.C. raging

because I don't want To murder Franco. & iggurance as/a/granite cliff I never got yr other letter—or if so it was lost in fog-blurr & black out books can be got but I have insatiable thirst for personal news—to take my mind out of this place To make a world beyond the wall. Greetings to yr. mother

Moore–William Carlos Williams Correspondence

7 Dec. 1936 (V:77:25)
"Miss Bishop said she felt she must now read all you have written and has been giving much thought to your anti-sonnet theory of form, as I have also; we being, however, animals with a little different markings from yours."

Moore–Bryher Correspondence

4 Aug 1921 (V:08:05)
"My brother's joy in my poems does something toward reconciling me to the stirring of the pool."

16 Jan 1923 (V:08:06)
"The Botticelli arrived some days before Christmas and its burnished contours are like nothing but themselves.

"Your corduroy dress sounds delightful. I like corduroy and especially grey.

"Yes, differences in the detail of speech fascinate me. . . .

"If I smoked cigarettes, I have no doubt I should like cigars better. Doesn't a hookah take hold of your imagination?"

Moore–Elizabeth Bishop Correspondence

From Moore to Bishop
9 Feb 1937 (V:04:31)
"Your considerateness in wondering how things may be regarding another's choice of occupation is much felt by me, but you should let me see all you do."

10 February (probably) 1938 (V:04:31)
"It was very independent of you to submit your prize story without letting me see it. If it is returned with a printed slip, that will be why."

7 March 1937 (V:04:31)
"Your things have the insidiousness of creativeness, in that the after impression is stronger than the impression while reading, but you are menaced by the goodness of your mechanics. One should, of course, have the feeling, this is ingeniously contrived; but a thing should make one feel after reading it, that one's life has been altered or added to. When I set out to find fault with you, there are so many excellences in your mechanics that I seem to be commending you instead, and I wish to say, above all, that I am sure good treatment is a

handicap unless along with it, significant values came out with an essential baldness. I hope the unessential baldness of this attack will not make it seem that I am against minutiae."

Oct 16 1940 (V:05:01)
"Regarding the water-closet, Dylan Thomas, W.C. Williams, E E Cummings, and others feel that they are avoiding a duty if they balk at anything like unprudishness, but I say to them, 'I can't care about all things equally, I have a major effect to produce, and the heroisms of abstinence are as great as the heroisms of courage, and so are the rewards.' I think it is to your credit, Elizabeth, that when I say you are not to say 'water closet', you go on saying it a little (like Donald in National Velvet), and it is calculated to make me wonder if I haven't mistaken a cosmetic patch for a touch of lamp-black, but I think not. The trouble is, people are not depersonalized enough to accept the picture rather than the thought. You saw with what gusto I acclaimed 'the mermaid's pap' in Christopher S. but few of us, it seems to me, are fundamentally rude enough to enrich our work in such ways without cost. If I tell Mother there is a feather on her dress and she says, 'On my back?' I am likely to say, 'No, On your rump," alluding to Cowper's hare that 'swung his rump around.' But in my work, I daren't risk saying, 'My Mother had a feather on her rump.' "

From Bishop to Moore
21 May 1936 (V:04:30)
"Your careful appreciation of my post-cards always shames me. I'm afraid that I won't really have made this trip at all until I have lured you into commenting on every bit of pictorial evidence I can produce."

5 Feb. 1940 (V:04:30)
"I think Louise must have told you all the 'news'—and I know she went to you with all my problems, because she wrote me *everything* you said, word for word. . . . She has been so good, going to all this trouble for me, writing the latest developments almost daily—and you surpassed her. Thank you so much."

19 Feb. 1940 (V:04:30)
"I don't know how, without seeing Key West, you managed to do it, but what you said about it being a 'kind of ten commandments in vegetable-dye color printing' is the best description yet. . . . I find it alternately inspirational and depressing to think that I should come so far and try so hard and achieve nothing but approximation, while you stay home and hit the Key West lighthouse right on the head. . . . And thank you for the helpful comments on The Fish. I did as you suggested about everything . . . except [one word]. . . ."

Moore–Louise Crane Correspondence

From a thank-you note for a piece of "primitive art," a paper nautilus
21 Feb 1937 (V:12:27)

"This large but weightless thing, with a glaze like ivory on the entrance and even on the sides. How curious the sudden change of direction in the corrugations, and the transparent oyster white dullness of the 'pupes' The wings are so symmetrical I should not know any part had been broken if you had not said so."

7 March 1939 (V:12:27)
"The nectarines lent gaiety to our misery, Mother having despised nectarines; and when I have bought nectarines in season never having been willing to take one. Risking no questions I cut a very red one in half and put it on the luncheon tray on a little Chinese saucer with flowers on it the color of the nectarine and waiting vigilantly saw her try it. She said 'Delicious. What flavor' ". . . .

10 Jan 1939 (V:12:27)
"The olives in their euphonious can, puts our American produce to shame, do they not? Overcoming my tendency to stand things on a high shelf as an ornament for the mere meal, I've opened everything—like the overexcited Chimpanzee in Rango—though not the guava jelly just yet. The almond nougat is beyond belief. It is so good."

For a May basket
9 May 1940 (V:12:27)
"Your tiny pink roses and pink bachelor's buttons and daisies white and pink, and bouvardia and grape hyacinths and lilacs above the pale pink of the basket, are such beauty and romance and fragrance, no amount of looking or nearness makes us used to them."

From Mary Warner Moore for the May basket
(V:12:22)
"Each flower that enters the group conveys its own message of spirit erectness, and tenderness Two qualities that seldom go together. The wee radiant-rosebuds;—the pink daisies, each with an eye of hope, whispering "Be of good cheer," and so softly one perforce takes heart even in these anguishing times; the lilacs so erect, so pure in their unworldly beauty, the nonchalant white daisies declaring that there's nothing but fun in the world, and the little grapes standing on end replying, 'Yes there is; but be beautiful anyhow!' Is it any wonder I want to learn faith and trust and truth over again!"

If I Were Sixteen Today

When I was sixteen—in fact thirteen—I felt as old as I have ever felt since; and what I wish I could have been when sixteen is exactly what I am trying to do now, to know that to be hindered is to succeed. If one cannot strike when the iron is hot, one can strike *till* the iron is hot (Lyman Abbott).

With every reason to feel confident—except that we were in straitened circumstances financially (my mother, brother, and I)—I felt insecure, and took a day at a time, not because I knew it was best but because I had to. I regarded myself as a wall-flower; I did not like my face, and not many of my clothes. I was an introvert.

However, I experienced society vicariously, my brother was not introspective, or brooding, or too diffident; he abounded in invitations. He did not exalt "the power of life to renew itself"; he exemplified it. He did not foresee his own later warning to a boy who had completed preparatory-school work, whose mania was dancing. "Remember, every girl has one question: 'Is he going to marry me?' and every man: 'How safe am I?' "

I received the present of a bicycle—a maroon Reading Standard. Was I delighted? Not at all. I would have to learn to ride; riding itself was work. Little did I anticipate sweeping down smooth roads lined by tassels of waving locust-blossoms, or pausing on a little bridge over a brook to drop leaves and see them whirled away as minnows veered or hung motionless.

If I could alter my attitude retroactively, I would say as my brother says, "Be confident; burn your bridges behind you. . . . You may have to get tough in a good cause. A bear has paws and teeth and sometimes has to use them." And, taking the advice of James Stern in a *Times Book Review* section, beware of "the uncertain approach"; of objecting to what you object to "in no small degree"; of belonging to a school which the late George Orwell once described as "that of the not ungreen grass."

I would, if I could, let little things be little things—would be less susceptible to embarrassment. David Seabury says, "When you are saying, 'I can't be calm, I can't be calm,' you *can* be calm." Don't relive bad moments, or *revive them for others,* or be expecting more of them. To postponers, I would say, DO IT NOW; and to firebrands of impatience, ROME WAS NOT BUILT IN A DAY. "Superiority" is at the opposite pole from insight. Fashion can make you ridiculous; style, which is yours to control individually, can make you attractive—a near siren. What of chastity? It confers a particular strength. Until recently, I took it for granted—like avoiding *"any drugs."*

Instead of hating an over-heavy curriculum and applying jest about the army—"the incompetent teaching the indifferent the irrelevant," I would give thought to the why rather than merely the what of my subjects. Progressive forms in mathematics have unity-structure. You may not like arithmetic; my aplomb suffers a trifle when a bank teller says, "Yes; it's all right; I just changed a 6 to a 7." Arithmetic demands of memory a very exact kind of co-ordination; and in school, I found geometry a relief; Smith's advanced algebra, easier than arithmetic; it exerted a certain fascination. Caesar's Commentaries are—it is true—unostentatiously skillful, not traps for a drudge. Xenophon on dogs and in his treatise on horsemanship, is an expert.

1. Whatever you do, put all you have into it.

2. Go to the trouble of asking, "What good does it do?" "Why Portuguese? I may never use it."

3. Give "culture" the benefit of the doubt; don't look on art as effeminate, and museums as "the most tiring form of recreation there is."

4. I would, like Sir Winston, refuse to let a betrayal rob me of trust in my fellow man.

5. One should above all, learn to be silent, to listen; to make possible promptings from on high. Suppose you "don't believe in God." Talk to someone very wise, who believed in God, did not, and then found that he did. The cure for loneliness is solitude. Think about this saying by Martin Buber: "The free man believes in destiny and that it has need of him." Destiny, not fate.

And lastly, ponder Solomon's wish: when God appeared to him in a dream and asked, "What wouldst thou that I give unto thee?" Solomon did not say fame, power, riches, but an understanding mind, and the rest was added.

The Complete Prose of Marianne Moore. Ed. Patricia C. Willis. New York: Viking Penguin, 1986. 502–504.

Charlotte Brontë

Mr. Benson wishes, in his life of Charlotte Brontë, to give us a portrait "in the round." That his Piltdown regressive excites surprise rather than pleasure, and represents a departure from the genial verisimilitude of other portraiture by him, need not change one's regard for him nor estrange one from Charlotte Brontë.

A Scotland Yard aptitude for clues is not negligible in biography, and Mr. Benson bristles with accuracies. It is curious to note the portentous significance found by him in the fact that a line by Charlotte Brontë which was, for Swinburne, the epitome of her genius, was not by her. She had taken it "verbatim from one of Mr. Brontë's poems." We are glad, however, to be persuaded that Branwell Brontë did not deteriorate so early as is generally thought, and that he had a part in the writing of *Wuthering Heights*. And we agree with Mr. Benson that Mrs. Gaskell sacrificed individuality by omitting the letters concerning Miss Celia Amelia—the Rev. William Weightman. Mr. Benson evidently thinks Charlotte Brontë's regard for M. Heger is more than regard, a disgrace; and he attaches guilty importance to Mrs. Gaskell's "suppressions" in this connection—risked in the belief that they "would never be disclosed. The odds in her favor were enormous," says Mr. Benson, "but the hundred-to-one chance went against her." A suggestion, however, gives as strong an impression as an assertion, and we could not fail to infer from such extracts as Mrs. Gaskell gave, and from the novels, an emotional cataclysm; also that it was one-sided. If Charlotte Brontë could speak now, one feels that she would wish to be without certain faults Mr. Benson enumerates; and would wish to take back the look which

Branwell says "struck him like a blow in the mouth"; but one dares to think it possible that, reviewing her second Brussells visit, which she mistrusted in advance, she might have the courage to let it remain.

Charlotte Brontë's father, Patrick Brunty, peasant schoolmaster, was a person of easy conscience when he usurped "the noble surname" Brontë, Mr. Benson thinks; though to the dull conscience of some it is like the kiss requested of Anna by the circuit-rider in Hardy's story. It would do her no harm and it would do him a great deal of good. And Currer Bell's referring to "my brothers" and receiving a letter addressed "C. Brontë, Esq.," are to her biographer, cheating. If "longing to be considered male was indeed an obsession with her," it is also true, as Mr. Benson says, "it was no use wishing anything of the sort."

Did Charlotte Brontë as "a burglar" discover Emily's poems, and deliberately sacrifice their sale by letting them be "sandwiched" between worthless ones? Mr. Benson says she called men "coarse." No word could be plainer of interpretation apparently, nor in her use of it is psychologically more complex. Also, she exemplifies, though not in its flower, the Celtic tendency to express affection disguised as abuse as in the comment: "Man is, indeed, an amazing piece of mechanism when you see, so to speak, the full weakness of what he calls his strength."

Mr. Benson's synopsis of *Jane Eyre* makes one pause. Beside his iron-maiden *et seq.*, his asterisk of commendation does not wholly suggest an authoress "pale with the secret war of feeling"—the scene, indoors or out, assisting the mood; "the falling fir-cones," the "quiet dust" on mirrors and "darkly-polished old mahogany" in the red room. This self-taught author "followed no one," as Professor Saintsbury says, "and many have followed her." Nevertheless, the implied question—would her novel be at once accepted now—is of interest, for the school-taught man adds schooling to what the self-taught man teaches himself.

In explaining Mr. Brontë's seeming lack of hospitality, "Charlotte wrote just the letter that would have made Jane Austen's eyes twinkle," Mr. Benson thinks. Perhaps so, for the urbanities of Bath and compelled facilities of Yorkshire were no more like, than a master-confectioner's product of finebolted flour is like, the roots and kernel of the wheat that makes the flour. And our disadvantaging advantages in these days make it all but impossible for us to know the peculiar weight of the last straw. The over-serious letter, however, might not have made Cowper's eyes twinkle—nor Lamb's. As for Charlotte Brontë being "incapable of appreciating" Miss Austen, Mr. Benson no doubt, is in the main, right; yet one recalls the remark: "She does her business of delineating the surface lives of genteel English people curiously well. There is a Chinese fidelity, a miniature delicacy in the painting."

A novelist "all to bits with the strain of her accomplished work," able to give her fiancé "a good wigging" and "resounding smacks" to uncongenial reviewers, suggests Bret Harte's re-strike of Mr. Rawjester and Miss Mix. We do value, however, the allusion to her literary instinct as flame, "kindled, after long ash-covered smouldering," and the narrative becomes intent when it visualizes the intentness of the three sisters:

> . . . as in the darkness of the hive the unseen and furious industry of the bees generates the curtains of wax on which are built the honey-cells, so in the dining-room of the sequestered parsonage and round the kitchen fire the weaving of dreams and the exercise of imagination were their passionate preoccupations.

This halcyon moment of enjoyment—in contemplating the bees—prompts civility, and we think of the rule in yachting, "Give room at marks." *Up and Down. Our Family Affairs*. . . . We recall, in *Up and Down*, the memorable words, referring to pleasure, there are so many things one doesn't want. We delay over these books, and agree with Gertrude Stein "it is very difficult in quarreling to be certain in either one what the other one is remembering." Then, over-sanguine—returning to Charlotte Brontë—to love, honor, and be gay, in the narrow shaft of sunlight, her marriage—we find her satirically presented. Is one to protest it, or be rammed, or give room?

Complete Prose. 286–288.

Well Moused, Lion

It is not too much to say that some writers are entirely without imagination—without that associative kind of imagination certainly, of which the final tests are said to be simplicity, harmony, and truth. In Mr. Stevens' work, however, imagination precludes banality and order prevails. In his book, he calls imagination "the will of things," "the magnificent cause of being," and demonstrates how imagination may evade "the world without imagination"; effecting an escape which, in certain manifestations of *bravura*, is uneasy rather than bold. One feels, however, an achieved remoteness as in Tu Muh's lyric criticism: "Powerful is the painting . . . and high is it hung on the spotless wall in the lofty hall of your mansion." There is the love of magnificence and the effect of it in these sharp, solemn, rhapsodic elegant pieces of eloquence; one assents to the view taken by the author, of Crispin whose

> . . . mind was free
> And more than free, elate, intent, profound.

The riot of gorgeousness in which Mr. Stevens' imagination takes refuge, recalls Balzac's reputed attitude to money, to which he was indifferent unless he could have it "in heaps or by the ton." It is "a flourishing tropic he requires"; so wakeful is he in his appetite for color and in perceiving what is needed to meet the requirements of a new tone key, that Oscar Wilde, Frank Alvah Parsons,

Tappé, and John Murray Anderson seem children asleep in comparsion with him. One is met in these poems by some such clash of pigment as where in a showman's display of orchids or gladiolas, one receives the effect of vials of picracarmine, magenta, gamboge, and violet mingled each at the highest point of intensity:

> In Yucatan, the Maya sonneteers
> Of the Caribbean amphitheatre
> In spite of hawk and falcon, green toucan
> And jay, still to the nightbird made their plea,
> As if raspberry tanagers in palms,
> High up in orange air, were barbarous.

One is excited by the sense of proximity to Java peacocks, golden pheasants, South American macaw feather capes, Chilcat blankets, hair seal needlework, Singalese masks, and Rousseau's paintings of banana leaves and alligators. We have the hydrangeas and dogwood, the "blue, gold, pink, and green" of the temperate zone, the hibiscus, "red as red" of the tropics.

> . . . moonlight on the thick cadaverous bloom
> That yuccas breed . . .
>
> . . . with serpent-kin encoiled
> Among the purple tufts, the scarlet crowns.

and as in a shot spun fabric, the infinitude of variation of the colors of the ocean:

> . . . the blue
> And the colored purple of the lazy sea,

the emerald, indigos, and mauves of disturbed water, the azure and basalt of lakes; we have Venus "the center of sea-green pomp" and America "polar purple." Mr. Stevens' exact demand, moreover, projects itself from nature to human nature. It is the eye of no "maidenly greenhorn" which has differentiated Crispin's daughters; which characterizes "the ordinary women" as "gaunt guitarists" and issues the junior-to-senior mandate in "Floral Decorations for Bananas":

> Pile the bananas on planks.
> The women will all be shanks
> And bangles and slatted eyes.

He is a student of "the flambeaued manner,"

> . . . not indifferent to smart detail . . .
> . . . hang of coat, degree
> Of buttons. . . .

One resents the temper of certain of these poems. Mr. Stevens is never inadvertently crude; one is conscious, however, of a deliberate bearishness—a shadow of acrimonious, unprovoked contumely. Despite the sweet-Clementine-will-you-be-mine nonchalance of the "Apostrophe to Vincentine," one feels oneself to be in danger of unearthing the ogre and in "Last Looks at the Lilacs," a pride in unserviceableness is suggested which makes it a microcosm of cannibalism.

Occasionally the possession of one good is remedy for not possessing another as when Mr. Stevens speaks of "the young emerald, evening star," "tranquillizing . . . the torments of confusion." "Sunday Morning" on the other hand—a poem so suggestive of a masterly equipoise—gives ultimately the effect of the mind disturbed by the intangible; of a mind oppressed by the properties of the world which it is expert in manipulating. And proportionately, aware as one is of the author's susceptibility to the fever of actuality, one notes the accurate gusto with which he discovers the Negro, that veritable "medicine of cherries" to the badgered analyst. In their resilience and certitude, the "Hymn from a Watermelon Pavilion" and the commemorating of a Negress who

> Took seven white dogs
> To ride in a cab,

are proud harmonies.

One's humor is based upon the most serious part of one's nature. "Le Monocle de Mon Oncle"; "A Nice Shady Home"; and "Daughters with Curls": the capacity for self-mockery in these titles illustrates the author's disgust with mere vocativeness.

Instinct for words is well determined by the nature of the liberties taken with them, some writers giving the effect merely of presumptuous egotism—an unavoided outlandishness; others, not: Shakespeare arresting one continually with nutritious permutations as when he apostrophizes the lion in *A Midsummer Night's Dream*—"Well moused, lion." Mr. Stevens' "junipers shagged with ice," is properly courageous as are certain of his adjectives which have the force of verbs: "the spick torrent," "tidal skies," "loquacious columns"; there is the immunity to fear, of the good artist, in "the blather that the water made." His precise diction and verve are grateful as contrasts to the current vulgarizations of "gesture," "dimensions" and "intrigue." He is able not only to express an idea with mere perspicuity; he is able to do it by implication as in "Thirteen Ways of Looking at a Blackbird" in which the glass coach evolved from icicles; the shadow, from birds; it becomes a kind of aristocratic cipher. "The Emperor of Icecream," moreover, despite its not especially original theme of poverty enriched by death, is a triumph of explicit ambiguity. He gets a special effect with those adjectives which often weaken as in the lines:

> . . . That all beasts should . . .
> . . . be beautiful
> As large, ferocious tigers are

and in the phrase, "the eye of the young alligator," the adjective as it is perhaps superfluous to point out, makes for activity. There is a certain bellicose sensitiveness in

I do not know which to prefer . . .
The blackbird whistling
Or just after,

and in the characterization of the snow man who

. . . nothing himself, beholds
The nothing that is not there and the nothing that is.

In its nimbleness *con brio* with seriousness, moreover, "Nomad Exquisite" is a piece of that ferocity for which one values Mr. Stevens most:

As the immense dew of Florida
Brings forth

The big-finned palm
And green vine angering for life.

Poetic virtuosities are allied—especially those of diction, imagery, and cadence. In no writer's work are metaphors less "winter starved." In "Architecture" Mr. Stevens asks:

How shall we hew the sun, . . .
How carve the violet moon
To set in nicks?

Pierce, too, with buttresses of coral air
And purple timbers,
Various argentines

and "The Comedian as the Letter C," as the account of the craftsman's un"simple jaunt," is an expanded metaphor which becomes as one contemplates it, hypnotically incandescent like the rose tinged fringe of the night blooming cereus. One applauds those analogies derived from an enthusiasm for the sea:

She scuds the glitters,
Noiselessly, like one more wave.

The salt hung on his spirit like a frost,
The dead brine melted in him like a dew.

In his positiveness, aplomb, and verbal security, he has the mind and the method of China; in such controversial effects as:

Of what was it I was thinking?
So the meaning escapes,

and certainly in dogged craftsmanship. Infinitely conscious in his processes, he says

> Speak even as if I did not hear you speaking
> But spoke for you perfectly in my thoughts.

One is not subject in reading him, to the disillusionment experienced in reading novices and charlatans who achieve flashes of beauty and immediately contradict the pleasure afforded by offending in precisely those respects in which they have pleased—showing that they are deficient in conscious artistry.

Imagination implies energy and imagination of the finest type involves an energy which results in order "as the motion of a snake's body goes through all parts at once, and its violation acts at the same instant in coils that go contrary ways." There is the sense of the architectural diagram in the disjoined titles of poems with related themes. Refraining for fear of impairing its litheness of contour, from overelaborating felicities inherent in a subject, Mr. Stevens uses only such elements as the theme demands; for example, his delineation of the peacock in "Domination of Black," is austerely restricted, splendor being achieved cumulatively in "Bantam in Pine-Woods," "The Load of Sugar-Cane," "The Palace of the Babies," and "The Bird with the Coppery Keen Claws."

That "there have been many most excellent poets that never versified, and now swarm many versifiers that never need answer to the name of poets," needs no demonstration. The following lines as poetry independent of rhyme, beg the question as to whether rhyme is indispensably contributory to poetic enjoyment:

> There is not nothing, no, no, never nothing,
> Like the clashed edges of two words that kill

and

> The clambering wings of black revolved,
> Making harsh torment of the solitude.

It is of course evident that subsidiary to beauty of thought, rhyme is powerful in so far as it never appears to be invented for its own sake. In this matter of apparent naturalness, Mr. Stevens is faultless—as in correctness of assonance:

> Chieftain Iffucan of Ascan in caftan
> Of tan with henna hackles, halt!

The better the artist, moreover, the more determined he will be to set down words in such a way as to admit of no interpretation of the accent but the one intended, his ultimate power appearing in a selfsufficing, willowy, firmly contrived cadence such as we have in "Peter Quince at the Clavier" and in "Cortège for Rosenbloom":

> . . . That tread
> The wooden ascents
> Of the ascending of the dead.

One has the effect of poised uninterrupted harmony, a simple appearing, complicated phase of symmetry of movements as in figure skating, tight-rope dancing, in the kaleidoscopically centrifugal circular motion of certain medieval dances. It recalls the snake in *Far Away and Long Ago,* "moving like quicksilver in a rope-like stream" or the conflict at sea when after a storm, the wind shifts and waves are formed counter to those still running. These expertnesses of concept with their nicely luted edges and effect of flowing continuity of motion, are indeed

> . . . pomps
> Of speech which are like music so profound
> They seem an exaltation without sound.

One further notes accomplishment in the use of reiteration—that pitfall of half-poets:

> Death is absolute and without memorial,
> As in a season of autumn,
> When the wind stops. . . .
> When the wind stops.

In brilliance gained by accelerated tempo in accordance with a fixed melodic design, the precise patterns of many of these poems are interesting:

> It was snowing
> And it was going to snow

and the parallelism in "Domination of Black" suggest the Hebrew idea of something added although there is, one admits, more the suggestion of mannerism than in Hebrew poetry. Tea takes precedence of other experiments with which one is familiar, in emotional shorthand of this unwestern type, and in "Earthy Anecdote" and in the "Invective against Swans," symmetry of design is brought to a high degree of perfection.

It is rude perhaps, after attributing conscious artistry and a severely intentional method of procedure to an artist, to cite work that he has been careful to omit from his collected work. One regrets, however, the omission by Mr. Stevens of "The Indigo Glass in the Grass," "The Man Whose Pharynx Was Bad," "La Mort du Soldat Est Près des Choses Naturelles (5 Mars)" and "Comme Dieu Dispense de Graces":

> Here I keep thinking of the primitives—
> The sensitive and conscientious themes
> Of mountain pallors ebbing into air.

However, in this collection one has eloquence. "The author's violence is for aggrandizement and not for stupor"; one consents therefore, to the suggestion that when the book of moonlight is written, we leave room for Crispin. In the event of moonlight and a veil to be made gory, he would, one feels, be appropriate in this legitimately sensational act of a ferocious jungle animal.

Complete Prose. 91–98.

Archaically New

In trying to reveal the clash of elements that we are—the intellectual, the animal; the blunt, the ingenious; the impudent, the imaginative—one dare not be dogmatic. We are a many-foliaged tree against the moon; a wave penetrated by the sun. Some authors do not muse within themselves; they "think"—like the vegetable-shredder which cuts into the life of a thing. Miss Bishop is not one of these frettingly intensive machines. Yet the rational considering quality in her work is its strength—assisted by unwordiness, uncontorted intentionalness, the flicker of impudence, the natural unforced ending.

Mere mysteriousness is useless; the enigma must be clear to the author, not necessarily to us.

> Such curious Love, in constant innocence,
> Though ill at ease,

has the right air, and so has this:

> —Sure of my love, and Love; uncertain of identity.

The specific is judiciously interspersed with generality, and the permitted clue to idiosyncrasy has a becoming evasiveness. We are willing to be apprised of a secret—indeed glad to be—but technique must be cold, sober, conscious of self-justifying ability. Some feminine poets of the present day seem to have grown horns and to like to be frightful and dainty by turns; but distorted propriety suggests effeteness. One would rather disguise than travesty emotion; give away a nice thing than sell it; dismember a garment of rich aesthetic construction than degrade it to the utilitarian offices of the boneyard. One notices the deferences and vigilances in Miss Bishop's writing, and the debt to Donne and Gerard Hopkins. We look at imitation askance; but like the shell which the hermit-crab selects for itself, it has value—the avowed humility, and the protection. Miss Bishop's ungrudged self-expenditure should also be noticed—automatic, apparently, as part of the nature. Too much cannot be said for this phase of self-respect.

We cannot ever be wholly original; we adopt a thought from a group of notes in the song of a bird, from a foreigner's way of pronouncing English, from the weave in a suit of clothes. Our best and newest thoughts about color have been known to past ages. Nevertheless an indebted thing does not interest us unless there is originality underneath it. Here, the equivalence for rhyme, achieved by the coming back again to the same word, has originality; and one feels the sincerity, the proportionateness, and the wisdom of superiority to snobbery—the selectiveness.

One asks a great deal of an author—that he should not be haphazard but considered in his mechanics, that he should not induce you to be interested in what is restrictedly private but that there should be the self-portrait; that he should pierce you to the marrow without revolting you. Miss Bishop's sparrows ("Valentine I") are not revolting, merely disaffecting. It is difficult, moreover, not to allow vigilance to fluctuate; an adjective or an "and" easily eludes one, and a mere shadow of the unintentionally mechanical deflects interest. Some phrases in these pieces of Miss Bishop's work are less live than others, but her methodically oblique, intent way of working is auspicious; one is made aware of the kind of refraction that is peculiar to works of art, that is in accordance with a good which is communicated not purveyed.

Complete Prose. 327–329.

Hymen

Dr. Mahaffy says in his essay "The Principles of the Art of Conversation," that artificiality is an evidence of some kind of dishonesty. Undoubtedly respect for the essence of a thing makes expression simple and in reading the present collection of poems by H. D., the hasty mind is abashed by the measure of intention and the exacting sincerity which prevail from the beginning to the end of the volume. Mr. Glenway Wescott praises the sternness of H. D.'s translations. "No race of men ever subsisted on sweet rhetorical distinction," he says and in her work, it is life denuded of subterfuge—it is the clean violence of truth that we have. Only as one isolates portions of the work, does one perceive the magic and compressed energy of the author's imagination, actuality in such lines as the following, being lost in the sense of spectacle:

> dark islands in a sea
> of gray olive or wild white olive
> cut with the sudden cypress shafts;

fingers

> wrought of iron
> to wrest from earth

secrets; strong to protect,
strong to keep back the winter.

One recognizes here, the artist—the mind which creates what it needs for its own subsistence and propitiates nothing, willing—indeed wishing to seem to find its only counterpart in the elements; yet in this case as in the case of any true artist, reserve is a concomitant of intense feeling, not the cause of it. In H. D.'s work, there is not so much reserve as insistence upon certain qualities; nature in its acute aspects is to her, a symbol of freedom. A liking for surf for instance, makes the contemplation of still water seem like loathing as in Swinburne when one recalls his comparison of Childe Harold and Don Juan:

> They are like lake water and sea water; the one is yielding, fluent, invariable: the other has in it a life and pulse, a sting and swell, which touch and excite the nerves like fire or like music; the ripple flags and falls in loose lazy lines, the foam flies wide of any mark, and the breakers collapse here and there in sudden ruin and violent failure. But the violence and weakness of the sea are preferable to the smooth sound and equable security of a lake.

In the following lines as in H. D.'s work throughout, wiry diction, accurate observation and a homogeneous color sense are joint phases of unequivocal faithfulness to fact:

Though Sparta enter Athens,
Thebes wreck Sparta,
each changes as water,
salt, rising to wreak terror
and fall back;

a broken rock
clatters across the steep shelf
of the mountain slope,
sudden and swift
and breaks as it clatters down
into the hollow breach
of the dried water course.

Color and careful detail may arrest without commanding, but here—physical beauty emends other beauties and H. D.'s concept of color makes it hard to disassociate ideas from the pageant that we have of objects and hues—Egyptian gold and silver work, a harmonious, tempera-like procession of dyes and craftsmanship—of these "flecks of amber on the dolphin's back," "white cedar and black cedar," "the shore burned with a lizard blue," "the light shadow print cast through the petals of the yellow iris flower," in "the paved parapet" on which "you will step carefully from amber stones to onyx." In this instinctive ritual of beauty, at once old and modern, one is reminded of the supernatural yellows of China—of an aesthetic consciousness which values simultaneously, ivory and the chiseled ivory of speech, finding "in the hardness of jade, the firmness of the intelligence; in its sound with the peculiarity of ceasing abruptly, the emblem of music, in the sharpness of its angles, justice; in its splendor, the sky and in its substance, the earth." "Beauty is set apart," H. D. says:

Beauty is cast by the sea
a barren rock,
beauty is set about
with wrecks of ships,
upon our coast, death keeps
the shadows—death waits
clutching toward us
from the deeps.

In the bleakness as in the opulence of "The Islands" from which the above lines are taken, one remembers Ezekiel's Tyre, "a barren rock, a place for the spreading of nets in the midst of the sea—" the Tyre which commanded with her wares, "emeralds, purple and broidered work, fine linen, coral and rubies, horses, war-horses, wine and white wool, bright iron, casia and calamus, precious cloths for riding, horns of ivory and ebony, wares in wrappings of blue and broidered work and in chests of rich apparel bound with cords and made of cedar—replenished and made very glorious in the heart of the seas."

Talk of weapons and the tendency to match one's intellectual and emotional vigor with the violence of nature, give a martial, an apparently masculine tone to such writing as H. D.'s, the more so that women are regarded as belonging necessarily to either of two classes—that of the intellectual freelance or that of the eternally sleeping beauty, effortless yet effective in the indestructible limestone keep of domesticity. Woman tends unconsciously to be the aesthetic norm of intellectual home life and preeminently in the case of H. D., we have the intellectual, social woman, non-public and "feminine." There is, however, a connection between weapons and beauty. Cowardice and beauty are at swords' points and in H. D.'s work, suggested by the absence of subterfuge, cowardice and the ambition to dominate by brute force, we have heroics which do not confuse transcendence with domination and which in their indestructibleness, are the core of tranquillity and of intellectual equilibrium.

Complete Prose. 79–82.

17
Ezra Pound (1885–1972)

Introduced and Edited by Ronald Bush

Ezra Pound's place in a feminist anthology of modern writing? Marianne Moore posed the problems succinctly. In 1918 and still unknown, she sent Pound a sample of her poetry. He replied (in a letter reprinted below) with encouraging criticism and asked her to tell him something about her life. She did (Marilyn Brownstein quotes from her reply, written 9 January 1919, in the introduction to the Moore section, **16**), and he showed genuine interest. But along with continued support and criticism, his second letter included a sequence of doggerel (also printed below) so outrageous one might view it as a bizarre joke did Pound not use it as the basis for an important statement of poetics (in his postscript to Remy de Gourmont's *The Natural Philosophy of Love*[1]) and then for a striking passage in Canto XXIX.[2] Taken together, the three texts (the doggerel is given here for the first time in its unexpurgated form) announce a theme that runs through Pound's middle and later work: that "the female is a chaos," the male a principle of form and order.

Moore's return letter has not been preserved, but, reviewing *A Draft of XXX Cantos* in *Poetry* in 1931, she articulated obvious dismay. Pound's poem, she testified, "has a power that is mind and is music; it comes with the impact of centuries and with the impact of yesterday." And yet, she added, "is not the view of women expressed by the Cantos older-fashioned than that of

Siam and Abyssinia? knowledge of the femaleness of *chaos,* of the *octopus,* of *Our Mulberry leaf, woman* appertaining more to Turkey than to a Roger Ascham?" (*Complete Prose* 272).

After more than half a century, it is hard to disagree. Despite the fact that Pound helped launch the careers of women whose talents were as diverse as Moore (see his essay on Moore and Loy in "Others," printed below), H. D., Iris Barry, Nancy Cunard, and Mary Barnard and that all of them (as well as Rebecca West, May Sinclair, and others) wrote about him with appreciation and gratitude, there is no question that his work flaunted machismo, and that he frequently characterized both modernist style and culture itself as masculine achievements.[3]

Worse, there is something genuine in the argument that Pound's energetic sponsorship of women was one more expression of his will to power. Take the case of Pound's efforts on the part of the magazine that Dora Marsden began in 1911 as the *Freewoman: A Weekly Feminist Review.* As the *Egoist: An Individualist Review,* the publication achieved a kind of literary immortality when it published James Joyce's *Portrait of the Artist as a Young Man.* These events are portrayed in a recent account by K. K. Ruthven as pure sexual politics—"a paradigmatic instance of the subordination of women by a male-dominated modernism." In Ruthven's words, what happened was this: Rebecca West, the literary subeditor of the *Freewoman* (in June 1913 renamed the *New Freewoman*), was "aware of [Pound's] activities as literary talent scout for *Poetry* (Chicago)" and sought him out. "For Pound, it was an opportune moment to use the *New Freewoman* in the same way as he was using *Poetry* (Chicago), that is, as a base from which to campaign on behalf of the Imagist movement in general and the Pound version of it in particular. . . . He was willing to assume editorial duties which . . . Rebecca West was in no fit state to take on," and in a very short time he and four other "self-styled men of letters" had changed the journal's name and changed its course. Thus, "by a conjuncture of feminist insouciance [and] masculine opportunism . . . the gender-specific *New Freewoman* was erased from patriarchal memory" and "*The Egoist* consolidated its position in androcentric literary history" (Ruthven 1278).[4]

Yet it seems to me there is something terribly reductive in Ruthven's characterizations. Reifying tendencies in men's and women's writing, he creates pure strains of androcentric and gynocentric modernism and then narrates the story of how one was imposed upon the other. Yet Pound, Marsden, West, and their contemporaries were enmeshed in the same powerful and sometimes contradictory historical forces, and it is as inadequate to sum up Pound's modernism by way of his swagger as it is to forget the power of nonsexually based cultural rebellion in the work of West. The case of the *Freewoman* is, I think, instructive.

Marsden started the *Freewoman* in reaction against the Pankhursts' singular concentration on the achievement of women's suffrage. According to one history of the movement, she began as "an energetic WSPU member," and was arrested several times in Manchester, "once for heckling Churchill from a glass roof—only a policeman catching her ankle saved her from falling to an early death." But having strategic and then philosophical differences with the WSPU, she sought to start a revolutionary paper in which the issue of the vote was superseded by reflection on marriage, sexuality, and a new moral and political order. Most strikingly, in contrast to suffragist literature, which "took meticulous care to avoid any charges of immorality for fear of damaging the campaign for votes," Marsden encouraged articles reevaluating the "relationship between sexual morality and the oppression of women" (Garner 61, 67). Describing herself as "philosophical anarchist" (Marsden 295), she immersed herself in a community of Nietzscheans, Fabians, syndicalists, theosophists, and anarchists and more and more inclined toward the position of "individualism," a position in which men's and women's emotional and spiritual liberation counted for more than any political reform. Thus she rehearsed what the historian Jonathan Rose has called the Edwardian obsession with Life, an obsession that "could mean the surrogate religion of vitalism, the worship of the life process as a spiritual force. It could specificially mean the creation of new life, an erotic impulse breaking out of Victorian constraints and sometimes worshipped as a religion in itself. Life could also be a mysterious spiritual quality that endowed human beings with identity, consciousness, a moral sense, and free will—a vital spark very like the Christian concept of the soul" (Rose 74). According to Harriet Weaver's biographers, it was Marsden who was responsible for subtitling the *New Freewoman* (the *first* reincarnation of the *Freewoman*) *An Individualist Review,* and it was she who proposed the journal's third name, the *Egoist* (Lidderdale and Nicholson 75).

Nor was Marsden the only one in her circle to link the struggle of feminism to the goal of liberating the life principle in every human being. May Sinclair, in a now difficult to obtain 1912 pamphlet entitled *Feminism,* wrote in response to the self-proclaimed "scientific" objections to feminism of a bacteriologist named Sir Almroth Wright that "the sublime enthusiasm and self-devotion and self-sacrifice of the suffragists spring from the same root"—the "stream of the Life-Force of which Woman is pre-eminently the reservoir" and which is associated with the "dawn of womanhood" and sexual passion (Sinclair 32, 30–31).

In this milieu Pound's contemporary attitudes look less eccentric, though they were to become coarser and more confused as his career progressed. Pound, it should be recalled, was befriended by Sinclair as early as 1909, and it was she who introduced him to Ford Madox Ford and Ford's companion, Violet Hunt (see Stock 62, 68). Hunt was herself involved in the suffragette movement, and during their time together Ford published a profeminist pamphlet in the same series as Sinclair's.[5] At their literary parties on Campden Hill "les jeunes" met one another and breathed the air of the new age. In the summer of 1913 Hunt introduced Pound to West, and soon after West approached Pound about writing for the *New Freewoman.* Pound responded enthusiastically, albeit with no little thought to his own agenda. Unquestionably he helped reorient the journal toward literature, and (as he wrote to James Joyce) he thought the journal's title "unsuitable." (*Pound and Joyce* 17). And yet the poetry and commentary he produced for the journal followed much of West's "programme"—"the revolt of women, philosophic anarchism, and a general whip-round for ideas that would reform simultaneously life and art."[6] Consider the 1914 essay "Suffragettes," written under the pseudonym of "Bastien von Helmholtz" and reprinted below. In it he mimed the voice of a "Male mind" "outside the struggle" while he boldly attacked Sinclair's opponent, Sir Almroth Wright. And if in the article he made light of the value of the women's vote, it was from a perspective close to that of the journal itself; no less than Marsden or West he considered a "just" demand for the vote less important than the aim of advancing Life—"keeping alight the flame of science and knowledge and the arts, and . . . setting a fine example of living."

The same desire to effect the liberation of all men and women drives most of Pound's early poetry and essays. There is a direct line from his 1912 essay, "Psychology and the Troubadors," in which he speaks of the vibration of sexual tensions that "gives light" and coincides with the "general object" of "all ecstatic religions" ("to stimulate a sort of confidence in the life-force"),[7] to Canto IV, whose conclusion notes the futility of imprisoning Danae and admonishes that natural energy can never be appropriated as political or sexual property ("No wind is the king's wind"), to Canto VI, which in its original version concerns the futile enclosure of Eleanor of Aquitaine and the revolutionary force of free love in a society of arranged marriages.[8] None of these texts is free of Pound's fascination with masterful heros, but all share the *New Freewoman*'s insistence on upsetting (for the good of men *and* women) the stifling conventions of traditional sexual mortality. So *Hugh Selwyn Mauberley,* which sums up British society in an antifeminist epigraph ("an old bitch gone in the teeth"),[9] also includes the sequence "Yeux Glauques," with its sympathetic focus on Elizabeth Siddell, a woman misused by sanctimonious Victorian and bohemian aesthete alike.

Unquestionably, though, after 1919 (the year of his letter to Moore) political and personal strains amplified Pound's ideological contradictions and strengthened the darker side of his religion of Life. Near despair about the war and its aftermath and suspecting that both were symptoms of bourgeois English society, Pound, in his search for radical solutions, turned to the "volitional" stance of Mussolini's fascism and to the associated theme (cf. the postscript to *The Natural Philosophy of Love*[10]) of renewing the chaotic and feminine morass of Western culture through male hierarchical order. As the twenties wore on, Pound created a new mystification of natural force and protested a "natural" pattern in human affairs corresponding to the age-old practices of an agricultural patriarchy. Certainly by the thirties he had come to regard the restoration of patriarchal culture as a radical conservation of the "natural," a conservation in which (As Robert Casillo has perceptively observed) "the violence which man does to nature—and to his own instincts" must be "disguised and concealed." Hence, Casillo notes, the Mussolini of the *Cantos* "figures not so much as a dictator as an *artifex* reverently educing the inward spirit of his people as the sculptor reveals the shape concealed with the stone; or, as [Canto 74] says, the stone must know "the form which the carver imparts it.' " (Casillo 299, 300).

This hierarchical sense of "natural" social and sexual relations would dominate the *Cantos* for as long as Pound worked on them. Yet it is important to remember that the poem never completely rejected its *New Freewoman* faith in the anarchic yet rejuvenating power of sexual energy (see the Na Khi stories of lovers' suicides in *Drafts and Fragments*). Existing in tandem, these opposing impulses fuel the contradictions of Pound's sexual ideology and of his literary procedures. From one point of view, the *Cantos* correspond to Sandra Gilbert's assessment of modernism as a conscious attempt to reincarnate "the patriarchal power of Homer's classical Greek in a new and equally difficult language which functioned (just as surely as Homer's had until the mid–nineteenth century) to occult and authenticate the high cultural 'yarns' of the father as against the commoner 'yearns' of the mother."[11] But from another viewpoint the poem looks very different. To Marjorie Perloff, the form of the *Cantos* remains quintessentially open, as resistant to the inherited structures of literary authority as the Dadaist poets (176ff). And Kathryne Lindberg identifies the poem with its celebration of the anarchic energy of Dionysus, whose presence "signals transformation and the survival of an ecstatic and intoxicating poetic force beyond the destruction of various forms" (207).

Which perspective is more accurate? Are the *Cantos* the work of Mussolini's follower or May Sinclair's friend? Or is there some way we can manage to think of Pound's epic as both—the product of contradictory impulses, competing ideologies?[12]

NOTES

1. Pound suggests that the brain, primarily a source of new forms and images, is in fact "in origin and development, only a great clot of genital fluid held in suspense or reserve." Pound finds confirmation of this hypothesis "in the symbolism of phallic religions, man really the phallus or spermatozoide charging, head-on, the female chaos." And he adds, "Even oneself has felt it, driving any new idea into the great passive vulva of London, a sensation analogous to the male feeling in copulation."

2. The passage begins:

> Wein, Weib, TAN AOIDAN
> Chiefest of these the second, the female
> Is an element, the female
> Is a chaos
> An octopus
> A biological process

3. For statements of the women Pound encouraged, see H. D., *End to Torment: A Memoir of Ezra Pound* (New York: New Directions, 1979); Iris Barry, "The Ezra Pound

Period," *The Bookman* 74 (October 1931): 159–171; Mary Barnard, *Assault on Mount Helicon: A Literary Memoir* (Berkeley: U of California P, 1984); May Sinclair, "The Reputation of Ezra Pound," *North American Review* 211(May 1920): 658–668; and the letters of Natalie Barney, quoted in "Ezra Pound: Letters to Natalie Barney," edited with commentary by Richard Sieburth, *Paideuma* 5.2 (1976): 279–295. The most poignant and the most ambivalent of these statements may be Nancy Cunard's last letter to Pound, included in this anthology. Pound in 1921 helped Cunard with some poetry and in 1930 she returned the favor by publishing his *Draft of XXX Cantos* in her Hours Press. The two were close friends and dancing partners, and when Cunard began a relationship with the black American musician Henry Crowder, Pound supported her against the opposition of her mother and frequently accompanied the lovers to Parisian clubs. But starting with the Spanish Civil War Cunard and Pound were politically at odds. After he was incarcerated in 1945 she wrote him a letter of gratitude, outrage and farewell from Gourdon in France (which Cunard had discovered through Pound). In it Cunard protests, "I cannot understand how the integrity that was so much you in your writing can have chosen the enemy of all integrity."

4. Ruthven's account depends upon Jane Lidderdale and Mary Nicholson, *Dear Miss Weaver* and on Bonnie Kime Scott, *Joyce and Feminism*. Ruthven distorts both, however, by relying on the interpretation advanced by Michael Levenson in *A Genealogy of Modernisms: A Study of English Literary Doctrine 1908–1922* (Cambridge: Cambridge University Press, 1984).

5. *This Monstrous Regiment of Women* (London: Women's Freedom League, 1912).

6. Quoted in Scott 86.

7. Reprinted in the amplified version of *The Spirit of Romance* (New York: New Directions, 1952); see 97, 95.

8. *The Cantos* now prints a version of Canto VI revised in the late twenties that indicates Pound's changing sexual politics by way of a new, bawdy opening. For the version published in *A Draft of XVI Cantos* (1925), see Bush (310–313).

9. See Gilbert and Gubar, *No Man's Land* 235.

10. "Without any digression on feminism . . . one offers woman as the accumulation of hereditary aptitudes . . . but to man, given what we have of history, the 'inventions,' the new gestures . . . merely because in him occurs the new up-jut, the new bathing of the cerebral tissues in the residuum, in *la mousse* of the life sap. . . . In his growing subservience to, and adoration of, and entanglement in machines, in utility, man rounds the circle almost into insect life, the absence of flesh; and may have need even of horned gods to save him, or at least a form of thought which permits them" (150–151).

11. Gilbert was speaking of *Ulysses*. See her essay, "Woman's Sentence, Man's Sentencing: Linguistic Fantasies in Woolf and Joyce," in *Virginia Woolf and Bloomsbury: A Centenary Celebration*, edited by Jane Marcus (London: Macmillan, 1987), 221. See also Gilbert and Gubar chap. 5.

12. For a criticism of recent reductionist accounts of modernism, see Ronald Bush, "But Is It Modern? T. S. Eliot in 1988," *Yale Review* 77.2(Winter 1988): 193–206.

WORKS CITED

Bush, Ronald. *The Genesis of Ezra Pound's Cantos*. Princeton: Princeton UP, 1976.

Casillo, Robert. "Nature, History, and Anti-Nature in Ezra Pound's Fascism." *Papers on Language and Literature* 22.3(1986):299, 300.

Garner, Les *Stepping Stones to Women's Liberty: Feminist Ideas in the Women's Suffrage Movement 1900–1918*. Rutherford, N.J.: Fairleigh Dickinson UP, 1984.

Gilbert, Sandra M., and Susan Gubar. *No Man's Land*. Vol. 1. *The War of the Words*. New Haven: Yale UP, 1988.

Lidderdale, Jane, and Mary Nicholson. *Dear Miss Weaver.* New York: Viking P, 1970.
Lindberg, Kathryne. *Reading Pound Reading.* New York: Oxford UP, 1987.
Marsden, Dora. *Freewoman* 19 Aug. 1912:295.
Moore, Marianne. *The Complete Prose of Marianne Moore.* Ed. Patricia C. Willis. New York: Viking Penguin, 1986.
Perloff, Marjorie. *The Poetics of Indeterminacy: Rimbaud to Cage.* Princeton: Princeton UP, 1981.
Pound, Ezra. *The Cantos.* New York: New Directions, 1970.
———. *Personae: The Collected Shorter Poems.* New York: New Directions, 1949.
———. Translator's Postscript. In Remy de Gourmont, *The Natural Philosophy of Love.* 1922. New York: Collier, 1961.
Pound, Ezra, and James Joyce. *Pound/Joyce.* Ed. Forrest Reid. New York: New Directions, 1967.
Rose, Jonathan. *The Edwardian Temperament 1895–1919.* Athens: Ohio UP, 1986.
Ruthven, K. K. "Ezra's Appropriations." *Times Literary Supplement* 20–26 November 1987:1278, 1300–1301.
Scott, Bonnie Kime. *Joyce and Feminism.* Bloomington: Indiana UP, 1984.
Sinclair, May. *Feminism.* London: Women Writers' Suffrage League, 1912.
Stock, Noel. *The Life of Ezra Pound.* New York: Pantheon, 1970.

Letter to Marianne Moore, 16 December 1918

London, 16 December

Dear Miss Moore: The confounded trouble is that I have come to the end of my funds, and can not pay for any more mss. for *The Little Review.*

I think the poems too good to print without paying for them: I know you have contributed to *The Egoist* unpaid. And I have myself done a deal of unpaid work: too much of it.

I hope to start a quarterly here before long (part of the funds are in hand); and to be able to pay contributors: at least to pay them something; and to give them the satisfaction of being in good company. I will either hold over your two poems for the quarterly and try to pay; or print them in *The L.R.* . . . as you choose or permit.

There are one or two details I should like to ask about. (Yeats and Eliot and various other people have had similar queeries leveled at them, and our friendships have weathered the strain, so don't take it ill of me.)

?Are you quite satisfied with the final cadence and graphic arrangement of same in "A Graveyard"? The ends of the first two strophes lead into the succeeding strophe, rightly. The ending

"it is
neither with volition nor consciousness"

closes the thing to my ear. Perhaps you will find a more drastic change suits you better. I do not offer an alternative as dogma or as a single and definite possibility. Very likely you are after a sound-effect which escapes me. But I don't quite see what it is, and I know that a critic often finds the wrong point in a verse when he can not say why it is wrong, and when his first proposals regarding it are useless.

Comme on est ridicule. I have copied your own order, instead of the thing that came into my head this P.M., namely: "Consciousness nor volition."

Hang'd if I now know which I thought better. But I think the eye catches either cadence rather better if you break the line at *is*.

I haven't analyzed the metric of the whole; but find it satisfactory.

I want to know, relatively, your age, and whether you are working on Greek quantitative measures or on René Ghil or simply by ear (if so a very good ear).

In "Old Tiger":

I am worried by "intentioned." It is "not English"; in French it is *intentionné,* and I have no objection to gallicisms if done with distinction, and obviously and intentionally gallicisms for a *purpose.* But "intentioned" is like a lot of words in bad American journalese, or like the jargon in philosophical text-books. It is like a needless file surface (to me—and will upset the natives here much more than it does me). You know, possibly, that I don't mind the natives' feelings, *but* I think when giving offence one should always be *dead* right, not merely defensible.

Pneumatic is le mot juste, but Eliot has just preempted it in Grishkin's "pneumatic bliss." This is not a final argument, but in so close a circle (you are in it willy nilly, by the mere fact of writing verse for the members of the reading public capable of understanding). Also T.S.E. has jaguar'd—quite differently, but still . . . we *must* defend the camp against the outer damnations.

T.S.E. first had his housemaids drooping like the boas in my "Millwins," and it was only after inquisition of this sort that he decided, to the improvement of his line, to have them sprout.

(Atque: I am rejecting imitators of T.S.E. who would be only too ready to rend anyone they might think at their preserve.) In the words of W.L. send us one to catch our fleas.

Do you want "its self" or "itself" at the end of 12 strophe? There is a slight, or rather a very considerable, difference. Whether the tail has a metaphorical ψυχη inside it.

And as for "peacock": is it the best word? It means peacock-green???

Do you see any signs of mental life about you in New York? I still retain curiosities and vestiges of early hopes, though I doubt if I will ever return to America, save perhaps as a circus.

How much of your verse *is* European? How much Paris is in it? This is, I think, legitimate curiosity on my part. IF I am to be your editor, and as I am still interested in the problem of how much America can do on her own. (Political divisions NOT mattering in the ultimate, but . . .)

I oughtn't to be too lazy to analyze your metric; but . . . I very often don't analyze my own until years after. . . . AND time, and one's energy. . . . At any rate, it is (yr. metric) a progress on something I (more or less, so far as English goes) began. . . . Whether my beginnings had anything to do with yr. metric is another matter. ONLY I am curious.

Syllabic, in stanzas, same shape per stanza.

1st work written A.D.???

1st work published????

Answers NOT for publication in small biographical note, as used in Tschaikago.

At any rate, the quarterly IF it comes off offers you a spiritual roof or habitation; question of its being domus, home, hearth, must be left to you.

DOES your stuff "appear" in America?

Or peacock-blue or p.b. green? Peacock has feet and other colours such as brown in its ensemble???

Also when you break words at end of line, DO you insist on caps. at beginning of next line? Greeks didn't, nor does Ghil. Not categorical inhibition, but . . .

Now, to be more amiable, have you a book of verse in print? And, if not, can I get one into print for you? My last and best work *Propertius* has just dodged two publishers, one of whom wants to print half the book, leaving out the best of it. Dopo tant' anni, I am not yet in the position of a Van Dyke or a Tennyson; but still, I have got Joyce, and Lewis, and Eliot and a few other comforting people into print, by page and by volume. At any rate, I will buy a copy of your book IF it is in print, and if not, I want to see a lot of it all together. You will never sell more than five hundred copies, as your work demands mental attention. I am inclined to think you would "go" better in bundles about the size of Eliot's *Prufrock and Observations*.

For what it is worth, my ten or more years of practice, failure, success, etc. in arranging tables of contents, is à votre service. Or at any rate unless you have a definite scheme for a sequence, I would warn you of the very great importance of the actual order of poems in a booklet. (I have gone right and gone wrong in this at one time or another and know the results.)

Your stuff holds my eye. Most verse I merely slide off of (God I do ye thank for this automatic selfprotection), BUT my held eye goes forward very slowly, and I know how simple many things appear to me which people of supposed intelligence come to me to have explained.—/—/

Thank God, I think you can be trusted not to pour out flood (in the manner of dear Amy and poor Masters).

I wish I knew how far I am right in my conjecture of French influence; you are nearer to Ghil than to Laforgue, whose name I think I used in *The Future*. My note in the *L.R.* was possibly better.————

O what about your age; how much more youngness is there to go into the work, and how much closening can be expected?

And what the deuce of your punctuations? I am puzzled at times: How much deliberate, and therefore to be taken (by me) with studious meticulousness?? How much the fine careless rapture and therefore to be pot-shotted at until it assumes an wholly demonstrable or more obvious rightness????

ANYHOW I will keep the poems for my quarterly unless you want to have them rushed into the *L.R. at once,* and unless you have something better for the Quarterly. No reason which they shouldn't appear simultaneously in both (only it will be the quarterly's proposed and hoped-for purse that will pay).

And are you a jet black Ethiopian Othello-hued, or was that line in one of your *Egoist* poems but part of your general elaboration and allegory and designed to differentiate your colour from that of the surrounding menageria?

I can't fit in the prose paragraph anywhere, so return it. Or rather, no. I will hold it and give it to the *Egoist,* if you so direct.

The Letters of Ezra Pound. Ed. D. D. Paige. New York: Harvest, 1950. 141–144.

Doggerel Section of Letter to Marianne Moore

[London, 1 February 1919]

The female is a chaos ,

the male

is a fixed point of stupidity, but only the female
can content itself with prolonged conversation
with but one sole other creature of its own sex and
of its own unavoidable specie

the male

is more expansive
and demands other and varied contacts ;

hence its combattiveness ,
hence its discredit for " taking up cudgels "
hence its utter failure to receive credit
for the ninety and nine unjust times
when it refrained from taking up cudgels
and was done in the eye
by the porcine and uncudgled ££££££££££££ circumbelliferous ;

hence
the debacle of its ££££ temper ,
£££££ hence

its slow recovery and recuperance from the ££ yaller janders
hence also its more wide-spread insistencies ,
hence its exposure to stings and mud-slings of the
ungodly and unco-decrous
etc. and ad infinitum .

You , my dear correspondent ,
are a stabilized female ,
I am a male who has attained the chaotic fluidities ;

our mutual usefulness
is open to the gravest suspicions of non-existence, but
nevertheless , also , and notwithstanding all this ,
I am glad that you are red-headed and not
woolled , dark , ethiopian .

It would have been a test case :
you dark , nubian ethiopian : could I
have risen to it ; could I ,
perceiving the intelligence from a distance,
have got over the Jim Crow law ;
could I have bridged the gap
from the distinguished Bengal to Ethiopia
and asserted the milk-whiteness of souls
laved in a Mithriac liquid ,
or disinfected with laneline

The most beautiful wrist-bones I have ever encountered

were those of young Bengali ;

race : the squareness of ivory and the Japanese
have sent two friends from their census :
O, O ,Ethiopia !
Could I have transcended into Ethiopia : true
I have at last found a bearable Russian , I have
dissipated that gravy-like thickness of the middle country
Baku and the Armenian thickness
which is
more Ethiopian than any blackness of Benares ;
could I have stood Ethiopia :
Could I
at three thousand miles distance have contemplated
without squeams the possibility of
meeting a compatriote of San Zeno :

Out of your Nathaniel Hawthorne frigidities can you ---
I think not ---

stand for my temple to Pallas Athene and for my cult of
other ancient and less prohibitive deities :
for my preference of Omar to Melancthon ;
of Anacreon to John Calvin;
for my Mediterranean colouring ;

for my spices of Araby ; for my perfumes and deyed stuffs
for £££££ Ceserea Phillipae

£££
for my Tyrrian and my Coan ;
for my nard and Libyan incense:

No . I had better leave you to Mr Kreymborg and Bill William
and leave off meddling in American matters

But I am so " confounded polygamous "
That exquisite cockleshell calls at so many ports ;
the Cytheraean carries my postbag ;
and extra half yard of mind ,
and extra millimetre of eye-lash : and behold me

even upon the threshold of you Presbyterian stair-turn

my lechery
capable of all altitudes ;
no cerebrality being too tenuous
no heights of the Paradiso too frigid ;
no air too vitreous , too discrete ,
too separatist in its tendency.

I , Manichean ; you a Malthusian of the intellect.

I so the confounded intruder and disturber of
the Hortus Inclusus ;

Zagreus at the door of the parsonage .
Keeping a carbon copy . "We must not"
writes a contemporary Church of England theological author
" give up Parthenogenesis ; it is the outpost of Incarnation "

Custer's last fight for the Trinity !
Eight Hinch sans-serif on the posters
" Ggawd deont dew bizniss thaat waye ! "))
" St. Paul was a Gentleman "
no reflection
on the habits of your particular family
but they are not alone in their clerical functions.I have seen
Savonarola still swinging a crucifix ,
down from Salo for the week-end and exhorting

the back-sliders of Venice ; and the Reverend Cavaliere ££££££
Dottore Alessandro
Robertson denouncing the Babylonian woman
and the Rrrroman reliegion
with fervour ::: O my Christ with fervour and sincerity
and cinviction. I have seen

the inhibitions of seventeen sects
and the dangers of national internationalism , Eloi , Eloi .

(Also Voltaire on the Elohim) .
And the wildreness iwll not be healed
either by fletcherizing or by a diet of locusts .

Splendours of vintages ;
Guido in accented imabics .

Chere Marianne. So much for the Muses (precedant)
The rest of your statements . . . .

Letters. 146–147. Supplemented by the original in the Beinecke Library, Yale University.

"Others"

Among other books received for review is a sequence by Moireen Fox, a new book of short poems by Joseph Campbell, and the "Others" Anthology for 1917. This last gives I think the first adequate presentation of Mina Loy and Marianne Moore, who have, without exaggerated "nationalism", without waving of banners and general phrases about Columbia gem of the ocean, succeeded in, or fallen into, producing something distinctly American in quality, not merely distinguishable as Americans by reason of current national faults.

Their work is neither simple, sensuous nor passionate, but as we are no longer governed by the *North American Review* we need not condemn poems merely because they do not fit some stock phrase of rhetorical criticism.

(For example an infinitely greater artist than Tennyson uses six "s" 's and one "z" in a single line. It is one of the most musical lines in Provencal and opens a poem especially commended by Dante. Let us leave the realm of promoted typists who quote the stock phrases of text-books.)

In the verse of Marianne Moore I detect traces of emotion; in that of Mina Loy I detect no emotion whatever. Both of these women are, possibly in unconsciousness, among the followers of Jules Laforgue (whose work shows a great deal of emotion). It is possible, as I have written, or intended to write elsewhere, to divide poetry into three sorts; (1.) melopoeia, to wit, poetry which moves by its music, whether it be a music in the words or an aptitude for, or suggestion of, accompanying music; (2.) imagism, or poetry wherein the feelings of painting and sculpture are predominant (certain men move in phantasmagoria; the images of their gods, whole countrysides, stretches of hill land and forest, travel with them); and there is, thirdly, logopoeia or poetry that is akin to nothing but language, which is a dance of the intelligence among words and ideas and modification of ideas and characters. Pope and the eighteenth-century writers had in this medium a certain limited range. The intelligence of Laforgue ran through the whole gamut of his time. T. S. Eliot has gone on with it. Browning wrote a condensed form of drama, full of things of the senses, scarcely ever pure logopoeia.

One wonders what the devil anyone will make of this sort of thing who has not in their wit all the clues. It has none of the stupidity beloved of the "lyric" enthusiast and the writer and reader who take refuge in scenery description of nature, because they are unable to cope with the human. These two contributors to the "Others" Anthology write logopoeia. It is, in their case, the utterance of clever people in despair, or hovering upon the brink of that precipice It is of those who have acceded with Renan "La bêtise humaine est la seule chose qui donne une idée de l'infini." It is a mind cry, more than a heart cry. "Take the world if thou wilt but leave me an asylum for my affection" is not their lamentation, but rather "In the midst of this desolation, give me at least one intelligence to converse with."

The arid clarity, not without its own beauty, of le tempérament de l'Americaine, is in the poems of these, I think, graduates or post-graduates. If they have not received B. A. 's or M. A. 's or B. Sc-s they do not need them.

The point of my praise, for I intend this as praise, even if I do not burst into the phrases of Victor Hugo, is that without any pretences and without clamours about nationality, these girls have written a distinctly national product, they have written something which would not have come out of any other country, and (while I have before now seen a deal of rubbish by both of them) they are, as selected by Mr. Kreymborg, interesting and readable (by me, that is. I am aware that even the poems before me would drive numerous not wholly unintelligent readers into a fury of rage-out-of-puzblement.) Both these poetrial have said a number of things not to be found in the current numbers of *Everybody's*, the *Century* or *McClure's*. "The Effectual Marriage", "French Peacock", "My Apish Cousins" have each in its way given me pleasure . Miss Moore has already prewritten her counterblast to my criticism in her poem "To a Steam Roller".

SUPPLEMENT: MARGARET ANDERSON'S ANNOTATION

Ezra and I disagreed about this poet. This is how I would express my disagreement today:

It is almost impossible for me to express, with moderation, my dislike of intellectual poetry. It is an anomaly. I can't read it without impatience. It can enrage me.

My position needs no defense—the simplest statement defends it: INTELLECTUAL POETRY IS NOT POETRY.

Poetry is not made from, nor read with, the mind. It arises in another center of man. You shouldn't have to THINK when you read a poem. Instead, "un monde vous frappe dans la poitrine et abolit tout ce qui n'est pas lui."

There is no idea in intellectual poetry that cannot be better expressed in prose. There is no emotion in intellectual poetry that springs from the affirmed permanent emotions of mankind.

Eliot is a poet—he uses his mind to reveal the life of his emotions. Marianne Moore is an intellectual—she uses the life of her mind as her subject-matter. Some subject-matters are proper to poetry; some are not. The difference is always between the verbal and the formal.

The Marianne Moores live in, and write from, the phenomenal world. Poets live in, and write from, the noumenal world.

"A List of Books." *Little Review* 4.11 (March 1918): 56–58. Anderson's Annotation, *The Little Review Anthology*. Ed. Margaret Anderson. New York: Horizon, 1953. 187–188.

Suffragettes

There is perhaps nothing more enjoyable, nothing so sustaining to the inner sense of one's own nobility than to suffer martyrdom or exile for the sake of a cause or of an idea which one believes noble. Miss Christabel Pankhurst has about as much intellect as a guinea-pig but she has a sense of values, of subjective emotional values, which is sound beyond question. And Sylvia, her sister, is also getting a lot out of life. It is glorious and stimulating to ride on a stretcher at the head of a loyal mob. I do not pity these young ladies. I regard them with envy, at least they "will have lived," they will always have that to look back upon if they survive it.

As to "the cause," it is just—and in a sense absurd. I mean there is only one valid argument against the suffrage. The clique which runs this country must, oh, at all costs, *must* keep up the fiction that the *vote* is of some use.

They fear presumably that if the masses should ever find out or begin to believe in the incompetence of the vote, they would then begin to act. We suppose that they would be shot? Let us cease to talk about "ifs." It suits the convenience of our rulers that we should believe in voting, in suffrage as a universal panacea for our own stupidities. As a syndicalist, somewhat atrabilious, I disbelieve vigorously in any recognition of political institutions, of the Fabian Society, John Galsworthy, and so on.

The duty of literate men and of all women is to keep alight some a spark of civilisation at the summit of things. It is the duty of everyone who is intelligent enough to read this paper to spend his or her energies setting some model of life to the rabble and to ages to come. It is not our duty to fuss about Sunday closing or minimum wage or any other attempt to make hell less hell-like for the lower classes.

Economics are not the muddle that they are made out to be. Were it not for the hideous immoralities preached by the established churches we should go at this matter somewhat straighter. States are not run by paternosters. Economics are pragmatical. And simple. If a family of two have two hundred or even one hundred pounds a year of more or less regular income, they can live as befits rational literate animals. If they have children, or if they have too many, they sink.

The rich are those who do not have too many children. The poor are those who do have too many children. It take a generation or so to establish the classes.

A sensible man or woman attempts to earn food, and not to have more wives, husbands, and children than he or she can support.

He or she will not waste his or her energy in mucking with politics or economics but in keeping alight the flame of science and knowledge and the arts, and in setting a fine example of living.

It is only the discoveries of science and of genius that remain. You can preach till you are blue about the iniquitous folly of being taxed to support a few war-trusts, a few factories that provide war gear and war scares. You have half a billion sterling set up against you. Submarines, and Ulivi if he perfects his machine, do the job before or without you. The needs pass. Politics are fit for a certain type of arrested man. A mediæval king was a sort of high sheriff. No one now cares a hang about mediæval kings and no one wants to be chief of police.

Only a few people, and those not of the nicest, have any hankering after the job of Prime Minister. Some one ought to be employed to look after our traffic and sewage, one grants that. But a superintendence of traffic and sewage is not the sole function of man. Certain stupid and honest people should, doubtless, be delegated for the purpose. There politics ends for the enlightened man.

The enlightened man should foregather with other enlightened men and plot for the preservation of enlightenment. That is to say, he should form his syndicat. The joiners, etc., who have interests in common should form their syndicats.

These syndicats should work on things as they are, on inevitable and implacable hostilities, on various forms of sloth and avarice. One puts up with the infamy of an over-stocked government service, and a lot of lazy over-paid parsons, etc., etc., because life is too short to waste it reforming or trying to reform this inferno.

As for feminine suffrage in its relations to present conditions.

We have to do not with justice, not with truth—no barrister, no judge, no politician deals with, or searches for these things. We have to do with something like the laws of bridge-whist, which do not pretend to be a research after justice and the primal verities.

We have a set of more or less competent, more or less avaricious, more or less well-meaning persons who "must," or at least will, under all circumstances, think about their own preservation, and advantage. They are in charge of a mechanism called the "state." They run it by chicane and catch-words. The catch-words are a very powerful part of chicane. The catch-words are limitedly capable of both good and evil. They may even run away with their inventors. I mean a man who gets on by bawling "justice" may in rare cases get himself caught in a nasty corner where he has to play according to whatever catch-word he has used or invented. He may even respect the words, and they may be a part of his "better nature."

Now there is no known definition of "justice" as that term is used in representative governments, limited monarchies, constitutional monarchies, etc., which can be used against the present demand for the enfranchisement of women. Their demand is irrevocably just.

Any minister, any man impassioned for "justice" must grant that the demand for suffrage is just.

On the other hand it is foolish. It is foolish because it is a demand for a shadow, a useless thing, but it is a thing to which the women have every "right."

The suffragettes as a body are foolish, not only because they demand a shadow, but because of their tactics. They seem to have very little intellect back of their campaign, and yet the proposition before them is so difficult they they have need of a very great deal of intellect if they are to win out.

I don't mean that they are all utter imbeciles. Their position is very difficult. It is quite possible that if all the "male" "intellect" in the country went over to their side they would not even then hold the cards for a win.

As for their actions of late: It is rot to say "we deplore violence"; we all like the violence so long as they don't smash our own windows. We all like to see big headlines. We like the papers to have racy bits of news in 'em. We like to read of bombs and explosions. The undergraduate in all of us survives up to that extent—unless we have property or interests in danger.

To be logical, however, the suffragettes should destroy only national property. They are, strictly speaking, outlaws. They are, however, outlaws enjoying as much protection from the state by which they are outlawed as do the active members of that state, *i.e.*, the voters. It may not be the height of prudence to forfeit that even incomplete protection from violence and some other sorts of annoyance. They are outlaws under a truce, under a truce which they have every "right" to forfeit if they choose.

Their right to attack in that case is the right to attack national property, national pictures, etc., not pictures belonging to Mr. Sargent. Their smashing of national treasures is more commendable, for instance, than would be a smashing of Mr. Asquith, who is not a national treasure, but only the treasure of a faction. So that in so far as they have refrained from assassinations, etc., they have been wise. They have been more just than their opponents.

Their attack on a hospital doctor would seem also logical. No man is by virtue of his contract as prison surgeon bound to take part in tortures worthy of a mediæval dungeon. The surgeon would seem to be exceeding the functions demanded of him by his state or syndicat. It is natural that a hostile syndicat should single him out for a particular vendetta. I doubt if that wretched male had anyone's sympathy.

The practical question is not one of "justice"; it is simply, will the country give the vote to women out of sheer boredom?

Will exaggerated ennui and exasperation drive "the ruling syndicat" to a just act. These maligned women (who are for the most part misrepresented by the Press), are they foolish beyond measure? A revolution is a successful rebellion. If the ruling syndicat recognises the outlawry and withdraws its tacit habitual protection of the outlaws, have they any chance of success sufficient to warrant their war?

I mean simply that a general who takes certain risks in war is courtmartialled if he fails.

Personally I want them to vote. They have played a sporting game. If men like Balfour of Burleigh have a "right" to play a certain silly form of tip-cat called voting, then women who are willing to die for an idea (however stupid) have an equal right to spend a few minutes a year in a stuffy polling booth.

"Ultimately" . . . one says, "they must win." Ideas, however stupid, that people are willing to suffer for, always "win." I mean they get a run for their money, they rule, sooner or later, for an indefinite period. Those who oppose the suffrage lay up for themselves a period of future infamy. That much they can promise themselves. A certain number of people will spit upon their tombs.

I write from outside the struggle. It is all one to me whether these women want to vote about district inspection of milk-cans, or whether they want the right to walk on shepherds' stilts.

The forces against them are sufficiently discussed elsewhere. They have for them, boredom, the weariness of "the unjust judge." They have the mob's tacit approval of violence, of anything that causes excitement, they have their own conviction, their own love of adventure, their hatred of traditional forms of feminine ennui, they have the force of male sentimentality or chivalry working in their favour. They have the "justice" of their cause, for whatever that bagatelle may be worth. The intellectuals' hatred of politicians and of politics is in their favour, this is only the passive favour of spectators who will do nothing for them save talk now and then.

They have the passionate fury that official caddishness or the spectacle of Sir Almroth Wright stirs up in the intelligent mind.

The *Male* mind does not want to be bothered with Asquith or Wright or their kind. Politics is unfit for men, it may be good enough for women, we doubt it. The male mind does not want a state run by women, or by "old women." Torture disgusts the male mind. The male parent disturbed by a row is apt to chastise all the disturbers quite impartially.

In the middle ages the "affairs" were, we suppose, in the hands of Jews and lawyers. The male muddled. He fought and occasionally won castles and lost them by chicane. If the control of the state were in "male" control, women would have the vote for the asking . . . and it would do them no good.

This argument, like all political arguments, runs in a circle. Unlike political arguments it confesses its circularity.

[I.]

As for the anti-militants, tax-resisters, etc., nothing has at any time prevented these people from summoning a women's parliament. It would have no legal status but it could deliberate, and its decisions, if they were at all sensible, would carry weight. They could recommend laws to the House of Commons. The opening of polls for delegates, suffrage, anti-suffrage and all, would force the women who "do not want votes" to vote for delegates to the women's congress or else to see "feminine opinion" effectually recorded against them. Mrs. Humphry Ward, for whom permit me to express my contempt in passing, would have to appear in such a contest, or else keep quiet.

[II.]

One supposes the talk about deadlock is all humbug, but even if there were a deadlock nothing would prevent the present ministry from instituting a women's chamber (women elected by woman's vote) and giving it the right to initiate legislation on questions of woman's labour, and such other matters as concern women in particular. Such powers could be slowly increased if the chamber proved competent.

That would do away with the objection to giving the suffrage to a lot of untrained voters.

A division of the houses of government into a male and female is far more in accord with contemporary ideas than a division of the houses into "commons" and "lords." One would, of course, hate to abolish that picturesque relic "The Lords," though the thought of being even slightly controlled by a body containing bishops is both painful and ridiculous.

Bastien von Helmholtz.

Egoist 1.13 (July 1914): 254–256.

18
Jean Rhys (1890–1979)

Introduced and Edited by Coral Ann Howells

Jean Rhys would seem to challenge the date limits of this anthology for several reasons: her most celebrated novel, *The Wide Sargasso Sea,* was not published until 1966; the interviews with her and her own writing about her work appeared in the 1960s and 1970s; her unfinished autobiography, *Smile Please,* was published in 1979. Nonetheless, Rhys began writing in the 1920s and was seventy-six when *The Wide Sargasso Sea* was published. Rhys's first short story was published in Ford Madox Ford's *transatlantic review* in 1924, and a collection, *The Left Bank and Other Stories,* appeared in 1927, to be followed by *Quartet* (1928), *After Leaving Mr Mackenzie* (1930), *Voyage in the Dark* (1934), and *Good Morning, Midnight* (1939). After *Good Morning, Midnight* Rhys disappeared from the literary scene, and her books went out of print.

Rhys was discovered living in Devon in 1957 when a dramatized version of *Good Morning, Midnight* was performed on the BBC Third Programme. John Lehmann published one of her stories, "Till September, Petronella," in the *London Magazine* of January 1960. *The Wide Sargasso Sea* won the Royal Society of Literature and the W. H. Smith Awards. It was followed by two other collections of stories, *Tigers Are Better Looking* (1969) and *Sleep It Off, Lady* (1976), and a collection of three essays, *My Day.* In 1967 André Deutsch reissued *Good Morning, Midnight* and *Voyage in the Dark,* followed by *Quartet* and *After Leaving Mr Mackenzie* in 1969. All the novels and short story collections are currently available in Penguin paperback editions. Rhys was made a Fellow of the Royal Society of Literature in 1966 and a CBE (Commander of the Order of the British Empire) in 1978. The three selections appearing here are chosen from the period 1924–1939 and show Rhys's feminized version of urban modernist fiction.

Jean Rhys, born in Dominica as Ella Gwendoline Rhys Williams, went to England in 1907 to go to school in Cambridge and returned only once to the Caribbean, twenty-nine years later. Breaking completely with her family, she worked as a chorus girl in a touring company, had her first traumatic love affair in 1910, and shortly after the First World War married Jean Lenglet. After four restless years spent in Holland, Vienna, and Paris, Lenglet was arrested for fraudulent currency dealings and extradited to Holland.

Rhys became Ford Madox Ford's protégée and existed on the periphery of the international modernist set in Paris. Their romantic and literary entanglement ended with the breakup of her marriage, and Rhys returned to England in 1927 to find a publisher for her first novel. She married again in 1932, and a third time in 1947.

Much of her work published in the 1960s and 1970s was written in draft during the 1940s and 1950s. It was only with the determined encouragement of Francis Wyndham and Diana Athill of André Deutsch that Rhys began publishing again. *The Wide Sargasso Sea* is a radical revision of a version written before 1939 and then destroyed. At the time of her third husband's death in 1966, she realized in a dream of giving birth that her novel was finished and at last agreed to its publication.

Rhys, as a white woman from Dominica living in England and Europe, was a modernist expatriate-exile figure. Her Caribbean background provides the dimension in which to ground her sense of dispossession and unbelonging. Her short stories and novels are for the most part urban European fictions that repress her Caribbean inheritance, though their fragmented form and pervasive sense of rootlessness figure an irreplacable absence.

Rhys's fiction is not explicitly feminist. Instead, she writes about women as victims of their own and male romantic fantasies, with a focus on female silence and suffering. Her protagonists are all women alone in Paris or London, working as mannequins, artists' models, or prostitutes, or not working at all but still reliant on men for economic survival. Yet within this, Rhys records these women's jagged moments of insight into their dependent condition, their resentments, and their silent crises of rage, just as she shows their emotional withdrawal into secret places within themselves.

"Vienne," Rhys's first published short story, appears here in its original version. It was later expanded for *The Left Bank* collection, then reprinted with minor changes in *Tigers Are Better Looking*. This version, without the embellishments that transformed it into a continuous narrative, is quintessential modernist writing with a feminized perspective. It consists of three fragments, all sketches about women as male fantasy objects. Rhys sketches an urban demimonde existence in postwar Vienna, with its chic nightclubs, cafés, restaurants, hotels, cars and golf courses, as a patriarchal world dominated by money, where women are luxury items to be bought and discarded. They are defined entirely as objects of the male gaze: to be "raved about" or "coveted" like the dancer at the Parisien with her Kirchner girl's legs; to be stalked and flirted with by men like Fischyl ("well, a man had only to choose"); or to be dressed with "rings and a string of pearls and as many frocks as I liked." The female narrator comments on the pervasive chilliness of such an existence and on the "cold eyes" of men.

The three sketches form a disrupted sequence in a female narrative about women's secret fears, their dependence on men, and their expendability. There is an unwritten connection between the danseuse who disappears from Vienna to marry a barber in Budapest and the anecdote of the young Russian girl who shot herself in a restaurant, thereby making the only kind of heroic gesture available to women whose existence depends wholly on pleasing men. As fragmented narrative it is told with marked shifts in perspective. "The Dancer" is presented from an entirely external view; in "Fischyl" the narrator combines the masculine view of Fischyl himself as "An Important Person" with her own resistant feminine perspective; in "The Spending Phase" an interiorized perspective is adopted, with the narrator voicing her sardonic criticism of masculine values, together with her fears of poverty and rejection. The ending juxtaposes an uncomprehending masculine view of women's behavior with a wry celebration of the Russian girl's courage in destroying herself when she becomes a useless object. The final phrase, "when your good time was over," is an implicit evaluation of what "good times" mean for women and a recognition of a woman's fate in a male-dominated world.

Ford's Preface to *The Left Bank* presents the masculine viewpoint which Rhys was writing against. Indeed, it enacts male dominance by occupying twenty-four of its twenty-seven pages with Ford's own reminiscences of Paris, and only then introducing Jean Rhys as an exotic and passionate woman writer "coming from the Antilles, with a terrifying insight and a terrific—almost a lurid—passion for stating the case of the underdog" (Ford 24). Even his comments on her "instinct for form," "possessed by singularly few writers of English and by almost no English women writers" (25), is double edged.

Contemporary reviewers echoed Ford's point of view, beginning almost invariably with praise for "Mr. Ford's interesting Preface" and contrasting his "easy authoritativeness" with Rhys's tentativeness (*Times Literary Supplement*). An American reviewer commented that "these anecdotes and sketches are so slight, so flashing, that their impression on the mind scarcely survives the reading" (*Saturday Review of Literature*).

Reviews of Rhys's subsequent fiction show a distinct moral bias against her "sordid" subject matter, together with a grudging admiration of her style: "It is a waste of talent" (*Times Literary Supplement* 5 March 1931) but "Within the limits of her subject, Miss Rhys has done a very nearly perfect job" (*Saturday Review of Literature* 16 March 1935). Such contradictory responses are highlighted in the reviews of *Good Morning, Midnight*. The *Times Literary Supplement* recommended it as First Choice in Novels of the Week while asserting that the only difficulty with the book was its heroine (22 April 1939). The *New Statesman and Nation* begins, "It is Miss Rhys's misfortune that she so brilliantly achieves the effect she intended," and ends, "though her book left me despondent, I found it quite remarkably impressive." Twenty-seven years later, the *Times Literary Supplement* review of *The Wide Sargasso Sea*, titled "A Fairy-Tale Neurotic," is recognizably working within the same tradition, commenting that "all her novels are about the injustice done by cruel men to lovely women" and concluding with one sentence praising her style, "a rare synthesis of the baroque and the precise, the coolly empirical and lushly pretty, and most of the poetry, of course, belongs with Antoinette."

The original ending of *Voyage in the Dark* reprinted here is the one Rhys agreed to change under pressure from her male publisher. As she wrote to Evelyn Scott, "I suppose I shall have to give in and cut the book and I'm afraid it will make it meaninglesss. The worst is that it is precisely the last part which I am most certain of that will have to be mutilated" (*Letters* 33). Despite her regret and resentments, Rhys did not try to restore the original ending when Deutsch republished the novel over thirty years later.

The "mutilated" ending was only the last in a series of casualties that beset this novel, the origins of which lay in Rhys's record of her personal casualty. The novel derives from notebooks written by Rhys after a traumatic love affair in London in 1910. These notebooks surfaced in Paris in 1923 and were instrumental in bringing her to Ford Madox Ford's attention. Rhys had lent them to Mrs. George Adam, wife of a *Times* correspondent, who typed them, adapted them, and sent the typescript to Ford. He did not publish them, and Rhys returned to the notebooks several years later to write *Voyage in the Dark*. It was published in 1934 after three publishers' refusals and with the revised ending. A comparison between the published version of part IV and the much longer original version shows a radical change in the narrative. Instead of ending with Anna Morgan's death from her bungled abortion, the published version ends with her return to consciousness in time to hear the words of the male doctor whose skill has saved her life: "She'll be alright," he said. "Ready to start all over again in no time, I've no doubt."

The original ending is Anna's interior monologue, with Anna as subject recording her own dying up to the moment of death. (Interestingly, Rhys resurrected from this vanished ending the first words, "Smile please," and the incident with the photographer in the title and opening of her autobiography, published shortly after her death.) The monologue interweaves Anna's present sensations with a rush of memories about her Caribbean childhood and her London love affair. In her hallucinatory state her Caribbean inheritance surfaces as dream. Everything is presented as double sided; carnival masks almost conceal "the malevolent idiot at the back of everything," though "a slobbering tongue" sticks out, and her lover's caring for her is limited by his prudential reminder that she must leave his house at four o'clock. Sensations of giddiness and pain fuse with childhood memories of falling off a horse as the monologue moves via a series of rapid transformations toward silence and blackness. Characteristic modernist features of the text include its registration of psychic fragmentation, its multivoicedness, and its dissolution of time. Anna dies as the victim of her own biology and of men, a colonial in the gendered and political senses of that word.

"Ghost Writing," also included here, is one of Rhys's rare portrayals of a woman writer, as Sasha Jansen tells her story of ghost writing fairy tales for a rich woman at Antibes. In 1925 Rhys, on Ford's recommendation, went to the French Riviera to ghost a book for a Mrs. Huenot, but after a short time she was dismissed and returned to Paris. It is characteristic of Rhys to use autobiographical materials and then reshape them as fiction, voicing her muted defiance and rebellion in a fierce self-satire, for Sasha's account is as self-lacerating as it is socially satiric. This passage from *Good Morning, Midnight* is typical of Rhys's fiction of the 1920s and 1930s, with its metropolitan Paris scenario and its deliberately shabby revision of the female romantic fantasy indulged in by an aging woman with a gigolo. It deals with brittle surfaces and social masks, but there are also sudden shifts that reveal the female narrator's vulnerability and hint at the possibility of intimacy between two such socially marginal figures as Sasha and René. Nevertheless, she inevitably retreats from personal contact into isolation, in a wry contemplation of her self-image in the underground fairy-tale world of magic mirrors that reflect the ghosts of past selves. Sasha's anecdote ends with her ironic awareness that all this happens in the lavatory of the Deux Magots café and in the precarious interval "when drink makes you look nice, before it makes you look awful."

The title, *Good Morning, Midnight,* is taken from a poem by Emily Dickinson, and Rhys's last novel is a revisionary reading of *Jane Eyre.* In an unstated and nontheoretical way, Rhys appears to be situating her fiction in a female writing tradition. In her letters she refers to her rather unsystematic reading of contemporary fiction by women, including Eliot Bliss (a white Jamaican novelist writing in England in the 1930s), Elizabeth Jenkins, Katherine Mansfield, and Stevie Smith. Rhys always saw herself as an isolated figure, however, and her letters reveal her sense of loneliness and marginality, indeed her resistance to being part of any literary group. She wrote her opinion of groups in a letter to her daughter Maryvonne in 1958: "Yes I think groups of children can be horrible. So can all groups. I hate them and fear them like I hated termites' nests at home. . . . These things build *huge* nests and little roads going from one nest to another . . . and *hell* to them. Well that is a Group to me" (*Letters* 155). Rhys's letters also reveal her desire for confidantes and show an extraordinary mixture of self-satire and self-pity. Though she writes sometimes about her fiction, it is in a completely nontheoretical way, always focusing on her subjective involvement with the process of writing and its significance to her as the only way toward her own sense of self-recognition and her only justification as a human being.

WORKS CITED

Ford, Ford Madox. Preface. In Jean Rhys, *The Left Bank and Other Stories.*
New Statesman and Nation. Review of *Good Morning, Midnight.* 22 April 1939:614.
Rhys, Jean. *After Leaving Mr Mackenzie.* London: Deutsch, 1969; New York: Harper and Row, 1972. Rpt. in *Jean Rhys: The Early Novels.*
———. *Good Morning, Midnight.* London: Deutsch, 1967; New York: Harper and Row, 1970. Rpt. in *Jean Rhys: The Early Novels.*
———. *Jean Rhys Letters 1931–1966.* London: Deutsch, 1984.
———. *Jean Rhys: The Early Novels.* London: Deutsch, 1984.
———. *The Left Bank and Other Stories.* New York: Books for Libraries P, 1970.
———. *My Day.* Vermont: Stinehour Press, 1975.
———. *Quartet.* London: Deutsch, 1969; New York: Harper and Row, 1971. Rpt. in *Jean Rhys: The Early Novels.*
———. *Sleep it Off, Lady.* London: Deutsch; New York: Harper and Row, 1976.
———. *Smile Please.* London: Deutsch; New York: Harper and Row, 1979.
———. *Voyage in the Dark.* London: Deutsch, 1967; New York: Norton, 1968. Rpt. in *Jean Rhys: The Early Novels.*
———. *The Wide Sargasso Sea.* London: Deutsch, 1966; New York: Norton, 1967.
Saturday Review of Literature. Review of *The Left Bank.* 5 November 1927:287.
———. Review of *Voyage in the Dark.* 16 March 1935:556.
Times Literary Supplement. Review of *After Leaving Mr Mackenzie.* 5 March 1931:180.
———. Review of *Good Morning, Midnight.* 22 April 1931:231.
———. Review of *The Left Bank.* 5 May 1927: 320.
———. Review of *Wide Sargasso Sea.* 17 November 1966:1039.

SELECTED CRITICISM

Angier, Carole. *Jean Rhys.* New York: Viking, 1985.
Harrison, Nancy R. *Jean Rhys and The Novel as Women's Text.* Chapel Hill and London: U of North Carolina P, 1988.
Nebeker, Helen. *Jean Rhys: Woman in Passage.* Montreal: Eden P, 1981.
O'Connor, Teresa F. *Jean Rhys: The West Indian Novels.* New York and London: New York UP, 1986.
Roe, Sue. "The Shadow of Light: The Symbolic Underworld of Jean Rhys." In *Women Reading Women's Writing,* ed. Sue Roe. Brighton: Harvester, 1987.

Vienne

I THE DANCER

Funny how it's slipped away, Vienne. Nothing left but a few snapshots—
Not a friend, not a pretty frock—nothing left of Vienna.
Hot sun, my black frock, a hat with roses, music, lots of music—

The little dancer at the "Parisien" with a Kirchner girl's legs and a little faun's face.

She was so exquisite that girl that it clutched at one, gave one a pain that anything so lovely could ever grow old, or die, or do ugly things—

A fragile child's body, a fluff of black skirt ending far above the knee. Silver straps over that beautiful back, the wonderful legs in black silk stockings and little satin shoes, short hair, cheeky little face.

She gave me the *songe bleu*—Four, five feet she could jump and come down on that wooden floor without a sound—

Her partner, an unattractive individual in badly fitting trousers, could lift her with one hand, throw her in the air, catch her, swing her as one would a flower.

At the end she made an adorable little "gamine's" grimace.

Ugly humanity, I'd always thought—I saw people differently afterwards—because for once I'd met sheer loveliness with a flame inside, for there was "it"—the spark, the flame in her dancing.

John (a dam good judge) raved about her. André also, though cautiously, for he was afraid she would be too expensive.

All the French officers coveted her—night after night the place was packed.

Finally she disappeared. Went back to Buda Pest where afterwards we heard of her.

Married to a barber

Rum!

Pretty women, lots.

How pretty women here are—

Lovely food.

Poverty gone, the dread of it—going.

II. "FISCHYL"

I met him at the Tabarin.

The Tabarin when we were in Vienna was the *chic* night café, though I did'nt think it as amusing as the Parisien—

Simone, Germaine, John, me, a rum Viennese who wore a monocle and was supposed to live on his very charming wife, two Italians.

Fischyl arrived to "kiss the hand"; froze on to me and asked if I'd come to play golf next morning.

The links are near the Prater—and we sat in the nice little house-place—drinking hot wine before we started.

It was dam cold for golf.

Also Fischyl said my hat was too big and insisted on my taking it off and putting on a sort of mosquito-net thing made of green gauze which covered my face up and fastened at the back.

He wore a white sweater and huge boots—

We sallied out and he started to show me how to hold my club but all I could think of was how to get at my nose which I wanted to blow.

Also I'd left my handkerchief in the club house.

However I explained (after two sniffs) to Fischyl.

He was quite a sport undid the mosquito net and lent me his enormous hanky.

Then he said that he was dying to kiss the back of my neck.

It was amusing golf—and we played several times.

He was tall and large with a bushy moustache and a beaky nose, old or oldish.

He talked incessantly of flirting, of London (which he hated) of English people (who amazed him) of himself—of Women.

I always remember one long discourse about some place where he'd been in some official capacity.

He talked French and though my French was improving there were blanks.

So I only gathered that it was in the Orient.

Turkey perhaps—or Asia Minor. Could it have been Smyrna?

Anyway there was Fischyl. An Important Person.

And every evening he would promenade along the principal street or place or whatever it was and choose a woman.

They sat at windows and passed in carriages.

For all the women were beautiful there—and all were . . . well, a man had only to choose.

I imagined Fischyl walking along, trousers rather tight, moustaches fiercely curling, chest well out—Choosing.

As a matter of fact I am not being fair to Fischyl for he was like most Viennese, charming, and clever as hell.

He was fearfully interested in the air raids over London—wanted to know if I remembered the one of such and such a date.

Was there any damage done? And where?

Afterwards I found out that he'd been in Germany during the war and was in some way connected with the air service.

I wonder if he'd anything to do with the bomb that fell so close to the Cavour that night I was with Kinsky?

Golf was too dam cold for the winter I decided.

III. THE SPENDING PHASE.

I'd noticed people growing more and more deferential to John and incidentally to me. I'd noticed that he seemed to have money—a good deal—a great deal.

He made it on the change he told me.

Then one day in the spring of 1921 we left the flat in Favoritenstrasse for a suite in the Imperial : a bedroom, sitting room and bathroom.

We sent off the cook and D—, promoted to be my maid came with us.

Nice to have lots of money—nice, nice.

Good to have a car, a big chauffeur, rings and a string of pearls and as many frocks as I liked.

Good to have money, money. All the flowers I wanted. All the compliments I wanted. Everything everything.

Oh great god money—you make possible all that's nice in life—Youth and beauty, the envy of women, and the love of men—

Even the luxury of a soul, a character and thoughts of one's own you give, and only you!—To look in the glass and think I've got what I wanted!

I gambled when I married and I've won—

As a matter of fact I wasn't so exalted really, but it was exceedingly pleasant.

Spending and spending And there was always more—

. . . .

One day I had a presentiment.

John gave an extra special lunch to the Japanese officers, Miyake, Hayashi, Oshima and Co.

We lunched in a separate room which started my annoyance for I preferred the restaurant especially with the Japanese who depressed me.

It was rather cold and dark and the meal seemed interminable—

Miyake in the intervals of eating enormously told us a long history of an officer in Japan who "hara-kari'd" because his telephone went wrong during manœuvres.

Rotten reason I call it but Miyake seemed to think him a hero.

Escaped as soon as I could upstairs.

I was like Napoleon's mother suddenly "Provided it lasts."

And if it does not? Well, thinking that was to feel the authentic "cold brand clutching my heart"

And a beastly feeling too let me tell you.

So damned well I knew that I could never be poor again with courage or dignity.

I did a little sum, translated what we were spending into francs—into pounds—I was appalled—(When we first arrived in Vienne the crown was 13 to the franc—at that time it was about sixty).

As soon as I could I attacked John—

First he laughed then he grew vexed.

"Ella I tell you it's all right. How much am I making? A lot.

"How much exactly? Can't say. How? You won't understand.

"Don't be frightened, it—brings bad luck. You'll stop my luck.

I shut up. I know so well that presentiments, fears, are unlucky.

"Don't worry" said John "soon I will pull it quite off and we will be rich, rich—

We dined in a little corner of the restaurant.

At the same table a few days before a Russian girl 24 years of age had shot herself.

With her last money she had a decent meal and then bang. Out—

And I made up my mind that if ever it came to it I should do it too.

Not to be poor again.

No and No and No—

So darned easy to plan that—and always at the last moment—one is afraid. Or cheats oneself with hope.

I can still do this and this. I can still clutch at that or that.

So and so will help me.

How you fight, cleverly and well at first, then more wildly—then hysterically.

I can't go down, I won't go down. Help me, help me.

Steady—I must be clever—So and so will help.

But so and so smiles a worldly smile.

You get nervous. He doesn't understand. I'll make him—

But so and so's eyes grow cold. You plead.

Can't you help me, won't you please? It's like this and this—

So and so becomes uncomfortable, obstinate—

No good—

I mustn't cry. I won't cry—

And that time you don't—You manage to keep your head up, a smile on your face.

So and so is vastly relieved. So relieved that he offers at once the little help that is a mockery, and the consoling compliment.

In the taxi still you don't cry.

You've thought of someone else—

But at the fifth or sixth disappointment you cry more easily—

After the tenth you give it up—You are broken—No nerves left—

And every second-rate fool can have their cheap little triumph over you—judge you with their little middle-class judgment.

Can't do anything for them. No good.

C'est rien—c'est une femme qui se noie—

But two years, three years afterwards. *Salut* to you little Russian girl who had pluck enough and enough knowledge of the world, to finish when your good time was over.

transatlantic review. Ed. Ford Madox Ford, 1924; New York: Kraus Reprint, 1967.

Voyage in the Dark

Part IV (Original Version)

Smile please the man said not quite so serious

He dodged out from behind the black cloth

You tell her to madam

He had a long black-yellow face with pimples on his chin he dodged in again under the black cloth

I looked down at my legs and the white socks coming half-way up my legs and the black shoes with a strap over the instep and the doll in my lap it could say Maman Papa and shut its eyes for Dodo.

Show her the picture-book Aunt Jane said

Now smile darling Mother said look at the pretty picture and smile

The trees in the picture were so tidy and the little girl so round and plump and the wall so high and you kept wondering what was beyond it and you couldn't imagine anything

Now the man said from behind the black cloth

Now keep quite still Mother said

I tried but my hand shot up of its own accord

Oh what a pity she moved now it'll have to be done all over again

I began to cry

Now now now the man said

A big girl like you I'm ashamed of you Mother said just one second and you are ten years older Meta was fanning her with a palm leaf fan to keep the flies away and she was too young to die Meta said with tears running down her face but I was only thinking of my new white dress and the wreath I would carry

The song went
  Ma belle ka di maman li
  Petit ke vini gros
I can play that tune on the piano

She can she picks out all the nigger tunes by herself

But that one's very melancholy Hester said and the words don't seem to me to make any sense.

I said it means My beautiful girl is singing to her mother The little ones grow old The little ones [grow] old

[A] very melancholy tune Hester said a very melancholy tun [It as]tonishes me how melancholy some of these negro tunes are I [thought th]ey were gay tunes

I dislike that song Hester said but I was hiding behind the oleander bushes the oleander trees singing it and singing all the songs I knew twenty songs one after the other all the songs I knew and my voice went thin thin but I went on singing until the steamer started to whistle I looked back from the boat and the lights were bobbing up and down Now all good times I leave behind Adieu sweetheart adieu I began to cry and it rolled down my face and splashed into the sea

That's Morne Anglais over there and that's Morne Piton over there and that's Diablotin bewitched where the devils are and that's the Crête over there

You hear me you come out from under there Meta said what you doing under there

That's the Crète brown right in the sun without any shade without any trees and the saddest place I know sadder than the doves cooing sadder than the sound of humming that never stops sadder than that sadder than the day he said while the grass is growing the horse is starving grass always takes too long to grow by God it does and by the time the grass has grown the poor old horse has starved his lips looked blue (your father's going to die your father's got heart disease his lips are blue it's not true he isn't going to die yes he is you look at him you look at his lips his lips are blue he's going to die I wasn't saying a thing she just flew at me she just flew at him and scratched him like that she's a dreadful girl what's going to become of that girl I wonder but there you are what can you expect)

He said by the time the grass has grown the poor old horse has starved and I looked at him and I saw that his lips were blue

Oh nonsense Hester said it's not like you to be so melancholy

Where's the child gone

She's rushed away somewhere she's a funny child

You leave her alone she'll be all right Father said

The horse was waiting outside

You come out from under there Meta said hiding under that bed always hiding

She caught hold of my foot you come out now I kicked my shoe came off she caught hold of my ankle and dragged I held on to the bed-post but I felt my hands slipping you come out from under that bed she said I said you let me go you damned black devil you let me go you woolly-haired devil I'll tell my father he'll send you packing she said I'll show you black devil I'll show you black devil she started shaking me and my teeth shook and my hair shook and my flesh shook on my bones and I kept on saying black devil black devil and still she shook me and I felt it starting in my stomach very gently and I said take care take care

It started very gently; and I thought 'Well, that's that, now it'll be all right.'

I got up and did everything she had told me ('You've got to be careful when it happens'), and I thought 'So this is what it's like. Well, it's not so bad.'

Then I lay down again and it was so still—so still and lovely, no gramophone or talking, and I thought 'I'm glad nobody's here because I hate people.'

'I'll be all right,' I thought and I was glad it had happened when nobody was there.

I looked at the clock. It was a quarter-to four. There was a long ray of light coming in from under the door and I knew I must have forgotten to put out the light in the passage, but I couldn't be bothered to get up and put it out. I could hear the clock ticking.

And the clock was ticking he said do you mind that clock I'm rather fond of it I've had it for years ever since I was at Eton and now I rather like it

Not from every angle I said certainly not he said but it's never from every angle

I like to put my hand here and feel your heart jump do you like it when I make love to you tell me I like it now I used not to but I like it now I said weights on your arms weights on your legs only your heart beating and not being able to breathe I like it now I said and he said my darling mustn't be sad my darling mustn't worry and the clock was ticking it's nearly four o'clock perhaps you ought to be I like it now I said and the front door always clicked behind me so gently and always as if it was for the last time

And another clock was ticking I lay there watching him and the dog in the picture *Loyal Hearts* and I could hear him breathing and see his chest going in and out he said well I told you I would didn't I I always told you I would didn't I and you never believed that I really would did you I said stop stop but softly so that Ethel wouldn't hear I'm too old for this sort of thing he said it's bad for the heart he laughed and it sounded funny les emotions fortes he said I said stop please stop I knew you'd say that he said

Mrs Polo said 'It was like this when I come, and then the young lady said something about Miss Gaynor, and I didn't know what to do, so I rung you up, miss. And I don't want to be mixed up with a thing like this.'

'Why ring me up,' Laurie said, 'it's nothing to do with me. You ought to get a doctor.'

Mrs Polo said 'I thought she wouldn't want a doctor here asking questions.'

Laurie said 'Cheer up, kid. It's all right, the worst part's over now. You'll be all right.'

'But look at that mattress,' Mrs. Polo said. 'What about that mattress? There's going to be a row about this.'

'Oh, don't be a fool,' Laurie said. 'Give me those pillows and pile them at the end of the bed . . . Now, you put your feet on them,' she said. 'You'll see, it'll be all right. It'll stop in a minute.'

'They die sometimes,' Mrs Polo said.

'Are you all right?' Laurie said.

I'm not here I'm there I'm not here I'm there they die sometimes

Are you afraid of dying Beatrice said no I said I don't believe I am are you yes she said I am but I never think about it I said haven't you ever wanted to die you know when you look down into deep water and see the trees upside down haven't you ever wanted to quickly like that Beatrice said that's a sin to want to kill yourself the nuns say that's a sin but there are only two sins presumption and despair what's to happen to anybody who's sinned them both

And I kept saying stop stop please stop will you stop and he said I thought you'd say that and he laughed and it sounded funny and his face was very white and his nostrils going in and out

Come and look at the masks Hester said some of them are really well done some of them are almost lovely look at the costumes I wouldn't have believed niggers could dress up like that why some of these costumes are quite perfect

Last year the Governor gave a prize for the best one Uncle Bo said

Damned half-French monkey somebody said of course he would go and do a thing like that

They passed under the window singing and they were dressed in every colour of the rainbow and we were watching them from between the slats of the jalousies because it wouldn't have done to have had the window quite open and there were perhaps twenty of them in each group and three musicians at the head a man with a concertina and another with a triangle and another with a chak-chak playing *Charlie Lulu* and *There's a Brown Girl in a Ring* and after the musicians a lot of little boys in their shirt-tails and perhaps the crown of a straw hat turning and twisting and dancing and others dragging kerosene-tins along and beating them with sticks and then the masks with clothes all colours of the rainbow sometimes the men didn't wear masks they just painted themselves with black or red paint the Darkies or the Red-Ochres or they wore masks a crude pink with the eyes squinting black near together squinting but the masks the women wore were made of close-meshed wire covering the whole face and tied at the back of the head and the handkerchief that went over the back of the head hid the strings and the masks were more like their faces than their own faces were and the masks were flesh-coloured and over the slits for the eyes mild blue eyes were painted and then there was a small straight nose and a little red heart-shaped mouth and under the mouth another slit so that they could put their tongues out at you

Father said a pretty useful mask watch it and a slobbering tongue comes out do you know I believe the whole damned business is like that don't you think the idea of a malevolent idiot at the back of everything is the only one that fits the facts

Hester said Gerald the child's listening

Oh no she isn't Father said she's looking out of the window and quite right too that's what it is he said a mask and you watch it and the slobbering tongue of an idiot sticks out

I could smell the bottle of eau-de-cologne on the dressing-table we were all there watching them because sometimes it was a very picturesque sight and they went about in crowds each crowd with musicians at the head when two crowds met you could almost hear a bang and then there was a lot of shouting and the women saying Hrrrrrrr Hrrrrrrr and then the two lots would thread their ways through and form up on the other side it was all colours of the rainbow when you looked down at it and the sky so blue

The colours are marvellous Hester said

It's all very well the colours are marvellous but this isn't a decent and respectable way to go on and it ought to be stopped

Why some of those men are almost naked it's not decent or respectable it ought to be stopped

Oh it'll be stopped Father said they're trying to stop it now but they can play my God they can and can't some of those little beggars dance

Oh they play all right somebody said

You look at the one Father said can't he dance do you see there's not one step out of time

I could hear them banging kerosene-tins

'Get a basin,' Laurie said, 'and some water.'
'Here's the water, miss,' Mrs Polo said.

They ought to stop them banging the kerosene-tins Aunt Jane said because it's an awful noise but I don't see why they should stop the Masquerade they've always had Masquerade ever since I was a girl they've always had their three days Masquerade ever since I can remember Aunt Jane said why should they want to stop it now some people want to stop everything

They were dancing along dressed in red and blue and yellow the women with their dark necks and arms covered with white powder dancing along to concertina-music dressed in red and blue and yellow and I knew what they were singing they were singing defiance to I don't know what but singing it all the same I knew what they were singing

You can't expect niggers to behave like white people all the time Uncle Bo said it's asking too much of human nature

It ought to be stopped Hester said it's not decent and all these Roman Catholic priests and nuns in an English island ought to be stopped too

You don't know anything about it Uncle Bo said it keeps them quiet

Now then Simon Legree Father said

A fat lot you people know about it don't you Uncle Bo said not that that'll stop you talking a fat lot you know about it I'd like to see the rich English give up their slaves without any compensation like we did

Without any compensation Hester said I don't know the figures but you were voted a large sum in compensation

Voted Uncle Bo said voted Oh yes it may have been voted all right but we never got it it all stayed in the good old home coop and if you like to come and have a look at things I can prove that to you easily enough if you'd like to come and have a look

Slavery was a wicked thing Aunt Jane said and God Almighty frowned on it and so it had to stop you can't threat human beings as if they were bits of wood it had to stop

English people don't think like that Uncle Bo said they may talk like it but they don't think like it

Their voices went up and down and I was looking out of the window and I knew why the masks were laughing

Look at that old fat woman Hester said just look at her

Oh yes she's having a go too Uncle Bo said they all have a go they don't mind

But I knew why they were laughing they were laughing at the idea that anybody black would want to be white

I knew and so I was dancing and the concertina was going and he said just kissing is silly only babies of about ten just kiss

I said I think so too if I kissed anybody I'd do everything but what's everything

Don't you know what everything is shall I show you what everything is

'Try not to be sick,' Laurie said.

I was being sick because his hands had such a lot of hair on them

You're a worrier Aunt Jane said it's a pity but you are

But there's such a lot to worry about this business about God and this business about children and what happens when you sleep with men and as if that's not enough this business about ladies and gentlemen and common people and some people having everything and others having nothing and their voices and their eyes when they speak to people who answer them back in a quavering voice and not a soul to tell you anything about it that makes any sense it's such a lot to worry about

My darling mustn't worry my darling mustn't be sad

And I thought say it again say darling again

And he said well it's nearly four o'clock perhaps you ought to be going

The concertina-man is very black he sits sweating his legs wide apart and the contertina goes forwards and backwards forwards and backwards one two three one two three pourquoi ne pas aimer bonheur suprême and the triangle-man kept time with his triangle and with his foot tapping his broad foot but the little man who played the chak-chak smiled with his eyes fixed

That's a chak-chak it's music niggers play do you like it

The thing like seeds being shaken

Yes that's a chak-chak do you like it

Well it's only nigger music but it does make you want to dance

Pourquoi ne pas aimer bonheur suprême

I'm giddy I said I'm awfully giddy but we went on whirling round and round rhythm of seeds of seed

'I'm awfully giddy,' I said.

'Are you?' Laurie said. 'It's all right; it'll stop in a minute.'

Stop stop stop

I thought you'd say that he said

Give me one of your coat-buttons I said as a souvenir because I collect them I've got nearly twenty

The one I kept separate belonged to Dr North he was on HMS *Invincible* I liked him best he had a black beard

Oh certainly he said it was awfully nice of you to invite us it's a lovely dance

We always do here I said if a man-of-war's in the harbour we send an invitation and any of the officers who like can come and my father always said he'd give a dance for me when I was fourteen that's my father over there the one with the red moustache and the curly grey hair

Father waved at me he said t'en fais pas mon petit c'est une vaste blague

Oh I see he said to tell you the truth I was wondering who my host was

I'm longing to go to London I said

Are you he said I wonder if you'd like it

Not like London Maudie said what an idea these funny people I [can] tell them in a minute I'm very sensitive that way

I'm awfully giddy I said

The horse was waiting outside

It was waiting for me under the sandbox-tree there was a man's saddle on and when I saw it I said I can't ride a man's saddle I'm used to a side-saddle I tried to hang back but it was useless and the next moment I was up my legs on each side of the horse groping for the stirrups but there weren't any stirrups no stirrups no bridle I balanced myself in the saddle trying to grip with my knees

The horse went forward with an exaggerated swaying lilting motion like a rocking horse I felt very sick I heard the concertina-music playing behind me all the time and the noise of the people's feet dancing he went up a street behind the house then up Coronation Hill and that was in a greenish shadow I saw the rows of small niggers' houses on each side of the street in front of one of them there was a woman cooking fishcakes on a coal pot and then the bridge and the sound of the horse's hoofs on the wooden planks and then the savannah the road goes along by the sea do you turn to the right or the left the left of course the horse started to go faster and faster at that turning the shadow was always the same shape it was the shadow of a huge tree quite black in the moonlight with every branch and every twig black in the moonlight shadows are ghosts you look at them and you don't see them you look at everything and you don't see it only sometimes you see it like now I see now I see I see the moon looking down on stones where nobody is the trees and the moon looking down on a place where nobody is there was a cold moon looking down on a place where nobody is full of stones where nobody is

I thought I'm going to fall nothing can save me now but still I clung desperately with my knees feeling very sick and the waves of pain going through me like the sea I always knew it was like waves and like the sea I always knew it was like waves and like the sea Now I'm beyond the trees and beyond the stones

Now he's galloping beside a precipice and far beneath I can see dead rotting leaves and soft earth the soft red earth I shall fall on

Mrs Polo said 'I'm clearing out. I don't want to be mixed up in this. Look at those sheets. And it isn't stopping. And her wanting the gramophone played. I never heard of such a thing. I don't want to be here when the doctor comes. And look at that mattress.'

Laurie said 'Go, damn you, if you want to. I'll stay.'

She said 'You're listening, aren't you? The doctor's coming. Say you fell downstairs. That's all you've got to say.'

The horse stopped dead and shot me right over his head

I was falling for a long time so long that before I touched the earth I had time to say I'm not afraid I'm not afraid I'm not afraid

'She fell,' Laurie said, 'early this morning.'

He put his ear down close to my mouth to listen.

I thought 'Why does he do that?'

I said 'I fell of the horse.'

He said 'You fell off the horse, did you? Stop that gramophone.'

'She liked it,' Laurie said. 'She asked me to play it.'

It stopped.

It was as if they weren't there. I knew they were talking but their voices sounded small like doll's voices.

And the concertina-music stopped and it was so still so still and lovely like just before you go to sleep   and it stopped   and there was the ray of light along the floor like the last thrust of remembering before everything is blotted out and blackness comes . . .

"Jean Rhys and *Voyage in the Dark*." Ed. and intro. by Nancy Hemond Brown. *London Magazine* 2.1, 2 (April/May 1985): 40–59.

Ghost Writing

The café is not very full. I choose a table as far away from everyone else as possible. We order two brandies.

He has told me that he is twenty-six, but I think he is older than that—he's about thirty. And he doesn't look like a gigolo, not at all like a gigolo.

Suddenly I feel shy and self-conscious. (How ridiculous! Don't let him see it, for God's sake.) I drink half my brandy-and-soda and start talking about the last time I was in the Deux Magots and how I had been staying at Antibes and how I came back very brown and on top of the world and with some money too, and all the rest.

'Money I had earned. Sans blague. It was too funny. I wrote up fairy stories for a very rich woman. She came to Montparnasse looking for somebody and of course there was a rush. She chose me because I was the cheapest. The night I got back to Montparnasse—very rich—we celebrated. We started up in this café because I was staying at a hotel near here.'

What with the brandy-and-soda and going back to the Deux Magots, the whole thing is whirling nicely round in my head. She would come into my room very early in the morning in her dressing-gown, her hair hanging down in two plaits, looking rather sweet, I must say. 'Are you awake, Mrs Jansen? I've just thought of a story. You can take it down in shorthand, can't you?' 'No, I'm afraid I can't.' (Cheated! For what I'm paying she ought to know shorthand.) 'But if you'll tell me what you want to say I think I can get it down.' Off she'd go. 'Once upon a time there was a cactus—' Or a white rose or a yellow rose or a red rose, as the case might be. All this, mind you, at six-thirty in the morning. . . . 'This story,' she would say, looking anxious, 'is an allegory. You understand that, don't you?' 'Yes, I understand.' But she was never very explicit about the allegory. 'Could you make it a Persian garden?' 'I don't see why not.' 'Oh, and there's something I want to speak to you about, Mrs Jansen. I'm afraid Samuel didn't like the last story you wrote.' Oh God, this awful sinking of the heart—like going down in a lift. I knew this job was too good to be true. 'Didn't he? I'm sorry. What didn't he like about it?' 'Well, I'm afraid he doesn't like the way you write. What he actually said was that, considering the cost of these stories, he thinks it strange that you should write them in words of one syllable. He says it gets monotonous, and don't you know any long words, and if you do, would you please use them? . . . Madame Holmberg is most anxious to collaborate with me. And she's a real writer—she's just finished the third volume of her Life of Napoleon.' After this delicate hint she adds: 'Samuel wished to speak to you himself, but I told him that I preferred to do it, because I didn't want to hurt your feelings. I said I was sure, if I told you his opinion, you'd try to do better. I should hate to hurt your feelings because in a strange way I feel that we are very much alike. Don't you think so?' (No, I certainly don't think so, you pampered chow.) 'I'm awfully sorry you didn't like the story,' I say.

Sitting at a large desk, a white sheet of paper in front of me and outside the sun and the blue Mediterranean. Monte Carlo, Monte Carlo, by the Med-it-er-rany-an sea-ee, Monte Carlo, Monte Carlo, where the boy of my heart waits for me-ee. . . . Persian garden. Long words. Chiaroscuro? Translucent? . . . I bet he'd like cataclysmal action and centrifugal flux, but the point is how can I get them into a Persian garden? . . . Well, I might. Stranger things have happened. . . . A blank sheet of paper. . . . Once upon a time, once upon a time there lived a lass who tended swine. . . . Persian gardens. Satraps—surely they were called satraps. . . . It's so lovely outside, and music has started up somewhere. . . . Grinding it out, oh God, with all the long words possible. And the music outside playing *Valencia*. . . . 'Are you still there, Mrs Jansen? You haven't gone out? I've just thought of a new story. Once upon a time there lived. . . .'

Shrewd as they're born, this woman, hard as a nail, and with what a sense of property! She'd raise hell if a spot of wine fell on one of her Louis Quinze chairs. Authentic Louis Quinze, of course they were.

They explain people like that by saying that their minds are in water-tight compartments, but it never seemed so to me. It's all washing about, like the bilge in the hold of a ship, all washing around in the same hold—no water-tight compartments. . . . Fairies, red roses, the sense of property—Of course they don't feel things like we do—Lilies in the moonlight—I believe in survival after death. I've had personal proof of it. And we'll find our dear, familiar bodies on the other side—Samuel has forgotten to buy his suppositoires—Pity would be out of place in this instance—I never take people like that to expensive restaurants. Quite unnecessary and puts ideas into their heads. It's not *kind,* really—Nevertheless, all the little birdies sing—Psycho-analysis might help. Adler is more wholesome than Freud, don't you think?—English judges never make a mistake—The piano is quite Egyptian in feeling. . . .

All washing around in the same hold. No water-tight compartments. . . .

Well, I am trying to tell René about all this and giggling a good deal, when he stops me.

'But I know that woman. I know her very well. . . . Again you don't believe me. This time you shall believe me. Listen, she was like this—' He describes her exactly. 'And the house was like this—' He draws a little plan on the back of an envelope. 'Here are the palm trees. Here are the entrance steps. That terrible English butler they had—do you remember? The two cabinets here with jade, the other two cabinets with a collection of china. The double circular staircase—do you remember how they used to come down it at night?'

'Yes,' I say. ' "I know how to walk down a staircase, me." '

'Which bedroom did you have? Did you have the one on the second floor with the green satin divan in the ante-chamber to the bathroom?'

'No. I had a quite ordinary one on the third floor. But what an array of scent-bottles! I dream of them sometimes.'

'It was a ridiculous house, wasn't it?'

'I was very much impressed,' I say. 'It's the only millionaire's house I've ever stayed in in my life.'

'I've stayed in much richer ones than that. I've stayed in one so rich that when you pulled the lavatory-plug it played a tune. . . . Rich people—you have to be sorry for them. They haven't the slightest idea how to spend their money; they haven't the slightest idea how to enjoy themselves. Either they have no taste at all, or, if they have any taste, it's like a mausoleum and they're shut up in it.'

'Well you're going to alter all that, aren't you?'

Of course, there's no doubt that this man has stayed in this house and does know these people. One would think that that would give us more confidence in each other. Not at all, it makes us suspicious. There's no doubt that a strict anonymity is a help on these occasions.

When did all this happen, and what is his story? Did he stay in France for a time, get into trouble over here and then join the Legion? Is that the story? Well, anyway, what's it matter to me what his story is? I expect he has a different one every day.

I say: 'Excuse me a minute,' primly, and go down to the lavatory.

This is another lavatory that I know very well, another of the well-known mirrors.

'Well, well,' it says, 'last time you looked in here you were a bit different, weren't you? Would you believe me that, of all the faces I see, I remember each one, that I keep a ghost to throw back at each one—lightly, like an echo—when it looks into me again?' All glasses in all lavabos do this.

But it's not as bad as it might be. This is just the interval when drink makes you look nice, before it makes you look awful.

Good Morning, Midnight. London: Deutsch, 1967. 138–142.

19
Dorothy Richardson (1873–1957)

Introduced and Edited by Diane F. Gillespie

"Why not say," Miriam Henderson asks herself in Dorothy Richardson's *The Tunnel* (1919), "man . . . is the male of woman? If women had been the recorders of things from the beginning it would all have been the other way round" (*Pilgrimage* 2:251). In *Deadlock* (1921) Miriam explains what "it" includes: "It was history, literature, the way of stating records, reports, stories, the whole method of statement of things from the beginning that was on a false foundation" (3:218). The way Richardson presents Miriam is the product of similar perceptions. *Pilgrimage* is an attempt, begun in 1913 and extended ultimately to thirteen separate novels or chapters, to provide what Richardson called the "feminine equivalent of the current masculine realism" (Foreword; reprinted below).[1]

Although reviewers of *Pilgrimage* and historians of the novel, from Richardson's contemporaries to those of the present day, recognize her as one of the pioneers in psychological fiction, the charges of inconsequence, dullness, obscurity, and formlessness have, until recently, overbalanced any praise for the integrity and intense reality of the work. Richardson, nonetheless, has had admirers. An early one, John Cowper Powys, produced a book-length study. Several other men wrote books on Richardson in the 1960s and 1970s (Blake, Gregory, Rosenberg, Staley). In the 1970s and 1980s women began to analyze Richardson's presentation of a feminine consciousness (Gillespie,

Hanscombe, Kaplan, Rose). Gloria Fromm's bibliography and biography also appeared.

While most of these studies discuss, mention, or at least list some of Richardson's many writings apart from *Pilgrimage,* few students of modernism ever encounter them. Richardson published, under her own name, a pseudonym, or anonymously, several translations, over thirty sketches and short stories, a dozen or so poems, and about 150 reviews, essays, and column contributions. The selections reprinted here help to explain more fully Richardson's outspokenly feminine version of modernism and her relationships with several other experimenters of her time.

In 1906 Richardson was reading H. G. Wells's novels and finding, for the first time, "a portentous silent reality" ("In the Crank's Library," reprinted below). Richardson met Wells in 1896 and spent two decades both admiring him and disputing with him. Eventually he was the model for Hypo Wilson in *Pilgrimage.* No doubt Richardson felt responsible for some of the changes in Wells's writing. Her review, however, challenges him to further improvements. Evenutally, she hopes, he will produce books where "womanhood shall be as well as manhood." She means, as a later essay explains, that man must recognize woman's "synthetic consciousness." It "has always made its own world, irrespective of circumstances," while men have gone on their futile quests for peace and wholeness. Richardson means too that man must recognize woman as "companion and fellow pilgrim" rather than as "hated and loved . . . mother nature" or "feared and adored . . . Queen of Heaven." Finally, she means that man must abandon the specialized role of "fighter, in warfare, in trade, and in politics" and see, with woman, "the life of the world as one life" ("The Reality of Feminism"; see below).

To do so requires that men acknowledge the "genius that exists potentially in every woman and is sometimes found in men." Richardson defines "talent" as "that which does" as opposed to "genius" or "that which sees." Both are necessary to the individual, to the artist, and to the community. Without talent, genius will find no expression, yet talent can also stifle genius, as it has among the women who have tried to imitate men.

Richardson thinks, optimistically, that "feminine genius is finding its way to its own materials" at last in both art and in the community ("Talent and Genius"; see below). While some men welcome women in spheres beyond the home, Richardson says, they still misjudge them. Men do not perceive that "feminine egoism" often differs from "masculine selfishness." Distinguishing between the increasing numbers of "man-trained women," those now free to pursue pleasures similar to men's, and the "womanly" women, Richardson admires the latter. The womanly woman does not have the "incomplete individuality" of a man, "that subtle form of despair which is called ambition, and accounts for his apparent selfishness." On the contrary, "only a completely self-centered consciousness can attain to unselfishness" and "only a complete self . . . can go out, perfectly, to others, move freely in any direction." This type of woman, Richardson thinks, with "her gift of imaginative sympathy, her capacity for vicarious living, for being simultaneously in all the warring camps," will have, if she is recognized and valued, the greatest impact upon society ("Women and the Future" 39–40; see below).

Richardson does not think, therefore, that women have in any essential way been damaged because they have been barred from public life; male-dominated societies, on the contrary, have been marred by their exclusion of women's values. She is not disturbed either by the charge that women have not produced great art. "Quiet, and solitude in the sense of freedom from preoccupations," Richardson wrote in 1925, "are the absolute conditions of artistic achievement," and most women have never been freed from "the human demand" long enough to pursue art ("Women in the Arts," reprinted below). Besides, the criteria for great art have been established by ambitious men and are the products of their incompleteness, of talent rather than genius. Women, as Miriam Henderson's comments in *Pilgrimage* indicate, have exercised their genius in private, not public, spheres and have used people, not paints or pens, as their medium. Women, Miriam says, are preeminent in "the art of making atmospheres. . . . Most women can exercise it, for reasons, by fits and starts. The best women work at it the whole of the time. Not one man in a million is aware of it. It's like air within the air. . . . At its best it is absolutely life-giving" (3:257).

Miriam and her creator want to make men aware of women's genius and the art of creating atmospheres in which they excel. To do so, however, they must use words and put them together into genres that can be recognizably labeled and evaluated according to established criteria. But while women like Richardson must produce something more tangible than an atmosphere, they must do so in ways that do not destroy or contradict it. At the same time, they must not write in ways that reinforce men's stereotypes of women. Richardson, therefore, consciously looked for a way to get beyond what she considered the "irrelevance" of men's writing, to express the "woman-consciousness" and its intense awareness of "life in its own right at first hand" (Morgan 400).

When she began *Pilgrimage,* Richardson realized that she was "telling *about* Miriam, describing her. There she was as I first saw her, going upstairs. But who was *there* to *describe* her?" (Morgan 400). The implied answer is no one. So Richardson experimented with eliminating the traditional, usually male, authorial voice which, to varying degrees, condescends to an inferior reader and coerces him or her to see the character as he does. At the same time, this voice makes a parade of its verbal cleverness and intellectual insight. "Always, for charm or repulsion, for good or ill," she says, "one was aware of the author and applauding, or deploring, his manipulations" ("Data" 19). Instead, Richardson posited a reader equal to the task of collaborating with her to discover the quality of life as it is being lived by her character. She strove, in addition, to make her style inseparable from that of her character's consciousness.

When she wrote her Foreword to *Pilgrimage* in 1938, Richardson acknowledged that her "lonely track" had become "a populous highway." Entering it with her were "a woman mounted upon a magnificently caparisoned charger" as well as "a man walking, with eyes devoutly closed, weaving as he went a rich garment of new words wherewith to clothe the antique dark material of his engrossment." In addition to this oblique reference to living writers Virginia Woolf and James Joyce, Richardson acknowledges Proust, now dead like Balzac and James, previous experimenters with a "single observer." Perhaps because, as Fromm suggests, Richardson was irritated by the frequent comparisons between her work and Woolf's, by Woolf's more privileged background, and by her elegant prose, Richardson declined to review *The Years* when it appeared in 1937 (*Dorothy Richardson* 318–319).

She did review, however, Joyce's *Finnegans Wake*. Richardson and Joyce were not constantly linked, as she and Woolf, as women writers, were; moreover, *Finnegans Wake* was unique. To Richardson it erases the line between poetry and the novel. The reader moves "within a medium whose close texture, like that of poetry, is everywhere significant" ("Adventure for Readers," reprinted below). The number of improvised words, however, requires more concentration from the reader than even imagist poetry does. To describe the burden placed upon the reader, Richardson amuses herself by producing a sentence nearly thirty lines long. Even when the reader begins to comprehend what is going on in the novel, he or she is once again "caught in impenetrable undergrowths, and his head assailed by missiles falling thicker and faster than before, hurled by one obviously in silent ecstasies as he watches the flounderings of his victim." She concludes that the reader of *Finnegans Wake* must forgo all "literary preoccupations and prejudices . . . and plunge, provisionally, here and there; *enter* the text and look innocently about." The reader who does so will experience "sheer delight" and discover "inexhaustible entertainment" as Joyce mocks but also looks, with a wistfulness Richardson finds primarily in male poets, at his creation.

Woolf had been excited by the intense reality and honesty of Richardson's characterization of Miriam Henderson in the volume of *Pilgrimage* that appeared in 1919, but she had reservations about the aesthetic significance of the experiment (Woolf, "The Tunnel" 122). When she reviewed *Revolving Lights* in 1923, she said Richardson had consciously developed "the psychological sentence of the feminine gender" capable of capturing not "states of doing" but "states of being." Such a sentence is "of a more elastic fibre than the old, capable of stretching to the extreme, of suspending the frailest particles, of enveloping the vaguest shapes." Woolf is not specific, and ultimately she describes Richardson's style as appropriate to a shift in values from public to private lives, from objects and events to atmospheres (Woolf, "Romance and the Heart" 124–125).

The shift requires different choices about point of view, as Richardson and Woolf both knew. Richardson also defines the shift in part as a matter of punctuation. "Feminine prose, as Charles Dickens and James Joyce have delightfully shown themselves to be aware, should properly be unpunctuated, moving from point to point without formal obstructions," she says in her Foreword to *Pilgrimage.* Her own first departures from conventional usage were unconscious, she says, then consciously justified. In "About Punctuation" (1924, reprinted below), Richardson says that the modern "machinery of punctuation and type" has reduced reader collaboration and "devitalized the act of reading," making it "less organic, more mechanical." Interested in the experiments of male writers but perhaps unwilling to reinforce the masculine view of feminine prose, Richardson defines herself as neither purist nor rebel. She advocates the "organic adaptation" of punctuation to suit the material.

Perhaps totally unpunctuated prose suggests too closely the stream metaphor Richardson rejects as a description of her writing. "Stream of consciousness," she says, is a label that "stands alone, isolated by its perfect imbecility." Richardson prefers the image of a tree to describe consciousness because "its central core, luminous point, (call it what you will, its names are legion) tho more or less continuously expanding from birth to maturity, remains stable, one with itself thruout life" (Kunitz 562; Richardson, "Novels," reprinted below; Rose, "The Unmoving Center" 367–371). The self, in other words, is more than a passive receiver of impressions that are constantly changing; it is active and creative, unified and continuous.

The value Richardson places on author-reader collaboration emerges again in her remarks on silent versus sound films. The silent film could be both "nowhere in the sense of having more intention than direction and more purpose than plan," and "everywhere by reason of its power to evoke, suggest, reflect, express from within its moving parts and in their totality of movement, something of the changeless being at the heart of all becoming." Its quality was "essentially feminine. In its insistence on contemplation it provided a pathway to reality" ("Continuous Performance"; see below). Similarly, literature is valuable according to "its ability to rouse and to concentrate the reader's contemplative consciousness," as Richardson says elsewhere. Although she suggests on this occasion that reader collaboration may be achieved either by "the author leading, visible and audible, all the time" or by an invisible and inaudible author who is "present . . . only in the attitude towards reality, inevitably revealed: subtly by his accent, obviously by his use of adjective, epithet, and metaphor" (Kunitz 562), her own preference is consistently for the latter.

"Life makes artists of us all," Richardson wrote in 1966. As the years accumulate behind us, we gain the perspective that reveals patterns and the detachment that frees from "intolerance and exclusions and fixities" ("Old Age" 25). The professional writer, however, can detect and reveal life's patterns by subordinating himself or herself to their evolution in a character's consciousness. Richardson thus rejects art as male-dominated societies have defined it. She relies on the reader's willingness to collaborate with the author in the discovery of whatever structure the work of art has.

Some of Richardson's readers have been willing to collaborate; many have not. May Sinclair, although she used a label for the novels that Richardson did not like, responded enthusiastically and began her own experiments along the same lines. Katherine Mansfield admired Richardson's powers of observation but concluded, like Virginia Woolf, that the work was inadequate as art ("Three Women Novelists" 4; see excerpt in this anthology). Art, however, is just what modernist writers, often with great excitement, were trying to redefine, by exploring the limitations of each genre and medium and by defining boundaries beyond which experimentation could not fruitfully proceed. Richardson, in her shift in emphasis from facts and objects to atmospheres, from prose to poetry, from talent to genius, from coercive to collaborative author-reader relationships, from masculine to feminine values and methods suitable for expressing them, helped to define some of these boundaries. If the modernist " 'meanderings' of the 'masculine fist' " ("Adventure for Readers"; see below) culminated in *Finnegans Wake,* then Richardson's *Pilgrimage,* along with her many related comments on women in society and in art, was an equivalent feminine challenge to traditional definitions of the novel.

NOTE

1. The eleven portions of *Pilgrimage* published separately were *Pointed Roofs* (1915), *Backwater* (1916), *Honeycomb* (1917), *The Tunnel* (1919), *Interim* (1919), *Deadlock* (1921), *Revolving Lights* (1923), *The Trap* (1925), *Oberland* (1927), *Dawn's Left Hand* (1931), and *Clear Horizon* (1935). A twelfth, *Dimple Hill,* appeared with the first collected edition, published by Dent in Great Britain and Knopf in the United States in 1938. A thirteenth, *March Moonlight,* appeared with the Dent reissued edition in 1967. *Pilgrimage* has been reissued in four volumes with an introduction by Gillian E. Hanscombe (London: Virago, 1979).

WORKS CITED

Blake, Caesar R. *Dorothy Richardson.* Ann Arbor: U of Michigan P, 1960.

[Fromm] Glikin, Gloria. "Dorothy M. Richardson: An Annotated Bibliography of Writings about Her." *English Literature in Transition* 8:1(1965):12–35.

Fromm, Gloria G. *Dorothy Richardson: A Biography.* Urbana: U of Illinois P, 1977.

Gillespie, Diane F. "Political Aesthetics: Virginia Woolf and Dorothy Richardson." In *Virginia Woolf: A Feminist Slant,* ed. Jane Marcus. Lincoln: U of Nebraska P, 1983:132–151.

Gregory, Horace. *Dorothy Richardson: An Adventure in Self-Discovery.* New York: Holt, Rinehart and Winston, 1967.

Hanscombe, Gillian E. *The Art of Life: Dorothy Richardson and the Development of Feminist Consciousness.* Athens: Ohio UP, 1982.

Kaplan, Sydney Janet. *Feminine Consciousness in the Modern British Novel.* Urbana: U of Illinois P, 1975, 8–46.

Kunitz, Stanley, ed. "Dorothy M. Richardson." *Authors Today and Yesterday.* New York: H. W. Wilson, 1933, 562–564.

Mansfield, Katherine. "Three Women Novelists" (1919) and "Dragonflies" (1920). In *Novels and Novelists*, ed. John Middleton Murry. Boston: Beacon, 1959.
Morgan, Louise. "How Writers Work: Dorothy Richardson." *Everyman* 22 Oct. 1931: 395–396, 400.
Richardson, Dorothy. "About Punctuation." *Adelphi* 1.11(April 1924):990–996.
———. "Adventure for Readers." *Life and Letters* 22(July 1939):45–52.
———. "Continuous Performance: The Film Gone Male." *Close Up* 9.1(March 1932):36–38.
———. "Data for Spanish Publisher." Ed. Joseph Prescott. *London Magazine* 6.6(June 1959):14–19.
———. Foreword. *Pilgrimage.* 4 vols. London: Dent, 1967.
———. "In the Crank's Library: *In the Days of the Comet.*" *Crank* 4.11(November 1906): 372–376.
———. "Novels." *Life and Letters* 56(March 1948):188–192.
———. "Old Age." *Adam: International Review* 31(1966):25–26.
———. *Pilgrimage.* 1915–1938. 4 vols. London: Dent, 1967; Virago, 1979.
———. "The Reality of Feminism." *Ploughshare* n.s.2.8(September 1917):241–246.
———. "Talent and Genius: Is Not Genius Actually Far More Common Than Talent?" *Vanity Fair* 21.2(October 1923):118, 120.
———. "Women in the Arts: Some Notes on the Eternally Conflicting Demands of Humanity and Art." *Vanity Fair* 24.3(May 1925):47, 100.
———. "Women and the Future: A Trembling of the Veil Before the Eternal Mystery of 'La Giaconda.' " *Vanity Fair* 22.2(April 1925):39–40.
Rose, Shirley. "Dorothy Richardson's Focus on Time." *English Literature in Transition* 17(1974):163–172.
———. "Dorothy Richardson's Theory of Literature: The Writer as Pilgrim." *Criticism* 12.1(Winter 1970):20–37.
———. "The Unmoving Center: Consciousness in Dorothy Richardson's *Pilgrimage.*" *Contemporary Literature* 10.3(Summer 1969):366–382.
Rosenberg, John D. *Dorothy Richardson, the Genius They Forgot: A Critical Biography.* New York: Knopf, 1973.
Staley, Thomas F. *Dorothy Richardson.* Boston: Twayne, 1976.
Woolf, Virginia. "The Tunnel" (13 Feb. 1919) and "Romance and the Heart" (19 May 1923). In *Contemporary Writers.* New York: Harcourt Brace Jovanovich, 1965.

From "In the Crank's Library": *In the Days of the Comet**

In the preface to *A Modern Utopia,* Mr Wells announced his return to imaginative writing, and this announcement was, surely, matter for rejoicing to all his readers.

Mr Wells has come at last to his own, has set about the serious business of his art. He has arrested his exuberant career among things; he has looked round

*By H. G. Wells. London: Macmillan and Co., Ltd.

on life, has criticised and analysed, has said, "Lo, here!" and again, "Lo, there!" and then at last has discovered the underlying reality, the Kingdom of Heaven that is neither "here" nor "there," but within the human heart. He has discovered humanity. There is, in this new book, an emotional deepening, a growth of insight and sympathy, that is startling; there is the direct human appeal to half-willing laughter and sharp-wrung tears; there is for the first time that indefinable quality that fine literature always yields, that sense of a vast something behind the delicate fabric of what is articulated—a portentous silent reality.

The book takes the form of a vision of two worlds—the world in whose sad twilight we grope to-day, and that world transfigured by love. Substantially it is a dream of anarchy, of human love set free, working everywhere its goodwill, knowing no other law. The story is told by the hero, who has known, as a poor young clerk, the world as we know it to-day, and who lives through the Change (brought about characteristically enough by a Comet which envelops the Earth in a green vapour, putting all life to sleep), and comes out to rejoice with transformed humanity on the other side—to look back with them amazed—shamed and contrite at the things that were before the Dawn of the new time. . . .

One comes away from the reading of the book infinitely refreshed and wondering a little. Wondering whether Mr Wells will shake himself free from the limitations that still beset him and rise to his full height—whether he will produce, as one feels now convinced he is capable of producing, a work of art that shall be *whole,* a broad, powerful movement of the spirit, a thing of simple, stately beauty. One hopes for a book where womanhood shall be as well as manhood. So far he has not achieved the portrayal of a woman, with the one exception of Leadford's mother. His women are all one specimen, carried away from some biological museum of his student days, dressed up in varying trappings, with different shades of hair and proportions of freckles, with neatly tabulated instincts and one vague smile between them all.

One hopes he may get rid of this rather irritating dummy and, along with her, of all his stage machinery—his men in towers, and men with voices, and men at writing-desks—and begin directly, without either apology or explanation,—laborious and altogether obstructive attempts to establish a rapport between himself and his readers.

One wonders, too, whether he will ever learn to find for his books the names which belong to them—and for his characters.

Well, he has already given us rich treasure, book after book to read again and again, and still to return to for refreshment, and with this new promise in our hands we may watch and hope.

Crank 4.11 (November 1906):372–376.

The Reality of Feminism

We commend our contributor's important essay to the attention of our readers; it passes in review several recent books, namely: "Towards a Sane Feminism," by Wilma Meikle (Grant Richards); "Woman and the Church," by the Rev. B. H. Streeter (T. Fisher Unwin); "Women in the Apostolic Church," by T. B. Allworthy (W. Heffer & Sons, Ltd.); "Woman's Effort," by A. E. Metcalfe (B. H. Blackwell).

During the first few decades of its existence, English feminism was the conscious acceptance by women of the diagnosis of the cynics and an attempt to deal with this diagnosis by placing upon environment the major part of the responsibility for feminine "failings." It declared that the faults of women were the faults of the slave, and were due to repressions, educational and social. Remove these repressions, and the failings would disappear. Feminists of both sexes devoted themselves to securing for women educational and social opportunities equal to those of men. The "higher" education of women was their watchword, the throwing open of the liberal professions their goal, and the demonstration of the actual equality of women and men the event towards which they confidently moved. It followed that only a very small number of women was affected. Only one class of women, the class well-dowered by circumstance, could be counted upon to supply recruits for the demonstration of the intellectual "quality" of women. This feminism was, therefore, in practice, a class feminism—feminism for ladies. In principle much had been gained. The exclusively sexual estimate of women had received its death-blow. But it soon became apparent that academic education and the successful pursuit of a profession implied a renunciation of domesticity. The opening heaven of "emancipation" narrowed to the sad and sterile vista—feminism for spinsters. From that moment public opinion see-sawed between the alternatives of discrediting domesticity and of dividing women into two types—"ordinary" women, who married, and "superior" women, who did not. But for at least one whole generation the belief in academic distinction as the way of emancipation for women was unclouded by any breath of doubt. The reaction which was later on to produce the formula of "university standards in home training" had barely set in when the whole fabric of feminist theory was challenged by the appearance of Charlotte Stetson's "Women and Economics." Opening her attack with a diagnosis of the female sex, which outdoes all the achievements of the cynics, she joined the earlier feminists in laying the responsibility for the plight of womanhood at the door of circumstance; but in a much more thorough-going fashion and with a backward and forward sweep which not only lifted the question out of the dimensions of an empirical problem and related it to the development of life as a whole, but purged it of the note of antagonism that characterises the bulk of feminist literature.

Woman as a purely sexual product, said this American feminist, is a quite recent development in the western world; and it is commerce that has produced her. Woman was a differentiated social human being earlier than man. The "savage" woman who first succeeded in retaining her grown son at her side, invented social life. Up to the era of machinery, *i.e.*, during the agricultural and civic centuries, the home was the centre of productive service. The scientific development of industry, while it did much to humanise the male—even though his commerce was as aggressive as his flint implements and his fleets of coracles—worked upon the female as a purely desocialising influence. By driving the larger industries from the homestead, it forced her either to follow them into the factory and workshop, to the destruction of home life, or to remain in a home that was no longer a centre of vital industries, but an isolated centre of consumption and destruction on a scale regulated entirely by the market value of its male owner. She became either an industrial pawn or a social parasite. Success on the part of the man completed her parasitic relationship to life by turning her into an increasingly elaborate consumer. Henceforth her sole asset was her sex, her sole means of expression her personal relationship to some specific male—father, brother, husband or son. She lived on her power to "charm." Sentiment flourished like a monstrous orchid. Home-life, over-focussed and over-heated, was cut off finally from the life of the world. Men kept their balance by living in two spheres, but the two spheres, "the world" and "the home" were so completely at variance that he could realise himself fully in neither, and was condemned to pose in each, to the annulling of his manhood. The average female, living by and through sex, missed womanhood, but achieved a sort of harmony by a thorough-going exploitation of sex. The home, all over-emphasised femininity, and the world, all over-specialised maleness, cancelled and nullified each other.

The way through this *impasse,* said Mrs. Stetson, was for women to follow the commercialised home industries into the world and to socialise them. Armies of women have been driven perforce into the industrial machine, heavily handicapped underlings, working under conditions they have been powerless to alter. They must now advance in a body, boldly and consciously, taking their old rank as producers, administrators, doing the world's housekeeping in the world. In order that they may do this, "homelife" as we know it, must be reorganised. The millions of replicas of tiny kitchens and nurseries, served by isolated women, must disappear. The world must become a home. In it women will pursue socially valuable careers, responsible to the community for their work, assured by the community of an economic status clear of sex and independent of their relationship to any specific male. They will spend their days at the work they can do best, whether nursery work, education, or mechanical engineering, finding their places in the social fabric as freely as do their brothers. Houses, communally cleansed and victualled, will remain as meeting-places for rest and recreation.

It was impossible to ignore Mrs. Stetson's facts. Her challenge left English feminists in two distinct groups, the one standing for the sexual and economic independence of all women, irrespective of class, and working towards the complete socialisation of industry, the other ignoring or deprecating the industrial activities of women and standing for the preservation of the traditional insulated home; seeking to improve the status of women by giving them votes, solving woman's economic problem by training her in youth to earn her living, "if need be."

These two mutually exclusive groups were caught up into the suffrage campaign; the one with the motive of transforming the conditions of female labour, the other because the capture of political power was part of the process of securing the recognition of the essential equality of women and men. The war has played into the hands of both parties by demonstrating the social efficiency of women and by giving an unprecedented urgency to the problem of woman in industry. The "equality" suffragists have secured a partial victory on the score of the proven ability of women to act as substitutes for men. The industrial suffragists rejoice in the spectacle of the disintegrated home, the inauguration of the municipal kitchen, and the fact that the promoters of infant welfare are more and more insistently emphasising the necessity for the municipal crèche.

Mrs. Stetson's forecast appears to be on the way to fulfilment, and those who are looking to the co-operation of women as the decisive factor in the achievement of the industrial revolution joyously welcome the independent and powerful restatement of Mrs. Stetson's main proposition that has recently come from the pen of Miss Wilma Meikle. Miss Meikle is a very thorough-going feminist, and the vigour and beauty of her work—by far the best attempt at constructive feminism which has yet appeared in England—is obviously the product of a profound faith. She evidently sympathises with the militant phases of the suffrage movement in its spirit of pure revolt and self-assertion rather than with the aspects represented by "women delicately unaware of the kitchen side of politics, genteelly unacquainted with the stupendous significance of commerce, women who had been bred in drawing-rooms where the ruling class posed as men whose power was based upon culture and oratory," women for whom "life was bowdlerised into a Mary Ward novel"; and she sympathises with the men who reach Parliament through sheer individual worth in public life rather than "obscure men like Thomas Babington Macaulay and Benjamin Disraeli, who had been rushed into social eminence by their flowing rhetoric at Westminster." But she is only incidentally a suffragist. The main argument of her book is a recantation of the whole of the suffrage movement. She is entirely sceptical as to the value of a parliamentary franchise which leaves the industrial masses at the mercy of political legislation, and believes that the way to political power is through industrial power, through the trades union and the power of the worker to transform his environment and make his own terms. Women must build up their power upon the basis of industrial organisation. "They must serve and work, and they must join the workers' surging revolt against the denial of things that make existence life, their hunger for knowledge and their desire for leisure, and their determination to have both." It follows that "the lady," "delicately sympathetic, alluringly reticent, consistently courteous and skilfully environed," must go. She is, even at her best, comparable to the Circassian, bred charmingly from her infancy to be the light of some good man's harem. Her caprices were an incentive to industrial enterprise, she helped the troubadours to invent "manners," she provided a market for the wares of the artist. But science and commerce and art are now no longer dependent on her greed. She is an anachronism. Home life must be re-organised to set her free to work.

> "The great Domestic Cant of Good Wifehood and Good Motherhood has tied the average woman into such a tangle of hypocrisies that she cannot unravel herself sufficiently to be a distinct personality. . . . Before long she is exhausted by hypocrisy. Her self-distrust lashes her to a duster, her determining to appear what she is not is a magnet that keeps her inextricably fastened to her servants or her cooking stove . . . her nerves are racked by the effort to live up to the Good Mother ideal. There is no fun left in her."

With the Great Domestic Cant weighing our women down under "the absurdly complicated organisation of the family there remains no cause for wonder that in spite of higher education, in spite of feminism, original thought amongst women is almost non-existent." Her financial independence must be secured. She must learn to think her own thoughts and form her own judgments in contact with actuality. All the freedoms there are can be claimed by her without the vote once she demonstrates her industrial indispensability and organises her ranks against those who would exploit her. Parliamentary life will follow rather than precede feminine emancipation. Finally, women in the mass, set free from their dependence upon a single masculine pocket for everything they desire in addition to food and clothing, will find it possible to live a full life,

> "and the old restlessness which has almost universally lowered the value of their work will at last be stilled . . . and with the full and final accomplishment of women's lives will come the end of feminism by its ultimate absorption into the common cause of humanity."

To many minds this vision of homeless womanhood caught equally with man in the industrial machine, interested equally with man in "earning a living," differentiated from man only by her occasional evanescent relationship to an infant, will bring nothing but dismay. They will see life shorn of roses and turned into a workshop. They will see the qualities that are "far above rubies" and can never be paid for, going by the board. In other words, they attach more importance to environment than to humanity. They have no faith in the qualities they wish to "preserve." They have no faith in womanhood. The apparent over-preoccupation of the feminists with environment is a very different thing. It is based on faith in womanhood, although both its reasoning and its demands make it appear that they regard women as potential men, obstructed by the over-elaborated machinery of the home.

But the fact of woman remains, the fact that she is relatively to man, *synthetic.* Relatively to man she sees life whole and harmonious. Men tend to fix life, to fix aspects. They create metaphysical systems, religions, arts, and sciences. Woman is metaphysical, religious, an artist and scientist in life. Let anyone who questions the synthetic quality of women ask himself why it is that she can move, as it were in all directions at once, why, with a man-astonishing ease, she can "take up" everything by turns, while she "originates" nothing? Why she can grasp a formula, the "trick" of male intellect, and the formula once grasped, so often beat a man at his own game? Why, herself "nothing," she is such an excellent critic of "things"? Why she can solve and reconcile, revealing the points of unity between a number of conflicting males—a number of embodied theories furiously raging together. Why the "free lance," the woman who is independent of any specific male, does this so excellently, and why the one who owes subsistence to a single male is usually loyally and violently partisan in public, and the wholesome opposite in private? And let him further ask himself why the great male synthetics, the artists and mystics, are three-parts woman? That women are needed "in the world" in their own right and because of their difference to men is clearly recognised in Canon Streeter's book on "Woman in the Church." But for him difference constitutes inferiority. He confesses that the present bankruptcy of the church is largely owing to the exclusion of women, and he calls for a cautious and partial admission of women into the ministry. It is not, he thinks, advisable that they should be admitted to the priesthood as long as the priest stands in a position of authority. In a democratised church system women as priests might, in time, be thinkable. For the present, the completion of the male church might be brought about by a large co-operation of women in the work and the deliberations of the church. Incidentally, it occurs to him that such a recognition of the feminine element in religion would act as a curb to the heresy of Mariolatry. In other words, women are to be admitted into a carefully regulated share in the working of a divine institution because during the centuries of their exclusion it has become progressively impotent, but they are to be excluded from its full powers and privileges because there is no divine principle in womanhood. Canon Streeter has never asked himself why Mariolatry has established itself tyrannously at the very heart of the liveliest system of man-made theology. He has made nothing of the fact that a male priesthood, having usurped authority and driven women from the early position of workers side by side with men, ordained priests equally with men by the laying on of hands, immediately reinstated her, enthroned above them as the Queen of Heaven. The Hebrew Jehovah, imagined as male, could not satisfy them. The deifying of Mary was an unconscious expression of their need to acknowledge the feminine element in Godhead. Canon Streeter is the male Protestant, caught in the Protestant cul-de-sac "he for God only, she for God in him." The acknowledgment reached unconsciously in Mariolatry has been reached consciously by the "heresy" of Quakerism. The early Quakers, wrapped as they were as "men" in secular fear and distrust of "woman," did not dare to deny her her human heritage of divine light and bravely took in the dark the leap of admitting her to full ministry. Only the Protestants have left her out altogether. Canon Streeter may reply that Quakerism is a democratised faith, and is heretical in its exclusion of priest and sacrament, thus underlining his dilemma. There is no alternative. Woman springs to the centre of an aristocratic church system—because men will have her there.

She walks into a democratic church system, man's equal, in her own right. If Anglicanism, to save its life, democratises itself and admits women to full fellowship, it will leave Catholicism in possession of the field as the typical classical church with Mariolatry a part of its system, the memorial for all time of the emptiness of the dream of male supremacy. A similar begging of the whole question of women in the ministry distinguishes Mr. T. B. Allworthy's recent valuable contribution to the history of women in the Apostolic church. He accounts for the activities of women in the early church by the fact that this church was social and not separated. Let the church once more become an integral part of social life and women will achieve their proper share in church life. How, one would like to ask, is the church to achieve the becoming an integral part of social life save by the free admission of women in their own right? The last book on our list is a résumé of all that women have done and suffered in their contest with the idea that a woman cannot be a legislator. Its author is of opinion that political enfranchisement is an essential part of feminine education, and Mr. Houseman, who contributes a preface, agrees in the sense that the great need of women is the need of a corporate consciousness, that such a consciousness was unattainable by her during the years of artificial segregation, and that it has been achieved by means of the agitation which has arisen for the ending of this segregation.

Taken together, these four books are a fairly inclusive statement of feminist thought to date. They are, in spite of their common tendency to contrast a "dark" past with a "bright" future, to separate environment from life and to regard environment as the more potent factor, a very remarkable convergence of recognition, coming from minds differing as to the why and wherefore, the ways and means of "feminism" upon the divine-human fact of womanhood. This is the essential thing. A fearless constructive feminism will re-read the past in the light of its present recognition of the synthetic consciousness of woman; will recognise that this consciousness has always made its own world, irrespective of circumstances. It can be neither enslaved nor subjected. Man, the maker of formulæ, has tried in vain, from outside, to "solve the problem" of woman. He has gone off on lonely quests. He has constructed theologies, arts, sciences, philosophies. Each one in turn has stiffened into lifelessness or become the battle-ground of conflicting theories. He has sought his God in the loneliness of his thought-ridden mind, in the beauty of the reflex of life in art, in the wonder of his analysis of matter, in the curious maps of life turned out by the philosophising intellect. Woman has remained curiously untroubled and complete. He has hated and loved and feared her as mother nature, feared and adored her as the unattainable, the Queen of Heaven; and now, at last, nearing the solution of the problem, he turns to her as companion and fellow pilgrim, suspecting in her relatively undivided harmonious nature an intuitive solution of the quest that has agonised him from the dawn of things. At the same moment his long career as fighter and destroyer comes to an end; an end that is the beginning of a new glory of strife. In the pause of deadly combat he sees the long past in a flash. He had ceased in principle to be a fighter before the war. With the deliberate conscious ending of his role of fighter, with his deliberate renunciation of the fear of his neighbour will come the final metamorphosis of his fear of "woman." Face to face with the life of the world as one life he will find it his business to solve not the problem of "woman" who has gained at last the whole world for her home, but of man the specialist; the problem of the male in a world where his elaborate outfit of characteristics as fighter, in warfare, in trade, and in politics, is left useless on his hands.

Ploughshare n.s.2.8(September 1917):241–246.

Talent and Genius

When Plato was planning his ideal commonwealth, he found the poets would not fit the pattern and proposed running them out of the town. Today, the poets, once discovered, run of their own accord. But genius, though its prestige has grown enormously since Plato's day, is still a thorn in the side of authority. It is also the central problem of modern psychology; and in their efforts to draw a circle round the phenomenon the psychologists have given the genius worshipping capacity of modern society some severe shocks. There was a bad quarter of an hour at the end of the century when they discovered its streak of madness, and the pundits of Decadence followed with much slaughtering of heroes.

A little later we began to hear of the subconscious. Uncanny but comforting, a capacious hold-all for mysteries. And common humanity, discovered in possession of this amazing *arrière-boutique,* was more interesting than ever. Hidden away within the workaday being of every one of us, unchanging, illimitable, and ever new, was the source of art, love and religion; the smiling kingdom of Heaven. We had heard this before. But here was the science for it. Science and faith had kissed each other. We could rejoice in peace.

We rejoiced. Until we were startled by the announcement that someone had found the way into the subconscious, investigated the premises and discovered all our activities at their single simple source. His report was humiliating, until we realized that we were hearing, not bad news about humanity, but good news about sex. If not only our "genius", art, philosophy and religion, but every one of our activities, is a sublimation of—or a failure to sublimate—the sex impulse, we are not less wonderful, but sex much more wonderful than we had supposed. And psychology, in shifting the smile of the sphinx, is as far as ever from solving her riddle.

There was once an irritable man of genius who brushed the problem away. Tush, said he, genius is a plain and simple thing. Genius is an infinite capacity for taking pains. His formula has deservedly held its own. It fulfils the one demand of a good definition. It defines. But it does not define genius. It defines talent, which is something far rarer.

THE SECRET OF DARWIN

It defines the ants, amongst the humbler orders of consciousness the most talented. It defines the great Darwin. We are accustomed to speak of the mighty genius of Darwin. Because his theory shattered our world, and rebuilt it, very far away from our hearts' desire. It forced us to live, until the genius of Samuel Butler set Darwin's facts in their right order in the context of reality, in a gloomy and uncertain twilight. Looking back to the sunshine of earlier days, we were tempted to wish that Darwin had never been born to enlighten our minds and sadden our hearts. Between whiles we were inordinately proud of him; hard-headed Darwinians with no nonsense about us. What a Titan England had produced! A Colossus, bestriding the world!

Then the human documents began to appear. His life and letters, the lives and letters of those who had known him. And the Colossus was nowhere to be found. In the whole record there is not a trace of any one of the characteristics of genius. From first to last not a single eccentricity. Nothing in the least gey ill to live with. And so distressed was this sweet and simple soul over the moral earthquake he had produced, so far from desiring to change the placid little world of his day, that he flouted his own theory to the extent of saying that it need not interfere with religious belief.

Our Darwin was no genius. He was a supremely talented naturalist. A naturalist with an infinite capacity for taking pains. With the enormous, unflagging industry of the semi-invalid, he collected and observed in his own small field; and presently there stood before his eyes his theory, ready-made.

THE MIDWIFE OF GENIUS

But in regarding genius as ordinary, Carlyle was right. If anything can be called ordinary, genius can. To say that genius is universal, that we all have it more or less, is to give utterance to a truism that has never had a night out. But more specifically, we may assert that genius is very ordinary and talent rare; that genius exists potentially in every woman and is sometimes found in men; that many men and a few women have talent.

But though separable, talent, that which does, and genius, that which sees, ought never to be separated. Talent, though the more independent of the two and able, given sufficient specialist knowledge, without possessing a scrap of wisdom, to make a tremendous noise in the world and draw down much limelight, does its best with genius behind it. Genius is helpless without talent. If anything is to be born of it there must be conscious laborious work on the original inspiration. Talent is the midwife of genius. Unschooled genius is apt to reel to its doom, dealing out destruction as it goes. The gift of genius in the individual is nothing for human boasting. Its only righteousness is in the development of the talents that belong to it.

What then of Jane Austen, producing a masterpiece, a perfect balance of genius and talent, in girlhood? What of Shakespeare?

Well, in the first place, we are all, even though we may not lisp in numbers, born within the medium of literary art, and begin our struggle with it even before we can speak. And the phenomenon of Jane Austen's masterpiece produced casually in a few weeks has recently been changed to the normal spectacle of long patient labor upon the original conception. Shakespeare is admittedly inexplicable. A child essayist described him the other day as "a man who wrote plays with a marvelous command of highflown language".

The "highflown" language could be picked up in the fifteenth century almost anywhere. A poet of simple birth, by frequenting the best circles, would find himself swimming in it. But the command, the intensive culture, the perfect gentlemanly sophistication—these things together in a casual barn-strutter, a man humbly reared, and excluded from the best circles by what, in his day, was held to be a low trade, have so shocked our sense of probability that many minds have clutched willingly at any theory, no matter how grotesque, that offered escape from the outrage on common sense. And now there is Mr. Looney, whose careful, unflustered observation of the surrounding facts, has at last unearthed and given to the world the simple, obvious, astounding explanation.

THE ABUSE OF TALENT

There is, of course, the other side of the picture. Genius either in the community or in the individual, may be stifled by talent. See the havoc played with the synthetic stupor of woman when first she emerged, in numbers, into the analytic partisan fighting world of men.

The feminine intelligentsia, the product of fifty years "higher education", are usually brilliant creatures. There is a great show of achievement in the arts and sciences to their credit. Almost none of it bears the authentic feminine stamp. Almost the whole could be credited to men. But this blind docility, so disastrous to women, and still more disastrous to the men who mould them, is a phase already passing. Feminine genius is finding its way to its own materials.

Of the lack of balance between talent and genius in the individual, there is a painfully perfect example in a man whose work is a permanent battle-ground of *doctrinaires,* Gustave Flaubert. Lack of balance is always comic, to the spectator. But comedy is tragedy standing on its head. And the comedy of Gustave Flaubert is like all other comedies, exasperating the spectacle of needless tumult.

Flaubert's genius was a passion for pure form. It gave birth to the now famous stylistic dogma of statement without commentary. But his magnificent talents, his infinite capacity for taking literary pains, were too much for him. His lifelong struggle leaves us *Salammbô* a pure exotic and one of the sacred books of the aesthetes; *Saint Antoine*, his masterpiece *manqué*, a grand conception reduced to nullity by too much scholarliness; *Madame Bovary*, a study from a living model chosen for him by brother artists to keep his literary genius within bounds, and chosen later by the reading public to represent him. Here his genius and his talent run neck to neck, and his friends stand justified in their choice. But an examination *de haut en bas* of a "small soul" is not great literature.

Then there is the neglected document of the *Education Sentimentale*, the unfinished cynical extravaganza, *Bouvard el Pécuchet* and three short stories, two of which, *St. Julien* and *Un Cœur Simple*, are miniature masterpieces, perhaps the most perfect miniatures in literature. They stand also the decisive test of great literature; the wayfaring man, though a fool, shall not err therein.

One man, two small masterpieces. What more, it may be asked, is needed? But one cannot get away from the pity of the limitation of Flaubert's production, from the waste of his life, the vanity of his sufferings. With the whole document before us in his most self-revealing letters, his letters to George Sand, the trouble is insipidly lucid. His loathing of humanity, his continuous depression, his lauding of his martyrdom to the skies, all cry aloud his mishandling of his genius.

George, she who was all genius and precious little talent, might have freed him if she had been younger and had had him for a while under her thumb. She would have cured his spinsterish inability to leave his work alone, to refrain from niggling over it until it went stale on his hands. As it was, she sat amongst her family and friends at Nohant, pouring out her novels on the backs of envelopes and tradesman's bills, and begged him to refrain from bitterness, to come out into life and enlarge himself. It was his method, not his life, that needed enlarging. "Try", he writes to George, "to have a great deal of talent, and even genius if you can". *Try* to have genius. These words epitomize his life.

GENIUS AND LIFE

In life, as in art, our achievements are born of the marriage of genius and talent. The driving force behind success is genius. The name of the firm is Vision & Practical Ability, Inc.

The personal records of great public men almost invariably reveal feminine genius in the background. Yet, so far in our history, it is obvious that the balance has been weighted on the side of talent. That specialist knowledge, the ability to do, has been divorced from wisdom, the ability to see. It is not for nothing that men have been defined as those who look without seeing and women as those who see without looking. Again and again civilization, that proud achievement of the talents of men, getting ahead of vision, has led with monotonous reiteration, down to disaster. Each picture has been proudly hung, but the surrounding household has been wrecked in the process. And though nothing is more foolish than to cry up one sex at the expense of the other, and to imagine that the single genius of woman will "save the world", it is perhaps not quite unreasonable to suppose that the vicious circle will be broken by the inclusion, in public affairs, of the dynamic power that has been, so far, almost universally short-circuiting in the home.

Vanity Fair 21.2(October 1923):118, 120.

Women and the Future

Most of the prophecies born of the renewed moral visibility of woman, though superficially at war with each other, are united at their base. They meet and sink, in the sands of the assumption that we are, today, confronted with a new species of woman.

Nearly all of the prophets, nearly all of those who are at work constructing hells, or heavens, upon this loose foundation, are men. And their crying up, or down, of the woman of today, as contrasted to the woman of the past, is easily understood when we consider how difficult it is, even for the least prejudiced, to *think* the feminine past, to escape the images that throng the mind from the centuries of masculine expressiveness on the eternal theme: expressiveness that has so rarely reached beyond the portrayal of woman, whether Madonna, Diana, or Helen, in her moments of realtionship to the world as it is known to men.

Even the pioneers of feminism, Mill, Buckle, and their followers, looked only to woman as she was to be in the future, making, for her past, polite, question-begging excuses. The poets, with one exception, accepted the old readings. There is little to choose between the visions of Catholic Rossetti and Swinburne the Pagan. Tennyson, it is true, crowns woman, elaborately, and withal a little irritably, and with much logic-chopping. But he never escapes patronage, and leaves her leaning heavily, albeit most elegantly, upon the arm of man. Browning stands apart, and Stopford Brooke will not be alone in asking what women themselves think of Browning's vision of woman as both queen and lord, outstripping man not only in the wisdom of the heart, but in that of the brain also.

And there is Meredith—with his shining reputation for understanding; a legend that by far outruns his achievement. Glimpses of woman as a full cup unto herself, he certainly had. And he reveals much knowledge of men as they appear in the eyes of such women. This it is that has been accounted unto him for righteousness. He never sees that he is demanding the emancipation of that which he has shown to be independent of bonds. Hardy, his brother pagan and counterpart, is Pereus hastening to Andromeda, seeking the freedom of the bound.

Since the heyday of Meredith and Hardy, batallions of women have become literate and, in the incandescence of their revelations, masculine illusions are dying like flies. But, even today, most men are scarely aware of the searchlight flung by these revelations across the past. These modern women, they say, are a new type.

It does not greatly matter to women that men cling to this idea. The truth about the past can be trusted to look after itself. There is, however, no illusion more wasteful than the illusion of beginning all over again; nothing more misleading than the idea of being divorced from the past. It is, nevertheless, quite probable that feminine insistence on exhuming hatchets is not altogether a single-hearted desire to avoid waste and error.

Many men, moreover, are thoroughly disconcerted by the "Modern Woman". They sign for ancient mystery and inscrutability. For La Giaconda . . . And the most amazing thing in the history of Leonardo's masterpiece is their general failure to recognize that Lisa stands alone in feminine portraiture because she is centered, unlike her nearest peers, those dreamful, passionately blossoming imaginations of Rossetti, neither upon humanity nor upon the consolations of religion.

THE ESSENTIAL EGOIST

It is because she is so completely *there* that she draws men like a magnet. Never was better artistic bargain driven than between Leonardo and this lady who sat to him for years; who sat so long that she grew at home in her place, and the deepest layer of her being, her woman's enchanted domestication within the sheer marvel of existing, came forth and shone through the mobile mask of her face. Leonardo of the innocent eye, his genius concentrated upon his business of making a good picture, caught her, unawares, on a gleeful, cosmic holiday. And in seeking the highest, in going on till he got what he wanted, he reaped also the lesser things. For there is in Lisa more than the portrayal of essential womanhood. The secondary life of the lady is clearly visible. Her traffic with familiar webs, with her household and the external shapings of life. When Pater said that her eyelids were a little weary, he showed himself observant. But he misinterpreted the weariness.

On the part of contemporary artists, there are, here and there, attempts to resuscitate man's ancient mystery woman, the beloved-hated abyss. The intensest and the most affrighted of these essayists are D. H. Lawrence and Augustus John. Perhaps they are nearer salvation than they know.

For the essential characteristic of women is egoism. Let it at once be admitted that this is a masculine discovery. It has been offered as the worst that can be said of the sex as a whole. It is both the worst and the best. Egoism is at once the root of shameless selfishness and the ultimate dwelling place of charity. Many men, of whom Mr. Wells is the chief spokesman, read the history of woman's past influence in public affairs as one long story of feminine egoism. They regard her advance with mixed feelings, and face her with a neat dilemma. Either, they say, you must go on being Helens and Cinderellas, or you must drop all that and play the game, in so far as your disabilities allow, as we play it. They look forward to the emergence of an army of civilized, docile women, following modestly behind the vanguard of males at work upon the business of reducing chaos to order.

Another group of thinkers sees the world in process of feminisation, the savage wilderness, where men compete and fight, turned into a home. Over against them are those who view the opening prospect with despair. To them, feminism is the invariable accompaniment of degeneration. They draw back in horror before the oncoming flood of mediocrity. They see ahead a democratized world, overrun by hordes of inferior beings, organized by majorities for material ends; with primitive, uncivilizable woman rampant in the midst.

Serenely apart from these small camps is a large class of delightful beings, the representatives of average masculinity at its best, drawing much comfort from the spectacle of contradictory, mysterious woman at last bidding fair to become something recognizably like itself. Women, they say, are beginning to take life like men; are finding in life the things men have found. They make room for her. They are charming. Their selfishness is social, gregarious. Woman is to be the jolly companion; to co-operate with man in the great business of organizing the world for jollity. But have any of these so variously grouped males any idea of the depth and scope of feminine egoism? Do they not confound it with masculine selfishness? Do they realize anything of the vast difference between these two things?

It is upon the perception of this difference that any verdict as to the result of woman's arrival "in the world" ultimately rests. Though, it is true, certain of these masculine forecasts are being abundantly realized. There is abroad in life a growing army of man-trained women, brisk, positive, rational creatures with no nonsense about them, living from the bustling surfaces of the mind; sharing the competitive partisanships of men; subject, like men, to fear; subject to national panic; to international, and even to cosmic panic. There is also an army let loose of the daughters of the horse-leech; part of the organization of the world for pleasure. These types have always existed. The world of the moment particularly favours them. But their egoism is as nothing to the egoism of the womanly woman, the beloved-hated abyss, at once the refuge and the despair of man.

For the womanly woman lives, all her life, in the deep current of eternity, an individual, self-centered. Because she is one with life, past, present, and future are together in her, unbroken. Because she thinks flowingly, with her feelings, she is relatively indifferent to the fashions of men, to the momentary arts, religions, philosophies, and sciences, valuing them only in so far as she is aware of their importance in the evolution of the beloved. It is man's incomplete individuality that leaves him at the mercy of that subtle form of despair which is called ambition, and accounts for his apparent selfishness. Only completely self-centered consciousness can attain to unselfishness—the celebrated unselfishness of the womanly woman. Only a complete self, carrying all its goods in its own hands, can go out, perfectly, to others, move freely in any direction. Only a complete self can afford to man the amusing spectacle of the chameleon woman.

Apart from the saints, the womanly woman is the only human being free to try to be as good as she wants to be. And it is to this inexorable creature, whom even Nietzsche was constrained to place ahead of man, that man returns from his wanderings with those others in the deserts of agnosticism. She is rare. But wherever she is found, there also are found the dependent hosts.

But is not the material of this intuitive creature strictly limited? Is she not fettered by sex? Seeking man, while man, freed by nature for his divine purpose, seeks God, through blood and tears, through trial and error, in every form of civilization? He for God only, she for God in him? She is. She does. When man announces that the tree at the door of the cave is God, she excels him in the dark joy of the discovery. When he reaches the point of saying that God is a Spirit and they that worship him must worship him in spirit and in truth, she is there waiting for him, ready to parrot any formula that shows him aware of the amazing fact of life.

And it is this creature who is now on the way to be driven out among the practical affairs of our world, together with the "intelligent" woman; i.e., with the woman who is intelligible to men. For the first time. Unwillingly. The results cannot be exactly predicted. But her gift of imaginative sympathy, her capacity for vicarious living, for being simultaneously in all the warring camps, will tend to make her within the council of nations what the Quaker is within the council of religions.

WOMEN IN THE FUTURE

Public concerted action must always be a compromise. But there is all the difference between having things roughly arranged *ad hoc* by father, however strong his sense of abstract justice, and having them arranged by father prompted by mother, under the unseen presidency of desire to do the best regardless, in the woman's regardless, unprincipled, miracle-working way, for all concerned.

The world at large is swiftly passing from youthful freebooting. It is on the way to find itself married. That is to say, in for startling changes. Shaken up. Led by the nose and liking it. A question arises. How will his apparently lessened state react on man? In how far has he been dependent on his illusion of supremacy? Perhaps the answer to this is the superiority of men in talent, in constructive capacity. It is the talent of man, his capacity to *do* most things better than women, backed up by the genius of woman. The capacity to *see* that is carrying life forward to the levels opening out ahead.

Vanity Fair 22.2(April 1924):39–40.

About Punctuation

Only to patient reading will come forth the charm concealed in ancient manuscripts. Deep interest there must be, or sheer necessity, to keep eye and brain at their task of scanning a text that moves along unbroken, save by an occasional full-stop. But the reader who persists finds presently that his task is growing easier. He is winning familiarity with the writer's style, and is able to punctuate unconsciously as he goes . . . It is at this point that he begins to be aware of the charm that has been sacrificed by the systematic separation of phrases. He finds himself *listening*. Reading through the ear as well as through the eye. And while in any way of reading the ear plays its part, unless it is most cunningly attacked it co-operates, in our modern way, scarcely at all. It is left behind. For as light is swifter than sound so is the eye swifter than the ear. But in the slow, attentive reading demanded by unpunctuated texts, the faculty of hearing has its chance, is enhanced until the text *speaks* itself. And it is of this enhancement that the strange lost charm is born. Quite modest matter, read thus, can arouse and fuse the faculties of mind and heart.

Only the rarest of modern prose can thus arouse and affect. Only now and again, to-day, is there any strict and vital relationship between the reader and what he reads. Most of our reading is a superficial swift gathering, as we loll on the borderland between inertia and attention, of the matter of a text. An easy-going collaboration, with the reader's share reduced to the minimum. So much the better, it may be said. Few books, ancient or modern, are worth a whole self. Very few can call us forth to yield all we are and suffer change. Yet it is not to be denied that the machinery of punctuation and type, while lifting burdens from reader and writer alike and perfectly serving the purposes of current exchange, have also, on the whole, devitalized the act of reading; have tended to make it less organic, more mechanical.

There is no discourtesy, since punctuation has come to be regarded as invariable, in calling it part of the machinery of book production. An invisible part. For so long as it conforms to rule punctuation is invisible. After the school years it is invisible; its use, for most people, as unconscious as the act of breathing. Most of us were taught punctuation exactly as we were taught rule of three. Even if we were given some sense of the time-value of the stop and its subdivisions, the thing that came first and last, the fun of the game, was the invariability of the rules. And so charming is convention, so exhilarating a deliberate conformity to tradition, that it is easy to forget that the sole aim of law is liberty; in this case, liberty to express.

It is not very long since an English gentleman's punctuation was as romantic as his spelling. The formal law was strictly observed only by scholars. Not until lately have infringements, by the ordinary, been regarded as signs of ill-breeding. And in high places there have always been those who have honoured the rules in the breach, without rebuke. Sterne, for example, joyously broke them all, and it has been accounted unto him for righteousness. Beside him stands Rabelais, wielding form as Pantaloon wields his bladder. Were they perhaps castigated for their liberties by the forgotten orthodox of the period? Or is it that the stickler for stereotyped punctuation makes his first appearance in our own time? Why, in either case, have Mr. Wells's experiments, never going further than a reinforcement of the full-stop and a free use of the dash, been dragged into the market-place and lynched, while the wholesale depredations of

Sterne and Rabelais are merely affectionately hugged? Is it because their rows and rows of dots, their stars, and their paragraphs built of a single word are so very often a libidinous digging of the reader's ribs? Because their stars wink? It is noteworthy that so long as his dots were laughter Mr. Wells was not called over the coals for mannerism. There was no trouble until those signs were used to italicize an idea or drive home a point; until they became pauses for reflection, by the reader. From that time onwards there have been, amongst his opponents, those who take refuge in attack on his method. Scorn of the dot and the dash has come forward to play its part in the business of answering Mr. Wells. Sterne and Rabelais and the earlier Wells, genially aware of the reader and with nothing to fear from him, offer open hospitality on their pages, space, while their wit detonates, for the responsive beat of the reader's own consciousness. The later Wells, usually the prey of dismay, anger or despair, handles the resources of the printed page almost exclusively as missiles, aimed full at the intelligence alone.

Of the value of punctuation and, particularly, of its value as pace-maker for the reader's creative consciousness, no one has had a keener sense than Mr. Henry James. No one has more sternly, or more cunningly, secured the collaboration of the reader. Along his prose not even the most casual can succeed in going at top-speed. Short of the casting off of burdens, the deep breath, the headlong plunge, the sustained steady swimming, James gives nothing at all. To complete renunciation he offers the recreative repose that is the result of open-eyed concentration. As aesthetic exercise, with its peculiar joys and edifications, the prose of James keeps its power, even for those in utmost revolt against his vision, indefinitely. It is a spiritual Swedish Drill. Gently, painlessly, without shock or weariness, as he carries us unhasting, unresting, over his vast tracts of statement, we learn to stretch attention to the utmost. And to the utmost James tested, suspending from the one his wide loops, and from the other his deep-hung garlands of expression, the strength of the comma and the semi-colon. He never broke a rule. With him, punctuation, neither made, nor created, nor begotten, but proceeding directly from its original source in life, stands exactly where it was at its first discovery. His text, for one familiar with it, might be reduced, without increase of the attention it demands, to the state of the unpunctuated scripts of old time. So rich and splendid is the fabric of sound he weaves upon the appointed loom, that his prose, chanted to his punctuation, in an unknown tongue, would serve as well as a mass—in D minor.

Yet even James, finding within bonds all the freedom he desired, did not quite escape the police. Down upon almost his last written words came the iron hand of Mr. Crosland, sternly, albeit most respectfully, recommending a strait-jacket in the shape of full-stops to be borrowed—from Mr. Bart Kennedy. Whose stops are shouts. A pleasant jest. Relieving no doubt a long felt desire for the presence in Mr. James of a little ginger. But Crosland is austere. Sternly, with no intervals for laughter, he drags us headlong, breathless, belaboured, from jest to jest with never a smile or pause. It is his essential compactness that makes him a so masterly sonneteer. His sonnets gleam, now like metalled ships, now like jewels. Prose, in his sense, might be written like a sonnet. First the form, a well-balanced distribution of stops for each paragraph, and then the text. An interesting experiment.

As interesting as that now on trial in a prose that is a conscious protest against everything that has been done to date by the hand of talent at work upon inspiration. But the dadaists, in so far as they are paying to law the loud tribute of anarchy, are the counterparts of the strictly orthodox.

Meanwhile, for those who stand between purists and rebels, the rules of punctuation are neither sacred, nor execrable, nor quite absolute. No waving of the tablets of the law has been able to arrest organic adaptation. The test of irregularities is their effectiveness. Verbless phrases flanked by full-stops, the use of *and* at the beginning of a sentence, and kindred effective irregularities, are safe servants, for good, in the cause of the written word. And always there has been a certain variability in the use of the comma. As the shortest breath of punctuation it is allowed, without controversy, to wander a little.

Yet the importance of the comma cannot be exaggerated. It is the angel, or the devil, amongst the stops. In prose, everything turns upon its use. Misplaced, it destroys sense more readily than either of its fellows. For while their wanderings are heavy-footed, either at once obvious, or easily traceable, the comma plays its pranks unobtrusively. Used discreetly, it clears meaning and sets both tone and pace. And it possesses a charm denied to other stops. Innocence, punctuating at the bidding of a prompting from within, has the comma for its darling. Spontaneous commas are as delightful in their way as spontaneous spelling; as delightful as the sharp breath drawn by a singing child in the middle of a word.

Experiment with the comma, as distinct from recourse to its recognised variability, is to be found, since the stereotyping of the rules, only here and there and takes one form: its exclusion from sequences of adjectives. This exclusion suggests an awareness of the power of the comma as a holder-up, a desire to allow adjectives to converge, in the mind of the reader, as swiftly as possible upon their object. But one would expect to find, together with such awareness, discrimination. And, so far as I know, the exclusion of the comma when it is practised at all, is unvarying; the possibilities are missed as surely here, as they are in conformity to the letter of the law.

The use of the comma, whether between phrases or in sequences of adjectives, is best regulated by the consideration of its time-value. If, for example, we read:—

> "Tom went singing at the top of his voice up the stairs at a run that ended suddenly on the landing in a collision with the sweep,"

we are brought sensibly nearer to sharing the incident than if we read:—

> "Tom went, singing at the top of his voice, up the stairs, at a run that ended, suddenly, on the landing, in a collision with the sweep."

Conversely, if we read :—

> "Tom stupid with fatigue fearing the worst staggered without word or sign of greeting into the room,

we are further off than in reading :—

> "Tom, stupid with fatigue, fearing the worst, staggered, without word or sign of greeting, into the room."

Even more obvious is the time-value of the comma in sequences of adjectives :—

> "Suave low-toned question-begging excuses"

bears the same meaning as :—

> "Suave, low-toned, question-begging excuses."

But the second is preferable.

> "Huge soft bright pink roses"

may be written :—

> "Huge, soft, bright, pink roses."

But the first wins.

It is a good plan, in the handling of phrases, to beware of pauses when appealing mainly to the eye, and to cherish them when appealing to reflection. With sequences of single words, and particularly of adjectives, when the values are concrete, reinforcing each other, accumulating without modification or contradiction upon a single object of sight, the comma is an obstruction. When the values are abstract, qualifying each other and appealing to reflection, or to vision, or to both vision and reflection at once, the comma is essential. If there is a margin of uncertainty, any possibility of ambiguity or misapprehension, it is best, no matter what is sacrificed of elasticity or of swiftness, to load up with commas. Or the reader may pay tax. And it is dangerous in these days of hurried readings to ask for the re-scanning even of a single phrase.

But there is woe in store, unless he be a prince of proof-readers, for the writer who varies his punctuation. The kindly hands that regulate his spelling will regulate also his use of stops; and, since hands are human, they will regulate irregularly. The result, when the author has altered the alterations, also irregularly, sometimes reading punctuation on to the page when it is not there—is chaos.

Adelphi 1.11(April 1924):990–996.

Women in the Arts

It is only lately that the failure of women in the fine arts has achieved pre-eminence in the *cause célèbre*, Man versus Woman, as a witness for the prosecution. In the old days, not only was art not demanded of women, but the smallest sign of genuine ability in a female would put a man in the state of mind of the lady who said when she saw the giraffe: "I don't believe it."

Thus Albrecht Dürer, travelling through the Netherlands in 1521 and happening upon the paintings of Susanne Horebout, makes appreciative notes in his diary, but is constrained to add: "Amazing that a she-creature should accomplish so much." And some three hundred years later, Gustave Flaubert, standing at the easel of Madame Commanville, smiles indulgently and murmurs: "Yes, she has talent; it is *odd*."

But today, under pressure of the idea that women in asserting equality, have also asserted identity with men, the demand for art as a supporting credential has become the parrot-cry of the masculinists of both sexes. A cry that grows both strident and hoarse. For this pre-eminent witness for the prosecution is, poor fellow, shockingly over-worked. And not only over-worked but also a little uneasy. Feeling no doubt, since most of his fellows have been hustled away in disgrace and those that remain are apt to wilt in the hands of defending counsel, that his own turn may be at hand.

But though towering a little insecurely still he towers, at once the last refuge of all who are frightened by anything that disturbs their vision of man as the dominant sex, and the despair of those feminists who believe fine art to be the highest human achievement.

There are of course many, an increasing band, who flatly deny that art is the highest human achievement and place ahead of it all that is called science, which they are inclined to regard as the work of humanity's post-adolescence. But it is a curious and notable fact, a fact quite as curious and notable as the absence of first-class feminine art, that all these people, whenever they want to enlighten the layman on the subject of the scientific imagination, are at pains to explain that the scientific imagination, at its best, is the imagination of the artist. It is not less odd that the man of science if he is masculinist, will, when hard-pressed, seize, to belabour his opponent, not the test-tube, but the mahlstick. (It is of course to be remembered that while the mahlstick is solid and persists unchanging, the test-tube is hollow and its contents variable.) And the rush for the mahlstick goes on in spite of the fact that the witness for science does not, on the whole, have a bad time. He has perhaps lost a little of his complacency. But he can still, when counsel for the defense reminds the jury how recently women have had access to scientific material and education, point to the meagre, uninstructed beginnings of some of the world's foremost men of science.

Side by side with the devotees of science we find those who count religion the highest human achievement. They are a house divided. In so far as they set in the van the mystic—the religious genius who uses not marble or pigment or the written word, but his own life as the medium of his art—they supply a witness for the defense who points to Catherine and Teresa walking abreast with Francis and Boehme. But their witness is always asked what he makes of the fact that Jesus, Mahomed, and Buddha are all of the sex male. His prompt answer: that he looks not backward but ahead, leaves things, even after he has pointed to Mrs. Eddy and Mrs. Besant, a little in the air. For Catholic feminists there is always the Mother of God. But they are rare, and as it were under an editorial ban. Privately they must draw much comfort from the fact that the Church which, since the days of its formal organization has excluded woman from its ultimate sanctities, is yet constrained to set her above it, crowned Queen of Heaven.

Last, but from the feminist point of view by no means least of those who challenge the security of the one solidly remaining hope of the prosecution, are the many who believe, some of these having arrived at feminism via their belief, that the finest flowers of the human spirit are the social arts including the art of dress. In vain is their witness reminded of the man modiste, the pub and the club. He slays opposition with lyrics, with idylls of the Primitive Mother forming, with her children, society, while father slew beasts and ate and slept. And side by side with the pub at its best he places the salon at its best, and over against Watt and his dreamy contemplation of the way the light steam plays with the heavy lid of the kettle—a phenomenon, thunders the prosecution, that for centuries countless women have witnessed daily in animal stupidity—he sets Watt's mother, seeing the lifting lid as tea for several weary ones.

But in all this there is no comfort for the large company of feminists who sincerely see the fine arts as humanity's most godlike achievement. For them the case, though still it winds its interminable way, is settled. There is no escape from the verdict of woman's essential inferiority. The arraignment is the more flawless because just here, in the field of art, there has been from time immemorial, a fair field and no favour. Always women have had access to the pen, the chisel and the instrument of music. Yet not only have they produced no Shakespeare, no Michelangelo and no Beethoven, but in the civilization of today, where women artistis abound, there is still scarcely any distinctive feminine art. The art of women is still on the whole either mediocre or derivative.

There is, of course, at the moment, Käthe Kollwitz, Mother and Hausfrau to begin with, and, in the estimation of many worthy critics, not only the first painter in Europe today but a feminine painter—one that is to say whose work could not have been produced by a man. She it may be is the Answer to Everything. For though it is true that one swallow does not make a summer, the production by the female sex of even one supreme painter brings the whole fine arts argument to the ground and we must henceforth seek the cause of woman's general lack of achievement in art elsewhere than in the idea that first-class artistic expression is incarnate in man alone.

Let us, however suppose that there is no Käthe Kollwitz, assume art to be the highest human achievement, accept the great arraignment and in the interest of the many who are driven to cynicism by the apparent impossibility of roping women into the scheme of salvation, set up the problem in its simplest terms. Cancel out all the variable factors; the pull of the home on the daughter, celibacy, the economic factor and the factor of motherhood, each of which taken alone may be said by weighting the balance to settle the matter out of court and taken all together make us rub our eyes at the achievements of women to date—cancel out all these and imagine for a moment a man and a woman artist side by side with equal chances and account if we can for the man's overwhelming superiority.

There is before we can examine our case one more factor to rule out—isolated here because it grows, in the light of modern psychological investigation, increasingly difficult to state, and also because as a rule it is either omitted from the balance, or set down as a good mark to the credit of one party. This elusive and enormously potent factor is called ambition. And its definition, like most others, can never be more or less than a statement of the definer's philosophy of life. But it may at least be agreed that ambition is rich or poor. Childishly self-ended or selflessly mature. And a personal ambition is perhaps not ill-defined as the subtlest form of despair—though a man may pass in a lifetime from the desire for personal excellence, the longing to be sure that either now or in the future he shall be recognized as excellent, to the reckless love of excellence for its own sake, leaving the credit to the devil—and so on to becoming, as it were behind his own back, one with his desire. And though the ambition of the artist need not of necessity be personal, he is peculiarly apt to suffer in the absence of recognition—and here at once we fall upon the strongest argument against fine art as the highest human achievement. These are altitudes. But we are discussing high matters. And though the quality of a man's ambition takes naught from the intrinsic value of his work, an ambition to the extent that it remains a thirst to be recognized as personally great, is a form of despair. And it is a form of despair to which men are notoriously more liable than are women. A fact that ceases to surprise when one reflects that, short of sainthood, a man must do rather than be, that he is potent not so much in person as in relation to the things he makes.

And so with ambition ruled out and our case thus brought down to the bare bones of undebatable actuality, back to our artists of whom immediately we must enquire what it is that they most urgently need for the development of their talents, the channels through which their special genius is to operate. The question has been answered by genius—on its bad days and always to the same effect. Da Vinci, called simultaneously by almost everything that can attract the mind of man, has answered it. Goethe, the court official, answered it. And by way of casting a broad net we will quote here the testimonies of an eleventh century Chinese painter and a modern writer, a South African.

"Unless I dwell in a quiet house, seat myself in a retired room with the window open, the table dusted, incense burning and the thousand trivial thoughts crushed out and sunk, I cannot have good feeling for painting or beautiful taste, and cannot create the you" (the mysterious and wonderful—Fennelosa's translation) Kakki.

"It's a very wise curious instinct that makes all people who have imaginative work (whether it's scientific or philosophic thinking, or poetry, or story-making, of course it doesn't matter so it's original work, and has to be spun out of the *texture of the mind itself*) try to creep away into some sort of solitude." . . . . "It's worry, tension, painful emotion, anxiety that kills imagination out as surely as a bird is killed by a gun." Olive Schreiner.

Quiet, and solitude in the sense of freedom from preoccupations, are the absolute conditions of artistic achievement. Exactly, it may be answered, and your male artist will pay for these things any price that may be asked. Will pay health, respectability, honour, family claims and what not. And keep fine. And there are in the world of art women who make the same payments and yet do not achieve supremacy and, indefinably, do not remain fine. What is the difference? Where is it that the woman breaks down? She should with a fair field and her fascinating burdensome gift of sight, her gift for expansive vicarious living, be at least his equal? She should. But there are, when we come down to the terms of daily experience, just two things that queer the pitch. One abroad and one at home. For the woman, and particularly the woman painter, going into the world of art is immediately surrounded by masculine traditions. Traditions based on assumptions that are largely unconscious and whose power of suggestion is unlimited. Imagine the case reversed. Imagine the traditions that held during a great period of Egyptian art, when women painters were the rule—the nude male serving as model, as the "artist's model" that in our own day is the synonym for nude femininity.

But even the lifting away from our present gropings after civility in the world at large of the diminishing shadow of that which, for want of a more elegant term, is being called menstate mentality, would do nothing towards the removal of the obstruction in the path of the woman artist at home. She would still be left in an environment such as has surrounded no male artist since the world began. For the male artist, though with bad luck he may be tormented by his womankind, or burdened by wife and family, with good luck may be cherished by a devoted wife or mistress, or neglectful char, by someone, that is to say, who will either reverently or contemptuously let him be. And with the worst of luck, living in the midst of debt and worry and pressure, still somehow he will be tended and will live serenely innocent of the swarming detail that is the basis of daily life.

It is not only that there exists for the woman no equivalent for the devoted wife or mistress. There is also no equivalent for the most neglectful char known to man. For the service given by women to women is as different from that given by women to men as is chalk from cheese. If hostile, it will specialize in manufacturing difficulties. If friendly, it will demand unfaltering response. For it knows that living sympathy is there. And in either case service is given on the assumption that the woman at work is in the plot for providing life's daily necessities.

And even vicarious expansion towards a multitude of details, though it may bring wisdom, is fatal to sustained creative effort.

Art demands what, to women, current civilization won't give. There is for a Dostoyevsky writing against time on the corner of a crowded kitchen table a greater possibility of detachment than for a woman artist no matter how placed. Neither motherhood nor the more continuously exacting and indefinitely expansive responsibilities of even the simplest housekeeping can so effectively hamper her as the human demand, besieging her wherever she is, for an inclusive awareness, from which men, for good or ill, are exempt.

Vanity Fair 24 (May 1925):47, 100.

Continuous Performance: The Film Gone Male

Memory, psychology is to-day declaring, is passive consciousness. Those who accept this dictum see the in-rolling future as living reality and the past as reality entombed. They also regard every human faculty as having an evolutionary history. For these straight-line thinkers memory is a mere glance over the shoulder along a past seen as a progression from the near end of which mankind goes forward. They are also, these characteristically occidental thinkers, usually found believing in the relative *passivity* of females. And since women excel in the matter of memory, the two beliefs admirably support each other. But there is memory and memory. And memory proper, as distinct from a mere backward glance, as distinct even from prolonged contemplation of things regarded as past and done with, gathers, can gather, and pile up its wealth only round universals, unchanging, unevolving verities that move neither backwards nor forwards and have neither speech nor language.

And that is one of the reasons why women, who excel in memory and whom the cynics describe as scarely touched by evolving civilisation, are humanity's silent half, without much faith in speech as a medium of communication. Those women who never question the primacy of "clear speech", who are docile disciples of the orderly thought of man, and acceptors of theorems, have either been educationally maltreated or are by nature more within the men's than within the women's camp. Once a woman becomes a partisan, a representative that is to say of one only of the many sides of question, she has abdicated. The batallions of partisan women glittering in the limelit regions of to-day's world, whose prestige is largely the result of the novelty of their attainments, communicating not their own convictions but some one or other or a portion of some one or other of the astonishing varieties of thought-patterns under which men experimentally arrange such phenomena as are suited to the process, represent the men's camp and are distinguishable by their absolute faith in speech as a medium of communication.

The others, whom still men call womanly and regard with emotion not unmixed with a sane and proper fear, though they may talk incessantly from the cradle onwards, are, save when driven by calamitous necessity, as silent as the grave. Listen to their outpouring torrents of speech. Listen to village women at pump or fireside, to villa women, to unemployed service-flat women, to chatelâines, to all kinds of women anywhere and everywhere. Chatter, chatter, chatter, as men say. And say also that only one in a thousand can *talk*. Quite. For all these women use speech, with individual differences, alike: in the manner of a facade. Their awareness of being, as distinct from man's awareness of becoming, is so strong that when they are confronted, they must, in most circumstances, snatch at words to cover either their own palpitating spiritual nakedness or that of another. They talk to banish embarrassment. It is true they are apt to drop, if the confrontation be prolonged, into what is called gossip and owes both its charm and its poison to their excellence in awareness of persons. This amongst themselves. In relation to men their use of speech is various. But always it is a façade.

And the film, regarded as a medium of communication, in the day of its innocence, in its quality of being nowhere and everywhere, nowhere in the sense of having more intention than direction and more purpose than plan, everywhere by reason of its power to evoke, suggest, reflect, express from within its moving parts and in their totality of movement, something of the changeless being at the heart of all becoming, was essentially feminine. In its insistence on contemplation it provided a pathway to reality.

In becoming audible and particularly in becoming a medium of propaganda, it is doubtless fulfilling its destiny. But it is a masculine destiny. The destiny of planful becoming rather than of purposeful being. It will be the chosen battle-ground of rival patterns, plans, ideologies in endless succession and bewildering variety.

It has been declared that it is possible by means of purely aesthetic devices to sway an audience in whatever direction a filmateur desires. This sounds menacing and is probably true. (The costumiers used Hollywood to lengthen women's skirts. Perhaps British Instructional, with the entire medical profession behind it, will kindly shorten them again). It is therefore comforting to reflect that so far the cinema is not a government monopoly. It is a medium, or a weapon, at the disposal of all parties and has, considered as a battlefield a grand advantage over those of the past when civil wars have been waged disadvantageously to one party or the other by reason of inequalities of publicity, restrictions of locale and the relative indirectness and remoteness of the channels of communication. The new film can, at need, assist Radio in turning the world into a vast council-chamber and do more than assist, for it is the freer partner. And multitudinous within that vast chamber as within none of the preceding councils of mankind, is the unconquerable, unchangeable eternal feminine. Influential.

Weeping therefore, if weep we must, over the departure of the old time films gracious silence, we may also rejoice in the prospect of a fair field and no favour. A field over which lies only the shadow of the censorship. And the censorship is getting an uneasy conscience.

Close Up 9.1(March 1932):36–38.

Adventure for Readers*

Having defined poetry as "*the result of* passion recollected in tranquillity" (the opening words are here apologetically italicized because, though their absence makes the definition meaningless, they are almost invariably omitted), Wordsworth goes on to describe what happens when the poet, recalling an occurrence that has stirred him to his depths, concentrates thereon the full force of his imaginative consciousness; how there presently returns, together with the circumstances of the experience, something of the emotion that accompanied it, and how, in virtue of this magnetic stream sustained and deepened by continuous concentration, there comes into being a product this poet names, with scientific accuracy, an "effusion".

In Wordsworth's own case, the product can itself become the source of further inspiration, and the presence upon the page of offspring set beneath parent and duly entitled "Effusion on Reading the Above", affords a unique revelation of the subsidiary workings of an emotion tranquilly regathered.

And while this enchanted enchanter and his successors (the greatest of whom, dead e'er his prime, produced for our everlasting adoration, effusions inspired by the reading of Lemprière's Dictionary) sang to the spirit their immortal ditties, our novelists, following the example of their forbears, those wandering minstrels who told for the delight of the untravelled, brave strange tales from far away, wove stories whose power to enthrall resided chiefly in their ability to provide both excitement and suspense; uncertainty as to what, in the pages still to be turned, might befall the hero from whom, all too soon, returning to "the world of everyday", the reader must regretfully take leave.

With vain, prophetic insight Goethe protested that action and drama are for the theatre, that the novelist's business is to keep his hero always and everywhere onlooker rather than participant and, "by one device or another," to slow up the events of the story so that they may be seen through his eyes and modified by his thought.

The first novelist fully to realize his ideal was Henry James and, by the time James had finished his work, something had happened to English poetry.

*FINNEGANS WAKE. JAMES JOYCE. Faber. 25*s*.

How, or just why, or exactly when the shift occurred from concentration upon the various aspects of the sublime and beautiful to what may be called the immediate investigation of reality, it is not easy to say, though a poet-novelist, Richard Church, in his recent address to the Royal Society of Literature, made, one feels, some excellent guesses as to the practical reasons for the changeover. Whereunto may be added the widespread application, for some time past, of Pope's injunction as to the proper study of mankind.

Whatever the combination of incitements, certain of our poets have now, for decades past, produced short stories rather than lyrics and, in place of the epic and foreshadowed by *The Ring and the Book,* so very nearly a prose epic, have given us, if we exclude *The Testament of Beauty,* rearing a nobly defiant head in the last ditch of the epic form, the modern novel.

The proof, if proof be needed, of the transference may be found in a quality this new novel, at its worst as well as at its best, shares with poetry and that is conspicuously absent from the story-telling novel of whatever kind. Opening, just anywhere, its pages, the reader is immediately engrossed. Time and place, and the identity of characters, if any happen to appear, are relatively immaterial. Something may be missed. Incidents may fail of their full effect through ignorance of what has gone before. But the reader does not find himself, as inevitably he would in plunging thus carelessly into the midst of the dramatic novel complete with plot, set scenes, beginning, middle, climax, and curtain, completely at sea. He finds himself within a medium whose close texture, like that of poetry, is everywhere significant and although, when the tapestry hangs complete before his eyes, each portion is seen to enhance the rest and the shape and the intention of the whole grows clear, any single strip may be divorced from its fellows without losing everything of its power and of its meaning.

Particularly is this true of the effusions of Marcel Proust and of James Joyce. For while every novel, taken as a whole, shares with every other species of portrayal the necessity of being a signed self-portrait and might well be subtitled Portrait of the Artist at the Age of—where, in the long line of novelists preceding these two, save, perhaps, in Henry James as represented by the work of his maturity, shall we find another whose signature is clearly inscribed across his every sentence?

Reaching *Finnegans Wake* we discover its author's signature not only across each sentence, but upon almost every word. And since, upon the greater number of its pages, nearly every other word is either wholly or partially an improvisation, the would-be reader must pay, in terms of sheer concentration, a tax far higher even than that demanded by Imagist poetry. And be he never so familiar with the author's earlier work, and in agreement with those who approve his repudiation of the orthodoxies of grammar and syntax, finding, when doubt assails, reassurance in the presence of similar effective and, doubtless, salutary heresies in the practice of the arts other than literature, the heavily-burdened reader of *Finnegans Wake,* hopefully glissading, upon the first page, down a word of a hundred letters—representing the fall that carried Finnegan to his death—into pathless verbal thickets, may presently find himself weary of struggling from thicket to thicket without a clue, weary of abstruse references that too often appear to be mere displays of erudition, weary of the mélange of languages ancient and modern, of regional and class dialects, slangs and catchwords and slogans, puns and nursery rhymes, phrases that are household words phonetically adapted to fresh intentions, usually improper, sometimes side-splitting, often merely facetious, incensed in discovering that these diverse elements, whether standing on their heads or fantastically paraphrased, apparently succeed each other as the sound of one suggests that of the next rather than by any continuity of inward meaning, and are all too frequently interspersed by spontaneous creations recalling those produced by children at a loss, bored to desperation by lack of interest and seeking relief in shouting a single word, repeating it with a change of vowel, with another change and another, striving to outdo themselves until they reach, with terrific emphasis, onomatopœia precipitating adult interference.

Meanwhile the author, presumably foreseeing the breakdown of even the most faithful Joycian as likely to occur in the neighbourhood of the hundredth page, comes to the rescue in the name of Anna Livia, invoked by a parody of a well-known prayer ("Annah the Allmaziful, the everliving, Bringer of Plurabilities, haloed be her eve, her singtime sung, her rill be run, unhemmed as it is uneven"), with a chapter on the allied arts of writing and reading, here and there exceptionally, and most mercifully, explicit, preluded by a list of the hundred and sixty-three names given to Annah's "untitled mamafesta memorializing the Mosthighest" (including *Rockabill Booby in the Wave Trough, What Jumbo made to Jalice and What Anisette to Him,* and *I am Older nor the Rogues among Whist I Slips and He calls me his Dual of Ayessha*), and one day perhaps to be translated, annotated, and issued as a Critique of Pure Literature and an Introduction to the Study of James Joyce.

The impact of this chapter, a fulfilment of the author's prescription—"Say it with missiles, and thus arabesque the page"—is tremendous, its high purpose nothing less than the demand that the novel shall be poetry. A grouped selection of caught missiles and fragments of missiles produces the following relatively coherent mosaic: "About that original hen . . . the bird in this case was Belinda of the Dorans, a more than quinque-gentarian . . . and what she was scratching looked like a goodish-sized sheet of letter-paper. . . . Well, almost any photoist . . . will tip anyone asking him the teaser that if a negative of a horse happens to melt enough while drying . . . what you get is . . . a positively grotesque distorted macromass of all sorts of horsehappy values . . . well, this freely is what must have occurred to our missive . . . by the sagacity of a lookmelittle likemelong hen. . . . Lead, kindly Fowl! . . . No, assuredly they are not justified these gloompourers who grouse that letters have never been quite their old selves again since Biddy Doran looked ad literature. . . . Who, at all this marvelling, but will press . . . to see the vaulting feminine libido . . . sternly controlled . . . by the uniform matteroffactness of a meandering masculine fist? . . . To concentrate solely on the literal sense or even the psychological content of any document . . . is . . . hurtful to sound sense."

Quite as far goes Mr. Walter de la Mare, who has recently declared that "When poetry is most poetic, when its sounds, that is, and the utterance of them, and when its rhythms rather than the words themselves are its real if cryptic language, any other meaning, however valuable it may be, is only a secondary matter".

Primarily, then, are we to *listen* to *Finnegans Wake*? Not so much to what Joyce says, as to the lovely way he says it, to the rhythms and undulating cadences of the Irish voice, with its capacity to make of every spoken word a sentence with parentheses and to arouse, in almost every English breast, a responsive emotion?

Consulting once more the author's elucidatory chapter, we find our instructions: "Closer inspection of the *bordereau* would reveal a multiplicity of personalities . . . and some prevision of virtual crime or crimes might be made by anyone unwary enough before any suitable occasion for it or them had so far managed to happen along. In fact . . . the traits featuring the chiaroscuro coalesce, their contrarieties eliminated, in one stable somebody. . . ." We are urged also to be patient, to avoid "anything like being or becoming out of patience. . . . So holp me Petault, it is not a misaffectual whyacinthinous riot . . . it only looks as like it as damn it . . . cling to it as with drowning hands, hoping against hope all the while, that by the light of philophosy . . . things will begin to clear up a bit one way or another within the next quarrel of an hour".

Thus encouraged, with this easily decipherable chapter's rich treasure in hand and perceptions exalted and luminous, the reader presses hopefully onward; only to find his feet once more caught in impenetrable undergrowths, and his head assailed by missiles falling thicker and faster than before, hurled by one obviously in silent ecstasies as he watches the flounderings of his victim. Scanning and re-scanning the lines until their rhythm grows apparent, presently acquiring ease in following cadence and intonation as he goes, the reader again finds himself listening to what appears to be no more than the non-stop patter of an erudite cheapjack. Weariness returns. So what? Weeks of searching for the coalescence and the somebody?

Let us take the author at his word. Really release consciousness from literary preoccupations and prejudices, from the self-imposed task of searching for superficial sequences in stretches of statement regarded horizontally, or of setting these upright and regarding them pictorially, and plunge, provisionally, here and there; *enter* the text and look innocently about.

The reward is sheer delight, and the promise, for future readings, of inexhaustible entertainment. Inexhaustible, because so very many fragments of this text now show themselves comparable only to the rider who leapt into the saddle and rode off in all directions. The coalescence and the somebody can wait. Already, pursuing our indiscriminate way, we have discovered coherencies, links between forest and forest, and certain looming forms, have anticipated the possibility of setting down upon "a goodish-sized sheet of letterpaper" the skeleton of the long argument. For the present, for a first reading, the "meanderings" of the "masculine fist" are a sufficient repayment. Even a tenth reading will leave some still to be followed up; and many to be continuously excused.

Do we find it possible, having thus "read" the whole and reached the end, a long, lyrically wailing, feminine monologue, to name the passion whose result is this tremendous effusion? Finnegan, the master-mason, and his wife Annie and their friends may symbolize life or literature or what you will that occasionally call for mourning. For their creator they are food for incessant ironic laughter (possibly a screen for love and solicitude), mitigated only here and there by a touch of wistfulness that is to reach at the end a full note. Shall we remind ourselves that most of our male poets have sounded wistful? And the women? Well, there is Emily Brontë, who, by the way, would have delighted, with reservations, in *Finnegans Wake*.

Life and Letters 22(July 1939):45–52.

Foreword to *Pilgrimage*

Although the translation of the impulse behind his youthful plan for a tremendous essay on *Les Forces humaines* makes for the population of his great cluster of novels with types rather than with individuals, the power of a sympathetic imagination, uniting him with each character in turn, gives to every portrait the quality of a faithful self-portrait, and his treatment of backgrounds, contemplated with an equally passionate interest and themselves, indeed, individual and unique, would alone qualify Balzac to be called the father of realism.

Less deeply concerned with the interplay of human forces, his first English follower portrays with complete fidelity the lives and adventures of inconspicuous people, and for a while, when in the English literary world it began its career as a useful label, realism was synonymous with Arnold Bennett.

But whereas both Balzac and Bennett, while representing, the one in regard to a relatively concrete and coherent social system, the other in regard to a society already showing signs of disintegration, the turning of the human spirit upon itself, may be called realists by nature and unawares, their immediate successors possess an articulate creed. They believe themselves to be substituting, for the telescopes of the writers of romance whose lenses they condemn as both rose-coloured and distorting, mirrors of plain glass.

By 1911, thought not yet quite a direct supply of documentary material for the dossiers of the *cause célèbre*, Man versus conditions impeached as the authors of his discontent, realist novels are largely explicit satire and protest, and every form of conventionalized human association is being arraigned by biographical and autobiographical novelists.

Since all these novelists happened to be men, the present writer, proposing at this moment to write a novel and looking round for a contemporary pattern, was faced with the choice between following one of her regiments and attempting to produce a feminine equivalent of the current masculine realism. Choosing the latter alternative, she presently set aside, at the bidding of a dissatisfaction that revealed its nature without supplying any suggestion as to the removal of its cause, a considerable mass of manuscript. Aware, as she wrote, of the gradual falling away of the preoccupations that for a while had dictated the briskly moving script, and of the substitution, for these inspiring preoccupations, of a stranger in the form of contemplated reality having for the first time in her experience its own say, and apparently justifying those who acclaim writing as the surest means of discovering the truth about one's own thoughts and beliefs, she had been at the same time increasingly tormented, not only by the failure, of this now so independently assertive reality, adequately to appear within the text, but by its revelation, whencesoever focused, of a hundred faces, any one of which, the moment it was entrapped within the close mesh of direct statement, summoned its fellows to disqualify it.

In 1913, the opening pages of the attempted chronicle became the first chapter of "Pilgrimage," written to the accompaniment of a sense of being upon a fresh pathway, an adventure so searching and, sometimes, so joyous as to produce a longing for participation; not quite the same as a longing for publication, whose possibility, indeed, as the book grew, receded to vanishing point.

To a publisher, nevertheless, at the bidding of Mr J. D. Beresford, the book was ultimately sent. By the time it returned, the second chapter was partly written and the condemned volume, put away and forgotten, would have remained in seclusion but for the persistence of the same kind friend, who acquired and sent it to Edward Garnett, then reading for Messrs Duckworth. In 1915, the covering title being at the moment in use elsewhere, it was published as "Pointed Roofs."

The lonely track, meanwhile, had turned out to be a populous highway. Amongst those who had simultaneously entered it, two figures stood out. One a woman mounted upon a magnificently caparisoned charger, the other a man walking, with eyes devoutly closed, weaving as he went a rich garment of new words wherewith to clothe the antique dark material of his engrossment.

News came from France of one Marcel Proust, said to be producing an unprecedentedly profound and opulent reconstruction of experience focused from within the mind of a single individual, and, since Proust's first volume had been published and several others written by 1913, the France of Balzac now appeared to have produced the earliest adventurer.

Finally, however, the role of pathfinder was declared to have been played by a venerable gentleman, a charmed and charming high priest of nearly all the orthodoxies, inhabiting a softly lit enclosure he mistook, until 1914, for the universe, and celebrated by evolving, for the accommodation of his vast tracts of urbane commentary, a prose style demanding, upon the first reading, a perfection of sustained concentration akin to that which brought it forth, and bestowing, again upon the first reading, the recreative delights peculiar to this form of spiritual exercise.

And while, indeed, it is possible to claim for Henry James, keeping the reader incessantly watching the conflict of human forces through the eye of a single observer, rather than taking him, before the drama begins, upon a tour amongst the properties, or breaking in with descriptive introductions of the players as one by one they enter his enclosed resounding chamber where no plant grows and no mystery pours in from the unheeded stars, a far from inconsiderable technical influence, it was nevertheless not without a sense of relief that the present writer recently discovered, in "Wilhelm Meister," the following manifesto:

> In the novel, reflections and incidents should be featured; in drama, character and action. The novel must proceed slowly, and the thought-processes of the principal figure must, by one device or another, hold up the development of the whole. . . . The hero of the novel must be acted upon, or, at any rate, not himself the principal operator. . . . Grandison, Clarissa, Pamela, the Vicar of Wakefield, and Tom Jones himself, even where they are not acted upon, are still retarding personalities and all the incidents are, in a certain measure, modelled according to their thoughts.

Phrases began to appear, formulae devised to meet the exigencies of literary criticism. "The Stream of Consciousness" lyrically led the way, to be gladly welcomed by all who could persuade themselves of the possibility of comparing consciousness to a stream. Its transatlantic successors, "Interior Monologue" and "Slow-motion Photography," may each be granted a certain technical applicability leaving them, to this extent, unhampered by the defects of their qualities.

Lives in plenty have been devoted to the critic's exacting art and a lifetime might be spent in engrossed contemplation of the movements of its continuous ballet. When the dancers tread living boards, the boards will sometimes be heard to groan. The present writer groans, gently and resignedly, beneath the reiterated tap-tap accusing her of feminism, of failure to perceive the value of the distinctively masculine intelligence, of pre-War sentimentality, of post-War Freudianity. But when her work is danced upon for being unpunctuated and therefore unreadable, she is moved to cry aloud. For here is truth.

Feminine prose, as Charles Dickens and James Joyce have delightfully shown themselves to be aware, should properly be unpunctuated, moving from point to point without formal obstructions. And the author of "Pilgrimage" must confess to an early habit of ignoring, while writing, the lesser of the stereotyped system of signs, and, further, when finally sprinkling in what appeared to be necessary, to a small unconscious departure from current usage. While meeting approval, first from the friend who discovered and pointed it out to her, then from an editor who welcomed the article she wrote to elucidate and justify it, and, recently, by the inclusion of this article in a text-book for students of journalism and its translation into French, the small innovation, in further complicating the already otherwise sufficiently complicated task of the official reader, helped to produce the chaos for which she is justly reproached.

For the opportunity, afforded by the present publishers, of eliminating this source of a reputation for creating avoidable difficulties, and of assembling the scattered chapters of "Pilgrimage" in their proper relationship, the author desires here to express her gratitude and, further, to offer to all those readers who have persisted in spite of every obstacle, a heart-felt apology.

D. M. R.

Trevone, 1938.

Pilgrimage. London: Dent, 1967. 9–12.

Novels

"Let us leave it to the reviewers to abuse such effusions of fancy at their leisure and over every new novel to talk in threadbare strains of the trash with which the press now groans. Let us not desert one another: we are an injured body. Although our productions have afforded more extensive and unaffected pleasure than those of any other literary corporation in the world, no species of composition has been so much decried. From pride, ignorance, or fashion, our foes are almost as many as our readers; and while the abilities of the nine-hundredth abridger of the History of England, or of the man who collects and publishes in a volume some dozen lines of Milton, Pope, and Prior, with a paper from the *Spectator,* and a chapter from Sterne, are eulogized by a thousand pens, there seems almost a general wish of decrying the capacity and undervaluing the labour of the novelist, and of slighting the performances which have only genius, wit, and taste to recommend them. 'I am no novel-reader—I seldom look into novels—do not imagine that *I* often read novels—it is really very well for a novel!' Such is the common cant. 'And what are you reading Miss——?' 'Oh!, it is only a novel!' replies the young lady, while she lays down her book with affected indifference or momentary shame. 'It is only *Cecilia,* or *Camilla,* or *Belinda,*' or in short, only some work in which the creative powers of the mind are displayed, in which the most thorough knowledge of human nature, the happiest delineation of its varieties, the liveliest effusion of wit and humour are conveyed to the world in the best chosen language. Now, had the young lady been engaged with a volume of the *Spectator,* instead of such a work, how proudly she would have produced the book and told its name!"

Encountering in *Northanger Abbey*—Jane Austen's sly dig at the contemporary thriller—this impassioned defence of the novel, one is moved to wonder whether, could she come among us to-day, she might presently be found defending its characteristic fiction, the detective novel, and might substitute in the case of a reader discovered immersed in a Sayers or an Innes, for "a volume of the *Spectator*", a novel by Proust, Joyce, or Virginia Woolf?

For assuredly, turning at last from the clamour of her astonishing surroundings to the quietude of the printed page, Jane would come in due course upon these pioneers; would wander bewildered through a chapter of Proust (are not then the French writers any longer explicit, direct, and clear?), glissade incredulously down a page or two of *Finnegan's Wake* (this Mr. Joyce is after all an Irishman), seek in *The Waves* for the emergence of recognizable narrative and at last, hoping for a clue to the novel's extraordinary metamorphosis, would take refuge with the essayists. Only to find "composure" (for her the prerequisite of all the virtues, and for whose recovery, whenever life produced emotional disturbance, the liveliest of her heroines is always prepared to pay the price of half an hour's quiet reflection in her own room), already severely shaken, fly off beyond recapture before the assaults of an amazing discovery. For her, amongst the names of giants appearing in steady succession ever since her own day and whose works have given to fiction its present status, stands her own name. Not only considered worthy—even by appreciative assessors of the strange new varieties—of mention among the elect of the long series, but set by certain critics in lofty isolation above them all. Set gravely; respectfully; even affectionately: "dear Jane."

Sooner or later she would inevitably encounter the label supplied by the critics for the group of novels so deeply bewildering her: *The Stream of Consciousness*, and might possibly discover its origin: the borrowing, for the purpose of summarizing the work of a writer she found both novel and interesting, by Miss May Sinclair from the epistemologists, of this more than lamentably ill-chosen metaphor, long since by them discarded but still, in literary criticism, pursuing its foolish way.

Sure, we may feel, that no authority of whatever eminence, would succeed in persuading her to regard consciousness as a stream; nor, it may be, would any amount of trumpet-blowing send her back for further investigation of the alleged waters, at any rate until she had pursued her investigations as far as the present moment. As far as these stories pouring from the press in ever-increasing numbers and eagerly read, she learns, by gentle and simple alike, albeit many of the former, like the young lady reading a mere novel, acknowledge their addiction a little shamefacedly. Selections made for her by an experienced guide turn out to be novels indeed: "performances which have genius, wit, and taste to recommend them." Terrible, they are. Each one a revelation of human depravity. Yet in none of them is there any conscious employment, *exploitation* as these moderns appear to call it, of horror for the sake of horror. And, indeed, from the writer's point of view, the power of the ever-present shadow of evil to throw into relief and pin into the memory every incident in the story is most remarkable—akin to the deep shadows in the pictures of that Dutch artist, Mr. Rembrandt. And women no less than men excel in the writing of these strange tales, even so, my guide tells me, outdo them on account of the capacity for imaginative sympathy and vicarious living that enables them to bring their characters to life as persons rather than as types, so that in reading their stories one suffers enlargement of one's personal experience. Wealth of enlightenment, too, is to be reaped as to to-day's changed opinions in regard to matters one had believed settled for ever in the minds of all right-thinking persons, and in regard also to every aspect of this strange new world, wide general knowledge and, what is surely more important and valuable, insight into human problems making some of these books, without endangering their quality as enthralling stories, admirable essays in social, political, and even religious criticism.

Yes, indeed, dear Jane, in absorbing a selection of to-day's detective stories you have experienced invaluable conducted tours.

And is not every novel a conducted tour? First and foremost into the personality of the author who, willy-nilly, and whatever be his method of approach, must present the reader with the writer's self-portrait. He may face his audience after the manner of a lecturer, tell his tale, interpolate the requisite information, descriptions, explanations; or, walking at his side, letting the tale tell itself, come forward now and again to make a comment or drive home a point; or, remaining out of sight and hearing may, so to speak, project his material upon a screen. In either case he will reveal whether directly or by implication, his tastes, his prejudices, and his philosophy. And thus it is, the revealed personality of the writer that ultimately attracts or repels. An unchallenged masterpiece, a miracle of collaboration between genius and talent, will be explored as it makes its way down the centuries, by generation after generation of entranced tourists, even by those in utmost revolt against the vision of the conductor; but, for these last, will never gain the wholehearted allegiance secured by conductors whose personality, while breaking none of the bonds of artistic orthodoxy, carries the tourist far beyond the selected bounds. And, indeed, in the interest of such vital company, even violations of the dogmas of artistic orthodoxy will either remain unnoticed or, if they are perceived, will be readily condoned.

This conviction implies, however, no sort of agreement with readers who scorn all novels save those that are either openly or inferentially social, moral, or religious treatises. Yet on behalf of these humanists and moralists one may allow their prejudices to be firmly grounded upon a half-conscious critical awareness of the vast discrepancy between the actuality of life as experienced and the dramatic fatalism, shared in spite of its relative freedom from the time-limit, by the orthodox novel with the stage; the way, akin to that of science, it must not only lift its selected material from the context of reality but what is even more decisively restrictive, must ignore, in order to supply a story complete with beginning, middle, climax, and curtain, the always unique modifications of contingency.

However we elect to regard "the novel", whether with the eyes of the high-priest we consider it as predestined to remain within a framework for ever established or, with the prophet, see its free development implied from the beginning, the novel will remain a tour of the mind of the author, the decisive factor his attitude towards phenomena. He may be what is called "romantic," inclined on the whole to concentrate on qualities and ignore defects, or "realist", deliberately, by way of corrective, emphasizing defects; so that in a sense the two, like the twins known as optimist and pessimist, cancel each other out. Either of these again may be a poet, his work signed all over. To-day there are novels wherein the interest of any single part is no longer dependent for the reader upon exact knowledge of what has gone before or upon a frothy excitement (a prime source of the moralist's condemnation) as to what next will happen. Such novels may be entered at any point, read backwards, or from the centre to either extremity and will yet reveal, like a mosaic, the interdependence of the several parts, each one bearing the stamp of the author's consciousness.

And all the variously branching diversities of the novel of to-day, the humanist novel, tending to drama in a resounding box, the psychological novel tending, in concentration upon the intimate trickeries of the mind, to fatalistic exploitation of unconscious motive, the secular novel, whether constructively or destructively critical, and the religious novel, whether symbolic, denominational, or expressive of the mystical awareness potential in every man, are to be found in the ranks of detective fiction. And every detective novel, like every other novel, remains a tour guide and tourist, whether congenial or at variance, engaged in a collaboration whose outcome is immeasurable.

Life and Letters 56(March 1948):188–192.

20
May Sinclair (1863–1946)

Introduced and Edited by Diane F. Gillespie

May Sinclair aptly defined, enthusiastically practiced, and vigorously defended modernist innovations in fiction and poetry. Well known during her lifetime, Sinclair published her many novels and stories in the United States as well as in England, and her essays appeared in both American and English periodicals. For decades, however, her books were unavailable until a few hardcover reprints appeared in the late 1960s and early 1970s. In the early 1980s Virago of London republished in paperback *Mary Olivier* (1919), *The Life and Death of Harriett Frean* (1922), and *The Three Sisters* (1914). A biography of Sinclair and an annotated bibliography of writings about her appeared in 1973 (Boll; Robb) and a useful Twayne introduction in 1976 (Zegger). While her work is receiving more attention, her role as a knowledgeable and effective champion of the experimental artists of her day also deserves recognition. The selections reprinted here reveal her in this role.

Sinclair's 1918 reference to Miriam Henderson's "stream of consciousness going on and on" in the early volumes of *Pilgrimage* ("The Novels of Dorothy Richardson," reprinted below) did not please Richardson (Kunitz 562; Richardson, "Novels," reprinted in section **19**), but the metaphor, borrowed from William James, has become commonplace in the vocabulary of literary criticism. Sinclair, a student of philosophy who published two books on the subject (*A*

Defense of Idealism, 1917; *The New Idealism,* 1922), recognized the imprecision of the term. *Stream,* on one hand, connotes unity and continuity and suggests an active, creative self; on the other hand, it evokes multiplicity and change and a view of the self as a passive receiver of impressions. Richardson objected to the latter connotation, which she thought predominated (Gillespie, "May Sinclair").

Probably because she too emphasized a unified, active self, Sinclair abandoned the term except as part of her characterization of a novelist in *Far End* (1926). His name, Christopher Vivart, suggests the vivid nature of his art, and he describes his experiment as "presentation, not representation." He presents only "a stream of consciousness, going on and on: it's life itself going on and on" (83).

Sinclair's own similar experiment, a female *Bildungsroman* entitled *Mary Olivier,* appeared in 1919. Often compared to *Pilgrimage, Mary Olivier* is the primary focus of the recent critics who discuss Sinclair's work (e.g., Kaplan). Like Richardson, Sinclair in *Mary Olivier* tries to present quotidian reality as directly as possible. In the face of many obstacles, including a mother with very traditional notions about woman's role, the main character struggles to develop her intellectual and artistic potential. Although Sinclair called this novel her "favorite" and "best book" (Steell 513), she did not consistently immerse herself in the consciousness of a single character in subsequent novels. Nor did she define her choices about point of view or her punctuation as "feminine," as Richardson did. Yet Sinclair had an abiding interest in the suffrage movement and its implications for women's roles in society (Gillespie, " 'The Muddle' "), and in 1912 she wrote a pamphlet called *Feminism* for the Women Writer's Suffrage League.

As a scholar Sinclair was almost entirely self-taught. Preoccupied with self-transcendence as well as with the integrity and full development of the individual, Sinclair read mystical literature and reflected it in her writing (Underhill; Neff, "New Mysticism"). She also read psychoanalytic literature, and in 1913 she was one of the founders of the Medico-Psychological Clinic of London. These interests, closely related to her philosophical pursuits, emerge in several of her novels, including *The Life and Death of Harriett Frean.* Frequently Sinclair explores cases in which heredity and environment affect individual consciousnesses and prevent people, particularly women, from realizing their full potential. She reveals how the institutions of marriage and the family, idealized by the Victorians, as well as the stereotypes of women as spiritual, asexual, and at the same time purely reproductive, can thwart, even destroy, people of either sex.[1] *The Creators* (1910) combines her examination of domestic life and women's roles with an exploration of the problems faced by both male and female artists.

One such problem is the hostility with which an uncomprehending public greets artistic experimentation. Sinclair, as her review in 1917 of T. S. Eliot's *Prufrock: And Other Observations* (reprinted below) illustrates, knew and approved of imagist and other avant-garde poetry of her day. Eliot may present what is ugly and unpleasant, she says, but he has every right to do so because he allows neither soothing euphemisms nor elaborate language to obscure the reality he sees. Prufrock is her major example, and her praise of Eliot's method anticipates her comments on Richardson a year later and her own experiment in *Mary Olivier.* Eliot gives us reality, she says, by giving us direct access to "Prufrock's mind, jumping quickly from actuality to memory and back again, like an animal, hunted, tormented, terribly and poignantly alive." Such poetry is meaningful to readers who define the primary concern of poetry as reality and admit ideas only to the extent that they are "realities and not abstractions."

What Sinclair means by her continual references to "reality" is clear in the context of her similar observations about the imagist poets. In addition to "real," the words Sinclair and the artist-characters in her fiction use to describe such poetry are "stripped," "naked," "clean," "clear," "pure," and "hard." Reality is neither the temporal world nor a denial of it. A fresh perception of the external world constitutes reality. In an essay on F. S. Flint in 1921, Sinclair associates the imagists with Wordsworth and says that the aim of both is "to restore the innocence of memory as Gauguin restored the 'innocence of the eye.' " To this end the imagist abandons traditional rhetorical language and intellectual abstractions and responds directly to experience. Sinclair defines poetry, in fact, as "the rhythmic expression of an intense personal emotion produced by direct contact with reality" and associates these qualities with prose as well ("The Poems of F. S. Flint" 7, 13).

She finds it easier, however, to define imagist poetry initially by describing what it is not, an approach she uses again when she tries to describe Richardson's prose method. Imagism, Sinclair insists in one of her essays on H. D., "is not Symbolism." Nor is it "image-making." "Presentation not Representation is the watchword of the school. The Image, I take it, is Form. But it is not pure form. It is form *and* substance." She compares the Victorian poets to Protestants who believe that the bread and wine symbolize the body and blood of Christ and contrasts them to the imagists whom she compares to Catholics. They believe that the bread and wine actually are the body and blood, not substitutes for it ("The Poems of 'H. D.' "; see below).

This identity of form and substance often results in charges of obscurity from uncomprehending critics and reviewers. Sinclair tries various methods of combating such charges, not by denying them altogether but by explaining and justifying and by distinguishing among different kinds of obscurity. In the essay on H. D., for instance, Sinclair distinguishes between the obscure thought that is the product of intellectual superficiality and the obscure feeling that is so because "emotion at a certain depth *is* obscure" (339–340). In the case of Eliot she distinguishes among various kinds of obscurity that "may come from defective syntax, from a bad style, from confusion of ideas, from involved thinking, from irrelevant association, from sheer piling on of ornament." Eliot's obscurity, however, is the result of none of these. Nor is it H. D.'s obscurity of feeling. Eliot's obscurity results either from references to unfamiliar objects or from very rapid and erratic movements among familiar ones. In the latter case, his poetry presents, not the mind perceived according to the rules of logic or literary tradition, but the lively way in which his particular mind actually works (" 'Prufrock: And Other Observations' ").

References to the intentions of various kinds of free verse poets, reflecting her acquaintance with the work of Eliot and the imagists, as well as references to the critical controversy raging around them, recur in Sinclair's fiction. The involvement of the visual as well as the verbal arts, the influence of aesthetic developments on the Continent, and the threat to art of the First World War all form part of the picture. Although *The Rector of Wyck* (1925) is of interest in this regard, most representative is Sinclair's novel *The Tree of Heaven* (1917). Michael Harrison, a young poet, finds confirmation for his experiments with "live verse" among his contemporaries in France. He also belongs to a group of English writers and artists whose theories might be associated with those of vorticism. "The Vortex," in fact, is the title of the second section, which deals both with Harrison's involvement in revolutionary art and with his sister's in revolutionary women's politics. Sinclair reproduces, in part, one of the many discussions about the arts occurring among the members of Harrison's group. They disagree on many points, such as whether past works of art ought to be destroyed, but they are united in their abhorrence of artists who imitate other artists in their desire to produce works of art that cannot be imitated and in their aim to present directly not the temporal world of appearances but the reality they perceive through it. "We're out against the damnable affectations of naturalism and humanism," says one of the visual artists. The more representational the work, the bigger the artist's lie. The reality most of them perceive is energy, movement, and rhythm (244). These theories apply to the verbal as well as to the visual arts. If a writer breaks up traditional syntactical patterns just as the painter or sculptor decomposes figures or groups of figures, then there will emerge not only new, freer prose forms but also freedom from the sterile abstract ideas that these syntactical patterns perpetuate.

Three years after the publication of *The Tree of Heaven*, Sinclair defended Ezra Pound, whose reputation had suffered in part from his association with little magazines, such as the vorticists' *Blast*, that shocked and offended people. Now, she notes with irony, almost "every serious and self-respecting magazine is closed to this most serious and self-respecting artist" ("The Reputation of Ezra Pound," reprinted below). Pound could easily have been a popular poet, she observes, but he rightly chose to go his own way. He has admirably defended Henry James against the petty criticisms that obscure the importance of his unrelenting attacks on personal oppression. With integrity and selflessness Pound also has worked to advance the reputations of other experimental writers and visual artists. He deserves, Sinclair implies, similar treatment. She acknowledges and disputes, therefore, the charge that Pound's poetry is derivative by examining some of his "violently individual" early poems. She challenges the conclusion that he is "finished" by noting the new clarity, "vividness and precision," as well as "concentration" of his more recent Chinese-influenced work. No uncritical flatterer, however, Sinclair notes with humor and wit how Pound's weaknesses coexist with his strengths in the three Cantos written thus far. Impressed by "Homage to Sextus Propertius," however, she identifies with Pound because in his poetry he seeks and finds "himself, a salient, abrupt, unmistakable entity through all his transformations."

In her fiction too Sinclair recreates the thrust and parry of this period of rapid change in which editors and critics attack and defend artistic innovations with equal conviction. In "The Return" (1921), for example, reviewers disagree about a free-verse poet whose aims are very like those of the imagists, but the poet's own family dismisses him totally as incompetent and obscure (693, 700). In *The Allinghams* (1927) one reviewer disparages Stephen Allingham's "Epithalamion" as inept, irritating, and eccentric and refuses to call poems such barbaric works that defy all poetic traditions. Another critic, however, insists that Allingham has substituted subtle for marked rhythms and simplicity for ornamentation (338–340).

In all these cases, actual and fictional, Sinclair closely associates aesthetic innovation with the metaphysical position she calls the "new idealism." Rejecting traditional linguistic and literary structures and themes is parallel, in philosophical discussion, to stripping away the abstract ideas about reality associated with traditional idealism. Directly presenting reality in such a way that manner cannot be separated from matter parallels apprehending ultimate reality, in a fresh and immediate way, through the temporal world.

Criticism, moreover, must comply. "Only a live criticism can deal appropriately with a live art," Sinclair declares ("The Novels of Dorothy Richardson"). The old distinctions and terms do not suffice when confronting a novel in which "Nothing happens, and yet everything that really matters is happening. . . . What really matters is a state of mind, the interest or the ecstasy with which we close with life." Sinclair soon evolved her own terminology. In 1921 she defined the "analytic" psychological novelist who analyzes the thoughts and emotions of his or her characters. The "synthetic" psychological novelist, on the other hand, refuses to play "God Almighty" and presents those thoughts and emotions directly ("The Future of the Novel," reprinted below). As with the imagist poets, form and substance are one. The labels Sinclair uses here create fewer confusions than does the "stream of consciousness" metaphor, although it, ironically, is the term that has survived.

A prolific professional writer, Sinclair produced work of varying quality. It reflects, however, most of the intellectual, artistic, and social interests of the modern period. At its best, her fiction renders effectively the inner lives of her characters. She is especially sensitive to women who must deal with discrepancies between restrictive social roles and intellectual or creative potential and to artists of both sexes whose experiments perplex and outrage their conventional audiences. Her essays also reveal her critical ability. She could articulate and defend modernist innovations for her contemporaries as well as for her successors.

NOTE

1. See, for example, *Superseded* (1901), *The Helpmate* (1907), *The Judgment of Eve* (1907), *Kitty Tailleur* (1908), and *The Combined Maze* (1913).

WORKS CITED

Boll, T. E. M. *Miss May Sinclair, Novelist: A Biographical and Critical Introduction.* Rutherford, N.J.: Fairleigh Dickinson U P, 1973.

Gillespie, Diane F. "May Sinclair and the Stream of Consciousness: Metaphors and Metaphysics." *English Literature in Transition* 21.2(1978):134–142.

———. " 'The Muddle of the Middle': May Sinclair on Women." *Tulsa Studies in Women's Literature* 4.2(Fall 1985):235–251.

Kaplan, Janet Sydney. *Feminine Consciousness in the Modern British Novel.* Urbana: U of Illinois P, 1975, 47–75.

Kunitz, Stanley, ed. *Authors Today and Yesterday.* New York: H. W. Wilson, 1933, 562–564.

Neff, Rebeccah Kinnamon. "May Sinclair's *Uncanny Stories* as Metaphysical Quest." *English Literature in Transition* 26.3(1983):187–191.

———. " 'New Mysticism' in the Writings of May Sinclair and T. S. Eliot." *Twentieth Century Literature* 26(1979):82–108.

Richardson, Dorothy. "Novels." *Life and Letters* 56(March 1948):188–192.

Robb, K. A. "May Sinclair: An Annotated Bibliography of Writings about Her." *English Literature in Transition* 16.3(1973):177–231.

Sinclair, May. *The Allinghams.* New York: Macmillan; London: Hutchinson, 1927.

———. *Anne Severn and the Fieldings.* London: Hutchinson; New York: Macmillan, 1922.

———. *The Combined Maze.* London: Hutchinson; New York: Harper, 1913.

———. *The Creators: A Comedy.* London: Constable; New York: Century, 1910.

———. *A Defense of Idealism: Some Questions and Conclusions.* London and New York: Macmillan, 1917.

———. *The Divine Fire.* London: Constable; New York: Holt, 1904.

———. *Far End.* New York: Macmillan; London: Hutchinson, 1926.

———. *Feminism.* London: Women Writers Suffrage League, 1912.

———. *The Helpmate.* London: Constable; New York: Holt, 1907.

———. *The Judgment of Eve.* London: Supplement to the Lady's Realm, 1907; New York: Harper, 1908.

———. *Kitty Tailleur.* London: Constable. *The Immortal Moment: The Story of Kitty Tailleur.* New York: Doubleday, 1908.

———. *The Life and Death of Harriett Frean.* 1922. London: Virago, 1980.

———. *Mary Olivier: A Life.* 1919. London: Virago, 1980.

———. *The New Idealism.* London and New York: Macmillan, 1922.

———. "The Novels of Dorothy Richardson." *Egoist* 5(April 1918):57–59. Rpt. *Little Review* 4(April 1918):3–11 and as Introduction to Richardson, *Pointed Roofs,* New York: Knopf, 1919.

———. "The Poems of F. S. Flint." *English Review* 32(January 1921):6–18.

———. "The Poems of 'H. D..' " *Fortnightly Review* 121(March 1927):329–340.

———. " 'Prufrock: And Other Observations': A Criticism." *Little Review* 4.8(December 1917):8–14.

———. *The Rector of Wyck.* London: Hutchinson; New York: Macmillan, 1925.

———. "The Reputation of Ezra Pound." *English Review* 30(April 1920):326–335.

———. "The Return." *Harper's* 142(May 1921):693–703.

———. *The Three Brontes.* London: Hutchinson; New York: Houghton Mifflin, 1912.

———. *The Three Sisters.* 1914. London: Virago, 1982.

———. *The Tree of Heaven.* New York, Macmillan, 1919; London: Cassell, 1917.

———. "Two Notes: I. On H.D. II. On Imagism." *Egoist* 2(1 June 1915):88–89.
———. *Two Sides of a Question: The Cosmopolitan and Superseded.* London: Constable; New York: Taylor, 1901.
Steell, Willis. "May Sinclair Tells Why She Isn't a Poet." *Literary Digest International Book Review* 2(June 1924):513, 559.
Underhill, Evelyn. " 'The Cant of Unconventionality:' A Rejoinder to Lady Robert Cecil." *Living Age* 256(8 Feb. 1908):323–329.
Zegger, Hrisey Dimitrakis. *May Sinclair.* Boston: Twayne, 1976.

The Novels of Dorothy Richardson*

I do not know whether this article is or is not going to be a criticism, for so soon as I begin to think what I shall say I find myself criticizing criticism, wondering what is the matter with it and what, if anything, can be done to make it better, to make it alive. Only a live criticism can deal appropriately with a live art. And it seems to me that the first step towards life is to throw off the philosophic cant of the nineteenth century. I don't mean that there is no philosophy of Art, or that if there has been there is to be no more of it; I mean that it is absurd to go on talking about realism and idealism, or objective and subjective art, as if the philosophies were sticking where they stood in the eighties.

In those days the distinction between idealism and realism, between subjective and objective was important and precise. And so long as the ideas they stand for had importance and precision those words were lamps to the feet and lanterns to the path of the critic. Even after they had begun to lose precision and importance they still served him as useful labels for the bewildering phenomena of the arts.

But now they are beginning to give trouble; they obscure the issues. Mr. J. B. Beresford in his admirable Introduction to *Pointed Roofs* confesses to having felt this trouble. When he read it in manuscript he decided that it "was realism, was objective." When he read it in typescript he thought: "This . . . is the most subjective thing I have ever read." It is evident that when first faced with the startling "newness" of Miss Richardson's method, and her form, the issues did seem a bit obscure to Mr. Beresford. It was as if up to one illuminating moment he had been obliged to think of methods and forms as definitely objective or definitely subjective. His illuminating moment came with the third reading, when *Pointed Roofs* was a printed book. The book itself gave him the clue to his own trouble, which is my trouble, the first hint that criticism up till now has been content to think in *clichés,* missing the new trend of the philosophies of the twentieth century. All that we know of reality at first hand is given to us through contacts in which those interesting distinctions are lost. Reality is thick and

**Pointed Roofs, Backwater, Honeycomb.* Duckworth and Co.

deep, too thick and too deep, and at the same time too fluid to be cut with any convenient carving-knife. The novelist who would be close to reality must confine himself to this knowledge at first hand. He must, as Mr. Beresford says, simply "plunge in." Mr. Beresford says that Miss Richardson is the first novelist who has plunged in. She has plunged so neatly and quietly that even admirers of her performance might remain unaware of what it is precisely that she has done. She has disappeared while they are still waiting for the splash. So that Mr. Beresford's Introduction was needed.

When first I read *Pointed Roofs* and *Backwater* and *Honeycomb* I too thought, like Mr. Beresford, that Miss Richardson has been the first to plunge. But it seems to me rather that she has followed, independently, perhaps unconsciously, a growing tendency to plunge. As far back as the eighties the de Goncourts plunged completely, finally, in *Sœur Philomène, Germinie Lacerteux,* and *Les Frères Zemgann.* Marguerite Audoux plunged in the best passages of *Marie Claire.* The best of every good novelist's best work is a more or less sustained immersion. The more modern the novelist the longer his capacity to stay under. Miss Richardson has not plunged deeper than Mr. James Joyce in his *Portrait of the Artist as a Young Man.*

By imposing very strict limitations on herself she has brought her art, her method, to a high pitch of perfection, so that her form seems to be newer than it perhaps is. She herself is unaware of the perfection of her method. She would probably deny that she has written with any deliberate method at all. She would say : "I only know there are certain things I mustn't do if I was to do what I wanted." Obviously, she must not interfere; she must not analyse or comment or explain. Rather less obviously, she must not tell a story or handle a situation or set a scene; she must avoid drama as she avoids narration. And there are some things she must not be. She must not be the wise, all-knowing author. She must be Miriam Henderson. She must not know or divine anything that Miriam does not know or divine; she must not see anything that Miriam does not see. She has taken Miriam's nature upon her. She is not concerned, in the way that other novelists are concerned with character. Of the persons who move through Miriam's world you know nothing but what Miriam knows. If Miriam is mistaken, well, she and not Miss Richardson is mistaken. Miriam is an acute observer, but she is very far from seeing the whole of these people. They are presented to us in the same vivid but fragmentary way in which they appeared to Miriam, the fragmentary way in which people appear to most of us. Miss Richardson has only imposed on herself the conditions that life imposes on us all. And if you are going to quarrel with those conditions you will not find her novels satisfactory. But your satisfaction is not her concern.

And I find it impossible to reduce to intelligible terms this satisfaction that I feel. To me these three novels show an art and method and form carried to punctilious perfection. Yet I have heard other novelists say that they have no art and no method and no form, and that it is this formlessness that annoys them. They say that they have no beginning and no middle and no end, and that to have form a novel must have an end and a beginning and a middle. We have come to words that in more primitive times would have been blows on this subject. There is a certain plausibility in what they say, but it depends on what constitutes a beginning and a middle and an end. In this series there is no drama, no situation, no set scene. Nothing happens. It is just life going on and on. It is Miriam Henderson's stream of consciousness going on and on. And in neither is there any grossly discernible beginning or middle or end.

In identifying herself with this life, which is Miriam's stream of consciousness, Miss Richardson produces her effect of being the first, of getting closer to reality than any of our novelists who are trying so desperately to get close. No attitude or gesture of her own is allowed to come between her and her effect. Whatever her sources and her raw material, she is concerned and we ought to be concerned solely with the finished result, the work of art. It is to Miriam's almost painfully acute senses that we owe what in any other novelist would be called the "portraits" of Miriam's mother, of her sister Harriet, of the Corries and Joey Banks in *Honeycomb,* of the Miss Pernes and Julia Doyle, and the North London school-girls in *Backwater,* of Fräulein Pfaff and Mademoiselle, of the Martins and Emma Bergmann and Ulrica and "the Australian" in *Pointed Roofs.* The mere "word-painting" is masterly.

> . . . Miriam noticed only the hoarse, hacking laugh of the Australian. Her eyes flew up the table and fixed her as she sat laughing, her chair drawn back, her knees crossed—tea was drawing to an end. The detail of her terrifyingly stylish ruddy-brown frieze dress, with its Norfolk jacket bodice and its shiny leather belt, was hardly distinguishable from the dark background made by the folding doors. But the dreadful outline of her shoulders was visible, the squarish oval of her face shone out—the wide forehead from which the wiry black hair was combed to a high puff, the red eyes, black now, the long, straight nose, the wide, laughing mouth with the enormous teeth.

And so on all round the school tea-table. It looks easy enough to "do" until you try it. There are thirteen figures round that table, and each is drawn with the first few strokes, and so well that you see them all and never afterwards can you mistake or confuse them.

You look at the outer world through Miriam's senses, and it is as if you had never seen it so vividly before. Miriam in *Backwater* is on the top of a bus, driving from North London to Piccadilly:

> On the left a tall grey church was coming towards them, spindling up into the sky. It sailed by, showing Miriam a circle of little stone pillars built into its spire. Plumy trees streamed by, standing large and separate on moss-green grass railed from the roadway. Bright, white-faced houses with pillared porches shone through from behind them and blazed white above them against the blue sky. Wide side streets opened, showing high balconied houses. The side streets were feathered with trees and ended mistily.
>
> Away ahead were edges of clean, bright masonry in profile, soft, tufted heads of trees, bright green in the clear light. At the end of the vista the air was like pure saffron-tinted mother-of-pearl.

Or this "interior" from *Honeycomb:*

> . . . the table like an island under the dome of the low-hanging rose-shaded lamp, the table-centre thickly embroidered with beetles' wings, the little dishes stuck about, sweets, curiously crusted brown almonds, sheeny grey-green olives; the misty beaded glass of the finger-bowls—Venetian glass from that shop in Regent street—the four various wine glasses at each right hand, one on a high thin stem, curved and fluted like a shallow tulip, filled with hock; and floating in the warmth amongst all these things the strange, exciting, dry sweet fragrance coming from the mass of mimosa, a forest of little powdery blossoms, little stiff grey—the arms of railway signals at junctions—Japanese looking leaves—standing as if it were growing, in a shallow bowl under the rose-shaded lamp.

It is as if no other writers had ever used their senses so purely and with so intense a joy in their use.

This intensity is the effect of an extreme concentration on the thing seen or felt. Miss Richardson disdains every stroke that does not tell. Her novels are novels of an extraordinary compression, and of an extenuation more extraordinary still. The moments of Miriam's consciousness pass one by one, or overlapping; moments tense with vibration, moments drawn out fine, almost to snapping-point. On one page Miss Richardson seems to be accounting for every minute of Miriam's time. On another she passes over events that might be considered decisive with the merest slur of reference. She is not concerned with the strict order of events in time. Chapter Three of *Pointed Roofs* opens with an air of extreme decision and importance: "Miriam was practising on the piano in the larger of the two English bedrooms," as if something hung on her practising. But no, nothing hangs on it, and if you want to know on what day she is practising you have to read on and back again. It doesn't matter. It is Miriam's consciousness that is going backwards and forwards in time. The time it goes in is unimportant. On the hundredth page out of three hundred and twelve pages Miriam has been exactly two weeks in Hanover. Nothing has happened but the infinitely little affairs of the school, the practising, the *vorspielen,* the English lesson, the *raccommodage,* the hair-washing. At the end of the book Fräulein Pfaff is on the station platform, gently propelling Miriam "up three steps into a compartment marked *Damen-Coupé.* It smelt of biscuits and wine." Miriam has been no more than six months in Hanover. We are not told and Miriam is not told, but we know, as Miriam knows, that she is going because Pastor Lahmann has shown an interest in Miriam very disturbing to Fräulein Pfaff's interest in him. We are not invited to explore the tortuous mind of the pious, sentimental, secretly hysterical Fräulein; but we know, as Miriam knows, that before she can bring herself to part with her English governess she must persuade herself that it is Miriam and not Mademoiselle who is dismissed because she is an unwholesome influence.

In this small world where nothing happens "that dreadful talk with Gertrude," and Fräulein's quarrel with the servant Anna, the sound of her laugh and her scream, "Ja, Sie Können Ihre paar Groschen haben! Ihre paar Groschen!" and Miriam's vision of Mademoiselle's unwholesomeness, stand out as significant and terrifying; they *are* terrifying, they *are* significant; through them we know Gertrude, we know Fräulein Pfaff, we know Mademoiselle as Miriam knows them, under their disguises.

At the end of the third volume, *Honeycomb,* there is, apparently a break with the design. Something does happen. Something tragic and terrible. We are not told what it is; we known, as Miriam knows, only by inference. Miriam is sleeping in her mother's room.

> Five o'clock. Three more hours before the day began. The other bed was still. "It's going to be a magnificent day," she murmured, pretending to stretch and yawn again. A sigh reached her. The stillness went on and she lay for an hour tense and listening. Some one else must know. . . . At the end of the hour a descending darkness took her suddenly. She woke from it to the sound of violent language, furniture being roughly moved, a swift, angry splashing of water . . . something breaking out, breaking through the confinements of this little furniture-filled room . . . the best gentlest thing she knew openly despairing at last.

Here Miss Richardson "gets" you as she gets you all the time—she never misses once—by her devout adhesion to her method, by the sheer depth of her plunge. For this and this alone is the way things happen. What we used to call the "objective" method is a method of after-thought, of spectacular reflection. What has happened has happened in Miriam's bedroom, if you like; but only by reflection. The first-hand, intimate and intense reality of the happening is in Miriam's mind, and by presenting it thus and not otherwise Miss Richardson seizes reality alive. The intense rapidity of the seizure defies you to distinguish between what is objective and what is subjective either in the reality presented or the art that presents.

Nothing happens. In Miriam Henderson's life there is, apparently, nothing to justify living. Everything she ever wanted was either withheld or taken from her. She is reduced to the barest minimum on which it is possible to support the life of the senses and the emotions at all. And yet Miriam is happy. Her inexhaustible passion for life is fed. Nothing happens, and yet everything that really matters is happening; you are held breathless with the anticipation of its happening. What really matters is a state of mind, the interest or the ecstasy with which we close with life. It can't be explained. To quote Mr. Beresford again: "explanation in this connexion would seem to imply knowledge that only the mystics can faintly realize." But Miss Richardson's is a mysticism apart. It is compatible with, it even encourages such dialogue as this:

> "Tea!" smiled Eve serenely.
> "All right, I'm coming, damn you, aren't I?"
> "Oh, Mimmy!"
> "Well, damn *me,* then. Somebody in the house must swear. I say, Eve!"

> "What?"
> "Nothing, only I *say.*"
> "Um."

It is not wholly destroyed when Miriam eats bread and butter—thus:

> When she began at the hard thick edge there always seemed to be tender places on her guns, her three hollow teeth were uneasy and she had to get through worrying thoughts about them—they would get worse as the years went by, and the little places in the front would grow big and painful and disfiguring. After the first few mouthfuls of solid bread a sort of padding seemed to take place and she could go on forgetful.

This kind of thing annoys Kensington. I do not say that it really matters, but that it is compatible with what really matters. Because of such passages it is a pity that Miss Richardson could not use the original title of her series: "Pilgrimage," for it shows what she is really after. Each book marks a stage in Miriam's pilgrimage. We get the first hint of where she is going to in the opening of the tenth chapter of *Pointed Roofs:* "Into all the gatherings at Waldstrasse the outside world came like a presence. It removed the sense of pressure, of being confronted and challenged. Everything that was said seemed to be incidental to it, like remarks dropped in a low tone between individuals at a great conference." In *Backwater* the author's intention becomes still clearer. In *Honeycomb* it is transparently clear:

> Her room was a great square of happy light . . . happy happy. She gathered up all the sadness she had ever known and flung it from her. All the dark things of the past flashed with a strange beauty as she flung them out. The light had been there all the time; but she had known it only at moments. Now she knew what she wanted. Bright mornings, beautiful bright rooms, a wilderness of beauty all round her all the time—at any cost.

And yet not that:

> Something that was not touched, that sang far away down inside the gloom, that cared nothing for the creditors and could get away down and down into the twilight far away from the everlasting accusations of humanity. . . . Deeper down was something cool and fresh—endless—an endless garden. In happiness it came up and made everything in the world into a garden. Sorrow blotted it out; but it was always there, waiting and looking on. It had looked on in Germany and had loved the music and the words and the happiness of the German girls, and at Banbury Park, giving her no peace until she got away.
>
> And now it had come to the surface and was with her all the time.

There are two essays of Remy de Gourmont in *Promenades Littéraires,* one on "l'Originalité de Maeterlinck," one on "La Leçon de Saint Antoine." Certain passages might have been written concerning the art of Dorothy Richardson.

> Si la vie en soi est un bienfait, et il faut l'accepter comme telle, ou la nier, la fait même de vivre le contient tout entier, et les grands mouvements de la sensibilité, loin de l'enricher, l'appauvrissent au contraire, en concentrant sur quelques partis de nous-mêmes, envahies au hasard par la destinée, l'effort d'attention qui serait plus uniformement reparti sur l'ensemble de notre conscience vitale. De ce point de vue une vie où il semblerait ne rien se passer que d'elementaire et quotidien serait mieux remplie qu'une autre vie riche en apparence d'incidents et d'aventures. . .
> Il y a peut-être un sentiment nouveau a créer, celui de l'amour de la vie pour la vie elle-même, abstraction faite des grandes joies qu'elle ne donne pas à tous, et qu'elle ne donne peut-être à personne. . . Notre paradis, c'est la journée qui passe, la minute qui s'envole, le moment qui n'est déjà plus. Telle est la leçon de Saint Antoine.

Egoist 5 (April 1918):57–59.

"Prufrock: And Other Observations": A Criticism

So far I have seen two and only two reviews of Mr. Eliot's poems: one by Erza Pound in *The Egoist,* one by an anonymous writer in *The New Statesman.* I learn from Mr. Pound's review that there is a third, by Mr. Arthur Waugh, in the *Quarterly.*

To Mr. Ezra Pound Mr. Eliot is a poet with genius as incontestable as the genius of Browning. To the anonymous one he is an insignificant phenomenon that may be appropriately disposed of among the "Shorter Notices." To Mr. Waugh, quoted by Mr. Pound, he is a "drunken Helot." I do not know what Mr. Pound would say to the anonymous one, but I can imagine. Anyhow, to him the *Quarterly* reviewer is "the silly old Waugh." And that is enough for Mr. Pound.

It ought to be enough for me. Of course I know that genius does inevitably provoke these outbursts of silliness. I know that Mr. Waugh is simply keeping up the good old manly traditions of the *Quarterly,* "so savage and tartarly," with its war-cry: " 'Ere's a stranger, let's 'eave 'arf a brick at 'im!" And though the behaviour of *The New Statesman* puzzles me, since it has an editor who sometimes knows better, and really ought to have known better this time, still *The New Statesman* also can plead precedent. But when Mr. Waugh calls Mr. Eliot "a drunken Helot," it is clear that he thinks he is on the track of a tendency and is making a public example of Mr. Eliot. And when the anonymous one with every appearance of deliberation picks out his *"Boston Evening Transcript,"* the one insignificant, the one neglible and trivial thing in a very serious volume, and assures us that it represents Mr. Eliot at his finest and his best, it is equally clear that we have to do with something more than mere journalistic misadventure. And I think it is something more than Mr. Eliot's genius that has terrified *The Quarterly* into exposing him in the full glare of publicity and *The New Statesman* into shoving him and his masterpieces away out of the public sight.

For "The Love-Song of J. Alfred Prufrock", and the "Portrait of a Lady" are masterpieces in the same sense and in the same degree as Browning's "Romances" and "Men and Women"; the "Preludes" and "Rhapsody on a Windy Morning" are masterpieces in a profounder sense and a greater degree than Henley's "London Voluntaries"; "La Figlia Che Piange" is a masterpiece in its own sense and in its own degree. It is a unique masterpiece.

But Mr. Eliot is dangerous. Mr. Eliot is associated with an unpopular movement and with unpopular people. His "Preludes" and his "Rhapsody" appeared in *Blast*. They stood out from the experimental violences of *Blast* with an air of tranquil and triumphant achievement; but, no matter; it was in *Blast* that they appeared. That circumstance alone was disturbing to the comfortable respectability of Mr. Waugh and *The New Statesman*.

And apart from this purely extraneous happening, Mr. Eliot's genius is in itself disturbing. It is elusive; it is difficult; it demands a distinct effort of attention. Comfortable and respectable people could see, in the first moment after dinner, what Mr. Henley and Mr. Robert Louis Stevenson and Mr. Rudyard Kipling would be at; for the genius of these three travelled, comfortably and fairly respectably, along the great high roads. They could even, with a little boosting, follow Francis Thompson's flight in mid-air, partly because it was signalled to them by the sound and shining of his wings, partly because Thompson had hitched himself securely to some well-known starry team. He was in the poetic tradition all right. People knew where they were with him, just as they know now where they are with Mr. Davies and his fields and flowers and birds.

But Mr. Eliot is not in any tradition at all; not even in Browning's and Henley's tradition. His resemblances to Browning and Henley are superficial. His difference is twofold; a difference of method and technique; a difference of sight and aim. He does not see anything between him and reality, and he makes straight for the reality he sees; he cuts all his corners and his curves; and this directness of method is startling and upsetting to comfortable, respectable people accustomed to going superfluously in and out of corners and carefully round curves. Unless you are prepared to follow with the same nimbleness and straightness you will never arrive with Mr. Eliot at his meaning. Therefore the only comfortable thing is to sit down and pretend, either that Mr. Eliot is a "Helot" too drunk to have any meaning, or that his "Boston Evening Transcript" which you do understand is greater than his "Love Song of Prufrock" which you do not understand. In both instances you have successfully obscured the issue.

Again, the comfortable and respectable mind loves conventional beauty, and some of the realities that Mr. Eliot sees are not beautiful. He insists on your seeing very vividly, as he sees them, the streets of his "Preludes" and "Rhapsody." He insists on your smelling them.

> "Regard that woman
> Who hesitates towards you in the light of the door
> Which opens on her like a grin.
> You see the border of her dress
> Is torn and stained with sand,
> And you see the corner of her eye
> Twists like a crooked pin.
>
> Remark the cat which flattens itself in the gutter,
> Slips out its tongue
> And devours a morsel of rancid butter."

He is

> "aware of the damp souls of housemaids
> Sprouting despondently at area gates."

And these things are ugly. The comfortable mind turns away from them in disgust. It identifies Mr. Eliot with a modern tendency; it labels him securely "Stark Realist", so that lovers of "true poetry" may beware.

It is nothing to the comfortable mind that Mr. Eliot is

> ". . . moved by fancies that are curled
> Around these images, and cling:
> The notion of some infinitely gentle
> Infinitely suffering thing."

It is nothing to it that the emotion he disengages from his ugliest image is unbearably poignant. His poignancy is as unpleasant as his ugliness, disturbing to comfort.

We are to observe that Mr. Eliot's "Observations" are ugly and unpleasant and obscure.

Now there is no earthly reason why Mr. Eliot should not be ugly and unpleasant if he pleases, no reason why he should not do in words what Hogarth did in painting, provided he does it well enough. Only, the comfortable mind that prefers So and So and So and So to Mr. Eliot ought to prefer Hogarth's "Paul Before Felix" to his "Harlot's Progress". Obscurity, if he were really obscure, would be another matter. But there was a time when the transparent Tennyson was judged obscure; when people wondered what under heaven the young man was after; they couldn't tell for the life of them whether it was his "dreary gleams" or his "curlews" that were flying over Locksley Hall. Obscurity may come from defective syntax, from a bad style, from confusion of ideas, from involved thinking, from irrelevant association, from sheer piling on of ornament. Mr. Eliot is not obscure in any of these senses.

There is also an obscurity of remote or unusual objects, or of familiar objects moving very rapidly. And Mr. Eliot's trick of cutting his corners and his curves makes him seem obscure where he is clear as daylight. His thoughts move very rapidly and by astounding cuts. They move not by logical stages and majestic roundings of the full literary curve, but as live thoughts move in live brains. Thus "La Figlia Che Piange:"

> "Stand on the highest pavement of the stair—
> Lean on a garden urn—
> Weave, weave the sunlight in your hair—
> Clasp your flowers to you with a pained surprise,
> Fling them to the ground and turn
> With a fugitive resentment in your eyes:
> But weave, weave the sunlight in your hair.
>
> So I would have had him leave,
> So would have had her stand and grieve,
> So he would have left
> As the soul leaves the body torn and bruised,
> As the mind deserts the body it has used.
> I should find
> Some way incomparably light and deft.
> Some way we both should understand,
> Simple and faithless as a smile or a shake of the hand.
>
> She turned away, but with the autumn weather
> Compelled my imagination many days,
> Many days and many hours,
> Her hair over her arms and her arms full of flowers.
> And I wonder how they should have been together!
> I should have lost a gesture and a pose.
> Sometimes these cogitations still amaze
> The troubled midnight and the moon's repose."

I suppose there are minds so comfortable that they would rather not be disturbed by new beauty and by new magic like this. I do not know how much Mr. Eliot's beauty and magic is due to sheer imagination, how much to dexterity of technique, how much to stern and sacred attention to reality; but I do know that without such technique and such attention the finest imagination is futile, and that if Mr. Eliot had written nothing but that one poem he would rank as a poet by right of its perfection.

But Mr. Eliot is not a poet of one poem; and if there is anything more astounding and more assured than his performance it is his promise. He knows what he is after. Reality, stripped naked of all rhetoric, of all ornament, of all confusing and obscuring association, is what he is after. His reality may be a modern street or a modern drawing-room; it may be an ordinary human mind suddenly and fatally aware of what is happening to it; Mr. Eliot is careful to present his street and his drawing-room as they are, and Prufrock's thoughts as they are: live thoughts, kicking, running about and jumping, nervily, in a live brain.

Prufrock, stung by a longing for reality, escapes from respectability into the street and the October fog.

"The yellow fog that rubs its back upon the window-panes,
The yellow smoke that rubs its muzzle on the window panes,
Licked its tongue into the corners of the evening,
Lingered upon the pools that stand in drains,
Let fall upon its back the soot that falls from chimneys,
Slipped by the terrace, made a sudden leap,
And seeing that it was a soft October night,
Curled once about the house and fell asleep."

Profrock has conceived the desperate idea of disturbing the universe. He wonders

"Do I dare
Disturb the universe?
In a minute there is time
For decisions and revisions which a minute will reverse.

For I have known them all already, known them all:
Have known the evenings, mornings, afternoons;
I have measured out my life with coffee spoons;
I know the voices dying with a dying fall
Beneath the music from a farther room.
    So how should I presume?"

Prufrock realises that it is too late. He is middle-aged. The horrible drawing-room life he has entered has got him.

"And the afternoon, the evening, sleeps so peacefully!
Smoothed by long fingers,
Asleep . . . tired . . . or it malingers,
Stretched on the floor, here between you and me.
Should I, after tea and cakes and ices,
Have the strength to force the moment to its crisis?
But though I have wept and fasted, wept and prayed,
Though I have seen my head (grown slightly bald) brought
    in upon a platter,
I am no prophet—and here's no great matter;
I have seen the moment of my greatness flicker,
And I have seen the eternal Footman hold my coat and
    snicker,
And, in short, I was afraid."

His soul can only assert itself in protests and memories. He would have had more chance in the primeval slime.

"I should have been a pair of rugged claws
Scuttling across the floors of silent seas."

As he goes downstairs he is aware of his futility, aware that the noticeable thing about him is the "bald spot in the middle of my hair". He has an idea; an idea that he can put into action:—

> "I shall wear the bottoms of my trousers rolled."

He is incapable, he knows that he is incapable of any action more momentous, more disturbing.

And yet—and yet—

> "I have heard the mermaids singing, each to each.
>
> I have seen them riding seaward on the wave
> Combing the white hair of the waves blown back
> When the wind blows the water white and black.
> We have lingered in the chambers of the sea,
> By sea-girls wreathed with seaweed red and brown
> Till human voices wake us and we drown."

Observe the method. Instead of writing round and round about Prufrock, explaining that his tragedy is the tragedy of submerged passion, Mr. Eliot simply removes the covering from Prufrock's mind: Prufrock's mind, jumping quickly from actuality to memory and back again, like an animal, hunted, tormented, terribly and poignantly alive. The Love-Song of Prufrock is a song that Balzac might have sung if he had been as great a poet as he was a novelist.

It is nothing to the *Quarterly* and to the *New Statesman* that Mr. Eliot should have done this thing. But it is a great deal to the few people who care for poetry and insist that it should concern itself with reality. With ideas, if you like, but ideas that are realities and not abstractions.

Little Review 4.8(December 1917):8–14.

The Poems of "H. D."

I

I am reminded by "H. D.'s" poems of a certain discussion that once started (in the columns of *The Egoist*) as to the importance of what is called Imagism. For the one poet who represents that movement at its perfection is "H. D."

It was in 1915, when Imagism, as a contemporary manifesto, was still young. Mr. Harold Monro, I believe, gave the first provocation when he complained that "the Imagists have not at any time taken the trouble to make themselves clear." This, I think, was because he was then concerned with their theory rather than their practice; but, even as theorists, the Imagists of 1914–15 were fairly hoarse with trying to make themselves clear.

Mr. Monro's main contention seems to be that if Imagism is anything at all it is not a new thing.

I am not sure that I know any better than Mr. Monro what Imagism is. But I am pretty certain which of several old things it is *not*. It is not Symbolism. It has nothing to do with image-making. It abhors Imagery. Imagery is one of the old worn-out decorations the Imagists have scrapped.

The Image is not a substitute; it does not stand for anything but itself. Presentation, not representation, is the watchword of the school. The Image, I take it, is Form. But it is not pure form. It is form *and* substance.

It may be either the form of a thing—you will get Imagist poems which are as near as possible to the naked presentation of a thing, with nothing, not so much as a temperament or a mood between you and it (good examples are Miss Amy Lowell's "The Bath," Mr. Flint's "Swan," and Mr. Richard Aldington's "Tube")—or it may be the form of a passion, an emotion or a mood, as in "H. D.'s" "Oread" and "Mid-Day."

Take "Oread":

Whirl up, sea—
Whirl your pointed pines,
Splash your great pines
On our rocks,
Hurl your green over us,
Cover us with your pools of fir.

And from "Mid-Day":

The shrivelled seeds
Are spilt on the path—
The grass bends with dust,
The grape slips
Under its crackled leaf:
Yet far beyond the spent seed-pods,
And the blackened stalks of mint,
The poplar is bright on the hill,
The poplar spreads out
Deep-rooted among trees.

The point is that the passion, the emotion, or the mood is never given as an abstraction. And in no case is the Image a symbol of reality (the object); it is reality (the object) itself. You cannot distinguish between the thing and its image. You can, I suppose, distinguish between the emotion and its image, but only as you distinguish between substance and its form.

What the Imagists are "out for" is direct, naked contact with reality. You must get closer and closer. Imagery must go. Symbolism must go. There must be nothing between you and your object. For "H. D." the tossing pines are not the symbol of her "Oread" mood. They are the image of her mood. The "shrivelled seeds," the "spent seed-pods," the "blackened stalks of mint" are the image of her drought. But they are not its symbol. The fusion, the identity, is complete.

I am trying to state the Imagist position as far as I understand it. But there are difficulties. Who is to say where the Image ends and Imagery begins? When Dante says he saw the souls of the damned falling like leaves down the banks of Acheron:

> Comme d'autonno si levan le foglie
> L'una appresso dell' altra, infin che'l ramo
> Rende alla terra tutte le sue spoglie,

it is an image, and it is also imagery. It makes no difference whether he says they *are* leaves or merely *like* leaves. The flying leaves are the perfect image of the damned souls. Only the identity is incomplete.

But when Sir John Suckling says his lady's feet peep in and out like small mice when she walks about (or whatever he *did* say) he is only using imagery. The mice are not a perfect image of his lady's feet, only a partial and imperfect image of their appearance.

When Milton sees Satan perched like a cormorant he has got something between imagery and the image.

When Keats sees

> Magic casements opening on the foam
> Of perilous seas in fairylands forlorn,

he is in one sense a perfect Imagist, since his Image *is* the thing he sees. In another he is hardly an Imagist at all. He gets his thrill, not directly through his Images, his casements and his foam and his seas and fairylands, but tortuously and surreptitiously through adjectives which Imagists would die rather than use—not because they would deny that those two lines are supremely beautiful, but because that sort of thing has become mush in the hands of its imitators. A true Image cannot lend itself to mush.

But—it is difficult.

You cannot draw a hard and fast line except perhaps between Keats and Sir John Suckling. It is all a question of closeness, more or less closeness. And Mr. Monro is right. Imagism is not a new thing. But in aiming at closeness, in discarding imagery, in rejecting every image that is not close enough, the Imagists are doing for the first time, consciously and deliberately and always, what the Victorian poets, at any rate, only did once or twice in a blue moon.

The Imagists may abhor my point of view and repudiate this statement of their case. I am not sure that the strict Imagist formula recognises moods. But Imagist practice knows better. Amy Lowell tries for the direct presentation of the Bath. But she cannot get rid of the poet in the bath-tub. Richard Aldington presents his compartment in the Tube railway carriage with the most brutal directness. But the whole point of the presentation is in the last three lines:

> I surprise the same thought
> In the brasslike eyes:
> 'What right have you to live?'

His mood is hostile to the Tube. And in his bitter poem it is the hostility, the mood, that counts. It is the Tube *"à travers un tempérament,"* in spite of the formula. Almost anybody else can do the "brown woodwork pitted with brass nails" and "the flickering background of fluted dingy tunnel" for him.

But if you ask whether it is not always the emotion, the mood, the temperament, and not the Image that counts, the answer to that is that you cannot have the one without the other.

That is why Imagism and Imitation are incompatible. The Imagists have been depreciated as imitators. This because they are following the formula, obeying the rules of the game. But, properly speaking, the Imagist who *is* an Imagist cannot imitate. It is fancy, not imagination, that is concerned with symbols and with imagery. You can analyse its processes. You can also imitate them. But Imagination which alone creates Images is an indivisible act. For each imagination its image is ultimate and unique. No other Imagist's Image will serve its turn. But the novelty of the form makes superficial resemblances striking and obscures the profoundest differences. I know that when I read the first Imagist Anthology I thought "But they're all doing the same thing. For the life of me I can't tell the difference between 'H. D.' and Richard Aldington." Only Ezra Pound stood out as an individual. For the simple reason that I knew his poems by heart already.

Well, they *are* all doing the same thing, but doing it with such a difference that I wonder now at the vastness of the formula that includes Richard Aldington and "H. D.," to say nothing of the others.

I am tired of these charges and countercharges. For all poets, old and new, the poetic act is a sacramental act with its rubric and its ritual. The Victorian poets are Protestant. For them the bread and wine are symbols of reality, the body and the blood. They are given "in remembrance." The sacrament is incomplete. The Imagists are Catholic; they believe in Transubstantiation. For them the bread and wine are the body and the blood. They are given. The thing is done. *Ite, missa est.* The formula may lead to some very ugly ritual, but that is the fault of the Imagist, not of Imagism.

II

Imagism, then, is more than a method, it is a state of soul. To see what may be wrung from it by pure genius, we must turn to the work of "H. D."

I remember winding up my little scrap with Mr. Monro on what now appears an absurd note of caution; thus: "Sometimes I wish that they (the Imagists) would leave off theorising and practise till they are perfect."

Well, well, "H. D." has been doing nothing else. In the face of her achievement the behaviour of some of her critics is instructive. I have little doubt that Mr. Harold Monro, for example, would revise the opinions he expressed in 1915; but even then his attitude was interesting. And as it is typical of much that is still being said, we might do worse than look at it again.

It is always interesting to watch a man on a sharp fence trying to preserve a sane and dignified equilibrium. Mr. Monro excites sympathy. He is so sincerely anxious to appear balanced before he slithers irrevocably down into the field where the Imagists are not; so innocently eager to be supported in his attitude by Ben Jonson, Dryden, Addison, Burke, Samuel Johnson, Coleridge, Wordsworth, and "even Matthew Arnold." He must trot them all out before he can make up his mind to praise the poetry of "H. D."; poetry that for sheer emotion, for clean-cut and perfect beauty, stands by itself in its own school.

It is as if he asked himself, "Now I wonder what Samuel Johnson would have said to 'H. D.'s' 'Oread'?" He is just going to be passably polite about it when he pulls himself up—"Yet I remember that sentence of Lowell's: 'Imagination,' et cetera." You see, he thinks that Lowell would say "H. D." hadn't got any.

He quotes "Oread":

Whirl up, sea—
Whirl your pointed pines,
Splash your great pines
On our rocks,
Hurl your green over us,
Cover us with your pools of fir.

"That," says Mr. Monro, "is all. It can be said in one minute before lunch."

And he finds fault with "H. D.," not because she gives him images, but because she has only given him "*one* image."

Has he never been on a hill, in or under a pine-wood, when it is tossed about by the wind? Doesn't he see that in this one image there are many things—colour, movement, sound and energy, the whole appearance and the passion of the pine-wood and the wind, that there are at least three passions and three agonists, the pine-wood, the wind, and the "Oread" who desires to be covered with the pine-waves, to be splashed, to play with the tumult of the pine-wood and the wind?

The miracle is that "H. D." has got it all into six lines, into twenty-six words. And Mr. Monro, instead of thanking his gods for the miracle, counts the number of lines and the number of words and says there aren't enough of them: "It is petty poetry; it is minutely small; it seems intended to be. Such images should appear by the dozen in poetry. Such reticence denotes either poverty of imagination or needlessly excessive restraint." He admits that "H. D." is "the truest Imagist of the group, but its future work will scarcely develop along the lines of her example. Her poems have a slight flavour of brine; they are fragile as sea-shells. If I came too near them I should be afraid of crushing them into the sand with my clumsy feet."

His fear is groundless. They are quite unbreakable. And it is precisely "along the lines of her example" that Imagism *has* developed.

Mr. Monro seems to doubt whether "H. D." has enough imagination to sustain her through a longer poem than "Oread." Well, there was, even then, "Hermes of the Ways," which is longer by a score of lines.

Mr. Flint has said: "The poetry of 'H. D.' has been described as a kind of 'accurate mystery.' . . . . The more you attempt to reason about it the less will you get out of it. It must work on you as an evocation."

We shall get no nearer to her secret than that. "Accurate mystery." It is in her earliest poems; it is in her latest. Always her scene (I quote Mr. Flint again) "is one that you can place in no country. The thing seems to have happened in eternity."

Take (from the collection of 1914) the well-known "Hermes of the Ways":

The hard sand breaks
and the grains of it
are clear as wine.
Far over the leagues of it,
the wind,
playing on the wide shore,
piles little ridges,
and the great waves
break over it.

But more than the many-foamed ways
of the sea,
I know him
of the triple path-ways,
Hermes,
who awaits.

Dubious,
facing three ways,
welcoming wayfarers,
he whom the sea-orchard
shelters from the west,
from the east
weathers sea-wind;
fronts the great dunes.

Wind rushes
over the dunes,
and the coarse salt-crusted grass
answers.

Heu,
it whips round my ankles!

Small is
this white stream,
flowing below ground,
from the poplar-shaded hill,
but the water is sweet.

(Note the thin minor sound of the vowels, and then the closing return to the major.)

. . .
. . .
. . .

Hermes, Hermes,
the great sea foamed,
gnashed its teeth about me;
but you have waited
where sea-grass tangles with
shore-grass.

I can add nothing to Mr. Flint's praise of this poem. I can only say that if "H. D." had never written anything else this would be enough to place her among the small, the very small, number of poets who have once in their lives achieved perfection. If you are sworn to admire nothing but Swinburne, or Rossetti, or Mrs. Browning, or Robert Browning and their imitators for ever and ever, you may reject the "Hermes" because there is no "passion" in it.

But why, in Heaven's name, should there be passion in it? Haven't we had enough of passion and of the sentiment that passed for passion all through the nineteenth century? We can't hope to escape the inevitable reaction. And isn't it almost time to remind ourselves that there is a beauty of restraint and stillness and flawless clarity? The special miracle of those Victorian poets was that they contrived to drag their passion through the conventional machinery of their verse, and the heavy decorations that they hung on it.

I do not know how anybody who does not feel the beauty of "H. D.'s" poem is to be shown it. I do not know by what test you can tell whether any verse is poetry or not. I think it is a question of magic. And if you cannot feel in these verses the sense of enchantment, of grave things not known and about to be, the *frisson* of immortality impending, then (I am afraid) you are past praying for.

To me "H. D." remains the most significant of the Imagists, the one for whom Imagism has most triumphantly come off. It is not necessary for poetry to prove anything; but, even to my ignorance, and I first approached the Imagists with a profound ignorance, she has demonstrated the power of the clean, naked, sensuous image to carry the emotion with rhyme—*not* without rhythm; the best imagist poems have a very subtle and beautiful rhythm—and always without decoration.

"H. D.'s" poems do not lend themselves to convenient classification as Poems of Passion and Emotion, Poems of Reflection, Poems of the Imagination, and Poems Descriptive, and so on. In all of them passion, emotion, reflection and the image, the sharp, vivid image that does the work of description, are fused together in the burning unity of beauty. One or more element (it is hardly ever reflection) may predominate, but it is never alone. You may call "The Tribute," "Pygmalion," "Eurydice," "The Cities," "The Look-Out," "The Cliff Temple" poems of reflection if you like. They are few, and in none of them is the concept thinned away to an abstraction. "H. D." invariably presents her subtlest, most metaphysical idea under some living, sensuous image solid enough to carry the emotion. The air we are given to breathe may be rarefied to the last degree, yet we are moving always in a world of clear colours and clear forms. Like every devout Imagist she is intolerant of thinness. Look where you will you find everywhere the same joy in vigorous movement, the same adoration of divine visible beauty. Beauty of the young athlete in "The Contest":

> The ridge of your breast is taut,
> and under each the shadow is sharp,
> and between the clenched muscles
> of your slender hips.
>
> From the circle of your cropped hair
> there is light,
> and about your male torse
> and the foot-arch and the straight ankle.
>
> . . . . .
>
> . . . . .
>
> The narcissus has copied the arch
> of your slight breast:
> your feet are citron flowers,
> your knees, cut from white ash,
> your thighs are rock-cistus.

Beauty of flowers from "Sea-Gods":

> But we bring violets,
> great masses—single, sweet,
> wood-violets, stream violets,
> violets from a wet marsh.
>
> Violets in clumps from hills,
> tufts with earth at the roots,
> violets tugged from rocks,
> blue violets, moss, cliff, river-violets
>
> Yellow violets' gold,
> burnt with a rare tint—

violets like red ash
among tufts of grass.

We bring
deep-purple, bird-foot violets.

We bring the hyacinth violet,
sweet, bare, chill to the touch—
and violets whiter than the inrush
of your own white surf.

Beauty of Evening:

The light passes
from ridge to ridge
from flower to flower—
the hepaticas, wide-spread
under the light
grow faint—
the petals reach inward,
the blue tips bend
toward the bluer heart
and the flowers are lost.

The cornel muds are still white,
but shadows dart
from the cornel-roots—
black creeps from root to root,
each leaf
cuts another leaf on the grass,
shadow seeks shadow,
then both leaf
and leaf shadows are lost.

Could rhyme do more for this verse than is done, in the one poem by the sheer musical reiteration of one sound, by the sheer visible reiteration of one thing: or in the other poem by the recurrence of the one word "lost" at the close of each strophe?

"H. D." has been reproached for her obscurity. She is certainly not afraid of the dark when darkness serves her purpose, where it is the essence of her subject or her mood. We must distinguish here between obscurity of thought and obscurity of feeling. Whereas unclarified thought means shallow thinking, emotion at a certain depth *is* obscure. It is only in her maturer work, if anywhere, that we find this quality. Her earlier poems have all the finite Greek perfection. Nothing can be added to or taken away from them. Every stroke is laid on with a hand that never hovers, never hesitates. Now, when a writer achieves formal perfection he is in danger either of standing still, repeating his finest effects till he becomes his own irreproachable plagiarist, or of going back and back in a horrible decline. The test of an enduring talent is its power to survive this moment. Technical perfection exists at the mercy of the unfolding spirit. At any minute a flash of metaphysical vision can destroy it.

"H. D." has escaped this disaster.

After the lucid, sharp simplicity of "Sea Roses," "Sitalkas," and "Hermes of the Ways," we have the comparative intricacy of "The Tribute," the comparative obscurity of "Egypt," the largeness and mystery of "Demeter." The first-named are poems of transition, and they may well have these transitional defects. Nothing easier than to insist on such blemishes; and nothing more unprofitable, since they are of the kind the casual reader may be trusted to discover for himself. When they begin to appear in the work of a poet distinguished for the opposite qualities, the plain business of the critic is to search for the causes of the change, and decide whether it signals the break-up of a talent or some process of new birth.

Now, not one of "H. D.'s" earlier poems shows any tendency to vagueness and obscurity. She has been, from the first, the perfect imagist. And if the critic will go further and actually take the trouble to find out what she is trying to express in these later forms, the obscurity he complains of will vanish. He will see that, at the worst, under the stress of a profounder vision, she is trying to put into the image more than it can well convey.

But for the most part her medium, plastic and utterly obedient, adapts itself. There is nothing tentative and experimental about these last poems. They may stand for the final, accomplished expression of "H. D." Comparing them with her earlier work, even admitting that they have lost something of its sharp simplicity, one sees that she has gained immeasurably in depth and range.

Talents have died before now of their own growth for lack of a form that allows expansion. I don't want to raise again the question whether good verse is, as Mr. Flint and Wordsworth maintain, nothing but good prose. Only whereas with the writer of good prose, however uninspired, language and meaning go evenly together, the purely lyric poet who rhymes and metres is apt to be overtaken by a dark rush of winged words before he is aware of his meaning. For he is at the mercy of rhyme and metre. Not so the *vers librist*. He is free to follow his thoughts in their own movement. Instead of twisting themselves in unnatural inversions or halting for the cadence and the rhyme, his thoughts are free. Before the dangerous inspiration is upon her, "H. D." has clarified her thought to its last transparency, and her future work should stand as high or higher than her past.

The period between her earlier and her later poems is fairly represented by "The Gift," "The Shrine," "Loss," "The Cliff Temple," and "Sea-Gods" (published in 1916 in "Sea-Garden"). Also "The Tribute," "Eurydice," and "The Look-Out."

"Eurydice" is the challenge of the self-delivered, defiant soul sent up out of hell to Orpheus, the arrogant and ruthless, the white, would-be delivered—her challenge to death and hell.

. . . .
. . . .
. . . .

Fringe upon fringe
of blue crocuses,
crocuses, walled against blue of themselves,
blue of that upper earth,
blue of the depth upon depth of flowers—
lost!

Flowers—
if I could have taken once my breath of them,
enough of them—
more than earth,
even than the upper earth
had passed with me
beneath the earth.

. . . .
. . . .

At least I have the flowers to myself
and my thoughts—no god
can take that:
I have the fervour of myself for a presence
and my own spirit for light.

And my spirit with its loss
knows this:
though small against the black,
small against the formless rocks,
hell must break before I am lost.

Before I am lost,
Hell must open like a red rose
for the dead to pass.

If ever we thought of "H. D." as cultivating, exquisitely, a narrow plot, tied by her imagism, with these and her latest poems before us, we can have no misgiving as to her range. There is the pure imagism of "Evening" and the flower passage out of "Sea-Gods," which I have already given. And the elegiac pathos of "Loss." There are no tears in it; no subjective grief; but an agony of physical contemplation:

I am glad the tide swept you out,
O beloved,
you of all this ghastly host
alone untouched,
your white flesh covered with salt
as with myrrh and burnt iris.

. . . .
. . . .
. . . .
I have seen beautiful feet
but never beauty welded with strength.
I marvelled at your height.

You stood almost level
with the lance bearers,
and so slight.
And I wondered as you clasped
your shoulder strap
at the strength of your wrist
and the turn of your young fingers,
and the lift of your shorn locks,
and the bronze
of your sun-burnt neck.

. . . .
. . . .
I wonder if you knew how I watched,
how I crowded before the spearsmen—
but the gods wanted you,
the gods wanted you back.

There is the metaphysical passion of "The Cliff Temple," persistent, harsh with frustration. It is not presented as metaphysical, but as something sensuous, craving for a god in the flesh, a baffling, secret god, almost evil, cruel in his remorseless flight:

. . . .
. . . .
I said:
for ever and for ever, must I follow you
through the stones?
I catch at you—you lurch:
You are quicker than my hand-grasp.
I wondered at you.
I shouted—dear—mysterious—beautiful—
white myrtle—flesh.
. . . .
. . . .
. . . .
Shall I hurl myself from here,
Shall I leap and be nearer you?
Shall I drop, beloved, beloved,
ankle against ankle?
Would you pity me, O white breast?
. . . .
. . . .

"The Tribute" is "H. D.'s" sole contribution to the mass of War-Poems—tribute to the men who fought and the men who, for admirable reasons, refused to fight:

> And this we will say for remembrance,
> speak this with their names:
> Could beauty be done to death
> they had struck her dead
> in ages and ages past,
> could beauty be withered from earth,
> they had cast her forth,
> root and stalk
> scattered and flailed.
> . . . .;
> Could beauty be caught and hurt
> could beauty be rent with a thought,
> for a thrust of a sword
> for a piece of their money tossed up
> then beauty were dead
> long, long before we came to earth,
> long, long before we rent our hearts
> with this worship, this fear
> and this dread.

The *vers librists* have revived the trick of beautiful assonance as a substitute for rhyming. Observe its effect here. Is it not more satisfying than the tight, clipping, recurrent rhyme? It is a hint, a dawn of rhyme that hangs back, letting the rhythm pass on till the one closing rhyme clinches all.

This poem is marred by a certain diffuseness and a *tic* of ineffective repetition.

But there is her later volume, "Hymen."

I do not know which of these poems *The Times* critic was thinking of when in 1921 he "experienced a difficulty in extracting any meaning from many of them." He names but two: "Egypt" and "Not Honey." I do not see that they justify his complaint; but I confess that at a first hasty reading I found certain passages in "Demeter" obscure.

What puzzled me was Demeter's references to "her":

> She is slender of waist
> slight of breast, made of many fashions;
> they have set *her* small feet
> on many a plinth;
> she they have known,
> she they have spoken with
> she they have smiled upon,
> she they have caught
> and flattered with praise and gifts.

You will observe the obscurity was mine. It is clear as daylight that this is Aphrodite, and that Demeter, the Earth Goddess, is proclaiming herself older, more august and mysterious than the graceful Olympians:

Sleep on the stones of Delphi—
dare the ledges of Pallas
but keep me foremost,
keep me before you, after you, with you,
never forget when you start
for the Delphic precipice,
never forget when you seek Pallas
and meet in thought
yourself drawn out from yourself
like the holy serpent,
never forget
in thought or in mystic trance
I am greatest and least.

The baffling, cryptic touch is deliberate, a device for evoking magic, for suggesting the unspeakable mysteries.

This fine poem just misses perfection owing to the abruptness and comparative insignificance of its close.

But in the others there is nowhere any falling-off. I find it hard to choose among so many perfect things. For one you take you might have taken almost any other. I cannot pass over the vigorous "Sea-Heroes" with its sea-sound and sea-swell:

Crash on crash of the sea
straining to wreck men, sea-boards, continents,
raging against the world, furious,

with its tremendous, resonant chanting of Greek names:

Akroneos, Oknolos, Elatreus,
helm of boat, loosener of helm, dweller by sea,
Nauteus, sea-man. . . . . . .

And there is the slender song rhyming on one note, "The Whole White World." There are "Simaetha" and "Phaedra" and "She Rebukes Hippolyta." There is this:

At Baia.

I should have thought
in a dream, you would have brought
some lovely perilous thing,
orchids piled in a great sheath,
as who should say (in a dream)

I send you this
who left the blue veins
of your throat unkissed.
Why was it that your hands
(that never took mine)
your hands that I could see
drift over the orchids' heads
so carefully,
your hands, so fragile, sure to lift
so gently, the fragile flowerstuff—
ah, ah, how was it?

You never sent (in a dream)
the very form, the very scent,
not heavy, not sensuous,
but perilous—perilous—
of orchids, piled in a great sheath,
and folded underneath in a bright scroll
some word.

Flower sent to flower;
for white hands, the lesser white,
less lovely, of flower leaf.

Lover to lover, no kiss,
no touch, but forever and ever this.

These are the poems that the critic of *The Times* found meaningless, "deadening and monotonous," indistinguishable from "prose sentences capriciously cut into strips."

Only a slight effort of attention is needed to get at the magic and the significance of such poems as I have quoted.

The creator of strange new beauty has a right to demand so much from anybody who undertakes to pronounce judgment. Is it too much to ask? I don't imagine, for example, that my own flair for strange new beauty is special and extraordinary, a thing that could not be cultivated by any lover of old familiar beauty who honestly desires to cultivate it. For beauty is ageless, eternal and one, recognisable under all differences of form. Therefore it is inconceivable that any devout lover of it should miss the divine quality of "H. D.'s" poetry. There is certainly nothing in contemporary literature that surpasses these later poems, at first sight so splendidly dim, at last so radiant, so crystalline. An austere ecstasy is in them. They have the quick beat of birds' wings, the rise and fall of big waves, the slow, magical movement of figures in some festival of Demeter or Dionysos carrying the *sacra*.

As for her detractors—"Could beauty be done to death" they would have killed her long ago, when first she appeared among the Imagists.

Fortnightly Review 121 (March 1927):329–340.

The Reputation of Ezra Pound

If the views of some of our more conservative reviewers were immortal, posterity would have an odd idea of Ezra Pound. It would know him, if it were allowed to know him at all, as a literary mountebank; a masquerader looking for something to wear, ransacking the wardrobes of every century but his own; an impudent schoolboy letting off squibs in his back garden.

But what, after all, has Mr. Pound really done? It is true that he has let off squibs, lots of squibs, and some of them have hit one or two respectable persons in the eye. Mr. Pound is not a respecter of respectable persons. He has displayed a certain literary frightfulness in the manner of Laurent Tailhado. He has shown an arrogant indifference to many admired masterpieces of his day. And he has associated himself with unpopular movements. His appearance in *Blast* blasted him in the eyes of respectable persons not hitherto hostile to his manifestations. People become unpopular through association with him. In the interval between the disappearance of *Blast* and the re-emergence of *The Little Review* he published some negligible trifles, which were held up as representative of a trivial talent. Worse still, when various people were forming little groups and creating little organs of their own, Ezra Pound had the temerity to form a group and create an organ more or less his own.

If *The Little Review* had never printed anything but what came to it through its foreign editor it might by this time have ranked as an important international concern; unfortunately, it printed many things for which Mr. Pound was not responsible, and when it trespassed its iniquities were laid on him. Besides he gave opportunities. His critical manner was deceptive. When *The Little Review* announced its Henry James number with an article by Ezra Pound, some of us had visions of an irresponsible and agile animal shinning up a monument to hang by his feet from the top.

What actually happened?

I do not know any book yet written on Henry James of more solid value than Mr. Pound's "Brief Note" in *The Little Review.*

> "I am tired of hearing pettiness talked about Henry James's style. The subject has been discussed enough in all conscience, along with the minor James. What I have not heard is any word of the major James, of the hater of tyranny, book after early book against oppression, against all the sordid petty personal crushing oppression, the domination of modern life, not worked out in the diagrams of Greek tragedy, not labelled 'Epos' or 'Æschylus.' The outbursts in 'The Tragic Muse,' the whole of 'The Turn of the Screw,' human liberty, personal liberty, the rights of the individual against all sorts of intangible bondage. The passion of it, the continual passion of it in this man who, fools said, didn't 'feel.' I have never found a man of emotion against whom idiots didn't raise this cry. . . ."

Is not that admirable? Is it not the essential serious truth of his subject? For the sake of it one can forgive Mr. Pound his minor perversities: for example, his dismissal of the beautiful "Spoils of Poynton" as "all that damned fuss about furniture."

And in relation to his actual *confrères,* what has happened? No contemporary critic has done more than Ezra Pound for the work of Gaudier Brzeska, of Mr. James Joyce, of Mr. Wyndham Lewis, of Mr. T. S. Eliot, to admit only four of the names associated with him. For the last seven years he has been more concerned to obtain recognition for other people than to capture any sort of hearing for himself. In this he has shown an absolutely incorruptible devotion to his craft. He may have been guilty of a few blunders, a few indiscretions and impertinences, but he has rendered services to modern international art that in any society less feral than our own would have earned him the gratitude of his contemporaries.

They have not even earned him moderate protection against prejudice.

It has been said of this poet—almost, if not quite the most original, the most individual poet of the century—that he has no originality, no hot, inspired genius, only talent, only an uncanny and prodigious dexterity; that his sources are purely and coldly literary; that he speaks behind a mask, and without his mask he is nothing.

Well, Mr. Pound never denied his sources, and the author of "Personæ" would hardly disclaim his mask. There never was a poet more susceptible to influence, more sensitive to cadences, to the subtle flavours and flying gestures of words; never one who has so absorbed into his system three diverse literatures: of the langue d'Oc, of old China, of Augustan Rome. With a snatch at the Anglo-Saxon, at Sappho, at the Greek epigrammatists. But there is one literature that he rejects, that by no possibility could he assimilate: the literature of the Edwardian and Georgian eras.

As it happened, Mr. Pound's first poems, in "Personæ" and "Exultations," were so amazingly original, so violently individual, that nothing but violent individuality was expected of him. He wrote "La Fraisne."

> "By the still pool of Mar-nan-otha
> Have I found me a bride
> That was a dog-wood tree some syne,
> She hath called me from mine old ways,
> She hath hushed my rancour of council,
> Bidding me praise
>
> Nought but the wind that flutters in the leaves."

He wrote the beautiful "Praise of Ysolt."

> "Lo, I am worn with travail
> And the wandering of many roads hath made my eyes
> As dark red circles filled with dust.
> Yet there is a trembling upon me in the twilight,
> And little red elf words crying 'A song,'
> Little grey elf words crying, 'A song,'

> Little brown leaf words crying, 'A song,'
> Little green leaf words crying, 'A song,'
> The words are as leaves, old brown leaves in the spring-time,
> Blowing they know not whither, seeking a song."

He wrote the "Ballad of the Goodly Fere."

> "A master of men was the Goodly Fere,
> A man of the wind and sea,
> If they think they have slain our Goodly Fere
> They are fools eternally,
>
> I ha' seen him eat of the honey-comb
> Sin' they nailed him to the tree."

Here was a voice that had not been heard before. Here was a strange, foreign beauty. They made Mr. Pound's reputation.

Then followed the "Canzoni." In spite of "The Yearly Slain" and "The Vision," the "Canzoni." were a set-back to extravagant expectations. The elaborate form, the artificial sweetness, the dexterous technique, the sheer convention of the thing, were felt to be incompatible with unfettered, unpremeditative genius. Instead of warbling native wood-notes wild, Mr. Pound was thinking of his metric. Obviously, Mr. Pound was not a warbler.

There followed the "Sonnets and Ballate of Guido Cavalcanti" to suggest that Mr. Pound was a translator (not too accurate) rather than a poet. And to complete the disillusion people remembered that even in "Exultations" the influence of Mr. W. B. Yeats was discernible in at least four lines.

> "But if one should look at me with the old hunger in her eyes
> How will I be answering her eyes?"
>
> "And it's a deep hunger I have when I see them a-gliding
> And a-flickering there where the trees stand apart."

There followed "Ripostes." "Ripostes" with the grave, uncanny beauty of "The Tomb at Akr Çaar"; the poignant, almost unbearable passion of "The Return"; the magic of "Apparuit."

> "Green the ways, the breath of the fields is thine there,
> open lies the land, yet the steely going
> darkly hast thou dared and the dreaded æther
> parted before thee.
>
> . . . .
>
> "Clothed in goldish weft, delicately perfect,
> gone as wind! The cloth of the magical hands!
> Thou a slight thing, thou in access of cunning
> daredst to assume this?"

Undoubtedly "Ripostes" contains some of his very finest work. It also includes some *opusculi* not so fine which have been remembered against him. Then came his somewhat invidious connection with *Poetry* and his appearance in *Blast*. Mr. Pound there made himself sponsor for Vorticism, and from that day to this alternate fury and indifference have been his portion. Or if any favour comes his way it wears the cold air of controversy and reservation. And, with one exception, every serious and self-respecting magazine is closed to this most serious and self-respecting artist.

He has not been at any pains to open them. It would have been easy enough. He had only to leave Vorticism and every other "ism" alone: It would have been far the more profitable course. With his uncanny capacity for saturating himself with various styles, his genius for impersonation, he could, if he had chosen, have become one of the most popular poets of his day; he had only to stand on the alert, to snare the familiar sentimental lilt, the familiar charm, the odour and cadence and the sensual thrill; only to follow the strong trail of the bloody realist—you can imagine the exquisite dexterity with which he would have sustained the *rôle*—only to write war-songs, to catch the note—he could so easily have caught it—of delicate yearning, or of stark, frightful, abominable truth. Why not? It would have paid him a hundred times over in cash and credit, and he would never have been found out, or not till he was too old and cynical to care.

It is, to say the least, surprising that in the years that saw the publications of "Lustra" and "Cathay" one should have heard it said that Ezra Pound was "finished," so clear it seems that he was only just beginning, only just discovering the medium, plastic, yet capable of the hardness of crystal or of bronze, that was to serve him henceforth. You perceive that between "Lustra" and "Cathay" something has happened to him.

That something was his discovery through Ernest Fenollosa of the old literatures of China and Japan.

(Here again his paraphrases from Fenollosa's translation of the "Noh" plays would have made a noble reputation for any man less dogged by invidious misfortune.)

Of all the influences that he has come under, that of the Chinese poets has been the most beneficent. It has made for clearness, for vividness and precision, for concentration, for the more and more perfect realisation of his ideal, the finding of his ultimate self.

> "Go, my songs, seek your praise from the young and from the intolerant,
> Move among the lovers of perfection alone,
> Seek ever to stand in the hard Sophoclean light
> And take your wounds from it gladly."

Barring one or two poems in "Ripostes" there is nothing in his earlier work to compare with his translations—or are they paraphrases?—of Bunno and Mei-Sheng and Rihaku; of Kakuhaku. Rosoriu and T'ao Yuan Ming.

Take this: Rihaku's "Lament of the Frontier Guard."

> "By the North Gate, the wind blows full of sand,
> Lonely from the beginning of time until now!
> Trees fall, the grass grows yellow with autumn.
> I climb the towers and towers to watch out the barbarous land:
> Desolate castle, the sky, the wide desert.
> There is no wall left to this village.
> Bones white with a thousand frosts,
> High heaps covered with trees and grass;
> Who has brought this to pass?
> Who has brought the flaming imperial anger?
> Who has brought the army with drums and, with kettle-drums?
> Barbarous Kings.
> A gracious spring, turned to blood-ravenous autumn,
> A turmoil of wars—men spread over the middle kingdom,
> Three hundred and sixty thousand,
> And sorrow, sorrow like rain.
> Soroow to go, and sorrow, sorrow returning.
> Desolate, desolate fields,
> And no children of warfare upon them,
>   No longer the men for offence and defence.
> Ah, how shall you know the dreary sorrow at the North Gate,
> With Rihaku's name forgotten,
> And we guardsmen fed to the tigers."

Observe the certainty with which Mr. Pound gets his effect, by the placing of a copula,

> "And sorrow, sorrow like rain";

by the cadence of his repetitions,

> "Sorrow to go, and sorrow, sorrow returning";

by sheer plain statement,

> "There is no wall left to this village."

Observe the firm perfection of his own "Liu Ch'e," written, as if in anticipation, before Fenollosa's work came into his hands.

> "The rustling of the silk is discontinued,
> Dust drifts over the courtyard,
> There is no sound of foot-fall, and the leaves
> Scurry into heaps and lie still,
> And she, the rejoicer of the heart, is beneath them.
>
> A wet leaf that clings to the threshold."

Or his "Fan-Piece for Her Imperial Lord." It is but three lines.

"O fan of white silk,
Clear as frost on the grass blade,
You also are laid aside."

After "Cathay," *Quia Pauper Amavi* with his Three Cantos:

"Hang it all, there can be but the one Sordello,
But say I want to, say I take your whole bag of tricks,
Let in your quirks and tweeks and say the thing's an art form. . . ."

Imitating Browning now? Perhaps; but, feature for feature, the new mask fits. Ezra Pound was never more himself than in this "art-form." You can see him chuckling as the idea dawned on him. "At last I can do what I 'want to'!" The form gives scope to his worst qualities and his best; his obscurity, his inconsequence, his caprice; his directness, his ease in the attack, his quickness, the shining, darkening turn and return as of a bird in the air or a fish in water; the baffling play of a spirit flying between darkness and light; the resurgence of abrupt, surprising beauty:

". . . here the sunlight
Glints on the shaken waters, and the rain
Comes forth with delicate tread, walking from Isola Garda.
Lo Soleils plovil,
It is the sun rains, and a spatter of fire
Darts from the 'Lydian' ripples, *lacus undae,*
And the place is full of spirits" . . .

Mr. Pound has poured into his Cantos the contents of what he calls his "phantastikon." Anything may happen in this art-form. There are as yet but three Cantos published: there may be three hundred before Mr. Pound has done, and no reason beyond the reader's convenience why the endless rhapsody should be divided into Cantos at all. The third proceeds, with no intelligible transition, from

"John Heyden,
Worker of miracles, dealer in levitation,"

to a chunk of the *Odyssey,* translated so *incomparably* well that one wishes Mr. Pound would finish what he has begun.

You may pass over the *Mœurs Contemporaines.* The thing has been done better by Jules Laforgue and Laurent Tailhade. You might even pass the *Langue d'Oc,* but that it has something that the earlier translations lacked: a rough hardness, a twist, a sharp tang overlying the artificial sweetness. The translator has escaped from the first enchantment of this literature. He is at pains to show up its essential artifice. By every possible device—the use of strange words like "gentrice" and "plasmatour"—he throws it seven centuries back in time. It is to sound as different from modern speech as he can make it, because it belongs to a world that by the very nature of its conventions is inconceivably remote, inconceivably different from our own, a world that we can no longer reconstruct in its reality.

By this device, this thickening of the veil that hangs between us and the dead world of the Langue d'Oc, Mr. Pound sets in relief the reality, the modernity of his Propertius. It is as if he said, "There is the echoed falsetto of a voice that never rang quite true; here—a thousand years before it—is the voice of a live man, a man you might meet in Piccadilly to-day." There is no essential difference between Rome in the Augustan and London in the Georgian age.

> "Annalists will continue to record Roman reputations,
> Celebrities from the Trans-Caucasus will belaud Roman celebrities
> And expound the distentions of Empire,
> But for something to read in normal circumstance?
> For a few pages brought down from the forked hill unsullied?
>   I ask a wreath which will not crush my head.
>   And there is no hurry about it;
> I shall have, doubtless, a boom after my funeral" . . .

Mr. Pound gives light English for the light Latin. Propertius's Roman irony rings fresh and English, a modern irony that mocks at everything, at love and death:

> "Midnight and a letter comes to me from our mistress:
>   Telling me to come to Tibur, 'At once!'
> Bright tips reach up from twin towers,
>   Anienan spring water falls into flat-spread pools.
>
> "What is to be done about it?
>   Shall I entrust myself to tangled shadows
> Where bold hands may do violence to my person?
>
> . . . . . .
>
> "Yet if I postpone my obedience
>   because of this respectable terror
> I shall be prey to lamentations worse than a nocturnal assailant.
>
> "And I shall be in the wrong,
>   and it will last a twelvemonth,
> For her hands have no kindness me-wards. . . .
>
> "Nor is there anyone to whom lovers are not . . .
>   sacred at midnight
> And in the Via Sciro.
>
> . . . .
>
> "What if undertakers follow my track?
>   such a death is worth dying.

She would bring frankincense and wreaths to my tomb,
She would sit like an ornament on my pyre."

Again:

"When, when and whenever death closes our eyelids,

Moving naked upon Acheron,
Upon the one raft, victor and conquered together,
Marius and Jugurtha together,
one tangle of shadows.
Cæsar plots against India,
Tigris and Euphrates shall, from now on, flow
at his bidding,
Tibet shall be full of Roman policemen,
The Parthians shall get used to our statuary
and acquire a Roman religion;

"One raft on the veiled flood of Acheron,
Marius and Jugurtha together.
Nor at my funeral either will there be any long trail,
bearing ancestral lares and images;
No trumpets filled with my emptiness,
Nor shall it be on an Atalic bed;
the perfumed cloths shall be absent.
A small plebeian procession,
Enough, enough and in plenty
There will be three books at my obsequies
Which I take, my not unworthy gift, to Persephone."

His irony laughs equally at himself and at the conquests of Augustus.

"Oh, august Pierides! Now for a large mouthed product.

Thus:

'The Euphrates denies its protection to the Parthian
and apologies for Crassus,'
And 'It is, I think, India which now gives necks
to your triumph,'
And so forth, Augustus. 'Virgin Arabia shakes
in her inmost dwelling.'

. . . .

And I shall follow the camp, I shall be duly celebrated
for singing the affairs of your cavalry."

Or take "A Difference of Opinion with Lygdamus." Nor even the reference to the "other woman's" incantations disturbs the bright impression of modernity.

Nor should this surprise us. Our imperial politics bring us very near to Augustan Rome. Our intelligentsia, by its psychology, by its ironic detachment, its disenchantments, the melancholy that overlies its increasingly intellectual view of life, is nearer to the intelligentsia of the Augustan era than, say, to that of the Eighteenth Century. And Ezra Pound has never found a mask that fitted him better than his Propertius. In all his adventures he goes out to the encounter with himself; he maintains himself, a salient, abrupt, unmistakable entity through all his transformations.

On this account his translation is not to be recommended to students cramming Propertius for an exam. He has made blunders here and there that any schoolmaster would have avoided. His "night-dogs" for *nocturnæque canes* procured him a rating from at least one professorial chair. There always will be a certain number of inverted minds for which microscopic errors assume supreme importance. Mr. Pound is a poet and he knows that in a foreign poet the essential thing is not always his literal sense, nor yet the structure and agreeable cadence of his verse, but his manner, the way he says things, his gesture, his tone and accent. With rather more brusquerie in his manner, it is this living gesture and tone and accent that Mr. Pound's paraphrasing conveys. You know that it is right because you feel that it is alive; that this *is* an actual Propertius. Mr. Pound should be tried by a jury, not of professors, but of his peers: his defence should be to read aloud Odes VII. and IX. and X. "My happy night, night full of brightness."—"The twisted rhombs ceased their clamour of accompaniment."—"Light, light of my eyes, at an exceeding late hour I was wandering,

And intoxicated."

If he had never written anything else: if he had never appeared in *Blast*, never helped to edit *The Little Review*, never expressed his inmost opinion of his contemporaries, but had burst upon the town in innocence with his "Homage to Sextus Propertius," he would have achieved a reputation, a more solid and enduring reputation than he made by "Personæ" and "Exultations."

English Review 30(April 1920):326–335.

"The Future of the Novel": An Interview

Miss May Sinclair expressed the opinion that one of the most interesting developments of the psychological novel is the method employed by James Joyce and Dorothy Richardson; the method, namely, of proceeding from one consciousness, and seeing and feeling everything through that consciousness, the author never adopting the attitude of God Almighty as he used to do in the ordinary traditional novel.

"This method," said Miss Sinclair, "has its limitations, which perhaps those who use it best realise. That is to say, you are confined to one consciousness, you share its prejudices and its blindnesses, you know no more of the other people in the book than it knows, but you get a much more vivid and real presentation of that particular character's life than you would by standing outside it.

"There are ways of circumventing these awkwardnesses. All the time the author naturally does know more than his character, and he must present things so that they appear both as they really are and as they appear to the consciousness of his one subject.

"It may be said that this method could only be applied to one kind of novel—the novel of the one predominant character. It certainly remains to be seen whether it will be successful in dealing with groups of characters all equally important. The difficulty in this case will be to get an æsthetic unity; but it will be worth trying for.

"It has been objected that a novel of action could not be written from this standpoint, but that altogether depends on the kind of consciousness you start with. If you take the consciousness of a man of action, you will have all his actions in his consciousness—the only place where they immediately and intimately are. The method—whatever else may be said for it—provides a more thorough-going unity than any other, for there is nothing more fundamental than the unity of consciousness.

"I see no end to the psychological development of the novel on these lines, but the method might not lend itself, for example, to certain forms of comedy. The reason is that the very essence of the comic is the incongruity between things as they are and things as they appear to consciousness.

"The whole point of the comedy of 'The Egoist' is in the difference between Sir Willoughby Patterne, as he appeared to Clara Middleton and George Meredith, and Sir Willoughby as he appears to himself.

"And to uphold this difference the author must be the absolute spectator of the two Willoughbys; he must, in fact, be the absolute outside spectator of his own creations. That is the difference between comedy and tragedy. Comedy allows you to be slightly more diffuse, less concentrated, less intense, to play round and round your subject.

"It can be said that all this may be true, and that there is nothing very new in it. The novelists who know their business—the great novelists—have always worked from the inside of their characters, and have always been one with them, but they have also always been the outside spectator.

"And that attitude, so far as it is perceptible to the reader, interferes more or less with a direct presentment of the subject. You are aware of the author all the time. This is especially so with the analytic novel of the past. The modern novelist should not dissect; he should not probe; he should not write about the emotions and the thoughts of his characters. The words he uses must be the thoughts—be the emotions.

"I think that the analytic psychological novel is becoming a thing of the past; that the synthetic psychological novel is taking its place, and there can be little doubt that it has a future before it."

Starr, Meredith, ed. "May Sinclair." *The Future of the Novel: Famous Authors and Their Methods: A Series of Interviews with Renowned Authors.* Boston: Small, Maynard, 1921. 87–89.

21

Gertrude Stein (1874–1946)

Introduced and Edited by Marianne DeKoven

Gertrude Stein was one of the most prolific, important, and influential writers of this century, with twenty-five books published in her lifetime and approximately the same number, including anthologies, published posthumously.[1] She was at the center of three major modernist–avant-garde Parisian groups: the lesbian Left Bank documented by Shari Benstock, the bohemian Montmartre of Picasso and modernist painting described by Stein herself in vivid detail in *The Autobiography of Alice B. Toklas*, and the postwar scene of younger American expatriate modernists, most notably Hemingway, Fitzgerald, Anderson, and Wilder, who sat at Stein's feet at 27 rue de Fleurus. "You are all a lost generation," the quote Hemingway attributes to "Gertrude Stein in conversation" in an epigraph to *The Sun Also Rises*, generated one of the prime epithets for the literary twenties, rivaled only by Fitzgerald's "jazz age" and Eliot's "waste land."[2] Yet the fine, important pieces collected here, like dozens of others that are similarly important and fine, are extremely difficult to obtain, available only in some libraries and, when in print, in obscure, expensive clothbound editions.

Until, in the past decade, feminist and postmodernist criticism began to take Stein's writing very seriously, most studies of her were biographical, focusing on her myriad connections with other important modernist and avant-garde artists and writers rather than on her own remarkable productivity and the diversity and originality of her work. In fact, this originality was defined rather as eccentricity, most importantly by Edmund Wilson in his early, highly influential work on modernism, *Axel's Castle.* It was not until the avant garde gained wider currency as precursor of postmodernism, poststructuralism, and French feminism, and effected a general shift in our sense of the possible in literature, that the revolutionary character of Stein's work was rendered visible. She went a great deal further than anyone else in the modernist period in reinventing literary language in a way that undoes conventional, hierarchical, patriarchal modes of signification, substituting, in diverse stylistic modes, a rich, complex, open-ended syntactical and semantic polysemy.

She was well aware of what she was doing; she was eminently a literary theorist as well as a practitioner. (She launched her intellectual life as a student of William James at Harvard.) Her essays and extended meditations of the 1930s do a great deal more than explain her own literary practice—they treat standard preoccupations of literary theory, such as definitions of genre, accounts of periodization, and literary nationality, as well as more abstract questions of the nature of representation and of literary time.[3] While Stein seldom treats directly the question of gender in these essays, the unpretentiousness and whimsical informality of her style and the simplicity of her diction "do theory" in a way that is welcoming and suggestive for theoretically oriented feminists who find inimical the overbearing, obfuscating language of so much masculine theoretical discourse. At the same time, the quality and structures of her thought are profound, challenging, complex. As she says in "A Transatlantic Interview 1946," reprinted here, "After all, my only thought is a complicated simplicity. I like a thing simple, but it must be simple through complication."

Two of the three critical essays reprinted here have a somewhat ambiguous textual status. "How Writing Is Written" was a lecture delivered at the Choate School during 1934–1935, the year of Stein's triumphant return to America as a famous writer (she had left for Europe, in professional and erotic defeat and depression, in 1903 and had never before returned). The essay first appeared in the *Oxford Anthology of American Literature* in 1938 and was reprinted by Robert Bartlett Haas in *How Writing Is Written: Volume II of the Previously Uncollected Writings of Gertrude Stein* in 1974. This version (the only one ever printed) is the result of a transcription from notes taken at the lecture by Dudley Fitts, who admitted that he "had difficulties" (Bridgman 266).

"A Transatlantic Interview 1946," the year of Stein's death (she died of cancer in July), was originally published as "Gertrude Stein Talking—A Transatlantic Interview" in the *UCLAN Review* (Summer 1962, Spring 1963, and Winter 1964). The interview was arranged by mail from America by Haas, a friend of Stein's, and was conducted by a third person, William S. Sutton, a friend of Haas's.[4] The published version was based on two afternoons of conversation between Stein and Sutton at her Paris apartment in January 1946. Sutton recorded in shorthand Stein's answers to questions formulated by Haas; Haas transcribed and presumably edited Sutton's mailings: not a procedure to inspire great confidence in the accuracy of the final printed version, especially since it did not appear in print until sixteen years later. Haas published excerpts of the *UCLAN Review* version in *A Primer for the Gradual Understanding of Gertrude Stein*—the version reprinted here—and indicated in his introduction that Stein did at least see and approve some version of the interview: "She inscribed the typescript as follows: 'To Bobby Haas and his progeny forever. You got a scoop! Always, Gertrude Stein' " (14; the "forever" is touching in light of Stein's imminent death).

The textual status of "What Are Master-pieces and Why Are There So Few of Them," on the other hand, is firm. Stein wrote it to be delivered as a lecture at Oxford and Cambridge in 1936, exactly a decade after her Oxford-Cambridge lecture "Composition as Explanation" (still available in paperback in the crucial Carl Van Vechten anthology, *Selected Writings of Gertrude Stein*) initiated her career as lecturer and essayist. The 1936 lecture was first published in *What Are Master-pieces*, 1940, and reprinted in the very useful but unfortunately out-of-print paperback anthology, *Look at Me Now and Here I Am: Writings and Lectures, 1909–1945*.

As Richard Bridgman says, "How Writing Is Written" and "What Are Master-pieces and Why Are There So Few of Them" (subsequently referred to as HWIW and WAM) are "short, lucid statements" and therefore are "useful places to commence a study of Gertrude Stein" (264).[5] They condense, in concise, readily accessible but not, *pace* Bridgman, oversimplified or diluted form, a number of Stein's central critical and theoretical preoccupations. Moreover, they stand in a dialectical relationship to one another that in turn represents the central dialectic in Stein's thought: a dialectic of notions of writing and art in general as transcendent "ends in themselves" (WAM), on one hand, and as prime representations of contemporaneity (HWIW) on the other. Though the two seem to be contradictory—it would seem that art must be *either* a "pure" end in itself *or* a social representation—it is in representing contemporaneity that art transcends contingence, and in transcending contingence art represents contemporaneity.

Because it was delivered to an audience of teenagers, HWIW is Stein's most accessible theoretical essay. It clarifies and summarizes the complex arguments Stein had begun in "Composition as Explanation" and developed in *Narration*, which was written in 1935 and delivered as a series of lectures at the University of Chicago. She continued to pursue the theme in *Picasso* of 1938. Stein's central concern in HWIW is the issue of contemporaneity in art. She claims, simply, that everyone, including writers and artists, lives in the present, because there is no other time available to live in: the past "is gone" and the future does not yet exist.

Crucially, the writer who is truly expressing "the present" is outcast by her or his contemporaries precisely because they cannot recognize contemporaneity in art. "Contemporaries" live in the present and express and constitute it unconsciously and inevitably, but they do not have interpretive frameworks to account for and normalize it. What they understand and are "soothed" by are representations approximately two generations or forty years behind their own historical moment. Works of art genuinely contemporary with them appear "ugly" and are repudiated.

Clearly, this theory of contemporaneity was constructed in part to "soothe" Stein's own experience of rejection—the ridicule and indifference that greeted her work in the world outside her small circle of admirers until the success of *The Autobiography of Alice B. Toklas* in 1932—and to ally it with the experience of Picasso and the other modernist painters she identified with. But it was also influenced by William James's notion of time as a continual flow of present moments. Stein adapted this notion to a mode of writing with one's attention constantly focused on the present moment, which she calls (in "Composition as Explanation") writing in the "continuous present." She further developed her explanation in "The Gradual Making of *The Making of Americans*," in *Lectures in America*.

Stein also summarizes in HWIW more succinctly than anywhere else her crucial notion of the difference in "time-sense" between what she thinks of as the English nineteenth century and the American twentieth century. In the English nineteenth century, the time-sense was linear, diachronic; in the American twentieth century, founded by Walt Whitman and then Henry Ford, the time-sense is synchronic: "the whole thing assembled out of its parts" rather than "beginning at one end and ending at another." Stein does not spell out the implications for literature of these divergent time-senses, but evidently the synchrony of the twentieth century implies modes of juxtaposition and collage that annihilate the linearity of nineteenth-century narrative realism.

This synchrony has an internal dynamic, however: "the Twentieth Century gives of itself a feeling of movement." This movement is not teleological but highly abstract. Not only is it an end in itself; it is also "static," like Brownian motion; Stein defines it in opposition to what she calls "events." She argues that journalism has entirely cornered the market on events, making a literature of events pale by comparison. Literature should therefore concern itself with the excitement or "vitality" of "existence," making us see with shock of recognition not what is happening but what is "there."

Stein's peroration in HWIW includes a marvelously succinct summary:

> And so what I am trying to make you understand is that every contemporary writer has to find out what is the inner time-sense of his contemporariness. The writer or painter, or what not, feels this thing more vibrantly, and he has a passionate need of putting it down; and that is what creativeness does. . . . If he doesn't put down the contemporary thing, he isn't a great writer, for he has to live in the past.

Having made this passionate assertion of the importance of her own work, she is moved to a striking and sharply observed self-revelation: Speaking of the infinitesimal shifts from sentence to sentence in her early writing that she likens to movement from frame to frame in a film, she states: "You see, finally, after I got this thing as completely as I could, then, of course, it being my nature, I wanted to tear it down." This rare bit of psychological rather than purely literary-theoretical self-analysis provides insight into the chronological succession of radically diverse styles that characterizes Stein's career as an experimental writer.

The writing in WAM is more sophisticated than that in HWIW, but the essay is almost equally accessible. Stein's concern is not with contemporaneity or with the necessity of great writing to provide an adequate representation of its own historical moment but with the noncontingent qualities of "masterpieces," qualities that make them independent of their historical moment. Again, one of these qualities is, precisely, the adequacy of the representation of contemporaneity, but Stein does not treat this issue in WAM, and perhaps never fully made the connection for herself.

An understanding of WAM is enriched by, though not dependent upon, a familiarity with one of Stein's greatest works, *The Geographical History of America Or The Relation of Human Nature to the Human Mind,* published in 1935, and with the essay "Pictures" in *Lectures in America*. Stein divides the "human mind," or "entity," from "human nature," or "identity." The human mind is transcendent, independent of memory, the past, all forms of embeddedness in history and human relations, whereas human nature is contingent, imbued with self-consciousness and relatedness. Masterpieces, quite simply, emerge from the human mind and not from human nature. Here Stein allies herself with a predominant quasi-religious modernist credo of the transcendent supremacy of art, which endows art and the artist in the act of creation with the only power available to human beings to rise above daily life and thereby to give it meaning. Versions of this religion of art are also offered by Joyce, Proust, Eliot, Woolf.

Representation, in Stein's radically antirepresentational view here, is at best irrelevant, at worst an encumbrance. Objects, people, events must be used as springboards for art, but "fundamentally the minute one is conscious deeply conscious of these things as a subject the interest in them does not exist." Stein developed this theme with great explicitness in "Pictures" (*Lectures in America*), where she discusses the "annoyance" one feels at an oil painting being forced to exist in relation to the objects it represents. In WAM, she develops the theme in relation to "psychology," arguing that everyone, particularly women in villages, knows all there is to know about psychology. Therefore, such knowledge of human nature has nothing to do with the creation of masterpieces, which emerge only from the human mind, "a thing in itself and not in relation":

> It is not the way Hamlet reacts to his father's ghost that makes the masterpiece, he might have reacted according to Shakespeare in a dozen other ways and everybody would have been as much impressed by the psychology of it.

> But there is no psychology in it, that is not probably the way any young man would react to the ghost of his father and there is no particular reason why they should.

Since the state of entity, or pure existence beyond "relation and necessity" and wholly within the human mind, is extremely difficult to achieve, there are very few masterpieces: "Everything is against them. Everything that makes life go on makes identity and everything that makes identity is of necessity a necessity."

Interestingly, though Stein is squarely within the idealist tradition here, she is also moving toward poststructuralist feminist notions of a subversive writing subject that is different from, incompatible with, the identity of the coherent, separate, uniquely individuated bourgeois-patriarchal self. It is precisely this self that Stein has in mind when she talks about identity. "What woman say [is] truer than what men say" because women have a looser allegiance to a remembered, consistently structured and self-imposed identity. Similarly, Stein seems to anticipate Lacan's influential "mirror-stage" theory of the inherent alienation in all constructions of the self when she says that "identity consists in recognition and in recognizing you lose identity because after all nobody looks as they look like."

"A Transatlantic Interview 1946" is inevitably looser and more diverse than the two lecture-essays. Much of it, particularly the opening section, recapitulates material Stein had covered many times in her various accounts of the history of her writing life, offering to readers unfamiliar with these accounts an unusually consistent and coherent version (such a version is simultaneously useful and oversimplified). What is unique here is the section containing her responses to excerpts from *Tender Buttons*. These responses reveal the intense concentration and effort Stein's writing required of her, involving a continual application of complex principles of selection and evaluation, a continual rejection of words that did not do the work she wanted done. For critics who, perhaps in unconscious obedience to the stereotype of women as undisciplined and self-indulgent, dismiss her as an "automatic writer," simply putting on paper whatever came into her head, this section should be particularly enlightening.

This interview is also notable for its egalitarian politics: Stein connects to the crucial democratic idea of "one man one vote" her notion of the "twentieth-century composition" as a principle of organization that rejects the dominating center (another poststructuralist feminist concept) but in which each part is of equal importance. This section, like her tribute to the Resistance in "The Winner Loses: A Picture of Occupied France" and her dissection of the Fascist tyrant in her characterization of "Angel Harper" (Adolf Hitler) in *Mrs. Reynolds*, is an antidote to Stein's attacks on Roosevelt and to her embarrassing friendship with the Vichy collaborationist Bernard Faÿ.

The remaining selections are literary rather than critical writings. Two of them are from *Geography and Plays* (1922), one of Stein's most important and most difficult to obtain early anthologies. Its title, like that of *Portraits and Prayers,* makes evident Stein's intention to reinvent genre as well as writing itself. *Geography and Plays* contains the brief but fine introductory essay by Sherwood Anderson quoted by Haas in "Transatlantic Interview." It also contains several of the famous works anthologized by Van Vechten in *Selected Writings of Gertrude Stein:* "Miss Furr and Miss Skeene" (1908–1912), "Susie Asado" (1913), and the early plays "What Happened" of 1913 and "Ladies Voices" of 1916.

Many of the less known (because relatively unavailable) works in *Geography and Plays* are comparable in quality and interest to the works anthologized by Van Vechten. "Americans" and "White Wines," both of 1913, are fine instances of what I call Stein's "lively words" style (DeKoven 63–84), the prewar culmination of her early experimental career (the best known work in this style is *Tender Buttons*). In this period (roughly 1909–1913) Stein became interested in the vibrancy of word juxtapositions, generally within short pieces which she considered word-portraits or prose poems rather than in the mammoth accretions of steadily shifting repetition, using a flattened, radically reduced vocabulary, that characterize the extremely lengthy volumes, containing extremely lengthy sentences and paragraphs, of her earlier experimental work, most notably *The Making of Americans* (1906–1911).

"Americans," which could be considered portraiture as well as "geography," does not depend for its effect on referentiality. The reader who tries to find out from this piece what Stein thought of Americans will be disappointed. Rather, its effect is that of a polysemous verbal collage comprised of multiple semantic resonances, achieved by suggestive, "almost-meaning" juxtapositions, puns, and sound associations. Holding the idea "Americans" in one's mind as one reads augments the experience of the piece, much as the nonabstract titles of some abstract or cubist paintings add to them an extra dimension of referential possibility. I find "Americans" as "successful," to use Stein's own term in "Transatlantic Interview," as the best of the *Tender Buttons*—a semantic cornucopia of almost infinite suggestiveness, yet at the same time precise and sharply focused in its verbal juxtapositions. It would be an interesting exercise to apply Stein's criteria in her "Transatlantic Interview" responses to *Tender Buttons* to segments of "Americans."

"White Wines" is one of Stein's earliest plays and is, in fact, an object lesson in the thinking she did about dramatic writing. It is written in the "lively words" style, but with an important difference: the writing is divided into discernibly different voices and into declarative sentences of fairly uniform length and structure employing recognizable speech rhythms. Such structural features are more significant for Stein's dramatic writing than the "Three Acts" into which "White Wines" is divided or the repeated stage directions corresponding to the titles of these acts.

The dramatis personae of "White Wines" are "5 women," and the voices are recognizably feminine: "Cunning very cunning and cheap, at that rate a sale is a place to use type writing. Shall we go home." Many of Stein's plays, most notably "Ladies Voices," and the later operas *Four Saints in Three Acts* (1927) and *The Mother of Us All* (1945–1946), seem more concertedly interested in women than Stein's work generally is. Plays enacted for Stein her idea of the twentieth-century "composition" as dynamic movement, existing for its own sake, within an overall stasis that has no dominating center. Perhaps she felt that women's lives and consciousnesses came closer to embodying that composition than men's ("what women say is truer than what men say").

Portraits and Prayers (1934) is even more difficult to obtain than *Geography and Plays.* It spans the entire range of Stein's experimental career. In "Play," of 1909, we can see Stein's commitment to what Roland Barthes called "the magic of the signifier," and to its "free-play" in her writing. This piece is written in what I call Stein's "insistent" style (she distinguishes "insistence," or shifting repetition, from "repetition," or mechanical reiteration), and is an excellent exemplum of her contention that the gradual shift of meaning from sentence to sentence in this style is just like the barely perceptible movement from frame to frame in a film (DeKoven 46–62). Coming toward the end of this style, "Play" also demonstrates some of the features of the "lively words" style that immediately followed: it is short, sprightly, tightly structured, dependent on semantic polysemy and open-endedness.

"A Description of the Fifteenth of November: A Portrait of T. S. Eliot" of 1924 emerged from the uncomfortable relations between Stein and Eliot. Eliot, highly skeptical about Stein's work, offered to publish something of hers in *Criterion* on the condition that it be absolutely current.[6] Stein titled the piece with the date of its composition, associating Eliot himself, highly appropriately, with the pressure of time. Beyond its anecdotal interest to students of modernism, this piece encompasses several modes of writing Stein employed in the twenties: the repeated motif "the fifteenth of November" exemplifies Stein's new concern with structural cohesion; the opening paragraph employs a kind of verbose doubletalk Stein used to mock the Latinate pretentiousness of so much "serious" sense-making writing; and the sequences of lyrical, incantatory, complexly rhythmed repetition, most notably in the closing paragraph, put us powerfully in the realm of the pre-Oedipal and of ritual uses of language.

"Sitwell Edith Sitwell" of 1925 is a witty, engaging, and quasi-referential piece: it nods in the direction of referentiality, though, characteristic as it is of Stein's twenties' writing, it eludes conventional referentiality itself. It is of inherent interest in a work on the gender of modernism, for Sitwell was a professed admirer of Stein's work and her own work is perhaps more visibly indebted to Stein than anyone else's. Another of Stein's transatlantic women friends, the American Mabel Weeks, figures importantly throughout the piece in various puns. Moreover, the introductory tableau "when they sit around her" foreshadows St. Therese's position in the first "Act One" of *Four Saints in Three Acts*.[7]

"To Kitty or Kate Buss" of 1930 is, like its subject, an everywoman of Stein's world of discourse: one of her nearly innumerable portraits of one of her nearly innumerable friends. Like her writing in general, it is simultaneously remarkable, a brilliant and pungent piece, and ordinary, both because it is representative of an enormous amount of similar work and because it is unpretentious, doing its powerful and revolutionary work with a light touch.

NOTES

1. See Appendix C, "Key to the *Yale Catalogue* (of Stein's writings), Part 4," in Bridgman, 365–385, for an extremely helpful chronological list of all of Stein's works by date of composition.
2. See Mellow.
3. The most important of these writings, in addition to the essays reprinted here, are *Lectures In America,* 1934, *Narration,* 1935, *The Geographical History of America Or The Relation Of Human Nature To The Human Mind,* 1935, and *Picasso,* 1938 (years given are dates of composition rather than publication).
4. Haas's Introduction to "Transatlantic Interview," 13–14 in *A Primer for the Gradual Understanding of Gertrude Stein,* contains this information.
5. Bridgman warns that, "if taken uncritically," these two essays "can wrench one's understanding of (Stein's) literary work askew," because they tidy the "dishevelled" record of her oeuvre (264). However, the inaccessibility of these two essays makes it unlikely that they will be misused in that way.
6. See the last chapter of *The Autobiography of Alice B. Toklas* for Stein's version of this story (189–190 in *Selected Writings*).
7. "Saint Therese half in and half out of doors . . . Saint Therese seated and not surrounded" (*Selected Writings,* 586).

WORKS CITED

Benstock, Shari. *Women of the Left Bank: Paris, 1900–1940.* Austin: U of Texas P, 1986.
Bridgman, Richard. *Gertrude Stein in Pieces.* New York: Oxford UP, 1970.
DeKoven, Marianne. *A Different Language: Gertrude Stein's Experimental Writing.* Madison: U of Wisconsin P, 1983.
Hemingway, Ernest. *The Sun Also Rises.* New York: Scribner's, 1926.
Mellow, James R. *Charmed Circle: Gertrude Stein & Company.* New York: Avon, 1974.
Stein, Gertrude. *The Autobiography of Alice B. Toklas.* New York: Random House, 1933.
———. "Composition as Explanation." 1926. *Selected Writings,* 511–523.
———. *Four Saints in Three Acts.* 1927. *Selected Writings,* 577–612.
———. *The Geographical History of America Or The Relation Of Human Nature To The Human Mind.* New York: Random House, 1936.
———. *Geography and Plays.* 1922. New York: Something Else, 1968.
———. *How Writing Is Written: Volume II of the Previously Uncollected Works of Gertrude Stein.* Ed. Robert Bartlett Haas. Los Angeles: Black Sparrow P, 1974.
———. *Lectures in America.* New York: Random House, 1935.
———. *Look at Me Now and Here I Am: Writings and Lectures, 1909–1945.* Ed. Patricia Meyerowitz. Harmondsworth: Penguin, 1971.
———. *The Making of Americans.* 1925. New York: Something Else, 1966.
———. *The Mother of Us All.* 1946. *Last Operas and Plays.* New York: Random House, 1949, 52–88.

———. *Mrs. Reynolds and Five Earlier Novelettes (1931–1942)*. New Haven: Yale UP, 1952.
———. *Narration*. Chicago: U of Chicago P, 1935.
———. *Picasso*. 1938. Boston: Beacon, 1959.
———. *A Primer for the Gradual Understanding of Gertrude Stein*. Ed. Robert Bartlett Haas. Los Angeles: Black Sparrow P, 1971.
———. *Selected Writings of Gertrude Stein*. Ed. Carl Van Vechten. New York: Random House, 1946.
———. *Tender Buttons*. 1914. *Selected Writings*, 459–509.
———. *What Are Master-pieces*. Los Angeles: Conference, 1940.
———. "The Winner Loses: A Picture of Occupied France." *Selected Writings*, 613–637.
Wilson, Edmund. *Axel's Castle*. New York: Scribner's, 1931.

How Writing Is Written

What I want to talk about to you tonight is just the general subject of how writing is written. It is a large subject, but one can discuss it in a very short space of time. The beginning of it is what everybody has to know: everybody is contemporary with his period. A very bad painter once said to a very great painter: "Do what you like, you cannot get rid of the fact that we are contemporaries." That is what goes on in writing. The whole crowd of you are contemporary to each other, and the whole business of writing is the question of living in that contemporariness. Each generation has to live in that. The thing that is important is that nobody knows what the contemporariness is. In other words, they don't know where they are going, but they are on their way.

Each generation has to do with what you would call the daily life: and a writer, painter, or any sort of creative artist, is not at all ahead of his time. He is contemporary. He can't live in the past, because it is gone. He can't live in the future because no one knows what it is. He can live only in the present of his daily life. He is expressing the thing that is being expressed by everybody else in their daily lives. The thing you have to remember is that everybody lives a contemporary daily life. The writer lives it, too, and expresses it imperceptibly. The fact remains that in the act of living, everybody has to live contemporarily. But in the things concerning art and literature they don't have to live contemporarily, because it doesn't make any difference; and they live about forty years behind their time. And that is the real explanation of why the artist or painter is not recognized by his contemporaries. He is expressing the time-sense of his contemporaries, but nobody is really interested. After the new generation has come, after the grandchildren, so to speak, then the opposition dies out; because after all there is then a new contemporary expression to oppose.

That is really the fact about contemporariness. As I see the whole crowd of you, if there are any of you who are going to express yourselves contemporarily, you will do something which most people won't want to look at. Most of you will be so busy living the contemporary life that it will be like the tired businessman: in the things of the mind you will want the things you know. And too, if you don't live contemporarily, you are a nuisance. That is why we live contemporarily. If a man goes along the street with horse and carriage in New York in the snow, that man is a nuisance; and he knows it, so now he doesn't do it. He would not be living, or acting, contemporarily: he would only be in the way, a drag.

The world can accept me now because there is coming out of *your* generation somebody they don't like, and therefore they accept me because I am sufficiently past in having been contemporary so they don't have to dislike me. So thirty years from now I shall be accepted. And the same thing will happen again: that is the reason why every generation has the same thing happen. It will always be the same story, because there is always the same situation presented. The contemporary thing in art and literature is the thing which doesn't make enough difference to the people of that generation so that they can accept it or reject it.

Most of you know that in a funny kind of way you are nearer your grandparents than your parents. Since this contemporariness is always there, nobody realizes that you cannot follow it up. That is the reason people discover—those interested in the activities of other people—that they cannot understand their contemporaries. If you kids started in to write, I wouldn't be a good judge of you, because I am of the third generation. What you are going to do I don't know any more than anyone else. But I created a movement of which you are the grandchildren. The contemporary thing is the thing you can't get away from. That is the fundamental thing in all writing.

Another thing you have to remember is that each period of time not only has its contemporary quality, but it has a time-sense. Things move more quickly, slowly, or differently, from one generation to another. Take the Nineteenth Century. The Nineteenth Century was roughly the Englishman's Century. And their method, as they themselves, in their worst moments, speak of it, is that of "muddling through." They begin at one end and hope to come out at the other: their grammar, parts of speech, methods of talk, go with this fashion. The United States began a different phase when, after the Civil War, they discovered and created out of their inner need a different way of life. They created the Twentieth Century. The United States, instead of having the feeling of beginning at one end and ending at another, had the conception of assembling the whole thing out of its parts, the whole thing which made the Twentieth Century productive. The Twentieth Century conceived an automobile as a whole, so to speak, and then created it, built it up out of its parts. It was an entirely different point of view from the Nineteenth Century's. The Nineteenth Century would have seen the parts, and worked towards the automobile through them.

Now in a funny sort of way this expresses, in different terms, the difference between the literature of the Nineteenth Century and the literature of the Twentieth. Think of your reading. If you look at it from the days of Chaucer, you will see that what you might call the "internal history" of a country always affects its use of writing. It makes a difference in the expression, in the vocabulary, even in the handling of grammar. In Vanderbilt's amusing story in your *Literary Magazine,* when he speaks of the fact that he is tired of using quotation marks and isn't going to use them any more, with him that is a joke; but when I began writing, the whole question of punctuation was a vital question. You see, I had this new conception: I had this conception of the whole paragraph, and in *The Making of Americans* I had this idea of a whole thing. But if you think of contemporary English writers, it doesn't work like that at all. They conceive of it as pieces put together to make a whole, and I conceived it as a whole made up of its parts. I didn't know what I was doing any more than you know, but in response to the need of my period I was doing this thing. That is why I came in contact with people who were unconsciously doing the same thing. They had the Twentieth Century conception of a whole. So the element of punctuation was very vital. The comma was just a nuisance. If you got the thing as a whole, the comma kept irritating you all along the line. If you think of a thing as a whole, and the comma keeps sticking out, it gets on your nerves; because, after all, it destroys the reality of the whole. So I got rid more and more of commas. Not because I had any prejudice against commas; but the comma was a stumbling block. When you were conceiving a sentence, the comma stopped you. That is the illustration of the question of grammar and parts of speech, as part of the daily life as we live it.

The other thing which I accomplished was the getting rid of nouns. In the Twentieth Century you feel like movement. The Nineteenth Century didn't feel that way. The element of movement was not the predominating thing that they felt. You know that in your lives movement is the thing that occupies you most—you feel movement all the time. And the United States had the first instance of what I call Twentieth Century writing. You see it first in Walt Whitman. He was the beginning of the movement. He didn't see it very clearly, but there was a sense of movement that the European was much influenced by, because the Twentieth Century has become the American Century. That is what I mean when I say that each generation has its own literature.

There is a third element. You see, everybody in his generation has his sense of time which belongs to his crowd. But then, you always have the memory of what you were brought up with. In most people that makes a double time, which makes confusion. When one is beginning to write he is always under the shadow of the thing that is just past. And that is the reason why the creative person always has the appearance of ugliness. There is this persistent drag of the habits that belong to you. And in struggling away from this thing there is always an ugliness. That is the other reason why the contemporary writer is always refused. It is the effort of escaping from the thing which is a drag upon you that is so strong that the result is an apparent ugliness; and the world always says of the new writer, "It is so ugly!" And they are right, because it *is* ugly. If you disagree with your parents, there is an ugliness in the relation. There is a double resistance that makes the essence of this thing ugly.

You always have in your writing the resistance outside of you and inside of you, a shadow upon you, and the thing which you must express. In the beginning of your writing, this struggle is so tremendous that the result is ugly; and that is the reason why the followers are always accepted before the person who made the revolution. The person who has made the fight probably makes it seem ugly, although the struggle has the much greater beauty. But the followers die out; and the man who made the struggle and the quality of beauty remains in the intensity of the fight. Eventually it comes out all right, and so you have this very queer situation which always happens with the followers: the original person has to have in him a certain element of ugliness. You know that is what happens over and over again: the statement made that it is ugly—the statement made against me for the last twenty years. And they are quite right, because it *is* ugly. But the essence of that ugliness is the thing which will always make it beautiful. I myself think it is much more interesting when it seems ugly, because in it you see the element of the fight. The literature of one hundred years ago is perfectly easy to see, because the sediment of ugliness has settled down and you get the solemnity of its beauty. But to a person of my temperament, it is much more amusing when it has the vitality of the struggle.

In my own case, the Twentieth Century, which America created after the Civil War, and which had certain elements, had a definite influence on me. And in *The Making of Americans,* which is a book I would like to talk about, I gradually and slowly found out that there were two things I had to think about; the fact that knowledge is acquired, so to speak, by memory; but that when you know anything, memory doesn't come in. At any moment that you are conscious of knowing anything, memory plays no part. When any of you feels anybody else, memory doesn't come into it. You have the sense of the immediate. Remember that my immediate forebears were people like Meredith, Thomas Hardy, and so forth, and you will see what a struggle it was to do this thing. This was one of my first efforts to give the appearance of one time-knowledge, and not to make it a narrative story. This is what I mean by immediacy of description: you will find it in *The Making of Americans,* on page 284: "It happens very often that a man has it in him, that a man does something, that he does it very often that he does many things, when he is a young man when he is an old man, when he is an older man." Do you see what I mean? And here is a description of a thing that is very interesting: "One of such of these kind of them had a little boy and this one, the little son wanted to make a collection of butterflies and beetles and it was all exciting to him and it was all arranged then and then the father said to the son you are certain this is not a cruel thing that you are wanting to be doing, killing things to make collections of them, and the son was very disturbed then and they talked about it together the two of them and more and more they talked about it then and then at last the boy was convinced it was a cruel thing and he said he would not do it and the father said the little boy was a noble boy to give up pleasure when it was a cruel one. The boy went to bed then and then the father when he got up in the early morning saw a wonderfully beautiful moth in the room and he caught him and he killed him and he pinned him and he woke up his son then and showed it to him and he said to him 'see what a good father

I am to have caught and killed this one,' the boy was all mixed up inside him and then he said he would go on with his collection and that was all there was then of discussing and this is a little description of something that happened once and it is very interesting."

I was trying to get this present immediacy without trying to drag in anything else. I had to use present participles, new constructions of grammar. The grammar-constructions are correct, but they are changed, in order to get this immediacy. In short, from that time I have been trying in every possible way to get the sense of immediacy, and practically all the work I have done has been in that direction.

In *The Making of Americans* I had an idea that I could get a sense of immediacy if I made a description of every kind of human being that existed, the rules for resemblances and all the other things, until really I had made a description of every human being—I found this out when I was at Harvard working under William James.

Did you ever see that article that came out in *The Atlantic Monthly* a year or two ago, about my experiments with automatic writing? It was very amusing. The experiment that I did was to take a lot of people in moments of fatigue and rest and activity of various kinds, and see if they could do anything with automatic writing. I found that they could not do anything with automatic writing, but I found out a great deal about how people act. I found there a certain kind of human being who acted in a certain way, and another kind who acted in another kind of way, and their resemblances and their differences. And then I wanted to find out if you could make a history of the whole world, if you could know the whole life history of everyone in the world, their slight resemblances and lack of resemblances. I made enormous charts, and I tried to carry these charts out. You start in and you take everyone that you know, and then when you see anybody who has a certain expression or turn of the face that reminds you of some one, you find out where he agrees or disagrees with the character, until you build up the whole scheme. I got to the place where I didn't know whether I knew people or not. I made so many charts that when I used to go down the streets of Paris I wondered whether they were people I knew or ones I didn't. That is what *The Making of Americans* was intended to be. I was to make a description of every kind of human being until I could know by these variations how everybody was to be known. Then I got very much interested in this thing, and I wrote about nine hundred pages, and I came to a logical conclusion that this thing could be done. Anybody who has patience enough could literally and entirely make of the whole world a history of human nature. When I found it could be done, I lost interest in it. As soon as I found definitely and clearly and completely that I could do it, I stopped writing the long book. It didn't interest me any longer. In doing the thing, I found out this question of resemblances, and I found in making these analyses that the resemblances were not of memory. I had to remember what person looked like the other person. Then I found this contradiction: that the resemblances were a matter of memory. There were two prime elements involved, the element of memory and the other of immediacy.

The element of memory was a perfectly feasible thing, so then I gave it up. I then started a book which I called *A Long Gay Book* to see if I could work the thing up to a faster tempo. I wanted to see if I could make that a more complete vision. I wanted to see if I could hold it in the frame. Ordinarily the novels of the Nineteenth Century live by association; they are wont to call up other pictures than the one they present to you. I didn't want, when I said "water," to have you think of running water. Therefore I began by limiting my vocabulary, because I wanted to get rid of anything except the picture within the frame. While I was writing I didn't want, when I used one word, to make it carry with it too many associations. I wanted as far as possible to make it exact, as exact as mathematics; that is to say, for example, if one and one make two, I wanted to get words to have as much exactness as that. When I put them down they were to have this quality. The whole history of my work, from *The Making of Americans,* has been a history of that. I made a great many discoveries, but the thing that I was always trying to do was this thing.

One thing which came to me is that the Twentieth Century gives of itself a feeling of movement, and has in its way no feeling for events. To the Twentieth Century events are not important. You must know that. Events are not exciting. Events have lost their interest for people. You read them more like a soothing syrup, and if you listen over the radio you don't get very excited. The thing has got to this place, that events are so wonderful that they are not exciting. Now you have to remember that the business of an artist is to be exciting. If the thing has its proper vitality, the result must be exciting. I was struck with it during the War: the average dough-boy standing on a street corner doing nothing—(they say, at the end of their doing nothing, "I guess I'll go home")—was much more exciting to people than when the soldiers went over the top. The populace were passionately interested in their standing on the street corners, more so than in the St. Mihiel drive. And it is a perfectly natural thing. Events had got so continuous that the fact that events were taking place no longer stimulated anybody. To see three men, strangers, standing, expressed their personality to the European man so much more than anything else they could do. That thing impressed me very much. But the novel which tells about what happens is of no interest to anybody. It is quite characteristic that in *The Making of Americans,* Proust, *Ulysses,* nothing much happens. People are interested in existence. Newspapers excite people very little. Sometimes a personality breaks through the newspapers—Lindbergh, Dillinger—when the personality has vitality. It wasn't what Dillinger *did* that excited anybody. The feeling is perfectly simple. You can see it in my *Four Saints.* Saints shouldn't do anything. The fact that a saint is there is enough for anybody. The *Four Saints* was written about as static as I could make it. The saints conversed a little, and it all did something. It did something more than the theatre which has tried to make events has done. For our purposes, for our contemporary purposes, events have no importance. I merely say that for the last thirty years events are of no importance. They make a great many people unhappy, they may cause convulsions in history, but from the standpoint of excitement, the kind of excitement the Nineteenth Century got out of events doesn't exist.

And so what I am trying to make you understand is that every contemporary writer has to find out what is the inner time-sense of his contemporariness. The writer or painter, or what not, feels this thing more vibrantly, and he has a passionate need of putting it down; and that is what creativeness does. He spends his life in putting down this thing which he doesn't know is a contemporary thing. If he doesn't put down the contemporary thing, he isn't a great writer, for he has to live in the past. That is what I mean by "everything is contemporary." The minor poets of the period, or the precious poets of the period, are all people who are under the shadow of the past. A man who is making a revolution has to be contemporary. A minor person can live in the imagination. That tells the story pretty completely.

The question of repetition is very important. It is important because there is no such thing as repetition. Everybody tells every story in about the same way. You know perfectly well that when you and your roommates tell something, you are telling the same story in about the same way. But the point about it is this. Everybody is telling the story in the same way. But if you listen carefully, you will see that not all the story is the same. There is always a slight variation. Somebody comes in and you tell the story over again. Every time you tell the story it is told slightly differently. All my early work was a careful listening to all the people telling their story, and I conceived the idea which is, funnily enough, the same as the idea of the cinema. The cinema goes on the same principle: each picture is just infinitesimally different from the one before. If you listen carefully, you say something, the other person says something; but each time it changes just a little, until finally you come to the point where you convince him or you don't convince him. I used to listen very carefully to people talking. I had a passion for knowing just what I call their "insides". And in *The Making of Americans* I did this thing; but of course to my mind there is no repetition. For instance, in these early *Portraits,* and in a whole lot of them in this book (*Portraits and Prayers*) you will see that every time a statement is made about someone being somewhere, that statement is different. If I had repeated, nobody would listen. Nobody could be in the room with a person who said the same thing over and over and over. He would drive everybody mad. There has to be a very slight change. Really listen to the way you talk and every time you change it a little bit. That change, to me, was a very important thing to find out. You will see that when I kept on saying something was something or somebody was somebody, I changed it just a little bit until I got a whole portrait. I conceived the idea of building this thing up. It was all based upon this thing of everybody's slightly building this thing up. What I was after was this immediacy. A single photograph doesn't give it. I was trying for this thing, and so to my mind there is no repetition. The only thing that is repetition is when somebody tells you what he has learned. No matter how you say it, you say it differently. It was this that led me in all that early work.

You see, finally, after I got this thing as completely as I could, then, of course, it being my nature, I wanted to tear it down. I attacked the problem from another way. I listened to people. I condensed it in about three words. There again, if you read those later *Portraits,* you will see that I used three or four words instead of making a cinema of it. I wanted to condense it as much as possible and change it around, until you could get the movement of a human being. If I wanted to make a picture of you as you sit there, I would wait until I got a picture of you as individuals and then I'd change them until I got a picture of you as a whole.

I did these *Portraits,* and then I got the idea of doing plays. I had the *Portraits* so much in my head that I would almost know how you differ one from the other. I got this idea of the play, and put it down in a few words. I wanted to put them down in that way, and I began writing plays and I wrote a great many of them. The Nineteenth Century wrote a great many plays, and none of them are now read, because the Nineteenth Century wanted to put their novels on the stage. The better the play the more static. The minute you try to make a play a novel, it doesn't work. That is the reason I got interested in doing these plays.

When you get to that point there is no essential difference between prose and poetry. This is essentially the problem with which your generation will have to wrestle. The thing has got to the point where poetry and prose have to concern themselves with the static thing. That is up to you.

1935

How Writing Is Written: Volume II of the Previously Uncollected Works of Gertrude Stein. Ed. Robert Bartlett Haas. Los Angeles: Black Sparrow P, 1974. 151–160.

What Are Master-pieces and Why Are There So Few of Them

I was almost going to talk this lecture and not write and read it because all the lectures that I have written and read in America have been printed and although possibly for you they might even being read be as if they had not been printed still there is something about what has been written having been printed which makes it no longer the property of the one who wrote it and therefore there is no more reason why the writer should say it out loud than anybody else and therefore one does not.

Therefore I was going to talk to you but actually it is impossible to talk about master-pieces and what they are because talking essentially has nothing to do with creation. I talk a lot I like to talk and I talk even more than that I may say I talk most of the time and I listen a fair amount too and as I have said the essence of being a genius is to be able to talk and listen to listen while talking and talk while listening but and this is very important very important indeed talking has nothing to do with creation. What are master-pieces and why after all are there so few of them. You may say after all there are a good many of them but in any kind of proportion with everything that anybody who does anything is doing there are really very few of them. All this summer I meditated and wrote about this subject and it finally came to be a discussion of the relation of human nature and the human mind and identity. The thing one gradually comes to find out is that one has no identity that is when one is in the act of doing anything. Identity is recognition, you know who you are because you and others remember anything about yourself but essentially you are not that when you are doing anything. I am I because my little dog knows me but, creatively speaking the little dog knowing that you are you and your recognizing that he knows, that is what destroys creation. That is what makes school. Picasso once remarked I do not care who it is that has or does influence me as long as it is not myself.

It is very difficult so difficult that it always has been difficult but even more difficult now to know what is the relation of human nature to the human mind because one has to know what is the relation of the act of creation to the subject the creator uses to create that thing. There is a great deal of nonsense talked about the subject of anything. After all there is always the same subject there are the things you see and there are human beings and animal beings and everybody you might say since the beginning of time knows practically commencing at the beginning and going to the end everything about these things. After all any woman in any village or men either if you like or even children know as much of human psychology as any writer that ever lived. After all there are things you do know each one in his or her way knows all of them and it is not this knowledge that makes master-pieces. Not at all not at all not at all. Those who recognize master-pieces say that is the reason but it is not. It is not the way Hamlet reacts to his father's ghost that makes the master-piece, he might have reacted according to Shakespeare in a dozen other ways and everybody would have been as much impressed by the psychology of it. But there is no psychology in it, that is not probably the way any young man would react to the ghost of his father and there is no particular reason why they should. If it were the way a young man could react to the ghost of his father then that would be something anybody in any village would know they could talk about it talk about it endlessly but that would not make a master-piece and that brings us once more back to the subject of identity. At any moment when you are you you are you without the memory of yourself because if you remember yourself while you are you you are not for purposes of creating you. This is so important because it has so much to do with the question of a writer to his audience. One of the things that I discovered in lecturing was that gradually one ceased to hear what one said one heard what the audience hears one say, that is the reason that oratory is practically never a master-piece very rarely and very rarely history, because history deals with people who are orators who hear not what they are not what they say but what their audience hears them say. It is very interesting that letter writing has the same difficulty, the letter writes what the other person is to hear and so entity does not exist there are two present instead of one and so once again creation breaks down. I once wrote in writing *The Making of Americans* I write for myself and strangers but that was merely a literary formalism for if I did write for myself and strangers if I did I would not really be writing because already then identity would take the place of entity. It is awfully difficult, action is direct and effective but after all action is necessary and anything that is necessary has to do with human nature and not with the human mind. Therefore a master-piece has essentially not to be necessary, it has to be that is it has to exist but it does not have to be necessary it is not in response to necessity as action is because the minute it is necessary it has in it no possibility of going on.

To come back to what a master-piece has as its subject. In writing about painting I said that a picture exists for and in itself and the painter has to use objects landcapes and people as a way the only way that he is able to get the picture to exist. That is every one's trouble and particularly the trouble just now when every one who writes or paints has gotten to be abnormally conscious of the things he uses that is the events the people the objects and the landscapes and fundamentally the minute one is conscious deeply conscious of these things as a subject the interest in them does not exist.

You can tell that so well in the difficulty of writing novels or poetry these days. The tradition has always been that you may more or less describe the things that happen you imagine them of course but you more or less describe the things that happen but nowadays everybody all day long knows what is happening and so what is happening is not really interesting, one knows it by radios cinemas newspapers biographies autobiographies until what is happening does not really thrill anyone, it excites them a little but it does not really thrill them. The painter can no longer say that what he does is as the world looks to him because he cannot look at the world any more, it has been photographed too much and he has to say that he does something else. In former times a painter said he painted what he saw of course he didn't but anyway he could say it, now he does not want to say it because seeing is not interesting. This has something to do with master-pieces and why there are so few of them but not everything.

So you see why talking has nothing to do with creation, talking is really human nature as it is and human nature has nothing to do with master-pieces. It is very curious but the detective story which is you might say the only really modern novel form that has come into existence gets rid of human nature by having the man dead to begin with the hero is dead to begin with and so you have so to speak got rid of the event before the book begins. There is another very curious thing about detective stories. In real life people are interested in the crime more than they are in detection, it is the crime that is the thing the shock the thrill the horror but in the story it is the detection that holds the interest and that is natural enough because the necessity as far as action is concerned is the dead man, it is another function that has very little to do with human nature that makes the detection interesting. And so always it is true that the master-piece has nothing to do with human nature or with identity, it has to do with the human mind and the entity that is with a thing in itself and not in relation. The moment it is in relation it is common knowledge and anybody can feel and know it and it is not a master-piece. At the same time every one in a curious way sooner or later does feel the reality of a master-piece. The thing in itself of which the human nature is only its clothing does hold the attention. I have meditated a great deal about that. Another curious thing about master-pieces is, nobody when it is created there is in the thing that we call the human mind something that makes it hold itself just the same. The manner and habits of Bible times or Greek or Chinese have nothing to do with ours today but the master-pieces exist just the same and they do not exist because of their identity, that is what any one remembering then remembered then, they do not exist by human nature because everybody always knows everything there is to know about human nature, they exist because they came to be as something that is an end in itself and in that respect it is opposed to the business of living which is relation and necessity. That is what a master-piece is not although it may easily be what a master-piece talks about. It is another one of the curious difficulties a master-piece has that is to begin and end, because actually a master-piece does not do that it does not begin and end if it did it would be of necessity and in relation and that is just what a master-piece is not. Everybody worries about that just now everybody that is what makes them talk about abstract and worry about punctuation and capitals and small letters and what a history is. Everybody worries about that not because everybody knows what a master-piece is but because a certain number have found out what a master-piece is not. Even the very master-pieces have always been very bothered about beginning and ending because essentially that is what a master-piece is not. And yet after all like the subject of human nature master-pieces have to use beginning and ending to become existing. Well anyway anybody who is trying to do anything today is desperately not having a beginning and an ending but nevertheless in some way one does have to stop. I stop.

I do not know whether I have made any of this very clear, it is clear, but unfortunately, I have written it all down all summer and in spite of everything I am now remembering and when you remember it is never clear. This is what makes secondary writing, it is remembering, it is very curious you begin to write something and suddenly you remember something and if you continue to remember your writing gets very confused. If you do not remember while you are writing, it may seem confused to others but actually it is clear and eventually that clarity will be clear, that is what a master-piece is, but if you remember while you are writing it will seem clear at the time to any one but the clarity will go out of it that is what a master-piece is not.

All this sounds awfully complicated but it is not complicated at all, it is just what happens. Any of you when you write you try to remember what you are about to write and you will see immediately how lifeless the writing becomes that is why expository writing is so dull because it is all remembered, that is why illustration is so dull because you remember what somebody looked like and you make your illustration look like it. The minute your memory functions while you are doing anything it may be very popular but actually it is dull. And that is what a master-piece is not, it may be unwelcome but it is never dull.

And so then why are there so few of them. There are so few of them because mostly people live in identity and memory that is when they think. They know they are they because their little dog knows them, and so they are not an entity but an identity. And being so memory is necessary to make them exist and so they cannot create master-pieces. It has been said of geniuses that they are eternally young. I once said what is the use of being a boy if you are going to grow up to be a man, the boy and the man have nothing to do with each other, except in respect to memory and identity, and if they have anything to do with each other in respect to memory and identity then they will never produce a master-piece. Do you do you understand well it really does not make much difference because after all master-pieces are what they are and the reason why is that there are very few of them. The reason why is any of you try it just not to be you are you because your little dog knows you. The second you are you because your little dog knows you you cannot make a master-piece and that is all of that.

It is not extremely difficult not to have identity but it is extremely difficult the knowing not having identity. One might say it is impossible but that it is not impossible is proved by the existence of master-pieces which are just that. They are knowing that there is no identity and producing while identity is not.

That is what a master-piece is.

And so we do know what a master-piece is and we also know why there are so few of them. Everything is against them. Everything that makes life go on makes identity and everything that makes identity is of necessity a necessity. And the pleasures of life as well as the necessities help the necessity of identity. The pleasures that are soothing all have to do with identity and the pleasures that are exciting all have to do with identity and moreover there is all the pride and vanity which play about master-pieces as well as about every one and these too all have to do with identity, and so naturally it is natural that there is more identity that one knows about than anything else one knows about and the worst of all is that the only thing that anyone thinks about is identity and thinking is something that does so nearly need to be memory and if it is then of course it has nothing to do with a master-piece.

But what can a master-piece be about mostly it is about identity and all it does and in being so it must not have any. I was just thinking about anything and in thinking about anything I saw something. In seeing that thing shall we see it without it turning into identity, the moment is not a moment and the sight is not the thing seen and yet it is. Moments are not important because of course master-pieces have no more time than they have identity although time like identity is what they concern themselves about of course that is what they do concern themselves about.

Once when one has said what one says it is not true or too true. That is what is the trouble with time. That is what makes what women say truer than what men say. That is undoubtedly what is the trouble with time and always in its relation to master-pieces. I once said that nothing could bother me more than the way a thing goes dead once it has been said. And if it does it it is because of there being this trouble about time.

Time is very important in connection with master-pieces, of course it makes identity time does make identity and identity does stop the creation of master-pieces. But time does something by itself to interfere with the creation of master-pieces as well as being part of what makes identity. If you do not keep remembering yourself you have no identity and if you have no time you do not keep remembering yourself and as you remember yourself you do not create anybody can and does know that.

Think about how you create if you do create you do not remember yourself as you do create. And yet time and identity is what you tell about as you create only while you create they do not exist. That is really what it is.

And do you create yes if you exist but time and identity do not exist. We live in time and identity but as we are we do not know time and identity everybody knows that quite simply. It is so simple that anybody does know that. But to know what one knows is frightening to live what one lives is soothing and though everybody likes to be frightened what they really have to have is soothing and so the master-pieces are so few not that the master-pieces themselves are frightening no of course not because if the creator of the master-piece is frightened then he does not exist without the memory of time and identity, and insofar as he is that then he is frightened and insofar as he is frightened the master-piece does not exist, it looks like it and it feels like it, but the memory of the fright destroys it as a master-piece. Robinson Crusoe and the footstep of the man Friday is one of the most perfect examples of the non-existence of time and identity which makes a master-piece. I hope you do see what I mean but anyway everybody who knows about Robinson Crusoe and the footstep of Friday knows that it is true. There is no time and identity in the way it happened and that is why there is no fright.

And so there are very few master-pieces of course there are very few master-pieces because to be able to know that is not to have identity and time but not to mind talking as if there was because it does not interfere with anything and to go on being not as if there were no time and identity but as if there were and at the same time existing without time and identity is so very simple that it is difficult to have many who are that. And of course that is what a master-piece is and that is why there are so few of them and anybody really anybody can know that.

What is the use of being a boy if you are going to grow up to be a man. And what is the use there is no use from the standpoint of master-pieces there is no use. Anybody can really know that.

There is really no use in being a boy if you are going to grow up to be a man because then man and boy you can be certain that that is continuing and a master-piece does not continue it is as it is but it does not continue. It is very interesting that no one is content with being a man and boy but he must also be a son and a father and the fact that they all die has something to do with time but it has nothing to do with a master-piece. The word timely as used in our speech is very interesting but you can any one can see that it has nothing to do with master-pieces we all readily know that. The word timely tells that master-pieces have nothing to do with time.

It is very interesting to have it be inside one that never as you know yourself you know yourself without looking and feeling and looking and feeling make it be that you are some one you have seen. If you have seen any one you know them as you see them whether it is yourself or any other one and so the identity consists in recognition and in recognizing you lose identity because after all nobody looks as they look like, they do not look like that we all know that of ourselves and of any one. And therefore in every way it is a trouble and so you write anybody does write to confirm what any one is and the more one does the more one looks like what one was and in being so identity is made more so and that identity is not what any one can have as a thing to be but as a thing to see. And it being a thing to see no master-piece can see what it can see if it does then it is timely and as it is timely it is not a master-piece.

There are so many things to say. If there was no identity no one could be governed, but everybody is governed by everybody and that is why they make no master-pieces, and also why governing has nothing to do with master-pieces it has completely to do with identity but it has nothing to do with master-pieces. And that is why governing is occupying but not interesting, governments are occupying but not interesting because master-pieces are exactly what they are not.

There is another thing to say. When you are writing before there is an audience anything written is as important as any other thing and you cherish anything and everything that you have written. After the audience begins, naturally they create something that is they create you, and so not everything is so important, something is more important than another thing, which was not true when you were you that is when you were not you as your little dog knows you.

And so there we are and there is so much to say but anyway I do not say that there is no doubt that master-pieces are master-pieces in that way and there are very few of them.

Look at Me Now and Here I Am: Writings and Lectures, 1909–1945. Ed. Patricia Meyerowitz. Harmondsworth: Penguin, 1971. 148–156.

A Transatlantic Interview 1946

Sherwood Anderson wrote, "For me the work of Gertrude Stein consists in a rebuilding, an entire new recasting of life, in the city of words." Is this an adequate summation of what you are trying to do?

It is and it isn't. The thing was not so simple as all that. In the beginning you must remember that I have always been from my babyhood a liberal reader of all English literature. In San Francisco they had a Mechanics library. As it happened, it had an uncommonly good collection for an ordinary town, and they had a really marvelously complete Seventeenth and Eighteenth Century English Literature collection, and the early Nineteenth Century. And when I was a youngster I used to spend days and days reading things there, and that was my early contact. And then when I became a scientist and became a psychologist, I was only being a scientist for a while, but I did not really care for science. I then went to England and read Elizabethan plays extensively which were very rich in word value.

Everything I have done has been influenced by Flaubert and Cézanne, and this gave me a new feeling about composition. Up to that time composition had consisted of a central idea, to which everything else was an accompaniment and separate but was not an end in itself, and Cézanne conceived the idea that in composition one thing was as important as another thing. Each part is as important as the whole, and that impressed me enormously, and it impressed me so much that I began to write *Three Lives* under this influence and this idea of composition and I was more interested in composition at that moment, this background of word-system, which had come to me from this reading that I had done. I was obsessed by this idea of composition, and the Negro story ("Melanctha" in *Three Lives*) was a quintessence of it.

You see I tried to convey the idea of each part of a composition being as important as the whole. It was the first time in any language that anyone had used that idea of composition in literature. Henry James had a slight inkling of it and was in some senses a forerunner, while in my case I made it stay on the page quite composed. You see he made it sort of like an atmosphere, and it was not solely the realism of the characters but the realism of the composition which was the important thing, the realism of the composition of my thoughts.

After all, to me one human being is as important as another human being, and you might say that the landscape has the same values, a blade of grass has the same value as a tree. Because the realism of the people who did realism before was a realism of trying to make people real. I was not interested in making the people real but in the essence or, as the painter would call it, value. One cannot live without the other. This was an entirely new idea and had been done a little by the Russians but had not been conceived as a reality until I came along, but I got it largely from Cézanne. Flaubert was there as a theme. He, too, had a little of the feeling about this thing, but they none of them conceived it as an entity, no more than any painter had done other than Cézanne. They all fell down on it, because the supremacy of one interest overcame them, while the Cézanne thing I put into words came in the *Three Lives* and was followed by the *Making of Americans.*

In the *Making of Americans* I began the same thing. In trying to make a history of the world my idea here was to write the life of every individual who could possibly live on the earth. I hoped to realize that ambition. My intention was to cover every possible variety of human type in it. I made endless diagrams of every human being, watching people from windows and so on until I could put down every type of human being that could be on the earth. I wanted each one to have the same value. I was not at all interested in the little or big men but to realize absolutely every variety of human experience that it was possible to have, every type, every style and nuance. I have always had this obsession, and that is why I enjoy talking to every GI. I must know every possible nuance.

Conception of this has to be based on a real feeling for every human being. The surprises of it are endless. Still there are the endless surprises, the combination that you don't expect, the relation of men to character that you do not expect. It never ends. All the time in it you see what I am singling out is that one thing has the same value as another. There are of course people who are more important than others in that they have more importance in the world, but this is not essential, and it ceases to be. I have no sense of difference in this respect, because every human being comprises the combination form. Just as everybody has the vote, including the women, I think children should, because as soon as a child is conscious of itself, then it has to me an existence and has a stake in what happens. Everybody who has that stake has that quality of interest, and in the *Making of Americans* that is what I tried to show.

In writing the *Three Lives* I was not particularly conscious of the question of style. The style which everybody shouted about surprised me. I was only interested in these other things. In the beginning gradually I became more conscious of the way you did this thing and I became gradually more conscious of it and at that time particularly of a need for evenness. At this time I threw away punctuation. My real objection to it was that it threw away this balance that I was trying to get, this evenness of everybody having a vote, and that is the reason I am impatient with punctuation. Finally I got obsessed with these enormously long sentences and long paragraphs. All that was an effort to get this evenness, and this went on until it sort of exhausted itself.

On the *Making of Americans* I had written about one thousand pages, and I finished the thing with a sort of rhapsody at the end. Then I started in to write *Matisse, Picasso, and Gertrude Stein.* You will see in each one of these stories that they began in the character of *Making of Americans,* and then in about the middle of it words began to be for the first time more important than the sentence structure or the paragraphs. Something happened. I mean I felt a need. I had thought this thing out and felt a need of breaking it down and forcing it into little pieces. I felt that I had lost contact with the words in building up these Beethovian passages. I had lost that idea gained in my youth from the Seventeenth Century writers, and the little rhymes that used to run through my head from Shakespeare, who was always a passion, got lost from the overall pattern. I recognized and I recognize (if you look at the *Long Gay Book*) this something else I knew would guide that.

I began to play with words then. I was a little obsessed by words of equal value. Picasso was painting my portrait at that time, and he and I used to talk this thing over endlessly. At this time he had just begun on cubism. And I felt that the thing I got from Cézanne was not the last composition. You had to recognize words had lost their value in the Nineteenth Century, particularly towards the end, they had lost much of their variety, and I felt that I could not go on, that I had to recapture the value of the individual word, find out what it meant and act within it.

Also the fact that as an American my mind was fresher towards language than the average English mind, as we had more or less renewed the word structure in our language. All through that middle period the interest was with that largely, ending up with *Tender Buttons.* In this I think that there are some of the best uses of words that there are. The movement is simple and holds by little words. I had at the same time a new interest in portraiture. I began then to want to make a more complete picture of each word, and that is when the portrait business started. I wait until each word can intimate some part of each little mannerism. In each one of them I was not satisfied until the whole thing formed, and it is very difficult to put it down, to explain, in words.

While during that middle period I had these two things that were working back to the compositional idea, the idea of portraiture and the idea of the recreation of the word. I took individual words and thought about them until I got their weight and volume complete and put them next to another word, and at this same time I found out very soon that there is no such thing as putting them together without sense. It is impossible to put them together without sense. I made innumerable efforts to make words write without sense and found it impossible. Any human being putting down words had to make sense out of them.

All these things interested me very strongly through the middle years from about after the *Making of Americans* until 1911, leading up to *Tender Buttons,* which was the apex of that. That was the culmination. Then came the war, and through the war I was traveling a great deal.

After the war the form of the thing, the question of the play form, began to interest me very much. I did very little work during the war. As soon as the war was over I settled down and wrote the whole of the *Geography and Plays.* That turned into very strong interest in play form, and then I began to be slowly impressed by the idea of narration.

After all, human beings are interested in two things. They are interested in the reality and interested in telling about it. I had struggled up to that time with the creation of reality, and then I became interested in how you could tell this thing in a way that anybody could understand and at the same time keep true to your values, and the thing bothered me a great deal at that time. I did quite a few plays and portraits, and that ended roughly with the *Four Saints,* 1932. Most of the things that are in the *Useful Knowledge,* including a book of poetry which was not printed, were constant effort, and after that I was beginning the narration consisting in plays at first, ending with the *Four Saints.*

After the *Four Saints* the portrait narration began, and I went back to the form of narration, and at that time I had a certain reputation, no success, but a certain reputation, and I was asked to write a biography, and I said "No." And then as a joke I began to write the *Autobiography of Alice Toklas,* and at that moment I had made a rather interesting discovery. A young French poet had begun to write, and I was asked to translate his poems, and there I made a rather startling discovery that other people's words are quite different from one's own, and that they can not be the result of your internal troubles as a writer. They have a totally different sense than when they are your own words. This solved for me the problem of Shakespeare's sonnets, which are so unlike any of his other work. These may have been his own idea, undoubtedly they were, but the words have none of the violence that exists in any of the poems, in any of the plays. They have a roughness and violence in their juxtaposition which the sonnets do not have, and this brought me to a great deal of illumination of narrative, because most narrative is based not about your opinions but upon someone else's.

Therefore narrative has a different concept than poetry or even exposition, because, you see, the narrative in itself is not what is in your mind but what is in somebody else's. Plays use it less, and so I did a tour de force with the *Autobiography of Alice Toklas,* and when I sent the first half to the agent, they sent back a telegram to see which one of us had written it! But still I had done what I saw, what you do in translation or in a narrative. I had recreated the point of view of somebody else. Therefore the words ran with a certain smoothness. Shakespeare never expressed any feelings of his own in those sonnets. They have too much smoothness. He did not feel "This is my emotion, I will write it down." If it is your own feeling, one's words will have a fullness and violence.

Then I became more and more interested in the subject of narration, and my work since this, the bulk of my work since then, has been largely narration, and I had done children's stories. I think *Paris, France* and *Wars I Have Seen* are the most successful of this. I thought I had done it in *Everybody's Autobiography.* I worked very hard on that and was often very exhausted, but it is often confused and not clarified. But in *Wars I Have Seen* and in *Paris, France,* to my feeling, I have done it more completely.

I have done the narration, because in narration your great problem is the problem of time in telling a story of anybody. And that is why newspaper people never become writers, because they have a false sense of time. They have to consider not the time in which to write but the time in which the newspaper is coming out. Three senses of time to struggle with, the time the event took place, the time they are writing, and the time it has to come out. Their sense of time can not be but false. Hemingway, on account of his newspaper training, has a false sense of time. One will sooner or later get this falsity of time, and that is why newspapers cannot be read later out of their published time.

I found out that in the essence of narration is this problem of time. You have as a person writing, and all the really great narration has it, you have to denude yourself of time so that writing time does not exist. If time exists, your writing is ephemeral. You can have a historical time, but for you the time does not exist, and if you are writing about the present, the time element must cease to exist. I did it unconsciously in the *Autobiography of Alice Toklas,* but I did it consciously in *Everybody's Autobiography* and in the last thing *Wars I Have Seen.* In it I described something momentous happening under my eyes and I was able to do it without a great sense of time. There should not be a sense of time, but an existence suspended in time. That is really where I am at the present moment, I am still largely meditating about this sense of time.

Words hold an interest that you never lose, but usually at one moment one is more preoccupied with one thing than another, the parts mould into the whole. The narrative phase began in the middle thirties and has continued to the present time. Anderson was interested in the phase I was going through at the moment that he knew me. The thing that worried him the most was the narrative, and like other writers of that period he had not freed himself from the Nineteenth Century influence. He was sort of a cutout of the old into the new design. This is well illustrated in a little book he wrote about farmers.

Will you give an account of the results of your experimentation with writing since your lecture tour in the United States?

This has already been covered. There is one thing that impressed me a good many years ago. The characters in the novels of the Nineteenth Century lived a queer kind of way. That is to say people lived and died by these characters. They took a violent interest in them: the Dickens characters, the George Eliot characters, the Meredith characters. They were more real to the average human being than the people they knew. They were far more real, and they would discuss them and feel for them like people they knew. At the end of the Nineteenth Century that died out. Meredith was the last to produce characters who people felt were alive. In the characters of Henry James this is really very little true, the characters do not live very much. The ensemble lives, but nobody gets excited about the characters.

You see there really has been no real novel writing in that sense in the Twentieth Century. The most creative writings were western stories and detective stories, but these were not enough. The hero was usually a dead man in the beginning of the book, and the rest of it is largely a question of a system, one man's way of doing a thing or Scotland Yard's way. The individual that made the Nineteenth Century live practically does not live in the Twentieth Century, where the individual does not stick out enough for the people reading about him. Take Sherwood Anderson, Hemingway, Fitzgerald, in all these it is the title and the form of the book that you remember rather than the characters in the book. That is the reason that the novel has not been a successful form of the Twentieth Century. Proust did it the best, but he made an old-fashioned thing of it. You take the average novel that is written in America today. No character sticks out, and no women's club gets all het up and excited about the character in the latest novel they read, or very little, surely.

You realize how they did in the Nineteenth Century. People really worried about and felt for these characters. Now, you see, even the cinema doesn't do it for them. A few actors or actresses do, but not the characters they portray. As long as the novel has existed, the characters were dominant. Can you imagine any one today weeping over a character? They get excited about the book but not the character.

This has interested me very much. I think that is the reason why the novel as a form has not been successful in the Twentieth Century. That is why biographies have been more successful than novels. This is due in part to this enormous publicity business. The Duchess of Windsor was a more real person to the public and while the divorce was going on was a more actual person than anyone could create. In the Nineteenth Century no one was played up like that, like the Lindbergh kidnapping really roused people's feelings. Then Eleanor Roosevelt is an actuality more than any character in the Twentieth Century novel ever achieved.

To my mind the novel form has not been a successful affair in the Twentieth Century. There has been nothing that you can honestly call a novel. There has not been one in the Twentieth Century with the possible exception of Proust. That makes the novel scheme quite out of the question. One falls back on the thing like I did in *Ida,* where you try to handle a more or less satirical picture within the individual. No individual that you can conceive can hold their own beside life. There has been so much in recent years. Napoleon was, you might say, an ogre in his time. The common people did not know all the everyday things, did not know him intimately, there was not this enormous publicity. People now know the details of important people's daily life unlike they did in the Nineteenth Century. Then the novel supplied imagination where now you have it in publicity, and this changed the whole cast of the novel. So the novel is not a living form, and people try to get out of the difficulty by essay and short story form, and that is a feeble form at best.

The only serious effort that has been made is the detective story, and in a kind of way Wallace is the only novelist of the Twentieth Century. He failed in the same way. He created an atmosphere of crime and did not have characters that people worried about. You cannot say that there is a novel of the Twentieth Century. I mean a more or less creative writer has never written anything that could in any reasonable sense of the word be called a novel. I have created a lot of characters, but that is another story.

Have there been any new developments in your attitude toward poetry?

Poetry is understandable, and the best poetry is real. The children's books and some of that in *Tender Buttons* and in some of the children's plays. There have been no new developments in poetry farther than that.

How and when are poetry and prose separate things?

I did that pretty thoroughly in that book of poetry and prose, and since then what poetry I have done has been in the children's books, and that you might call spontaneous poetry, and in *Paris, France* there is quite a bit of it, but that is mainly dealing with children. Somehow or other in war time the only thing that is spontaneously poetic is children. Children themselves are poetry. The poetry of adults in wartime is too intentional. It is too much mixed up with everything else. My poetry was children's poetry, and most of it is very good, and some of it as good as anything I have ever done. *The World is Round* is being included in a new American anthology.

The early book, Tender Buttons, *was written in Spain in 1913 and was Gertrude Stein's first attempt to "express the rhythm of the visible world."* Tender Buttons *was, therefore, to Gertrude Stein's development what the "Demoiselles d'Avignon" was to Picasso's, a key work marked with the enormous struggle of creating a new value.*

The following readings were chosen at random from Tender Buttons *and are followed by Gertrude Stein's verbatim responses.*

A DOG

A little monkey goes like a donkey that means to say that means to say that more sighs last goes. Leave with it. A little monkey goes like a donkey.

"A little monkey goes like a donkey . . ." That was an effort to illustrate the movement of a donkey going up a hill, you can see it plainly. "A little monkey goes like a donkey." An effort to make the movement of the donkey, and so the picture hangs complete.

A WHITE HUNTER
A white hunter is nearly crazy.

"A white hunter is nearly crazy." This is an abstract, I mean an abstraction of color. If a hunter is white he looks white, and that gives you a natural feeling that he is crazy, a complete portrait by suggestion, that is what I had in mind to write.

A LITTLE GIRL CALLED PAULINE (excerpt)

A little called anything shows shudders.
Come and say what prints all day. A whole few
watermelon. There is no pope.

No cut in pennies and little dressing and choose wide soles and little spats really little spices.

A little lace makes boils. This is not true. . . .

"A little called anything shows shudders." This was another attempt to have only enough to describe the movement of one of those old-fashioned automobiles, an old Ford, the movement is like that automobile. This is an account of movement that is not always successful. For the most part it is successful and is rather interesting.

A LITTLE BIT OF A TUMBLER

A shining indication of yellow consists in there having been more of the same color than could have been expected when all four were bought. This was the hope which made the six and seven have no use for any more places and this necessarily spread into nothing. Spread into nothing.

I have used this idea in more places. I used to take objects on a table, like a tumbler or any kind of object and try to get the picture of it clear and separate in my mind and create a word relationship between the word and the things seen. "A shining indication of yellow . . ." suggests a tumbler and something in it. ". . . when all four were bought" suggests there were four of them. I try to call to the eye the way it appears by suggestion the way a painter can do it. This is difficult and takes a lot of work and concentration to do it. I want to indicate it without calling in other things. "This was the hope which made the six and seven have no use for any more places . . ." Places bring up a reality. ". . . and this necessarily spread into nothing," which does broken tumbler which is the end of the story.

A WAIST

A star glide, a single frantic sullenness, a single financial grass greediness.

Object that is in wood. Hold the pine, hold the dark, hold in the rush, make the bottom.

A piece of crystal. A change, in a change that is remarkable there is no reason to say that there was a time.

A woolen object gilded. A country climb is the best disgrace, a couple of practices any of them in order is so left.

"A star glide, a single frantic sullenness, a single financial grass greediness." This was probably an effort to express an emotion, another version of an "Ode to a Mistress's Eyebrows." "Object that is in wood. Hold the pine, hold the dark, hold in the rush, make the bottom. A piece of crystal. A change, in a change that is remarkable there is no reason to say that there was a time." This is fairly successful of what I knew up to that date. I did not have to call in other things to help. I do not like to do this, there is so much one must reject to keep the even smoothness of suggestion.

A PIECE OF COFFEE

More of double.

A place in no new table.

A single image is not splendor. Dirty is yellow. A sign of more in not mentioned. A piece of coffee is not a detainer. The resemblance to yellow is dirtier and distincter. The cleaner mixture is whiter and not coal color, never more coal color than altogether.

The sight of a reason, the same sight slighter, the sight of a simpler negative answer, the same sore sounder, the intention to wishing, the same splendor, the same furniture.

The time to show a message is when too late and later there is no hanging in a blight.

A not torn rose-wood color. If it is not dangerous then a pleasure and more than any other if it is cheap is not cheaper. The amusing side is that the sooner there are no fewer the more certain is the necessity dwindled. Supposing that the case contained rose-wood and a color. Supposing that there was no reason for a distress and more likely for a number, supposing that there was no astonishment, it is not necessary to mingle astonishment.

The settling of stationing cleaning is one way not to shatter scatter and scattering. The one way to use custom is to use soap and silk for cleaning. The one way to see cotton is to have a design concentrating the illusion and the illustration. The perfect way is to accustom the thing to have a lining and the shape of a ribbon and to be solid, quite solid in standing and to use heaviness in morning. It is light enough in that. It has that shape nicely. Very nicely may not be exaggerating. Very strongly may be sincerely fainting. May be strangely flattering. May not be strange in everything. May not be strange to.

"Dirty is yellow." Dirty has an association and is a word that I would not use now. I would not use words that have definite associations. This was earlier work and none of the later things have this. This early work is not so successful. It is an effort and does not come clean. "The time to show a message is when too late and later there is no hanging in a blight." There is too much phantasy here. "A not torn rose-wood color. If it . . . is not necessary to mingle astonishment." That is the image but it is not completely successful, but it is better than the first part. You see there is too much appeal to the eye.

"The settling of stationing . . . May not be strange to." There is too much effort. If an effort that you make is successful, if you do get what you want to create, the effort must not show. It should create a satisfaction in the mind of the reader but in the same image as the creation. In this the mind is distracted and that is not satisfactory and it is therefore a failure. Here I am groping. I have not mastered my material. Insofar as creation is successful a reader realizes it as a successful entity, and in this you can see how successfully you have mastered your material.

A BROWN

A brown which is not liquid not more so is relaxed and yet there is a change, a news is pressing.

"A brown which is not liquid . . ." The color is held within and there you see I was groping for the color.

PEELED PENCIL, CHOKE

Rub her coke.

That is where I was beginning and went on a gool deal after that period to make sound pictures but I gave that up as uninteresting.

EGGS

Kind height, kind in the right stomach with a little sudden mill.

Cunning shawl, cunning shawl to be steady.

In white in white handkerchiefs with little dots in a white belt all shadows are singular they are singular and procured and relieved.

No that is not the cows shame and a precocious sound, it is a bite.

Cut up alone the paved way which is harm. Harm is old boat and a likely dash.

"In white in white handkerchiefs with little dots in a white belt all shadows are singular . . ." There I used a lot of imagery and from what I was interested in it is not a success. It should allow imagery with it without troubling anybody.

SUGAR (excerpts)

A violent luck and a whole sample and even then quiet.

Water is squeezing, water is almost squeezing on lard. Water, water is a mountain and it is selected and it is so practical that there is no use in money. A mind under is exact and so it is necessary to have a mouth and eye glasses.

A question of sudden rises and more time than awfulness is so easy and shady. There is precisely that noise . . . .

Put it in the stew, put it to shame. A little slight shadow and a solid fine furnace.

The teasing is tender and trying and thoughtful . .

A canoe is orderly. A period is solemn. A cow is accepted. . . .

This is rather fine, looking at it dispassionately. "A violent luck . . . There is precisely that noise." I call that from my standpoint a successful poem. ". . . slight shadow and a solid fine furnace." You see a "little slight shadow" has poetical appeal, but it is not quite successful poetry.

"Water is squeezing, water is almost squeezing on lard." The imagery of that is really a perfect example of realism, there is enough there to a person looking at water that is realistic, there is enough use that is outside the image before your eyes. "A mind under is exact and so it is necessary to have a mouth and eyeglasses." That impresses any person, so to speak it is part of the water and is therefore valid. It is supposed to continue the actual realism of water, of a great body of water.

You must remember each time I took something, I said, I have got to satisfy each realistic thing I feel about it. Looking at your shoe, for instance, I would try to make a complete realistic picture of your shoe. It is devilish difficult and needs perfect concentration, you have to refuse so much and so much intrudes itself upon you that you do not want it, it is exhausting work.

MUTTONS (excerpts)

Mouse and mountain and a quiver, a quaint statue and pain in an exterior and silence more silence louder shows salmon a mischief intruder . . . A sign is the specimen spoken.

A meal in mutton, mutton, why is lamb cheaper, it is cheaper because so little is more. Lecture, lecture and repeat instruction.

"Mouse and mountain and a quiver . . ." Here you see I was wise enough not to hesitate and still I dominated. ". . . A sign is the specimen spoken." You see also here you have a very good example. You take a paragraph like that and the values are pretty steady though this seems difficult to a normal reader's understanding. This is pretty good because it is more abstract.

You see it is the people who generally smell of the museums who are accepted, and it is the new who are not accepted. You have got to accept a complete difference. It is hard to accept that, it is much easier to have one hand in the past. That is why James Joyce was accepted and I was not. He leaned toward the past, in my work the newness and difference is fundamental. Cézanne was my great influence though I never met him; he was an ailing man at that time.

This book is interesting as there is as much failure as success in it. When this was printed I did not understand this creation. I can see now, but one cannot understand a thing until it is done. With a thing in the process of doing, you do not know what you are doing until it is done, finished, and thus you cannot explain it. Until then you are struggling.

I was not interested in what people would think when they read this poetry; I was entirely taken up with my problems and if it did not tell my story it would tell some story. They might have another conception which would be their affair. It is not necessarily attached to the original idea I had when I wrote it.

Nobody enters into the mind of someone else, not even a husband and wife. You may touch, but you do not enter into each other's mind. Why should you? In a created thing it means more to the writer than it means to the reader. It can only mean something to one person and that person the one who wrote it.

What was the character of your first audience?

Well, Carl Van Vechten was the first person who published me, and Carl was a great believer in me from the very beginning. Then there was a group of young people in New York. I do not know what has become of them now. They were all friends of Carl Van Vechten. There was a man called Don Marquis, and he in the guise of making fun was very much interested in my work. Henry McBride said, "If you laugh with her you have more fun than laughing at her." Protestingly, he used pieces of my work in his paper. I was essentially a writer's writer. My audience in France, that was a perfect audience. The first person who ever printed anything of mine here was Jean Cocteau. That was in a book called *Potomac,* in 1913. He was the first one. He printed the *Portrait of Mabel Dodge,* which he heard read in a cafe. Then there was Edith Sitwell, who was my chief English contact. Harold Acton was another one. Then there was Bernard Fay, who printed a piece of *Melanctha,* and he lectured on my work a great deal at the Collège de France.

Will you trace for me something of the nature of the development of your acceptance?

I became fairly early in the game a writer's writer. Sherwood Anderson and people like that scattered all over the country were interested, and it gave them something to think about—Bromfield, Hemingway, Anderson, Wendell Wilcox—and it disseminated between one and another. When I was at a dinner party at Beverly Hills in Hollywood, there were a great many of the big vedettes of the cinema. After the dinner all these people were seated in front of me, and I did not know what it was all about or what they wanted, and finally one blurted out, "What we want to know is how do you get so much publicity?" So I told them, "By having such a small audience. Begin with a small audience. If that small audience really believes, they make a big noise, and a big audience does not make a noise at all."

What is your attitude toward lecturing?

Picasso and I were talking the other day. I always said I never minded living in France. I write with my eyes, not with my ears or mouth. I hate lecturing, because you begin to hear yourself talk, because sooner or later you hear your voice, and you do not hear what you say. You just hear what they hear you say. As a matter of fact, as a writer I write entirely with my eyes. The words as seen by my eyes are the important words, and the ears and mouth do not count. I said to Picasso, "When you were a kid you never looked at things." He seemed to swallow the things he saw but he never looked, and I said, "In recent years you have been looking, you see too much, it is a mistake for you." He said, "You are quite right." A writer should write with his eyes, and a painter paint with his ears. You should always paint knowledge which you have acquired, not by looking but by swallowing. I have always noticed that in portraits of really great writers the mouth is always firmly closed.

What about your relationship with Richard Wright?

Richard Wright I first encountered through his writings on my work. I was impressed by the quality of his writings. I think in the first place he has a great mastery of the English language, and I think, to my mind, he has succeeded in doing the most creative work that has been done in many a year. His *Black Boy* is a very masterly novel, and every time he writes there is a form. He dominates his language. He holds it. *Uncle Tom's Children* has a piece of consummate description in the first of the story. I do not think there has been anything done like it since I wrote *Three Lives.* There has not been anything so good in the English language since. The others are merely followers. Richard Wright is not a follower. He does admire my writing thoroughly. He did a criticism of *Wars I Have Seen.* I saw it in a newspaper and was astounded by the quality of the writing and asked who he was and was given some of his books. He writes very wonderful letters. His meditations on the American scene are the most interesting I have heard from anybody. I think he is a very, very interesting person.

In Esquire, *July 1945, Sinclair Lewis wrote: ". . . When the exhibitionist deliberately makes his rites as confusing as possible, he is permitted to go on only because so many people are afraid to blurt out, 'I don't know what it means.' For that same reason, Gertrude Stein, the Mother Superior of all that shoddy magic, is still extensively admired even though she is also extensively unread."*

The best answer to that is what Picasso said, a perfectly good answer. In the first place this is my answer. The facts of the case are that all these people, including myself, are people with a considerably large endowment, and most of us spent thirty years of our life being made fun of and laughed at and criticized and having no existence and being without a cent of income. The work needs concentration, and one is often exhausted by it. No one would do this merely for exhibitionism; there is too much bitterness. Picasso said, "You see, the situation is very simple. Anybody that creates a new thing has to make it ugly. The effort of creation is so great, that trying to get away from the other things, the contemporary insistence, is so great that the effort to break it gives the appearance of ugliness. Your followers can make it pretty, so generally followers are accepted before the master. The master has the stain of ugliness. The followers who make it pretty are accepted. The people then go back to the original. They see the beauty and bring it back to the original."

Sinclair Lewis would never accept, for instance, that the GI is an entirely different creature from the Sammy of the last war. It would never occur to him to enter into things. He follows the journalistic form and is a newspaperman with a gift for writing books. I have been accused of repetition, but that is not so, and Sinclair Lewis is talking as they talked thirty years ago. The young man and the GI of today would never come to talk to me if I was an exhibitionist or a repetitionist, because time would have killed that. These do not last through time. The point is that the repetition is in Lewis; it is not in me. Lewis is saying what they said thirty years ago about *Tender Buttons.* Anderson also was protesting against it. You see the thing I mean is very well stated in *Composition.* I do not consider that any creative artist is anything but contemporary. Only he is sensitive to what is contemporary long before the average human being is. He puts down what is contemporary, and it is exactly that. Sooner or later people realize it.

I remember one day in the rue Raspail I was walking with Picasso. There came down the street a camouflaged truck, and he stood absolutely still and stared at it and said, "That is what you and I have been doing for years. What is the matter with these people?" He had known fifteen years before they knew that it was contemporary. Picasso said that no one is capable of understanding you who is not capable of doing the same work himself.

Why have you not explained more generally what you are attempting to do?

You explain it to anybody that asks, but if the asking desire is not there, the explanation is useless. You can explain when there is contact, and that person who has made contact can explain to others. It is in *Wars I Have Seen* and *Everybody's Autobiography.* But the thing you have to remember is that it is what these people like, and what Sinclair Lewis cannot understand is that it lives and is ageless.

He is the perfect example of the false sense of time of the newspaper world. He lives in the past and present but not the future. They have no time other than false time. He makes *Main Street* as if time were the main thing, which it isn't. He does not see that *Main Street* is made up of clear accounts of things. He was always dominated by an artificial time when he wrote *Main Street.* After all, the average human being is selfish and as such is interesting, everybody is, and he gives a little character to it. All right, but that is a cliché. He did not create actual human beings at any time. That is what makes it newspaper. Sinclair Lewis is the typical newspaperman who writes novels as a newspaperman, and everything he says is newspaper. The difference between a thinker and a newspaperman is that a thinker enters right into things; a newspaperman is superficial.

When I was in America one day there were three young newspapermen and a photographer, and they had just come out of college and took themselves very seriously, but eventually we got talking about things in general. The only one of the four of them who understood my writing was the photographer. He said, "I don't have to remember what you say. I am not involved with the mechanics of remembering it, and so I can understand it. They are too busy trying to remember what you say."

Why did you answer questionnaires like those in Little Review *and* transition *cryptically, with a chip on your shoulder?*

That does not interest me; it is like the Gallup Poll. After all, my only thought is a complicated simplicity. I like a thing simple, but it must be simple through complication. Everything must come into your scheme; otherwise you cannot achieve real simplicity. A great deal of this I owe to a great teacher, William James. He said, "Never reject anything. Nothing has been proved. If you reject anything, that is the beginning of the end as an intellectual." He was my big influence when I was at college. He was a man who always said, "Complicate your life as much as you please, it has got to simplify."

Nothing can be the same thing to the other person. Nobody can enter into anybody else's mind; so why try? One can only enter into it in a superficial way. You have slight contacts with other people's minds, but you cannot enter into them.

Then why did you publish manuscripts that were really written only for yourself?

There is the eternal vanity of the mind. One wants to see one's children in the world and have them admired like any fond parent, and it is a bitter blow to have them refused or mocked. It is just as bitter for me to have a thing refused as for any little writer with his first manuscript. Anything you create you want to exist, and its means of existence is in being printed.

A Primer for the Gradual Understanding of Gertrude Stein. Ed. Robert Bartlett Haas. Los Angeles: Black Sparrow P, 1971. 15–35.

Americans

Eating and paper.

A laugh in a loop is not dinner. There is so much to pray.

A slight price is a potatoe. A slimness is in length and even in strength.

A capable extravagance that is that which shows no provision is that which when necessity is mild shows a certain distribution of anger. This is no sign of sin.

Five, five are more wonderful than a million. Five million, five million, five million, five are more wonderful than two together. Two together, two together.

A song, if a sad song is in unison and is sung, a sad song is singing. A sign of singing.

A gap what is a gap when there is not any meaning in a slice with a hole in it. What is the exchange between the whole and no more witnesses.

Press juice from a button, press it carelessly, press it with care, press it in a storm. A storm is so waiting and awful and moreover so much the worse for being where there is a storm that the use the whole use of more realization comes out of a narrow bridge and water faucets. This is no plain evidence of disaster. The point of it is that there is a strange straw being in any strange ice-cream.

A legal pencil a really legal pencil is incredible, it fastens the whole strong iron wire calender.

An inherent investigation, does that mean murder or does it only mean a railroad track with plenty of cinders.

Words that cumber nothing and call exceptionally tall people from very far away are those that have the same center as those used by them frequently.

Bale, bale is a thing that surrounding largely means hay, no hay has any more food than it needs to weigh that way henceforward and not more that most likely.

A soap, a whole soap, any piece of a whole soap, more whole soap and not mistily, all this is no outrage and no blessing. A precious thing is an oily thing. In that there is no sugar and silence.

A reason is that a curly house an ordinary curly house is exactly that, it is exactly more than that, it is so exactly no more than more than that.

Waiter, when is a waiter passive and expressed, a waiter is so when there is no more selection and really no more buckets altogether. This is what remains. It does. It is kindly exacted, it is pleased, it is anxious, it is even worthy when a material is like it. It is.

What is a hinge. A hinge is a location. What is a hinge necessarily.

When the butter cup is limited and there are radishes, when radishes are clean and a whole school, a real school is outrageous and more incensed, really more incensed and inclined, when the single satisfaction is so perfect and the pearl is so demure when all this is changed then there is no rattle there is hardly any rattle.

A and B and also nothing of the same direction is the best personal division there is between any laughing. The climate, the whole thing is surrounded, it is not pressed, it is not a vessel, it is not all there is of joining, it is a real anxious needful and it is so seldom circular, so more so than any article in the wire. The cluster is just the same ordinarily.

Supposing a movement is segregated and there is a piece of staging, suppose there is and the present is melted does that mean that any salt is bitter, would it change an investigation suddenly, when it would would it mean a long wide and not particular eddy. Would it and if it did would there be a change. A kind of exercise is hardest and the best excellence is sweet.

Finding a best hat with a hardy hat pin in midsummer is a reason for being blindly. A smell is not in earth.

A wonder to chew and to eat and to mind and to set into the very tiny glass that is tall. This is that when there is a tenement. All weights are scales.

No put in a closet, no skirt in a closet, no lily, no lily not a lime lily. A solving and learned, awake and highing and a throat and a throat and a short set color, a short set color and a collar and a color. A last degree in the kink in a glove the rest.

A letter to press, a letter to press is not rowdy, it is not sliding, it is not a measure of the increasing swindling of elastic and breaking.

The thread, the thread, the thread is the language of yesterday, it is the resolution of today, it is no pain.

What is pain, pain is so changing the climate and the best ever that it is a time, it is really only a time, it is so winding. It is even.

A warm banana is warm naturally and this makes an ingredient in a mixture which has banana in it.

Cooling in the chasing void, cooling more than milder.

Hold that ho, that is hold the hold.

Pow word, a pow word is organic and sectional and an old man's company.

Win, win, a little bit chickeny, wet, wet, a long last hollow chucking jam, gather, a last butter in a cheese, a lasting surrounding action.

White green, a white green. A looking like that is a most connected piece of example of what it is where there is no choking, no choking in any sign.

Pin in and pin in and point clear and point where.

Breakfast, breakfast is the arrangement that beggars corn, that shows the habit of fishes, that powders aches and stumblings, and any useful thing. The way to say it is to say it.

No counting, no counting in not cousins, no counting for that example and the number of thirty and thirteen and thirty six and thirty.

A blind hobble which makes distress. A place not to put in a foot, a place so called and in close color, a place best and more shape and really a thought.

Cousin why is there no cousin, because it is an article to be preparatory.

Was it green told, was it a pill, was it chased awake, will it sale per, peas are fish, chicken, cold ups, nail poppers, nail pack in hers extra. Look pase per. Look past per. Look past per. Look past fer. Look past fer. Look past fer.

No end in yours, knock puzzler palers, no beast in papers, no bird.

Icer cream, ice her steam, ice her icer ice sea excellent, excel gone in front excel sent.

Leaves of wet perfect sharpen setters, leaves of wet purr feet shape for seal weight for shirters.

Leaves of wet for ear pole ache sold hers, ears for sake heat purse change to meeters, change to be a sunk leave to see wet hers, but to why in that peace so not. Knot lot.

Please bell room please bell room fasten a character fasten a care in apter buttons fasten a care in such, in such. Fasten a care in, in in a in.

A lovely life in the center makes a mine in found a lovely pond in the water makes it just a space. A lovely seat in a day lump makes a set to collapse, a lovely light in a grass field makes it see just the early day in when there is a sight of please please please.

Due tie due to die due show the never less more way less. Do, weigh the more do way less.

Let us call a boat, let us call a boat.

Leave little grace to be. Leave little grace to bea, live little grace to bee.

Leave little grace. Leave little.

Leave little grace to be.

Near red reserve leave lavender acre bat.

Shout us, shout horse curve less.

Least bee, least bay alter, alter the sat pan and left all, rest in, resafe in article so fur.

A cannon ball a cigar and a dress in suits, a cannon ball a cigar and a dress suit case, a cannon ball a cigar and a dress suit case, a head a hand a little above, a shake in my and mines.

Let us leaves, moor itch. Bars touch.

Nap old in town inch chair, nap on in term on chain, do deal sack file in for, do bale send on and for, reset the pan old in for same and chew get that all baste for, nice nor call churches, meet by and boot send for in, last when with and by that which for with all do sign call, meet with like shall what shirs not by bought lest, not by bought lest in own see certain, in own so same excellent, excellent hairy, hairy, excellent not excellent not knot excellent, excellent knot.

B r, brute says. A hole, a hole is a true, a true, a true.

Little paper and dolls, little paper and row why, little paper and a thin opera extra.

No use to age mother, no whole wide able recent mouth parcel, no relief farther, no relief in loosens no relief abler, no relief, no relief pie pepper nights, no relief poor no relief or, no relief, or no relief.

America a merica, a merica the go leading s the go leading s cans, cans be forgot and nigh nigh is a niecer a niecer to bit, a niecer to bit.

It was a peach, it was a long suit, it was a heavy harsh singes.

Leave crack his leave crack his eats, all guest all guest a stove. Like bit.

Nuts, when and if the bloom is on next and really really really, it is a team, it is a left and all it cut, it is a so like that between and a shun a shun with a believer, a believer in the extra, extra not, extra a rechange for it more. No sir.

No it sir.

It was a tame in, it was a tame in and a a little vent made a whole simmer simmer a wish.

What is it not to say reach house. Coal mill. Coal mill well. It to lease house. Coal mill tell. Coal in meal tell.

A pill shape with a round center.

Color Cook color him with ready bbs and neat show pole glass and nearly be seen every day more see what all a pearly little not shut, no rail see her.

No peter no rot.

Poles poles are seeds and near the change the change pets are swimming swimming and a plate all a plate is reed pour for the grammar grammar of lake.

Lake in a sad old chimney last and needs needs needs needs needs needs needs, in the mutton and the meat there is a change to pork walk, with a walk mean clean and butter and does it show the feather bench does it mean the actual and not or does it light the cylinder. It is in choice and chosen, it is in choice and knee and knee and knee and just the same two bay.

To irregulate to irregulate gums.

America key america key.

It is too nestle by the pin grove shirr, all agree to the counting ate ate pall. Paul is better.

Vest in restraint in repute.

Shown land in constate.

I am sorry I am awfully sorry, I am so sorry, I am so sorry.

No fry shall it see c bough it.

Nibbling bit, nibbling bit, may the land in awe for.

It is not a particular lamp lights which absolutely so far pull sizes and near by in the change with it not in the behoof.

It was a singe, it was a scene in the in, it was a singe in.

Never sink, never sink sinker, never sink sinker sunk, sink sink sinker sink.

A cattle sheep.

By the white white white white, by the white white white white white white, by the white white white white by the white by the white white white white.

Needless in pins.

In the fence in the for instance, in the fence or how, hold chirp, hold chirp her, hold your paper, hope hop in hit it.

Extra successive.

Little beats of long saturday tileing.

No neck leg ticking.

Peel more such wake next stir day.

Peel heaps pork seldom.

Coiled or red bench.

A soled in a light is not waver. There is for much ash so.

In the second, in the second second second.

Pour were whose has. Pole sack sirs.

A neat not necklace neglect.

A neat not neglect. A neat.

A neat not neglect.

Put a sun in sunday. Sunday.

Geography and Plays. 1922. New York: Something Else, 1968. 39–45.

White Wines

THREE ACTS

1. All together.
2. Witnesses.
3. House to house.
   (5 women)

All together.

Cunning very cunning and cheap, at that rate a sale is a place to use type writing. Shall we go home.

Cunning, cunning, quite cunning, a block a strange block is filled with choking.

Not too cunning, not cunning enough for wit and a stroke and careless laughter, not cunning enough.

A pet, a winter pet and a summer pet and any kind of a pet, a whole waste of pets and no more hardly more than ever.

A touching spoon a real touching spoon is golden and show in that color. A really touching spoon is splendid, is splendid, and dark and is so nearly just right that there is no excuse.

The best way is to wave an arm, the best way is to show more used to it than could be expected.

Comfort a sudden way to go home, comfort that and the best way is known.

All together.

Hold hard in a decision about eyes. Hold the tongue in a sober value as to bunches. See the indication in all kinds of rigorous landscapes. Spell out what is to be expected.

Show much blame in order and all in there, show much blame when there is a breath in a flannel. Show the tongue strongly in eating. Puzzle anybody.

Violet and the ink and the old ulster, shut in trembling and a whole departure, flood the sunshine, terrorize the grown didy, mingle sweetness with communion.

All together.

Change the sucking with a little sucking.

Modify the brave gallant pin wheel. Show the shout, worry with wounds, love out what is a pendant and a choke and a dress in together.

Punish the grasshopper with needles and pins are plenty. Show the old chink.

All together.

Put the putty in before the door put the oil glass in with what is green. Put the mellow choice with all the test, rust with night and language in the waist. Praise the cat and show the twine the door, mention every scrap of linen carpet, see the eagle and behold the west, win the day light with the hat unpressed, show it in a shudder and a limp, make a best container with no speed, and a jacket and a choice and beets, beets are what there are when bets are less. Bets are less in summer.

SINGLE WITNESSES

(1). A spread out case is so personal it is a mountain of change and any little piece is personal, any one of them is an exchange. No forethought is removed. Nothing, hindrances, butter, a safe smooth, a safe why is a tongue a season, why is a loin large by way of spoiling. There is no cake in front. A choking is an example.

More witnesses.

It is true, it certainly is true and a coat any coat, any dress, all dress, a hat, many hats, all colors, every kind of coloring, all this makes shadows longer and birds, makes birds, just makes birds.

Not much limping is in the back, not much limping is in the front, not much limping is circular, a bosom, a candle, an elegant foot fall, all this makes daylight.

Single Witnesses.

(2). A blunder in a charger is blue. A high pocket not higher than the wrist and the elbow, the pocket is not added.

A clutch, a real clutch is merry and a joke and a baby, a real clutch is such a happy way. A real clutch is so soon worried so easily made the same, so soon made so.

[A real white and blue, blue and blue, blue is raised by being so and more much more is ready. At last a person is safe.

More witnesses.

Pile in the windows, freeze with the doors, paint with the ceiling, shut in the floors, paint with the ceiling, paint with the doors, shut in the ceiling, shut out the doors, shut in the doors, shut in the floors, shut in the floors, shut in the doors.

More witnesses.

Put the patient goat away, put the patient boat away, put away the boat and put it, the boat, put it, put away that boat. Put away the boat.

Single Witnesses.

(3). An army of invincible and ever ready mustaches and all the same mind and a way of winding and no more repertoire, not any more noise, this did increase every day.

A moon, a moon, a darkness and the stars and little bits of eels and a special sauce, not a very special sauce, not only that.

A wide pair that are not slippers, not a wide pair of slippers, not pressed to be any of that in that particular but surely, surely, surely a loan, surely every kind of a capital.

More Witnesses.

A splendid little charles louis philip, a splendid spout of little cups and colds, a splendid big stir, a splendid glass, a splendid little splinter, a splendid cluster.

Single Witnesses.

(4). Why should wet be that and cut, cut with the grass, why should wet be that and clut with the purse, why should wet be wet and the wet that wet. Why should wet be the time to class. Why should there be solemn cuppings.

The lean bark, that is the round and intense and common stop and in shouting, the left bark and the right bark and a belt, in that belt, in no belt and a corset, in a belt and chores, in a belt and single stitches, in more boys than enough, in all thin beer and in all such eggs, in all the pile and in all the bread, in the bread, in the bread, in the condition of pretty nearly saying that yesterday is today, and tomorrow, tomorrow is yesterday. The whole swindle is in short cake and choice cake is white cake and white cake is sponge cake and sponge cake is butter.

House to house.

(1). A habit that is not left by always screaming, a habit that is similar to the one that made quiet quite quiet and made the whole plain show dust and white birds and little plaintive drops of water, a habit which brightened the returning butter fly and the yellow weed and even tumbling, the habit which made a well choose the bottom and refuses all chances to change, the habit that cut in two whatever was for the use of the same number, the habit which credited a long touch with raising the table and the hour glass and even eye glasses and plenty of milk, the habit which made a little piece of cheese wholesome and darkness bitter and clanging a simple way to be solemn, a habit which has the best situation and nearly all the day break and the darkness a habit that is cautious and serious and strange and violent and even a little disturbed, a habit which is better than almost anything, a habit that is so little irritating, so wondering and so unlikely is not more difficult than every other.

(2). A change a real change is made by a piece by any piece by a whole mixture of words and likenesses and whole outlines and ranges, a change is a butt and a wagon and an institution, a change is a sweetness and a leaning and a bundle, a change is no touch and buzzing and cruelty, a change is no darkness and swinging and highness, a change is no season and winter and leaving, a change is no stage and blister and column, a change is no black and silver and copper, a change is no jelly and anything proper, a change is not place, a change is not church, a change is not more clad, a change is not more in between when there is that and the change is the kind and the king is the king and the king is the king and the king is the king.

(3). Could there be the best almost could there be almost the most, could there be almost almost, could there be the most almost. Could there be the most almost, could there be the most almost, could there be almost almost. Could there be almost, almost.

Can the stretch have any choice, can the choice have every chunk, can the choice have all the choice, can the stretch have in the choice. Can there be water, can there be water and water. Can there be water. Can there be.

(4). A cousin to cooning, a cousin to that and mixed labor and a strange orange and a height and a piece of holy phone and a catching hat glass and a bit of undertaking. All this makes willows and even then there is no use in dusting not in really redusting, not in really taking everything away. The best excuse for shadows is in the time when white is starched and hair is released and all the old clothes are in the best bag.

House to house.

A wet hurt and a yellow stain and a high wind and a color stone, a place in and the whole real set all this and each one has a chin. This is not a claim it is a reorganization and a balance and a return.

Geography and Plays. 1922. New York: Something Else, 1968. 210–214.

Play

Play, play every day, play and play and play away, and then play the play you played to-day, the play you play every day, play it and play it. Play it and remember it and ask to play it. Play it, and play it and play away. Certainly every one wants you to play, every one wants you to play away, to play every day, to play and play, to play the play you play every day, to play and remember it and ask to play it and play it and to play away and to play every day and to-day and all day. That's the way to play, to play every day and all day, to play away, to play and play and play, to play and to remember what you play and to play it the next day and to ask to play it another day and to play it and to play it every day, to play it to-day, to play it all day.

This is the way to play, every one wants them to play all day, to play away, to play to-day, to play all day, to play every day, always to play. Every one is very glad to have them play, to have them play all day, to have them play every day, to have them play and play and play.

Every one is certain that some of them are playing, playing and playing and playing every day and all day and to-day. Every one is certain that some of them are playing and remembering and playing again again what they were playing. Some of them are certainly playing, playing, playing. Every one is wanting some of them to be playing and playing and playing, to be playing to-day, to be playing all day, to be playing every day, to be playing away.

Some are certain that playing is good for them, good for some of them, playing all day, every day is good for them, good for some of them.

Some are going to be playing all day, playing every day. Some are going to be playing to-day, going to be playing away, going to be remembering to play and going to play every day, all day, going to play and play and play.

Some play every day, play all day, play every day and all day, play all day every day. Some play and play and play and play all day and play every day.

Some play and remember what they play and ask to play that again the next day and they play it again the next day and play it all day and play and play.

Some play every day. Some play all day. Some play to-day. Some play and play. Some play and play and play. Some play every day and all day. Some play away. Some play and play and play.

Portraits and Prayers. New York: Random House, 1934. 160–161.

A Description of the Fifteenth of November: A Portrait of T. S. Eliot

On the fifteenth of November we have been told that she will go either here or there and in company with some one who will attempt to be of aid in any difficulty that may be pronounced as at all likely to occur. This in case that as usual there has been no cessation of the manner in which latterly it has all been as it might be repetition. To deny twice. Once or twice.

On the fifteenth of November in place of what was undoubtedly a reason for finding and in this way the best was found to be white or black and as the best was found out to be nearly as much so as was added. To be pleased with the result.

I think I was.

On the fifteenth of November have it a year. On the fifteenth of November they returned too sweet. On the fifteenth of November also.

The fifteenth of November at best has for its use more than enough to-day. It can also be mentioned that the sixteenth and any one can see furniture and further and further than that. The idea is that as for a very good reason anything can be chosen the choice is the choice is included.

After contradiction it is desirable.

In any accidental case no incident no repetition no darker thoughts can be united again. Again and again.

In plenty of cases in union there is strength.

Can any one in thinking of how presently it is as if it were in the midst of more attention can any one thinking of how to present it easily can any one really partake in saying so. Can any one.

All of it as eagerly as not.

Entirely a different thing. Entirely a different thing when all of it has been awfully well chosen and thoughtfully corrected.

He said we, and we.

We said he.

He said we.

We said he, and he.

He said.

We said.

We said it. As we said it.

We said that forty was the same as that which we had heard.

It depends entirely upon whether in that as finally sure, surely as much so.

Please please them. Please please please them.

Having heard half of it.

Please having having had please having had please having had half of it.

Please please half of it.

Pleases.

Yes and a day.

A day and never having heard a thing.

Extra forty.

There is no greater pleasure than in having what is a great pleasure.

Happy to say that it was a mistake.

If at each part of one part and that is on the whole the best of all for what it provides and any satisfaction if at each part less less and more than usual it is not at all necessary that a little more has more added in a day. It is considerably augmented and further it settles it as well.

This makes mention more and more and mention to mention this makes it more and more necessary to mention that eighteen succeeds three. Can going again be startling.

On the fifteenth of November in increase and in increases, it increases it as it has been carefully considered. He has a son and a daughter and in this case it is important because although in itself a pleasure it can be a pleasure.

Fortunately replacing takes the place of their sending and fortunately as they are sending in this instance if there are there and one has returned and one is gone and one is going need there be overtaking. Overtaken. A usefulness to be.

Mentioned as a mistake. No mention not mentioned not mentioning not to be before and fortunately. It was very fortunate.

If calling had come from calling out, Come and call. Call it weekly.

In this case a description.

Forward and back weekly.

In this case absolutely a question in question.

Furnished as meaning supplied.

Further back as far back.

Considerably more.

Simply and simply and simply, simply simply there. Simply so that in that way, simply in that way simply so that simply so that in that way.

November the fifteenth and simply so that simply so that simply in that simply in that simply so that in that simply in that simply in that way simply so that simply so that in that way simply in that way, simply in that way so that simply so that simply so that simply simply in that, simply in that so that simply so that simply so that simply in that, so that simply in that way.

Actually the fifteenth of November.

Played and plays and says and access. Plays and played and access and impress. Played and plays and access and acquiese and a mistake. Actually the fifteenth of November. Let us lose at least three. You too. Let us lose at least three. You too. Let us lose at least three. Three and there makes made three and three made makes, there and three makes, fourteen is a few.

A few separated rather separated separately.

As readers make red as pallor and few as readers make red and so do you.

Very nearly actually and truly.

A bargain in much as much a bargain in as much as there is of it. Have had it in reserve. To have had it in reserve. And have had it in reserve. Or have had it in reserve. Or have had it in reserve. To have had it in reserve. Touch a tree touch a tree to it.

Irons make an iron here and there.

And do declare.

The fifteenth of November has happily a birthday. And very happily a birthday. And very happily a birthday. The fifteenth of November has, happily, a birthday and very happily a birthday, and very happily a birthday.

Not as yet and to ask a question and to ask a question and as yet, and as yet to as yet to ask a question to and as yet.

Not as yet and to ask a question and to ask a question and as not yet. As not yet and to as yet and to ask a question and to as yet and to wind as yet and to as yet and to ask a question and to as yet ask a question as not yet, as not yet and to ask as not yet, and as not yet to ask a question as yet, and to as yet to wind as not yet, as not yet to wind please wind as not yet to ask a question and to and not yet. Please wind the clock and as yet and as not yet. Please wind the clock and not yet, to please not yet as not yet.

He said enough.

Enough said.

He said enough.

Enough said.

Enough said.

He said enough.

He said enough.

Enough said.

He said enough.

Not only wool and woolen silk and silken not only silk and silken wool and woolen not only wool and woolen silk and silken not only silk and silken wool and woolen not only wool and woolen silk and silken not only silk and silken not only wool and woolen not only wool and woolen not only silk and silken not only silk and silken not only wool and woolen.

Portraits and Prayers. 68–72.

Sitwell Edith Sitwell

In a minute when they sit when they sit around her.

Mixed it with two who. One two two one two two. Mixed it with two who.

Weeks and weeks able and weeks.

No one sees the connection between Lily and Louise, but I do.

After each has had after each has had, after each has had had had it.

Change in time.

A change in time is this, if a change in time. If a change in time is this. If a change in time.

Did she come to say who.

Not to remember weeks to say and asking, not to remember weeks to-day. Not to remember weeks to say. Not to remember weeks to say and asking.

And now a bow.

When to look when to look up and around when to look down and around when to look down and around when to look around and around and altered.

Just as long as any song.

And now altogether different.

It was in place of places and it was here.

Supposing she had had a key supposing she had answered, supposing she had had to have a ball supposing she had it fall and she had answered. Supposing she had it and in please, please never see so.

As much even as that, even can be added to by in addition, listen.

Table table to be table to see table to be to see to me, table to me table to be table to table to table to it. Exactly as they did when when she was not and not and not so. After that perhaps.

She had a way of she had a way of not the name.

Little reaching it away.

As afternoon to borrow.

It made a difference.

This is most.

Introduces.

This is for her and not for Mabel Weeks.

She could not keep it out.
Introduces have and heard.
Miss Edith Sitwell have and heard.
Introduces have and had.
Miss Edith Sitwell have and had.
Introduces have and had introduces have and had and heard.
Miss Edith Sitwell have and had and heard.
Left and right.
Part two of Part one.
If she had a ball at all, if she had a ball at all too.
Fill my eyes no no.
It was and held it.
The size of my eyes.
Why does one want to or to and to, when does one want to and to went to.
To know it as well as all there.
If a little other more not so little as before, now they knew and that and so.
What in execute.
Night is different from bright.
When he was a little sweeter was he.
Part two.
There was a part one.
He did seem a little so.
Half of to mention it at all.
And now to allow literally if and it will if and it does if and it has if and it is.
Never as much as a way.
How does she know it.
She could be as she sleeps and as she wakes all day. She could be as she sleeps and as she wakes all day it is not so.
It leads it off of that.
Please carried at.
Twice at once and carry.
She does and care to and cover and never believe in an and being narrow.
Happily say so.
What is as added.
And opposite.
Now it has to be something entirely different and it is.
Not turned around.
No one knows two two more.
Lose and share all and more.
Very easily arises.
It very easily arises.
Absently faces and by and by we agree.
By and by faces apparently we agree.

Apparently faces by and by we agree.
By and by faces apparently we agree.
Apparently faces by and by we agree.

Portraits and Prayers. 92–95.

To Kitty or Kate Buss

It is in ingredients that mays are a measure.

Which they are when they are whichever they are.

It is made by a text. When this you see remember me, that mays are made an extremely urgent measure. They are used to measure whichever they are used for as it is for weights which are weights with which to measure.

They made them have lambs which are colored like dogs.

They did have with them what they had with them.

They were by themselves in a minute.

A minute is a long time in which to say yes.

Cingria said Kitty had a name
Fortune tellers a name
For which they came.
Kitty Buss had the name
Kitty Buss had the same
Kitty Buss is the same as Kitty which is a name.
Katy Buss came with her name.
This is why she asked a little name to blame.

She is to blame for the name Kate Buss is a name which could rhyme with game but does it all the same. Which is for it as with it a name.

She meant to be had as when they went to leave it as a Basket. A basket if it is mentioned dates it.

Do you see how I introduce dates. Dates a flower dates a fruit. She is made to have it mean Jasmine a muguet.

Excuse me for introducing French it is not my custom but it seemed a choice thanks so much.

Portraits and Prayers. 103–104.

22

Sylvia Townsend Warner (1893–1978)

Introduced and Edited by Jane Marcus

Appropriately for a leftist and a writer of folk and fairy tales, the English poet and novelist Sylvia Townsend Warner died on May Day, 1978, at the age of eighty-four, the author of seven novels, nine books of poetry, ten volumes of short stories, a biography of T. H. White, a translation of Proust's *Contre Sainte-Beuve,* and numerous essays and reviews.[1] The publication of some of her letters in 1982 by her editor at the *New Yorker,* William Maxwell, and *Collected Poems,* edited by Claire Harman in 1983, followed the feminist revival of her work in the 1978 reprint by the Women's Press in London of Warner's brilliant prize-winning 1926 novel, *Lolly Willowes.* Along with Rebecca West's *Harriet Hume,* this is an example of a form one might call feminist fantastic realism, the direct forerunner of Angela Carter's work.[2] Townsend Warner's letters, as dazzling as Virginia Woolf's, give some idea of the extraordinary range of her talent: "The day before yesterday, I appeased a life-long ambition: I held a young fox in my arms. . . . I held him in my arms & snuffed his wild geranium smell, and suddenly he thrust his long nose under my chin, and burrowed against my shoulder, and subsided into bliss. His paws are very soft, soft as raspberries. Everything about him is elegant—an Adonis of an animal."[3]

Like Antonia White, Warner was the daughter of a schoolmaster. She grew up at Harrow, enduring, like Woolf, the bliss and terror of an autodidact's self-education in her father's library. Starting her career as "that odd thing—a musicologist," she spent the decade 1917–1927 as one of four editors of the ten-volume Oxford University Press *Tudor Church Music*, "romantically engaged in tracing, scoring and collating Masses, Motets" and other pieces from manuscript sources. World War I changed the course of her life. Her intent was to compose, but the war shut off the chance of going to Germany to study with Schönberg. Her first published work was an essay on her job as a relief munitions worker in *Blackwoods Magazine* in 1916.[4] She claimed that she became a poet to fill up the leftover sheets of "beautiful smooth white photographic paper" on which she inscribed early musical texts. The very musicality of her poetry, the attention, like Edith Sitwell's, to rhythm and qualities of sound, coupled with a dry, bleak English pastoral irony which critics have likened to Hardy and to her close friend and fellow Dorset writer T. F. Powys, may suggest some of the reasons modernism has not claimed her as a major poet.

But, as Celeste Schenck argues, new definitions and the elasticizing of stylistic considerations, beyond valorizing the style of Eliot and Joyce, bring to light some dazzling uncanonized women poets.[5] The project of this volume is to expand the canon to include those puzzling writers, such as Warner, whose vertical lines of descent from other poets and horizontal lines of affiliation with writers of her own age zigzag across the history of twentieth-century writing on any path but the straight. "Scoured table, pray for me," Warner writes in "Woman's Song," "All things wonted, fleeting, fixed, / Stand me and myself betwixt, / Sister my mortality" (*Collected Poems*, 19, 20). The domestic scene, especially the hearth, grounds her poetry for tart and troubled deconstructions of family, state, and sexual ideologies. Politics are pursued on the plane of the fantastic in her elfin stories as diligently as her fellow Marxists exploited realism. In "Wish in Spring" from *The Espalier* (1927) Warner notes that writing is hard work. If it were as natural as leaves on trees "then I should have poems innumerable, / One kissing the other; / Authentic, perfect in shape and lovely variety, / And all of the same tireless green color . . . / But as I am only a woman / And not a tree, / With piteous human care I have made this poem, / And set it now on the shelf with the rest to be." Explicitly denying divine inspiration or the high calling of Eliot or Pound, Townsend Warner compares poems to cups and saucers and writing to domestic labor, valorizing, as Woolf does in her portraits of charwomen, women's daily work at the same time as she demystifies and undoes the "dignity" of art and artists.

In the introduction to *Collected Poems*, Claire Harmon, whose official biography was published in 1989, makes a case for the brilliance of *Opus 7* (1931), a long narrative satire in couplets reminiscent of Crabbe whose heroine is the hard-drinking Rebecca Random, forced by postwar poverty to sell flowers to pay for her gin. Revising modernism to include this poem unsettles definitions and sisters the critic's own mortality. If we privilege lyric fragmented voices from this period, what to do with this other tradition, the daughter of *Aurora Leigh?* Townsend Warner wrote the verse novel as well as Tudor metrical conceits, the dark and dramatic Hardyesque as well as the committed communist ballad. Her multivoicedness and creation of character in dramatic soliloquy calls out for a critical extension of Bakhtin's work on the novel to poetry. In the age of metropolitan modernism, Warner politicizes the pastoral. A storyteller at heart, she shaped poetry for story as she molded the short story and novel for lyric and for history, and she set all the forms at her disposal dancing to the tune of politics.

With her lover, poet Valentine Ackland (1906–1969), Warner in 1933 published *Whether a Dove or a Seagull,* dedicated to Robert Frost, a duet whose authorship was not attributed in individual poems as a protest from the Left, an "experiment in presentation" designed to unsettle ideas about individual genius and to question the social modes of canon formation, exactly as this anthology does. Destabilizing the comforts of attribution for the reader, *Whether a Dove or a Seagull* confronts contemporary critical concerns with subject positions, subjectivity, and authorial identity. When Ackland's poetry is collected—for she has received even less attention than Warner—the picture of "Sapphic modernism" sketched by Shari Benstock in *Women of the Left Bank* may be filled in somewhat.[6] Literary historians of the 1930s have largely left women out of Left history, and one of the most urgent projects of the revision of modernism must be the recording and revival of those voices. Politics, in particular the documentation of the work done by women writers who fought fascism in Spain, is beginning to receive the attention it deserves by Barbara Brothers and by Wendy Mulford in her fine study of Warner and Ackland.

Valentine Ackland's *For Sylvia: An Honest Account,* a moving lesbian autobiography, records Ackland's struggles with alcoholism as well as her childhood and brief and appalling experience in marriage. Her conversion to Catholicism adds to the growing list of modernist women, sometimes lesbian, sometimes bisexual, whose artistic and gender identities were bound up with a relationship to the church. Radclyffe Hall, Una Troubridge, Antonia White, Emily Coleman—they all ask us to consider the relationship of Catholicism to modernisms other than Joyce's. An interesting place to begin this inquiry is with Christopher St. John's *Hungerheart: The Story of a Soul.*[7] St. John was an early and active suffragette, a drama and music critic, the lover of Edy Craig (Ellen Terry's daughter, who was a feminist theatrical producer), one of the models for Miss LaTrobe in Woolf's *Between the Acts,* and the author of a biography of the composer Dame Ethel Smyth.

Beyond the scope of this volume but essential to its project is continuing study of modernist women in music, drama, and dance. What is the relation of female modernism to the struggle for the vote? The great outpouring of women's writing in feminist political pamphlets ought to be examined, as well as suffrage plays and novels. The peace movement and women's World War I novels deserve study, as well as the relationship of feminism to vorticism and surrealism. One large gap is being filled by Brothers's and Mulford's work on women and the Spanish Civil War. As Brothers points out, Warner's neglect occurs on many fronts. Left out of the literary histories of the Spanish Civil War presumably because she was a woman, she is left out of literary modernism because she was a communist and a lesbian. But she does not reappear in the *Norton Anthology of Literature by Women* or in Gilbert and Gubar's *No Man's Land.*

Brothers discusses Warner's Spanish Civil War poetry and her political novels, *After the Death of Don Juan* (1938) and *Summer Will Show* (1936). In "A Wilderness of One's Own" in Squier I discuss the fantastic realism of *Lolly Willowes* as a literary response to the failure of realism to imagine new gender possibilities after the suffrage movement and the war. *Mr. Fortunes's Maggot* (1927) and *The True Heart* (1929) have been reprinted by Virago; the latter is a Victorian Cupid and Psyche story about a determined servant and her beloved, a mentally retarded upper-class man. Warner was always turning fictional plots upside down. In *The Flint Anchor* (1954) it is a "patriarch" who is oppressed by the ideology of the family. *The Corner that Held Them* (1948), a brilliant recreation of life in a fourteenth-century convent, is like no other historical novel I have read. Umberto Eco's all-male world in *The Name of the Rose* might be simply a masculine version of convent life set in a different country. Can our present concepts of modernism expand from definitions of fragmented or lyrical fiction to include the feminist or Marxist historical novel as Warner conceived it?

Eleanor Perenyi sees Warner's historical novels as hallucinatory, the writing of dreams of lived past reality, original and compelling in this peculiar genre because history is presented as somehow more real than life. It is in *Summer Will Show* that Warner most fully confronts the question "What is the role of the bourgeois (and female) intellectual in making the revolution?" Set in Paris during the revolution of 1848, it imagines Marx himself answering the question; and in the love affair between the rich English gentlewoman, Sophia Willoghby, and Minna, her husband's beautiful revolutionary Jewish mistress, the novel rewrites the plot of the English novel (by women) as we know it and liberates the reader into a world of difference, racial, sexual and political, which is astonishing as well as disquieting. Minna tells a spellbinding tale of a pogrom that links racial and sexual otherness with revolutionary political activity and writing. Sophia's black nephew, the "issue" of Britain's slave trade, becomes the agent of French state forces against the radicals, killing the Jewish refugee as patriarchy refuses to recognize his paternity.

My choice of Warner's texts for this volume is eccentric. "Cottage Mantleshelf" is a World War I poem that contains in its attack on couples and coupling a radical critique of Western dualism and its structures of binary opposition. Suffused in rose light and contrary images of England and roses, like Woolf's *Mrs. Dalloway,* it overturns the homoerotic text of British poetry of this war with the instrument of class. Like Septimus, "young Osbert," the "nancy boy," is a "scapegoat," disowned by the nation for whom he gave his youth. This pink and black Art Deco portrait of the mantleshelf of the Home Front interrogates the reproductive ideology that underwrites the war narrative, critiquing the heterosexual plot and its cultural reproduction in the pairings on the working-class hearth, as well as parodying the patriotism of Laurence Binyon's "For the Fallen" and the love and war poetics of *Antony and Cleopatra.* Warner's work does not participate in Sandra Gilbert's paradigm of the sex war as the key to modernism.[8] In fact she sees through the limitations of that metaphor.

Warner's Peter Le Neve Foster lecture of 1959 ("Women as Writers") is included here because it clearly demonstrates that feminist criticism did not appear suddenly in the 1970s with no predecessors. At a low point in the history of Woolf's reputation as a writer, Warner's lecture revived interest in Woolf's then forgotten text, *A Room of One's Own,* specifically as the mother text of socialist-feminist criticism.

By allusion and deliberate intertextuality with *A Room,* Warner resurrected a dead text and playfully invented as companions for Judith Shakespeare her own fictional Joan Milton and Françoise Rabelais. Obstinacy and slyness are the characteristics of women writers, she says, continuing Woolf's connection of women writers as outsiders with Shakespeare: "It is a dizzying conclusion, but it must be faced. Women, entering literature, entered it on the same footing as William Shakespeare." She again intrudes the element of class into the analysis of writing and gender, longing for a woman Clare or Burns or Bunyan. Woolf's peroration argues that the woman Shakespeare will come from the working class. Warner discusses women as middle-class writers and tries to imagine a royal princess writing a play. She anticipates feminist critical discussions of the Victorian attribution of morality to women and also, tellingly, she sees the twentieth-century superwoman on the horizon. Her hilarious play on institutionalized misogyny resonates in the application of "MacHeath's Law": "She may invent but she may not write down. MacHeath's Law explains why the early women writers caused so little alarm. They only went off one at a time."

"Bluebeard's Daughter" is a fable from *The Cat's Cradle-Book* (1940), a collection that destabilizes the genre of fable and offers a fundamental moral challenge to humanism and its arrogant self-reflexivity by asserting that the origin of the storytelling impulse is in cats. Crossing the boundaries between the animal and the human, Warner, like Woolf in *Flush,* undoes the inescapability of all categorical imperatives, gender, nation, language and history. A witty critique of the scholarly pursuit of the Ur-language, cultural anthropology as a discipline, and all forms of textual scholarship, *The Cat's Cradle-Book* is the "text" of all the collated cat narratives collected by a man who is expiating his guilt at the death of his beloved Siamese, Haru, because he couldn't bear to let her out to mate when she was in heat nor could he consummate his own desire. Warner's narrator agrees that the art of narrative was invented by cats and, further, that the origin of narration is in lactation. It is mother cats who tell stories to their nursing kittens. Like modern critics collecting the tales of the Other, the collector brings a disease upon the subjects of his study, objectifying them in pursuit of his ideal pure text. The obvious lessons are not lost on the reader.

"Cat is not a recognized language," she writes. How are you to convince people that what is roughly a vocabulary of guttural and mew can convey such fine shades of meaning?" All marginalized literatures and peoples share this problem. They do not have the same grammar and syntax as the dominant language, and they are defined by difference (as the dominant define culture and language in their difference from those "gutturals and mews"). The reader of "Bluebeard's Daughter" is confronted by Warner's deconstructive urge. If Bluebeard was a bad husband, how do we know he was also a bad father? she asks, taking one of the most powerful myths of our culture and turning it upside down. Djamileh's mouth is stained blue like her hair of "deep butcher's blue." She is the daughter of the patriarchy, like all women as they inhabit the role of bluebeard's daughter. Their fathers have murdered their mothers for the sin of curiosity (otherwise known as the desire for history) in wanting to know the stories of women. Djamileh does not choose revenge. Behind the locked doors which her husband's curiosity wants to open is no mystery. She channels their desire to know into the mutual study of astronomy. This fable is an answer to Woolf's Shakespeare's sister, in which the martyr is replaced by the survivor.

Just as *The Cat's Cradle-Book* challenges the disciplines for robbing the subjectivity of the peoples and stories they study, so "Bluebeard's Daughter" gives us a feminist fable with a twist. Warner's text should be read against Béla Bartók's brilliant modernist opera *Bluebeard's Castle* (1911), which, like much male modernism, blames the victim and rewrites the legend to exonerate Bluebeard, whose last wife, significantly named Judith, is jealous of his previous relationships and greedily invades his privacy. George Steiner takes Bartok's revisionist misreading even further from questions of gender. His Bluebeard represents establishment culture, which will not come to terms with the holocaust or pay serious attention to science. Judith is not a woman. She stands for the human urge to open all doors. This appropriation of the oppressed victim as a representation of man's plight, as in Geoffrey Hartman's denial of gender in the Procne and Philomel myth in "The Voice of the Shuttle," is one of the characteristics of the modernist rewriting of history. Sylvia Townsend Warner's story tells us that the daughter of a monster is not herself a monster, that men are not necessarily the enemy. They can be educated to intellectual inquiry.

NOTES

1. Warner's ten volumes of short stories include fables, elfin tales, and realist fiction, spanning her whole career, many first published in the *New Yorker.*

2. See the discussion in my "Wilderness of One's Own."

3. Quoted in Perenyi.

4. An excellent discussion of Warner's politics is in Mulford. A reevaluation of women writers and World War I is under way. See the 1989 Feminist Press reprints of *Not So Quiet. . . .* by Helen Zenna Smith (Evadne Price) and *We That Were Young* by Irene Rathbone, with Afterwords by Jane Marcus.

5. See Schenck's introductions to Mew (section **15**) and Wickham (**25**) in this volume and her essay in *Women Writers in Exile,* ed. Broe and Ingram.

6. Wendy Mulford's book contains a good bibliography of Ackland's work. In addition to Benstock's book, see her chapter, "Expatriate Sapphic Modernism: Entering Literary History," in Glasgow and Jay.

7. For a discussion of *Hungerheart,* see Nina Auerbach, *Ellen Terry: Player in Her Time,* New York: Norton, 1987. On Catholicism and lesbianism, see Joanne Glasgow's essay in Glasgow and Jay (see n. 6). On Emily Coleman, see Mary Lynn Broe's essay on Hayford Hall in Broe and Ingram.

8. For a critique of Gilbert's "Soldier's Heart," see my "Asylums of Antaeus" and my Afterword to Smith; see also Tylee.

WORKS CITED

Ackland, Valentine. *For Sylvia: An Honest Account.* London: Chatto and Windus, 1985.

———. *The Nature of the Moment.* London: Chatto and Windus, 1973.

———, and Sylvia Townsend Warner. *Whether a Dove or a Seagull.* London: Chatto and Windus, 1934.

Bartók, Béla. *Bluebeard's Castle.* 1911. Libretto for opera by Béla Balasz. See notes to 1966 London recording.

Benstock, Shari. *Women of the Left Bank: Paris, 1900–1940.* Austin: U of Texas P, 1986.

Brothers, Barbara. "Writing against the Grain: Sylvia Townsend Warner and the Spanish Civil War." In *Women Writers in Exile,* ed. Mary Lynn Broe and Angela Ingram. Chapel Hill: U of North Carolina P, 1989.

———. "Summer will Show: The Historical Novel as Social Criticism." In *Women in History, Literature and the Arts,* ed. Lorrayne Baird-Lange and Thomas Copeland, 267–273. Youngstown: Youngstown State UP, 1989.

Feaver, Vicki. "Making a Stand against Habit." *Times Literary Supplement* 18 March 1983:278.

Glasgow, Joanne. "What's a Nice Lesbian Like You Doing in a Church of Torquemada? Radclyffe Hall and Other Catholic Converts." In Glasgow and Jay.

———, and Karla Jay, eds. *Radical Revisions: Lesbian Texts and Contexts,* New York: New York UP, forthcoming.

Marcus, Jane. "Still Practice, A W/rested Alphabet: Toward a Feminist Aesthetic." *Art and Anger* 21–249. Columbus: Ohio State UP, 1988.

———. "A Wilderness of One's Own." In Susan Squier, ed., *Women Writers and the City,* 134–160. Knoxville: U of Tennesse P, 1984.

———. "Alibis and Legends: The Ethics of Elsewhereness; Gender and Estrangement." In *Women Writers in Exile,* ed. Mary Lynn Broe and Angela Ingram, 172–187. Chapel Hill: U of North Carolina P, 1989.

———. "The Asylums of Antaeus: Women, War and Madness." In *The Difference Within: Feminism and Critical Theory,* ed. Elizabeth Meese and Alice Parker, 49–83. Amsterdam and Philadelphia: John Benjamins, 1988.

Mulford, Wendy. *This Narrow Place, Sylvia Townsend Warner and Valentine Ackland: Life, Letters and Politics, 1930–1951.* London: Pandora, 1988. With bibliography.

Perenyi, Eleanor. "The Good Witch of the West." *New York Review of Books* 18 July 1985:27–29.

Rathbone, Eleanor. *We That Were Young*. 1932. New York: Feminist Press, 1989.
St. John, Christopher. *Hungerheart: The Story of a Soul*. London: Methuen, 1915.
Smith, Helen Zenna. *Not So Quiet . . .* 1930. New York: Feminist Press, 1989. Afterword by Jane Marcus.
Steiner, George. *In Bluebeard's Castle*. New Haven: Yale UP, 1971.
Tylee, Claire. "Maleness Run Riot—The Great War and Women's Resistance to Militarism." *Women's Studies International Forum* 11.3(1988):199–210.
Warner, Sylvia Townsend. *Collected Poems*. Ed. and intro. Claire Harmon, with bibliography. Manchester: Carcanet, 1982.
———. *Letters*. Ed. William Maxwell. New York: Viking P, 1982.
———. *The Espalier*. London: Chatto and Windus, 1926.
———. *Lolly Willowes*. 1926. London: Women's Press, 1978.
———. *The True Heart*. London: Chatto and Windus, 1929. Rpt. London: Virago.
———. *Opus 7*. London: Chatto and Windus, 1931.
———. *Summer Will Show*. London: Chatto and Windus, 1936.
———. *The Corner That Held Them*. London: Chatto and Windus, 1948.
———. *The Cat's Cradle-Book*. New York: Viking P, 1940.
———. The Peter Le Neve Foster Lecture, 1959. In *Collected Poems*.
Woolf, Virginia. *A Room of One's Own*. New York: Harcourt Brace, 1929.
———. *Mrs. Dalloway*. New York: Harcourt Brace, 1925.
———. *Flush*. New York: Harcourt Brace, 1933.

Women as Writers

(The following is the text of the Peter Le Neve Foster Lecture which Sylvia Townsend Warner delivered to the Royal Society of Arts on 11 February 1959.)

When I received this invitation to lecture to the Royal Society of Arts on "Women as Writers" (and here let me express my thanks to the responsible committee, and to the shade of Peter le Neve Foster, whose family founded the lectureship, and to my Chairman)—when I received this invitation, it was the invitation that surprised me. The choice of subject did not. I am a woman writer myself, and it never surprises me. Even when people tell me I am a lady novelist, it is the wording of the allegation I take exception to, not the allegation itself. One doubt, it is true, crossed my mind. It was inevitable that I should remember a book called *A Room of One's Own*, by Virginia Woolf. What had I to add to that? But *A Room of One's Own*, I thought, is not so much about how women write as about how astonishing it is that they should have managed to write at all. As they have managed to, there might still be something I could add. But then I reread my invitation, and became the prey of uneasiness. Women as Writers. *Women* as Writers. Supposing I had been a man, a gentleman novelist, would I have been asked to lecture on Men as Writers? I thought it improbable.

Here was an implication I might or might not resent. Here, at any rate, was an obligation I couldn't dodge.

It would appear that when a woman writes a book, the action sets up an extraneous vibration. Something happens that must be accounted for. It is the action that does it, not the product. It is only in very rare, and rather non-literary instances, that the product—*Uncle Tom's Cabin,* say, or the *Memoirs of Harriet Wilson*—is the jarring note. It would also appear that this extraneous vibration may be differently received and differently resounded. Some surfaces mute it. Off others, it is violently resonated. It is also subject to the influence of climate, the climate of popular opinion. In a fine dry climate the dissonance caused by a woman writing a book has much less intensity than in a damp foggy one. Overriding these variations due to surface and climate is the fact that the volume increases with the mass—as summarised in Macheath's Law:

One wife is too much for most husbands to hear
But two at a time sure no mortal can bear.

Finally, it would appear that the vibration is not set up until a woman seizes a pen. She may invent, but she may not write down.

Macheath's Law explains why the early women writers caused so little alarm. They only went off one at a time. If a great lady such as Marie de France chose to give her leisure to letters instead of embroidery, this was merely a demonstration that society could afford such luxuries—an example of what Veblen defined as Conspicuous Waste. No one went unfed or unclothed for it. Nor could she be held guilty of setting a bad example to other women, since so few women were in a position to follow it. So things went on, with now and then a literate woman making a little squeak with her pen, while the other women added a few more lines to Mother Goose (about that authorship, I think there can be no dispute). It was not till the retreat from the Renaissance that the extraneous vibration was heard as so very jarring. By then, many women had learned to read and write, so a literate woman was no longer an ornament to society. Kept in bounds, she had her uses. She could keep the account books and transcribe recipes for horse pills. But she must be kept within bounds: she must subserve. When Teresa of Avila wrote her autobiography, she said in a preface that it had been written with leave, and "in accordance with my confessor's command". True, she immediately added, "The Lord himself, I know, has long wished it to be written"—a sentiment felt by most creative writers, I believe; but the woman and the Lord had to wait for permission.

The French have always allowed a place to Conspicuous Waste, it is one of the things they excel at; and Mme de La Fayette rewarded this tolerance by giving France the first psychological novel, *La Princesse de Clèves.* But Molière was probably a surer mouthpiece of public opinion when he made a game of literary ladies. It is more damning to be shown as absurd than to be denounced as scandalous. It is more damning still to be thought old-fashioned. Margaret, Countess of Newcastle, was derided not only as a figure of fun but as a figure out of the lumber-room. (Much the same condemnation fell on Lady Murasaki, a most eminent woman writer, whose nickname in the Japanese court of the early eleventh century was Dame Annals.) In eighteenth-century England, a woman of fashion wrote at her peril (I doubt if Pope would have laid so much stress on Lady Mary Wortley-

Montagu being dirty if she had not been inky.) A woman who wrote for publication—by then, a fair number did—sank in the social scale. If she wrote fiction, she was a demirep. If she wrote as a scholar, she was a dowdy. However, as men of letters had also gone down in the world, writing women gained more than they lost. They gained companionship, they approached a possibility of being judged on their merits by writers of the opposite sex.

Too much has been made of Dr. Johnson's opinion of women preachers, not enough of the fact that Mrs Chapone and Elizabeth Carter contributed to *The Rambler,* nor of his goodwill towards Mrs Lennox, and the hot apple pie he stuck with bay leaves in her honour. In the case of Fanny Burney, Johnson showed more than goodwill. He showed courage. Fanny Burney was his friend's daughter, and a virgin. And Fanny Burney had written a novel. Not even a romance. A novel.

The speed with which women possess themselves of an advantage is something astonishing. Such quantities of virtuous women turned to novel-writing that Jane Austen was able to pick and choose among them, to laugh at Ann Radcliffe and Mary Brunton, to admire Miss Edgeworth. It was an Indian summer, the last glow of the Age of Reason. Jane Austen could inscribe her title-page with that majestic, *By a Lady.* The Brontë sisters, not so. They were born too late. The barometer had fallen, the skies had darkened. They grew up in an age which had decided that women had an innate moral superiority. As almost everything was a menace to this innate moral superiority, it was necessary that women should be protected, protected from men, protected from life, protected from being talked about, protected from Euclid—Mary Somerville the mathematician has recorded how hard put to it she was to expose herself to Euclid—protected above all from those dangerous articles, themselves. You couldn't have women dashing their pens into inkpots and writing as if they knew about life and had something to say about it. Determined to write and to be judged on the merit of their writing, women put on men's names: Aurore Dudevant became George Sand, and Mary Ann Evans, George Eliot, and Emily Brontë consented to the ambiguity of Ellis Bell.

I think I can now venture a positive assertion about women as writers. It is a distinguishing assertion; if I were talking about Men as Writers I could not make it. Women as writers are obstinate and sly.

I deliberately make this assertion in the present tense. Though a woman writing today is not hampered by an attribution of innate moral superiority, she has to reckon with an attribution of innate physical superiority; and this, too, can be cumbersome. There is, for instance, bi-location. It is well known that a woman can be in two places at once; at her desk and at her washing-machine. She can practise a mental bi-location also, pinning down some slippery adverb while saying aloud, "No, not Hobbs, Nokes. And the address is 17 Dalmeny Crescent." Her mind is so extensive that it can simultaneously follow a train of thought, remember what it was she had to tell the electrician, answer the telephone, keep an eye on the time, and not forget about the potatoes. Obstinacy and slyness still have their uses, although they are not literary qualities.

But I have sometimes wondered if women are literary at all. It is not a thing which is strenuously required of them, and perhaps, finding something not required of them, they thank God and do no more about it. They write. They dive into writing like ducks into water. One would almost think it came naturally to them—at any rate as naturally as plain sewing.

Here is a non-literary woman writing in the nineteenth century. She wrote under her own name, for her sex was already notorious:

> There were three separate registers kept at Scutari. First, the Adjutant's daily Head-Roll of soldiers' burials, on which it may be presumed that no one was entered who was not buried, although it is possible that some may have been buried who were not entered.
>
> Second, the Medical Officer's Return, in regard to which it is quite certain that hundreds of men were buried who never appeared upon it.
>
> Third, the return made in the Orderly Room, which is only remarkable as giving a totally different account of the deaths from either of the others.

I should like to think that Florence Nightingale's work is not yet done. If it could be set as a model before those who write official reports, the publications of Her Majesty's Stationery Office might grow much leaner, much time and money might be saved. But this is by the way.

Here is another, writing in the seventeenth century:

> Take a pint of cream, three spoonfuls of rice flour, the whites of three eggs well beaten, and four spoonfuls of fine sugar. Stir these well into your cream cold; then take a few blanched almonds and beat them in a mortar with two spoonfuls of water, then strain them into your cream and boil it till it comes from the skillet. Then take it up and put in two spoonfuls of sack, and wet your cups with sack and put in your custard, and let it stand till it is cold.

From a cookery book, as you will have realised—but a piece of tight, clear, consecutive writing.

Here is a woman writing from Norwich in July 1453:

> And as for tidings, Philip Berney is passed to God on Monday last past with the greatest pain that ever I saw a man; and on Tuesday Sir John Heveningham went to his church and heard three masses and came home never merrier; and said to his wife that he would go say a little devotion in his garden and then dine; and forthwith he felt a fainting in his leg and slid down. This was at nine of the clock and he was dead ere noon.

Here is another Norfolk woman, writing, or possibly dictating, towards the close of the previous century:

And after this I saw God in a Point—that is to say, in my understanding; by which I saw he is in all things. I beheld and considered, seeing and knowing in sight, with a soft dread, and thought: What is sin?

I really have not cheated over these examples. The two notable women, the two women of no note, I chose them almost at random, and went to their writings to see what I would find. I found them alike in making themselves clear.

As far as I know, there is only one certain method of making things clear, and that is, to have plainly in mind what one wishes to say. When the unequivocal statement matches itself to the predetermined thought and the creative impulse sets fire to them, the quality we call immediacy results. Immediacy has borne other names, it has even been called inspiration—though I think that is too large a term for it. But immediacy has this in common with inspiration, that where it is present the author becomes absent. The writing is no longer propelled by the author's anxious hand, the reader is no longer conscious of the author's chaperoning presence. Here is an example; it is a poem by Frances Cornford:

> The Cypriot woman, as she closed her dress,
> Smiled at the baby on her broad-lapped knee,
> Beautiful in calm voluptuousness
> Like a slow sea.

One does not feel that the woman has been written about. She is there.

Women as writers seem to be remarkably adept at vanishing out of their writing so that the quality of immediacy replaces them. Immediacy is the word in *La Princess de Clèves,* that masterpiece of emotion laced up in the tight embroidered bodice of court dress. Madame de Cleves's heart is laid open before us, and we hang over it; not even pity is allowed to intervene between us and the demonstration. Immediacy is the word when Jane Austen keeps a bookful of rather undistinguished characters not only all alive at once but all aware of each other's existence. In *Wuthering Heights* immediacy makes a bookful of almost incredible characters fastened into a maddeningly entangled plot seem natural and inevitable, as if it were something familiar to us because of a dream. When the goblins fasten on Lizzie and press the fruit against her clenched teeth; when Orlando finds the man in Mrs Stewkley's room, the man who turned his pen in his fingers, this way and that; and gazed and mused; and then, very quickly, wrote half a dozen lines—and no more need be said, with our own eyes we have looked on William Shakespeare; when Murasaki's Genji takes Yugao to the deserted house where the ghost steals her away from him; when, at the close of Colette's *La Chatte,* the girl looks back from the turn of the avenue and sees the cat keeping a mistrustful eye on her departure and the young man playing, deftly as a cat, with the first-fallen chestnuts, it is not the writer one is conscious of. One is conscious of a happening, of something taking place under one's very nose. As for Sappho, I cannot speak. She rises in my mind like a beautiful distant island, but I cannot set foot on her because I haven't learned Greek. But I am assured that immediacy is the word for Sappho.

While all these splendid examples were rushing into my mind, I realised that a great many examples which could not be called splendid were accompanying them: that when the gust of wind flutters the hangings and extinguishes the solitary taper and Mrs Radcliffe's heroine is left in darkness, it is a darkness that can be felt; that in George Sand's writing, for all its exploitation and rhetoric, George Sand may suddenly be replaced by the first frost prowling under cover of night through an autumn garden; that the short stories of Mary Wilkins, a New England writer of the last century whose characters appear to be made out of lettuce, can remain in one's mind and call one back to a re-reading because one remembers a queer brilliant verisimilitude, the lighting of immediacy.

There is, of course, George Eliot. She makes herself admirably clear and her mind, such a fine capacious mind, too, is stored with things she wishes to say; but in her case, immediacy does not result. We remember scenes and characters, but do they ever haunt us? She dissects a heart, but something intervenes between us and the demonstration—the lecturer's little wand. There is a class of women writers, praiseworthily combining fiction with edification, and among them is Mrs Sherwood of *The Fairchild Family*, Mrs Gatty of *Parables from Nature*, Mrs Trimmer . . . it seems to me that George Eliot insisted upon being a superlative Mrs Trimmer.

Still, George Eliot apart—a considerable apart—I think one might claim that this quality of immediacy, though common to either sex, is proportionately of more frequent occurrence in the work of women writers. And though it is impossible in judging the finished product to pronounce on which pages were achieved with effort, which came easily, the fact that even quite mediocre women writers will sometimes wear this precious jewel in their heads seems to indicate that it is easier for a woman to make herself air and vanish off her pages than it is for a man, with his heavier equipment of learning and self-consciousness. Perhaps this is really so, and for a reason. Suppose, for instance, that there was a palace, which you could only know from outside. Sometimes you heard music playing within, and the corks popping, and sometimes splendid figures came to an open window and spoke a few words in a solemn chanting voice; and from time to time you met someone who had actually been inside, and was carrying away under his arm—it was always a man—a lute or a casket or the leg of a turkey. And then one day you discovered that you could climb into this palace by the pantry window. In the excitement of the moment you wouldn't wait; you wouldn't go home to smooth your hair or borrow your grandmother's garnets or consult the Book of Etiquette. Even at the risk of being turned out by the butler, rebuked by the chaplin, laughed at by the rightful guests, you'd climb in.

In something of the same way, women have entered literature—breathless, unequipped, and with nothing but their wits to trust to. A few minutes ago, or a few centuries ago, they were writing a letter about an apoplexy, or a recipe for custard. Now they are inside the palace, writing with great clearness what they have in mind to say—for that is all they know about it, no one has groomed them for a literary career—writing on the kitchen table, like Emily Brontë, or on the washstand, like Christina Rossetti, writing in the attic, like George Sand, or in the family parlour, protected by a squeaking door from being discovered at it, like Jane Austen, writing away for all they are worth, and seldom blotting a line.

Do you see what we are coming to?—I have put in several quotations to prepare you for it. We are coming to those other writers who have got into literature by the pantry window, and who have left the most illustrious footprints on the windowsill. It is a dizzying conclusion, but it must be faced. Women, entering literature, entered it on the same footing as William Shakespeare.

So if women writers have what might appear an unfairly large share of the quality of immediacy which is sometimes called inspiration—and in the case of Shakespeare we all agree to call it so—it is not, after all, original in them—like sin. It derives from their circumstances, not from their sex. It is interesting to see what other qualities, also deriving from circumstance, the circumstance of entering literature by the pantry window, they share with Shakespeare. I can think of several. One is their conviction that women have legs of their own, and can move about of their own volition, and give as good as they get. Lady Macbeth, and Beatrice, and Helena in *All's Well,* could almost be taken for women writers' heroines, they are so free and uninhibited, and ready to jump over stiles and appear in the drawing-room with muddy stockings, like Lizzie Bennet.

Another pantry window trait is the kind of workaday democracy, an ease and appreciativeness in low company. It is extremely rare to find the conventional comic servant or comic countryman in books by women. A convention is *pis-aller,* a stop-gap where experience is lacking. A woman has to be most exceptionally secluded if she never goes to her own back door, or is not on visiting terms with people poorer than herself. I have said before—but as the remark has only appeared in Russian I can decently repeat myself—Emily Brontë was fortunate in being the daughter of a clergyman, because the daughter of a clergyman, with her duty of parish visiting, has wonderful opportunities to become acquainted with human passions and what they can lead to. Another trait in common is a willing ear for the native tongue, for turns of phrase used by carpenters, gardeners, sailors, milliners, tinkers, old nurses, and that oldest nurse of all, ballad and folklore. Just as Mme de Sévigné was always improving her French by picking up words and idioms from her tenants at Les Rochers, Colette listened to every trade, every walk in life, and kept dictionaries of professional terms beside her desk—while Edith Sitwell's poetry reaches back through centuries of English poetical idiom to *Nuts in May* and Mother Goose.

These traits, as you will have noticed, are technical assets. They affect presentation, not content. Their absence may be deadening, but their presence does not make their possessor any more eligible to be compared with Shakespeare. The resemblance is in the circumstances. Women writers have shared his advantage of starting with no literary advantages. No butlers were waiting just inside the front door to receive their invitation cards and show them in. Perhaps the advantage is not wholly advantageous; but circumstances do alter cases. It was not very surprising that young Mr Shelley should turn to writing; it was surprising that young Mr Keats did, and his poetry reflects his surprise, his elation. It is the poetry of a young man surprised by joy. So is the poetry of John Clare. But though the male entrants by the pantry window possess the quality of immediacy just as women writers do, are at ease in low company and in the byways of their native language, they do not employ these advantages with the same fluency—I hesitate to use the word *exploit;* I will say, they are not so much obliged to them. I see a possible explanation for this, which I will come to presently.

But first I must come to the present day, when women, one might think, have so well established themselves as writers that the extraneous vibration must be hushed, and the pantry window supplanted as an entrance to literature by the Tradesman's Door. No woman writer should despise the Tradesman's Door. It is a very respectable entrance, the path to it was first trod by Mrs Aphra Behn, and many women have trodden it since, creditably and contentedly too. I should be failing my title if I did not remind you that we now have women newspaper reporters working in such vexed places as Cyprus—a signal advance. Yet, when we use the term *backwriter,* we still feel that it must apply to a man; that a woman is once and for always an amateur. In the same spirit, if she happens to make a great deal of money by a book, well and good, it is one of those lucky accidents that happen from time to time, no one is the worse for it, and she is unexpectedly the better. But if she earns her living by her pen, we are not so ready to accept the idea. If we are polite enough to dissemble our feelings we say that it is a pity that with so much talent she should be reduced to this sort of thing. If we are candid and pure-souled, we say that it's outrageous and that she ought to become a hospital nurse. If she marries—again it's a pity—a polite pity that she will have to give up her writing. So much pity is ominous.

And in fact, the vibration may start up at any moment. Macheath's Law still holds; not for numbers, perhaps, but for area. It is admitted that women may write very nearly what they please, just as, within limits, they may do what they please: though I suppose it will be a long time before they can enter the priesthood or report football matches on the BBC. But this liberty is zoned. It applies to women belonging to the middle classes. You know those shiny papers one reads in waiting-rooms, and how, every week, they show a photograph of a woman of the upper clases, with a little notice underneath. One has just come out. One has recently married. One wins prizes with her Shetland ponies, another has a charming pair of twins, another is an MFH. But despite Edith Sitwell and Dorothy Wellesley, one does not expect to read below the photograph that the lady is a poet. Take it a step higher. Suppose that a royal princess would not tear herself from the third act of her tragedy in order to open a play-centre. People would be gravely put out, especially the man who had been building the play-centre, men who have taught their wives to know their place, and who expect princesses to be equally dutiful.

A working-class woman may be as gifted as all the women writers I have spoken of today, all rolled into one; but it is no part of her duty to write a masterpiece. Her brain may be teeming, but it is not the fertility of her brain she must attend to, perishable citizens is what her country expects of her, not imperishable Falstaffs and Don Quixotes. The Lord himself may long have wished for her books to be written; but leave has yet to be granted. Apart from one or two grandees like Mme de La Fayette, women writers have come from the middle class, and their writing carries a heritage of middle-class virtues; good taste, prudence, acceptance of limitations, compliance with standards, and that typically middle-class merit of making the most of what one's got—in other words, that too-conscious employment of advantages which I mentioned a few minutes ago, and which one does not observe in Clare, or Burns, or Bunyan. So when we consider women as writers, we must bear in mind that we have not very much to go on, and that it is too early to assess what they may be capable of. It may well be that the half has not yet been told us: that unbridled masterpieces, daring innovations, epics, tragedies, works of genial impropriety—all the things that so far women have signally failed to produce—have been socially, not sexually, debarred; that at this moment a Joan Milton or a Françoise Rabelais may have left the washing unironed and the stew uncared for because she can't wait to begin.

Cottage Mantleshelf

On the mantleshelf love and beauty are housed together.
There are the two black vases painted with pink roses,
And the two dogs carrying baskets of flowers in their jaws.
There are the two fans stencilled with characters from Japan,
The ruby glass urns each holding a sprig of heather,
And the two black velvet cats with bead eyes, pink noses, and white cotton
claws.

All these things on the mantleshelf are beautiful and are married:
The two black vases throb with their sympathetic pink roses,
The puss thinks only of her tom and the dog of his bitch.
On the one fan a girl is coquetting and on the other a man,
Out of the same vein of fancy the urns were quarried,
Even the sprigs of heather have been dried so long you can't tell 'tother from
which.

But amid this love and beauty are two uncomely whose sorrows
Isled in several celibacy can never, never be mated,
One of them being but for use and the other useful no more.
With a stern voice rocking its way through time the alarm clock
Confronts with a pallid face the billowing to-morrows
And turns its back on the enlarged photograph of young Osbert who died at
the war.

Against the crumpled cloth where the photographer's fancy
Has twined with roses the grand balustrade he poses,

His hands hang limp from the khaki sleeves and his legs are bent.
His enormous ears are pricked and tense as a startled hare's,
He smiles—and his beseeching swagger is that of a nancy,
And plain to see on the picture is death's indifferent rubber stamp of assent.

As though through gathering mist he stares out through the photo's
Discolouring, where the lamp throws its pink-shaded echo of roses
On the table laid for supper with cheese and pickles and tea.
The rose-light falls on his kin who sit there with a whole skin,
It illumines through England the cottage homes where just such ex-voto
Are preserved on their mantleshelves by the living in token that they are not as
he.

Uncomely and unespoused amid the espousals of beauty.
The cats with their plighted noses, the vases pledging their roses,
The scapegoat of the mantleshelf he stands and may not even cleave
To the other unpaired heart that beats beside him and apart;
For the pale-faced clock has heard, as he did, the voice of duty
And disowns him whom time has disowned, whom age cannot succour nor the
years reprieve.

Collected Poems, ed. Claire Harmon. Manchester: Carcanet 1982. 21–22.

Bluebeard's Daughter

Every child can tell of his ominous pigmentation, of his ruthless temper, of the fate of his wives and of his own fate, no less bloody than theirs; but—unless it be here and there a Director of Oriental Studies—no one now remembers that Bluebeard had a daughter. Amid so much that is wild and shocking this gentler trait of his character has been overlooked. Perhaps, rather than spoil the symmetry of a bad husband by an admission that he was a good father, historians have suppressed her. I have heard her very existence denied, on the grounds that none of Bluebeard's wives lived long enough to bear him a child. This shows what it is to give a dog a bad name. To his third wife, the mother of Djamileh, Bluebeard was most tenderly devoted, and no shadow of suspicion rested upon her quite natural death in childbed.

From the moment of her birth Djamileh became the apple of Bluebeard's eye. His messengers ransacked Georgia and Circassia to find wet-nurses of unimpeachable health, beauty, and virtue; her infant limbs were washed in nothing but rosewater, and swaddled in Chinese silks. She cut her teeth upon a cabochon emerald engraved with propitious mottoes, and all the nursery vessels, mugs, platters, ewers, basins, and chamber-pots were of white jade. Never was there a more adoring and conscientious father than Bluebeard, and I have sometimes thought that the career of this much-widowed man was inevitably determined by his anxiety to find for Djamileh an ideal stepmother.

Djamileh's childhood was happy, for none of the stepmothers lasted long enough to outwear their good intentions, and every evening, whatever his occupations during the day, Bluebeard came to the nursery for an hour's romp. But three days before her ninth birthday Djamileh was told that her father was dead; and while she was still weeping for her loss she was made to weep even more bitterly by the statement that he was a bad man and that she must not cry for him. Dressed in crape, with the Bluebeard diamonds sparkling like angry tears beneath her veils, and wearing a bandage on her wrist, Fatima came to Djamileh's pavilion and paid off the nurses and governesses. With her came Aunt Ann, and a strange young man whom she was told to call Uncle Selim; and while the nurses lamented and packed and the governesses sulked, swooned, and clapped their hands for sherbet, Djamileh listened to this trio disputing as to what should be done with her.

"For she can't stay here alone," said Fatima. "And nothing will induce me to spend another night under this odious roof."

"Why not send her to school?"

"Or to the Christians?" suggested Selim.

"Perhaps there is some provision for her in the will?"

"Will! Don't tell me that such a monster could make a will, a valid will. Besides, he never made one."

Fatima stamped her foot, and the diamond necklace sidled on her stormy bosom. Still disputing, they left the room.

That afternoon all the silk carpets and embroidered hangings, all the golden dishes and rock-crystal wine-coolers, together with the family jewels and Bluebeard's unique collection of the Persian erotic poets, were packed up and sent by camel to Selim's residence in Teheran. Thither travelled also Fatima, Ann, Selim, and Djamileh, together with a few selected slaves, Fatima in one litter with Selim riding at her side, doing his best to look stately but not altogether succeeding, since his mount was too big for him, Ann and Djamileh in the other. During the journey Ann said little, for she was engaged in ticking off entries in a large scroll. But once or twice she told Djamileh not to fidget, and to thank her stars that she had kind friends who would provide for her.

As it happened, Djamileh was perfectly well provided for. Bluebeard had made an exemplary and flawless will by which he left all his property to his only daughter and named his solicitor as her guardian until she should marry. No will can please everybody; and there was considerable heartburning when Badruddin removed Djamileh and her belongings from the care of Fatima, Ann, and Selim, persisting to the last filigree egg-cup in his thanks for their kind offices toward the heiress and her inheritance.

Badruddin was a bachelor, and grew remarkably fine jasmines. Every evening when he came home from his office he filled a green watering pot and went to see how they had passed the day. In the latticed garden the jasmine bush awaited him like a dumb and exceptionally charming wife. Now he often found Djamileh sitting beneath the bush, pale and silent, as though, in response to being watered so carefully, the jasmine had borne him a daughter.

It would have been well for Djamileh if she had owed her being to such an innocent parentage. But she was Bluebeard's daughter, and all the girl-babies of the neighbourhood cried in terror at her father's name. What was more, the poor girl could not look at herself in the mirror without being reminded of her disgrace. For she had inherited her father's colouring. Her hair was a deep butcher's blue, her eyebrows and eyelashes were blue also. Her complexion was clear and pale, and if some sally of laughter brought a glow to her cheek it was of the usual pink, but the sinister parental pigmentation reasserted itself on her lips, which were deep purple as though stained with eating mulberries; and the inside of her mouth and her tongue were dusky blue like a well-bred chow-dog's. For the rest she was like any other woman, and when she pricked her finger the blood ran scarlet.

Looks so much out of the common, if carried off with sufficient assurance, might be an asset to a modern miss. In Djamileh's time taste was more classical. Blue hair and purple lips, however come by, would have been a serious handicap for any young woman—how much more so, then, for her, in whom they were not only regrettable but scandalous. It was impossible for Bluebeard's badged daughter to be like other girls of her age. The purple mouth seldom smiled; the blue hair, severely braided by day, was often at night wetted with her tears. She might, indeed, have dyed it. But filial devotion forbade. Whatever his faults, Bluebeard had been a good father.

Djamileh had a great deal of proper feeling; it grieved her to think of her father's crimes. But she had also a good deal of natural partiality, and disliked Fatima; and this led her to try to find excuses for his behaviour. No doubt it was wrong, very wrong, to murder so many wives; but Badruddin seemed to think that it was almost as wrong to have married them, at any rate to have married so many of them. Experience, he said, should have taught the deceased that female curiosity is insatiable; it was foolish to go on hoping to find a woman without curiosity. Speaking with gravity, he conjured his ward to struggle, as far as in her lay, with this failing, so natural in her own sex, so displeasing to the other.

Djamileh fastened upon his words. To mark her reprobation of curiosity, the fault which had teased on her father to his ruin, she resolved never to be in the least curious herself. And for three weeks she did not ask a single question. At the end of the third week she fell into a violent fever, and Badruddin, who had been growing more and more disquieted by what appeared to him to be a protracted fit of sulks, sent for a doctoress. The doctoress was baffled by the fever, but did not admit it. What the patient needed, she said, was light but distracting conversation. Mentioning in the course of her chat that she had discovered from the eunuch that the packing-case in the lobby contained a new garden hose, the doctoress had the pleasure of seeing Djamileh make an instant recovery from her fever. Congratulating herself on her skill and on her fee, the old dame went off, leaving Djamileh to realize that it was not enough to refrain from asking questions, some more radical method of combating curiosity must be found. And so when Badruddin, shortly after her recovery, asked her in a laughing way how she would like a husband, she replied seriously that she would prefer a public-school education.

This was not possible. But the indulgent solicitor did what he could to satisfy this odd whim, and Djamileh made such good use of her opportunities that by the time she was fifteen she had spoilt her handwriting, forgotten how to speak French, lost all of her former interest in botany, and asked only the most unspeculative questions. Badruddin was displeased. He sighed to think that the intellectual Bluebeard's child should have grown up so dull-witted, and spent more and more time in the company of his jasmines. Possibly, even, he consulted them, for though they were silent they could be expressive. In any case, after a month or so of inquiries, interviews, and drawing up treaties, he told Djamileh that, acting under her father's will, he had made arrangements for her marriage.

Djamileh was sufficiently startled to ask quite a number of questions, and Badruddin congratulated himself on the aptness of his prescription. His choice had fallen upon Prince Kayel Oumarah, a young man of good birth, good looks, and pleasant character, but not very well-to-do. The prince's relations were prepared to overlook Djamileh's origin in consideration of her fortune, which was enormous, and Kayel, who was of a rather sentimental turn of mind, felt that it was an act of chivalry to marry a young girl whom other young men might scorn for what was no fault of hers, loved her already for being so much obliged to him, and wrote several ghazals expressing a preference for blue hair.

> "What wouldn't I do, what wouldn't I do,
> To get at that hair of heavenly blue?"

(the original Persian is, of course, more elegant) sang Kayel under her window. Djamileh thought this harping on her hair not in the best of taste, more especially since Kayel had a robust voice and the whole street might hear him. But it was flattering to have poems written about her (she herself had no turn for poetry), and when she peeped through the lattice she thought that he had a good figure and swayed to and fro with a great deal of feeling. Passion and a good figure can atone for much; and perhaps when they were man and wife he would leave off making personal remarks.

After a formal introduction, during which Djamileh offered Kayel symbolical sweetmeats and in her confusion ate most of them herself, the young couple were married. And shortly thereafter they left town for the Castle of Shady Transports, the late Bluebeard's country house.

Djamileh had not set eyes on Shady Transports since she was carried away from it in the same litter as Aunt Ann and the inventory. It had been in the charge of a caretaker ever since. But before the wedding Badruddin had spent a few days at the village inn, and under his superintendence the roof had been mended, the gardens trimmed up, all the floors very carefully scrubbed, and a considerable quantity of female attire burned in the stable yard. There was no look of former tragedy about the place when Djamileh and Kayel arrived. The fountain plashed innocently in the forecourt, all the most appropriate flowers in the language of love were bedded out in the parterre, a troop of new slaves, very young and handsomely dressed, stood bowing on either side of the door, and seated on cushions in stiff attitudes of expectation Maya and Moghreb, Djamileh's favourite dolls, held out their jointed arms in welcome.

Tears came into her eyes at this token of Badruddin's understanding heart. She picked up her old friends and kissed first one and then the other, begging their pardon for the long years in which they had suffered neglect. She thought they must have pined, for certainly they weighed much less than of old. Then she recollected that she was grown up, and had a husband.

At the moment he was not to be seen. Still clasping Maya and Moghreb, she went in search of him, and found him in the armoury, standing lost in admiration before a display of swords, daggers, and cutlasses. Djamileh remembered how, as a child, she had been held up to admire, and warned not to touch.

"That one comes from Turkestan," she said. "My father could cut off a man's head with it at a single blow."

Kayel pulled the blade a little way from the sheath. It was speckled with rust, and the edge was blunted.

"We must have them cleaned up," he said. "It's a pity to let them get like this, for I've never seen a finer collection."

"He had a splendid collection of poets, too," said Djamileh. "I was too young to read them then, of course, but now that I am married to a poet myself I shall read them all."

"What a various-minded man!" exclaimed Kayel as he followed her to the library.

It is always a pleasure to explore a fine old rambling country house. Many people whose immediate thoughts would keep them tediously awake slide into a dream by fancying that such a house has—no exact matter how—come into their possession. In fancy they visit it for the first time, they wander from room to room, trying each bed in turn, pulling out the books, opening Indian boxes, meeting themselves in mirrors. . . . All is new to them, and all is theirs.

For Kayel and Djamileh this charming delusion was a matter of fact. Djamileh indeed declared that she remembered Shady Transports from the days of her childhood, and was always sure that she knew what was round the next corner; but really her recollections were so fragmentary that except for the sentiment of the thing she might have been exploring her old home for the first time. As for Kayel, who had spent most of his life in furnished lodgings, the comfort and spaciousness of his wife's palace impressed him even more than he was prepared to admit. Exclaiming with delight, the young couple ransacked the house, or wandered arm in arm through the grounds, discovering fishponds, icehouses, classical grottoes, and rustic bridges. The gardeners heard their laughter among the blossoming thickets, or traced where they had sat by the quantity of cherry-stones.

At last a day came when it seemed that Shady Transports had yielded up to them all its secrets. A sharp thunderstorm had broken up the fine weather. The rain was still falling, and Kayel and Djamileh sat in the western parlour playing chess like an old married couple. The rain had cooled the air, indeed it was quite chilly; and Kayel, who was getting the worst of the game, complained of a draught that blew on his back and distracted him.

"There can't really be a draught, my falcon," objected Djamileh, "for draughts don't blow out of solid walls, and there is only a wall behind you."

"There is a draught," persisted he. "I take your pawn. No, wait a moment, I'm not sure that I do. How can I possibly play chess in a whirlwind?"

"Change places," said his wife, "and I'll turn the board."

They did so and continued the game. It was now Djamileh's move; and as she sat gazing at the pieces Kayel fell to studying her intent and unobservant countenance. She was certainly quite pretty, very pretty even, in spite of her colouring. Marriage had improved her, thought he. A large portrait of Bluebeard hung on the wall behind her. Kayel's glance went from living daughter to painted sire, comparing the two physiognomies. Was there a likeness—apart, of course, from the blue hair? Djamileh was said to be the image of her mother; certainly the rather foxlike mask before him, the narrow eyes and pointed chin, bore no resemblance to the prominent eyes and heavy jowl of the portrait. Yet there was a something . . . the pouting lower lip, perhaps, emphasized now by her considering expression. Kayel had another look at the portrait.

"Djamileh! There *is* a draught! I saw the hangings move." He jumped up and pulled them aside. "What did I say?" he inquired triumphantly.

"Oh! Another surprise! Oh, haven't I a lovely Jack-in-the-Box house?"

The silken hangings had concealed a massive stone archway, closed by a green baize door.

Kayel nipped his wife's ear affectionately. "You who remember everything so perfectly—what's behind that door?"

"Rose-petal conserve," she replied. "I have just remembered how it used to be brought out from the cupboard when I was good."

"I don't believe it. I don't believe there's a cupboard, I don't believe you were ever good."

"Open it and see."

Beyond the baize door a winding stair led into a small gallery or corridor, on one side of which were windows looking into the park, on the other, doors. It was filled with a green and moving light reflected from the wet foliage outside. They turned to each other with rapture. A secret passage—five doors in a row, five new rooms waiting to be explored! With a dramatic gesture Kayel threw open the first door. A small dark closet was revealed, perfectly empty. A trifle dashed, they opened the next door. Another closet, small, dark, and empty. The third door revealed a third closet, the exact replica of the first and second.

Djamilech began to laugh at her husband's crestfallen air.

"In my day," she said, "all these cupboards were full of rose-petal conserve. So now you see how good I was."

Kayel opened the fourth door.

He was a solemn young man, but now he began to laugh also. Four empty closets, one after another, seemed to these amiable young people the height of humour. They laughed so loudly that they did not hear a low peal of thunder, the last word of the retreating storm. A dove who had her nest in the lime tree outside the window was startled by their laughter or by the thunder; she flew away, looking pale and unreal against the slate-coloured sky. Her flight stirred the branches, which shook off their raindrops, spattering them against the casement.

"Now for the fifth door," said Kayel.

But the fifth door was locked.

"Djamileh, dear, run and ask the steward for the keys. But don't mention which door we want unfastened. Slaves talk so, they are always imagining mysteries."

"I am rather tired of empty cupboards, darling. Shall we leave this one for the present? At any rate till after tea? So much emptiness has made me very hungry, I really need my tea."

"Djamileh, fetch the keys."

Djamileh was an obedient wife, but she was also a prudent one. When she had found the bunch of keys she looked carefully over those which were unlabelled. They were many, and of all shapes and sizes; but at last she found the key she had been looking for and which she had dreaded to find. It was a small key, made of gold and finely arabesqued; and on it there was a small dark stain that might have been a bloodstain.

She slipped it off the ring and hid it in her dress.

Returning to the gallery, she was rather unpleasantly struck by Kayel's expression. She could never have believed that his open countenance could wear such a look of cupidity or that his eyes could become so beady. Hearing her step, he started violently, as though roused from profound absorption.

"There you are! What an age you have been—darling! Let's see now. Icehouse, Stillroom, Butler's Pantry, Winecellar, Family Vault . . . I wonder if this is it?"

He tried key after key, but none of them fitted. He tried them all over again, upside-down or widdershins. But still they did not fit. So then he took out his pocketknife, and tried to pick the lock. This also was useless.

"Eblis take this lock!" he exclaimed. And suddenly losing his temper, he began to kick and batter at the door. As he did so there was a little click; and one of the panels of the door fell open upon a hinge, and disclosed a piece of parchment, framed and glazed, on which was an inscription in ancient Sanskrit characters.

"What the . . . Here, I can't make this out."

Djamileh, who was better educated than her husband in such worthless studies as calligraphy, examined the parchment and read aloud: "CURIOSITY KILLED THE CAT."

Against her bosom she felt the little gold key sidle, and she had the unpleasant sensation which country language calls: "The grey goose walking over your grave."

"I think," she said gently, "I think, dear husband, we had better leave this door alone."

Kayel scratched his head and looked at the door.

"Are you sure that's what it means? Perhaps you didn't read it right."

"I am quite sure that is what it means."

"But, Djamileh, I do want to open the door."

"So do I, dear. But under the circumstances we had better not do anything of the sort. The doors in this house are rather queer sometimes. My poor father . . . my poor stepmothers . . ."

"I wonder," mused Kayel, "if we could train a cat to turn the lock and go in first."

"Even if we could, which I doubt, I don't think that would be at all fair to the cat. No, Kayel, I am sure we should agree to leave this door alone."

"It's not that I am in the least inquisitive," said Kayel, "for I am not. But as master of this house I really think it my duty to know what's inside this cupboard. It might be firearms, for instance, or poison, which might get into the wrong hands. One has a certain responsibility, hang it!"

"Yes, of course. But all the same I feel sure we should leave the door alone."

"Besides, I have you to consider, Djamileh. As a husband, you must be my first consideration. Now you may not want to open the door just now; but suppose, later on, when you were going to have a baby, you developed one of those strange yearnings that women at such times are subject to; and suppose it took the form of longing to know what was behind this door. It might be very bad for you, Djamileh, it might imperil your health, besides birth-marking the baby. No! It's too grave a risk. We had much better open the door immediately."

And he began to worry the lock again with his penknife.

"Kayel, please don't. *Please* don't. I implore you, I have a feeling—"

"Nonsense. Women always have feelings."

"—as though I were going to be sick. In fact, I am sure I am going to be sick."

"Well, run off and be sick, then. No doubt it was the thunderstorm, and all those strawberries."

"I can't run off, Kayel. I don't feel well enough to walk; you must carry me. Kayel!"—she laid her head insistently on his chest—"Kayel! I felt sick this morning, too."

And she laid her limp weight against him so firmly that with a sigh he picked her up and carried her down the corridor.

Laid on the sofa, she still kept a firm hold on his wrist, and groaned whenever he tried to detach himself. At last, making the best of a bad job, he resigned himself, and spent the rest of the day reading aloud to her from the erotic Persian poets. But he did not read with his usual fervour; the lyrics, as he rendered them, might as well have been genealogies. And Djamileh, listening with closed eyes, debated within herself why Kayel should be so cross. Was it just the locked door? Was it, could it be, that he was displeased by the idea of a baby with Bluebeard blood? This second possibility was highly distressing to her, and she wished, more and more fervently, as she lay on the sofa keeping up a pretence of delicate health and disciplining her healthy appetite to a little bouillon and some plain sherbet, that she had hit upon a pretext with fewer consequences entailed.

It seemed to her that they were probably estranged for ever. So it was a great relief to be awakened in the middle of the night by Kayel's usual affable tones, even though the words were:

"Djamileh, I believe I've got it! All we have to do is to get a stonemason, and a ladder, and knock a hole in the wall. Then we can look in from the outside. No possible harm in that."

All the next day and the day after, Kayel perambulated the west wing of Shady Transports with his stonemasons, directing them where to knock holes in the walls; for it had been explained to the slaves that he intended to bring the house up to date by throwing out a few bow-windows. But not one of these perspectives (the walls of Shady Transports were exceedingly massy) afforded a view into the locked closet. While these operations were going on he insisted that Djamileh should remain at his side. It was essential, he said, that she should appear interested in the improvements, because of the slaves. All this while she was carrying about that key on her person, and debating whether she should throw it away, in case Kayel, by getting possession of it, should endanger his life, or whether she should keep it and use it herself the moment he was safely out of the way.

Jaded in nerves and body, at the close of the second day they had a violent quarrel. It purported to be about the best method of pruning acacias, but while they were hurrying from sarcasm to acrimony, from acrimony to abuse, from abuse to fisticuffs, they were perfectly aware that in truth they were quarrelling as to which of them should first get at that closet.

"Laterals! Laterals!" exclaimed Djamileh. "You know no more of pruning than you know of dressmaking. That's right! Tear out my hair, do!"

"No, thank you." Kayel folded his arms across his chest. "I have no use for *blue hair.*"

Pierced by this taunt, Djamileh burst into tears. The soft-hearted Kayel felt that he had gone too far, and made several handsome apologies for the remark; but it seemed likely that his apologies would be in vain, for Djamileh only came out of her tears to ride off on a high horse.

"No, Kayel," she said, putting aside his hand, and speaking with exasperating nobility and gentleness. "No, no, it is useless, do not let us deceive ourselves any longer. I do not blame you; your feeling is natural and one should never blame people for natural feelings."

"Then why have you been blaming me all this time for a little natural curiosity?"

Djamileh swept on.

"And how could you possibly have felt anything but aversion for one in whose veins so blatantly runs the blood of the Bluebeards, for one whose hair, whose lips, stigmatize her as the child of an unfortunate monster? I do not blame you, Kayel. I blame myself, for fancying you could ever love me. But I will make you the only amends in my power. I will leave you."

A light quickened in Kayel's eye. So he thought she would leave him at Shady Transports, did he?

"Tomorrow we will go *together* to Badruddin. He arranged our marriage, he had better see about our divorce."

Flushed with temper, glittering with tears, she threw herself into his willing arms. They were still in all the raptures of sentimental and first love, and in the even more enthralling raptures of sentiment and first grief, when they set out for Teheran. Absorbed in gazing into each other's eyes and wiping away each other's tears with pink silk handkerchiefs, they did not notice that a drove of stampeding camels was approaching their palanquin; and it was with the greatest surprise and bewilderment that they found themselves tossed over a precipice.

When Djamileh recovered her senses she found herself lying in a narrow green pasture, beside a watercourse. Some fine broad-tailed sheep were cropping the herbage around, and an aged shepherdess was bathing her forehead and slapping her hands.

"How did I come here?" she inquired.

"I really cannot tell you," answered the shepherdess. "All I know is that about half an hour ago you, and a handsome young man, and a coachman, and a quantity of silk cushions and chicken sandwiches appeared, as it were from heaven, and fell amongst us and our sheep. Perhaps as you are feeling better you would like one of the sandwiches?"

"Where is the young man? He is not dead?"

"Not at all. A little bruised, but nothing worse. He recovered before you, and feeling rather shaken he went off with the shepherds to have a drink at the inn. The coachman went with them."

Djamileh ate another sandwich, brooding on Kayel's heartlessness.

"Listen," she said, raising herself on one elbow. "I have not time to tell you the whole of my history, which is long and complicated with unheard-of misfortunes. Suffice it to say that I am young, beautiful, wealthy, well-born, and accomplished, and the child of doting and distinguished parents. At their death I fell into the hands of an unscrupulous solicitor who, entirely against my will, married me to that young man you have seen. We had not been married for a day before he showed himself a monster of jealousy; and though my conduct has been unspotted as the snow he has continually belaboured me with threats and reproaches, and now has determined to shut me up, for ever, in a hermitage on the Caucasus mountains, inherited from a woman-hating uncle (the whole family are very queer). We were on our way thither when, by the interposition of my good genius, the palanquin overturned, and we arrived among your flocks as we did."

"Indeed," replied the aged shepherdess. "He said nothing of all that. But I do not doubt it. Men are a cruel and fantastic race. I too have lived a life chequered with many strange adventures and unmerited misfortunes. I was born in India, the child of a virtuous Brahmin and of a mother who had, before my birth, graced the world with eleven daughters, each lovelier than the last. In the opinion of many well-qualified persons, I, the youngest of her children, was even fairer——"

"I can well believe it," said Djamileh. "But, venerable Aunt, my misfortunes compel me to postpone the pleasure of hearing your story until a more suitable moment. It is, as you will see, essential that I should seize this chance of escaping from my tyrant. Here is a purse. I shall be everlastingly obliged if you will conduct me to the nearest livery-stables where I can hire a small chariot and swift horses."

Though bruised and scratched Djamileh was not the worse for her sudden descent into the valley, and following the old shepherdess, who was as nimble as a goat, she scrambled up the precipice, and soon found herself in a hired chariot, driving at full speed towards the Castle of Shady Transports, clutching in her hot hand the key of the locked closet. Her impatience was indescribable, and as for her scruples and her good principles, they had vanished as though they had never been. Whether it was a slight concussion, or pique at hearing that Kayel had left her in order to go off and drink with vulgar shepherds, I do not pretend to say. But in any case, Djamileh had now but one thought, and that was to gratify her curiosity as soon as possible.

Bundling up a pretext of having forgotten her jewelry, she hurried past the house steward and the slaves, refusing refreshment and not listening to a word they said. She ran into the west parlour, threw aside the embroidered hangings, opened the green baize door, flew up the winding stair and along the gallery.

But the door of the fifth closet had been burst open.

It gave upon a sumptuous but dusky vacancy, an underground saloon of great size, walled with mosaics and inadequately lit by seven vast rubies hanging from the ceiling. A flight of marble steps led down to this apartment, and at the foot of the steps lay Kayel, groaning piteously.

"Thank heaven you've come! I've been here for the last half-hour, shouting at the top of my voice, and not one of those accursed slaves has come near me."

"Oh, Kayel, are you badly hurt?"

"Hurt? I should think I've broken every bone in my body, and I know I've broken my collar-bone. I had to smash that door in, and it gave suddenly, and I pitched all the way down these steps. My second fall today. Oh!"

As she leaned over him the little golden key, forgotten and useless now, slid from her hand.

"My God, Djamileh! You've had that key all this time. And so *that* was why you came back?"

"Yes, Kayel. I came back to open the door. But you got here before me."

And while that parry still held him she hastened to add:

"We have both behaved so shockingly that I don't think either of us had better reproach the other. So now let us see about your fracture."

Not till the collar-bone was mending nicely; not till the coverlet which Djamileh had begun to knit as she sat by her husband's bedside, since knitting is so soothing to invalids, was nearly finished; not till they had solved the last of the acrostics sent to them by a sympathizing Badruddin, did they mention the affair of the closet.

"How could I have the heart to leave you—you, looking so pale, and so appealing?" said Kayel suddenly.

"And the lies I told about you, Kayel, the moment I came to . . . the things I said, the way I took away your character."

"We must have been mad."

"We were suffering from curiosity. That was all, but it was quite enough."

"How terrible curiosity is, Djamileh! Fiercer than lust, more ruthless than avarice. . . ."

"Insatiable as man-eating tigers. . . ."

"Insistent as that itching-powder one buys at low French fairs. . . . O Djamileh, let us vow never to feel curiosity again!"

"I made that vow long ago. You have seen what good it was."

They meditated, gazing into each other's eyes.

"It seems to me, my husband, that we should be less inquisitive if we had more to do. I think we should give up all our money, live in a village, and work all day in the fields."

"That only shows, my dearest, that you have always lived in a town. The people who work all day in the fields will sit up all night in the hopes of discovering if their neighbour's cat has littered brindled or tortoise-shell kittens."

They continued to interrogate each other's eyes.

"A man through whose garden flowed a violent watercourse," said Djamileh, "complained one day to the stream: 'O Stream, you have washed away my hollyhocks, swept off my artichokes, undermined my banks, flooded my bowling-green, and drowned my youngest son, the garland of my grey head. I wish, O Stream, that you would have the kindness to flow elsewhere.' 'That cannot be,' replied the stream, 'since Allah has bidden me to flow where I do. But if you were to erect a mill on your property, perhaps you would admit that I have my uses.' In other words, Kayel, it seems to me that, since we cannot do away with our curiosity, we had best sublimate it, and take up the study of a science."

"Let it be astronomy," answered Kayel. "Of all sciences, it is the one least likely to intervene in our private life."

To this day, though Bluebeard's daughter is forgotten, the wife of Kayel the astronomer is held in remembrance. It was she whose sympathetic collaboration supported him through his researches into the Saturnian rings, it was she who worked out the mathematical calculations which enabled him to prove that the lost Pleiad would reappear in the year 1963. As time went on, and her grandchildren came clustering round the telescope, Djamileh's blue hair became silver;

but to the day of her death her arched blue brows gave an appearance of alertness to her wrinkled countenance, and her teeth, glistening and perfect as in her girlhood, were shown off to the best advantage by the lining of her mouth, duskily blue as that of a well-bred chow-dog's.

The Cat's Cradle-Book. London: Chatto & Windus, 1960. 157–180.

23
Rebecca West (1892–1983)

Introduced and Edited by Bonnie Kime Scott

When nineteen-year-old Cicely Fairfield renamed herself Rebecca West in 1912, the twentieth century gained a unique and forceful female interpreter, who has yet to be adequately heeded. She had begun writing in earnest for the radical suffragist journal the *Freewoman* and dropped her original name to spare her sister Lettie professional embarrassment over this association. The name she hastily chose partakes of the fresh, rebellious spirit of the new woman that Ibsen brought to the theatre near the end of the nineteenth century and suits West's taste for the dramatic. She studied acting in London before taking up journalism and once played the role of Ibsen's Rebecca West. She pointed out that she was not at all like the "very gloomy" heroine of *Rosmersholm* ("Bookshelf"), and she certainly had better powers of survival than that suicidal heroine. West was still reviewing books, working on manuscripts, and writing about what it felt like to be ninety in 1982 (Glendinning 248).

Though West claimed aristocratic Anglo-Irish ancestors in County Kerry through her father, she inherited poverty and insecurity from a man she adored but lost when he deserted the family in 1901. Charles Fairfield was an antisocialist, antisuffragist journalist (she says a talented one) and a compulsive speculator with family fortunes. The rise and fall of fortunes in a male-structured commercial world became an abiding theme with her. From her mother, Isabella Campbell Mackenzie, West imbibed Edinburgh traditions, a love of music that would serve her literary metaphors, and the character type of a brave, though stern, female provider. West's two older sisters, Lettie (later a physician, with whom she frequently argued) and Winnifred (who had the ability to soothe her), were born in Australia. Rebecca began and ended in London but spent much of her childhood in Edinburgh. Her fictionalized portrait of family life in *The Fountain Overflows* shows parents who stimulated the intellect of their children while they were themselves isolates, regarded as strange to outsiders. West was to express feelings of marginality even after she had been made Dame Rebecca in 1959 (Scott interview). The education in "lady-likeness" that West received through age fifteen at a working women's college in Edinburgh was maddening to a young woman whose convictions included "votes for women" (see her analysis, *Young Rebecca* 154–157). She shares restless female ambition with her autobiographical heroines Adela (in an unpublished manuscript of 1905 vintage), Ellen Melville of *The Judge* (1922), and the much later Rose Aubrey of *The Fountain Overflows* (1956). Travel is an escape for the spirit, an antidote for rage over the situation at home, to the young journalist of the 1913 narrative "Trees of Gold," included below.

West's ability to argue for socialism and to review books with cutting wit proved attractive to literary men, including George Bernard Shaw, Max Beerbohm, D. H. Lawrence, and H. G. Wells. She met Shaw in Fabian socialist circles, and her book jackets still bear his statement that "Rebecca West could handle a pen as brilliantly as ever I could and much more savagely" (*Young Rebecca*). Beerbohm's Shavian cartoon image of her (imaginary, since he had not seen her) was surrounded by the text of a letter that included a list of the Shavian qualities he detected in her work: "curt, frank, breezy, trenchant, vain, swift, stern, frivolous, incorruptible, kind, accurate." Lawrence wrote to encourage her as "a real good squaw for scalps" at a time when "there are such a lot of scalps ripe for taking."

It was her harsh criticism of H. G. Wells's novel *Marriage* that brought on Wells and their ten-year liaison. She called him "the old maid among novelists" and said "the sex obsession that lay clotted on *Ann Veronica* and *The New Machiavelli* like cold white sauce was merely old maids' mania, the reaction towards the flesh of a mind too long absorbed in airships and colloids" (*Young Rebecca* 64). West had a flexible concept of gender that admitted men to the category of old maid or spinster; she felt that the spinster's idolizing of the opposite sex was a disadvantage in writing.[1] Anthony, the child she had by Wells in 1914, would provide West's most sustained torment, first as she found herself rusticated from her literary environment for the birth and finally as both she and her son mythologized the family triangle after Wells's death.[2] West's youthful brashness and beauty and her free-love relationship to the married Wells could dominate over her literary merits in the public imagination.[3] She had a paragraph about the circumstances of Anthony's birth deleted from a 1947 *Time* magazine article and refused profits from writing on Wells (Glendinning 199–200). When in 1981 an interviewer asked if it would be "insensitive" to mention Wells, West replied, "I cannot be bothered with this any longer"; she had no response to his evocation of people's references to her "great beauty" ("Bookshelf").

The vast corpus of West's writing defies usual categories of genre and period. In the critical introduction to a West anthology produced in the 1970s, Samuel Hynes noted that "Dame Rebecca's work has not fused with the critics," identifying the wide "interstices between her books" as a problem to her literary reputation (Hynes xviii). A number of her works written through the 1920s can be related to canonical modernism, even though they have not been canonized. *The Return of the Soldier, The Judge, Harriet Hume,* and the fictionalized essay "The Strange Necessity" have modernist traits such as stream of consciousness narrative, a concern with the unconscious developed on psychoanalytic lines, and surreal fantasy sequences. The inadequacy of genre designations is clear in "The Strange Necessity" and in her much-praised *Black Lamb and Grey Falcon* (1941), a work that might be labeled sociohistorical travel narrative. Her book reviews quickly become explorations on equality of employment or documents in critical theory, the latter being the case in "What Is Mr. T. S. Eliot's Authority as a Critic?" included here. Journalism typically does not count toward a literary reputation, and a great deal of West's energy flowed into this form, which offered necessary financial support, even though she valued it less than her novels. West's writing on social issues and the literary scene helps contextualize modernism, and her longevity moves us historically into the anti-Communist, cold war era. After 1940, West did extensive trial and crime reportage, specializing in themes relating to treason that seem very distant from her modernist tendencies and her early socialist feminism.

Gender study offers a rich approach to the entire West canon and helps explain her literary fortunes. A number of male critics, showing their discomfort with West's bold feminism, have attempted to relegate it and her use of a feminine style to her early writing. N. Gordon Ray offers this excuse: "If she . . . expounded feminist doctrine with an assurance amounting to fanaticism, this was after all what subscribers to the *Freewoman* expected for their three pennies; no doubt she had her private reservations" (8). In "The Strange Necessity," Samuel Hynes finds West "acting out her liberation from the stereotypes of her sex, and showing us how a free mind might play upon ideas." His representative of female stereotype is Virginia Woolf; the preferred attitudes are "intellectual toughness and knowledge" (xii). Hynes is comfortable, however, with an androgynous designation for West. Harold Orel says that West "wishes to discuss" fewer women authors "than feminists may wish" (32).[4] Such remarks suggest that the politics of gender have asserted themselves in West studies.

Remarks on feminism, accurate or not, do not fully explore the flexible field of gender. Constructions of gender—including virility (to use a favorite term for West) and femininity—vary in history, in cultures, in the life span of the individual. Thus we might hypothesize that her own youth and the conditions of history surrounding modernism evoked a more feminist and feminine identification in West in her early writing; the 1950s and her approach to late middle age elicited a more masculine side. Another aspect of gender is that its constructions are always interconnected. Thus in "The World's Worst Failure" (included here), where West describes in great detail a very feminine woman, she must make a connection to the woman's intended audience, a husband killed in the Great War, and a lover removed by financial ruin; she must study the rules of a cultural system of the chic. She sees shades of difference and an underlying "instinct for elegance" in two other women, an American of slightly greater personal ambition and her own literary persona.

West wrote a lot on men—monograph-length studies of Henry James, D. H. Lawrence, Saint Augustine, and Arnold Bennett and a set of lectures that center on Shakespeare (*The Court and the Castle*). But even here she is constantly aware of the forces of gender in men's development and thought. Saint Augustine, for example, assumes maternal and paternal orientations in successive stages of his life. She notes that his colonial and racial status set certain challenges that the young Augustine "could have accepted as ultimately he did. . . . They were all associated with his father, or at least the male side of life." But he opted first for the maternal side, which offered a "haven of calm" quite apart from the rewards of civilization in Christian immortality (*Essential RW* 170–171). West compares the introspective field of Saint Augustine's writings to the focus of the moderns (*Essential RW* 165), and it is this achievement that she admires in both Woolf and Lawrence (see "High Fountain of Genius" and "What Is Mr. T. S. Eliot's Authority" below). *The Return of the Soldier* (1918) qualifies as war literature, but it is set on a feminized home front. West tells the soldier's story from the perspective of Jenny, Chris's cousin, whose narrative powers include the capacity to fantasize her way into battlefield settings (see Stetz). The spiritual, vital center of the novel is Margaret, a lower-class, worn woman, devoid of style. The shell-shocked Chris has reverted in memory to their idyllic youthful love in a setting by the Thames. This peaceful, classless, semiotic setting remains a resource to characters in West's final fiction, *Cousin Rosamund.* Margaret is a favorite character type for West—the revitalizing female. We are left doubting whether the restoration of Chris to his materialistic, modern wife and the economies and mechanics of war is a happy ending and regretting a social order that could provide no other. Even one of West's most appreciated crime stories, "Mr. Setty and Mr. Hume," juxtaposes an oblivious woman to its supposed concerns: activities of the alleged murderer, detective work, courtroom drama, and West's own reportage, things that "will exist only on the printed page." Mrs. Hume, wife of the supposed murderer, goes about the business of tending to a new baby with West's endorsement of her difference: "Women of her type resemble artists in their failure to feel surprise at the exceptional event." Her work was renewal: "The snarl in Hume's genetic line would be untangled" (*Essential RW* 318–319).

Female centering is more obvious in *The Judge* (1922), *Harriet Hume*

(1929), *The Harsh Voice* (1935), *The Thinking Reed* (1936), and *The Fountain Overflows* (1956). These titles were brought back into print by the feminist Virago Press. Both Virago's *Young Rebecca* and the *Norton Anthology of Literature by Women* include "Indissoluble Matrimony," first published in 1914. In its depiction of sex war between a devitalized, insecure, puritanical husband and his sensuous, socialist, outgoing wife, the story fulfills the central paradigms of Sandra Gilbert and Susan Gubar's view of modernism.[5] West's 1913 narrative, "Trees of Gold," demonstrates a whole range of concerns in a young woman narrator—from fending off the sexism of male fellow passengers on a train to countering the doctrine of Christian sacrifice with an aesthetic of ultimate beauty, read in an exotic landscape. *The Judge* begins with a restive young heroine working as a secretary in Edinburgh. The novel takes on new scope through her marriage to Richard Yaverland, whose masculine, worldly experience includes residence and land ownership in South America and success in the munitions industry. It is the story of his origin as the illegitimate son of Marion Yaverland that takes the novel into the mythic range of vital maternal instinct, caught in destructive cultural strictures and evil deeds. *Harriet Hume* is a lighter "fantasy" novel that sets the male ambition to rise in political endeavors against feminine art. The heroine has a magical ability to read the spiritual lapses of a mind invested in masculine patterns of success. Cassandralike figures continue to appear in *The Thinking Reed* and *The Fountain Overflows*. West reads patterns of male and female failure in the relationships described in *The Harsh Voice*.

Love of women is constant in West's work. She richly textualizes the female body and apparel, though she carefully distances herself from any lesbian identification and sometimes decries what she has carefully described. "Trees of Gold" offers a restrained love of women in ritual, with its description of Spanish nuns. Her second essay written in Spain, "Nana," is more erotic, taking the female perceiver back to early nurture from a female caretaker. She admires a performer in a disreputable cafe:

> I love shiny things: the glossy tiles in the corridors of the tubes, the gleam of the water as it slides to the weir, well-polished boots. So I love this lady. In all directions she presented smooth white surfaces and pleasant bulges; her hair rose from bright low forehead like a solid and newly-blackleaded iron fender; her shoulder beamed like a newly-enamelled bath. And this amazing incandescence was only the glittering facade of an attractiveness whose rich texture pleased the eye as the pile of a Benares carpet pleases the finger. . . . A sudden generous smile of the big brilliant mouth showed it to be something of the very dearest charm. For about her glowed the rarest warmth in the world, the comfortable warmth of hot bread-and-milk consumed beside the nursery fire: and in that bosom which should have been sheathed in starched linen one would certainly find the sympathy that gives its kisses freely and barges no price of repentance.

Relentless diagnosis of feminine adornment and postures is offered in "The World's Worst Failure." West's continued concern with the operations of gender and a troubled grappling with sexual orientation are major features of her late fiction. *The Fountain Overflows* and the two posthumous volumes, *This Real Night* and *Cousin Rosamund,* offer a female-dominated family epic spanning the years from the turn of the century into the Depression. This work has been compared in form to Dickens but will reward treatment alongside one of Woolf's least studied works, *The Years.*

West's feminist and socialist journalism gave thoroughgoing consideration to the operation of gender in the social and cultural systems of her day. A fine selection of these writings through 1917 is included by Jane Marcus in *The Young Rebecca. "The Freewoman"* included below is a sample of West's efforts to give a balanced appraisal of the contributions of the Pankhursts, acknowledging their unintelligent moments and lapses in taste but applauding them for bringing subjects such as venereal disease to public attention. The *Freewoman,* analogously, opened up the subject of "sex," and "shattered the romantic conception of women" which suggested that they could adapt to anything, "that they were in a bland state of desireless contentment which, if they were beautiful, reminded the onlooker of a goddess, and when they were plain . . . cabbage." West took up such issues as equal pay for women teachers (mentioned again in her reply to Lawrence's "Good Boy Husbands"), conditions for women factory workers, female access to unions, property rights, divorce, women's education and nutrition, and the limitations of the public schoolboy attitudes toward women visible in the House of Commons and the Labour party. Part of the exhilaration of being a journalist was that she was a working woman, a position in life vastly preferable to the parasitic woman cultivated in patriarchal society.

In her accounts of the evolution of the *Freewoman* into the increasingly literary *New Freewoman* and *Egoist* (*"The Freewoman"* and "Spinster to the Rescue," included below), West assumes the confident, judgmental tone that is typical of many of her narrators, in fiction as well as journalism. Readers may feel maneuvered into a position they cannot share, such as West's inability to see any logic in Harriet Shaw Weaver's late loyalty to the Communist party.[6] Both essays acquaint us with the personalities and historical contexts of women who were essential to the founding and survival of the journals—the prime mover, Dora Marsden, whose later metaphysical concerns gave rise to doubt in West, and the supportive "saint" Harriet Shaw Weaver. West rose quickly to an assistant editorship of the *New Freewoman,* where she began to do regular book reviews. The value she placed on literature as a complement to the political concerns of the *New Freewoman* is seen in her recruitment of Ezra Pound as literary editor for the journal. She met Pound at the home Violet Hunt shared with Ford Madox Ford. It was common to praise Ford's role in advancing younger writers, but West salutes both Ford and Hunt as "those untiring nurses of talent." West offers an innocuous if amusing description of Pound; "He dressed like a provincial American dandy in the previous century and something about the luminous quality of his skin and his red hair made him look as if he had been dipped in marmalade." But she mentions his "steely ambition . . . —an ambition which he extended to benefit his friends"

("Spinster"). It is not a pure statement of benevolence. West did not number herself among those friends. In correspondence West said harsher things that she did not want published. Pound was more willing that West to shove Marsden aside, and he failed to give West credit for the authors she suggested bringing to the journal. He spoke unkindly of her to others, undermining her with people she admired, such as Richard Aldington. Like H. D. and T. S. Eliot, Aldington served in the literary department of the *Egoist* (West, Letter to Jane Lidderdale). West did write an introduction of "imagisme," incorporating material from *Poetry* magazine, to preface Pound's poetry in the August 15, 1913, issue of the *New Freewoman.*

West made her own way in the changing world of literary and political journalism. She became a regular writer for the *New Republic,* where "The World's Worst Failure" appeared, followed by four sequels, each on a different sort of woman. This variety is typical of her sensitivity to the difference in women's difference. West's reviews began to appear in titled columns: a theatre column in the popular women's magazine *Time and Tide,* "Notes on Novels" in the *New Statesman,* "A Letter from Abroad" and "London Letter" in *Bookman,* and "I Said to Me" in the *New York American.* Her regular writing for the *New Yorker* became the capstone on her popularity in the United States—a phase of her career embarked on in 1924 after the Wells affair. She continued to earn her own way after her 1930 marriage to Henry Andrews, whose usual identification as a banker might lead people to think the contrary. The quiet, cultured, amorous relationship she had hoped for seems to have lasted only about five years, though the marriage persisted until his death and only close friends knew about her unhappiness and the ways the marriage inhibited her work. For friends, West had a collection of editors, critics, and writers, both men and women, with whom she shared her craft and her personal troubles in voluminous correspondence, which has yet to be published. Some of the most interesting connections in the 1920s and 1930s were with American drama critic Alexander Woollcott, journalists Janet Flanner and Emily Hahn, editor Harold Ross at the *New Yorker,* and novelist G. B. Stern, whose work bears comparison to West's later novels centered on female family life. E. M. Hutchinson, her bibliographer, provided an important connection to Yale in the 1950s. He was aware of the sexual politics that had led to her neglect in academic circles. Yale University and the University of Tulsa now house her papers.

A large number of critical articles and reviews by West record her reactions to modernist writers. Selections in this anthology relate to Lawrence, Woolf, Eliot, and (indirectly) James Joyce. West can also be consulted for her views on Dorothy Richardson, Katherine Mansfield, Violet Hunt, May Sinclair, Wyndham Lewis, Marcel Proust, and Colette, among others.[7]

In "Spinster to the Rescue," West acknowledges that "Stephen Dedalus and Leopold Bloom . . . have found their way into the world's mind." Her most extensive observations on Joyce appear in the title essay of *The Strange Necessity,* where she analyzes Stephen and Bloom in terms of one of her favorite binaries, spirit and matter. She celebrates the revivifying life force of Molly Bloom, whom she calls "Marion," the name she was to give the mother figure of *The Judge*.

West reviewed many of Woolf's notable works, including *Jacob's Room, A Room of One's Own, Orlando,* and *The Waves*. In "High Fountain of Genius" she connects Woolf's prose in *Orlando* to a time-honored poetic tradition of language and her form to music: it "should be read like a Beethoven sonata." She embraces Woolf's project of arriving at an understanding of modern consciousness that is historically informed, yet not realistic. "Mrs. Woolf gives us certain poetic statements which convey to us the sum of the relationship between the *donnée* of each age and Orlando's fine perceptions." She finds hope that "the genuinely creative spirit" can survive in "our critical age." West framed the letter of appreciation that Woolf wrote in response to this review: "I cant tell you how it exhilarates me to feel your mind working along where mine tried to go (what a lot more of my meaning you have guessed than anybody else) and expanding and understanding, making Everything ten times more important than it seemed before."

In "What Is Mr. T. S. Eliot's Authority as a Critic?" West is determined not to give Eliot the final word on tradition and the modern. Considering his present stature, readers may be shocked by her bold pronouncement that "the years this American has spent in England have inflicted damage on our literature from which it will probably not recover for a generation" and her charges that he sometimes masks a lack of industry with an authority of manner, his "sober and seemly form." West assesses his American contexts, focusing on the humanism of Irving Babbitt and Paul Elmer More. Though they properly encourage respect for tradition, they are wary of "intellectual faults likely to arise in a community where all things are new," and they have reduced humanism "to propaganda for a provincial conception of metropolitan gentility." She wearies of Eliot's repeated invoking of formulas "invented for a different society" and detrimental to "vital creation."

In the close of her essay on Eliot, West demonstrates a typical enthusiasm for Lawrence's writing, focusing on works from supposedly minor genres: letters and travel literature. In both it is an "order within himself" as opposed to a demand for the external order of law that allows nature "a surface that could take such clear impressions." Her personal "Elegy" on Lawrence takes off from a shared landscape outside Florence, where they had strolled together, and appreciated Lawrence's ability to make such experiences, not naturalistic fiction, but a symbol for the state of his soul (*Essential RW* 389–393). West was always able to point out inaccuracies in his political arguments and to supply missing perspectives on gender issues, as she does in the responses to "Good Boy Husbands." Lawrence gives her a pretext to take up provocative themes, such as equal opportunities for women in the work force, the value of female sexual experience in assessing the value of "virility," and the differing levels of conflict with a "primitive self" experienced by modern women as compared to modern men.

Despite her appreciation of their work, West expressed feelings of marginality to canonized modernists. Wyndham Lewis had published her feminist story, "Indissoluable Matrimony," in *Blast*, but this revolutionary vorticist journal was short-lived. Though they went to restaurants together, she found him uncomfortably mute. Her relation to Pound had gone badly, perhaps out of a spirit of competition, as noted above. Lawrence died early. The contact with Woolf was sporadic, even though it did involve one publication by Hogarth Press ("A Letter to a Grandfather"). In her diary Woolf wrote "unkind" observations on West that hurt her. "We were not twin souls," West said (Scott interview). West felt that she lacked the sort of promotion that was available through a connection to Eliot, though the article on Eliot contained here suggests that West could not have agreed with Eliot's basic philosophies on literary tradition. *The Court and the Castle* (1957) provides a discussion of stream of consciousness in Richardson, Woolf, Lawrence, and Joyce, viewing all of them outside of the arena of state politics (215–223), an area that she ventured into regularly, beginning with her early journalism and continuing with the legal reportage in the 1940s and 1950s.

Woolf used West to represent the modern woman writer in *A Room of One's Own*, noting her effect on a male contemporary: "Z, most human, most modest of men, taking up some book by Rebecca West and reading a passage in it, exclaimed: 'The arrant feminist! She says that men are snobs.' " Woolf explains this as "the infringement of his power to believe in himself" (35). As we come to know her texts again in this generation, Rebecca West still has power as an iconoclast, but also as a model of belief in oneself and one's perceptions, regardless of sex. Her interrupted influence helps us rewrite modernism.

NOTES

I am grateful to Jane Marcus for locating several of the items anthologized in this section and for providing the photograph (see illustrations), a gift to her from Rebecca West.

1. "Spinsters and Art" (*Young Rebecca* 42–47) makes a related argument.
2. Victoria Glendinning attempts to give both sides of this troubled relationship in her biography of West and catches both participants in nasty responses. She observes, notably, "Anthony had the same problem in coming to terms with Rebecca that most males, related or not, have in coming to terms with exceptionally forceful people who are women. He dealt with it sometimes by ridiculing and denying her powers, sometimes by exaggerating them and seeing them as 'evil,' and building a black legend around her name. Rebecca retaliated by doing exactly the same thing to him." (176) For a compendium of materials relating to the Wells relationship, see Ray. Anthony West's works blasting his mother are listed in Works Cited.
3. Regrettably the pattern continues in Fay Weldon's *Rebeccca West* in the Penguin "Lives of Modern Women" series.

4. See my "Strange Necessity of Rebecca West" for a discussion of West's relation to women authors.

5. See *No Man's Land* 96–100.

6. West's anticommunism is probably the most difficult aspect of her political self for many feminists to fathom. See Ferguson. On her tone of authority, see Marcus, "Rebecca West: A Voice of Authority."

7. She also appreciated Emily and Charlotte Brontë, whose works undoubtedly influenced *The Judge* (Marcus, Introduction, *The Judge*), and Jane Austen (*The Court and the Castle* 113–114).

WORKS CITED

Beerbohm, Max. Letter to G. B. Shaw. 28 June 1918. In *The Young Rebecca,* plate 9.
"Bookshelf." Tape of program 12 Jan. 1981. U of Tulsa.
Ferguson, Moira. "Feminine Manicheanism: Rebecca West's Unique Fusion." *Minnesota Review* 15:53–60.
Glendinning, Victoria. *Rebecca West: A Life.* London: Weidenfeld and Nicolson, 1987.
Hutchinson, G. E. "The Dome." *The Itinerant Ivory Tower: Scientific and Literary Essays,* 241–255. New Haven: Yale UP, 1953.
———. *A Preliminary List of the Writings of Rebecca West 1912–1951.* New Haven: Yale UP, 1957.
Hynes, Samuel. "In Communion with Reality." In *The Essential Rebecca West,* ix–xix.
Lawrence, D. H. Letter to Rebecca West. 15 April 1929. MS., U of Tulsa.
Marcus, Jane. Editor's Introduction. In West, *The Young Rebecca,* 3–11.
———. Introduction. In West, *The Judge.*
———. "Rebecca West: A Voice of Authority." In *The Faith of a (Woman) Writer,* ed. Alice Kessler-Harris and William McBrien, 237–246. Westport, Conn.: Greenwood P, 1988.
Orel, Harold. *The Literary Achievement of Rebecca West.* London: Macmillan, 1986.
Ray, N. Gordon. *H. G. Wells and Rebecca West.* New Haven: Yale UP, 1974.
Scott, Bonnie Kime. Unpublished interview with Rebecca West, 17 Oct. 1981.
———. "The Strange Necessity of Rebecca West." In *Women Reading Women's Writing,* ed. Sue Roe, 263–286. Brighton: Harvester, 1987.
Stetz, Margaret Diane. "Drinking 'The Wine of Truth': Philosophical Change in West's *The Return of the Soldier. Arizona Quarterly* 43.1(1987):63–78.
Weldon, Fay. *Rebecca West.* Harmondsworth: Penguin, 1985.
West, Anthony. *H. G. Wells: Aspects of a Life.* London: Hutchinson, 1984.
———. *Heritage.* London: Secker and Warburg, 1984.
West, Rebecca. *The Court and the Castle.* New Haven: Yale UP, 1957.
———. *The Essential Rebecca West.* Harmondsworth: Penguin, 1983.
———. *The Fountain Overflows.* Harmondsworth: Penguin, 1985.
———. *Harriet Hume.* London: Virago, 1980.
———. *The Harsh Voice.* London: Virago, 1982.
———. *The Judge.* London: Virago, 1980.
———. Letter to Jane Lidderdale. 29 Jan. 1967. MS., U of Tulsa.
———. "Nana." *New Freewoman* 1.2(1913):26–27.
———. *The New Meaning of Treason.* New York: Viking P, 1964.
———. *The Strange Necessity: Essays by Rebecca West.* New York: Doubleday, 1928.
———. *The Thinking Reed.* London: Virago, 1984.
———. *The Young Rebecca: Writings of Rebecca West 1911–1917.* Ed. Jane Marcus. London: Virago, 1982.
Woolf, Virginia. MS. letter to Rebecca West. 10 Nov. 1928. U of Tulsa.

Trees of Gold

The collection of toothbrushes which I keep in my bedroom looks untidy: but it will have to stay as it is until I write my autobiography, because the only record of my spiritual life consists of the chemist's marks on the handles. For when I find myself consumed by any passion (which is usually rage) I fling myself out of London into some little place. And always I forget to take a toothbrush and have to buy a new one: hence I have accumulated a hoard of those boney reminders of the temperament. Sometimes they do not earn their keep, for they do not tell me why I went to Eastbourne. That was a horrible place, ravaged by a wind that made one look as though one had been drawn by Walter Sickert and that drove me dishevelled into a Ballad Concert where two fat men played a Chopin concert for twenty-five minutes. They might have been Belloc and Chesterton eternally discoursing of the Jews. . . . And I wonder why I went to Poole. I spent a jolly afternoon there in an old long-profaned Chapel on the quay, sitting on plump, crepitant sacks that exuded the sleepy scent of grain, while against a milk-white sea clucking machinery most entertainingly dropped coal into a dissolute little tramp steamer and fetched up sleek mud from the harbour bottom. That was what I really liked: dying a little death and dropping my life behind me, and giving to pleasant little plans when I could contemplate the innocent activities of the natives as a virgin martyr new to Heaven might survey the gambols of the Cherubim. But it has suddenly come about that England is no place for a respectable virgin martyr; It blunts the fine edge of the sword of the soul to live in a peace maintained by the torture of women. If I had stayed in England any longer I should have become as satisfied as any proprietor of a slaughter-house that God's in His Heaven, all's right with the world. So I looked round for a country that was not given over to the devil, who is the eternal fomenter of law and order. The news that King Alfonso was being specially guarded drove me to Spain: happy is the country where they know at whom to throw their bombs.

To recover this certainty of which I had been robbed by our great free Parliamentary institutions, I crossed the Pyrenean frontier one Sunday in May. My body was hot with fatigue, and the discussion of Votes for Women, which I was carrying on with a Basque wine-merchant, the King of Spain's photographer, and a German commercial traveller, lacked coherence because I cannot speak more than ten words of any foreign language grammatically. This is not a defect but a penalty attached to an active mind. How could I, who have been busy all my life debating on the nature of things, possibly spare the time to master a different and unenlightening system of naming things? Nevertheless, I leaped into a river of language and emerged, dripping with irregular verbs and wagging my tail with pride, to lay at their feet a declaration that things being as they are I want a vote. They gazed on me as one might gaze on a rebellious chocolate-cream. I should have left it at that: but my fundamental honesty, distressed at receiving this moist and benevolent glance on false pretences, moved me to explain that I was not a luxury but a journalist.

It was a brutal thing to do. They sat in a quiet large-eyed row and looked at me as a London crowd will look all day at a house where murder has been done, while their imaginations reconstructed the crime whereby the quivering morsel of femininity that must surely have been born in me was clubbed to death. Oddly enough, I felt guilty and unbeautifully raddled with intellectual passions: so that I appreciated the kindness of the German commercial traveller in bringing out his samples to divert the conversation. With a half-hearted hope of resuscitating my womanliness he surrounded me with miles and miles of galoon. I took the stiff ribbon in my hands, and with determination smiled delightedly at the raised chocolate and magenta flowers: and I recovered the sense of my innocence. For this German, staggering from capital to capital to seduce immortal souls into the purchase of galoon, was given up to blacker, more unsensuous sensuality than I should ever touch in staggering from Poole to Eastbourne, or even from idea to idea. I discovered where the emotion of modern Europe was spending itself one day last winter when, misdirected by Exchange, a voice asked me through the telephone to quote my lowest price for earthenware stoves (size D.). Never before had I been asked any question with such passion. The man who spoke was, like this German, one of a more hot-eyed and disordered multitude than was ever led by drink or the basest kinds of love, who desire to spread Axminster carpets on the Muscovian steppes and gild the South Sea lands with Waterbury watches as their forefathers desired to feed the whole earth with the body of Christ. Our enemy is commerce: The frenetic distribution and exchange of ugly things made by unhappy people confuses the earth. I thanked God that I had no hand in peace and prosperity and handed back the galoon.

We passed out of the Pyrenean mists and I looked out to find that we had left that damnable smiling green which makes France fit for nothing but a bleaching-ground. Quite quickly I realized that I had come to something that was as important to me as my birth. We had passed into a broad valley that was burned: not by the sun, for in these parts it was hardly more than early Spring, but by some deep passion of the earth that might have burst through the fields and light the air to flame had it not been that kind of passion that loves to feed upon itself. The red soil crumbled, the grass was young yet consumed. A fire ran up the poplars and discoloured the leaves that were rustling in a cold wind: and beside them a river flowed thinly as though leeched of its fulness by this ravening country. The land throbbed like a bared heart, and here and there a graveyard was the symbol of the valley's desperation. There were four high walls that were not white but pallid like terrified flesh: and above them spread black cypresses, calm as nothing else in that land was calm, without doubt rising from miraculously cold, wet roots. The ravaged earth had set itself to prison death, who yet sucked to its prison all the life its passion could create. The mind could grasp that struggle, but not the war between the valley and the naked limestone mountains that marched up from the east and west as proudly as befitted the raw material, the untainted substance of the earth. The land broke into a surf of burnt green trees against these cliffs, which were so stripped and shining that its veins of snow seemed warm and human: it became a hot and narrow gorge twisting upwards against this coldness. Rage shivered the mountain into peaks and deep distortions so beautiful that it strained this consciousness to perceive them: one could not fully grasp its beauty because of the limitations of this humanity. To enter into it one would need to be a mountain. It was exactly what I had always expected life to be like. Until now I had always been a little disappointed with things.

The train slid haltingly up an incline against a roaring wind into a tunnel full of little blue-clad navvies, who shouted and waved lamps from deep trenches. And I realised that I was feeling horribly ill. I had left London with the kind of fatigue that easily becomes a frenzy, and I had not passed unscathed by the flatness of France and the blunt ugliness of its women. But this was a grimmer kind of physical misery. I was a grey and disgusting object: I felt as though I was going to die, and I knew that my corpse would be most offensive to the eye. And not only was I distressed by my body but I felt concerned about my soul. For my illness was due, not to the long journey nor even to those galoons, but to the beauty of the burning valley and the naked hills. I was shattered by excitement. I had a right to be excited. This really was an important occasion in my life: before I had always worshipped this violent and courageous beauty, which I had never found in people and rarely in art, without any certainty that it existed. All the same, that it should shatter me condemned my life. I cared for nothing really deeply except this beauty. But I could not express it. And if I could make anything which had that quality of fierce splendour I could not make people like it. They would turn their backs on ravaged and distorted Spain and go to Switzerland to be pleased by the unsurprising beauty of the sunshine on the snow. I might, of course, ascend to a region where I would be content to make beauty without praise or company. But beauty is so dangerous. One has to use flame to burn the galoons from Europe and the tame squalor from life, and in the end one may so eaily turn this weapon of fire on itself. By the heat of its desires and adorations the mind may become like hot wax: incapable of receiving the sharp impressions which are all it lives for. The fire by whose blaze the soul meant to lighten the world may burn it down to its foundations and leave it a smoking ruin, as unlovely as any factory or building designed from the first for base uses. The fervent purpose may destroy its instrument and die frustrated. It brings not only personal disaster but it is a treachery against the orderly procession of generation after generation, which we call life. The poor hurt the community in which they live: they fall into ugly ways of life, they spread disease, they leech the stores of the kind. So too the tragic hurt the community: they live impulsively, they spread excitement, they make preposterous demand on the patience and service of those of good-will. They wreck the peace for which the race must seek for the sake of the future.

But all the fine things that grow out of life, like beauty or love or pride, demand this ritual of rashness and cruelty. If one loves them we must pardon those whose dignity it is to perform the ritual; it is worth while. At Burgos I walked to the Chapel of a palace, which eight hundred years ago a Castilian King gave to the most aristocratic order of Cistercian nuns. I saw the thirty sisters celebrate mass as they might have performed a slow court dance before the throne, and bow to the altar with such reverence as the daughters of the most mighty houses of Spain might decently pay to the son of a carpenter. Each of their bodies was as proud as a walled city full of towers. To cultivate their pride they had fenced their bodies in the spotless decency of an ordered life among women: they had folded away their minds in the cold casket of the love of Christ. Without doubt they might have governed their country haughtily or borne children to inherit their power: but in that life they might have been chipped and broken by contacts with insubordinate persons and uncoercible desires. They turned their backs on life and gave it an inspiring masterpiece, for that mass gave one the power to defy the earth and to defy it beautifully. If Christ had so abandoned himself to his genius for grace he might have sweetened the world. But he chose to save it, not by a gentle life-time spent sunnily among children and fishermen, but by the nine hours of His passion on the Cross: so he damned it by accustoming it to the sight of pain. Here in Spain the contemplation of his torn and bleeding body has perverted the people into a habit of indecency and the enjoyment of bull-fights. To this desire to save the world we still fall. To secure peace in our time we insist on "character," meaning an absence of characteristics, in our schools and produce an eventempered and disciplined population, that might as well have never been born. Our writers totter into sociology to tidy things up, and benevolently design new and improved workhouse dietaries instead of new stars. They will make life easy to live. But life itself is nothing: it is the trimmings that matter, the pride and honour and beauty.

That is why I face unashamed the disaster that the worship of my kind of beauty may bring on me and on my neighbours. On the Castilian heights above Burgos there were trees of gold. They thrust shining leaves into the quivering cloudless skies, and their slim trunks were the glowing metal itself. They shivered in a wind that came down from the snow and the light throbbed through their bodies. The secret of their beauty was a lichenous growth that gnawed inwards as it glowed outwards. Yet they were better, so gilded and diseased, than the healthy tree whereof they cut the mischievous cross of Christ.

New Freewoman. 15 June 1913:5–7.

The "Freewoman"

I have been asked to write an account of the "Freewoman," and those who asked me were wise, for that paper, unimportant as it was in content, and amateurish in form, had an immense effect on its time. But unfortunately, I have forgotten nearly everything about it. It must have lived about 14 or 15 years ago, because I know I was about 17 or 18 years of age; and in the intervening years I have done so much else and have so completely lost touch with the other persons involved, that the details are fogged in my mind.

The paper was the creation of Dora Marsden, who was one of the most marvellous personalities that the nation has ever produced. She had, to begin with, the most exquisite beauty of person. She was hardly taller than a child, but she was not just a small woman; she was a perfectly proportioned fairy. She was the only person I have ever met who could so accurately have been described as flower-like that one could have put it down on her passport. And on many other planes she was as remarkable. In her profession she had been more than ordinarily successful. Though she was still under thirty, she was head of a training college for teachers. She was one of the fighting suffragettes under Mrs. Pankhurst, and in the course of her activities she had shown courage that even in that courageous company seemed magnificent. She had been to prison more than once, and had behaved with what would have been amazing heroism in any woman, but which was something transcendent in her case, since she was physically fragile and the victim of a tiresome form of ill-health.

She conceived the idea of starting the "Freewoman" because she was discontented with the limited scope of the suffragist movement. She felt that it was restricting itself too much to the one point of political enfranchisement and was not bothering about the wider issues of Feminism. I think she was wrong in formulating this feeling as an accusation against the Pankhursts and suffragettes in general, because they were simply doing their job, and it was certainly a whole time job. But there was equally certainly a need for someone to stand aside and ponder on the profounder aspects of Feminism. In this view she found a supporter in Mary Gawthorpe, a Yorkshire woman who had recently been invalided out of the suffrage movement on account of injuries sustained at the hands of stewards who had thrown her out of a political meeting where she had been interrupting Mr. Winston Churchill. Mary Gawthorpe, was a merry militant saint who had travelled round the provinces, living in dreary lodgings on $15 or $20 a week, speaking several times a day at outdoor meetings, and suffering fools gladly (which I think she found the hardest job of all), when trying to convert the influential Babbits of our English zenith cities. Occasionally she had a rest in prison, which she always faced with a sparrow-like perkiness. She had wit and common sense and courage, and each to the point of genius. She lives in the United States now, but her inspiration still lingers over here on a whole generation of women.

These two came together and planned this paper, but Dora Marsden played the chief part in organizing and controlling it throughout the whole of its life, for at that time Mary Gawthorpe was sick almost unto death.

Dora Marsden came to London with her devoted friend Grace Jardine, who was Martha to her Mary, and they found a publisher to finance them. At this point I had better remind my readers that again and again radical movements find themselves obliged to be financed by the insane. Radicals may take comfort in reflecting that the same is true of non-radical movements, but that the fact is so serious because there is no striking antithesis between such movements and their financiers. This particular gentleman financed not only the "Freewoman," but Chesterton and Belloc's "The Eye Witness," and a fashionable illustrated paper which was tended by a beautiful lady with red gold hair and decorative footwear. Her slippers gleam undimmed across the gulf of time; I have not been able to forget them. The movies had not come into their own, but she anticipated the *anima* of Mr. Cecil de Mille. He also published his own poetry, which consisted of Wordsworthian nature verse and Browningish monologues about the soul. One I remember particularly was a touching lament by St. Augustine on his own celibacy. And this gentleman also published, with the utmost generosity of terms, various books by young lions. For example, he brought out Katherine Mansfield's first volume of short stories "In a German Pension." So we started in: or rather they did. I did not join them till later; in fact, I never wrote for the "Freewoman" till it had got such a bad name for its candour that I was forbidden to read it by my family, and thus I came to adopt my present pseudonym. The initial group consisted of Dora Marsden, Grace Jardine and a glorious red-haired bachelor of science, who had been in and out of gaol for the cause, named Rona Robinson. They went at first for all the conventional Feminist articles of faith. In their early numbers I fancy they represented as nearly as possible the same program as the National Woman's Party. That programme had certainly been accepted by English women of this subsequent period with an extraordinary completeness. I think there are probably hardly any subscribers to the quiet orthodox woman's weekly of to-day, TIME AND TIDE, who do not take it for granted that it is degrading to woman, and injurious to the race to leave the financing of the mother and her children to the double-barrelled caprice of the father and the father's employer. They may differ regarding the specific remedies they propose to end this state of affairs, but hardly any of them would defend it. I am convinced that this change of outlook is partly due to the strong lead given by the "Freewoman." But the greatest service that the paper did its country was through its unblushingness. It paralleled the achievement of Miss Christabel Pankhurst, who did an infinite service to the world by her articles on venereal disease. The content of them was not too intelligent. It blamed the impurity of men for the state of affairs to which the impurity of women and the social system are also contributory causes. But it mentioned venereal diseases loudly and clearly and repeatedly and in the worst possible taste: so that England fainted with shock, and on recovering listened quite calmly when the experts came forward and said that since the subject had at last been mentioned they might urge that the state could do this and that to prevent these diseases. Even so, the "Freewoman" mentioned sex loudly and clearly and repeatedly, and in the worst possible taste; and likewise the content was not momentous. Those who laugh at Freud and Jung should turn back to those articles and see how utterly futile and blundering discussions on these points used to be even when they were conducted by earnest and intelligent people. But the "Freewoman" by its candour did an immense service to the world by shattering, as nothing else would, as not the mere cries of intention towards independence had ever done, the romantic conception of women. It pointed out that lots of women who were unmated and childless resented their condition. It pointed out that there were lots of women who were mated and who had children who found elements of dissatisfaction in their position. It even mentioned the existence of abnormalities of instinct. In fact, it smashed the romantic pretence that women had as a birthright the gift of perfect adaptation: that they were in a bland state of desireless contentment which, when they were beautiful, reminded the onlooker of goddesses, and when they were plain were more apt to remind him of cabbage. If this romantic conception had been true, there would have been no reason for the emancipation of women, since as they could be happy anywhere and anyhow, there was never any need to alter their environment. It had to be admitted that women were vexed human beings who suffered intensely from male-adaptation to life, and that they were tortured and dangerous if they were not allowed to adapt themselves to life. That admission is the keystone of the modern Feminist movement.

Dora Marsden made her point with unique effectiveness, considering the length of the paper's life. Nevertheless the paper was coming to an end psychically when it came to an end physically. Its psychic death was due to the fact that Dora Marsden started on a train of thought which led her to metaphysics. She began to lose her enthusiasm for bringing women's industry on equal terms with men, because it struck her that industrialism destroyed more in life than it produced. She began to be sceptical of modern civilisation and this led her to preaching a kind of Tolstoyism which would have endeavoured to lead the world back to primitive agriculture. I waged war with her on this point in a correspondence that the curious might hunt down in the files. I signed myself therein Rachel East. I got no chance to convince her, for already she had retreated to further remoteness and was developing an egoistic philosophy on the lines foreshadowed by Max Stirner. About this time the brick fell. Our publisher fled suddenly to North Africa, with the lady of the shoes and a considerable sum of money which an unfortunate gentleman had entrusted him as an investment in the business. It then turned out that he was a criminal of singular type: really a naïve moral imbecile. After various financial fantasias and a number of carelessly conceived and executed bigamies he had settled down as a publisher not a mile from our police department offices at Scotland Yard, and had there flourished for two years: and no doubt would have done so for many more years had not the young lions been so expensive and the lady with the shoes so desirous of foreign travel.

He was brought back and sent to a place of seclusion for some years. Mr. Chesterton and Mr. Belloc and Dora Marsden and her flock were homeless for a time. Then odd people turned up and financed it, and it was reissued as "The Egoist," of which paper I was literary editor. That did not last long. My position seemed to be impossible. The routine of the office was not impeccable. There was an *arrivist* American poet who intended to oust me, and his works and those of his friends continually appeared in the paper without having passed me. This was unbearably irritating, particularlry at that age. And Dora Marsden, more and more remote in her ether of speculation, could not understand it when I objected to articles which did not come up to a certain standard of taste and literary skill. So I quit. I am quite sure that she never understood why. An argument that there is relation between the expression and what is expressed, and that if the one is coarse the other is unlikely to be authentic, seemed to her a far away babble, for it was becoming less and less imperative for her to express herself. Hers was now to be rather than to do.

The paper lived some time after I left. It did a magnificent thing for literature in publishing James Joyce's "Portrait of the Artist as a Young Man." Of its last days I cannot speak, for about that time ill-health fell on me and for long I was out of things. I have heard nothing of Dora Marsden for ten years or so. It may be that the wisdom she has obtained is not communicable, but I am sure to some far peak of wisdom she must have attained, and I cannot think that it is not good for the race when some of its component atoms reach projection, even if they cannot transmit it to their fellows. At any rate, Dora Marsden left us a heritage in the unembarrassed honesty of our times.

Time and Tide. 16 July 1926:648–649.

Spinster to the Rescue

Harriet Shaw Weaver is known to students of literature as the St. Bernard in human form who kept on and on rescuing James Joyce from the continuous Alpine storm of misfortune which raged around him.

So great were her services to him that it can fairly be said to be doubtful whether Stephen Dedalus and Leopold Bloom would have found their way into the world's mind had it not been for this delicate and restrained spinster, whose manners were exquisite, whose vocabulary was pure, and whose spirit was so austere that angry tears came to her eyes and her evening was spoiled because of a joking accusation that she was tipsy.

How this happened is told in great detail in *Dear Miss Weaver* (Faber, 90s.), a biography by her cousin Jane Lidderdale, and by Mary Nicholson. It is an odd story.

It began in 1911 with Miss Weaver's contact with a feminist journal called the *Freewoman,* which must be pronounced a remarkable periodical, even by this reviewer, who is striving to keep a proper detachment since she was, at the age of 19, the assistant editor.

It was edited by Dora Marsden, a graduate of Manchester University, who had been to prison as a suffragette and had hunger-struck and been forcibly fed. She was brilliant in mind and saintly in character and, as a photograph in this volume shows, exquisitely lovely.

The literary editor, recruited by the assistant editor on the recommendation of those untiring nurses of talent, Ford Madox Ford and Violet Hunt, was an American poet and scholar in his late twenties, named Ezra Pound.

He was remarkable in appearance; he dressed like a provincial American dandy in the previous century and something about the luminous quality of his skin and his red hair made him look as if he had been dipped in marmalade. He was also remarkable for his steely ambition, as "Dear Miss Weaver" shows—an ambition which he extended to benefit his friends.

There was in the offing—also found through Ford Madox Ford and Violet Hunt—a marvellously gifted boy of 19 called Richard Aldington.

The programme of the paper consisted of the revolt of women, philosophic anarchism and a general whip-round for ideas which would reform simultaneously life and art. More, no doubt, we would have taken on, had there been time. In at the door came Miss Harriet Weaver, the *Freewoman* being exactly what she thought she needed.

She was 35 years old, the daughter of a country doctor whose wife had inherited a fortune from her cotton-spinning father, upon which he had brought his family down from the North and settled in one of the most beautiful houses in Hampstead. He abandoned his profession and became a conspicuous figure in religious circles, and when his daughter grew to adult years and asked permission to study medicine he refused and set her down to teach Sunday School.

At 25 she would teach Sunday School no more, and went into the slums and was for many years a devoted social worker among children—but not from piety. She was a natural revolutionary and wanted nothing except to change the basis of society.

She was now orphaned and independent, and therefore proposed to set about doing just that—change the basis of society.

She was asexual: as the authors of "Dear Miss Weaver" rather oddly put it, she felt "a total lack of interest in the other sex, except as human beings." But her mother had sent her to her room when she found her reading "Adam Bede," and feeling unable to soil her lips with reference to the iniquities of George Eliot, sent for the vicar to do a rush job, as she might have sent for the plumber.

Miss Weaver was therefore exhilarated by the feminist gospel even when it referred to sexual liberation (which it very vaguely did). And she was deeply moved by a series of articles on economics by Mr. Arthur Kitson of the Banking and Currency League who denounced investments as a form of usury, and therefore confirmed her suspicion that she had no right to her income because it was unearned and usurious.

From the horse's mouth, it can be affirmed that this was the only proof the *Freewoman* ever had that any reader ever read any of Mr. Kitson's articles, or even any part of any of them. But the single proof was earthshaking. Miss Weaver became backer of the *Freewoman,* which presently became the famous *Egoist*.

She became the backer of the editor, and sheltered the composition of all, and the publication of some, of the treatises by which Miss Marsden, blending theology with philosophy and social science, sought to solve all problems.

She listened to Ezra Pound when he spoke of an unpublished genius named James Joyce, and saw to it that "A Portrait of the Artist as a Young Man" was serialised in the *Egoist*, and then became his agent, his publisher, his friend, his banking account, and the bearer of all his burdens which could possibly be shared. Getting on in years, she even took charge of his afflicted daughter.

She was more than a patron, she was a patron saint. Constantly, and in his last years finally, he turned against her. As the authors of "Dear Miss Weaver" put it:

> "She promised to tide him over until 'Work in Progress' was published, and he accepted this help from her, as he had accepted her help in the past, as the outward and visible sign of his inward and invisible 'grace.' "

Her sweetness was not shaken; but it is well to be understood that for her last dedication she chose not a person but a party. She was a faithful member of the Communist party for the last 25 years or so of her life.

It is correctly mentioned in the biography that I, the assistant editor, met Miss Weaver only once. It was a touching encounter, for it was at the family house in Hampstead, which Miss Weaver was leaving after 22 years in order that she could give away the shameful unearned income, and as she looked around her at the cedar trees in the garden, it could be seen that this was a real sacrifice. But the encounter was unhappy.

Miss Weaver was obviously not stupid, but there seemed a lack of complete comprehension, an intellectual deafness. Of her, the great giver, it could truly be said that it was a shame to take her money.

The proof lies in the incompatibility of the objects to which she offered up her devotion. She gave admiration alike to James Joyce and Dora Marsden; and though Miss Marsden's mind was once a miracle, the mainspring broke and the end was darkness. Long before that her treatises read as if they were dictated by spirits at seances. But Miss Weaver did not jib till the final decline, when the last treatise was announced as being the Book of Truth, an analysis of Heaven's Covenant with Creation, and of it the author wrote:

> "Now Deity has enabled you to help me with such spectacular help and in so many ways during an almost *full half century* that it seems probable that she will help you to complete the full 50 years . . ."

It is equally strange that Miss Weaver so easily, and for such naïve reasons as are given by her biographers, became a Communist, if the philosophic anarchism of the *Freewoman* had ever meant anything to her. Nor does it seem consistent that she should have shown no distress at the involvement with Mussolini of her friend and collaborator of long standing, Ezra Pound.

But obviously what mattered was her protection of Joyce, and it is ironical that, when her career is set before us by this biography, it should furnish such a glorious disproof of Mr. Arthur Kitson's argument which sent her into the offices of the *Freewoman* and started it all.

Of course there ought to be unearned incomes. They are in harmony with the random universe, and allow our eccentrics to go hither and thither, picking up this and that, and occasionally finding something that is, near enough, the philosopher's stone.

Sunday Telegraph. November 11, 1970:12.

The World's Worst Failure

The Frenchwoman who was dining at the central table struck a note of the highest possible pitch of physical refinement. She was reflected an infinite number of times in the mirrors that made tunnels of light into the hotel dining-room's walls, and all these little images, even to the glimmer of shoulders furthest away in the recesses of the twilight, caught up this note and sustained it so that it filled the air like a high nasal tone on a violin. It appears to be a point of honor with Frenchwomen who devote themselves to elegance to start with as few good looks as possible, and she was no exception. The touch of Jewish blood that had crinkled her light brown hair and given aquiline intensity to her discreetly tinted face had lent her all the distinction she possessed. Yet she was an achievement as delicate, as deliberately selective of the soft and gracious things, as difficult a piece of craftsmanship, as a Conder fan. Her body was not the loosely articulated thing of arrested and involuntary movements that serves as the fleshly vehicle of most of us, but was very straight and still, with the grace of flowers arranged by a florist, within a dress so beautiful that one imagined it hard and permanent like a jewel, yet so supple of texture that one could have crushed it into a handful. It was the aim of her fragility to rouse such thoughts of violence.

As she sat there she made a harmony out of prudent gestures of whose restraint she was without doubt inwardly conscious and proud; one could divine her thinking, "I hardly moved my hand an inch that time, yet I flatter myself the movement could not easily have been bettered." Her little shoes of soft leather, which had a bloom on them like a peach, stayed quite still under the table because they were already in the prettiest position imaginable. She did not move in her chair because the straight stem of her back grew from the foliage of her skirts with a grace that could not have been surpassed by any alteration. She had trained like an athlete for this elegance, and her feats deserved more than a moment's attention. It was strange that in spite of her tremendous and successful concentration upon her person she aroused no interest in her personality.

One found in her that association of vividness of presence and absence of individuality which one finds in non-Europeans. When one meets the lithest and most beautiful of Hindus one speculates not about his personality but about the system of which he is manifestly a part and a product. And even so one forgot the soul that doubtless inhabited the Frenchwoman, that doubtless knew ardours and loneliness, in her fitness and conspicuousness as part of the system of the *chic.*

For a week she remained as uncommunicative as a picture. One night she intimated by gently levelling her appearance at me that she wanted to speak with me, and said in a low yet nasal and tremulous voice that Maidenhead was not *gai.* She wrinkled her nose at the unlit asphalt roads which led to neither casino nor café in a way that suggested that in a happier world she might have been a very agreeable little street-boy. I pointed out that on the river one can always row. But she did not row well and feared people would laugh at her attempts. I assured her that there were so many boats on the Thames that people would not look at her. She fell into an impatient silence which intimated a state of things in which people did not look at her was too like death to be considered, and relapsed from humanity into her elegance again. One perceived in her discomfort that there must be many sorts of pain of which no cognisance is taken in this world: the anguish of the chair on which nobody sits, the wine that is not drunk, the woman bred to please when there is no one at hand to be pleased.

It was at noon one day, gripped by the horror of neurasthenia, that she sent for me.

Her room was dark save for the twilight of many mirrors and the austere glitter which made her dressing-table look like the bench of a laboratory. She had got into bed, and pressed her face into the pillow while I rubbed the cold hands of which the nails were no longer pink. Yes, she had seen a doctor and he had given her medicine, but she did not like taking medicine. I turned to the glittering dressing-table, but found nothing there but a silver and crystal arsenal of those weapons with which the elegant wage war upon the imperfections of the human appearance.—"They are very bright."—"This place is so *triste,* I spend hours polishing them."—I found the medicine at last, not yet released from its brown paper, amongst the seven bottls of hair-lotion. I gave her as stiff a dose as I dared, but for some time before she slept she receded into a drowsiness in which she was again possessed by horrible thoughts and looked out at me desperately. Once she put her hand to her chest as though she was going to tell me that she had weak lungs and said, *"Voyez-vous, je suis feminine, très feminine."*

And when I came out of the dining-room that night she was waiting for me in the hall, panoplied again in her elegance. In a white frock of great art her body was stiff like a gardenia; on her long hands there were rosy nails again, and her mouth was braced to smallness and a pout. She thanked me for my attentions of the morning, and drawing close to me, poured out little weak, desolated sentences that were more touching because she preserved her air of invincible self-possession and worldliness. "You are kind, please come into my room, I will tell you the story of my life." But instead she showed me her hats and dresses, and it seemed to do the poor soul as much good. And then she mounted on a chair, showing high white satin boots tied round the knee with silver ribbons, and brought down piles of photographs from the top of the wardrobe. She seemed to have spent much of the ten months which had elapsed since she fled before the Prussians from her country villa in posing to London photographers. Then she grew flushed and dimpled at hearing that I had been to Biarritz, and tossed out of her memory, like a girl rummaging for pretty dresses in a forgotten chest, the triumphant toilettes with which she had ravished and infuriated the *beau monde* of those parts.

One saw, as she rolled up and down the room in imitation of a stout Russian princess under the influence of passion, that a very jolly and human grotesque had been wasted when she became a part of what was, it appeared before I left the room, an even more ancient and relentless system than the *chic.* For as I said goodnight my eyes fell on a couple of large photographs on the mantlepiece which represented two very similar little bearded Frenchmen. And the Frenchwoman, following my eyes, clutched at my arm. "*Figurez-vous,* my husband is killed in the war, and by the same post I hear that my lover has lost all his money and can no longer marry me."

The more complicated a tragedy is the more comic it appears. I gaped for a moment and then remembered the appetite of the Latin races for sententiousness. "Madame, it is the fate of all sensitive souls to discover that life would be simple if it were not for sex." "*Mademoiselle, vous êtes une vraie philosophe. . . .*" Indeed, it was sad to think that there was now no one to look at those photographs, those white satin boots.

The next night I found her coiled in a red plush armchair in the hotel drawing-room, so preoccupied by her misery that her elegance sat absurdly on her like a smart hat worn on one side, attending only deafishly to a sallow girl from Chicago. And suddenly she began to talk about love. It was not that she was ill-bred and without reticence, but she was wandering in the windy corridors that lead to madness and the cloak of reserve had been blown from her. "When I love," she was telling us soon, "*c'est une catastrophe. . . .*" She gave us various illustrations of her conduct when the worse for passion, culminating in an anecdote about a trunk impetuously abandoned on the platform at Lyons. "I can think of nothing but the beloved. Yes, it is a complete interruption of my life." It was obvious that for long she had lived entirely that her life might be interrupted. "Women are like that," she said with a certain pride.

The American dissented. It was her opinion that a woman ought to preserve her general interests and take part in the world's work, though she admitted it was necessary that we should retain the fragility which makes us worshipful. "We must still strike," she said thoughtfully, "the feminine note." In the brooding look on her sharp face there was the calculating coquetry which explains the failure of women in industry and the professions. She and her kind took up work not because they loved the world but in order that they might offer an appearance of strength which some man would find virile satisfaction in breaking down to weakness, an appearance of independence which some man would be proud to see exchanged for dependence upon him. And their half-hearted work made women workers cheap and ill-esteemed.

Both these women were keeping themselves apart from the high purposes of life for an emotion that, schemed and planned for, was no better than the made excitement of drunkenness. One ought to pass into love reluctantly for life's sake, as one goes up into the mountains because he's very sick and to live longer on the plain means death. And once there, braced by the new air, he turns to work. If it should befall that he has to leave the country of love he goes forth brave with eternal health, a soundness that no later sickness can corrupt. It is impossible that he should appear as a frustrated schemer or a broken bankrupt.

It was midnight, and they had been talking about love for hours. Fatigue had given me a delirium, so that when I looked across the room our images in the great cheval mirror seemed fantastic pictures of our souls. The Frenchwoman, her pinched little face grievous above her cloth-of-silver gown, her pink painted nails unnatural on her limp hands, appeared as a starved child bedizened for some bad purpose; and perhaps that was all she pitifully was. The Chicago girl held her head like a queen but pursed her mouth peevishly and anxiously, like a characterless schoolmistress trying to enforce discipline; and indeed there was nothing more dignified in this woman who lived and worked that she might be worshipful, and yet, because she did nothing disinterestedly, made nothing within herself that a man could worship.

And I—I was a black-browed thing scowling down on the inkstain that I saw reflected across the bodice of my evening dress. I was immeasurably distressed by this by-product of the literary life. It was a new evening dress, it was becoming, it was expensive. Already I was upsetting the balance of my nerves by silent rage; I knew I would wake up in the night and magnify it with an excited mind till it stained the world; that in the end I would probably write some article I did not in the least want to write in order to pay for a new one. In fact I would commit the same sin that I loathed in these two women. I would waste on personal ends vitality that I should have conserved for my work. And I was sinning for the same reason, for what could make me drape myself in irrelevant and costly folds of petunia satin, and what could make me forfeit my mental serenity at their defacement, if it were not for some deep and overlaid but sturdy instinct for elegance? I perceived suddenly that in every woman there is just such an instinct which urges her, just so far as it is not resisted by her intelligence and education, towards an existence such as that of the Frenchwoman, who now, comically desolate as a mateless monkey, was murmuring, "*Une femme doit plaire—c'est son bonheur.*" That is why woman is the world's worst failure.

New Republic 5.62(January 8, 1916):242–244.

Reply to D. H. Lawrence's "Good Boy Husbands"

There have been times when I wonder why we fought to get women the vote, instead of fighting to take it away from men, and one of these times was when I read Mr. D. H. Lawrence's article on "Goodboy Husbands" in last week's *Sunday Dispatch*.

Rarely have I seen such a tangle as his arguments save when a kitten has got hold of a ball of wool; and wool does not snap so easily when tested as some of Mr. Lawrence's remarks.

For example, take his statement: "It may be that men nowadays are all grown-up babies. But if they are, it is because they were delivered over in their tenderest years, poor little devils, to absolute petticoat rule; mothers first, then schoolmistresses."

Now, who in the world does Mr. Lawrence want to take charge of babies "in their tenderest years"? Are fathers now going to give up working and stay at home and nurse their babies? Are young men, instead of going into business to study as Norland Nurses and nurse their babies?

I cannot believe that this change will be greeted by Mr. Lawrence's sex with any enthusiasm, for I have known but few fathers who longed to take sole charge of their young children, and hardly any men who enjoyed the close companionship of infants not their own.

And is it now to be the case that not only are men allowed the first pickings of jobs in industry and commerce and the professions, but that they are to drive women, married and unmarried, out of the work that has till now been acknowledged as their right; the work of child-rearing?

And what, pray, is the point of that word "nowadays"? Surely Mr. Lawrence does not think that in the days of Merrie England archers applied for leave on the field of Agincourt so that they could go home and mind their babies?

Does he believe that Nelson's sailors, disbanded at the end of the Napoleonic wars by sea, expressed pleasure because they would now be able to go to training college and learn how to teach little toddlers?

As a matter of fact, if he had looked back into the past far enough in the direction of the virility he so much admires, he would find some startling evidence that petticoat government in youth of the most absolute sort was the very finest training for it. For in some of the savage tribes in which men are as mighty warriors as the human race knows the boys are kept with the womenfolk and hardly see an adult male until they are adolescent.

The best thing Mr. Lawrence can do with this extraordinary remark is to tie it up in a brown paper parcel and drop it over London Bridge at midnight and deny all knowledge of it, if the Thames Conservancy people ask questions.

I have exhumed it and examined its decomposing remains only because it is a superb example of the way that there is an inherent tendency in men to talk abusive nonsense about women, which is purely a way of letting off emotional steam and need not be taken seriously intellectually.

I have no doubt that it was a wet day where Mr. Lawrence lives, and that he had meant to prune the roses, and that he felt disappointed, and there was a nice new writingpad in the house; and hence, quite illogically, he evolved this remarkable theory that men are being deprived of their virility through being caught young by spinster schoolmistresses and taught to be good little mommy's darlings.

I do not know what could be done about it if his theory was correct. For it is not feminine intrusiveness that causes so much of the world's schoolteaching to be done by women, but economic necessity. The State does not spend enough on education to be able to offer salaries that will tempt men away in large numbers from the jobs offered them in industry or commerce or the professions; however, those salaries do attract women, who have nothing like the same opportunities of employment elsewhere.

But in any case these spinster schoolmistresses cannot have the effect that Mr. Lawrence fears, for a reason which ought to be familiar to him, since he is a great novelist and knows human nature inside out, and must therefore understand the workings of the spinster mind. He ought to know that the very last thing a spinster schoolmistress is likely to do with a boy is to turn him into a mammy's darling.

How can a woman who has had experience of men invariably detect the woman who has had no experience of men? By her chidlike trust in the ideal of virility.

The woman who has had experience of men knows that though there are a certain number of men who are made in the mould that is traditionally called manly—that is, who are courageous, spirited, indifferent to hardship, experimental, and forthright, there are not nearly enough to go round; just as there are not nearly enough Madonnas who are perfectly beautiful in mind and body to go round among all the men who want wives.

She knows that there are quite a lot of men who, on the contrary, are timid, lacking in initiative, firmly attached to civilisation, conventional, and evasive.

She does not grieve over this state of affairs very much, because if she keeps her eyes open she will see that a man may conform closely to the ideal masculine type and yet, in modern conditions, be nothing but a curse to his family and the community; and that a man may depart from it as widely as may be, and yet be a very decent fellow.

For it sometimes turns out that a man who is a hero on the field of battle or a fearless explorer is a bully and a wastrel and a nit-wit; and a man who is content to live out his life as a bank clerk in Surbiton, and regards his hot water bottle as an essential of existence, may be a very fine fellow with a good mind, a loyal soul, and a loving heart. In fact, she has learned that it takes all sorts to make a world.

But the woman who has had no experience of men believes that all men, save the pitiful weaklings of the flock, are cast in the traditional manly mould.

She imagines the male just as the old ballads and legends and sagas see him, in the guise of the conquering hero who fights immense armies and swims torrents and defies the lightning.

There is no harm in her doing this. In fact, it is excellent that she should do so, since the human race must eventually perish off the earth if the majority of men do not possess these virile qualities.

But if the spinster happens to be a nurse or a schoolmistress this element makes her inclined to err in the opposite direction from the one alleged by Mr. Lawrence. It makes her apt positively to over-value manliness in her pupils.

Surely we have all heard nurses say, "Oh, I don't like Tommy very much. He's good, but he's just a little milk-sop. I like Jacky. He's naughty, but I like a boy to have a bit of spirit in him." In the same way schoolmistresses often show a distinct tendency to favour those of their pupils who belong to the bullet-headed, pugnacious type. "Jimmy is stupid, but he is such a little man!" they say tolerantly.

Indeed, I have sometimes wondered whether if there is a charge to be laid against the average schoolmistress it is that they expect too much from their boy pupils in the way not of softness but of toughness. They expect a boy to be heroic when he is hardly grown to a boy from a baby.

I am not at all sure that there is not such a thing as being taught a little too early not to cry when one is hurt; and perhaps the tendency of men to make much more fuss over their ailments than women is due to an unconscious determination to get their own back for not having been allowed to work out their feelings in the same way that little girls are allowed to do.

But this is a very indirect effect, and I am sure that on the whole the type of boy whom the schoolmistress encourages is much more likely to be mammy's little terror than mammy's little darling.

For proof of what I say I ask Mr. Lawrence to think in what part of society this change in men that he deplores is most noticeable. He seems to think it a lack of virility. I would not go so far; but I would admit that a certain amount of young men do go about nowadays behaving more like lilies than heroes.

But these do not belong to the classes which are taught by schoolmistresses. It is not the working man who got his education at an elementary school that seems languid and effete. It is, as a rule, the man, who got his education at a preparatory school and a public school from male teachers.

The mass of men are all right, just as the mass of women are all right. But, of course, it is not as easy for a man to be a man to-day as it is for a woman to be a woman. Most women of this age are doing exactly what women were doing in primitive times—being wives and mothers. There is, therefore, little division between woman and her primitive self, the bundle of instincts with which she is born.

But primitive man was a hunter and a fighter, and the life he lived when he hunted and fought bred in him all sorts of habits of mind and body that modern mechanised civilisation has no use for in his descendant. The hunter and fighter had to use his courage and his initiative; his descendant is often forbidden to use them. Even the War called more for obedience in its soldiers than for aggression and independence.

Consequently there is a great deal of conflict between modern man and his primitive self. Many men resolve this conflict by making the most of the life they have to live—pursuing beauty, or justice, or wisdom as fearlessly as if it were the wild boar in the jungle.

But sometimes even the most gifted men find it too much for them, and then they kick and scream; and very often their kicking and screaming takes the form of writing gratuitous attacks on women, nervously declaring that they aren't women, that women are awful, that they wouldn't be found dead being a woman, and so on, to the destruction of logic.

For what a mess that article by Mr. Lawrence was! He wanted to prove that spinster schoolmistresses tame the young male. So then he told us about his father, who was taught by a spinster schoolmistress and wasn't tamed. Then he told us about his own generation, which was taught by a schoolmaster and was tamed.

This seemed pretty queer evidence for his case. Then we came on this astounding statement: "They were the first generation to be really tamed. *With what result?* They went down the pit, but even the pit was no more the happy subterranean warren it used to be. Down pit everything was made to run on lines, too—new lines, up-to-date lines; and the men became ever, less men, more mere instruments.

Now you might have thought that machinery was put into the mines because of late years the coal-owners had to strain every nerve to compete with their rivals of America and on the Continent. But you were wrong. It was because the miners had been taught by spinster schoolmistresses. So now you know.

Truly, I sometimes wonder if men ought to have the vote.

Unpublished. Sent to *Sunday Dispatch*, 7 May 1929.

What Is Mr. T. S. Eliot's Authority as a Critic?

Selected Essays. By T. S. Eliot (Faber. 12s 6d.)
Mr. Eliot Among the Nightingales. By Louis Grudin. (Joiner and Steele. 6s.)
The Poetry of T. S. Eliot. By Hugh Ross Williamson (Hodder and Stoughton. 5s.)
The Letters of D. H. Lawrence. Edited by Aldous Huxley (Heinemann. 21s.)
Etruscan Places. By D. H. Lawrence. (Secker. 15s.)

Many who open the new volume of Mr. T. S. Eliot's "Selected Essays," put forth in such sober and seemly form by Messrs. Faber and Faber, and who recognise the sober and seemly quality of its balanced sentences, may be incredulous if told that, to my mind at least, the years this American author has spent in England have inflicted damage on our literature from which it will probably not recover for a generation.

His appointment to the Chair of Poetry at Harvard will probably inflict damage on American literature which will be only less because of the lesser time he intends to occupy it. Readers will be the more incredulous if they remember his poetry, which is indeed true and splendid poetry; and if they have read the section on Dante, which has been published separately and is of unsurpassed excellence in its field.

Yet the case against Mr. Eliot is strong. He came over here about the time of the war, when English criticism was at its low ebb, when—perhaps because politics exercised such a compelling force on many able minds—it was purely arbitrary and impressionist; and he came over with a defined position.

He had been born in the Middle West where all things are new. He had been to Harvard and fallen under the influence of Professor Irving Babbitt and Professor Paul Elmer More, who have developed a movement known as Humanism, which attempts to correct the intellectual faults likely to arise in a community where all things are new.

HUMANISM

This movement very properly attempts to create as lively a respect as possible for the tradition and achievements of the past, and it is unfortunate that the limitations of its founders, which are so considerable as to counterbalance their undoubted learning, have reduced it to propaganda for a provincial conception of metropolitan gentility.

Its character can be deduced from the fact that Professor Irving Babbitt considers it a sign of naughty modernity to admire the pictures of Cézanne; and that Professor Paul Elmer More once counted the reference to women's hair in the poetry of Mr. W. B. Yeats and came to the conclusion that they were so numerous as to be unwholesome. Reading their works, one feels those who like to call trousers unmentionables have turned their attention to higher things.

But from these teachers Mr. Eliot learned certain facts; that no artist can be isolated, and none can hope to comprehend the present save in the light of the past, and that violence, confusion, and the presentation of unanalysed emotion are poor artistic technique. He was, throughout a period lasting some years, a most useful influence in English criticism.

He put forward certain fundamental truths which had been overlooked, and by his appearance of deliberation and trenchancy he encouraged others to cultivate these virtues in reality.

In recent years, however, Mr. Eliot's influence on English letters has been pernicious, for several reasons, which are manifest in this volume. He has made his sense of the need for authority and tradition an excuse for refraining from any work likely to establish where authority truly lies, or to hand on tradition by continuing it in vital creation.

AUTHORITATIVE AIR

He registers himself as fastidious by crying out against violence, confusion, and the presentation of unanalysed emotion. But he appears unable to distinguish between these vices and vigour, the attempts to find new and valid classifications in place of old ones which have proved invalid, and the pressing of the analysis of emotion to a further stage; and there seems as often as not to be no discriminative process whatsoever working behind these repetitions of his formulæ.

The sober form of his sentences bears no relation to their content, which, as "Selected Essays" shows, often betrays lack of industry and flippancy, superficiality, and even vulgarity of thought.

It must be recorded that these defects are found in Mr. Eliot's work either together or not at all. When he has been industrious, as in his studies of Marlowe, Middleton, Heywood, Tourneur, Ford, and Massinger, he is serious, helpful, and sensitive. But there are a number of essays in this volume which, since they are framed with an authoritative air, appear to propound meagreness as a standard of excellence.

In his essay on "Wilkie Collins and Dickens" he records portentously the not surprising fact that, like the rest of God's creatures, he finds the thrillers of Wilkie Collins truly thrilling, though inferior as works of art to Dickens's novels; and in his three pages on Marie Lloyd he does nothing but explain sententiously and with a trimming of innaccurate sociological generalisation that she was a low comedian.

We may wish to test our feeling and guard against the possibility that we owe it in part to the disparity between the excessive promise held out by Mr. Eliot's authoritative manner and a performance which is perhaps not below the normal; and there are two essays in this volume which permit us to apply a test. We can compare his essay on Swinburne with the essay Mr. W. J. Turner contributed to a recently published volume on "The Great Victorians"; and we can compare his essay on Baudelaire with the essays on the same subject by Monsieur Paul Valéry and Mr. Aldous Huxley.

In each case it is as if we had taken a valuable watch into a watchmaker's shop and laid it on the counter, and a clever man with an impressive manner had picked it up and made some comment on its obvious qualities; and if, later, the watchmaker, making a close and careful examination, had reported in the light of his technical knowledge on its condition. Mr. Eliot is not the watchmaker.

CLASSICAL DONS

That the vacuum left by his lack of industry is filled in too often by flippancy is proved on many pages, as when in a patronising paper on "Arnold and

Pater" he remarks of "Marius the Epicurean" that "its content is a hodge podge of the learning of the classical don, the impressions of the sensitive holiday visitor to Italy, and a prolonged flirtation with the liturgy."

One may judge just how silly an attack on "Marius" this is by considering how silly an attack it is to make on any book.

What is the matter with the learning of the classical don? In an ignorant world it does not come amiss. What is the matter with sensitiveness, or holidays, or visitors, or Italy? One might, if one chose, describe Dante's Inferno as the impressions of a sensitive holiday visitor to Hell. And one might, if one chose, apply not less roguish terms than flirtation to Mr. Eliot's own essay in religious controversy, "Thoughts after Lambeth."

How flippancy is forced on Mr. Eliot by his lack of industry and his reliance on formulæ we may see in his dialogue on dramatic form, in which he takes as specimen modern dramatists, Mr. Arlen and Mr. Coward. It is not very clear why he selects Mr. Arlen for this purpose in face of his marked disinclination to write plays; and it is even less clear why he should say Mr. Coward's drama is one of "pure amusement" without an ethical motive.

There is possibly no other playwright, and few writers except Jeremiah and the author of Ecclesiastes, who are more inveterately didactic than Mr. Coward. His farces are tense with rage at the ill-mannered wastrels that enact them; he has never written a revue which is not interlarded with songs against the world, the flesh, and the devil as directly stated as any of Dr. Watts's hymns. One is forced to conclude that Mr. Eliot has written about Mr. Coward without knowing much, or indeed anything, about him, and that he has simply gambled on the Babbitt-More formula that the present day is inferior in seriousness to the past.

This procedure is not legitimate; and its distorting effects can be judged from another essay, where Mr. Eliot sneers at the late William Archer for believing in the idea of progress.

He plainly implies that this proves Mr. Archer a crude and tasteless person of the sort that thinks a power station superior to Chartres Cathedral. But William Archer's idea of progress was something so profound and so shaped by spiritual effort that one would hardly expect the author of these facile essays to sympathise with it.

He believed that while it was the duty of every man to subject his will to any discipline which seemed likely to serve the higher aims of humanity, he must prevent himself from dominating the wills of any other human beings, lest they should be deprived from seeking their salvation in their own way; and he supposed—and it is not at all an unreasonable supposition—that it was easier for a man to prevent himself from committing this sin now than it has been in the past.

If we allow Mr. Eliot to dismiss this attitude with a sneer we are sacrificing our knowledge of real moral achievement for formulæ which can give us nothing in return, because they were invented for a totally different society.

That can be judged from the passage where Mr. Eliot triumphantly writes:

> "Someone said: 'The dead writers are remote from us because we know so much more than they did.' Precisely, and they are that which we know."

The retort is very neat, but who made the imbecile remark that provoked it? What lettered person in England imagines that it is not profitable to read dead writers and is unaware that many of these are superior to the living? Our error lies rather in the other direction, towards ancestral worship.

But there are people in the Middle West (though mercifully not many, and in diminishing numbers) who do talk like this, who honestly believe that Mr. Galsworthy must write better than Chaucer because he was born to enjoy the benefits of electric lights and the automobile. To them, and not to us, Mr. Eliot should address his repetitions of formulæ, which have, indeed, no value whatsoever save for these localised heretics.

In "Mr. Eliot Among the Nightingales" Mr. Louis Grudin ably exposes the fundamental confusions of thought that prevent Mr. Eliot arriving at any valid critical conclusions; but this lively author presently passes into a discussion of aesthetics which, though it is fascinating to any adept in the subject, is discouraging to the lay mind.

The reader of this volume may take up with profit Mr. Hugh Ross Williamson's "The Poetry of T. S. Eliot," where an able writer examines Mr. Eliot the poet with a sense and sensibility which Mr. Eliot the critic could never rival.

It is a relief to turn to writers who care not a fig for claiming authority, but who humbly perform the kind of task of discovery and analysis that continues the tradition of English literature.

LAWRENCE'S LETTERS

Here are the "Letters of D. H. Lawrence," with a preface by Aldous Huxley which persuades one to give truce to one's feeling that it is time we all stopped reading about Lawrence and started reading Lawrence, so wise an exploration is it into the sources of a fountain of genius. Here are the letters themselves that are interesting not only in their glimpses of Lawrence as a creature that passed among ordinary human beings like an angel, sometimes with a sword, sometimes with a blessing. We see that the irascibility and suspicion which have been over-emphasised in some accounts of him were more than balanced by serenity and good sense.

But what makes the letters specially interesting is their revelation of how spontaneous in him was his sense of the beauty in nature.

It was pure, and utterly without that self-gratulatory tone which makes so many English poets seem to exclaim, "What a good boy am I!" as they put their thumbs in the pie of the countryside and pull out a hedge or a duckpond.

Lawrence did not cry out for law and order, and he could contemplate phases of disorder as a necessary part of growth. But he must have had a greater measure of order established within himself than most of us can claim when he could offer to nature a surface that could take such clear impressions as the exquisite landscapes in the letters, or in "ETRUSCAN PLACES," the record of his visit to the remains of the rich and vital civilisation that was wiped out by the Romans. It is a book which, if only for its description of the grey sea at Ladispoli, must be read by anybody who cares for living words.

Daily Telegraph. 30 September 1932:6.

High Fountain of Genius

For once the important historical event is not happening two blocks away in time and space from where one is. One has to admit that to an observer on another star a person reviewing Virginia Woolf's "Orlando" must be in much the same position as those who went to their editors' offices and condescendingly offered to write a piece on this or that volume, if the space could be spared, as they thought well of this Keats, that Shelley. There does not seem any reason at all to doubt that in this book has been issued a poetic masterpiece of the first rank; that is, a work which illuminates an important part of human experience by using words to do more than describe the logical behavior of matter, by letting language by its music and its power to evoke images convey meanings too subtle and too profound to be formulated in intellectual statements. It is written in prose; but that is a matter of the way marks fall on a page. Exploratory beauty, turning dark jungle into a safe habitation for the spirit, is here as it is in the work of the greatest of those who in the past used verse for their medium.

This is an important justification for our age, for it proves that there is nothing about the mental habit of the present generation which breaks the poetic tradition. For here is Virginia Woolf, most thoroughgoing of all skeptics, the archetype of self-consciousness, whose left lobe (which is critical) is obviously without cease letting her right lobe (which is creative) know what it doeth; and we find her committing herself to a theme which is as ambitious as any that author ever tackled in the great ages of faith when the truth was understood to lie no deeper under the surface of the earth than a man with Christian principles could dig and to have been buried that deep not from malignity of Providence but lest humanity should be deprived of its good medicinal work. Natural enough it would have been to choose it in those days, when it was believed that a stupid man could dig up so much truth, and a clever man could dig up so much more and a great man could bring up great sizable chunks of it at a time; and that people were getting cleverer and greater all the time, so that in due course we should all have the truth stored in the library just as the apples and potatoes are stored in the cellar. But to choose such a theme to-day is a heroism that one did not know could be performed.

For consider Mrs. Woolf as we know her, and reckon the forces that must have opposed that choice. She is fastidious, she is scholarly; she has infallible design, she is aware of all such designs as one might reasonably call perfect, she would not break her delightful occupation of contemplating such designs to create one of her own unless it forced her by its life to let it live. She knows, moreover, that such designs can be constructed out of trifles light as air, that Constant made "Adolphe" out of the couplings of two troublesome donkeys, that Chardin painted six pothecary bottles on a deal table, that Coupenni's enduring music is made of sounds as non-indicative of permanence as the tinkle of ice against glass that breaks. Indeed, she knows that to insist on such laxity of subject is an excellent prophylactic against failure, since it involves the artist in no intellectual discussion, seduces him into the service of no moral propaganda. Owing to certain trouble in the human family of late years she has no faith that the movements of its spirit lead up any staircase of progress. Man has more force than sense, and when he goes into the garden like as not he never goes near the truthbed but ceremonially uncovers some dead cat of dangerous myth that has been carried round the town a score of times already and on each procession killed scores with its unsanitary emanations. Nor is one sorry, seeing what a fool he is, and so insanitary in his ways that maybe the cat is his true emblem and associate. Let us turn our eyes away to that Chinese painting, that Queen Anne sofa table, let us listen to the music of Scarlatti or Arvic.

What would be a more ineluctable condemnation to the minor?—or, worse still, to such disorderly conflicts with their own creativeness as have temporarily overcome Mr. Aldous Huxley? Notoriously the most fair-minded and honorably disposed person to his fellow man, he nevertheless continually makes statements about his own invented characters which have the poisonous quality of an anonymous letter. His individual creativeness forces him to invent these people and a good three dimensional world for them to inhabit and all would be beautiful and enduring art if it were not that the disillusionment which has been implanted in him by the age makes him loathe himself for adding quantitatively to life, for increasing the horrid sum of experience. Like the poor crazed anonymous letter-writer, he will not walk in the sunshine with his fellows, but dashes indoors, sits down in a back room and writes accounts of them full of fulminations over the undoubted fact that at certain times they are not a General Grant in full uniform. If a talent as fine as Mr. Huxley's can be so handicapped by this age one might well have the greatest apprehensions as to the fate of literature until the philosophical barometer changes. But "Orlando" shows that the waters of genius, subjected to great pressure make a high fountain in the air.

"Orlando" is the story of a human being born in the days of Queen Elizabeth, who is alive to-day and is about thirty-six years of age; and feels no ill consequences from having round about the middle of the eighteenth century changed from a man to a woman. This is fantasy, but those who object to it can go and knock on Shelley's tombstone and ask him to give an account of the percentage and early years of the Witch of Atlas in the conscientious manner of Mr. Archibald Marshall. To make this character Mrs. Woolf has compressed the successive generations of a famous family who still hold one of the most beautiful historic homes in England; and by making it she has been able to write an account of human experience during that period which historians call modern history: the last few hundred years, which are near enough for us to recognize their parentage of us. It was in the days of Queen Elizabeth that the contemplation of life as a whole became a possibility for our civilization. The political situation had settled down sufficiently for it no longer to be necessary for superior men to dedicate themselves wholly to action on the field or to scholarship within the Church; so there was their engendered the ideal of an aristocrat who could master life by participation in all of its noble activities, who fought, governed and was a patron of the arts. The battle between Nominalism and Realism had resulted in a working basis for philosophy; there were now enough concepts established in the mind of Europe to afford a basis for speculative thought and social action. The Reformation had, in a certain sense, brought peace to Europe by opposing channels to two different types of mind so that their floods no longer boiled together in the same tideway. Sheep's wool and wheat turned into gold with an alchemic efficiency not know before, and more flowed without need for alchemy from over the sea. The sum of things said "Go!" to man and he started on a race that is described in "Orlando."

But this is no rhymed Buckle's "History of Civilization." A wine gives no factual information about the number of vines in the vineyard, where it was grown, or the ownership of the clos, or the process in the vats. Simply, it has a certain flavor, a certain fragrance, a certain body, which is the result of a certain inter-relation between grapes, rain, the sun and the human will. Even so Mrs. Woolf gives us certain poetic statements which convey to us the sum of the relationship between the *donnee* of each age and Orlando's fine perceptions. There is the quintessence of the Elizabethan age in the opening chapter that shows young Orlando in the attic of his gigantic house practicing the art of slicing at the mummified head of a Moor that his ancestor had brought home from the Crusades which still hung from the rafters; writing poetry in a copybook, and strolling out among the fields and oak-forests to a high place which is described by Mrs. Woolf with the frankest contempt for realism, with the profoundest reality. It is no photograph, it is as inexact a copy of appearances as tapestry, and one can see the stitches. Only it leaves in the mind a picture of Elizabethan England, which once apprehended will be incorporated in one like one's own experience. Standing on that high place he looks down on the dark congeries of his house, which has a room for every day in the year, and sees lights, hears trumpets, and runs down to meet the Queen, ricketty, brocaded, jeweled, smelling like a cupboard in which clothes are kept in camphor, royal, coming on an avaricious visit. As he runs, as he hurries to the banquet hall to kneel before her with a bowl of rosewater, as he afterwards enjoys her crabbed and languishing favors, as she looks on him through deluded and penetrating eyes, there is made visible the torture of Elizabethan life, the margin beside

Elizabethan drama, the parchment on which all the complicated deeds of Elizabethan politics were signed by intriguers. It was like that, for one who lived sensitively to be living then. There was then that ideal of making life magnificent by ceremonial, by hanging gorgeousness on the wall and supporting the splendid arras by certain contrivances of negotiation, that passed later into a robust yet more cynical programme for existence, that here is told in the passage concerning the Great Frost. The Thames was frozen at Greenwich from bank to bank; the ice was laid out with arbors and alleys and drinking booths at the royal expense, and in an inclosure railed off by a silken rope, walked the court. Through the crystal by London Bridge one could look down on a bumboat woman sitting with her lap full of apples in a sunken wherry, her soul in another world. The ice broke one night. On a yellow flood ice floes carried cursing and praying citizens to doom. Interwoven with this account, which has the chapbook vision of prodigious nature, is the story of Orlando's passion for a Muscovite princess who was infinitely delicate and infinitely involved with the gross, who seemed finer than the women of his own country, who was akin to creatures of grease and lust and cruelty such as were never seen against the primness of green fields. The content of innumerable seventeenth century novels and memoirs is precipitated in this intricate pattern suggesting a society at once as matter-of-fact as saddle-of-mutton, round-mouthed at marvel, and in touch with barbarities of foreign courts that were as outcrops of the primitive soil of being. We know it was then that Defoe was writing; as we know when Orlando becomes a woman, runs out to the moors and there in a transport at the winds, the heath, the scent of the bog myrtle, falls asleep with the wet feathers of a storm-tossed bird falling on her face, we know that this was the nature of human experience at the time when the Romantic movement was born, when Emily was conceiving "Wuthering Heights."

It is an epitome of all of us, it leaves us impaled, as we all are, on the mystery of the present moment. Mrs. Woolf enquires deeply into fundamentals and never more deeply than when she is most frivolous in form. People who like literalism will be most irritated, no doubt, by the passages in which Orlando changes her sex. But it is there that Mrs. Woolf shows exactly the magnificence of her power of transacting complex thought and perception on a plane of artistic creation. She is debating in these passages how far one's sex is like a pair of faulty glasses on one's nose; where one looks at the universe, how true it is that to be a woman is to have a blind spot on the North Northwest, to be a man is to see light as darkness East by South. She plays with the thought and its implications uncovering the existence of the absolute, the off-chance of there being an independent universe so that it is like a fall of fine lace at a lady's bosom, a tortoise shell tea-caddy inlaid with silver and ivory in which she dips her fine silver spoon that there may be something to pour into the Lowestoft teacup. One is present, as one rarely is in literature, at the spectacle of a human being who can keep its power of expression running alongside its power of perception. There could be no more beautiful expression of this mystery of the present moment, our destiny never to be able to understand what is going on in the one moment when our will is called into play as we understand what happened in the past which our will cannot touch, than the presentation at the end of Orlando and her lover in purely romantic terms. They have been seen till then with the eyes of the author, with her individual vision, as individual beings. But on the last page, when they arrive at the present they are suddenly presented not as individuals but as types. For romantic art presents men and women simply, superficially as we see them in one dazed moment of contact with reality before reflection sets in, flatteringly, as we see them under the influence of our hope that the contact will not lead to harm, that every thing will turn out well.

The book is full of minute beauties; it is full of explanations of phases of being that have not before been visited by the writer. It demands careful reading and the completest consent to receive novelty. In fact, it has got to be read as conscientiously and as often as one would play over a newly discovered Beethoven sonata before one is satisfied one had got everything out of it that the composer had put in; which is a demand that literature is usually too humble to make. But if one complies with it one will have no anxiety about the effect of our critical age on the genuinely creative spirit.

New York Herald Tribune Books. 21 October 1928:1, 6.

24
Antonia White (1899–1980)

Introduced and Edited by Jane Marcus

Antonia White's four autobiographical novels, *Frost in May* (1933), *The Lost Traveller* (1950), *The Sugar House* (1952), and *Beyond the Glass* (1954), constitute a whole discourse on the writing woman's life in the twentieth century. The revival of White's reputation with the reprinting of her work was one of the first projects undertaken by Carmen Callil at Virago Press in London. White wrote her life as she lived it in a series of fictions and an enormous series of diaries drawn upon by her two daughters for their heartbreakingly hostile memoirs (Chitty; Hopkinson). "The House of Clouds" is reprinted here from White's volume of short stories, *Strangers* (1954). *The Hound and the Falcon* (1965) is the story of her reconversion to Catholicism. From 1949 to 1967 she translated thirty-four novels from the French; her version of Maupassant's *Une Vie* won the Clairoun Prize, and she translated many of the works of Colette. Like Colette, she loved cats and wrote about them in *Minka and Curdy* and *Living with Minka and Curdy.* In 1983, after her death, her daughter Susan Chitty published *As Once in May,* which contains a four-part sequel to the *Frost in May* quartet, five sections of another novel, sixteen chapters of her autobiography up to age six, stories, essays, and poems.

The daughter of Christine White and Cecil Botting, the head of the Classics Department of St. Paul's School in London, Antonia White was named Eirene Botting. Her father, a convert to Catholicism, sent her at age nine to the Convent of the Sacred Heart at Roehampton, the setting for *Frost in May.* (A memoir, "A Child of the Five Wounds," is reprinted in *As Once in May,* and it is interesting to compare the two.) Expelled at fifteen, like Nanda in her book, for having written a novel, she discovered only at the end of her life that the nuns had not in fact expelled her. Her father, around whose approval her whole life seems constructed, had removed her on his own and sent her to a secular school. She was married three times; two of the marriages were annulled.

Where does White belong in the feminist revision of modernism? Mary Lynn Broe places her in the context of Hayford Hall, an alternative English salon, with her friends Djuna Barnes, Peggy Guggenheim, and Emily Coleman. We might also see her as different from her peers in that she was a working woman who had to support her children as an advertising copy writer and journalist, shuttling between versions of high and low modernism, the world of makeup, fashion, and the daily press and the world of serious writing—though here I would question what these divisions mean in terms of canon formation.

After the initial recuperation begun by Virago, White's extraordinary work threatens to be inundated by the swamp of her daughters' biographical script, which figures her, not as a writer, but as a bad mother—much as Rebecca West's reputation, revived by 1970s feminism, was reinscribed by biography into the bad mother posture created by her son and his defenders or the wronged mistress posture in which she is defined by her relation to H. G. Wells. White's career was a lifelong attempt to write her life as a woman, and her contribution to modernism is a major redefinition of female autobiographical forms. Her particular contribution is the suppression of the "I-narrative" common to women diarists and the appropriation of the authoritative third person for the female voice. Thus her work might be read in terms of the theoretical approaches to women's autobiography redefined be Bella Brodski, Celeste Schenck, and Shari Benstock.

One way to read *Frost in May* in the context of the revision of modernism is to set it next to Joyce's *Portrait of the Artist as a Young Man,* since it was consciously written as a gendered reply to that work. Reading intertextually (a good method for our project) we will need to take Joyce's novel off its canonical pedestal and read it not as a classic or "universal" text but as a Catholic boys' school novel, a male autobiographical fiction. Both works show the ways in which gendered subjectivity is formed by church law and conceptions of virtue and sin and how the artist transforms the rich heritage of symbolic language and cultural tradition for his or her art. In both novels the dogmatic issue is free will, and Stephen is encouraged by his priests and teachers to exert authority and to fashion his art out of the whole cultural apparatus of the Catholic church. Nanda, whose nuns are agents of the patriarchal arm of the church, must submit to the systematic breaking of her will and adapt to a sadomasochistic spirituality congruent with the church's notion of woman. She is taught to inflict pain on both body and soul, to suppress self and internalize an ethic of self-sacrifice, to regard her own creative spirit as the enemy within, sinful and socially unacceptable.

White's gender anxiety appears to be enacted in narrative structure. Unlike other women modernists, she does not open her text for co-making by the reader. *Frost in May* is cold and distant in narrative stance, and the third-person authoritative narrator effaces the teller in the telling. The events of Nanda's education, her invitation as a convert into the Edenic garden of the convent and her expulsion after she has been trained to submit her will to the rules of a strict authoritarian regime, are told without emotion, as if still participating in the idealized order of the Order. It is the reader in the world who judges Mr. Grey and the Mother Superior as evil. A Catholic reader could read the breaking of Nanda's spirit as a triumph of ideology. Elizabeth Bowen identifies in White's style a cool exactness and a lack of "kindness," and Samuel Hynes expands this definition by calling the writing "icily objective" and "heartless." She seems to know that one slip into narrative sympathy for this oppressed child will send her subject sailing into sentimentality, one plea for pity will exile the autobiographical fictions to the shelves of the unread. Even now, all of Antonia White is out of print in the United States.

Frost in May and its sequels, *The Sugar House* and *Beyond the Glass*, are constructed autobiographically as participants in and subverters of the two overlapping discourses of "confession," the Catholic church discourse, and the discourse of popular women's magazine and fictional "confessions," dismissed from the canon because they are "personal." The novels and *The Hound and the Falcon* also participate in the conventional discourse of spiritual autobiography as confession, from Augustine to Rousseau. White's narrative suppression of the "I," inside the very discourses in which subjectivity and I-narratives are the accepted form, is a splendid subversion of the trap that catches the woman writer in narcissism or complaint and then renders her discourse trivial. The third person narration of personal tragedy dignifies the story by usurping and speaking from the position of God, not the humble petitioner for mercy. White shows no narrative mercy. That is what this coldness and distance are all about. She enacts Stephen Dedalus's aesthetic, remaining indifferent and above her story. She also creates a feminist form for confession by eliminating its element of formal closure as a speech act, contrition.

Scholars of church history have shown that individual confession to a priest was a replacement of public confession and absolution of the congregation during the mass in order to control and define female sexuality. Foucault argues that the church consolidated its discursive power by making confession a sacrament in the Fourth Lateran Council of 1215, thereby shifting the search for "truth" in collective witness from inside the speaker to the listener (the priest who could control the narrative by means of questions). In this lies the enormous power over discourse enjoyed by the church as well as the influence of these structures on literary forms. Like the medieval Italian mystics studied by Phyllis Culham, White denies the power of the listening priest in the female confessional narrative and reinvests the speaker with the authority to explain herself, to control her own discourse, and to write herself back into the public sphere. The brilliance of White's strategy lies in its refusal to ask the reader for absolution.

Joyce appropriates the confessional mode through the creations of "homely little confiteors," using the forms of "Peaching, Confessing and Admitting" (Culleton). He wants a woman reader of his sexual fantasies and a male betrayer (Lowe-Evans)—a melodramatic structure closer to the confessions of popular literature and in contrast to the Big Public Confiteors of White.

The resistance to dialogue with the listener is, in this case of Catholic discourse, a conscious feminist literary strategy, not a retreat to traditional form, but the recovery of a lost public subject position for writers marginalized and privatized by Catholicism and patriarchy. The critical balance achieved by recent feminist Joycean readings of the personal and autobiographical is strengthened by analyzing Catholic female modernism in White as an elimination of the authority of the listener-reader position in autobiographical narrative as a form of confession. What seems like a traditional form, in the way that Kristeva would dismiss women writers and valorize Joyce for subverting the symbolic with the semiotic, is in fact a different kind of subversion because the assumptions about women's writing are different. One cannot call *Frost in May* a monologic novel in Bakhtin's terms, because it becomes increasingly clear that his terms are male and have to do with masculine fiction. The female monologic may in fact be liberating in a history of women's writing while dialogism is the practice of men.

But there is another subversive discourse in *Frost in May.* Though White, her critics, and her daughters maintain that she was crippled by an intellectually and psychologically incestuous relationship with her father (see Broe), Nanda's non-Catholic mother, like White's own, offered another set of values for the female artist. The subtext of lesbianism in the masquerade of "the Prince," in Nanda's love for Leonie, in the horrific tales of the French nuns outside of the classroom study of saints, with ghastly details of martyrdom and death, the exaltation of pain, discipline, and punishment are models for Nanda's own novel of conversion—a long tale of sin and depravity that lacks the requisite ending of confession and absolution. She is expelled because of this. *Frost in May* itself, like its heroine's first fiction, ends without confession and absolution, as Nanda enters the chapel without genuflecting, without crossing herself with holy water. Trained in the prayerful discourse of supplication, in the woman's position of speaking from abjection on her knees, she rises to assume the stance of speaking subject.

The storytelling nuns have a rich tradition of Catholic gothic—the story of the bride, lost in the cellars of her own house on her wedding day, found many years later to frighten another bride away from marriage, the story of the poor outsider let into Lippington Convent to join the elite for first communion, who suffered through the whole service with a safety pin in her ear, thinking it was part of the sacrament as the nun pinned on her veil. Despite the fact that their text of Dante is bowdlerized and what they read in the classroom is edited by the nuns as agents of patriarchy, Mother Poitier, who knits and tells stories and is compared to Scheherazade, offers a grand example of women's Catholic oral traditions which act as counterexamples to patriarchal teaching. Sister Francis is a modern Diana, an amazon whose body is trained in sports, and she subverts the order of suppression, repression, and shame, which is the convent's offical line. *Frost in May* creates its own tradition for a Catholic female narrative, pleasure and conversion (the story of the continental aristocratic girls) or transgression and expulsion from the fold (Nanda's story). As firmly as the daughter's tale is embedded in the Father's and the church's, a subtext of female solidarity and mythology ironically undercuts the master plot.

The novel opens with Nanda and her father traveling on a horse-bus, with an old Irishwoman named Bridget Mulligan blessing her and suggesting that she offer her life to God in thanks for her father's conversion. This is in fact the plot, Agamemnon sacrificing Iphigenia, refigured by Catholic folklore. The enclosed carriage is enveloped in fog, with Nanda's legs and arms tightly bound by gaiters and muff. The old woman coughs and is answered dismissively by Mr. Grey. But in the course of her questioning, Nanda begins to realize what is happening to her. Bridget Mulligan is the clown or holy fool, agent of this knowledge. She wears a velvet cap and a man's overcoat (this man's overcoat turns up again in "The House of Clouds") and recalls Joyce's Buck Mulligan and another scene of ritual as well as invoking the Irish Bridget, virgin as muse, giver of civilization, enchantress. She asks if Nanda knows when the Feast of the Purification is, unsettling her and making her realize at some level what is happening. Other abject figures appear in this novel as holy fools. Monica, the obsessive artist, cannot learn doctrine but draws dogs and is expelled for giving them the features of the nuns. Mrs. Grey, muted and eclipsed by her husband, an embarrassment to the Nanda who wants to fit into the Catholic world, never ceases to remind her that the nuns have stolen the power of words (the relation of sign to signified) to envelop the children in a counteruniverse (a private language that excludes outsiders and that the girls speak as a sign of their belonging) by calling rooms by the names of saints, not their functions, and taking a word such as *dispensation* and giving it a new meaning for initiates only. Her mother's commonsense critique of this powerful discourse gives Nanda the power to write outside the magic ritualistic "language" of the convent.

In "Asylums of Antaeus" I have argued that Antonia White's short stories "Surprise Visit" and "The House of Clouds" constitute a challenge to the argument made by Sandra Gilbert in "Soldier's Heart" and subsequently to the controlling metaphor in Gilbert and Susan Gubar's *No Man's Land*. White's stories offer a brilliant fictional examination of the ways women were not empowered by war, but driven mad by it. Julia Tye in "Suprise Visit" is a publisher's assistant in London who returns to Bedlam, the madhouse in which she was incarcerated during the war, to find that it is now the Imperial War

Museum. She remains in control until she sees the figure of a nurse among the statues of soldiers and tanks and guns. As a child Antonia had been taught to recite in Greek the first line of the *Iliad.* "Sing, oh Goddess, the wrath of Achilles. . . ." In the story she equates war with Helen's plight and women's madness, and the nurse recalls women's role in the social intimidation and control of other women as the policewomen of patriarchy.

"The House of Clouds" (1928, reprinted below) interrogates male valor in wartime by depicting Helen's madness as a mimicry of the deaths of soldiers. Like Emily Coleman's *Shutter of Snow* the narrative of the madwoman is lyrically surreal in its conjunction of motherhood with male violence or war. Helen has visions of terrifying matriarchal nurses who are also, like the matriarchs in *Mrs. Dalloway,* mothers who proudly give their sons to war and enforce patriarchal patriotism. Helen fears her father, the doctor and the state: "They were going to take her away to use her as an experiment. Something about the war." She wears a man's overcoat when whisked away to the asylum, and under drugs she speaks in male voice: "Morphia, mo-orphia, put an 'M' on my forehead." The M marks her for motherhood and nursing, the only roles allowed women in wartime. She is Orphia-Ophelia, the madwoman and poet, Helen in London, the fairy horse ridden to death. The forcible feeding scene conflates women's suffrage and madness, the punishment of women who struggle for freedom and those who want to commit suicide without producing cannon fodder for the next war. This written description matches the violence (it was clearly a form of rape) of the famous suffrage posters and forces the reader to relate women's war experiences to the prior history of their struggle for freedom, a struggle subsumed by mobilization for war. White's fiction reinforces the urge to study women writers in relation to their own history, a narrative in which what are called the prewar years are in fact the high point of fifty years of struggle for equality. The war crushed this powerful movement, and their writing often articulates ambivalence about the reproductive or nurturing roles demanded of women. It is ironic that Antonia White's daughters fix her reputation as a bad mother, reproducing the cultural prescriptions that were ideological torture for women modernists.

WORKS CITED

Benstock, Shari. *The Private Self: Theory and Practice of Women's Autobiography.* Chapel Hill: U of North Carolina P, 1988.

Bowen, Elizabeth. Introduction. In White, *Frost in May* (1982):7–12.

Broe, Mary Lynn. "My Art Belongs To Daddy: Incest as Exile: The Textual Economics of Hayford Hall." In *Women Writers in Exile,* ed. Mary Lynn Broe and Anglea Ingram, 42–85. Chapel Hill: U of North Carolina P, 1989.

Brodski, Bella, and Celeste Schenck. *Life/Lines: Theorizing Women's Autobiography.* Ithaca, N.Y.: Cornell UP, 1989.

Chitty, Susan. *Now to My Mother.* London: Weidenfeld and Nicolson, 1985.

Culham, Phyllis. "Pouvoir, Savior and Negotiated Discourse: Mediated Autobiography and Female Mystics of Medieval Italy." Paper delivered at International Feminist Theory Conference, Dubrovnic, 1988.

Culleton, Claire. "The Indispensable Informer: Peaching, Confessing, Admitting in *A Portrait of the Artist as a Young Man.*" Ph.D diss., U of Miami.

Foucault, Michel. *History of Sexuality.* Vol. 1. New York: Random House, 1980.

Gilbert, Sandra. "Soldier's Heart: Literary Men, Literary Women and the Great War." *Signs* 8:422–450.

———, and Susan Gubar. *No Man's Land.* Vols. 1 and 2. New Haven: Yale UP, 1988–1990.

Hopkinson, Lyndall P. *Nothing to Forgive.* London: Chatto and Windus, 1988.

Hynes, Samuel, "Antonia White." *Times Literary Supplement* 7 March 1969:733.

Joyce, James. *A Portrait of the Artist as a Young Man.* New York: Penguin, 1982.

Kavan, Anna. *Asylum Piece.* 1940. New York: Michael Kesend, 1981.

Lowe-Evans, Mary. "Confession in The Joyce Canon: Some Historical Parallels." *Journal of Modern Literature,* forthcoming.

Marcus, Jane. "The Asylums of Antaeus: Women, War and Madness." In *The Difference Within: Feminism and Critical Theory,* ed. Elizabeth Meese and Alice Parker, 49–83. Amsterdam and Philadelphia: John Benjamins, 1988.

White, Antonia. *Frost in May.* 1933. New York: Dial, 1982.

———. *The Lost Traveller.* 1950. New York: Dial, 1980.

———. *The Sugar House.* 1952. New York: Dial, 1981.

———. *Beyond the Glass.* 1954. New York: Dial, 1981.

———. *The Hound and the Falcon.* 1965. London: Virago, 1980.

———. *Strangers.* 1954. London: Virago, 1981. Includes "The House of Clouds" and "Surprise Visit."

———. *As Once in May.* Ed. Susan Chitty. London: Virago, 1983.

Woolf, Virginia. *Mrs. Dalloway.* New York: Harcourt Brace, 1925.

The House of Clouds

The night before, Helen had tried to drown herself. She did not know why, for she had been perfectly happy. The four of them, she and Robert and Dorothy and Louis, had been getting supper. Louis had been carrying on one of his interminable religious arguments, and she remembered trying to explain to him the difference between the Virgin Birth and the Immaculate Conception as she carried plates out of the kitchen. And then, suddenly, she had felt extraordinarily tired and had gone out into the little damp courtyard and out through the gate into the passage that led to the Thames. She wasn't very clear what happened next. She remembered that Robert had carried her back to Dorothy's room and had laid her on the bed and knelt beside her for a long time while neither of them spoke. And then they had gone back into the comfortable noise and warmth of Louis's studio next door, and the others had gone on getting supper exactly as if nothing had happened. Helen had sat by the fire, feeling a little sleepy and remote, but amazingly happy. She had not wanted any supper, only a little bread and salt. She was insistent about the salt, because salt keeps away evil spirits, and they had given it to her quietly without any fuss. They were gentle with her, almost reverent. She felt they understood that something wonderful was going to happen to her. She would let no one touch her, not Robert even. It was as if she were being charged with some force, fiery and beautiful, but so dangerous that a touch would explode it,

She did not remember how she got home. But today had been quite normal, till at dinner-time this strong impulse had come over her that she must go to Dorothy's, and here, after walking for miles in the fog, she was. She was lying in Dorothy's bed. There was a fire in the room, but it could not warm her. She kept getting up and wandering over to the door and looking out into the foggy courtyard. Over and over again, gently and patiently, as if she were a child, Dorothy had put her back to bed again. But she could not sleep. Sometimes she was in sharp pain; sometimes she was happy. She could hear herself singing over and over again, like an incantation:

O Deus, ego amo te
Nec amo te ut salves me
Nec quia non amantes te
Aeterno punis igne.

The priest who had married her appeared by her bed. She thought he was his own ghost come to give her the last sacraments and that he had died at that very moment in India. He twisted his rosary round her wrist. A doctor came too; the Irish doctor she hated. He tried to give her an injection, but she fought him wildly. She had promised someone (was it Robert?) that she would not let them give her drugs. Drugs would spoil the sharpness of this amazing experience that was just going to break into flower. But, in spite of her fighting, she felt the prick of the needle in her arm, and sobbing and struggling still, she felt the thick wave of the drug go over her. Was it morphia? Morphia, a word she loved to say, lengthening the first syllable that sounded like the note of a horn. "Morphia, moorphia, put an 'M' on my forehead," she moaned in a man's voice.

Morning came. She felt sick and mortally tired. The doctor was there still; her father, in a brown habit, like a monk, sat talking to him. Her father came over to the bed to kiss her, but a real physical dislike of him choked her, and she pushed him away. She knew, without hearing, what he and the doctor had been talking about. They were going to take her away to use her as an experiment. Something about the war. She was willing to go; but when they lifted her out of bed she cried desperately, over and over again, for Robert.

She was in a cab, with her head on a nurse's shoulder. Her father and two other men were there. It seemed odd to be driving through South Kensington streets in broad daylight, dressed only in one of Dorothy's nightgowns and an old army overcoat of Robert's. They came to a tall house. Someone, Louis, perhaps, carried her up flights and flights of steps. Now she was in a perfectly ordinary bedroom. An old nurse with a face she liked sat by the fire; a young one, very pink and white and self-conscious, stood near her. Helen wandered over to the window and looked out. There went a red bus, normal and reassuring. Suddenly the young nurse was at her elbow, leading her away from the window.

"I shouldn't look out of the window if I were you, dear," she said in a soft hateful voice. "It's so ugly." Helen let herself be led away. She was puzzled and frightened; she wanted to explain something; but she was tired and muddled; she could not speak. Presently she was in bed, alone but for the old nurse. The rosary was still on her wrist. She felt that her parents were downstairs, praying for her. Her throat was dry; a fearful weariness weighed her down. She was in her last agony. She must pray. As if the old nurse understood, she began the "Our Father" and "Hail Mary". Helen answered. Decade after decade they recited in a mechanical rhythm. There were cold beads on Helen's forehead, and all her limbs felt bruised. Her strength was going out of her in holy words. She was fighting the overpowering sleepiness that she knew was death. "Holy Mary, Mother of God," she forced out in beat after beat of sheer will-power. She lapsed at last. She was dead, but unable to leave the flesh. She waited, light, happy, disembodied.

Now she was a small child again and the nurse was the old Nanny at the house in Worcestershire. She lay very peacefully watching the nurse at her knitting under the green lamp. Pleasant thoughts went through her head of the red-walled kitchen garden, of the frost on the rosemary tufts, of the firelight dancing in the wintry panes before the curtains were drawn. Life would begin again here, a new life perfected day by day through a new childhood, safe and warm and orderly as this old house that smelt of pines and bees-wax. But the nightmares soon began. She was alone in a crypt watching by the coffin of a dead girl, an idiot who had died at school and who lay in a glass-topped coffin in her First Communion dress, with a gilt paper crown on her head. Helen woke up and screamed.

Another nurse was sitting by the green lamp.

"You must be quiet, dear," said the nurse.

There were whispers and footsteps outside.

"I hear she is wonderful," said a woman's voice.

"Yes," said another, "but all the conditions must be right, or it will be dangerous for her."

"How?"

"You must all dress as nurses," said the second voice, "then she thinks she is in a hospital. She lives through it again, or rather, they do."

"Who . . . the sons?"

"Yes, The House of Clouds is full of them."

One by one, women wearing nurses' veils and aprons tiptoed in and sat beside her bed. She knew quite well that they were not nurses; she even recognized faces she had seen in picture papers. These were rich women whose sons had been killed, years ago, in the war. And each time a woman came in, Helen went through a new agony. She became the dead boy. She spoke with his voice. She felt the pain of amputated limbs, of blinded eyes. She coughed up blood from lungs torn to rags by shrapnel. Over and over again, in trenches, in field hospitals, in German camps, she died a lingering death. Between the bouts of torture, the mothers, in their nurses' veils, would kiss her hands and sob out their gratitude.

"She must never speak of the House of Clouds," one said to another.

And the other answered:

"She will forget when she wakes up. She is going to marry a soldier."

Months, perhaps years, later, she woke up in a small, bare cell. The walls were whitewashed and dirty and she was lying on a mattress on the floor, without sheets, with only rough, red-striped blankets over her. She was wearing a linen gown, like an old-fashioned nightshirt, and she was bitterly cold. In front of her was the blank yellow face of a heavy door without a handle of of any kind. Going over to the door, she tried frantically to push it open. It was locked. She began to call out in panic and to beat on the door till her hands were red and swollen. She had forgotten her name. She did not know whether she were very young or very old; a man or a woman. Had she died that night in Dorothy's studio? She could remember Dorothy and Robert, yet she knew that her memory of them was not quite right. Was this place a prison? If only, only her name would come back to her.

Suddenly the door opened. A young nurse was there, a nurse with a new face. As suddenly as the door had opened, Helen's own identity flashed up again. She called wildly, "I know who I am. I'm Helen Ryder. You must ring up my father and tell him I'm here. I must have lost my memory. The number is Western 2159."

The nurse did not answer, but she began to laugh. Slowly, mockingly, inch by inch, though Helen tried with all her strength to keep it open, she closed the door.

The darkness and the nightmare came back. She lost herself again; this time completely. For years she was not even a human being; she was a horse. Ridden almost to death, beaten till she fell, she lay at last on the straw in her stable and waited for death. They buried her as she lay on her side, with outstretched head and legs. A child came and sowed turquoises round the outline of her body in the ground, and she rose up again as a horse of magic with a golden mane, and galloped across the sky. Again she woke on the mattress in her cell. She looked and saw that she had human hands and feet again, but she knew that she was still a horse. Nurses came and dragged her, one on each side, to an enormous room filled with baths. They dipped her into bath after bath of boiling water. Each bath was smaller than the last, with gold taps that came off in her hands when she tried to clutch them. There was something slightly wrong about everything in this strange bathroom. All the mugs were chipped. The chairs had only three legs. There were plates lying about with letters round the brim, but the letters never read the same twice running. The nurses looked like human beings, but Helen knew quite well that they were wax dolls stuffed with hay.

They could torture her for all that. After the hot baths, they ducked her, spluttering and choking, into an ice-cold one. A nurse took a bucket of cold water and splashed it over her, drenching her hair and half-blinding her. She screamed, and nurses, dozens of them, crowded round the bath to laugh at her. "Oh, Nelly, you naughty, naughty girl," they giggled. They took her out and dried her and rubbed something on her eyes and nostrils that stung like fire. She had human limbs, but she was not human; she was a horse or a stag being prepared for the hunt. On the wall was a looking-glass, dim with steam.

"Look, Nelly, look who's there," said the nurses.

She looked and saw a face in the glass, the face of a fairy horse or stag, sometimes with antlers, sometimes with a wild, golden mane, but always with the same dark, stony eyes and nostrils red as blood. She threw up her head and neighed and made a dash for the door. The nurses caught and dragged her along a passage. The passage was like a long room; it had a shiny wooden floor with double iron tracks in it like the tracks of a model railway. The nurses held her painfully by the armpits so that her feet only brushed the floor. The passage was like a musty old museum. There were wax flowers under cases and engravings of Queen Victoria and Balmoral. Suddenly the nurses opened a door in the wall, and there was her cell again. They threw her down on the mattress and went out, locking the door.

She went to sleep. She had a long nightmare about a girl who was lost in the dungeons under an old house on her wedding-day. Just as she was, in her white dress and wreath and veil, she fell into a trance and slept for thirty years. She woke up, thinking she had slept only a few hours, and found her way back to the house, and remembering her wedding, hurried to the chapel. There were lights and flowers and a young man standing at the altar. But as she walked up the aisle, people pushed her back, and she saw another bride going up before her. Up in her own room, she looked in the glass to see an old woman in a dirty satin dress with a dusty wreath on her head. And somehow, Helen herself was the girl who had slept thirty years, and they had shut her up here in the cell without a looking-glass so that she should not know how old she had grown.

And then again she was Robert, endlessly climbing up the steps of a dark tower by the sea, knowing that she herself was imprisoned at the top. She came out of this dream suddenly to find herself being tortured as a human being. She was lying on her back with two nurses holding her down. A young man with a signet ring on his finger was bending over her, holding a funnel with a long tube attached. He forced the tube down her nose and began to pour some liquid down her throat. There was a searing pain at the back of her nose: she choked and struggled, but they held her down ruthlessly. At last the man drew out the tube and dropped it coiling in a basin. The nurses releashed her, and all three went out and shut the door.

This horror came at intervals for days. She grew to dread the opening of the door, which was nearly always followed by the procession of nurses and the man with the basin and the funnel. Gradually she became a little more aware of her surroundings. She was no longer lying on the floor, but in a sort of wooden manger clamped to the ground in the middle of a cell. Now she had not even a blanket, only a kind of still canvas apron, like a piece of sail-cloth, stretched over her. And she was wearing, not a shirt, but a curious enveloping garment, very stiff and rough, that encased her legs and feet and came down over her hands. It had a leather collar, like an animal's, and a belt with a metal ring. Between the visitations of the funnel she dozed and dreamt. Or she would lie quietly, quite happy to watch, hour after hour, the play of pearly colours on the piece of sailcloth. Her name had irrevocably gone, but whole piece of her past life, people, episodes, poems, remained embedded in her mind. She could remember the whole of "The Mistress of Vision" and say it over to herself as she lay there. But if a word had gone, she could not suggest another to fill the gap, unless it was one of those odd, meaningless words that she found herself making up now and then.

One night there was a thunderstorm. She was frightened. The manger had become a little raft; when she put out her hand she could feel waves lapping right up to the brim. She had always been afraid of water in the dark. Now she began to pray. The door opened and a nurse, with a red face and pale hair and lashes, peered round the door, and called to her:

"Rosa Mystica."

Helen called back:

"Turris Davidica."

"Turris Eburnea," called the nurse.

"Domus Aurea," cried Helen.

And so, turn by turn, they recited the whole of the Litany of Our Lady.

One day she discovered that, by standing up in the manger, she could see through a high window, covered with close wire-netting, out into a garden. This discovery gave her great pleasure. In the garden women and nurses were walking; they did not look like real people, but oddly thin and bright, like figures cut out of coloured paper. And she could see birds flying across the sky, not real birds, but bird-shaped kites, lined with strips of white metal that flew on wires. Only the clouds had thickness and depth and looked as clouds had looked in the other world. The clouds spoke to her sometimes. They wrote messages in white smoke on the blue. They would take shape after shape to amuse her, shapes of swans, of feathers, of charming ladies with fluffy white muffs and toques, of soldiers in white busbies.

Once the door of her cell opened and there appeared, not a nurse, but a woman with short, frizzy hair, who wore a purple jumper, a tweed skirt, and a great many amber beads. Helen at once decided that this woman's name was Stella. She had a friendly, silly face, and an upper lip covered with dark down.

"I've brought you a pencil," she announced suddenly. "I think you're so sweet. I've seen you from the garden, often. Shall we be friends?"

But before Helen could answer, the woman threw up her head, giggled, shot Helen an odd, sly look, and disappeared. With a sudden, sharp, quite normal horror, Helen thought, "She's mad."

She thought of the faces she had seen in the garden, with that same sly, shallow look. There must be other people in the place, then. For the first time, she was grateful for the locked door. She had a horror of mad people, of madness. Her own private horror had always been that she would go mad.

She was feeling quiet and reasonable that day. Her name had not come back to her, but she could piece together some shreds of herself. She recognized her hands; they were thinner and the nails were broken, but they were the hands she had had in the life with Dorothy and Robert and the others. She recognized a birthmark on her arm. She felt light and tired, as if she had recovered from a long illness, but sufficiently interested to ask the nurse who came in:

"What is this place?"

The nurse, who was young and pretty, with coppery hair and green eyes, looked at Helen with pity and contempt. She was kindly, with the ineffable stupid kindliness of nurses.

"I'm not supposed to tell you anything, you know."

"I won't give you away," promised Helen. "What is it?"

"Well it's a hospital, if you must know."

"But what *kind* of a hospital?"

"Ah, that'd be telling."

"What *kind* of a hospital?" persisted Helen.

"A hospital for girls who ask too many questions and have to give their brains a rest. Now go to sleep."

She shook a playful finger and retreated.

It was difficult to know when the episode of the rubber room took place. Time and place were very uncertain, apt to remain stationary for months, and then to dissolve and fly in the most bewildering way. Sometimes it would take her a whole day to lift a spoon to her mouth; at other times she would live at such a pace that she could see the leaves of the ivy on the garden wall positively opening and growing before her eyes. The only thing she was sure of was that the rubber room came after she had been changed into a salmon and shut up in a little dry, waterless room behind a waterfall. She lay wriggling and gasping, scraping her scales on the stone floor, maddened by the water pouring just beyond the bars that she could not get through. Perhaps she died as a salmon as she has died as a horse, for the next thing she remembered was waking in a small, six-sided room whose walls were all thick bulging panels of grey rubber. The door was rubber-padded too, with a small red window, shaped like an eye, deeply embedded in it. She was lying on the floor, and through the red, a face, stained red too, was watching her and laughing.

She knew without being told, that the rubber room was a compartment in a sinking ship, near the boiler room, which would burst at any minute and scald her to death. Somehow she must get out. She flung herself wildly against the rubber walls as if she could beat her way out by sheer force. The air was getting hotter. The rubber walls were already warm to touch. She was choking, suffocating: in a second her lungs would burst. At last the door opened. They were coming to rescue her. But it was only the procession of nurses and the funnel once more.

The fantasies were not always horrible. Once she was in a cell that was dusty and friendly, like an attic. There were spider-webs and an old ship's lamp on the ceiling. In the lamp was a face like a fox's mask, grinning down at her. She was sitting on a heap of straw, a child of eleven or so, with hair the colour of straw, and an old blue pinafore. Her name was Veronica. With crossed legs and folded arms she sat there patiently making a spell to bring her brother Nicholas safe home. He was flying back to her in a white aeroplane with a green propeller. She could see his face quite clearly as he sat between the wings. He wore a fur cap like a cossack's and a square green ring on his little finger. Enemies had put Veronica in prison, but Nicholas would come to rescue her as he had always come before. She and Nicholas loved each other with a love far deeper and more subtle than any love between husband and wife. She knew at once if he were in pain or danger, even if he were a thousand miles away.

Nicholas came to her window and carried her away. They flew to Russia, and landed on a plain covered with snow. Then they drove for miles in a sledge until they came to a dark pine forest. They walked through the forest, hand in hand, Veronica held close in Nicholas's great fur cape. But at last she was tired, dazed by the silence and the endless trees, all exactly alike. She wanted to sit down in the snow, to sleep.

Nicholas shook her: "Never go to sleep in the snow, Ronnie, or you will die."

But she was too tired to listen, and she lay down in the snow that was soft and strangely warm, and fell into an exquisite dreamy torpor. And perhaps she did die in the snow as Nicholas had said, for the next thing she knew was that she was up in the clouds, following a beautiful Indian woman who sailed before her, and sifting snow down on the world through the holes in her pinafore.

Whenever things became too intolerable, the Indian woman would come with her three dark, beautiful sons, and comfort her. She would draw her sweet-smelling yellow veil over Helen and sing her songs that were like lullabies. Helen could never remember the songs, but she could often feel the Indian woman near, when she could not see her, and smell her sweet, musky scent.

She had a strange fantasy that she was Lord of the World. Whatever she ordered came about at once. The walls of the garden outside turned to blue ice that did not melt in the sun. All the doors of the house flew open and the passages were filled with children dressed in white and as lovely as dreams. She called up storms; she drove ships out of their courses; she held the whole world in a spell. Only herself she could not command. When the day came to an end she was tired out, but she could not sleep. She had forgotten the charm, or never known it, and there was no one powerful enough to say to her, "Sleep."

She raved, she prayed, but no sleep came. At last three women appeared.

"You cannot sleep unless you die," they said.

She assented gladly. They took her to a beach and fettered her down on some stones, just under the bows of a huge ship that was about to be launched. One of the three gave a signal. Nothing could stop it now. On it came, grinding the pebbles to dust, deafening her with noise. It passed, slowly, right over her body. She felt every bone crack; felt the intolerable weight on her shoulders, felt her skull split like a shell. But she could sleep now. She was free from the intolerable burden of having to will.

After this she was born and re-born with incredible swiftness as a woman, as an imp, as a dog, and finally as a flower. She was some nameless, tiny bell, growing in a stream, with a stalk as fine as hair and a human voice. The water flowing through her flower throat made her sing all day a little monotonous song, "Kulallah, Kulallah." This happy flower-life did not last long. Soon there came a day when the place was filled with nurses who called her "Helen." She did not recognize the name as her own, but she began to answer it mechanically as a dog answers a familiar sound.

She began to put on ordinary clothes, clumsily and with difficulty, as if she had only just learned how, and to be taken for walks in a dreary yard; an asphalt-paved square with one sooty plane-tree and a broken bench in the middle. Wearily she would trail round and round between two nurses who polished their nails incessantly as they walked and talked about the dances they had been to. She began to recognize some of her companions in the yard. There was the woman with the beads, the Vitriol woman, and the terrible Caliban girl. The Caliban girl was called Micky. She was tall and rather handsome, but Helen never thought of her except as an animal or a monster, and was horrified when Micky tried to utter human words. Her face was half-beautiful, half-unspeakable, with Medusa curls and great eyes that looked as if they were carved out of green stone. Two long, yellow teeth, like tiger's fangs, grew right down over her lip. She had a queer passion for Helen, who hated and feared her. Whenever she could, Micky would break away from her nurses and try to fondle Helen. She would stroke her hair, muttering, "Pretty, pretty," with her deformed mouth. Micky's breath on her cheek was hot and sour like an animal's, her black hair was rough as wire. The reality of Micky was worse than any nightmare; she was shameful, obscene.

The Vitriol woman was far more horrible to look at, but far less repulsive. Helen had heard the nurses whispering how the woman's husband had thrown acid at her. Her face was one raw, red, shining burn, without lid or brow, almost without lips. She always wore a neat black hat and a neat, common blue coat with a fur collar. Everyone she met she addressed with the same agonized question: "Have you seen Fred? Where's Fred? Take me to Fred!"

On one of the dirty walls someone had chalked up:

"Baby."

"Blood."

"Murder."

And no one had bothered to wipe it out.

The yard was a horror that seemed to have no place in the world, yet from beyond the walls would come pleasant ordinary noises of motors passing, and people walking and bells ringing. Above the walls, Helen could see a rather beautiful, slender dome, pearl-coloured against the sky, and tipped with a gilt spear. It reminded her of some building she knew very well but whose name, like her own, she had forgotten.

One day, she was left almost alone in the yard. Sitting on the broken bench by the plane-tree was a young girl, weeping. Helen went up to her. She had a gentle, bewildered face; with loose, soft plaits falling round it. Helen went and sat by her and drew the girl's head on to her own shoulder. It seemed years since she had touched another person with affection. The girl nestled against her. Her neck was greenish-white, like privet; when Helen touched it curiously, its warmth and softness were so lovely that tears came into her eyes. The girl was so gentle and defenceless, like some small, confiding animal, that Helen felt a sudden love for her run through all her veins. There was a faint country smell about her hair, like clover.

"I love you," murmured Helen, hardly knowing what she said.

But suddenly a flock of giggling nurses were upon them with a chatter of:

"Look at this, will you'?" and,

"Break away there."

She never saw the country girl again.

And so day after day went past, punctuated by dreary meals and drearier walks. She lived through each only because she knew that sooner or later Robert must come to fetch her away, and this hope carried her through each night. There were messages from him sometimes, half-glimpsed in the flight of birds, in the sound of a horn beyond the walls, in the fine lines ruled on a blade of grass. But he himself never came, and at last there came a day when she ceased to look for him. She gave up. She accepted everything. She was no longer Helen or Veronica, no longer even a fairy horse. She has become an Inmate.

Strangers. London: Virago, 1981. 45–66.

25
Anna Wickham (1884–1947)

Introduced and Edited by Celeste M. Schenck

Anna Wickham, like her exact contemporary Charlotte Mew, has lapsed into obscurity for reasons that have everything to do with the form of her verse and the manner of her dress—Harold Acton, for example, found her poetry as unfashionable as her person (Smith, in Wickham 2). Unlike Mina Loy, whose elegance after four babies was continually remarked, Wickham was large and haphazard in appearance. She once deliberately wore a wool jumper to an affair where Edith Sitwell was sure to show up in gold brocade. Wickham was prolific (nearly 1,400 poems in twenty years) where Mew was spare, yet both wrote overtly feminist poetry that has escaped notice for its failure to adhere to the experimentalist demands of a masculinist modernism. Thomas Hardy called Mew "far and away the best living woman poet—who will be read when others are forgotten" (Fitzgerald 174), and Anna Wickham had by 1932 an international reputation. Anthologies of the day printed more of her poems than those of de la Mare, Graves, and, in some volumes, even Yeats (Smith, in Wickham 23).

Neither Wickham nor Mew came from literary families or had anything like a formal education, and neither studied poetry formally, although Wickham's father apparently made her promise to become a poet. Mew destroyed everything that might constitute a record of her life except for the few pieces that make up her *Collected Poems* and some stories, and most of

Wickham's papers and letters were lost in the 1943 bombing of her Hampstead home. Both Wickham and Mew questioned the Catholic church, but whereas Wickham's revisionary supplication of the feminized deity poignantly redresses banishment—"In nameless, shapeless God found I my rest, / Though for my solace I built God a breast"—Mew's resignation, in "Madeleine in Church," is complete—"I do not envy Him His victories, His arms are full of broken things" (Mew 26). Finally, both Wickham and Mew committed suicide. The indignity of Mew's death by the ingestion of disinfectant was matched only by the carelessness of her obituary: "Charlotte New [sic], said to be a writer" (Monro, in Mew xii). Wickham's fate is as banal: The *London Picture Post* did a feature on her in 1946 called "The Poet Landlady" (Smith, in Wickham 28).

A closer look at the life's work of the colorful Wickham, a free-spirited, half working-class Australian emigrée who began her career as an opera singer, then divided her life between London and Paris, might cause us to agree with Stanley Kunitz that the neglect of Anna Wickham is "one of the great mysteries of contemporary literature."[1] A pacifist who nonetheless supported the Great War effort, a deprived and unhappy wife who remained faithful to her husband during the entire course of their tumultuous relationship until his death, an acquaintance of Ezra Pound, Djuna Barnes, Natalie Barney, D. H. Lawrence, and Dylan Thomas who was as comfortable in a London pub as she was on the fashionable Left Bank, a staunch feminist and supporter of women's rights who harbored a masochistic sexuality founded in mother-lack and Catholic education, Wickham was an exciting mass of contradictions of which her poetry is the record. Her Australian childhood offered freedoms unavailable to Englishwomen, and it seems to have stamped Wickham as well with a robust sense of sexual entitlement, a view of social inequality, and an authentic personal voice, all of which set her apart from other women poets of that period. For all the exhilaration of her Australian exile, however, the return to England and her sensitivity to inequalities of class heightened her sense of herself as an outsider. The social rivalry between her mother's and father's families finds its way into poems such as "Descent of Dorelia" and "The Little Old House." And her own marriage into a family of aristocratic origins initiated her into the oppression of Victorian femininity.

Like Charlotte Mew's, Wickham's formal conventionality is often the very vehicle of her politics: her forced rhymes are meant to be funny and irreverent and to set off the political conflicts of which her poetry is made; they should not be read as merely unsophisticated concessions to the popular conventions of the day. "Meditation at Kew," outlining a poignant but humorous utopian program for marital reform, is the poetic version of her 1938 feminist manifesto, *The League for the Protection of the Imagination of Women. Slogan: World's Management by Entertainment.*

> Alas! for all the pretty women who marry dull men,
> Go into the suburbs and never come out again,

Who lose their pretty faces and dim their pretty eyes,
Because no one has skill or courage to organize.

What do pretty women suffer when they marry?
They bear a boy who is like Uncle Harry,
A girl who is like Aunt Eliza, and not new,
Those old dull races much breed true.

I would enclose a common in the sun,
And let the young wives out to laugh and run;
I would steal their dull clothes and go away,
And leave the pretty naked things to play. (Wickham 45)

In "Nervous Prostration," a poem analyzing the politics of marriage into the upper class, the rhyme scheme and alternating meter sets off rather than contains the rage driving the poem.

I married a man of the Croydon class
When I was twenty-two.
And I vex him, and he bores me
Till we don't know what to do!
And as I sit in his ordered house,
I feel I must sob or shriek,
To force a man of the Croydon class
To live, or to love, or to speak! (210)

There is defiance in the emphasis of the rhyme scheme, and in its metrical regularity not a little irony. In fact the poem is closer to folk balladry than to the genteel metrics of the Croydon class; we might even term it deliberately low-bred, even doggerel, a formal as well as political spoof on bourgeois values. This poem and "Dedication of the Cook," "The Angry Woman," "Definition," "The Wife," "All Men to Women," "Divorce," and "The Song of the Low-Caste Wife" criticize prevailing domestic politics, especially in their analysis of sexual difference within the culture that Wickham, marginalized by caste and country as well as gender, could see clearly as triple outsider.

When Wickham writes at the head of her extraordinary autobiography, "I am a woman artist and the story of my failure should be known" (52), she compels the kind of rereading the inclusion within this anthology guarantees, one which accounts not only for her disappearance from modernism's archives but also for the politics of feminist collusion in that exile.[2] Wickham's poems of class consciousness are a salutary addition to a modernist canon insufficiently concerned with the differentials of class and ethnicity. Her poems range from feminist pieces on marital relations and on the conflict between mothering and writing to analyses of the domination of one class by another, as in "Laura Gray," "Comments of Kate the Cook," "The Butler and the Gentleman," "Daughter of the Horse-Leech," and "Woman to a Philosopher." "Song of the Low-Caste Wife," unlike "Meditation at Kew," is rhythmically uneven and unrhymed, but it is no less than revolutionary in its dramatization of the rift between herself and the women of her husband's family and class, its claim for "new myths" conceived by the "new men" mothered by underclass women, its valorization of lust and energy, change and growth, over "old glories" and "dead beauty" (165). "The Angry Wife" is similarly unremarkable in its formal aspects, but trenchant in its analysis of motherhood as both experience and institution. The poem first describes marriage in political terms—"If sex is a criterion for power, and never strength / What do we gain by union?" (202)—and then protests the institutional version of parenting which issues from that sexual politics, necessitating the male child's revolt against the mother.

Finally, in a love poem called "The Mill," the concord of heart at one with specific, palpably felt environment is expressed by means of a regularized rhyme scheme, the purposive flowing of alternating rhyme into matched concluding couplets.

> I hid beneath the covers of the bed,
> And dreamed my eyes were lovers,
> On a hill that was my head.
> They looked down over the loveliest country I have seen,
> Great fields of red-brown earth hedged round with green.
> In these enclosures I could see
> The high perfection of fertility,
> I knew there were sweet waters near to feed the land,
> I heard the churning of a mill on my right hand,
> I woke to breathlessness with a quick start,
> And found my mill the beating of your heart. (48)

I do not mean to suggest that the enormously uneven Wickham corpus remains undiscovered as a pre-text of literary Modernism. Mew must be admitted to the canon as an undiscovered treasure, while Wickham remains important for reasons other than either experimentalism or formalism in verse. Still, the personal and material specificity of "The Mill" should have its history among our modernisms, reflecting—alongside Eliot's phlegmatic portrayals of deceptive lovers, Joyce's spoofs on the magazine romanticism of the day, Loy's send-ups of the masculine sexual principle, and Barnes's decadent New Women poems—its own particular vision, neither ironized nor sentimental, of the way we loved then.

NOTES

1. There is at present disappointingly little critical bibliography on Wickham. The notable exception is the excellent centenary volume published by Virago and edited and introduced by R. D. Smith, *The Writings of Anna Wickham: Free Woman and Poet*. The collection includes poetry, prose, her "Fragment of an Autobiography," and Smith's comprehensive memoir and introduction.

2. I do not mean to imply, by asking that we review the work of less experimental poets of the period, that radical critiques of power and status remained the exclusive province of nonexperimenters, but rather to include, within feminist rewriting of periodization, poets who were not compelled, stylistically speaking, to "make it new." My concern for the way in which an alternative canon—Barnes, Loy, H. D., Stein, Moore—might be positioned and coopted does not displace my recognition of the difficulty feminist critics faced in getting these poets into the canon in the first place. Restriction of feminist critical interest to the sentence-breaking, experimentalist women authors of this period may inadvertently work to reify Modernism as a term.

WORKS CITED

Fitzgerald, Penelope. *Charlotte Mew and Her Friends.* London: Collins, 1984.

Mew, Charlotte. *Charlotte Mew: Collected Poems and Prose.* Ed. and intro. Val Warner. Manchester: Carcanet (Virago), 1981.

Wickham, Anna. *The Writings of Anna Wickham.* Ed. and intro. R. D. Smith. London: Virago, 1984.

Song of the Low-Caste Wife

What have you given me for my strong sons?
O scion of kings!
In new veins the blood of old kings runs cold.
Your people thinking of old victories, lose the
 lust of conquest,
Your men guard what they have,
Your women nurse their silver pots,
Dead beauty mocks hot blood!
What shall these women conceive of their chill
 loves
But still more pots?

But I have conceived of you new men;
Boys brave from the breast,
Running and striving like no children of your
 house
And with their brave new brains
Making new myths.

My people were without while yours were kings,
They sang the song of exile in low places
And in the stress of growth knew pain.

The unprepared world pressed hard upon them,
Women bent beneath burdens, while cold struck
babes,
But they arose strong from the fight,
Hungry from their oppression.

And I am full of lust,
Which is not stayed with your old glories.
Give me for all old things that greatest glory,
A little growth.

Am I your mate because I share your bed?
Go then, find each day a new mate outside your
house.
I am your mate if I can share your vision.
Have you no vision king-descended?
Come share mine!
Will you give me this, for your sons?
O scion of kings!

The Writings of Anna Wickham. Ed. R. D. Smith. London: Virago, 1984. 165–166.

Divorce

A voice from the dark is calling me.
In the close house I nurse a fire.
Out in the dark cold winds rush free
To the rock heights of my desire.
I smother in the house in the valley below,
Let me out to the night, let me go, let me go.

Spirits that ride the sweeping blast,
Frozen in rigid tenderness,
Wait! for I leave the fire at last
My little-love's warm loneliness.
I smother in the house in the valley below,
Let me out to the night, let me go, let me go.

High on the hills are beating drums.
Clear from a line of marching men
To the rock's edge the hero comes

He calls me and he calls again.
On the hill there is fighting, victory or quick
 death,
In the house is the fire, which I fan with sick
 breath.
I smother in the house in the valley below,
Let me out to the dark, let me go, let me go.

Writings. 166–167.

The Angry Woman

I am a woman, with a woman's parts,
And of love I bear children.
In the days of bearing is my body weak,
But why because I do you service, should you call
 me slave?

I am a woman in my speech and gait,
I have no beard, (I'll take no blame for that!)
In many things are you and I apart,
But there are regions where we coincide,
Where law for one is law for both.

There is the sexless part of me that is my mind.

You calculate the distance of a star,
I, thanks to this free age can count as well,
And by the very processes you use.
When we think differently of two times two,
I'll own a universal mastery in you!—

Now of marriage,—
In marriage there are many mansions,
(This has been said of Heaven).
Shall you rule all the houses of your choice
Because of manhood or because of strength?
If I must own your manhood synonym for every
 strength,
Then must I lie.
If sex is a criterion for power, and never strength,

What do we gain by union?
I lose all, while nothing worthy is so gained by
you,
O most blessed bond!

Because of marriage, I have motherhood.
That is much, and yet not all!

By the same miracle that makes me mother
Are you a father.

It is a double honour!
Are you content to be from henceforth only
father,
And in no other way a man?
A fantastic creature like a thing of dreams
That has so great an eye it has no head.
I am not mother to abstract Childhood, but to my
son,
And how can I serve my son, but to be much
myself.

My motherhood must boast some qualities,
For as motherhood is diverse
So shall men be many charactered
And show variety, as this world needs.

Shall I for ever brush my infant's hair?
Cumber his body in conceited needle-work?
Or shall I save some pains till he is grown?
Show him the consolation of mathematics
And let him laugh with me when I am old?

If he is my true son,
He will find more joy in number and in laughter
Than in all these other things.

Why should dull custom make my son my enemy
So that the privilege of his manhood is to leave
my house?
You would hold knowledge from me because I
am a mother,
Rather for this reason let me be wise, and very
strong,—
Power should be added to power.—

And now of love!—
There are many loves.
There is love, which is physiology,
And love, which has no more matter in it than is
in the mind.
There is spiritual love, and there is good
affection.
All these loves women need and most of all the
last.

Kiss me sometimes in the light,
Women have body's pain of body's love.
Let me have flowers sometimes, and always joy.
And sometimes let me take your hand and kiss
you honestly
Losing nothing in dignity by frank love.
If I must fly in love and follow in life,
Doing both things falsely,
Then am I a *mime,*
I have no free soul.

Man! For your sake and for mine, and for the
sake of future men,
Let me speak my mind in life and love.
Be strong for love of a strong mate,
Do not ask my weakness as a sacrifice to power.
When you deny me justice
I feel as if my body were in grip of a cold
octopus,
While my heart is crushed to stone.

This rapture have I of pretence!

Writings. 202–204.

26

Virginia Woolf (1882–1941)

The Modern Tradition. *Introduced and Edited by Suzette Henke*

In an anthology entitled *The Gender of Modernism,* Virginia Woolf needs little introduction. Her name, associated with the London Bloomsbury group—with the aesthetics of Roger Fry and Clive Bell and with the poetics of E. M. Forster and T. S. Eliot—has become a watchword for the kind of modernist innovation illustrated in her major novels, *Jacob's Room, Mrs. Dalloway, To the Lighthouse, The Waves, The Years,* and *Between the Acts.* Her theoretical works of feminist interrogation, *A Room of One's Own* and *Three Guineas,* attest to a pervasive and passionate sensitivity, throughout her writing, to the problematics of gender and sexual difference.

"In or about December, 1910," Woolf declared in "Mr. Bennett and Mrs. Brown," "human character changed." This deliberately enigmatic assertion prophesies at the end of the Edwardian era a tumultuous revolution in literary aesthetics and the visual arts. Confronted with the post-Impressionist exhibition mounted by Roger Fry in London during those last months of 1910, artists and their audiences, Woolf implies, would never again be able to see themselves with the kind of naiveté that had once governed traditional mimetic representation.[1]

In the essays entitled "Modern Fiction" and "Mr. Bennett and Mrs.

Brown," included in this anthology, Woolf raises a clarion call to a new aesthetics of psychological realism. One cannot assume a natural evolutionary tendency in the growth of *Homo fictus* similar to the progressive development of *Homo sapiens.* Writers "keep moving," she observes, but often "with a circular tendency." H. G. Wells, Arnold Bennett, and John Galsworthy, under the attack of Woolf's seering irony and acerbic wit, sustain a critical drubbing as "materialists" who imperil the very soul of English literature: "It is because they are concerned not with the spirit but with the body that they have disappointed us" ("Modern Fiction"). Woolf's rhetoric in "Modern Fiction" is playful and vaguely coy. She treats these ponderous male authors, literary giants of the Edwardian drawing room, like lascivious-minded schoolboys—suitors whose obscene but prurient preoccupations make them unworthy of noble courtship. English fiction, personified as female and virginal, is bidden politely to scorn them: to draw up her skirts and flee to the desert, haughtily spurning such audacious and inappropriate contenders for her hand.

Wells is occasionally inspired, Woolf admits, but his genius is marred by a "great clod of clay" at the heart of his fictional representations—that materialism that makes him bury in a welter of ideas and scientific facts characters exuding "crudity and coarseness." In his utopian fantasies, "every citizen is generous and candid, manly and magnificent, and rather like Mr. Wells himself" ("Mr Bennett"). Galsworthy, in turn, proves to be far too preoccupied with polemical praxis—a social reformer "burning with indignation, stuffed with information, arraigning civilization" from an imaginary podium ("Mr Bennett"). Bennett, traducing his own literary potential (or potency), is "perhaps the worst culprit of the three": gifted, he has prostituted his talents to a craftsmanship that excludes life. His characters are automatons (or perhaps Frankensteins) whose electrical energies pulse with movement, but whose hearts and spirits have been doomed to mechanical asphyxiation. They are condemned, it seems, to "an eternity of bliss spent in the very best hotel in Brighton" ("Modern Fiction"). All three of these Edwardian writers "have looked very powerfully, searchingly, and sympathetically out of the window; at factories, at Utopias; . . . but never . . . at life, never at human nature" ("Mr Bennett").

In hurling at this triumvirate of unimaginative Edwardians the age-old epithet of "materialist," Woolf brings to bear on their masculine, patriarchal sensibilities the full weight of Judeo-Christian opprobrium. These sainted, idolized, and puffed-up members of the British literary establishment ought, she believes, to be exposed for wasting "immense skill and immense industry making the trivial and the transitory appear the true and the enduring" ("Modern Fiction"). In a flick of the eye, Woolf appeals to sacred Platonic categories that hark back to the millennial debate between Parmenides and Heraclitus, Plato and Aristotle. No Aristotelian she, Woolf demands that we accede to an ineffable Ideal, the "true and enduring." The questions that she raises are serious indeed and all the more crucial for their tacit conflation of moral, aesthetic, and ethical values. G. E. Moore and his search for the Ideal in *Principia Ethica* haunts the background of "Modern Fiction," imbued as it is with philosophical assumptions cultivated in the heart of Bloomsbury debate.

If a reader, putting down a novel, should be moved to ask "Is it worth while? What is the point of it all?" ("Modern Fiction"), then might this same reader not apply a similiar set of questions to his or her own life? Woolf perpetually teases her audience, both in fiction and in critical prose, by making use of obscure pronominal referents. The "it" in these queries might just as suitably refer to an existential life quest as to the Edwardian literary endeavor. Woolf's rhetorical thrust is moral and ponderous: if literature cannot represent the psychological verities of human experience, then perhaps life itself is not "worth while"? What, in other words, is the "point of it all"?[2] In Edwardian literary representation, life ineluctably "escapes; and perhaps without life nothing else is worth while." Woolf demands that modern literature provide nothing less than a transcendental signifier, "the thing we seek"—that vague, inarticulate fin in the waste of waters, that semimystical sign that valorizes human experience, whether "we call it life or spirit, truth or reality, this, the essential thing" ("Modern Fiction"). For Woolf, literature and life are one. And finding, dis-covering, re-presenting the truth of subjective consciousness is, for her, a redemptive and life-saving project.

In her powerful indictment of Edwardian literary technique, Woolf constructs an imaginary monster—a tyrant whose authority, buttressed by the conventions of mimetic art, forces the enslaved author "to provide a plot, to provide comedy, tragedy, love interest, and an air of probability embalming the whole." The writer, she suggests, has become an alienated laborer, forced by the constraints of popular opinion to deliver fictional placebos to a clamoring but infantile audience. The "powerful and unscrupulous tyrant" is none other than an immature reading public nurtured on the intellectual pabulum of scintillating plots and melodramatic action, Aristotelian comedy and tragic catharsis, all neatly resolved in a dramatic climax that offers both denouement and closure. And if such artificial resolutions do not, in fact, resemble quotidian experience? Well, no matter. Life is more easily lived if one is constantly soothed with fictive anodynes that erase from the chaos of indeterminacy the kinds of gaps, slippages, and disturbing emotional *aporias* that cling to the mind "from the beginning of consciousness to the end." Woolf challenges her readers to examine their consciences—to look within and ask the salient question: "Is life like this?" Do Edwardian novels reflect "an ordinary life on an ordinary day"? ("Modern Fiction"). The answer, quite clearly, is "no."

Like the nineteenth-century evangelical preacher, Woolf asks her auditors to consult their hearts, then confess to a shocking disparity between private experience and its public, fictional representation. "Look within," she implores, "and life, it seems, is very far from being 'like this.' Examine for a moment an ordinary mind on an ordinary day. The mind receives a myriad impressions—trivial, fantastic, evanescent, or engraved with the sharpness of steel." Enduring truth, residual in the subjective consciousness, manifests itself to all who would be saved. The ordinary mind to be examined is, of course, the reader's own; personal experience is the sole criterion for judging aesthetic mimesis. Like Pater before her, Woolf insists that we should wrench from the tablets of our elected literary representatives a recognizable reflection of those "myriad impressions" that impinge on consciousness in "an incessant shower of innumerable atoms." "Is it not the task of the novelist to convey this varying, this unknown and uncircumscribed spirit, whatever aberration or complexity it may display?" ("Modern Fiction"). For the psychological writer, the "overmastering impression" is all.[3]

The subjective, conditional clauses at the heart of Woolf's exhortations are strategically organized to challenge the literary status quo and pave the way for a genuine revolution of the artistic imagination. Woolf begs and cajoles us to release the "enslaved" author from popular demands of plot, comedy, tragedy, love interest, and catastrophe. "For us, those conventions are ruin, those tools death" ("Mr Bennett"). Implicit in her stirring diatribe is the assumption that the turn-of-the-century practice of formal realism was white, male, bourgeois, and patriarchal. "House property," she observes ironically, "was the common ground from which the Edwardians found it easy to proceed to intimacy" ("Mr Bennett"). Their photographic representations of life reflect an imperialism of the spirit buttressed by authorial omniscience and a "will to power" that ruthlessly controls a well-constructed, anatomically correct, but totally distorted and phallogocentric model of human experience. Such artistic commodities appeal, furthermore, to the received wisdom of patrons and publishers, reviewers and literary critics—almost, to a man, members of a white, ruling-class intelligentsia. Brashly, Woolf takes her case to the common people and pleads that they search their hearts for the "thing we seek." The Georgian writer will try to capture a new style of psychological verisimilitude contingent on fluid, evanescent impressions of a subjective life-world. Deconstructing the props of traditional fiction, Woolf calls for a reconstruction of art to reflect the semiotic dimensions of ordinary life. She tacitly invokes the chorus of Greek drama and urges that the common man or woman be foregrounded in modern fiction—that heroic activity be redefined, that the range of literary topoi be expanded to include the whole panoply of quotidian existence. "The proper stuff of fiction," she tells us, "does not exist; everything is the proper stuff of fiction" ("Modern Fiction").

For Woolf, art is a matter of life and death, and her rhetorical strategies, always personal and figurative, are stirring, evangelical appeals to an audience whose souls are in jeopardy from the perils of Edwardian materialism. Her impassioned plea for greater spirituality in artistic representation ushers in a new age of psychological fiction, a modernist era of technical daring that will require an educated public redeemed from its nineteenth-century addiction to the gratifications of formal realism. The contemporary British audience does, indeed, need saving: "it is a very suggestible and docile creature, which, once you get it to attend, will believe implicitly what it is told for a certain number of years" ("Mr. Bennett"). Woolf desperately wants her readers to grow up and grow into the exciting innovations offered by Georgian writers such as James Joyce, Joseph Conrad, E. M. Forster, and (always implied) Virginia Woolf herself. About to embark on an era of stylistic and technical experimentation, she is priming her audience for the rich, fluid ebullience of the multipersonal stream of consciousness she will introduce in *Mrs. Dalloway, To the Lighthouse,* and *The Waves.*[4]

"Modern Fiction" betrays the intensity of her aesthetic anxieties, her fears that an intransigent British public might not have sufficient courage or insight to respond to avant-garde fabulation. And so she takes pains to warn us that the most innovative of the moderns will seek to illumine those "dark places of psychology" hitherto excluded from literary representation, "difficult for us to grasp, incomprehensible to our predecessors." Couched in her tantalizing but fragmentary description of the paradigmatic Mrs. Brown are Woolf's own criteria for Georgian writing: a willingness to experiment; fidelity to a personal, controlling vision; and a commitment to the discovery of common ground between reader and author. If the pompous Edwardians were content to dictate a totalitarian world view, the pliable Georgian will attempt, instead, to share a rich, imaginative microcosm. The reader, in turn, must be eager to immerse his or her sensibilities in that "luminous halo" of consciousness, complete with gaps, slippages, chaos, disruption, perplexities, confusion, wonder, love, and a denial of satisfying closure. Such fiction, like our tantalizing impression of Mrs. Brown, will be characterized by a disconcerting undecidability; it will assume that "there is no answer, that if honestly examined life presents question after question which must be left to sound on and on after the story is over in hopeless interrogation" ("Modern Fiction"). One must keep the faith and remain staunchly convinced that life "is not a series of gig lamps symmetrically arranged; but a luminous halo, a semi-transparent envelope surrounding us from the beginning of consciousness to the end" ("Modern Fiction").

Woolf identifies as Georgian such authors as Forster, Lawrence, Eliot, and Joyce. She believes that, of the novelists, Forster and Lawrence "spoilt their early work because, instead of throwing away those [Edwardian] tools, they tried to use them. They tried to compromise" ("Mr. Bennett). Only Joyce and Eliot were willing to inaugurate in literature the kind of iconoclasm necessary to an age characterized by "the sound of breaking and falling, crashing and destruction" ("Mr. Bennett"). Despite a series of acerbic (even arrogant and satirical) comments about Joyce in oft-quoted diary entries, Woolf considered him a staunch compatriot in the fight for psychological realism. "Mr. Joyce is spiritual," she declares in "Modern Fiction": "he is concerned at all costs to reveal the flickerings of that innermost flame which flashes its messages through the brain" ("Modern Fiction").

Woolf apparently read the early episodes of *Ulysses* in the *Little Review* and, in a previously unpublished notebook devoted to "Modern Novels," recorded her initial appreciation of the book's startling experimental techniques.[5] She admired Joyce's "attempt to get thinking into literature," as well as the "occasional beauty of his phrases." "The thing is that he is attempting to do away with the machinery—to extract the marrow" ("Modern Novels"). And though Woolf complains about the purported obscenities of the novel in "Mr. Bennett and Mrs. Brown," she expresses greater responsiveness when, in her reading notes, she observes that "so much seems to depend on the *emotional* fibre of the mind it may be time that the subconscious mind dwells on indecency." Woolf praises Joyce's "desire to be more psychological" and "get more things into fiction." *Ulysses,* she observes, records the "inner thought" of the individual, "then the little scatter of life on top to keep you in touch with reality." Woolf was one of the first critics to recognize Joyce's innovative use of cinematic technique. His narrative, she suggests, is "possibly like a cinema that shows you very slowly, how a hare does jump; all pictures were a little made up before." It is unfair, she writes in a marginal note, "to approach Joyce by way of his 'method'; and that is on the surface startling." Comparing *Ulysses* to Laurence Sterne's *Tristram Shandy,* she remarks: "For all I know, every great book has been an act of revolution."

The essays by Woolf in this volume constitute nothing less than a passionate call to aesthetic arms, a rhetorical plea for modernist revolution. In a final peroration, Woolf urges her 1924 audience: "Tolerate the spasmodic, the obscure, the fragmentary, the failure. Your help is invoked in a good cause. For . . . we are trembling on the verge of one of the great ages of English literature" ("Mr. Bennett"). And so, indeed, we were.

NOTES

1. In her biography of Fry, Woolf records the impact of the first exhibition of post-Impressionist pictures, "Manet and the Post-Impressionists," mounted by Fry in the Grafton Galleries in November 1910. The paintings, she tells us, were considered "outrageous, anarchistic and childish. They were an insult to the British public" (*Roger Fry* 154). For Fry and his contemporaries, however, the event was nothing short of a "revelation." Fry was convinced that British art was "alive, and that a great age was at hand" (161).

2. In *Mrs. Dalloway,* Septimus Smith provokes the psychiatrist Sir William Bradshaw with a set of similar questions: 'Why live? . . . And perhaps, after all, there is no God? . . . In short, this living or not living is an affair of our own?" (153–154). Sir William, an emblem of the British establishment, mentally responds with a symbolic defense of the goddesses Proportion and Conversion, twin guardians of domestic, professional, and political imperialism.

3. Woolf is clearly echoing Walter Pater's Conclusion to *The Renaissance* throughout her essay on "Modern Fiction."

4. In a 1908 letter to Clive Bell, Woolf confessed: "I think a great deal of my future . . . how I shall re-form the novel and capture multitudes of things at present fugitive, enclose the whole, and shape infinite strange things" (*Letters* 1, 356).

5. "Modern Fiction" was originally published under the title "Modern Novels" in the *Times Literary Supplement,* April 10, 1919, and slightly revised prior to publication in the first *Common Reader.* Her reading notes for the essay are contained in an unpaginated notebook entitled "Modern Novels (Joyce)" and published here for the first time by

permission of Quentin Bell and the Henry W. and Albert A. Berg Collection of the New York Public Library, Astor, Lenox and Tilden Foundations. Woolf's initial responses to Joyce's *Ulysses* provide fascinating insight into her first attempts to grapple with the perplexing experimental techniques of this modernist competitor. More importantly, these reading notes challenge some of the notorious remarks culled from Woolf's private diary entries about Joyce's "he-goat" authorial persona. Nowhere else does Woolf express such admiration for the revolutionary strategies of *Ulysses*. I wish to thank Edward L. Bishop of the University of Alberta for his generous help in deciphering Woolf's spidery script. Errors and ellipses in the transcription are my own. In some cases I have regularized spelling and italicized book titles. The first paragraph of the essay is, I believe, Woolf's response to May Sinclair's 1918 review of Dorothy Richardson's *Pilgrimage*. The following editorial symbols and abbreviations appear in "Modern Novels (Joyce)":

[word] = a reading editorially supplied;
[*word*] = a deletion editorially restored;
[?word] = an uncertain reading;
[. . .] = an illegible word or words.

WORKS CITED

Pater, Walter. *The Renaissance*. 1873. New York: New American Library, 1959.
Woolf, Virginia. *The Letters of Virginia Woolf*. Vol. 1. Ed. Nigel Nicolson and Joanne Trautmann. New York and London: Harcourt Brace Jovanovich, 1975.
———. *Moments of Being*. Ed. Jeanne Schulkind. New York and London: Harcourt Brace Jovanovich, 1976.
———. "Modern Fiction." *The Common Reader*. 1925. New York: Harcourt Brace and World, 1953.
———. "Modern Novels (Joyce)." Second of two holograph notebooks, unnumbered. Henry W. and Albert A. Berg Collection, Astor, Lenox and Tilden Foundations, New York Public Library.
———. "Mr. Bennett and Mrs. Brown." *The Captain's Death Bed and Other Essays*. New York and London: Harcourt Brace, 1950.
———. *Mrs. Dalloway*. New York: Harcourt Brace and World, 1925.
———. *Roger Fry: A Biography*. 1940. New York and London: Harcourt Brace Jovanovich, 1976.

Modern Fiction

In making any survey, even the freest and loosest, of modern fiction it is difficult not to take it for granted that the modern practice of the art is somehow an improvement upon the old. With their simple tools and primitive materials, it might be said, Fielding did well and Jane Austen even better, but compare their opportunities with ours! Their masterpieces certainly have a strange air of simplicity. And yet the analogy between literature and the process, to choose an example, of making motor cars scarcely holds good beyond the first glance. It is doubtful whether in the course of the centuries, though we have learnt much about making machines, we have learnt anything about making literature. We do not come to write better; all that we can be said to do is to keep moving, now a little in this direction, now in that, but with a circular tendency should the whole course of the track be viewed from a sufficiently lofty pinnacle. It need scarcely be said that we make no claim to stand, even momentarily, upon that vantage ground. On the flat, in the crowd, half blind with dust, we look back with envy to those happier warriors, whose battle is won and whose achievements wear so serene an air of accomplishment that we can scarcely refrain from whispering that the fight was not so fierce for them as for us. It is for the historian of literature to decide; for him to say if we are now beginning or ending or standing in the middle of a great period of prose fiction, for down in the plain little is visible. We only know that certain gratitudes and hostilities inspire us; that certain paths seem to lead to fertile land, others to the dust and the desert; and of this perhaps it may be worth while to attempt some account.

Our quarrel, then, is not with the classics, and if we speak of quarrelling with Mr. Wells, Mr. Bennett, and Mr. Galsworthy it is partly that by the mere fact of their existence in the flesh their work has a living, breathing, every-day imperfection which bids us take what liberties with it we choose. But it is also true that, while we thank them for a thousand gifts, we reserve our unconditional gratitude for Mr. Hardy, for Mr. Conrad, and in a much lesser degree for the Mr. Hudson, of *The Purple Land, Green Mansions,* and *Far Away and Long Ago.* Mr. Wells, Mr. Bennett, and Mr. Galsworthy have excited so many hopes and disappointed them so persistently that our gratitude largely takes the form of thanking them for having shown us what they might have done but have not done; what we certainly could not do, but as certainly, perhaps, do not wish to do. No single phrase will sum up the charge or grievance which we have to bring against a mass of work so large in its volume and embodying so many qualities, both admirable and the reverse. If we tried to formulate our meaning in one word we should say that these three writers are materialists. It is because they are concerned not with the spirit but with the body that they have disappointed us, and left us with the feeling that the sooner English fiction turns its back upon them, as politely as may be, and marches, if only into the desert, the better for its soul. Naturally, no single word reaches the centre of three separate targets. In the case of Mr. Wells it falls notably wide of the mark. And yet even with him it indicated to our thinking the fatal alloy in his genius, the great clod of clay that has got itself mixed up with the purity of his inspiration. But Mr. Bennett is perhaps the worst culprit of the three, inasmuch as he is by far the best workman. He can make a book so well constructed and solid in its craftsmanship that it is difficult for the most exacting of critics to see through what chink or crevice decay can creep in. There is not so much as a draught between the frames of the windows, or a crack in the boards. And yet—if life should refuse to live there? That is a risk which the creator of *The Old Wives' Tale,* George Cannon, Edwin Clayhanger, and hosts of other figures, may well claim to have surmounted. His characters live abundantly, even unexpectedly, but it remains to ask how do they live, and what do they live for? More and more they seem to us, deserting even the well-built villa in the Five Towns, to spend their time in some softly padded first-class railway carriage, pressing bells and buttons innumerable; and the destiny to which they travel so luxuriously becomes more and more unquestionably an eternity of bliss spent in the very best hotel in Brighton. It can scarcely be said of Mr. Wells that he is a materialist in the sense that he takes too much delight in the solidity of his fabric. His mind is too generous in its sympathies to allow him to spend much time in making things shipshape and substantial. He is a materialist from sheer goodness of heart, taking upon his shoulders the work that ought to have been discharged by Government officials, and in the plethora of his ideas and facts scarcely having leisure to realise, or forgetting to think important, the crudity and coarseness of his human beings. Yet what more damaging criticism can there be both of his earth and of his Heaven than that they are to be inhabited here and hereafter by his Joans and his Peters? Does not the inferiority of their natures tarnish whatever institutions and ideals may be provided for them by the generosity of their creator? Nor, profoundly though we respect the integrity and humanity of Mr. Galsworthy, shall we find what we seek in his pages.

If we fasten, then, one label on all these books, on which is one word, materialists, we mean by it that they write of unimportant things; that they spend immense skill and immense industry making the trivial and the transitory appear the true and the enduring.

We have to admit that we are exacting, and, further, that we find it difficult to justify our discontent by explaining what it is that we exact. We frame our question differently at different times. But it reappears most persistently as we drop the finished novel on the crest of a sigh—Is it worth while? What is the point of it all? Can it be that owing to one of those little deviations which the human spirit seems to make from time to time Mr. Bennett has come down with his magnificent apparatus for catching life just an inch or two on the wrong side? Life escapes; and perhaps without life nothing else is worth while. It is a confession of vagueness to have to make use of such a figure as this, but we scarcely better the matter by speaking, as critics are prone to do, of reality. Admitting the vagueness which afflicts all criticism of novels, let us hazard the opinion that for us at this moment the form of fiction most in vogue more often misses than secures the thing we seek. Whether we call it life or spirit, truth or reality, this, the essential thing, has moved off, or on, and refuses to be contained any longer in such ill-fitting vestments as we provide. Nevertheless, we go on perseveringly, conscientiously, constructing our two and thirty chapters after a design which more and more ceases to resemble the vision in our minds. So much of the enormous labour of proving the solidity, the likeness to life, the story is not merely labour thrown away but labour misplaced to the extent of obscuring and blotting out the light of the conception. The writer seems constrained, not by his own free will but by some powerful and unscrupulous tyrant who has him in thrall to provide a plot, to provide comedy, tragedy, love interest, and an air of probability embalming the whole so impeccable that if all his figures were to come to life they would find themselves dressed down to the last button of their coats in the fashion of the hour. The tryant is obeyed; the novel is done to a turn. But sometimes, more and more often as time goes by, we suspect a momentary doubt, a spasm of rebellion, as the pages fill themselves in the customary way. Is life like this? Must novels be like this?

Look within and life, it seems, is very far from being "like this." Examine for a moment an ordinary mind on an ordinary day. The mind receives a myriad impressions—trivial, fantastic, evanescent, or engraved with the sharpness of steel. From all sides they come, an incessant shower of innumerable atoms; and as they fall, as they shape themselves into the life of Monday or Tuesday, the accent falls differently from of old; the moment of importance came not here but there; so that if a writer were a free man and not a slave, if he could write what he chose, not what he must, if he could base his work upon his own feeling and not upon convention, there would be no plot, no comedy, no tragedy, no love interest or catastrophe in the accepted style, and perhaps not a single button sewn on as the Bond Street tailors would have it. Life is not a series of gig lamps symmetrically arranged; but a luminous halo, a semi-transparent envelope surrounding us from the beginning of consciousness to the end. Is it not the task of the novelist to convey this varying, this unknown and uncircumscribed spirit, whatever aberration or complexity it may display, with as little mixture of the alien and external as possible? We are not pleading merely for courage and sincerity; we are suggesting that the proper stuff of fiction is a little other than custom would have us believe it.

It is, at any rate, in some such fashion as this that we seek to define the quality which distinguishes the work of several young writers, among whom Mr. James Joyce is the most notable, from that of their predecessors. They attempt to come closer to life, and to preserve more sincerely and exactly what interests and moves them, even if to do so they must discard most of the conventions which are commonly observed by the novelist. Let us record the atoms as they fall upon the mind in the order in which they fall, let us trace the pattern, however disconnected and incoherent in appearance, which each sight or incident scores upon the consciousness. Let us not take it for granted that life exists more fully in what is commonly thought big than in what is commonly thought small. Any one who has read *The Portrait of the Artist as a Young Man* or, what promises to be a far more interesting work, *Ulysses,* now appearing in the *Little Review,* will have hazarded some theory of this nature as to Mr. Joyce's intention. On our part, with such a fragment before us, it is hazarded rather than affirmed; but whatever the intention of the whole there can be no question but that it is of the utmost sincerity and that the result, difficult or unpleasant as we may judge it, is undeniably important. In contrast with those whom we have called materialists Mr. Joyce is spiritual; he is concerned at all costs to reveal the flickerings of that innermost flame which flashes its messages through the brain, and in order to preserve it he disregards with complete courage whatever seems to him adventitious, whether it be probability, or coherence or any other of these signposts which for generations have served to support the imagination of a reader when called upon to imagine what he can neither touch nor see. The scene in the cemetery, for instance, with its brilliancy, its sordidity, its incoherence, its sudden lightning flashes of significance, does undoubtedly come so close to the quick of the mind that, on a first reading at any rate, it is difficult not to acclaim a masterpiece. If we want life itself here, surely we have it. Indeed, we find ourselves fumbling rather awkwardly if we try to say what else we wish, and for what reason a work of such originality yet fails to compare, for we must take high examples, with *Youth* or *The Mayor of Casterbridge.* It fails because of the comparative poverty of the writer's mind, we might say simply and have done with it. But it is possible to press a little further and wonder whether we may not refer our sense of being in a bright yet narrow room, confined and shut in, rather than enlarged and set free, to some limitation imposed by the method as well as by the mind. Is it the method that inhibits the creative power? Is it due to the method that we feel neither jovial nor magnanimous, but centred in a self which, in spite of its tremor of susceptibility, never embraces or creates what is outside itself and beyond? Does the emphasis laid, perhaps didactically, upon indecency, contribute to the effect of something angular and isolated? Or is it merely that in any effort of such originality it is much easier, for contemporaries especially, to feel what it lacks than to name what it gives? In any case it is a mistake to stand outside examining "methods." Any method is right, every method is right, that expresses what we wish to express, if we are writers; that brings us closer to the novelist's intention if we are readers. This method has the merit of bringing us closer to what we were prepared to call life itself; did not the reading of *Ulysses* suggest how much of life is excluded or ignored, and did it not come with a shock to open *Tristram Shandy* or even *Pendennis* and be by them convinced that there are not only other aspects of life, but more important ones into the bargain.

However this may be, the problem before the novelist at present, as we suppose it to have been in the past, is to contrive means of being free to set down what he chooses. He has to have the courage to say that what interests him is no longer "this" but "that": out of "that" alone must he construct his work. For the moderns "that," the point of interest, lies very likely in the dark places of psychology. At once, therefore, the accent falls a little differently; the emphasis is upon something hitherto ignored; at once different outline of form becomes necessary, difficult for us to grasp, incomprehensible to our predecessors. No one but a modern, perhaps no one but a Russian, would have felt the interest of the situation which Tchekov has made into the short story which he calls "Gusev." Some Russian soldiers lie ill on board a ship which is taking them back to Russia. We are given a few scraps of their talk and some of their thoughts; then one of them dies and is carried away; the talk goes on among the others for a time, until Gusev himself dies, and looking "like a carrot or a radish" is thrown overboard. The emphasis is laid upon such unexpected places that at first it seems as if there were no emphasis at all; and then, as the eyes accustom themselves to twilight and discern the shapes of things in a room we see how complete the story is, how profound, and how truly in obedience to his vision

Tchekov has chosen this, that, and the other, and placed them together to compose something new. But it is impossible to say "this is comic," or "that is tragic," nor are we certain, since short stories, we have been taught, should be brief and conclusive, whether this, which is vague and inconclusive, should be called a short story at all.

The most elementary remarks upon modern English fiction can hardly avoid some mention of the Russian influence, and if the Russians are mentioned one runs the risk of feeling that to write of any fiction save theirs is waste of time. If we want understanding of the soul and heart where else shall we find it of comparable profundity? If we are sick of our own materialism the least considerable of their novelists has by right of birth a natural reverence for the human spirit. "Learn to make yourself akin to people. . . . But let this sympathy be not with the mind—for it is easy with the mind—but with the heart, with love towards them." In every great Russian writer we seem to discern the features of a saint, if sympathy for the sufferings of others, love towards them, endeavour to reach some goal worthy of the most exacting demands of the spirit constitute saintliness. It is the saint in them which confounds us with a feeling of our own irreligious triviality, and turns so many of our famous novels to tinsel and trickery. The conclusions of the Russian mind, thus comprehensive and compassionate, are inevitably, perhaps, of the utmost sadness. More accurately indeed we might speak of the inconclusiveness of the Russian mind. It is the sense that there is no answer, that if honestly examined life presents question after question which must be left to sound on and on after the story is over in hopeless interrogation that fills us with a deep, and finally it may be with a resentful, despair. They are right perhaps; unquestionably they see further than we do and without our gross impediments of vision. But perhaps we see something that escapes them, or why should this voice of protest mix itself with our gloom? The voice of protest is the voice of another and an ancient civilisation which seems to have bred in us the instinct to enjoy and fight rather than to suffer and understand. English fiction from Sterne to Meredith bears witness to our natural delight in humour and comedy, in the beauty of earth, in the activities of the intellect, and in the splendour of the body. But any deductions that we may draw from the comparison of two fictions so immeasurably far apart are futile save indeed as they flood us with a view of the infinite possibilities of the art and remind us that there is no limit to the horizon, and that nothing—no "method," no experiment, even of the wildest—is forbidden, but only falsity and pretence. "The proper stuff of fiction" does not exist; everything is the proper stuff of fiction, every feeling, every thought; every quality of brain and spirit is drawn upon; no perception comes amiss. And if we can imagine the art of fiction come alive and standing in our midst, she would undoubtedly bid us break her and bully her, as well as honour and love her, for so her youth is renewed and her sovereignty assured.

The Common Reader. 1925. New York: Harcourt Brace and World, 1953. 150–158.

From "Mr. Bennett and Mrs. Brown"

It seems to me possible, perhaps desirable, that I may be the only person in this room who has committed the folly of writing, trying to write, or failing to write, a novel. And when I asked myself, as your invitation to speak to you about modern fiction made me ask myself, what demon whispered in my ear and urged me to my doom, a little figure rose before me—the figure of a man, or of a woman, who said, "My name is Brown. Catch me if you can."

Most novelists have the same experience. Some Brown, Smith, or Jones comes before them and says in the most seductive and charming way in the world, "Come and catch me if you can." And so, led on by this will-o'-the-wisp, they flounder through volume after volume, spending the best years of their lives in the pursuit, and receiving for the most part very little cash in exchange. Few catch the phantom; most have to be content with a scrap of her dress or a wisp of her hair.

My belief that men and women write novels because they are lured on to create some character which has thus imposed itself upon them has the sanction of Mr. Arnold Bennett. In an article from which I will quote he says, "The foundation of good fiction is character-creating and nothing else. . . . Style counts; plot counts; originality of outlook counts. But none of these counts anything like so much as the convincingness of the characters. If the characters are real the novel will have a chance; if they are not, oblivion will be its portion. . . ." And he goes on to draw the conclusion that we have no young novelists of first-rate importance at the present moment, because they are unable to create characters that are real, true, and convincing.

These are the questions that I want with greater boldness than discretion to discuss tonight. I want to make out what we mean when we talk about "character" in fiction; to say something about the question of reality which Mr. Bennett raises; and to suggest some reasons why the younger novelists fail to create characters, if, as Mr. Bennett asserts, it is true that fail they do. This will lead me, I am well aware, to make some very sweeping and some very vague assertions. For the question is an extremely difficult one. Think how little we know about character—think how little we know about art. But, to make a clearance before I begin, I will suggest that we range Edwardians and Georgians into two camps; Mr. Wells, Mr. Bennett, and Mr. Galsworthy I will call the Edwardians; Mr. Forster, Mr. Lawrence, Mr. Strachey, Mr. Joyce, and Mr. Eliot I will call the Georgians. And if I speak in the first person, with intolerable egotism, I will ask you to excuse me. I do not want to attribute to the world at large the opinions of one solitary, ill-informed, and misguided individual.

My first assertion is one that I think you will grant—that every one in this room is a judge of character. Indeed it would be impossible to live for a year without disaster unless one practised character-reading and had some skill in the

A paper read to the Heretics, Cambridge, on May 18, 1924. Ellipses indicate portions cut for this anthology.

art. Our marriages, our friendships depend on it; our business largely depends on it; every day questions arise which can only be solved by its help. And now I will hazard a second assertion, which is more disputable perhaps, to the effect that in or about December, 1910, human character changed.

I am not saying that one went out, as one might into a garden, and there saw that a rose had flowered, or that a hen had laid an egg. The change was not sudden and definite like that. But a change there was, nevertheless; and, since one must be arbitrary, let us date it about the year 1910. The first signs of it are recorded in the books of Samuel Butler, in *The Way of All Flesh* in particular; the plays of Bernard Shaw continue to record it. In life one can see the change. . . . All human relations have shifted—those between masters and servants, husbands and wives, parents and children. And when human relations change there is at the same time a change in religion, conduct, politics, and literature. Let us agree to place one of these changes about the year 1910.

I have said that people have to acquire a good deal of skill in character-reading if they are to live a single year of life without disaster. But it is the art of the young. In middle age and in old age the art is practised mostly for its uses, and friendships and other adventures and experiments in the art of reading character are seldom made. But novelists differ from the rest of the world because they do not cease to be interested in character when they have learnt enough about it for practical purposes. They go a step further, they feel that there is something permanently interesting in character in itself. When all the practical business of life has been discharged, there is something about people which continues to seem to them of overwhelming importance, in spite of the fact that it has no bearing whatever upon their happiness, comfort, or income. The study of character becomes to them an absorbing pursuit; to impart character an obsession. . . .

. . . . I will tell you a simple story which, however pointless, has the merit of being true, of a journey from Richmond to Waterloo, in the hope that I may show you what I mean by character in itself; that you may realize the different aspects it can wear; and the hideous perils that beset you directly you try to describe it in words.

One night some weeks ago, then, I was late for the train and jumped into the first carriage I came to. As I sat down I had the strange and uncomfortable feeling that I was interrupting a conversation between two people who were already sitting there. Not that they were young or happy. Far from it. They were both elderly, the woman over sixty, the man well over forty. They were sitting opposite each other, and the man, who had been leaning over and talking emphatically to judge by his attitude and the flush on his face, sat back and became silent. I had disturbed him, and he was annoyed. The elderly lady, however, whom I will call Mrs. Brown, seemed rather relieved. She was one of those clean, threadbare old ladies whose extreme tidiness—everything buttoned, fastened, tied together, mended and brushed up—suggests more extreme poverty than rags and dirt. There was something pinched about her—a look of suffering, of apprehension, and, in addition, she was extremely small.

Her feet, in their clean little boots, scarcely touched the floor. I felt that she had nobody to support her; that she had to make up her mind for herself; that, having been deserted, or left a widow, years ago, she had led an anxious, harried life, bringing up an only son, perhaps, who, as likely as not, was by this time beginning to go to the bad. All this shot through my mind as I sat down, being uncomfortable, like most poeple, at traveling with fellow passengers unless I have somehow or other accounted for them. Then I looked at the man. He was no relation of Mrs. Brown's I felt sure; he was of a bigger, burlier, less refined type. He was a man of business I imagined, very likely a respectable corn-chandler from the North, dressed in good blue serge with a pocket-knife and a silk handkerchief, and a stout leather bag. Obviously, however, he had an unpleasant business to settle with Mrs. Brown; a secret, perhaps sinister business, which they did not intend to discuss in my presence.

"Yes, the Crofts have had very bad luck with their servants," Mr. Smith (as I will call him) said in a considering way, going back to some earlier topic, with a view to keeping up appearances.

"Ah, poor people," said Mrs. Brown. . . .

"What changes they're making in this part of the world," said Mr. Smith, looking out of the window, and looking furtively at me as he did so.

It was plain, from Mrs. Brown's silence, from the uneasy affability with which Mr. Smith spoke, that he had some power over her which he was exerting disagreeably. It might have been her son's downfall, or some painful episode in her past life, or her daughter's. Perhaps she was going to London to sign some document to make over some property. Obviously against her will she was in Mr. Smith's hands. . . .

"So about the matter we were discussing. It'll be all right? George will be there on Tuesday?"

"We shan't be late," said Mrs. Brown, gathering herself together with superb dignity.

Mr. Smith said nothing. He got up, buttoned his coat, reached his bag down, and jumped out of the train before it had stopped at Clapham Junction. He had got what he wanted, but he was ashamed of himself; he was glad to get out of the old lady's sight.

Mrs. Brown and I were left alone together. She sat in her corner opposite, very clean, very small, rather queer, and suffering intensely. The impression she made was overwhelming. It came pouring out like a draught, like a smell of burning. What was it composed of—that overwhelming and peculiar impression? Myriads of irrelevant and incongruous ideas crowd into one's head on such occasions; one sees the person, one sees Mrs. Brown, in the centre of all sorts of different scenes. . . .

. . . . The important thing was to realize her character, to steep oneself in her atmosphere. I had no time to explain why I felt it somewhat tragic, heroic, yet with a dash of the flighty and fantastic, before the train stopped, and I watched her disappear, carrying her bag, into the vast blazing station. She looked very small, very tenacious; at once very frail and very heroic. And I have never seen her again, and I shall never know what became of her. . . .

I believe that all novels begin with an old lady in the corner opposite. I believe that all novels, that is to say, deal with character, and that it is to express character—not to preach doctrines, sing songs, or celebrate the glories of the British Empire, that the form of the novels, so clumsy, verbose, and undramatic, so rich, elastic, and alive, has been evolved. To express character, I have said; but you will at once reflect that the very widest interpretation can be put upon those words. For example, old Mrs. Brown's character will strike you very differently according to the age and country in which you happen to be born. . . .

. . . . I think that after the creative activity of the Victorian age it was quite necessary, not only for literature but for life, that someone should write the books that Mr. Wells, Mr. Bennett, and Mr. Galsworthy have written. Yet what odd books they are! Sometimes I wonder if we are right to call them books at all. For they leave one with so strange a feeling of incompleteness and dissatisfaction. . . . But the Edwardians were never interested in character in itself; or in the book in itself. They were interested in something outside. Their books, then, were incomplete as books, and required that the reader should finish them, actively and practically, for himself.

Perhaps we can make this clearer if we take the liberty of imagining a little party in the railway carriage—Mr. Wells, Mr. Galsworthy, Mr. Bennett are travelling to Waterloo with Mrs. Brown. Mrs. Brown, I have said, was poorly dressed and very small. She had an anxious, harassed look. I doubt whether she was what you call an educated woman. Seizing upon all these symptoms of the unsatisfactory condition of our primary schools with a rapidity to which I can do no justice, Mr. Wells would instantly project upon the window-pane a vision of a better, breezier, jollier, happier, more adventurous and gallant world, where these musty railway carriages and fusty old women do not exist; where miraculous barges bring tropical fruit to Camberwell by eight o'clock in the morning; where there are public nurseries, fountains, and libraries, dining-rooms, drawing-rooms, and marriages; where every citizen is generous and candid, manly and magnificent, and rather like Mr. Wells himself. But nobody is in the least like Mrs. Brown. There are no Mrs. Browns in Utopia. Indeed I do not think that Mr. Wells, in his passion to make her what she ought to be, would waste a thought upon her as she is. And what would Mr. Galsworthy see? Can we doubt that the walls of Doulton's factory would take his fancy? There are women in that factory who make twenty-five dozen earthenware pots every day. There are mothers in the Mile End Road who depend upon the farthings which these women earn. But there are employers in Surrey who are even now smoking rich cigars while the nightingale sings. Burning with indignation, stuffed with information, arraigning civilization, Mr. Galsworthy would only see in Mrs. Brown a pot broken on the wheel and thrown into the corner.

Mr. Bennett, alone of the Edwardians, would keep his eyes in the carriage. He, indeed, would observe every detail with immense care. He would notice the advertisements; the pictures of Swanage and Portsmouth; the way in which the cushion bulged between the buttons; how Mrs. Brown wore a brooch which had cost three-and-ten-three at Whitworth's bazaar; and had mended both gloves— . . . . And so he would gradually sidle sedately towards Mrs. Brown, and would remark how she had been left a little copyhold, not freehold, property at Datchet, which, however, was mortgaged to Mr. Bungay the solicitor—. . . .

. . . . I have formed my own opinion of what Mr. Bennett is about—he is trying to make us imagine for him; he is trying to hypnotize us into the belief that, because he has made a house, there must be a person living there. With all his powers of observation, which are marvellous, with all his sympathy and humanity, which are great, Mr. Bennett has never once looked at Mrs. Brown in her corner. There she sits in the corner of the carriage—that carriage which is travelling, not from Richmond to Waterloo, but from one age of English literature to the next, for Mrs. Brown is eternal, Mrs. Brown is human nature, Mrs. Brown changes only on the surface, it is the novelists who get in and out—there she sits and not one of the Edwardian writers has so much as looked at her. They have looked very powerfully, searchingly, and sympathetically out of the window; at factories, at Utopias, even at the decoration and upholstery of the carriage; but never at her, never at life, never at human nature. And so they have developed a technique of novel-writing which suits their purpose; they have made tools and established conventions which do their business. But those tools are not our tools, and that business is not our business. For us those conventions are ruin, those tools are death.

. . . . So it is in literature. The writer must get into touch with his reader by putting before him something which he recognizes, which therefore stimulates his imagination, and makes him willing to co-operate in the far more difficult business of intimacy. And it is of the highest importance that this common meeting-place should be reached easily, almost instinctively, in the dark, with one's eyes shut. . . .

But now, if you will allow me to pull my own anecdote to pieces, you will see how keenly I felt the lack of a convention, and how serious a matter it is when the tools of one generation are useless for the next. The incident had made a great impression on me. But how was I to transmit it to you? All I could do was to report as accurately as I could what was said, to describe in detail what was worn, to say, despairingly, that all sorts of scenes rushed into my mind, to proceed to tumble them out pell-mell, and to describe this vivid, this overmastering impression by likening it to a draught or a smell of burning. To tell you the truth, I was also strongly tempted to manufacture a three-volume novel about the old lady's son, and his adventures crossing the Atlantic, and her daughter, and how she kept a milliner's shop in Westminster, the past life of Smith himself, and his house at Sheffield, though such stories seem to me the most dreary, irrelevant, and humbugging affairs in the world.

But if I had done that I should have escaped the appalling effort of saying what I meant. And to have got at what I meant I should have had to go back and back and back; to experiment with one thing and another; to try this sentence and that, referring each word to my vision, matching it as exactly as possible, and knowing that somehow I had to find a common ground between us, a convention which would not seem to you too odd, unreal, and far-fetched to believe in. I admit that I shirked that arduous undertaking. I let my Mrs. Brown slip through my fingers. I have told you nothing whatever about her. . . .

That is what I mean by saying that the Edwardian tools are the wrong ones for us to use. They have laid an enormous stress upon the fabric of things. They have given us a house in the hope that we may be able to deduce the human beings who live there. To give them their due, they have made that house much better worth living in. But if you hold that novels are in the first place about people, and only in the second about the houses they live in, that is the wrong way to set about it. Therefore, you see, the Georgian writer had to begin by throwing away the method that was in use at the moment. He was left alone there facing Mrs. Brown without any method of conveying her to the reader. But that is inaccurate. A writer is never alone. There is always the public with him—if not on the same seat, at least in the compartment next door. Now the public is a strange travelling companion. In England it is a very suggestible and docile creature, which, once you get it to attend, will believe implicitly what it is told for a certain number of years. If you say to the public with sufficient conviction: "All women have tails, and all men humps," it will actually learn to see women with tails and men with humps, and will think it very revolutionary and probably improper if you say: "Nonsense. Monkeys have tails and camels humps. But men and women have brains, and they have hearts; they think and they feel,"—that will seem to it a bad joke, and an improper one into the bargain.

But to return. Here is the British public sitting by the writer's side and saying in its vast and unanimous way: "Old women have houses. They have fathers. They have incomes. They have servants. They have hot-water bottles. That is how we know that they are old women. Mr. Wells and Mr. Bennett and Mr. Galsworthy have always taught us that this is the way to recognize them. But now with your Mrs. Brown—how are we to believe in her? We do not even know whether her villa was called Albert or Balmoral; what she paid for her gloves, or whether her mother died of cancer or of consumption. How can she be alive? No; she is a mere figment of your imagination."

And old women of course ought to be made of freehold villas and copyhold estates, not of imagination.

The Georgian novelist, therefore, was in an awkward predicament. There was Mrs. Brown protesting that she was different, quite different, from what people made out, and luring the novelist to her rescue by the most fascinating if fleeting glimpse of her charms; there were the Edwardians handing out tools appropriate to house building and house breaking; and there was the British public asseverating that they must see the hot-water bottle first. Meanwhile the train was rushing to that station where we must all get out.

Such, I think, was the predicament in which the young Georgians found themselves about the year 1910. Many of them—I am thinking of Mr. Forster and Mr. Lawrence in particular—spoilt their early work because, instead of throwing away those tools, they tried to use them. They tried to compromise. . . . Something had to be done. At whatever cost of life, limb, and damage to valuable property Mrs. Brown must be rescued, expressed, and set in her high relations to the world before the train stopped and she disappeared for ever. And so the smashing and the crashing began. Thus it is that we hear all round us, in poems and novels and biographies, even in newspaper articles and essays, the sound of breaking and falling, crashing and destruction. . . .

. . . . But, instead of being gloomy, I am sanguine. For this state of things is, I think, inevitable whenever from hoar old age or callow youth the convention ceases to be a means of communication between writer and reader, and becomes instead an obstacle and an impediment. At the present moment we are suffering, not from decay, but from having no code of manners which writers and readers accept as a prelude to the more exciting intercourse of friendship. The literary convention of the time is so artificial—you have to talk about the weather and nothing but the weather throughout the entire visit—that, naturally, the feeble are tempted to outrage, and the strong are led to destroy the very foundations and rules of literary society. Signs of this are everywhere apparent. Grammar is violated; syntax disintegrated; as a boy staying with an aunt for the weekend rolls in the geranium bed out of sheer desperation as the solemnities of the sabbath wear on. The more adult writers do not, of course, indulge in such wanton exhibitions of spleen. Their sincerity is desperate, and their courage tremendous; it is only that they do not know which to use, a fork or their fingers. Thus, if you read Mr. Joyce and Mr. Eliot you will be struck by the indecency of the one, and the obscurity of the other. Mr. Joyce's indecency in *Ulysses* seems to me the conscious and calculated indecency of a desperate man who feels that in order to breathe he must break the windows. At moments, when the window is broken, he is magnificent. But what a waste of energy! And, after all, how dull indecency is, when it is not the overflowing of a superabundant energy or savagery, but the determined and public-spirited act of a man who needs fresh air! Again, with the obscurity of Mr. Eliot. I think that Mr. Eliot has written some of the loveliest single lines in modern poetry. But how intolerant he is of the old usages and politenesses of society—respect for the weak, consideration for the dull! As I sun myself upon the intense and ravishing beauty of one of his lines, and reflect that I must make a dizzy and dangerous leap to the next, and so on from line to line, like an acrobat flying precariously from bar to bar, I cry out, I confess, for the old decorums, and envy the indolence of my ancestors who, instead of spinning madly through mid-air, dreamt quietly in the shade with a book. . . .

For these reasons, then, we must reconcile ourselves to a season of failures and fragments. We must reflect that where so much strength is spent on finding a way of telling the truth, the truth itself is bound to reach us in rather an exhausted and chaotic condition. Ulysses, Queen Victoria, Mr. Prufrock—to give Mrs. Brown some of the names she has made famous lately—is a little pale and dishevelled by the time her rescuers reach her. And it is the sound of their axes that we hear—a vigorous and stimulating sound in my ears—unless of course you wish to sleep, when, in the bounty of his concern, Providence has provided a host of writers anxious and able to satisfy your needs.

Thus I have tried, at tedious length, I fear, to answer some of the questions which I began by asking. I have given an account of some of the difficulties which in my view beset the Georgian writer in all his forms. I have sought to excuse him. May I end by venturing to remind you of the duties and responsibilities that are yours as partners in this business of writing books, as companions in the railway carriage, as fellow travellers with Mrs. Brown? . . . In one day thousands of ideas have coursed through your brains; thousands of emotions have met, collided, and disappeared in astonishing disorder. Nevertheless, you allow the writers to palm off upon you a version of all this, an image of Mrs. Brown, which has no likeness to that surprising apparition whatsoever. In your modesty you seem to consider that writers are different blood and bone from yourselves; that they know more of Mrs. Brown than you do. Never was there a more fatal mistake. It is this division between reader and writer, this humility on your part, these professional airs and graces on ours, that corrupt and emasculate the books which should be the healthy offspring of a close and equal alliance between us. Hence spring those sleek, smooth novels, those portentous and ridiculous biographies, that milk and watery criticism, those poems melodiously celebrating the innocence of roses and sheep which pass so plausibly for literature at the present time.

Your part is to insist that writers shall come down off their plinths and pedestals, and describe beautifully if possible, truthfully at any rate, our Mrs. Brown. You should insist that she is an old lady of unlimited capacity and infinite variety; capable of appearing in any place; wearing any dress; saying anything and doing heaven knows what. But the things she says and the things she does and her eyes and her nose and her speech and her silence have an overwhelming fascination, for she is, of course, the spirit we live by, life itself.

But do not expect just at present a complete and satisfactory presentment of her. Tolerate the spasmodic, the obscure, the fragmentary, the failure. Your help is invoked in a good cause. For I will make one final and surpassingly rash prediction—we are trembling on the verge of one of the great ages of English literature. But it can only be reached if we are determined never, never to desert Mrs. Brown.

The Captain's Death and Other Essays. New York: Harcourt Brace, 1950. 94, 102, 104–107, 109–119.

Modern Novels (Joyce)

Order of *Ulysses*
I claret red
II pale blue
III orange
IV dark green
V light green
VI green
VII dark blue

Miss Sinclair, *Little Review*

Reality is thick and deep. [The] novelist must confine himself to this knowledge at first hand: he must plunge in!

What we call the "objective method" is a method of after-thought, of spectacular reflection. By presenting what happens in the mind Miss R[ichardson] seizes reality alive. The ordinary life reaches then the extraordinary. The fabric of life—life itself. Rémy de Gourmont, *Promenades Littéraires.*

Ulysses, James Joyce

[I. Claret Red]
The undoubted occasional beauty of his phrases. It is an attempt to get thinking into literature—hence the jumble. Told in episodes. The repetition of words like rosewood and wetted ashes. Possibly one might write about the effect of reading something new—its queerness. Well, but it isn't so different after all—Perhaps it's unfair to consider the method so much—doesn't it limit one a good deal? But then every method has its limitations—things that can't be said. Question how far we now accept the old tradition without thinking.

April 1918

[II. Pale Blue]
["]On his wise shoulders through the checkerwork of leaves the sun flung spangles, dancing coins["]—It's very close, rather exquisite—but how without blood and flesh and brains? Perhaps it simply is the way one thinks if one holds a pen and writes on without coherence—interesting perhaps to doctors.

[*Ulysses* III. Orange]

Minor [. . .] minds lack quality—and as you get nothing *but* minor minds!—still an effort in the right direction—at least out of the first-class carriage line.

[*Ulysses* IV. Dark Green]

The first-class carriage that takes you to the best hotel in Brighton—that's true of Arnold B[ennett] though not quite so true of Wells. Still, there's a worldliness about them both. What's it all for?—as Henry James said. But the worst of Joyce & c. is their egotism—no generosity or comprehensiveness. Also seems to be written for a set in a back street. What does this come from? Always a mark of the second rate. Indifference to public opinion—desire to shock—need of dwelling so much on indecency.

[V. Light Green]

Whole question of indecency a difficult one. It should be colourless: but this we can't quite manage yet.

The thing is that he's attempting to do away with the machinery—to extract the marrow—It's quite true of course, that half of a writer's strength often goes in keeping up [the] illusion of reality "subject to [a] cold in the head?["] [The] object [is] that the reader shall never forget that these people are real. One must burke the question of what reality is. Why is an emotion more real than a cold in the head?

Our object is not to improve. The fact is that if we stand still we go backwards. The Victorians were moving on. Hardy is planted beyond reach of change; only seems desirable when we read novels *not* by Hardy. Always to keep moving our only chance.

Tristram Shandy.

Novels in letters.

The desire to be more psychological—get more things into fiction. Everything can go in.

Gertrude Stein.

[*Ulysses* VI. Green]

The inner thought, and then the little scatter of life on top to keep you in touch with reality.

Everyone worth the name always *has* selected.

The quite unjust sense that he's doing it on purpose to show off.

The—thrush—throstle—

Perhaps this method gets less into other people and too much into one. So much seems to depend on the *emotional* fibre of the mind it may be true that the subconscious mind dwells on indecency.

Queer jerking variety of thought—novels "composed" seemingly.

Funeral perhaps the best thing.

But isn't it always the same mind? [?Is] that true of everyone?

The interest is that this is psychology.

[*Ulysses* VII. Dark Blue]

Possibly like a cinema that shows you very slowly, how a hare does jump; all pictures were a little made up before. Here is thought made phonetic—taken to bits.

Dedalus now appears in the office. No introduction—meant to be in the swirl of moments, I suppose.

Stephen comes into the office, brings Deasy's letter. Certainly cuts out a lot that's dull, mainly an excuse for writing.

For all I know, every great book has been an act of revolution. But these people seem to try consciously (which makes us [?urgent]) not the gradual development which we see in H[enry] J[ames] or Conrad.

Tristram Shandy—Would my objections apply to *T[ristram] S[handy]*? Don Juan. I believe Johnson was outraged by *T[ristram] S[handy]*. *T[ristram] S[handy]* has a warmer temperature than *Ulysses.*

Sketch of Article

Nobody has any wish to abuse the ancients. We may envy them. Their air of flawless ease and accomplishment. No doubt it was nothing of the sort to them. But such as survive have an air of knowing what they want and doing it. Without wishing to fabricate ages and epochs, perhaps we are now at the end of an age. Yet one could always be saying that of any like art. We are discontented. Only means that we must go on; can't stand still; move on from our immediate past. A[rnold] Bennett and Wells. No wish to disparage them either; can't however see them as enviable or flawless, rather provincial and temporary. Haven't they explored one [*side*] path as far as it will go: the business of representation: colloquial modernity—the school of the cold in the head. It is from them we wish to start. We see how much fails to get into their books. Is it life itself that we miss? We get ideas and facts; the shapes of people somehow already a little elderly and out of date, but not life. What is life? That's the question. Something not necessarily leading to a plot. Burke the question of reality, in the absolute. Question only what is real to us. Something perhaps not dramatic nor humorous, not tragic: just the quality of the day.

Here we come to Joyce. And here we must make our position clear as bewildered, befogged. We don't pretend to say what he's trying to do. We know so little about the people.

Dispose of Joyce and come on to the [?measure] of our [?scope], by which we mean only that reality, or life, or interest, has come for us to lie rather in the emotions of people. We believe that we can say more about people's mind and feelings. Well then it becomes less necessary to dwell upon their bodies. [Side note] (At any rate. . . . Why not in fact leave out bodies?) All sorts of new situations become possible—the old misleading. New versions of beauty; demanding, of course, a new form. We see stories where people did not see them in the past. . . . Things do seem, suddenly for the most part, to compose a whole—the general wealth of matter. Must get out of the way of thinking that the novel is so and so. It is what one chooses to make it. And then the question of indecency. Must get out of the way of thinking that indecency is more real than anything else—a dodge now because of the veil of reticence, but a cheap one.

Then the summing up. The necessity of magnanimity and generosity. Trying to see as much of other people as possible, and not oneself—almost a school for character.

The bane of prejudice. . . .

Pendennis. It's a very queer convention that makes us believe that people talked or felt or lived as J[ane] A[usten] and Thackeray and Dickens make them—the only thing is that we're used to it—Mrs. Shandon cares for nothing but tea when her husband is away. Oh what varieties of pain do we not make our women suffer! And that leads to a charming apostrophe to the teapot—a kind of jolly abandonment of humour and life.

[Side Notes]
Bloom—editor of a paper. Dignam dies. Stephen Dedalus is the son of Mr. Dedalus. Mulligan is his friend—so what is the connection between Bloom and Dedalus?

It's possible that the novel to us is what the drama was to the Greeks. Therefore all the remarks here recorded are vague, discursive, and by no means are of finality. The quick darting mind painfully [?piling] up.

Unfair to approach Joyce by way of his 'method'; and that is on the surface startling.

Yet it seems just possible that the big things are the big things: love, death, jealousy and so on; but must be seen again, felt again; always, perpetually.

Yet Joyce is quite right, morally, not artistically, to do this.

Henry W. and Albert A. Berg Collection, Astor, Lenox and Tilden Foundations, New York Public Library.

Cultural Critique. *Introduced and Edited by Brenda R. Silver*

On November 18, 1940, in the midst of the bombing that had already destroyed both her houses in London, Virginia Woolf recorded in her diary a response to her male contemporaries spurred by her reading of Herbert Read's autobiography:

> Little boys making sand castles. This refers to H[erbert] Read; Tom Eliot; Santayana; Wells. Each is weathertight, & gives shelter to the occupant. . . . But I am the sea which demolishes these castles. I use this image; meaning that owing to Read's article on Roger, his self that built the castle is to me destructive of its architecture. A mean, spiteful Read dwells outside. What is the value of a philosophy which has no power over life? I have the double vision. I mean, as I am not engrossed in the labour of making this intricate word structure I also see the man who makes it. I should say it is only word proof not weather proof. . . . His selection from literature is: Flaubert, Henry James, Blake, Wordsworth. All we at the moment can do is to make these selections: like dogs seeking the grass that cures us. But of course, being a tower dweller, Read then walls them in, others out. . . . I am carrying on, while I read, the idea of women discovering, like the 19th century rationalists, agnostics, that man is no longer God. My position, ceasing to accept the religion, is quite unlike Read's, Wells', Tom's, or Santayana's. It is essential to remain

> outside; & realise my own beliefs: or rather not to accept theirs. A line to think out. (*Diary* 5:340).[1]

Five days later, Woolf noted that having just finished the novel she later entitled *Between the Acts*, her "thoughts turn, well up, to write the first chapter of the next book (nameless). Anon, it will be called" (*Diary* 5:340). The reference here to "Anon," the opening essay in the "Common History" of English literature that Woolf was writing at the time of her death, provides an apt juxtaposition to the previous entry.[2] Taken together, the two entries illustrate Woolf's emphasis at the end of her life on the project that had occupied her throughout: the construction of a cultural narrative that would deconstruct the history and the "traditions" that have empowered men to act like gods whose pursuit of their religions and beliefs threatened the very future of civilization itself. In Woolf's narrative, women, who have historically been outsiders and agnostics in relation to the institutions and beliefs that constitute the official version of culture, can write culture anew.

The most visible manifestations of Woolf's ongoing critique of her culture appear in her two major works of feminist polemic. *A Room of One's Own* (1929) provides an innovative history of women's creativity and literary tradition that serves as a corrective to T. S. Eliot's "Tradition and the Individual Talent"; and *Three Guineas* (1938) answers the question of how women can help to end war, by brilliantly dissecting the destructiveness inherent in patriarchal culture and its institutions. But her cultural critique began much earlier and permeated every aspect of her consciousness and her writing, fictional, critical, polemical alike, linking her exposure of the traditions that have imprisoned her male colleagues in their deadly word structures to her creation of a counterculture, a counterhistory, and a countertradition, associated with women and artists.[3]

The texts that appear below provide glimpses from the beginning, the middle, and the end of Woolf's career into the historical inscriptions of gender that characterize her revisionary project. The first section of "The Journal of Mistress Joan Martyn," a story written in 1906 when Woolf was twenty-four, sets out an agenda for rewriting history by including the details of daily life, in particular those of domestic life, which means writing the excluded history of women.[4] The selections from "Byron and Mr. Briggs" (1922), written in conjunction with Woolf's first book of criticism, *The Common Reader*, provide a genealogy and characteristics for her central figure of cultural authority, the "common reader."[5] In it, she represents Mr. Briggs and his descendants as lively participants in a dialogue that they create and continue through the acts of reading and talk. By 1940–1941, when Woolf was making her "Notes for Reading at Random" and writing "Anon" and "The Reader," the role of the reader in the creation of any kind of cultural story had become more problematic—and more urgent. Her "Common History," written under pressure of her own and her culture's death, not only articulates a cultural history rooted in the (unconscious) emotions and desires that generate creation and destruction but also posits a tradition that sets the creative instinct against the powers of barbarism and death so dominant at that time.[6] Within this tradition, both Anon—who is sometimes man, sometimes woman, but always outsider and critic—and the reader become metaphors for the potentially regenerative role of the artist and art.

For Woolf, as for her contemporaries who lived through World War I and the unfolding political and cultural crises of the interwar period, the question of tradition and cultural values had more than academic resonance. Recording a conversation in 1935 about religion, morality, communism, and writing with Eliot, J. M. Keynes, and her nephew Julian Bell, Woolf accuses the younger generation of having "no sense of tradition and continuity. I used to feel that the British Museum reading room was going on for ever" (*Diary* 4:208). "Tom," she adds, "agreed to most of this, but reserved his idea of God." This reservation is crucial, for the conversation was initiated by Eliot's publication of *After Strange Gods,* the work in which he calls most forcefully for a return to a "tradition" grounded in shared but exclusive religious and cultural beliefs ("right tradition") and the practice of "orthodoxy." As John Guillory has pointed out, what started in Eliot as a "violent revisionist impulse" in "Tradition and the Individual Talent" had been transformed by 1934 into "orthodoxy and the literary elite" (176, 184–185). It is here that Woolf differs most strongly from Eliot, as well as Pound and Yeats, all of whom turned, as she herself did during the thirties, to social and political commentary. Unlike these men, she does not locate the origins of the threat to civilization in the loss of Christianity or other forms of systemic belief. Instead she turns a critical eye on the discourses and the impact of a patriarchal culture dedicated to hierarchy, dominance, capitalism, imperialism, and war. The result is her rejection of the orthodoxies and authorities, including those associated with fascism, that so many of her male contemporaries came to accept and even to glorify as the solution to their culture's ills.

What distinguishes Woolf's perspective on tradition and cultural values from these men's is a divided consciousness, or double vision, that is inseparable from her consciousness of herself as a woman and her distrust of priestly male authority. On the one hand, Woolf shared with her male colleagues a sense of her cultural inheritance, the European literary and cultural tradition, that she had access to through her family—in particular her father, Leslie Stephen—and her social class, as well as through the act of reading.[7] On the other hand, Woolf was from the beginning acutely aware of the limited role that women had played—and continued to play—whether as artists and critics, in the creation and transmission of the tradition defined by men. She recognized early both women's marginality and exclusion. Even the British Museum reading room, Woolf's recurring image of the archives of traditional culture, made the message clear; Julia Hedge, struggling to write an essay of her own, stares at the names ringing the dome and asks, "why didn't they leave room for an Eliot or a Bronte?" (*Jacob's Room* 106). In a diary entry written when Woolf was twenty-one, the aspiring writer and critic vividly expresses the dual sense of inheritance and exclusion that constituted women's relationship to their culture. Reading in the country, she muses, "I think I see for a moment how our minds are all threaded together—how any live mind today is . . . of the very same stuff as Plato's and Euripides. It is only a continuation & development of the same thing—It is this common mind that binds the whole world together; & all the world is mind. . . . I feel as though I had grasped the central meaning of the world, & all these poets & historians & philosophers were only following out paths branching from that centre in which I stand." In the city, however, "I read—then I lay down the book—& say—what right have I, a woman, to read all these things that men have done? They would laugh if they saw me."[8]

Twenty-five years later this split consciousness had become for Woolf the source of both women's criticism and their vision. A passage in *A Room of One's Own* that has rightly become an icon of contemporary feminist thought describes how "if one is a woman one is often surprised by a sudden splitting off of consciousness, say in walking down Whitehall, when from being the natural inheritor of that civilisation, she becomes, on the contrary, outside of it, alien and critical" (101). For Woolf, the woman who is turned away from the libraries and chased off the turf at her culture's major universities experiences from within the alienation, or exile, that Edward Said associates with the ability to write a critical narrative of one's culture. Unlike Erich Auerbach, Said's example, whose exile to Turkey enabled him to escape the "authoritative and authorizing agencies" that would have prevented his audacious task of chronicling the whole of the Western cultural tradition, women experience this "critically important alienation" (8) while standing at its political and ideological centers: Whitehall, for example. If culture is equated with place, with "*belonging to* or *in a* place, being *at home in a place*," a form of possession, and the critic has to be "out of place," displaced, or homeless to acquire a critical consciousness (8), then women, denied a place in its public discourses, are among its most discerning critics. Forced into self-awareness and the isolated consciousness that comes from being divided—"out of place but very much *of* that place"—they have the potential to stand "consciously against the prevailing orthodoxy and very much for a professedly universal or humane set of values" (Said 15). In Woolf's perception, expressed most forcefully in *Three Guineas,* women not only can but must exploit the contradictions engendered by their liminality to reveal the partiality of the reigning truths. However "unpleasant it is to be locked out," she (under)states, "it is worse perhaps to be locked in" (*A Room* 24).

In exploring Woolf's inscription of this prophetic insight, I want to focus on her dialogue with Eliot about the location of cultural authority and its construction as a priesthood. I use here Said's analysis of the critic's cultural function and position, his plea for a "secular criticism," which focuses on the modernists and the shift in cultural authority they effected in the beginning of the twentieth century from filiation to affiliation. Rejecting the cultural inheritance handed down to them by their parents (filiation), writers and intellectuals turned instead to the production of alternate systems of relationship, alternate systems of cultural values and belief, that claimed their authority through "institutions, associations, and communities" founded on affiliation (Said 17). But in reauthorizing themselves through these affilations, the modernists reinstituted or reaffirmed a concept of authority that brought with it its own hierarchies, canons, and exclusiveness. One might say, as Eliot did when he chose to call his iconoclastic critical work *The Sacred Wood*—an allusion to the sacred grove where "the priesthood is secured only by murdering the previous encumbent" (Baldick 112)—"the priest is dead; long live the priest."

While Said assumes the participation of women in the modernist shift from filiation to affiliation, he offers no women as examples. But if gender is absent from his critique of this process of shifting authorities, it was only too present to Woolf. However much she agreed with Eliot that "tradition and continuity" were important, she reacted strongly and negatively to the continuing religious cast of his cultural authority and cultural critique, which she associated with patriarchal values and constraints. If Matthew Arnold perceived culture as the new religion and located it in the state and Eliot reclaimed the authority of religion itself for the new clergy, the literary and cultural critics (Guillory 184–185), Woolf wanted to reject the priestly, the religious model, wherever it appeared. In *Jacob's Room,* for example (as Christine Froula has illustrated), she juxtaposes the respectful male response to the authority of a university don to that of "a woman" who, "divining the priest, would, involuntarily, despise" (*Jacob's Room* 41; Froula 321–323).[9] In *Three Guineas,* she responds to her male colleague's request that she join a society pledged to "protect culture and intellectual liberty" with an analysis of how women's experience of these "abstract words" (88) has made her wary of all organized institutions and societies with their credo "shall not, shall not, shall not" (105). Instead, she calls upon women to remain a society of outsiders, preserving their duality of perspective—their critical difference—and using it to envision something new. In Woolf's Outsiders Society there will be no officers, no hierarchies, no authorities, no ceremonies or oaths—only the common goal women share with their brothers, to prevent dictatorship and war (105–106).

One other aspect of the shift from filiative to affiliative authority proved problematic for Woolf, as for other female modernists: the fact that they brought to their analysis of culture a mixed genealogy and had to come to terms not only with the tradition of the fathers but also with the tradition of the mothers that was just beginning to emerge.[10] However much Woolf may have struggled with her literary mothers, however ambiguous she may have been about their art, she was clear that to create a counterculture that could provide alternate values and beliefs to those still espoused by the cultural priests of her day, she had to recover the history of women and their creativity.

History is the key word in Woolf's revisionary project: "we cannot," she declared, "understand the present if we isolate it from the past" (*Pargiters* 8).

Here, as in her insistence in *A Room of One's Own* that literature is "attached to life at all four corners . . . to grossly material things, like health and money and the houses we live in" (43–44), she adopts the teachings of her father, often called the first sociological critic in England, to her own ends. Arguing that writers had to be placed in their social and political contexts, Stephen insists that texts such as letters, diaries, and state papers were as crucial to understanding literary and cultural history as fiction and poetry.[11] Where Woolf differs is in transforming these writings, considered even by Stephen to be of secondary importance, into primary inscriptions of women's creativity.

"The Journal of Mistress Joan Martyn," Woolf's early attempt to write women into culture, establishes many of her recurring themes. In the first section, which I have included below, the medieval historian Rosamond Merridew describes her method and her quarrels with her male colleagues and illustrates her point about the importance of domestic life by recounting her discovery of Joan Martyn's diary. Offered either the household accounts or the stud book by the present male owner of the manor house in Norfolk that had been Joan's home, the historian chooses instead to recuperate the diary of the young woman. This act of recuperation illustrates her methodological premise that reconstructions of daily life, even when an act of imagination is needed to make them, are more than digressions; they recreate the "reality" of the human beings of the period, which is only suggested by the documentary records that all too often omit women.

The diary itself (not reprinted here), which constitutes the second part of the story, records the activities and the thoughts of the women, children, and servants left at home while the father is off in London and the older brothers off at war. The war, at the center of traditional histories and a fact of life for the Martyns, becomes here context, not text. The family priest is present, but more as a companion than a law giver. What emerges are portraits of women who run the estate during the day and read or listen to stories at night. John Lydgate's *Palace of Glass* sets Joan and her mother dreaming of knights and ladies; an itinerant minstrel provides songs for both the gentry and the peasants who gather in the yard to listen to him; and Joan herself, in her last entry, contemplates writing about knights and ladies adventuring in strange lands but sets more store by another form of art: the storytelling of old women that surpasses what is written in books and that serves as a source of community and continuity:

> Such a woman was Dame Elsbeth Aske, who, when she grew too old to knit or stitch & too stiff to leave her chair, sat with clasped hands by the fire all day long, & you had only to pull her sleeve & her eyes grew bright, & she would tell you stories of fights & kings, & great nobles, & stories of the poor people too, till the air seemed to move & murmur. She could sing ballads also; which she made as she sat there. And men & women, old & young, came long distances to hear her; for all that she could neither write nor read. And they thought that she could tell the future too. (267)

Significantly, while both Joan and her father show great pride in the daughter's literacy—her ability to provide a written record for their descendants—the diarist acknowledges and even privileges an oral tradition associated with women. Equally significant, the figures who receive and transmit the cultural heritage are decidedly not authorities. It is not surprising, then, that when Woolf began to prepare her first book of critical essays in 1918, she read the major critics past and present, and acknowledged the scholar, but chose as her model the "common reader."[12] "Byron and Mr. Briggs," conceived as the introductory essay to her projected critical work, illustrates her persistent desire to link literature both to its current readers and to the audience for whom it was produced.

A word needs to be said about Woolf's usage of *common* here. Woolf is clear in "Byron and Mr. Briggs" that her common reader has a certain amount of education as well as access to a good library and contemporary publications. (The "very exceptional bank clerk" she admits to the company might well be a reference to Eliot.) In this sense *common* refers to what is shared by a certain class of individuals, not by the culture as a whole. She is also clear that while gender infuses the responses of men and women to the books they read—the reader-narrator admits that notice of the love interest in Byron's letters, not to mention the sentences, reveals her sex—it does not prohibit a reader's access to the books themselves or deserve particular note. (She does not in this essay address the question of the woman writer.) Finally, while her use of *common* might suggest what readers should share in common, i.e., universally, I would not, as Marianne DeKoven does, associate it with *The Book of Common Prayer;* this resonates more with Eliot's identification of *common* with an institutionalized belief than with Woolf's call for independent judgment and thought.[13] In fact, Woolf's representation of the iconoclastic role of the common reader presents a sharp contrast to the construction of the critic as priest already implicit in Eliot's *Sacred Wood.* What distinguishes old Mr. Briggs and his spiritual sons and daughters is exactly their disregard for the priestly function of critics such as Coleridge and Eliot.

By the time Woolf began to write "Anon" and "The Reader" in 1940, the critical consciousness attributed to the common reader had taken on ideological resonance. Whereas Eliot, appealing deliberately to the "uncommon reader," had declared himself as early as 1928 a classicist, a conservative, and an Anglo-Catholic (*For Lancelot Andrewes* ix), Woolf began to claim more and more forcefully her status as outsider, agnostic, and critic, and to search for a tradition grounded in the heterodox and the inclusive. As is clear from her diary and her letters, Woolf saw the preparation and the writing of her history as a way to counter the destruction occurring all around her. What she searches for, what she claims as common, is not the tradition associated with established institutions or authorities, but what she calls the "song making instinct" and identifies both with the desire to sing and the desire to listen. At the heart of this tradition lies a literature that enacts the mutual strivings of artist and audience rather than the word structures of the solipsistic male voice. "This is continuity," she adds in her "Notes" for "Anon," "certain emotions always in being: felt by people always." "Only when we put two and two together," she declares, "two pencil strokes, two written words, two bricks . . . do we overcome dissolution and set up some stake against oblivion" ("Anon").

One way to understand Woolf's emphatic rejection of Eliot's vision is through her choice of Hugh Latimore, the sixteenth-century Protestant preacher and martyr, as one of the carriers of the cultural tradition she privileges in her text. Eliot had also evoked Latimore in an early declaration of his creed—his essay on "Lancelot Andrewes" (1926)—but only to dismiss him. In Eliot's depiction, Andrewes, bishop of Winchester under James I, is credited with establishing the intellectual authority of the English church. "Compare a sermon by Andrewes," Eliot writes, "with a sermon by another earlier master, Latimer. It is not merely that Andrewes knew Greek, or that Latimer was addressing a far less cultivated public, or that the sermons of Andrewes are peppered with allusion and quotation. It is rather that Latimer . . . is merely a Protestant; but the voice of Andrewes is the voice of a man who has a formed visible Church behind him, who speaks with the old authority and the new culture" (*For Lancelot Andrewes* 18). For Edward Said, to whom this passage signifies Eliot's own claim to "the old authority and new culture," the "merely" is crucial; it denotes Eliot's rejection of the position and the language of "a protesting orphan" and places him, with Andrewes, squarely within the corporate structure of the new Church (18). Woolf, siding with the mere protestor, grants Latimer the critical consciousness essential to the destruction of the castles and towers that wall people in.

In Woolf's portrayal, Latimer speaks with the voice of the outsider and critic; he preaches by the roadside to the common people, uses the common English tongue, and criticizes the established authorities, including the king. "He is public crier," she comments in her reading notes, "also journalist: a kind of representative of the people—licensed to speak out against abuses—a weekly article in a left paper" ("A & R" 410). He belongs squarely in the line of singers and performers who constitute the tradition and the relationship to authority that she associates with Anon. In fact, it is Anon's social isolation and position as outcast that grant him or her the freedom to "say out loud what we feel, but are too proud to admit" ("Anon"); similarly, Anon's ability to tap the reservoir of common feeling and common belief results in tolerance, if not acceptance, by the otherwise divergent social classes who constitute his or her audience. Most important, perhaps, Anon's use, like Latimer's, of the common idiom, English, in contrast to the learned, or aristocratic, tongues—French, Greek, and Latin—speaks eloquently to Woolf's desire to establish the mother tongue as the medium for an alternate cultural discourse.[14]

While most of the producers and transmitters of the common voice named in the essay are men, "Anon" and the various fragments of "The Reader" also chronicle the various ways that women have contributed to the creation of a counterculture. A cryptic comment in her "Notes," "Semiramis—

more on Aspasia—witches and fairies," not only suggests her recurring emphasis on the pressures affecting women of genius but also points to their achievements. The juxtaposition of Semiramis and Aspasia, two women traditionally associated with intellectual and artistic accomplishment, with witches recalls her statement in *A Room of One's Own* that "when . . . one reads of a witch being ducked, of a woman possessed by devils, of a wise woman selling herbs, . . . then I think we are on the track of a lost novelist, a suppressed poet. . . . Indeed, I would venture to guess that Anon, who wrote so many poems without signing them, was often a woman" (50–51).[15] For Woolf, she was also a playwright, Miss La Trobe, the central artist figure in *Between the Acts,* the novel about history, community, continuity, and the role of the artist that Woolf was revising when she began her new critical book. Read in conjunction with the novel, Anon provides a historical ancestry for Miss La Trobe, who is often referred to as "Miss Whatshername" and whose gift for "getting things up"—for bringing out people's talents and for making individuals aware, however momentarily, of the emotions hidden beneath their public faces and roles—earns her acceptance in the community that otherwise scorns and ostracizes her. But even when not artists, women play a crucial role in Woolf's historical narrative as letter writers, as diarists, and, most important, as readers (just as they appear in *Between the Acts* as the playwright's most responsive audience and as voracious, creative readers). When Woolf wanted a figure to embody the birth of the reader, she turned almost instinctively to Lady Anne Clifford.[16]

Ultimately, the presence of an audience responsive to the ancestral memories evoked by Anon emerges as the primary focus of Woolf's speculative history. The traditional works written by university-trained "insiders" might "do a great service like Roman roads," but her "Common History" would pursue what they avoid: "the forests & the will o the wisps" (*Diary* 5: 333). "Try to write lit the other way round," she comments in her "Notes"; "define the influences: the affect; the growth; the surrounding, also the inner current." If one aim was to chart the growth of human consciousness and the desires that lie buried in the human psyche, another was to highlight the material conditions and the social and cultural discourses surrounding the production and reception of art. "Keep a running commentary upon the External," she enjoins herself ("Notes"); for the desire to sing, located at the origins of creation, depends upon the building of the hut, the preservation of the body and social interaction, for it to find a human voice.

By the end of March 1941 the external had become too pressing for Woolf. If her drafts for "The Reader," which are among the last things she wrote, assert that readers are still in existence, they also convey the devastating results of the reader's present absence or silence: "when his attention is distracted, in times of public crisis, the writer exclaims: I can write no more."[17] The powers of greed, evil, violence, and destruction, present even in the world of Anon, had become too strong. Although women, readers, and artists populate Woolf's revisionary cultural narratives and provide an alternate cultural script, the circumstances in 1941 prevented them, in Woolf's perspective, from translating their individual consciousness into action or art. ("Skip present day; A Chapter on the future": "Notes.") Like Robert Burton, author of *Anatomy of Melancholy,* she sat in her room thinking of suicide. But despite her despair, the interconnected images of author, reader, and text that dominate her history and inform even her final musings offer us, her descendants, a vision of inconclusiveness and liminality as powerful strategies for cultural criticism and change.

NOTES

1. Read had reviewed Woolf's biography of *Roger Fry* in the *Spectator,* August 2, 1940. For another analysis of art and exclusion see Woolf, "The Leaning Tower" (1940). I wish to thank Quentin Bell and Angelica Garnett, administrators of the Author's Literary Estate, for their generous permission to reprint the extracts from Woolf's writings that appear in this chapter. In addition, I wish to acknowledge *Twentieth Century Literature* for permission to reprint "The Journal of Mistress Joan Martyn" and sections of " 'Anon' and 'The Reader': Virginia Woolf's Last Essays"; and *Yale Review* for permission to reprint extracts from "Byron and Mr. Briggs."

2. Woolf "conceived" her "idea for a Common History book—to read from one end of lit. including biog; & range at will, consecutively" on September 12, 1940 (*Diary* 5:318). On September 18, she wrote "*Reading at Random/Notes*" at the top of a notebook, in which she recorded a number of ideas for structuring a work she called, tentatively, *Reading at Random* or *Turning the Page.* At the time of her death, she had written a more or less complete version of the first essay, "Anon," and several fragments of the opening of the second essay, "The Reader." The working notes, entitled "Notes for Reading at Random" (and cited here as "Notes"), as well as her reading notes and the drafts for the essays are now housed in the Berg Collection, New York Public Library, and the Monks House Papers, University of Sussex Library. A fuller edition of "Notes for Reading at Random," "Anon," and "The Reader" appear in Silver, " 'Anon' and 'The Reader': Virginia Woolf's Last Essays" (cited as "A & R").

3. In Gordon's biography of Woolf, "counter-history" is associated with "homemakers and artists—the creators of civilization" (161 ff). See also Johnston.

4. I am using the transcription of the story by Susan M. Squier and Louise A. DeSalvo that appears in *Twentieth Century Literature.* See also Susan Dick's edition.

5. I am using the clean copy version of the essay by Edward A. Hungerford that appeared in the *Yale Review.* See also Andrew McNeillie's fuller transcription.

6. Late in her life Woolf also started reading Freud, whose *Civilization and Its Discontents* may well be echoed here; see *Diary* 5:250. For a discussion of Freud's influence on the darkness of Woolf's later vision, see Elizabeth Abel.

7. See, for example, her essay " 'The Countess of Pembroke's Arcadia,' " where she adds her name and her perceptions to "the long succession of readers" extending back to 1655 before sending the book into the future (*CE* I: 19).

8. [Diary] No. 2. Berg Collection. Cited in Silver, *Reading Notebooks* 5–6.

9. Froula also notes that access to priestly or cultural authority is related to power, not sex, and that within this paradigm what defines "men" and "women" is their relation to and attitude toward cultural authority (322–323).

10. See, for example, Gilbert and Gubar's study of the "female affiliation complex."

11. While this belief is expressed in many of Stephen's writings, his lecture to schoolboys, "The Study of English Literature," provides a good source of comparison to Woolf's practice.

12. Woolf began to read criticism and critical theory for the book she originally called *Reading* or *Reading and Writing* at the end of 1918 and continued to read until the work was published as *The Common Reader* in 1925. For references and sources, see Silver, *Reading Notebooks.*

13. In addition to analyzing the use of *common,* DeKoven argues convincingly that the book itself is a "reader" and illustrates how Woolf undermines the authority of Dr. Johnson's pronouncement on the common reader by making her reader judge works by their representation of women.

14. It is worth noting in this respect that Andrewes was a principle translator of the Authorized Version of the Bible. In "Anon," Woolf identifies the lack of a useful, intimate common prose or speech with the influence of the biblical style.

15. Semiramis, patterned on a ninth-century Assyrian queen, was associated during the Hellenistic period with various works of law, literature, and architecture. Aspasia, a hetaira, or courtesan, in fifth-century Athens, was the highly educated companion of Pericles who later owned her own house of women; Plato credited her with writing Pericles' famous funeral oration (*Menexenus*). In *A Room of One's Own* Woolf cites Pericles' comment that "the chief glory of a woman is not to be talked of" in her discussion of how "anonymity runs in [women's] blood" (52).

16. Previously, Lady Anne Clifford and her diary had provided Woolf with details of Elizabethan material life and the education given to noblewomen in the sixteenth century that enabled them to be patrons but not poets; see "The Elizabethan Lumber Room" (1925) and "Donne after Three Centuries" (1932). In "Anon" and "The Reader" she emerges as a figure in her own right.

17. Gordon (259–262) reads "Anon" and "The Reader" as a study of the failure of the contemporary audience to be the kind of common reader that Woolf felt was necessary for creative interaction with the artist. Patricia Joplin explores the other side: the ability of artists, including Miss La Trobe, to incite violence, as in Nazi Germany.

WORKS CITED

This list includes works cited in the selections below.

Abel, Elizabeth. *Virginia Woolf and the Fictions of Psychoanalysis.* Chicago: Chicago UP, 1989.

Bacon, Francis. *Essays and Colours of Good and Evil.* Ed. W. Aldis Wright. London: Macmillan, 1862.

———. *The Letters and Life.* Ed. James A. Spedding. Vol. 1, "Lady Bacon at Gorhambury."

Baldick, Chris. *The Social Mission of English Criticism 1848–1932.* Oxford: Clarendon, 1983.

Chambers, E. K. *The Medieval Stage.* 2 vols. Oxford: Clarendon, 1903.

Chambers, E. K., and F. Sidgwick. *Early English Lyrics.* London: Sidgwick and Jackson, 1926.

Clifford, Lady Anne. *Diary.* Ed. V. Sackville-West. London: Heinemann, 1923.

DeKoven, Marianne. "Virginia Woolf as Critic in *The Common Reader.*" Presented to the Modern Language Association, 1987.

Eliot, T. S. *After Strange Gods: A Primer of Modern Heresy.* New York: Harcourt Brace, 1934.

———. *For Lancelot Andrewes: Essays on Style and Order.* London: Faber and Gwyer, 1928.

Evans, B. Ifor. *A Short History of English Literature.* Harmondsworth: Penguin, 1940.

Froula, Christine. "When Eve Reads Milton: Undoing the Canonical Economy." *Critical Inquiry* 10(1983):321–347.

Gilbert, Sandra, and Susan Gubar. " 'Forward into the Past': The Female Affiliation Complex." *No Man's Land,* vol. 1, 165–226. New Haven: Yale UP, 1988.

Gordon, Lyndall. *Virginia Woolf: A Writer's Life.* New York: Norton, 1984.

Guillory, John. "The Ideology of Canon-Formation: T. S. Eliot and Cleanth Brooks." *Critical Inquiry* 10(1983):173–198.

Harrison, G. B. *An Elizabethan Journal: 1591–1594.* London: Constable, 1928.

———. *Elizabethan Plays and Players.* London: Routledge, 1940.

Harrison, William. *Harrison's Description of England in Shakspere's Youth.* Ed. Frederick J. Furnivall. 2 vols. London: New Shakspeare Society, 1877.

Henslowe, Philip. *Diary.* Ed. Walter W. Greg. 2 vols. London: Bullen, 1904–1908.

Johnston, Judith L. "The Remediable Flaw: Revisioning Cultural History in *Between the Acts.*" In *Virginia Woolf and Bloomsbury: A Centenary Celebration,* ed. Jane Marcus. Bloomington: Indiana UP, 1987.

Joplin, Patricia Klindienst. "The Authority of Illusion: Feminism and Fascism in Virginia Woolf's *Between the Acts.*" *South Central Review* 6(1989):88–104.

Latimer, Hugh. *Fruitfull Sermons.* London: Cotes, 1635.

Malory, Sir Thomas. *Le Morte DArthur.* Including "Preface of William Caxton." Ed. Sir Edward Strachey. London: Macmillan, 1868.

Marlowe, Christopher. *Tamburlaine the Great. Part the First.* In *Elizabethan Tragedy: Six Representative Plays,* ed. George Rylands. London: Bell, 1933.

Newdigate-Newdegate, Lady. *Gossip from a Muniment Room; Being Passages in the Lives of Anne and Mary Fytton 1574 to 1618.* London: David Nutt, 1897.

Read, Herbert. *Annals of Innocence and Experience.* London: Faber and Faber, 1940.

Said, Edward. "Introduction: Secular Criticism." *The World, the Text, and the Critic.* Cambridge: Harvard UP, 1983.

Silver, Brenda R., ed. " 'Anon' and 'The Reader': Virginia Woolf's Last Essays." *Twentieth Century Literature* 25(1979):356–441. Cited in text as "A & R."

———. *Virginia Woolf's Reading Notebooks.* Princeton: Princeton UP, 1983. Cited in text as *Reading Notebooks.*

Spenser, Edmund. *Works.* 4 vols. Ed. J. Payne Collier. London: Bell and Daldy, 1862.

Stephen, Leslie. "The Study of English Literature." *Cornhill Magazine* n.s.8(1887):494–495.

Trevelyan, G. M. *History of England.* London: Longmans, Green, 1926.

Williamson, George C. *Lady Anne Clifford, Countess of Dorset, Pembroke & Montgomery. 1590–1676. Her Life, Letters, and Work.* Kendall: Titus Wilson, 1922.

Woolf, Virginia. Anon. Holograph fragments. Folders 1–3. Typescript fragments. Folders 4–10. Berg Collection, New York Public Library.

———. [Articles, essays, fiction and reviews.] v. 8 [1938–1939]. Berg Collection, New York Public Library.

———. *Between the Acts.* New York: Harcourt Brace, 1941.

———. [Between the Acts] Later typescript. Berg Collection, New York Public Library.

———. "Byron and Mr. Briggs." Ed. Edward A. Hungerford. *Yale Review* 68(1979):321–349.

———. "Byron and Mr. Briggs." Ed. Andrew McNeillie. *The Essays of Virginia Woolf.* Vol. 3: 1919–1924, 473–500. New York: Harcourt Brace Jovanovich, 1988.

———. *Collected Essays.* 4 vols. Harcourt Brace and World, 1966–1967.

———. *The Common Reader.* New York: Harcourt Brace, 1925.

———. *The Diary of Virginia Woolf.* Ed. Anne Olivier Bell. Vols. 4–5. New York: Harcourt Brace Jovanovich, 1982, 1984.

———. [Holograph reading notes] Notes for reading at random. Berg Collection, New York Public Library.

———. *Jacob's Room.* New York: Harcourt, 1922.

———. "The Journal of Mistress Joan Martyn." *The Complete Shorter Fiction,* ed. Susan Dick, 33–62. New York: Harcourt Brace Jovanovich, 1985.

———. "The Journal of Mistress Joan Martyn." Ed. Susan M. Squier and Louise A. DeSalvo. *Twentieth Century Literature* 25(1979):237–269.

———. *Letters.* Vol. 6. Ed. Nigel Nicholson and Joanne Trautmann. New York: Harcourt Brace Jovanovich, 1980.

———. Monks House Papers/A.24e; B.4; B.5c. University of Sussex Library.
———. "Notes for Reading at Random." In Silver, ed., " 'Anon' and 'The Reader,' " 369–379. Cited in text as "Notes."
———. *The Pargiters.* Ed. Mitchell A. Leaska. New York: New York Public Library & Readex Books, 1977.
———. [The Reader] Typescript fragments. Folders 1–5. Typescript fragment. Berg Collection, New York Public Library.
———. *A Room of One's Own.* New York: Harcourt, 1929.
———. T. L. (draft fragment) to Ben Nicholson. Berg Collection, New York Public Library.
———. *Three Guineas.* New York: Harcourt Brace, 1938.

The Journal of Mistress Joan Martyn

My readers may not know, perhaps, who I am. Therefore, although such a practise is unusual & unnatural—for we know how modest writers are—I will not hesitate to explain that I am Miss Rosamond Merridew, aged fortyfive—my frankness is consistent!—& that I have won considerable fame among my profession for the researches I have made into the system of land tenure in mediaeval England. Berlin has heard my name; Frankfurt would give a soireé in my honour; & I am not absolutely unknown in one or two secluded rooms in Oxford & in Cambridge. Perhaps I shall put my case more cogently, human nature being what it is, if I state that I have exchanged a husband & a family & a house in which I may grow old for certain fragments of yellow parchment; which only a few people can read & still fewer would care to read if they could. But as a mother, so I read sometimes not without curiosity in the literature of my sex, cherishes most the ugliest & stupidest of her offspring; so a kind of maternal passion has sprung up in my breast for these shrivelled & colourless little gnomes; in real life I see them as cripples with fretful faces, but all the same, with the fire of genius in their eyes. I will not expound that sentence; it would be no more likely to succeed than if that same mother to whom I compare myself took pains to explain that her cripple was really a beautiful boy, more fair than all his brothers. At any rate, my investigations have made a travelling pedlar of me; save that it is my habit to buy & not to sell. I present myself at old farm houses, decayed halls, parsonages, church vestries always with the same demand. Have you any old papers to show me? As you may imagine the palmy days for this kind of sport are over; age has become the most merchantable of qualities; & the state moreover with its Commissions has put an end for the most part to the enterprise of individuals. Some official, I am often told, has promised to come down & inspect their documents; & the favour of the "State" which such a promise carries with it, robs my poor private voice of all its persuasion.

Still it is not for me to complain, looking back as I can look back, upon some very fine prizes that will have been of real interest to the historian, & upon others that because they are so fitful & so minute in their illumination please me even better. A sudden light upon the legs of Dame Elizabeth Partridge sends its beams over the whole state of England, to the King upon his throne; She wanted stockings! & no other need impresses you in quite the same way with the reality of mediaeval legs; & therefore with the reality of mediaeval bodies, & so, proceeding upward step by step, with the reality of mediaeval brains; & there you stand at the centre of all ages: middle beginning or end. And this brings me to a further confession of my own virtues. My researches into the system of land tenure in the 13th 14th & 15th Centuries have been made doubly valuable, I am assured, by the remarkable gift I have for presenting them in relation to the life of the time. I have borne in mind that the intricacies of land tenure were not always the most important facts in the lives of men & women & children; I have often made so bold as to hint that the subtleties which delight us so keenly were more a proof of our ancestors negligence than a proof of their astonishing painstaking. For what sane man, I have had the audacity to remark, could have spent his time in complicating his laws for the benefit of half a dozen antiquaries who were to be born five centuries after he was in the grave?

We will not here discuss this argument on whose behalf I have given & taken many shrewd blows; I introduce the question merely to explain why it is that I have made all these enquiries subsidiary to certain pictures of the family life which I have introduced into my text; as the flower of all these intricate roots; the flash of all this scraping of flint.

If you read my work called "The Manor Rolls" you will be pleased or disgusted according to your temperament by certain digressions which you will find there.

I have not scrupled to devote several pages of large print to an attempt to show, vivdly as in a picture, some scene from the life of the time; here I knock at the serfs door, & find him roasting rabbits he has poached; I show you the Lord of the Manor setting out on some journey, or calling his dogs to him for a walk in the fields, or sitting in the high backed chair inscribing laborious figures upon a glossy sheet of parchment. In another room I show you Dame Elinor, at work with her needle; & by her on a lower stool sits her daughter, stitching too, but less assiduously. "Child, thy husband will be here before thy house linen is ready" reproves the mother.

Ah, but to read this at large you must study my book! The critics have always threatened me with two rods; first, they say, such digressions are all very well in a history of the time, but they have nothing to do with the system [of] mediaeval land tenure; secondly, they complain that I have no materials at my side to stiffen these words into any semblance of the truth. It is well known that the period I have chosen is more bare than any other of private records: unless you choose to draw all your inspiration from the Paston Letters you must be content to imagine merely, like any story teller. And that, I am told, is a useful art in its place; but it should be allowed to claim no relationship with the sterner art of the Historian. But here, again, I verge upon that famous argument which I carried on once with so much zeal in the Historians Quarterly; We must make way with our introduction, or some wilful reader may throw down the book & profess to have mastered its contents already: O the old story! Antiquaries Quarrels! Let me draw a line here then so ___________ & put the whole of this question of right & wrong, truth & fiction behind me.

On a June morning two years ago, it chanced that I was driving along the Thetford road from Norwich to East Harling. I had been on some expedition, a wild goose chase it was, to recover some documents which I believed to lie buried in the ruins of Caister Abbey. If we were to spend a tithe of the sums that we spend yearly upon excavating Greek cities in excavating our own ruins what a different tale the Historian would have to tell!

Such was the theme of my meditations; but nevertheless one eye, my archaeological eye, kept itself awake to this landscape through which we passed. And it was in obedience to a telegram from this that I leapt up in the carriage, at a certain point & directed the driver to turn sharply to the left. We passed down a regular avenue of ancient elm trees; but the bait which drew me was a little square picture, framed delicately between green boughs at the far end, in which an ancient doorway was drawn distinctly in lines of carved white stone.

As we approached the doorway proved to be encircled by low walls of buff coloured plaster; & on top of them, at no great distance was the roof of ruddy tiles, & finally I beheld in front of me the whole of the dignified little house, built like the letter E with the middle notch smoothed out of it.

Here was one of those humble little old Halls, then, which survive almost untouched, & practically unknown for centuries & centuries, because they are too insignificant to be pulled down or rebuilt; & their owners are too poor to be ambitious. And the descendants of the builder go on living here, with the curious unconsciousness that the house is in any way remarkable which serves to make them as much a part of it, as the tall chimney which has grown black with generations of kitchen smoke. Of course a larger house might be preferable, & I doubt not that they would hesitate to sell this old one, if they had a good offer. But that is the natural, & unselfconscious spirit which proves somehow how genuine the whole thing is. You can not be sentimental about a house you have lived in for 500 years. This is the kind of place, I thought, as I stood with my hand on the bell, where the owners are likely to possess exquisite manuscripts, & sell them as easily [to] the first rag man who comes along, as they would sell their pig wash, or the timber from the park. My point of view is that of a morbid eccentric, after all, & these are the people of healthy nature. Cant they write? they will tell me; & what is the worth of old letters? I always burn mine—or use them to tie over jampots.

A maid came, at last, staring meditatively at me, as though she ought to have remembered my face & my business. "Who lives here?" I asked her, "Mr Martyn" she gaped, as if I had asked the name of the reigning King of England. "Is there a Mrs Martyn, & is she at home, & might I see her?" The girl waved to me to follow, & led me in silence to a person who could, presumably, undertake the responsibility of answering my strange questions.

I was shown across a large hall, panelled with oak, to a smaller room in which a rosy woman of my own age was using a machine upon a pair of trousers. She looked like a housekeeper; but she was, the maid whispered, Mrs Martyn.

She rose with a gesture that indicated that she was not precisely a lady to receive morning calls, but was nevertheless the person of authority, the mistress of the house; who had a right to know my business in coming there.

There are certain rules in the game of antiquary, of which the first & simplest is that you must not state your object at the first encounter. "I was passing by your door; & I took the liberty—I must tell you I am a great lover of the picturesque, to call, on the chance that I might be allowed to look over the house. It seems to me a particularly fine specimen."

"Do you want to rent it, may I ask" said Mrs Martyn, who spoke with a pleasant tinge of dialect.

"Do you let rooms then?" I questioned.

"O no," rejoined Mrs Martyn decisively: "We never let rooms; I thought perhaps you wished to rent the whole house."

"It's a little big for me; but still, I have friends."

"Ah well, then," broke in Mrs Martyn, cheerfully, setting aside the notion of profit, & looking merely to do a charitable act; "I'm sure I should be very pleased to show you over the house—I dont know much about old things myself; & I never heard as the house was particular in any way. Still its a pleasant kind of place—if you come from London." She looked curiously at my dress & figure, which I confess felt more than usually bent beneath her fresh, & somewhat compassionate gaze; & I gave her the information she wanted. Indeed as we strolled through the long passages, pleasantly striped with bars of oak across the white wash, & looked into spotless little rooms with square green windows opening on the garden,—& I saw that the furniture was spare but decent, we exchanged a considerable number of questions & answers. Her husband was a farmer on rather a large scale; but land had sunk terribly in value; & they were forced to live in the Hall now, which would not let; although it was far too large for them, & the rats were a nuisance. The Hall had been in her husbands family for many a year, she remarked with some slight pride; she did not know how long, but people said the Martyns had once been great people in the neighbourhood. She drew my attention to the y. in their name. Still she spoke with the very chastened & clear sighted pride of one who knows by hard personal experience how little nobility of birth avails, against certain material drawbacks, the poverty of the land, for instance, the holes in the roof, & the rapacity of rats.

Now although the place was scrupulously clean, & well kept there was a certain bareness in all the rooms, a prominence of huge oak tables, & an absence of other decorations than bright pewter cups & china plates which looked ominous to my inquisitive gaze. It seemed as though a great deal must have been sold, of those small portable things that make a room look furnished. But my hostesses dignity forbade me to suggest that her house had ever been other than it was at present. And yet I could not help fancying a kind of wistfulness in the way she showed me into rooms that were almost empty, compared the present poverty to days of greater affluence, & had it on the tip of her tongue to tell me that "Things had once been better." She seemed half apologetic, too, as she led me through a succession of bedrooms, & one or two rooms that might have served for sitting rooms if people had had leisure to sit there, as though she wished to show me that she was quite aware of the discrepancy between such a house & her own sturdy figure. All this being as it was, I did not like to ask the questions that interested me most—whether they had any books? & I was beginning to feel that I had kept the good woman from her sewing machine long enough, when she suddenly looked out of the window, hearing a whistle below, & shouted something about coming in to dinner. Then she turned to me with some shyness, but an expression of true hospitality, & begged me to "Sit down to dinner" with them. "John, my husband, knows a sight more than I do of these old things of his, & I know he's glad enough to find some one to talk to. It's in his blood, I tell him" she laughed, & I saw no good reason why I should not accept the invitation. Now John did not fall so easily beneath any recognized heading as his wife did. He was a man of middle age & middle size, dark of hair & complexion, with a pallor of skin that did not seem natural to a farmer; & a drooping moustache which he smoothed slowly with one well shaped hand as he spoke. His eye was hazel & bright, but I fancied a hint of suspicion when its glance rested upon me. He began to speak however, with even more of a Norfolk accent than his wife; & his voice, & dress asserted that he was, in truth if not altogether in appearance, a solid Norfolk farmer.

He nodded merely when I told him that his wife had had the kindness to show me his house. And then, looking at her with a twinkle in his eye he remarked, "If she had her way the old place would be left to the rats. The house is too big, & there are too many ghosts. Eh Betty." She merely smiled, as though her share of the argument had been done long ago.

I thought to please him by dwelling upon its beauties, & its age; but he seemed little interested by my praises, munched largely on cold beef, & adding "ayes" and "noes" indifferently.

A picture, painted perhaps in the time of Charles the First, which hung above his head, has so much the look of him had his collar & tweed been exchanged for a ruff & a silk doublet, that I made the obvious comparison.

"O aye," he said, with no great show of interest, "that's my grandfather; or my grandfathers grandfather. We deal in grandfathers here."

"Was that the Martyn who fought at the Bogne" asked Betty negligently while she pressed me to take another slice of beef.

"At the Bogne" exclaimed her husband, with query and even irritation—"Why, my good woman, your thinking of Uncle Jasper. This fellow was in his grave long before the Bogne. His name's Willoughby," he went on speaking to me, as though he wished me to understand the matter thoroughly; because a blunder about such a simple fact was unpardonable, even though the fact itself might not be of great interest.

"Willouby Martyn: born 1625 died 1685: he fought at Marston Moor as Captain of a Troop of Norfolk men. We were always royalists. He was exiled in the Protectorate, went to Amsterdam; bought a bay horse off the Duke of Newcastle there; we have the breed still; he came back here at the Restoration, married Sally Hampton—of the Manor, but they died out last generation, & had six children, four sons & two daughters. He bought the Lower Meadow you know Betty" he jerked at his wife, to goad her unaccountably sluggish memory.

"I call him to mind well enough now" she answered, placidly.

"He lived here all the last part of his life; died of small pox, or what they called small pox then; & his daughter Joan caught it from him. They're buried in the same grave in the church yonder." He pointed his thumb, & went on with his dinner. All this was volunteered as shortly & even curtly as though he were performing some necessary task, which from long familiarity had become quite uninteresting to him; though for some reason he had still to repeat it.

I could not help showing my interest in the story, although I was conscious that my questions did not entertain my host.

"You seem to have a queer liking for these old fathers of mine" he commented, at last, with an odd little scowl of humorous irritation. "You must show her the pictures after dinner, John," put in his wife; "& all the old things."

"I should be immensely interested," I said, "but I must not take up your time."

"O John knows a quantity about them; he's wonderful learned about pictures."

"Any fool knows his own ancestors, Betty;" growled her husband; "still, if you wish to see what we have, Madam, I shall be proud to show you." The courtesy of the phrase, & the air with which he held the door open for me, made me remember the 'y' in his name.

He showed me round the Hall, pointing with a riding crop to one dark canvas after another; & rapping out two or three unhesitating words of description at each; they were hung apparently in chronological order, & it was clear in spite of the dirt & the dark that the later portraits were feebler examples of the art, & represented less distinguished looking heads. Military coats became less & less frequent, & in the 18th century the male Martyns were represented [in] snuff coloured garments of a homely cut, & were briefly described as "Farmers" or "him who sold the Fen Farm" by their descendant. Their wives & daughters at length dropped out altogether, as though in time a portrait had come to be looked upon more as the necessary appendage of the head of the house, rather than as the right which beauty by itself could claim.

Still, I could trace no sign in the man's voice that he was following the decline of his family with his riding crop, for there was neither pride nor regret in his tone; indeed it kept its level note, as of one who tells a tale so well known that the words have been rubbed smooth of meaning.

"Theres the last of them—my father" he said at length, when we had slowly traversed the four sides of the Hall; I looked upon a crude canvas, painted in the early 60ties I gathered, by some travelling painter with a literal brush. Perhaps the unskilful hand had brought out the roughness of the features; & the harshness of the complexion; had found it easier to paint the farmer than to produce the subtle balance which one might gather, blent in the father as in the son. The artist had stuffed his sitter into a black coat, & wound a stiff white tie round his neck; the poor gentleman had never felt at ease in them, yet.

"And now, M[r] Martyn," I felt bound to say, "I can only thank you, & your wife for . . ."

"Stop a moment," he interrupted, "we're not done yet. There are the books."

His voice had a half comic doggedness about it; like one who is determined, in spite of his own indifference to the undertaking, to make a thorough job of it.

He opened a door & bade me enter a small room, or rather office; for the table heaped with papers, & the walls lined with ledgers, suggested the room where business is transacted by the master of an estate. There were pads and brushes for ornament; & there were mostly dead animals, raising lifeless paws, & grinning, with plaster tongues, from various brackets & cases.

"These go back beyond the pictures;" he said, as he stopped & lifted a great parcel of yellow papers with an effort. They were not bound, or kept together in any way, save by a thick cord of green silk, with bars at either end; such as you use to transfix bundles of greasy documents—butchers bills, & the years receipts.

"Thats the first lot," he said ruffling the leaves with his fingers, like a pack of cards; "that's no 1:1480 to 1500:" I gasped, as anyone may judge: but the temperate voice of Martyn reminded me that enthusiasm was out of place, here; indeed enthusiasm began to look like a very cheap article when contrasted with the genuine thing.

"Ah indeed; that's very interesting; may I look?" was all I said, though my undisciplined hand shook a little when the bundle was carelessly dropped into it. M[r] Martyn indeed offered to fetch a duster before desecrating my white skin; but I assured him it was of no consequence, too eagerly perhaps, because I had feared that there might be some more substantial reason why I should not hold these precious papers.

While he bent down before a book case, I hastily looked at the first inscription on the parchment. "The Journal of Mistress Joan Martyn," I spelt out, "kept by her at Martyn's Hall, in the county of Norfolk the year of our Lord 1480."

"My grandmother Joans diary" interrupted Martyn, turning round with his arm full of books. "Queer old Lady she must have been. I could never keep a diary myself. Never kept one beyond the 10th of February, though I tried often. But here you see," he leant over me, turning the pages, & pointing with his finger, "here is January, February, March, April—so on—a whole twelve months."

"Have you read it, then?" I asked, expecting, nay, hoping that he would say no.

"O yes, I've read it;" he remarked casually, as though that were but a simple undertaking. "It took me some time to get used to the writing, & the old girls spelling—is odd. But there are some queer things in it. I learnt a deal about the land from her, one way & another." He tapped it meditatively.

"Do you know her history too?" I asked.

"Joan Martyn," he began in the voice of a showman, "was born 1495. She was the daughter of Giles Martyn. She was his only daughter. He had three sons though; we always have sons. She wrote this Diary when she was 25: She lived here all her life—never married. Indeed she died at the age of 30. I daresay you might see her tomb down there with the rest of them."

"Now this" he said, touching a thick book bound in parchment, "is more interesting to my mind. This is the household book of Jasper for the year 1583. See how the old gentleman kept his accounts; what they eat & drank; how much meat & bread & wine cost; how many servants he kept—his horses, carriages, beds, furniture, everything. There's method for you. I have a set of ten of them." He spoke of them with greater pride than I had heard him speak of any of his possessions yet.

"This one too makes good reading of a winters night" he went on, "This is the Stud book of Willoughby; you remember Willoughby."

"The one who bought the horse of the Duke, & died of small pox," I repeated glibly.

"That's so," he nodded. "Now this is really fine stuff this one." He went on, like a conoisseur, talking of some favourite brand of port. "I wouldn't sell this for £20. Here are the names & the pedigrees,—lives—values—descendants; all written out like a bible." He rolled some of the strange old names of these dead horses upon his tongue, as though he relished the sound like wine. "Ask my wife if I cant tell 'em all without the book" he laughed, shutting it carefully & placing it on the shelf.

"These are the Estate books; they go down to this year; there's the last of 'em. Here's our family history." He unrolled a long strip of parchment, upon which an elaborate genealogical tree had been inscribed, with many faded flourishes & extravagances of some mediaeval pen. The boughs spread so widely by degrees, that they were lopped unmercifully by the limits of the sheet—a husband depending, for instance, with a family of 10 children & no wife. Fresh ink at the base of all recorded the names of Jasper Martyn, my host, & his wife Elizabeth Clay: they had three sons. His finger travelled sagaciously down the tree, as though it were so well used to this occupation that it could almost be trusted to perform it by itself. Martyns voice murmured on as though it repeated a list of Saints or Virtues in some monotonous prayer.

"Yes," he concluded, rolling up the sheet & laying it by, "I think I like those two best. I could say them through with my eyes shut. Horses or Grandfathers!"

"Do you study here a great deal then?" I asked, somewhat puzzled by this strange man.

"I've no time for study, he returned, rather roughly, as tho' the farmer cropped up in him at my question. "I like to read something easy in the winter nights; & in the morning too, if I wake early. I keep them by my bed sometimes. I say them to send myself to sleep. It's easy to know the names of ones own family. They come natural. But I was never any good at book learning, more's the pity."

Asking my permission, he lit a pipe & began puffing forth great curls of smoke, as he ranged the volumes in order before him. But I kept No One, the bundle of parchment sheets, in my hand, nor did he seem to miss it from the rest.

"You would be sorry to part with any of these, I daresay?" I hazarded, at last, covering my real eagerness with an attempt at a laugh.

"Part with them?" he returned, "what should I part with them for?" The idea was evidently so remote that my question had not, as I feared, irritated his suspicions.

"No, no," he went on, "I find them far too useful for that. Why, Madam, these old papers have stood out for my rights in a court of law before now; besides, a man likes to keep his family round him; I should feel—well kind of lonely if you take my meaning, without my Grandfathers & Grandmothers, & Uncles & Aunts." He spoke as though he confessed a weakness.

"O" I said, "I quite understand—"

"I daresay you have the same feeling yourself Madam & down here, in a lonely place like this, company means more than you could well believe. I often think I should'nt know how to pass the time, if it were'nt for my relations."

No words of mine, or attempts at a report of his words, can give the curious impression which he produced, as he spoke, that all these "relations" Grandfathers of the time of Elizabeth, nay Grandmothers of the time of Edward the Fourth were just, so to speak, brooding round the corner; There was none of the pride of "ancestry" in his voice but merely the personal affection of a son for his parents. All generations seemed bathed in his mind in the same clear & equable light: it was not precisely the light of the present day, but it certainly was not what we commonly call the light of the past. And it was not romantic, it was very sober, & very broad & the figures stood out in it, solid & capable, with a great resemblance, I suspect, to what they were in the flesh.

It really needed no stretch of the imagination to perceive that Jasper Martyn might come in from his farm & his fields, & sit down here alone to a comfortable gossip with his "relations"; whenever he chose; & that their voices were very nearly as audible to him as those of the labourers in the field below, which came floating in, upon the level afternoon sunlight through the open window.

But my original intention of asking whether he would sell, almost made me blush when I remembered it now: so irrelevant & so impertinent. And also, strange though it may seem, I had lost for the time my proper antiquarian zeal; all my zest for old things, & the little distinguishing marks of age, left me, because they seemed the trivial & quite immaterial accidents of large substantial things. There was really no scope for antiquarian ingenuity in the case of Mr Martyn's ancestors, anymore than it needed an antiquary to expound the history of the man himself.

They are, he would have told me, all flesh & blood like I am; & the fact that they have been dead for four or five centuries makes no more difference to them, than the glass you place over a canvas changes the picture beneath it.

But on the other hand, if it seemed impertinent to buy it, it seemed natural, if perhaps a little simpleminded, to borrow.

"Well Mr Martyn," I said at length, with less eagerness & less trepidation than I could have thought possible under the circumstances, "I am thinking of staying for a week or so in this neighbourhood—at The Swan at Gartham indeed—I should be much obliged to you if you would lend me these papers to look through during my stay. This is my card. Mr. Lathom, (the great landowner of the place) will tell you all about me." Instinct told me that M[r] Martyn was not the man to trust the benevolent impulses of his heart.

"O Madam, theres no need to bother about that;" he said, carelessly, as though my request were not of sufficient importance to need his scrutiny. "If these old papers please you, I'm sure your welcome to 'em." He seemed a little surprised, however, so that I added,

"I take a great interest in family histories, even when they're not my own."

"It's amusing eno', I daresay, if you have the time" he assented politely; but I think his opinion of my intelligence was lowered.

"Which would you like" he asked, stretching his hand towards the Household Books of Jasper; & the Stud book of Willoughby.

"Well I think I'll begin with your grandmother Joan" I said; "I like beginning at the beginning."

"O very well," he smiled; "though I don't think you'll find anything out of the way in her; She was very much the same as the rest of us—as far as I can see, not remarkable—"

But all the same, I walked off with Grandmother Joan beneath my arm; Betty insisted upon wrapping her in brown paper, to disguise the queer nature of the package, for I refused to let them send it over as they wished, by the boy who took the letters—on his bicycle.

Ed. Susan M. Squier & Louise A. DeSalvo. *Twentieth Century Literature* 25 (1979): 240–251.

From "Byron and Mr. Briggs"

3.

We are on the brink of a serious argument; but with a little circumspection, it may be possible to keep on the outskirts. The qualities that a book should contain in the abstract, the qualities that it does contain in the flesh, have been discussed and analysed from the times of Aristotle to the present moment. Aristotle, Dryden, Addison, Johnson, Coleridge, Boileau, Keats, Sainte Beuve, Matthew Arnold, Taine, Anatole France, Remy de Gourmont—to go no further, have all said their say and said it (as one feels in reading them) with a conviction which is only roused in men's minds, and conveyed to the minds of others, when they have been looking on the truth. That this truth is never the same for two generations, or for two human beings,—let alone for two human beings of genius—is a fact which may be distressing, if you wish to get the matter settled once and for all; but has to be faced. At any rate differences of critical theory and differences of critical judgment are by this time sufficiently notorious. Any parrot can repeat the usual string of blunders. Johnson ridiculed Tristram Shandy. Arnold thought Shelleys letters better than his poetry. Coleridge fell prostrate at the feet of Mr Bowles. The parrot has said enough. Then, any pig can sort the critics into schools. There is the biographic; the psychological; the socio-political; the historical; the aesthetic; the impressionist; the scientific; the analytic. Doubtless there are more; but each can be traced back to some man of genius who was so convinced of the truth of what he saw that he imposed his conviction upon others. But the men who read in this way, with an overmastering bias in this that or the other direction, are the critics. Pelt them with volumes taken from each of the twenty seven divisions into which modern literature is divided and they will somehow order them into conformity with a principle arrived at by reading, and reasoning, and the light of individual genius. But the reviewer never penetrates deep enough to lay hold upon a principle. Like a man in a shooting gallery, he sees books move steadily past him. Bang! He lets fly. The rabbit is missed; but he has only just time to reload before taking aim at the pheasant.

Therefore it is useless to look in any scrap book of old reviews for a method. You may find a personality, but that is quite a different thing, and (with E. K. Sanders at the back of my mind) I should like to discover what the value of a reviewer is, taking it for granted that he has no method, but only a personality—that he is in short much nearer the ordinary reader, of whom there are multitudes, than the critic of whom, with great luck, there is one in a century.

4.

But the common reader is a person of great importance. Dr Johnson rejoiced "to concur with the common reader; for by the common sense of readers, uncorrupted with literary prejudices, after all the refinements of subtilty and the dogmatism of learning, must be finally decided all claim to poetical honours." In an age without a critic, [and there is none to be found in England at the moment,] literature both past and present must rest in the hands of the people who continue to read it. Milton is alive in the year 1922 and of a certain size and shape only because some thousands of insignificant men and women are holding his page at this moment before their eyes. But when Coleridge was lecturing about Shakespeare, or Dryden was writing about poetry, common opinion had an influence to guide it. You shut your Shakespeare and went to hear Coleridge; you read the preface to [long blank] and your judgment of poetry was shaped accordingly. But to have this effect, an influence must be powerful. Acting first upon the scholars and reviewers it must by them be spread abroad among the multitude. In our time there are scholars by the score and reviewers by the thousand; but there is no critic to point the way.

5.

General statements are convenient and no doubt sometimes they are true. But this one has in it obvious elements of falsehood should you descend from the general to the particular—should you look into the way in which reading is commonly done now, and not imagine how it was done a hundred years ago by old Mr Briggs who drove up from Kensington to hear Coleridge in snowy weather, only to find that Coleridge had forgotten to come.

The truth is that reading is kept up because people like reading. The common reader is formidable and respectable and even has power over great critics and great masterpieces in the long run because he likes reading and will not let even Coleridge do his reading for him. How many thousands I know not, but certainly there are many thousands who never pick up a book on a bookstall for half a minute without getting some kind of shock from it. Expose them to something violent, like King Lear, and the shock entirely obliterates Aristotle, Dryden, Addison, Johnson, Coleridge, Boileau, Diderot, Sainte-Beuve &c &c. The whole hierarchy is powerless to unseat the judgment of an ignorant boy or girl who has read the play to the end. It is all very well, when the impression has spent itself, to take down Coleridge and Coleridge will delight and instruct, but only in the margin of the mind. It is I who have read the play. I hold it in my brain. I am directly in touch with Shakespeare. No third person can explain or alter or even throw much light upon our relationship.

This then is the very heart of the business—it is this which sends the blood coursing through the whole of the old book & the new. It is this which raises libraries and draws up out of the air myriads upon myriad of new books. But it is an unguided passion, voluntary individual & lawless and thus capable of doing enormous harm as a glance at contemporary literature will prove. Take the case of Mr Briggs for example (1795–1859). He was convinced by the eloquent Mr Coleridge that Measure for Measure was the most painful of Shakespeares plays "like-wise degrading to the character of women"; but next time he read Measure for Measure he had forgotten what Coleridge said; or his own ideas seemed fresher or his wife bounced into the study & kissed him on the top of the head that very moment. At any rate Coleridges principles, eloquent, profound, and original as they were, applied to old poetry, to poetry in general, and Mr Briggs never once thought of Coleridge when he laid it down a few weeks later that this new book by Mr Keats was trash.

6.

And Briggs' grandchildren? This spectacle maker of Cornhill with his taste for literature and this loathing for Keats left a large number of descendants. Many have gone out into the world and fought and conquered and made money and died rather honourably in obscure Indian villages with nothing but a copy of

Dickens and or a little volume of Shakespeare to keep them company. A taste for reading is very hard to kill. At the same time, how are we to say what it amounts to in the flesh? Briggs the Colonel died with his Shakespeare; but never formulated his views upon the poetic drama. Briggs the stockbroker read Darwin; and burnt Swinburne. Mrs Briggs (who was a Grant from Dundee) knew the Waverley novels by heart but she could never abide George Eliot. Between them the different generations must have devoured half the London Library and the whole of Mudies. Silently, voraciously, like a locust or a caterpillar. As for leaving any record of their opinions save by crosses and notes of exclamation in the margin (which staffs of librarians are always engaged in rubbing out) that was, and that is, none of their business. They read then for pleasure; they read now for pleasure; and if you catch them laying down the law in private about Mr Wells' latest or Mr Joyce's most outrageous, they do it violently enough; but always with a sort of shrug of the shoulders as if to say "That's what I think. But who am I?"

It would be difficult to persuade the grandchildren of Briggs who knew Coleridge that Dr Johnson respected them: that they decide all claim to poetical honours: that their views matter so much as to be gone into at some length and made the subject of a book by a distant relation.

Yet that was the conclusion to which my reading of old newspaper articles finally led me. The views of the grandchildren of Briggs matter; and we reviewers are, almost all of us, [descended from the spectacle maker of Cornhill.] The genealogists may dispute this claim; but if one has waited for three weeks to get Byrons letters from the Library, then, according to my definition, one is a grandchild of Briggs.

[7.]
x x x x x x

Byron was a fine bold boy and wrote far better letters from abroad than his people had a right to expect. He should have stayed an undergraduate for ever, dominating his own group but strictly kept in order by Kinnaird & Hobhouse; also here are women; and he must needs be a man of the world, and learn the trade from that tight lipped hard faced prosaic peeress Lady Melbourne who soon brought out the worst of him,—the dancing master and dandy, so proud of his conquests though so obviously ashamed of his foot. Caroline Lamb, insane but generous, would have made a better wife than the mathematical Miss Milbanke. The big boy who limped off the field in a rage because he had been clean bowled for two or three runs needed what women call "managing." But what woman could give it him? He was dangerous; a treacherous lap dog. In the midst of sentiment down came the sledge hammer of fact. Who could be more unflinching and direct? Indeed one is inclined to wonder why he thought himself a poet. Presumably the fashion of the age dictated, and Byron was impressed by fashions. Yet his description of the Wedderburne affair proves, what his poetry hints, that prose was his medium; satire his genius. He goes to Venice, and is there a single phrase to show that he saw it? Does he even momentarily abstract himself from the Countesses and the Carnivals to think, on the Lido, as Wordsworth thought in rustic Cumberland, how she had held the gorgeous East in fee, and men must mourn when even the showod [*sic.* shadow?] of what once was great has passed away? No such phrase, with its aloofness, contemplation, and solicitude for the fate of mankind in general is possible from Byron. All is immediate, personal, and of this world. Yet it would be difficult to rank Don Juan much lower than the Prelude or to forget hours spent racing before the wind through Byrons Cantos, when Wordsworths stanzas lay cold, unruffled, shut in and shadowed by the rocks of his own self-centredness.

Byron was a novelist—that is to say he came at his conception through his observation of actual life; whereas a poet thinks of life in general, or so intensely of his own in particular as to include the general experience. This he expresses in language exact and enduring. Byron on the other hand writes the perfection of prose. Compare, for example, his letters with the stiff and stilted compositions by Shelley here, unfortunately, placed beside them. Sir Timothy's conduct is (for the first time) intelligible. To have this prig for one's son, to listen to his preachings intolerable. But Mary loved him. She can hardly write for fury that a servant girl should slander him, and meeting Mrs Hoppner in the street cut her dead. All this must have seemed rather extreme and a little bourgeois to Byron; whose range was so wide, whose grasp was so vigorous, whose blood was so blue. And so he frittered his life away; and grew very bitter before the end, which was in the grand style, as the death of Ajax was; fate bowling him out before he had made half the runs he should have made. And up fly our caps as he limps off the field in a rage.

x x x x x x

Let us pull this page to pieces observing that it was written quickly, not from notes but from recollection, and is an attempt to give an impression remaining in the mind an hour or two after finishing a book. Some reading is implied, more than could be expected of a working man, or of any but a very exceptional bank clerk. On the other hand, no Byron expert and no scholar could write so carelessly. A critic would have disregarded all the personalities and would have fixed upon the aesthetic problems here glimpsed and brushed aside. But it has, in spite of compression, one very marked and for our purposes very important characteristic. The reader has obviously from the first page to the last read with a view to forming a whole. As each page is turned you can see him hastily rigging up, from reading or experience, something to serve for background; roughly setting the characters in action, deciding, ordering their relations; making a dart at their qualities; hazarding a guess at the character of literature; and shaping the whole little world as it grows in his mind into likeness with some conception which he derives partly from his time (he is pagan, not Christian) partly from private experiences and qualities peculiar to himself. "He", do we say? But it is obvious from the shape of each sentence, from the tilt [& atmosphere & proportion of the whole] that he is a woman. "But Mary loved him". The cat is out of the bag, and since no one can put her back again had better be given the run of the house.

But the writer's sex is not of interest; nor need we dwell upon the peculiarities of temperament which make one person's reading of Byron's letters different from another's. It is the quality that they have in common that is interesting—that the reading of ordinary readers has in common, that is to say, for it is clear that scholars and critics read differently, in a way of their own.

8.

To make a whole—it is that which we have in common. Our reading is always urged on by the instinct to complete what we read, which is, for some reason, one of the most universal and profound of our instincts. You may see it at work any night among the passengers in a third class railway carriage. Is he related to the woman opposite? No they work in the same office. In love then? No; she wears a wedding ring. Going home then to the same suburb? Ah, yes. "We shall meet on Tuesday". A bridge party no doubt. . . . "I'm sure it would pay to start another hotel there" from which it appears that they belong to a group of people in the habit of going to St Andrews to play golf in the summer.

Everyone plays this familiar game. Everyone feels the desire to add to a single impression the others that go to complete it. Here a mans face catches the attention; instinctively you give him character, relationships, occupation, habits, desires, until some sort of completeness is achieved. There [must be] something disagreeable to the mind in allowing an impression of any force to remain isolated. It must at once [be] made habitable for others; one must, for ones own comfort, have a whole in ones mind: fragments are unendurable. So it is in reading Byron's letters. There too, in the impression quoted we see the same desire at work to complete, to supply background, relationship, motive, while we are rounding the whole with a running commentary which flings out at the end, "Fate bowled him unfairly. Up fly our caps, as he limps off the field in a rage."

The book is finished: so too, the train reaches Putney. Our fellow passengers get out, but not before we are fairly easy in our minds about them. They have their lives; they have their place in the scheme.—although we have to admit that our attention was intermittent, that we read a column in the evening newspaper, and that after the woman said "We shall meet on Tuesday" a glaring red theatre shot up on the right; a backstreet in Wandsworth was illuminated; so that the three dots which mark the interruption of this splendour and misery threw some strange significance upon the man's next remark that it would pay to start a hotel there.

It is hardly necessary to say that such wholes as these are extremely imperfect, & probably highly inaccurate. Very likely there was not a word of truth in our re-construction of the travellers lives. Certainly if we examine the fragment on Byrons letters we shall find slips enough in five hundred words to infuriate a scholar. Byron did not make "two or three runs"; Wordsworth did not live in "rustic Cumberland" when he wrote the sonnet On the Extinction of the Venetian Republic here misquoted; The Prelude is not strictly speaking written in stanzas; and the use of metaphors to convey critical judgments is generally an attempt to conceal under artificial flower vagueness and poverty of thought. That is all true; and to write of facts inaccurately is to impair the validity, even artistic value of the [writing] and no one would be so foolish as not to wish it otherwise. But given our conditions, given our education, it is inevitable; given above all those two instincts which are so deeply implanted in our souls—the instinct to complete; the instinct to judge. Give us a fragment and we will make a whole of it; give us a book and we will judge it for ourselves.

9.

Thus then in some such terms as this perhaps the common reader may be defined; but who shall say anything about his partner in the enterprise—this vast, bewildering, uncharted, perpetually increasing and changing volume of literature? Twenty seven divisions, we say, have been driven through the mass; but what if they are not water tight? if biography leaks through into history and history into fiction, and criticism is stained with the juice of them all? In what sense can we talk, even lazily over the fire, of making a whole? To make a whole even of one man, Lord Byron, must we not have read some three hundred volumes, and a good many papers still waiting to be published?

Ed. Edward A. Hungerford. *Yale Review* 68 (1979). 327–335.

Notes for Reading at Random

18th Sept 19[3]40

Reading at Random. or Turning the Page
Notes.

To begin with English country before Eth [Elizabeth]
The effect of country upon writers. Hall. Holingshed.[1]
The idea of the book is to find the end of a ball of
string & wind out. Let one book suggest another.
Keep to time sequence. Pass from criticism to biography.

Lives of people. Always follow the genuine scent—the
idea of the moment. No 'periods': No text book.
Read very widely Write rather from memory.

Oct 3rd
The Life of a Book.
Take a living book & trace, vanishing; its family:
But wh. book? But keep very free.
Harrisons State of England.[2]
His mastiff. Months with an R in them.
How many departments a person has: needing historians,
psychologists, poets &c. to interpret.
The forces telling on H. his attitude toward the court, the
Church. His regrets for logs of wood as pillows.
Squire Waterton. The continuity of tradition. The RC
Church as a carrier. Harrison seen by Furnivall. What F
paid for butter in 1878. The infection; also the medium.
The snatch of song: If I were in my castle of Boverly.
The song making instinct. The map of London.
Alfred Tennyson, Mrs GH Lewes had suggested: a
meeting was held in March . . . in Gower St. at 8.
This is continuity—the [*extension*] certain emotions always in
being: felt by people always.

---

for the 19th century. Aug. [Augustus] Hare. his mother (repulsive)
Scene illustrating Henry James's subject. Osbert on
Two Generations. Sitwell meets Hare.[3]

* * *

Crot, Ninn, & Pulley—the 3 influences.
Might <begin> be a fictitious review of a [*book*] hist. of Eng. Lit.
What it omits. Try to write lit the other way round.
define the influences: the affect; the growth; the
surrounding, also the inner, current all left out in
text books. Written for Pulley. Semiramis—more on
Aspasia—witches & fairies.
Division of novelists into ventriloquists: soliloquists.
What is creation? The [*old in*] Mr Fs aunt.
The virtue of our age that people dont rest on their
laurels. Perpetually broken up. Renewing. No
conclusions. Perhaps the necessary effect of coming

continuing after so many other writers: a great choice of models—examples. For instance, Reads admiration for Ruskin . .[4] Reviving the old fashions: No great poet. See Yeats. The times too big?—or too close to us—for great poetry.

Ideas for the shape of the book.
To begin with the country. The eye the youthful sense. Our floods. This brings back the wildness.
Out of doors. Indoors. no study no library.
Songs sung at the door.
The importance of the audience.
No public, in our sense.
Anonymity.
The song . . the call to our primitive instincts.
Rhythm—Sound. Sight.
Harrison: at the right distance, at last, to see England. No one looked before that.
Piers Ploughman. (after Chaucer)
This first chapter. [*Th*] Some single figure—Bess of Hardwick.[5]
The pageant. The Masque. The play.

* * *

The song singers. About Sh^{re} [Shakespeare]: the person is consumed: S^{re} never breaks the envelope. We dont want to know about him: Completely expressed. When the incantation ceases, we see the person.
That opera took over the poetic play?

---

separate article.
Goldsmith. The patron.
Congreve . . . The French. Madame de Sévigné.
Group: La R^{d}. [La Rochefoucauld] &c.
Gibbon . . .
Capt. Marryatt.[6]

19th Century. The scene fr. [from] which Henry James took his material. Memoirs
—Single figures. all cut off—compared with E^{thans}.

Coleridge.

[*The Fren*] The 19th Cent. to consist of outlines of people.
Skip present day.
A Chapter on the future.

* * *

From Duncan & Vanessa yesterday I got this idea. A
book explaining lit. from our common standpoint, to painters.
This wd. then be the angle. [*Our*] It would begin
from the writers angle . . That is: we all feel
the desire to create. The curiosity to know about
others in the same condition. This wd. lead to
an introduction: about the germ of creation: its
thwartings: our society: interruption: conditions.
Can we then see the others, in the same state—
I shd. therefore take a poem & build up round it
the society wh. [*c*] helps it. I shd. take a
very old anon. poem. I shd. distinguish between
the actual scene: the weather: the house; the
patron; society: make it chronological.
Often deviate. Bring in Latin. Italy—Greece.

The universality of the creative instinct . . .
Stone, wool, words paint. discuss words.
Always keep the writer in the foreground. Make out a
rough plan of the different helps & hindrances:
A sketch—a guess.

The patron. The girl at the door. The wind & the rain.

Evolve [on] the town: the Great house. Fill
England with people. Take samples. [*No*] Both of
art & of the outer pressure.
Then increase the number of figures.
Describe the growth of London. The small country town.
The audience at the play. At the fire side.
Keep a running commentary upon the External.
The "modern" . . the growth of articulateness.
The split into several languages for writers.

Advertisements. Reviews: travel. Society. Make a
sketch of 19th Cent. society . .

* * *

1. Anon.
2. [*The audience*] The ear & the eye.
3. The individual. 3. The audience.
4. Words?

[*The eye & the*]
The ear & the eye.

Music . . rhythm. The young ladies singing
[*The*] The chorus. The sound. The song coming in.
The nonsense. The Beauty. something very deep—
primitive. not yet extinct.
The eye. Spenser. The pictures.
Spenser. The Renaissance . . . looking across? at Italy.
Allegory—making thoughts visible . . .

The connection between seeing & writing:
Michael Angelo. Leonardo. Blake. Rossetti.
a twin gift. Wh. shall be born. depends on
Nin Crot & Pulley.
The writer never becomes a musician . . .
too technical?
What is "manner" in writing—Manners—the influence of the patron.

* * *

The big house where the book is read.
description of Penshurst. Of Lady Rich: Lady. Bess of Hardwick.
Sir P Sidney. Spenser.

The artist.
Language.
What [*works*] tells on an artist: the thing seen: the framework:
the eye. the ear: the senses:

the thing properly ended.
the individual. the soul.
The difference between reading & seeing: acting:
the word heard. Its solidity: its depths.
How an actor cuts deeper to the bone.
The anonymous element in the play.

Chaucer: the society he wrote for small & noble.
took his points. hit off real people.

Society.
The relation between the small house & the big.
The E^{than} psychology.
Witches.
The nimbus of ignorance. And no Eng^{sh} past.

The writer—[*the f*] what is his mark? That he
enjoys dispassionately: has a split in his consciousness?
The condition of the E^{tn} [Elizabethan] writer who had no
literary past; only read classics in translation
Did Sh^{re} [Shakespeare] read Chaucer?
Irresponsibility. Words without associations.
no conventions: no deference: cd. invent—

When [*di*] was the first theatre built?
The theatre for those who cant read.
brought in pit & gallery. But did the
nobles 'go to the play'?

* * *

Influence of the bible on prose. The biblical style limited
& emphatic.
The untaught wrote more as we do—the Bacon letters
She quotes Latin & Greek. The servant is racy

" 'Anon' and 'The Reader': Virginia Woolf's Last Essays." Brenda R. Silver. *Twentieth Century Literature* 25(1979):373–379.

NOTES

The title "Notes for Reading at Random" is written on a piece of tape stuck on the cover of the notebook in which Woolf recorded her ideas for her new book. Most if not all of the entries were made before Woolf started writing "Anon" on November 24, 1940; the title "or Turning the Page" was added after the original entry was made. The notes consist of seven unnumbered manuscript pages; the *** in the text indicates page breaks. The transcription of the entries approximates as closely as possible their appearance in the manuscript. The following editorial symbols and abbreviations appear in "Notes for Reading at Random," "Anon," and "The Reader":

[word]	= a reading editorially supplied;
[*word*]	= a deletion editorially restored;
< word >	= an insertion, usually above the line, made by Woolf;
< *word* >	= an insertion deleted but editorially restored;
[?word]	= an uncertain reading;
[. . .]	= an illegible word or words.

1. Possibly Edward Hall (*The Union of the Noble and Illustre Families of Lancastre and York*) and certainly Raphael Holinshed, both chroniclers of English life. Holinshed's *Chronicles* (1577) include the *Description of England* by William Harrison referred to later.

2. William Harrison's *Description of England in Shakspere's Youth,* ed. Furnivall.

3. Woolf's review of *Two Generations,* edited by Osbert Sitwell ("Georgiana and Florence"), was published in the *Listener,* October 31, 1940.

4. Herbert Read's autobiography, *Annals of Innocence* (1940), the impetus for Woolf's comments cited at the beginning of this chapter.

5. Elizabeth Hardwick, Countess of Shrewsbury, considered after the other Bess—Queen Elizabeth—the most extraordinary woman of her age. Asked by Vita Sackville-West to write a biography of Bess of Harwick, Woolf replied that she would "make her a Common Reader" (*Letters* 6:445).

6. With the exception of "The French . . .," all the writers listed here were the subjects of articles published by Woolf between 1934 and 1940: "Oliver Goldsmith" (1934), "Congreve's Comedies" (1937), "The Historian and 'The Gibbon' " and "Reflections at Sheffield Place" (1937), both about Gibbon, and "The Captain's Death Bed" (1935), the captain being Frederick Marryat. Woolf's essay "Madame de Sévigné" was written in May 1939, though she continued to read her letters through at least the end of 1940.

Anon

"For many centuries after Britain became an island" the historian says "the untamed forest was king. Its moist and mossy floor was hidden from Heavens eye by a close drawn curtain woven of innumerable tree tops".[1] On those matted boughs innumerable birds sang; but their song was only heard by a few skin clad hunters in the clearings. Did the desire to sing come to one of those huntsmen because he heard the birds sing, and so rested his axe against the tree for a moment? But the tree had to be felled; and a hut made from its branches before the human voice sang too.

By a bank as I lay
    Musing myself alone, hey ho!
A birdes voice
Did me rejoice,
    Singing before the day;
And me thought in her lay
She said, winter was past, hey ho!

The voice that broke the silence of the forest was the voice of Anon. Some one heard the song and remembered it for it was later written down, beautifully, on parchment. Thus the singer had his audience, but the audience was so little interested in his name that he never thought to give it. The audience was itself the singer; "Terly, terlow" they sang; and "By, by lullay" filling in the pauses, helping out with a chorus. Every body shared in the emotion of Anons song, and supplied the story. Anon sang because spring has come; or winter is gone; because he loves; because he is hungry, or lustful; or merry; or because he adores some God. Anon is sometimes man; sometimes woman. He is the common voice singing out of doors, He has no house. He lives a roaming life crossing the fields, mounting the hills, lying under the hawthorn to listen to the nightingale.

By shutting out a chimney or a factory we can still see what Anon saw—the bird haunted reed whispering fen, the down and the green scar not yet healed along which he came when he made his journeys. He was a simple singer, lifting a song or a story from other peoples lips, and letting the audience join in the chorus. Sometimes he made a few lines that exactly matched his emotion— but there is no name to that song.[2]

Then when the houses had come together in some clearing in a ring, and roads, often flooded, often deep in mud, led from the cottage to the Manor, from the Manor to the Church in the middle, minstrels came, jugglers, bear leaders, singing their songs at the back door to the farm hands and the maid servants in the uncouth jargon of their native tongue.

Icham for woing al forwake
Wery no water in wore

Up stairs they spoke French.[3] Anons words were as uncouth to the master and mistress as to us. Anon singing at the back door was despised. He had no name; he had no place. Yet, even if they felt contempt for the singer, whose body took its souls part in the song, they tolerated him. Even Kings and Queens the scholars tell us, must have their minstrel.[4]+ They needed his comment, his buffoonery. They kept him in the house, tolerating him, as we tolerate those who say out loud what we feel, but are too proud to admit. He used the outsiders privilege to mock the solemn, to comment upon the established. The church men [*feared*] and hated the anonymous singer. They did their best to < [. . .] >. They pressed him and his twin gift into the service of the church. He was to be found acting the Mass in the church; but, as he acted more and more his own art, he left the church, and staged his pageant in the churchyard, or later was given a pitch for his drama in the market place. Still he remained nameless, often ribald, obscene.

Yet during the silent centuries before the book was printed his was the only voice that was to be heard in England. Save for Anon singing his song at the back door the English might be a dumb race, a race of merchants, soldiers, priests; who left behind them stone houses, cultivated fields and great churches, but no words. It was Anon who gave voice to the old stories, who incited the peasants when he came to the back door to put off their working clothes and deck themselves in green leaves. He it was who found words for them to sing, when they went at the great seasons to do homage to the old pagan Gods. He taught them the songs they sung at Christmas and at midsummer. He led them to the haunted tree; to the well; to the old burial place where they did homage to the pagan gods. If we could see the village as it was before Chaucers time we should see tracks across the fields joining manor house to hovel, and hovel to church. Some of those paths of course were worn by soldiers and labourers. They must fight together and plough together if they were not to be conquered by man and nature. That connection as time goes on and [*the*] pen records the daily struggle, is still painfully recorded in old letter books and ledgers. It makes the staple of the old correspondence between the Pastons of Norfolk and the Betsons and Paycockes of Essex.[5] But there was also the other less visible connection—the common belief. That track between the houses in the village has been grown over,—like the track along which the pilgrims rode to Canterbury.—no one rides that way now.[6] But before Chaucers time it was trod daily. It led to the tree; to the well. In spring it led to the Maypole. At Midsummer they lit the bonfire on the hill. At Christmas the mummers acted Anons old play; and the boys came singing his wassailing song. The road led to the old graves, to the stones where in time past the English had done sacrifice. The peasants still went that way by instinct, in spring and summer and winter. The old Gods lay hidden beneath the new.[7] It was to them led by Anon that they did worship, in their coats of green leaves, bearing swords in their hands, dancing through the houses, enacting their ancient parts.[8]

It was the printing press that finally was to kill Anon. But it was the press also that preserved him. When in 1477 Caxton printed the twenty one books of the Morte DArthur he fixed the voice of Anon for ever. There we tap the reservoir of common belief that lay deep sunk in the minds of peasants and nobles. There in Malorys pages we hear the voice of Anon murmuring still. If Caxton himself doubted—King Arthur he objected never lived—there were still nobles and gentry who were positive. They said that you could see Gawaines skull at Dover; and the Round Table at Winchester; and "in other places Launcelots sword and many other things". So Caxton printed the old dream. He brought to the surface the old hidden world: It is a mixed world. There is London; and Carlisle; and St Albans; there is the Archbishop of Canterbury and St Pauls. The roads lead past London to castles where Knights lie enchanted; down the roads ride Queens on white mules; Morgan le Fay turns herself to stone; and a hand rises from a lake holding Excalibur. The story is told with a childs implicit belief.

It has a childs love of particularity. Everything is stated. The beauty is in the statement, not in the suggestion. "So he went in and searched from chamber to chamber, and found his bed, but she was not there; then Balin looked into a little garden, and under a laurel tree he saw her lie upon a quilt of green samite and a knight with her, and under their heads grass and herbs".[9] The world is seen without comment; did the writer know what beauty he makes us see?

But, save that self consciousness had not yet raised its mirror, the men and women are ourselves, seen out of perspective; elongated, foreshortened, but very old, with a knowledge of all good and all evil. They are already corrupt in this fresh world. They have evil dreams. Arthur is doomed; the Queens are lustful. There never was, it seems, a time when men and women were without memory; There never was a young world. Behind the English lay ages of toil and love. That is the world beneath our consciousness; the anonymous world to which we can still return. Of the writer the scholars can find something. But Malory is not distinct from his book. The voice is still the voice of Anon. telling his story about Kings and Queens who are base and heroic; vile and gentle, like ourselves, stripped of the encumbrances that time has wrapped about us.

Caxtons printing press foretold the end of that anonymous world; It is now written down; fixed; nothing will be added; even if the legend still murmers on, and still down in Somersetshire the peasants remember how "on the night of the full moon King Arthur and his men ride round the hill, and their horses are shod with silver". The printing press brought the past into existence. It brought into existence the man who is conscious of the past the man who sees his time, against a background of the past; the man who first sees himself and shows himself to us. The first blow has been aimed at Anon when the authors name is attached to the book. The individual emerges. His name is Holingshed; his name is also Harrison.[10] Harrison emerging from the past tells us that he has a library; that he owns a mastiff; that he digs up Roman coins. He tells us that he has never been more than forty miles from Radwinter in Essex. Anon is losing his ambiguity. The present is becoming visible. Harrison sees the present against the settled recorded past. The present looks degenerate, raw, against that past. There is too much comfort now; the pillow has taken the place of the old log with a dip in the middle; there are too many chimneys. The young Shakespeares and Marlowes are not the men their fathers were. They are tender and subject to rheumatism. Also they dress most fantastically compared with their ancestors.

He does not see the mummers and the wassailers; he does not hear the voice of Anon; he scarcely listens even to the song of Chaucers Canterbury pilgrims. For the English past as Harrison saw it, served only to show up the material change—the change that had come over houses, furniture clothing. There was no English literature to show up the change in the mind. Anons song at the back door was as difficult for him to spell out as for us. & more painful. for [it] reminded him of his lack of intellectual ancestry. His intellectual pedigree only reached back to Chaucer, to Langland to Wycliffe. In order to have ancestors by way of the mind he must cross the channel his ancestors by way of the mind are the Greeks and Romans. His page is burdened with these proofs of good breeding—Henricus Cornelius

Agrippa; Suetonius; Pliny, Cicero—he quotes them to prove his nobility of mind as we to prove ours quote the Elizabethans. He turns away from the present. He does not hear Anon singing at the back door; he ignores the actors who were acting their crude dramas in the market place. Upstairs he says in the great room "our ancient ladies of the court" are to be found reading histories and chronicles, the Greeks and the Latins as they sit at their needlework. And the scholars were reading the classics that were chained to the shelves in the college libraries. Yet in spite of the printed book, the common people were still at their lewd practices.

The preacher, going his round on horseback, from village to village found them at it and raised his voice in anger. "Riding on a journey homeward from London" Latimer about 1549 went to the Church to preach and found the door fast locked against him. For more than half an hour he waited; and at last "one of the parish came to me and said: Sir this is a busy day with us, we cannot hear you, it is Robin Hoods day. The parish are gone abroad to gather for Robin Hood. I was fain there to give place to Robin Hood. I thought my Rochet would have been regarded, though I were not: but it would not serve, it was fain to give place to Robin Hoods men. It is no laughing matter, my friends, it is a weeping matter, a heavy matter, under the pretence for gathering for Robin Hood, a Traitor, and a Thief, to put out a preacher. . . ."

Robin Hood was nothing but a thief to Latimer, and the peasants doing him honour were still blind with superstition. He himself had walked "in the shadow of death" till he was thirty. Then gentle master Bilney at Cambridge had opened his eyes. Now they saw through the old popish practices, the old Pagan customs. They saw England itself at this moment in its reality. When he walked trying to read his book in the Archbishop of Canterburys garden there was a knocking at the gate. And his man came and said "Sir, there is one that would speak with you". So he shut his book and went out among the poor; into the prisons, into the fields. "The cry of the workmen is come up into my eares" he said. He heard the "poor Labourers, gun makers, Powdermen, Bow makers, arrowmakers, smiths, carpenters soldiers and other crafts" crying that they were unpaid. He found the poor without a goose or a pig for the great were enclosing the fields. He went to the great man and found him still in bed, after his hawking and his hunting, and the hall full of poor suiters waiting to make their plaints. He saw the curates in their velvet shoes and slippers "meet to dance the morris dance". He saw the fine ladies dresses in vardigalls with their hair puffed out in tussocks under French hoods. He saw the young men, no longer shooting with the long bow, as his father had taught him to shoot, but bowling, drinking, whoring. And in the streets of London he saw the harlot going to execution, making merry as she went and crying, "that if good fellows had kept touch with her, she had not bin at this time in that case". He noted the smell of rotting bodies in the churchyard at St Pauls and foretold plague to come. And in every village he found the peasants going on pilgrimages, setting up candles, worshipping pigs bones, and following Robin Hood. How should they know better when there was no preaching in the pulpits, when the words they heard were in a tongue they could not understand?

So he went about England preaching in English, no matter if he preached on horseback or stood under a tree. + or preaching to the King in person. He did not moderate his words. He spoke to the King himself in a voice that stumbles, that repeats, that loses the thread of its argument—one can almost hear the fist striking the pulpit—no matter, he will bring before the King the real state of England. + He will unveil, show up, speak the truth, even if it brings him to the faggot as it brought his master, the gentle Mr Bilney. "who was for ever visiting prisoners and sick folk". There is only a short pace left him before he too will stand outside the Bocardo at Oxford and feel the flames on his own flesh. So he pours out his anger; So he lights up the state of England+ in a voice that stumbles, that uses the plain language of the farm from which he sprang. It is the voice of reason, of humanity, of common sense. There is an urgency in his preaching. It is not a learned voice; it is not a courtly voice; it is the voice of a plain man, whose tearing down superstition, + before he too goes to join Master Bilney at the faggot. And yet for all his urgency, his severity, he is a man of flesh and blood. He cracks his joke. He tells his story. He has a curious sympathy for the human. He is a man of the people, a man of humour, with a love of shooting, with a respect for the gentry.[11] But he sees, as the courtier cannot, as the poor cannot, what superstition and ignorance are rife in the land. It is for light and learning that he cries. Give the money, he implores that used to be spent on "pilgrimage matters, in trentalls and masses in purgatory matters" to poor mens sons so that they may become scholars. "There be now none but great mens sons in college". "It will come to pass there we shall have nothing but a little English divinity, that will bring the realm into a very barbarousness, and utter decay of learning". And while the peasants are starving, and continuing their gross superstitions, he sees everywhere the great houses rising. "All the affection of men now adays is in building gay and sumptuous houses, it is in setting up and pulling down, and never have they done building".

Both Latimer and Harrison the preacher and the chronicler, saw the great house rising on the ruins of [the] old. Each in his own way denounced its luxury, its immorality. There today, standing in its green island of park, separated often from the high road only by a dip in the ground and a low red wall[, it] dwarfs its [*neighbors*]. It looks incongruous, standing among the bungalows and the shops. With its conglomeration of chimneys chapels roofs it looks out of proportion, stranded, derelict. Inside all is kept as if Queen Elizabeth were still expected. The up right Elizabethan chairs stand round the walls. Their fringes and tapestries are not much faded. The great oak tables are heavy and polished. The carved cupboards and chests look brand new. Cut glass chandeliers hang down from the decorated plaster work on the ceiling. Even the knick knacks have survived—; the inlaid work box, the pear shaped lute on which the Queen once played. The furniture remains; stiff, ornate, angular and uncushioned. There are the very "vardigalls" that raised the preachers wrath.

Elizabethan clothes have had too much attention from the historical novelist, and too little from the psychologist.[12] What desire was it that prompted this extraordinary display? There must have been some protest, some desire to affirm something, behind the slashed cloaks; the stiff ruffs; the wrought chains and the loops of pearls. The cost was great; the discomfort appalling; yet the fashion prevailed. Was it perhaps, the mark of an anonymous, unrecorded age to enforce the individual; to make ones physical body as bright, as definite, as marked as possible? Fame must be concentrated in the body; since the other kind of fame, the publicity of the paper, of the photograph, was denied them. Did the eloquence of dress speak, when the art of verbal speech was still unformed?

The Elizabethans are silent. There is no little language nothing brief, intimate, colloquial. When they write the rhythm of the Bible is in their ears. It makes their speech unfamiliar. It is only expressive of certain emotions. Thus when Lady Ann Bacon writes to her son she is a preacher addressing a subordinate.[13] Fear of God and distrust of man surround her as with the walls of a dungeon. She admonishes; she exhorts. The actual object—it is a basket of strawberries is approached circuitously ceremoniously. Greek and Latin come as easily to her pen as a French phrase comes to ours. They [wrap themselves] about in a cumbrous garment when they [try] to talk. Then again we cannot hear the rough English voice that they heard at the back door. the voice of the mummer and the minstrel. Nor can we see the paths that led to the well and the tree. Robin Hood is gone with all his merry men. The gay and sumptuous house full of oaths and coarseness and also of learning, of courtesy, is silent; a house full of furniture and finery but without inhabitants.[14] Bright contrasted colours meet on their faces; scarlet and snow; ebony and gold; but there is no natural connection, no common complexion.[15]

The writer, who is distinct from the minstrel, whose words are printed in a book with his name to it, must be a poet. For when familiar letters are written in Biblical prose, there is a limit to what can be put into words. There is a barrier between the sayable and the unsayable. If he cannot talk, he must sing. But though at the beginning of the sixteenth century the printing press has given the poet a name, he is still unspecialised. He is not wholly writer, wholly musician or wholly painter.[16] It seems possible that the great English art may not be the art of words. He sees acutely what is before him without the shadow of reflection: his ear is stimulated by the sound of words spoken aloud. He must make words sonorous, rhythm obvious. since they are to be read out in company. "I spent most of my time" wrote Lady Ann Clifford "in playing at Glecko and hearing Moll Neville read the Arcadia . . . Rivers used to read to me in Montaignes Essays and Moll Neville in the Faery Queen". Further, words must move easily to the lilt of the singing voice, to the sound of lute and virginals. The English sang their songs then, or played them. When London was burning Pepys noted that "hardly one lighter or boat in three that had the goods of a house in it, but there was a pair of virginals in it".[17] Music moved beneath the words. No grammar bound them tightly together. They could be read aloud; danced to or sung to; but they could not follow the pace of the speaking voice. They could not enter into the private world.

Spenser then—"a little man with short hair, a small band and cuffs"[18] standing on the threshold of the "gay and sumptuous house" at Penshurst was separate from the minstrel; from the chronicler; and from his audience.[19] They no longer joined in the song and added their own verses to the poem. But the book that had given him a separate existence had brought into being a little group of readers. It had to find its way into the great room where the gentry sat at leisure when they had hunted and hawked and done the business of their estates. That audience at once began to exert its pressure.[20] What is the book that will please my patron Sir Philip Sidney? What is the theme that will recommend itself to the Queen? Whom must I praise, whom may I satirise? At once come into existence some of those innumerable influences that are to tug, to distort, to thwart; as also they are to stimulate and draw out. The poet is no longer a nameless wandering voice, but attached to his audience. tethered to one spot and played upon by outside influences. Some are visible to himself only; others show themselves only when time has past. As the book goes out into a larger, a more varied audience these influences become more and more complex. According to its wealth, its poverty, its education, its ignorance, the public demands what satisfies its own need—poetry, history, instruction, a story to make them forget+ their own drab lives. The thing that the writer has to say becomes increasingly cumbered. It is only to be discovered in a flash of recognition—Thus some say that their beards bristle when they come upon it; others that a thrill runs down the nerves of the thigh. To disengage the song from the effect of the audience becomes as time goes on a task for the critic—that specially equipped taster who was not yet in existence when the Faery Queen emerged from the depths of anonymity.

Those depths, those long years of anonymous minstrelsy, folk song, legend and words that had no name attached to them, lay behind him. Their confusion pressed upon him. He was conscious of them. "For why a Gods name" he exclaimed "may not we, as else the Greeks, have the kingdom of our own language . . ."?[21] He was word conscious; an artist; aware of his medium; that words are not paint, nor music; but have their possibilities; their limitations. To be thus aware the writer must have a past behind him. To Spenser the golden age was Chaucers. "Dan Chaucer, well of English undefiled . . ." He trusted that "the infusion sweet Of thine own spirit which doth in me survive" might help him. He looks back to Chaucer; he descends from Chaucer. It was Chaucer who gave him the standard by which to measure his own words. But where the modern writer attacks the actual work of some one of the generation that has just gone, making that book the starting point in another direction, Spensers revolt was against no particular writer—who was there writing English except Chaucer?—but against language itself, its decay, since Chaucer, its corruption. Perhaps Chaucers crudity served as an antidote to his own facility. Perhaps too he used the crabbed old words, not as we now might revert to them to rub sharp what much use has worn smooth; but to restrain what was to come. He was, as we cannot be, aware of the future. Everywhere, in ballads, in talk at the tavern, at the back door, he must have heard something rising, bursting up, from beneath. Was it partly to restrain the coming insurrection that he looked back to the Canterbury Pilgrims?[22]

As so often happens, it was the attraction of what is opposed that drew Spenser to Chaucer. For there is that connection between the Faery Queen and the Canterbury Tales but no other. The one is clear sharp definite; the other sensuous, sinuous, dallying. The one is direct, about this real man, this real woman, here and now. the other wanders through time which is neither past nor present, through lands that are neither known nor unknown. Unlike Malory, he has ceased to believe in giants. The faith that the nobles had in 1470 in the real existence of Arthur has turned to scepticism. His poem lacks some reality that Malory achieved unthinkingly. Malory too was behind him. Where Malory sees directly Spenser sees at a distance. He sees Knights and ladies with regret, with desire, but not with belief. There is no sharpness in his figures; no edge; no anguish; no sin;+ On the other hand he shows us as Malory cannot the world surrounding them. He realises time and change. And looking back, from a distance he sees them pictorially; grouped, like the figures in a fresco, with the flowers growing at their feet, behind them marble pillars, trees with bright birds, and the libbard and the lion roaming or couchant. There is no tension; no direction; but always movement, as the metre flings its curve of sound, to break, like a wave on the same place, and like a wave to withdraw, to fill again. Folded in this incantation we drowse and sleep; yet always see through the waters, something irradiated.[23]

Spenser standing on the threshold of the great house is half in shadow, half in light, Half is still unrealised for he cannot confine emotions within himself. He must symbolise, exteriorise. Jealousy is not a passion to issue on actual lips. He must float it outwards; make it abstract; give it a symbolical shape. He cannot speak through the mouths of individuals. The body containing within itself all the passions is still sunk in shadow. But the other half of him is in the light. He is aware of his art as Chaucer was not, nor Langland, nor Malory. His is no longer a wandering voice, but the voice of a man practising an art, asking for recognition, and bitterly conscious of his relation [to] the world, of the worlds scorn.

Had the poet remained in the great room, proferring his book to the little group of readers, English poetry might have remained book poetry, read aloud; a recollection; a reflection; something heard by the leisured listening in the great room. But there was the other voice; the voice at the back door. Spencer had heard it. He recalled the voice of "minstrels making goodly merriment, With wanton bards and rhymers impudent". He had been, it Is said, at the pageant at Kenilworth when, to amuse the Queen, an old story was staged. He had seen "the player dressed in green",+—the old play that the peasants acted when spring came and to placate the earth, the mummer hung himself with green leaves.[24]

But English was coming to court. Like other great people the Queen must have her diversion.[25] Whenever the Queen went to the great house, the minstrels acted before her in English. Ironically enough, the preacher who was for banishing Robin Hood had himself forged the very weapon that gave the old minstrels a new lease of life. When Latimer said the Lords prayer in English at the beginning and end of his sermons he was putting English into high places. He was rescuing it from the back door. He was teaching the nobles and the peasants to respect their mother tongue. He was making it possible for the gentry and the commons to sit together in one house listening to a play.

For the wandering minstrels, driven from the Church, now taking up their pitch in the market place or in the yard of an Inn had by 1576 somehow possessed themselves of a house.[26] It was a shadowy [. . .] lodging: at first; but by 1591 the playhouse in Southwark needed rebuilding. Planks and nails and hinges and timber were brought to the Rose. Carpenters and painters were hired. and the sums spent on the rebuilding were entered at last by Henslowe in his vellum covered book. It was a wooden house, part open to the air, part thatched. It stood in Southwark, next [to] the Barge the Bell and the Cock "recognised stews". The contrast between town and country, judging by Nordens map, was sharp.[27] There, in one fretted mass of spires and little streets, lay the City. But grass fields rose behind it. From Southwark there was a view of open country. Fields and hills came close down to the stews on the Bankside. And the Bankside was infested with hogs.

The house according to Dr. Greg, could hold three thousand people. Most paid one penny to stand in the open; twopence secured a seat; sixpence was the price of a seat under cover. The audience came flocking across the river. For what other amusement was there, a contemporary asked, of an afternoon for the "number of captains and soldiers about London"?[28] Only the amusements that the preachers so furiously denounced; carding, dicing, gaming, the following of harlots and drink. The common people came+ over the river from the crowded festering little streets round St Pauls, where the dead bodies smelt so strong. They came in defiance of peachers & magistrates. They came in such numbers that the watermen lived on their fares. The flag flew; the trumpets sounded, and at about half past two in the afternoon, the audience crowded into the playhouse. In cloud or in sun shine they saw the actors issue from the doors, richly dressed in the taffetas and tinsels, in the satin doublets and hose laid thick with gold lace that Henslowe entered in his book. or, according to one spectator, dressed in the cast off robes of the nobles sold by their servants. They were splendidly dressed. But there was no scenery. The sun beat or the rain poured upon the common people standing in the yard. Then the King spoke:

> Brother Cosroe, I find myself aggrieved,
> Yet insufficient to express the same;
> For it requireth a great and thundering speech.[29]

At last one man speaks in his own person. The wandering voices are collected, embodied. There is no abstraction any longer. All is visible, audible tangible in the light of the present moment. The world takes shape behind him. Egypt and Libya and Persia and Greece rise up. Kings and Emperors stride forth. Like great moths shaking their wings still damp and creased they unfurl the great sentences, the absurd hyperboles.

The spring is withered by your smothering host,
For neither rain can fall upon the earth
Nor sun reflex his virtuous beams thereon,
The ground is mantled with such multitudes.

The utmost stretch of words can scarcely give body to this vast universe that is struggling into being. Words mount; pile on top of each other; over balance and tumble. Great names clash their cymbals. If, blown on by this pressure, the poet veers aside

So poets say my lord
And 'tis a pretty toy to be a poet

he is urged on. There is no pause, no shade. Armies trample; horses neigh; Battles are fought. Blood flows. Over all the Gods are seated on their thrones. The Gods will exact tribute. Meanwhile let us boast:

Our souls, whose faculties can comprehend
The wondrous architecture of the world,
And measure every wandering planets course,
Still climbing after knowledge infinite,
And always moving as the restless spheres,
Will us to wear ourselves, and never rest . . .

Then suddenly the triumph parts asunder; the poet changes his tune

What is beauty, saith my sufferings then?
If all the pens that ever poets held,
Had fed the feelings of their masters thoughts . . .
If these had made one poems period,
And all combined in beautys worthiness
Yet should there hover in their restless heads
One thought, one grace, one wonder, at the least,
Which into words no virtue can digest.

There is a jolt at the points. Lovely as the words are, the mind slides on to another rail. To speak them the poet has separated himself from the actors. He cannot yet make Tamburlaine speak those words with his own lips. The play is still in part the work of the undifferentiated audience, demanding great names, great deeds, simple outlines, and not the single subtlety of one soul.[30]

The audience is silent. If we try to look at the audience off the stage in their private lives we see only wisps, passing phantoms. + There are the Fytton sisters, daughters of Sir Edward Fytton, knight of Gawsworth in Cheshire. Mary, the younger, became one of Elizabeths Maids of Honour.[31] She goes from her country home to the great world. Sir William Knollys, a person of great consequence there, promised her father that he will not fail "to fulfill your desire in playing the Good shepherd and will to my power defend the innocent lamb from the wolvish cruelty and foxlike subtlety of the tame beasts of this place. . . ." His words weave a veil through which nothing is seen in its actual shape.+ Silence falls. Then in involved metaphors, making use of the old images, speaking circumlocuitously of spring and summer and winter frost and flowers in a fair garden he reveals obliquely his illicit passion for the girl. Silence again descends. Then "one Mrs Martin who dwelt at the Chopping Knife near Ludgate" gossips that the young Maid of Honour has dressed up as a man in a large white cloak and gone to meet her lover, Lord Pembroke privately. Silence descends. Then we learn Mary has borne him a bastard, whom he refuses to acknowledge: And her father conveys her home. Silence again descends. It is broken later when some further intrigue makes her mother cry: "If it had pleased God when I did bear her that she and I had been buried it had saved me from a great deal of sorrow and grief and her from . . . such shame as never had Cheshire woman. . . . Write no more to me of her". But her passion, her disgrace, her humiliation are all acted in dumb show. They are hidden either by silence, or by flourishes and ornaments that amount to silence. Even a plain country squire once he takes pen in hand has recourse to poetry. Mr Beaumont, after trying to explain "My conceit of this triple love, of affection passion and conjunction" has recourse to poetry. He quotes Spenser to help him out. It is the poets still who speak for the squires. They have no serviceable language. Yet behind these florid decorations the wolves of the court pry prey and raven. Bastards are born. Reputations are ruined. There is something gross behind the flowers. Only the people themselves pass unseen. They too like the dramatists remain anonymous.[32]

And the play itself was still anonymous. The lack of Marlowes name, or of Kyds, shows how largely the play was a common product, written by one hand, but so moulded in transition that the author had no sense of property in it. It was in part the work of the audience. And the audience was a large one. Fifteen hundred people, Dr Greg computes was an average attendance, Of these the greater part were apprentices, citizens, soldiers, the common people seeking relief from the boredom of the afternoon. Their presence is obvious enough in the early plays. It is they who draw up the extravagance the hyperbole, as a sheet of paper draws up the fire. It was they who made the playwright capable of his great strides, of vast audacities beyond the reach of the solitary writer with his mind fixed upon the reader in the great room. If we could measure the effect of the audience upon the play we should have a hold which is denied us upon the play itself. But the audience, drawn though it is by an irresistable attraction to the play, is silent.

That silence is one of the deep gulfs that lies between us and the play. They come crowding across the river daily; but they sit there silent. They neither praise nor blame. We can compare this silence with our own silence at the Russian ballet or at the cinema in their early days. A new art comes upon us so surprisingly that we sit silent, recognising before we take the measure. But, while we have a measuring rod handy, our past[, and] a press that at once applies a standard, the Elizabethans had no literature behind them with which to compare the play, and no press to give it speech. To the Elizabethans the expressive power of words after their long inadequacy must have been overwhelming. Surprise must have kept them silent. There at the Globe or at the Rose men and women whose only reading had been the Bible or some old chronicle came out into the light of the present moment. They saw themselves splendidly dressed. They heard themselves saying out loud what they had never said yet. They heard their aspirations, their profanities, their ribaldries spoken for them in poetry. And there was something illicit in their pleasure. The preacher and the magistrate were always denouncing their emotion. That too must have given it intensity.

The play then owes its hyperbole to the audience in the penny seats. At their command it is violent; it is coarse; it is, like our own detective stories and best sellers a parody and a transformation of actual fact. It must have [been] a great temptation for the playwright to feed the desire of the audience in the penny seats. But in the seats in the covered part of the house there were nobles, rulers scholars. Lord Southampton and Lord Rutland, Rowland White wrote to Sir Robert Sidney "pass away their time in London, merely in going to plays every day". Yet they are silent too. A young poet dedicates his sonnets to Mr W.H. and none of them troubles to ask, Who is this patron? It is not a matter of interest in court circles. And this lack of curiosity is harder to explain. For they were readers; they had the Greeks and the Latins at the back of their minds. How can it have been that they said nothing about this astonishing new art, that they did not express that sense of outrage, of partisanship which seems to be the common reaction of the more cultivated part of the public when a new writer of genius appears? Perhaps Bacon in his Essays supplies a reason. "These things be but Toyes" he wrote in the essay called "Of Masques and Triumphs". To the aristocratic scholar the players were still only mountebanks, bear leaders and acrobats. They spoke in the vulgar tongue. Off the stage they lived in the heart of darkness. Marlowe lying on the bed at Deptford reached out and stabbed Ingram in the head; whereupon Ingram gave Marlowe a mortal wound over the right eye.[33] Ben Johnson ran Gabriel Spenser through the body with a sword that cost three and sixpence. Kempe, one of the actors, went dancing to Norwich.[34] If Tennyson had run Browning thru the body, or Sir Hen[ry] Irving had skipped over the steps in dancing shoes no doubt V^n [Victorian] society wd. have kept them at a distance. So complete was Bacons contempt for this underworld that he could be tolerant. "The Stage is more beholding to Love than the life of Man. . . . great spirits and great businesse do keep out of this weak passion." The proper place for the weak passion was the stage, for love "leads to speaking in a perpetual hyperbole".

The proper topics of discussion in the upper world was not the Play at the Bankside. The titles of the Essays enumerate the proper topics. "Of Truth. Of Death. Of Unity in religion. Of Revenge. Of Simulation and Dissimulation." These were the subjects that the rulers discussed at their high tables; and the play was a diversion with which to relax the mind after serious work. The sediment of that conversation is to be found in the rich deposits of the essays. He is concerned with the great world of action; with government; with the tortuous natures of Princes; with the arts by which Princes can sway, can coax, can suppress. He lives entirely in the world of great spirits and great business. The common people is contemptible. "The master of supersition is the people". Praise, "if it be from the common people, it is commonly false and naught. The lowest virtues draw praise from them; the middle virtues work in them astonish ment; and admiration; but of the highest vertues they have no sense or perceiving at all".

The soul that walked between delicate groves, now and then formulating a phrase to be taken down by the young secretary Thomas Hobbes, kept to a narrow path between hedges. While Montaigne ranged the world, indulging all curiosities, mixing garrulously with every one, Bacon kept to the narrow path. Yet even in the shade his thought is embodied. His deep meditations are given concrete form. "Nay retire men cannot when they would: neither will they when it were reason; but are impatient of privateness even in age and sickness which require the Shadow: Like old Townmen that will still be sitting at their street door, though thereby they offer Age to scorn". Even in the green shade thought is coloured. "The Colours that show best by candlelight, are: White, Carnation, and a kinde of Sea-Water Green". It only needs one poet for these thoughts to become people.

Bacons contempt was for hyperbole; not the for the art of speech. He was teaching the ranting players to speak slowly, closely, subtly. He was proving that there is another kind of poetry, the poetry of prose. He was bringing the prose of the mind into being. And thus by increasing the range of the poet, by making it possible for him to express more, he was making an end of anonymity.[35]

Anonymity was a great possession. It gave the early writing an impersonality, a generality. It gave us the ballads; it gave us the songs. It allowed us to know nothing of the writer: and so to concentrate upon his song. Anon had great privileges. He was not responsible. He was not self conscious. He is not self conscious. He can borrow. He can repeat. He can say what every one feels. No one tries to stamp his own name, to discover his own experience, in his work. He keeps at a distance from the present moment. Anon the lyric poet repeats over and over again that flowers fade; that death is the end. He is never tired of celebrating red roses and white breasts. The anonymous playwright has like the singer this nameless vitality, something drawn from the crowd in the penny seats and not yet dead in ourselves. We can still become anonymous and forget something that we have learnt when we read the plays to which no one has troubled to set a name.

But at some point there comes a break when anonymity withdraws. Does it come when the playwright had absorbed the contribution of the audience; and can return to them their own general life individualised in single and separate figures? There comes a point when the audience is no longer master of the playwright. Yet he is not separate from them. A common life still unites them; but there are moments of separation. Now we say, he is speaking our own thoughts. Now he is our selves. But this sense of individuality comes fitfully. The beauty which is so astonishingly revealed, is often a suspended derelict irrelevant beauty. There is no sequence. It does not connect; the parts are severed, and something runs to waste. For the anonymous playwright is irresponsible. He flouts truth at the bidding of the audience. he cares only for the plot. We are left in the end without an end. The emotion is wasted.

But gradually the audience is mastered by the playwright. The mist withdraws. So many dramatists are exploring tunnels that lead at last to some common discovery. So many private people are pressing their weight of unexpressed emotion upon the writers consciousness. Country squires are learning to speak what they feel without quoting Spenser. The curtain rises upon play after play. Each time it rises upon a more detached, a more matured drama. The individual on the stage becomes more and more differentiated; and the whole group is more closely related and less at the mercy of the plot. The curtain rises upon Henry the Sixth; and King John; upon Hamlet and Antony and Cleopatra and upon Macbeth. Finally it rises upon the Tempest. But the play has outgrown the uncovered theatre where the sun beats and the rain pours. That theatre must be replaced by the theatre of the brain. The playwright is replaced by the man who writes a book. The audience is replaced by the reader. Anon is dead.[36]

" 'Anon' and 'The Reader' " 382–424.

NOTES

The essay that Woolf entitled "Anon" in every version of the manuscript and typescript was left unfinished at the time of her death. The transcript of the essay included here consists of a more or less clear text of the last version of the essay, based on typescripts that include Woolf's manuscript corrections; when clear, these corrections have been silently incorporated into the text. The + signifies an incomplete clause that Woolf included in a subsequent sentence. Typographical errors have been corrected, and ellipses and quotations marks have been printed in conformity with Woolf's published writing. Punctuation, paragraphs, spelling, capitalization, and repetitions, however, have been left exactly as they appear in the original, reminding the reader that the essay was still very much a rough draft. Woolf would certainly have revised it before publication, perhaps including some of the material found in the earlier versions. In the notes I have identified Woolf's citations and added some passages from earlier drafts that amplify her thoughts. For a history of the different versions, textual variants, a textual apparatus, and further information about Woolf's sources and reading, see "A & R." But even that is incomplete; readers interested in experiencing Woolf's essay in full should consult the original manuscripts and typescripts.

1. The historian who provided this introduction, as well as a similar passage in *Between the Acts* (218), was G. M. Trevelyan (3), whose *History of England* Woolf was reading while planning her work. Trevelyan was also the source of her diatribe against "insider" history: *Diary* 5:333.

2. The first two paragraphs of this version of "Anon" are a drastic reduction of the original opening. The most significant difference in the original is that the description of Anon's desire to sing leads immediately to Anon's death:

> Anon died round about 147[8]<7>. It was the printed book with the authors name attached that killed him. After that the audience was separate from the singer. After that the song was attached to the singer. Anon gives place to Geoffrey or John or Peter; he lives in a house; and he has books.
>
> The heart of this vast proliferation of printed pages remains the song. The song has the same power over the reader in the 20th century as over the hearer in the 11th. To enjoy singing, to enjoy hearing the song, must be the most deep rooted, the toughest of human instincts comparable for persistency with the instinct of self preservation. It is indeed the instinct of self preservation. Only when we put two and two together—two pencil strokes, two written words, two bricks <notes> do we overcome dissolution and set up some stake against oblivion. The passion with which we seek out these creations and attempt endlessly, perpetually, to make them is of a piece with the instinct that sets us preserving our bodies, with clothes, food, roofs, from destruction.
>
> But the printing press brought into existence forces that cover over the original song—books themselves, and the readers of books. If science were so advanced that we could at this moment X ray the singers mind we should find a nimbus surrounding the song; a stream of influences. Some we can name—education; class; the pressure of society. But they are so many, and so interwoven and so obscure that it is simpler to invent for them nonsense names—say Nin Crot and Pully. Nin Crot and Pully are always at their work, tugging, obscuring, distorting. Some are visible only to the writer. Others only to the reader. More and more complex do they become as time passes. The song beneath is only to be discovered in a flash of recognition; Some say they feel it when their beards bristle; others that a thrill runs down the nerves of the thigh. But the song is there still.

The original opening also includes a description of one modern but vastly different embodiment of Anon: "Anon is only a voice. He has his representative today, When some procession passes, a hand will thrust a broadsheet on you in Cheapside. But you can see the author. Most often anonymity is used to conceal something on purpose from the audience. But the old Anon was not hiding for that reason."

3. In earlier descriptions of Anon's language and social status, Woolf had written, " 'English,' says the historian, 'had gone underground for two centuries . . .' " Woolf's source may have been Chambers, "Some Aspects of Medieval Lyric," or Trevelyan, who wrote that after the Conquest, "the Anglo-Saxon tongue . . . was exiled from hall and bower, from court and cloister, and was despised as a peasants' jargon, the talk of ignorant serfs. . . . There is no more romantic episode in the history of man than this underground growth and unconscious self-preparation of the despised island *patois* . . ." (131–132).

4. Most of the details in this and the next paragraph are taken from Chambers, *The Medieval Stage.*

5. For the Pastons, old friends of Woolf's, see *The Paston Letters;* Thomas Betson and Thomas Paycocke are the subjects of chapters in Power, *Medieval People.*

6. Earlier drafts of this passage suggest more explicitly the connection between the scars on the land and the scars in the mind, both of which link us to the past:

> Could we see [the great Elizabethan house] as it is said that the airman sees a village <field> from the air with the scars of other villages <old roads> and other houses on it. we should see the great house connected with the village. . . . But there was also the other connection—the common belief. That bond between the great house and the small has faded, till it is like one of those perhaps rather greener rides still to be found in England along which, antiquaries say the Pilgrims rode to Canterbury. So the scholars tell us of the roads now faded in the mind.

7. In earlier versions Woolf notes that "the desire to enact was coupled with the other desire—to make something useless; something unconnected with the daily struggle. to bring out into the day light embodied their own natural love of play."

8. Early drafts of this section contain a paragraph describing in great detail one aspect of the common belief shared by noble and peasant: superstition and a belief in witchcraft.

9. Woolf has misquoted here; the phrase "found his bed" should read "found her bed."

10. Woolf's source for this section was Harrison's *Description of England in Shakspere's Youth.* In other drafts, Harrison, described as a "representative man," provides a self-portrait of the new writer, his social position, and his audience:

> Even now when words are printed the great public is not the reader, or the paymaster. Written words must please a single man in the first place, and the Harrison's volume is ceremoniously tended tendered to a Lord Cobham in words as ornate as the carvings and decorations that shocked him in the fashionable Elizabethan house.

11. He begins to sound like Rev. Streatfield in *Between the Acts* (190–191).

12. The section on Elizabethan clothes was added late in the writing of the essay.

13. Earlier versions of the section on Lady Ann are fuller, emphasizing more her violence and suspicions and citing several passages from her letters to her sons, Anthony and Francis. One draft of this section includes a note to compare Lady Ann's letters to Madame de Sévigné's.

14. This sentence is all that remains of an elaborate metaphor comparing the Elizabethan house to a "convoluted iridescent shell," polished on the outside but silent and empty of human life within. Woolf made a trip to Penshurst, once the home of Sir Philip Sidney, on June 14, 1940, the day Paris fell (*Diary* 5:296–297).

15. Earlier versions are more explicit about the influence of the Bible on Elizabethan prose: "They can say nothing simple, nothing intimate. They are never subtle; they are never shaded."

16. This paragraph is the residue of one of the earliest ideas for "Anon": the interrelationship of the arts and the importance of the eye and the ear on early writers. In one version, this section concludes by evoking Anon and the Elizabethan play as the reason why the Elizabethan artist turned toward poetry rather than music or painting.

17. On January 1, 1941, Woolf wrote in her diary, "On Sunday night, as I was reading about the Great fire, in a very accurate detailed book, London was burning"; this book was almost certainly Pepys's *Diaries.*

18. Woolf found this description of Spenser in Collier, "The Life of Edmund Spenser," *Works* I:clv.

19. In an earlier attempt to define what made Spenser the first artist, Woolf wrote: "The artist—the person who stands outside, by some impulse desiring to observe and state <rather than to take part—>."

20. In one version, Woolf is more explicit, and more bitter, about the negative effects of both the printing press—"not a nice feeder"—and the public it created on Anon: "Only a few [writers] still persist in making words into works of art."

21. Letter to Gabriel Harvey, in *Works* I:clviii.

22. Earlier versions make the coming insurrection more explicitly linguistic.

23. In an earlier version Woolf noted, "It is the thing itself; it is the original design, from which Tennyson and Morris made their copies."

24. See *The Fairie Queene,* "Mutabilitie Cantos," vii.35.

25. An alternate version on the same page reads: "The Queen must have her minstrels."

26. Most of the details about the Elizabethan playhouse and audience are found in *Henslowe's Diary,* ed. Greg; Harrison, *Elizabethan Plays and Players;* and Evans.

27. John Norden's map of London (1593) appears both in *Harrison's Description of England,* where it is annotated, and in Harrison, *Elizabethan Plays and Players.*

28. Thomas Nashe, *Piers Penniless* (1592); quoted in Harrison, *Elizabethan Plays and Players* 100.

29. This and the following quotations are taken from Marlowe, *Tamberlaine the Great,* part I.

30. Earlier drafts of this passage emphasize more the distinction between the dramatist who wrote those startling lines of poetry and the anonymous playmaker who "lacks the little language to put on Kings lips" and who is still inspired by the "common voice" of the audience.

31. Mary Fytton, the mistress of William Herbert, Lord Pembroke, was at one time thought to be a possible model for the dark lady of the sonnets. The letters and documents that tell the story recorded here appear in Newdigate-Newdegate.

32. The original version of the Fytton section concludes with several reflections about the lack of a critical sense in the Elizabethan audience:

> Thus the early works of Shakespeare make no ripple in the pool of silence. No one protests that here is an upstart writer who is for throwing society into the melting pot. The great might be mocked—that was the ancient privilege of the court jester; or some scene from history re enacted. But the censor was quick to control irreverence. And in fact the dramatist was not destroying society. The indignation that, after the first silent surprise, that Ibsen for example stirred in London was partly the rage of those who felt that venerable institutions were being criticised. But the public at the Globe and the Rose could not feel as the public in the 19th century felt when Ghosts was acted that old humbugs were being shown up; and the rottenness of society. After all, when country squires must call in Spenser to express their meaning, prose was not yet serviceable; the critical spirit had no proper tool.

33. Woolf found the details of Marlowe's death in two works by Harrison: *Elizabethan Plays and Players* 124 and *An Elizabethan Journal* 243.

34. The story of Gabriel Spenser's death is told both by Harrison, *Elizabethan Plays and Players* 188–189, and by Greg, *Henslowe's Diary* II, 313. The story of Will Kempe's dance from London to Norwich is told by Harrison 225–227.

35. The effect of Bacon's criticisms, gravity, and prose on the play is explored in more detail in earlier versions of the Bacon section.

36. There are four different endings to "Anon," all of them heavily revised. What appears to be the first draft concludes:

> But anonymity is a great possession. . . . Nor is anon dead in ourselves. The crude early dramas still have the power to make us ask—as the audience asked—the childs question: what comes next? <a power denied to [Wordsworth] Coleridge Tennyson.>
>
> It is only later when the pressure of silent hoarded emotion had thrown up words, as the fingers of the man at the monotype machine cast letters from the bubbling lead, that we lost this general quality to gain—everything it seems. For the curtain goes on rising incessantly for fifty years. Now it rises on Henry the Fifth. . . . The stage has become too small to act this drama. Perhaps after centuries, the play will come to birth again, differently, in the Magic Flute, in Fidelio. But the play never again fitted the stage completely in England. The book after Shakespeare takes the place of the play. And Anon is dead for ever.

The Reader

The great house that Latimer deplored becomes solid and entire in the pages of Lady Anne Cliffords diary.[1] From her childhood she was tenacious of her hereditary rights—her father had the right to carry the Kings sword "and so it lineally descended to me". All her youth she fought, against kinsmen, husband and the king himself for her right to inherit the lands in Westmoreland. ". . . I would never part from Westmoreland while I lived upon any condition whatsoever" she told him. When the lands and the five castles were hers, she instantly began rebuilding; Not only the land was hers, but diamond buttons, rubies, fur cloaks.+ As if to solidify her possessions she wrote out inventories of them. Family love is in part the desire to hand on her property. She sends for her grandchildren in order that they may taste the delight of possession and so refresh her own satisfaction. The sense of the body permeates her pages. All movements become spectacular. Crowds attend her. Six bay horses drag the coach. The coach is lined with green cloth, and laced with green and black silk lace. She is for ever asserting her identity. She has her initials carved even over farm house walls. This is her property; this land is hers by right. Certain flesh and blood—that of the Stanleys, the Russells, the Cliffords, the Herberts and above all of the Cliffords has become like a precious stone not to be mixed with baser metal. When Lord Sheffield marries Anne Erwin it was "held a very mean match, and indiscreet on part of him." She believes in the immortality of the body as firmly as in the immortality of the soul.

Yet there were moments when even this carapace of possessions proved too heavy for her. "If I had not excellent Chaucer's book here to comfort me, I were in a pitiable case, having so many troubles as I have here, but when I read in that, I scorn and make light of them all, and a little part of his beauteous spirit infuses itself in me." She adds that postscript to a letter about a little cabinet and cup which she had left with Lady Kent when she borrowed a hundred pounds of her.

But it is only when she reads that she comments. When she goes to the play she says only "Supped with my Lord and Lady Arundel and after supper I saw the play of the Mad Lover . . ." or "We stood to see the Masque in the box with my Lady Ruthven." It was when the playhouses were shut presumably that the reader was born. The curious faculty of making houses and countries visible, and men and women and their emotions, from marks on a printed page was undeveloped+ so long as the play was dominant. The audience at the play house had to draw in the play with their eyes and ears. Without a book of the words they could not deepen and revise the impression left by the play, or ask those questions that are debated now in every newspaper. The lack of general reading accounts for the long pause between Shakespeares death and the 18th century when the plays of Shakespeare hung suspended, unrealised—even in 17 Morgann could say that Shakespeare still lacked half his proper fame.[2] The lack of a reading public accounts too for the scarcity of criticism and for the general nature of what criticism there is. Both Sidney and Jonson are writing for the small critical public, and thus deal with general questions, and not with particular books and persons.

The reader then comes into existence sometime at the end of the sixteenth century, and his life history could we discover it would be worth writing, for the effect it had upon literature. At some point his ear must have lost its acuteness; at another his eye must have become dull. Our own attempt when we read the early Elizabethan plays [to] supply the trumpets and the flags, the citizens and the apprentices is an effort to revert to an earlier stage. As time goes on the reader becomes distinct from the spectator. His sense of words and their associations develops. A word spelt in the old spelling brings in associations. + As the habit of reading becomes universal, readers split off into different classes. There is the specialised reader, who attaches himself to certain aspects of the printed words. Again there is the very large class of perfectly literate people who strip many miles of print yearly from paper yet never read a word. Finally there is the reader who, like Lady Anne Clifford read excellent Chaucers book when they are in trouble. "and a little part of his beauteous spirit infuses itself in me." And the curious faculty—the power to make places and houses, men and women and their thoughts and emotions visible on the printed page is always changing. The cinema is now developing his eyes; the Broadcast is developing his ear. His importance can be gauged by the fact that when his attention is distracted, in times of public crisis, the writer exclaims: I can write no more.

But the presence of the reader was felt even while the play was still on the stage. It was for him that Burton composed that extraordinary composition the Anatomy of Melancholy. It is there that the reader makes his first appearance, for it is there that we find the writer completely conscious of his relation with the reader. and He reveals himself. I am a bachelor. I am neither rich nor poor. I am a tumbler over of other mens books. I live in college rooms. I am a spectator not an actor. There is no playhouse audience forcing him to embody his meditations. The vast accumulations, of learning, that have filtered from books into the quiet college room meander over the page. He sees through a thousand green shades what lies immediately before him—the unhappy heart of man. The reflections serve to chequer the immediate spectacle. From books he has won the tolerant sense that we are not single figures but innumerably repeated. In pursuit of melancholy he travels over the whole world, though he has never left his college room. We are at a remove from the thing treated. We are enjoying the spectacle of melancholy, not sharing its anguish.

It is here that we develop faculties that the play left dormant. + Now the reader is completely in being. He can pause; he can ponder; he can compare; he can draw back from the page and see behind it a man sitting alone in the centre of the labyrinth of words in a college room thinking of suicide. He can gratify many different moods. He can read directly what is on the page, or, drawing aside, can read what is not written. There is a long drawn continuity in the book that the play has not. It give a different pace to the mind. We are in a world where nothing is concluded.

Addendum

[While the other versions of the opening of "The Reader" contain much of the material found in the fragment printed above, there are some passages that are worth extracting for their insights into Woolf's attempts to conceptualize the difference between the Elizabethan audience and the modern reader: what was lost, what was gained, the communal nature of the art, the importance of the body of the actor, how we can recapture the sense of the eye and the ear.]

* * *

This faculty, the power to make out of print men, countries, places houses & words & bodies, & their thoughts, is rare; It is not existent in great masses of the literate. It is different from the scholars gift or the critics.

But if we cease to consider the plays separately, but scramble them together as one common attempt; then we are able to make them serve as sketches for one masterpiece. And the darkness in which these plays lie helps the endeavour to conceive of that many nameless workers; and many private people were pressing their weight were discharging their emotion into that vast cauldron of seething matter which at last Shakespeare struck out into his plays.

We have lost the sound of the spoken word; all that the sight of the actors bodies suggests to the mind through the eye. We have lost the sense of being part of the audience. We miss a thousand suggestions that the dramatist conveyed by the inflection of voice, by gesture, by the placing of the actors bodies. This can still be proved by comparing our impression after seeing the play acted with our impression after reading the play alone. But as the actor imports much that is of his own day, and foreign to the past, so that there is still something in every Elizabethan play sunk beyond recall.

Presumably the earlier plays, in which the playwright and the audience were in closer cooperation, are the more damaged by reading them. The reader instinctively tries to be there in person. He tries to supply the trumpets and the flags; the citizens and the apprentices. He nourishes the inadequate emotion with a dip into Henslowe, with a dip into Holinshed. He labours to supply the sunk part of the play. He is perpetually rebuffed. He is apt to become not a reader but a student; a careful collector of old scattered bones. At some point however in Elizabethan drama the reader is born. When the dramatist becomes conscious of the play as a work of art; when he is able to unite the play by something in himself—his personality, his conception—it is then that, he brings the reader into being.

* * *

Letter.

You will complain very justly that this brittle and imperfect sketch with all its exaggerations, foreshortenings gives you nothing of the emotion which is presumably to be found in the books themselves. Here then let us make a transition from one kind of reader to another. In order to divest ourselves of the attitude which—Let us make certain confessions. . . . The first is that the critical attitude pinches the mind. It is no longer fitting. . . . it pinches; it compresses; it puts the mind in whalebones, like a stays, or pinches the foot like too tight shoes. Even to copy accurately a quotation breaks the stream of thought. The need of accuracy is again inimical. In short, the critic today is like a in the position of a body which feels the attraction of many magnets at one and the same time. To demagnetise ourselves we have to shut the book; If we can, let us be aware only of the and to seek if we can find it a state of mind that is propitious; that state of mind in which it seems possible to us to write the book, not to read it. In that state of mind full of impressions, uncoordinated, contradictory, in which so many senses seem to take part; and yet one or two gradually become significant. Here we are trying to discover what the source of the sunk impulse. And the hidden spring, the gush of water deep beneath the mud. Whether it holds true universally, or if not, the fi t [sic] instinct is to be . . .

* * *

Take a simple instance, the quotation. In order to copy out even one stanza of a play, it is necessary to open at the right page then to copy accurately. This at once breaks the stream of thought. Besides, there is always present the other critic—Let us see him in person—For ever so many years, he has not been later than nine at the Museum. Or, his lectures have been so regular that one cd find him at his place at the reading desk at four every Thursday. There is no need to discuss the effect of that prohibition. If we could evade all this, we should have to sink into a very dusky layer of the mind. to be able to put down the book or the paper & the pen, to free ourselves from all the impositions of authority & the dominion of what is customary.

Let us try then to recapture some actual experience, which seems to have a connection with the experience of reading these old books; to spring from poetry; to be interfused with the same emotion. If number 18 still runs, let us take it, when the owling time is at hand, down to London Bridge. There is a curious smell in this part of the world, of hops, it may be; & also a curious confraternity. A woman going one way hails a man going the other. Here there is no differentiation. The streets are drab enough. The sewer has a great turbulent swollen stream. The cranes are picking sacks from the holds of ships. There is a shiny slab of mud beneath the warehouses; & St Pauls rises. The gulls are swooping; & some small boys paddle in the pebbles. Above the sky is huddled & crowded with purple streamers. We are still thinking of the plays, because it was here that the Globe stood. Now let us give way to the imagination. The roar & the chaos; the grind of wheels; the general diffusion: all soon breed a great desire for statement. Such was one of the elements in the drama. Here is the unwritten poem. In this disorder, this sound the difficulty of keeping away from the statement. A roar, a general incoherence. The pressure of light, & gestures; some singing: an attitude. Leaning over the river, losing ones way in some alley; there rises the curious nameless [*desire to express*]

It is equally important, to the understanding of the poem, not to read at all, to dip now & again into the [*inchoate*] & to talk, with many elisions, much left out.

This is particularly true today; when the economic force is cutting the critic into a special form.

For then we revive the reader—a very important person. For the reader was born when the playhouse closed.

" 'Anon' " and 'The Reader' " 427–435.

NOTES

1. Descriptions and quotations are found in *The Diary of Lady Anne Clifford,* ed. Sackville-West, and Williamson, *Lady Anne Clifford.*

2. Possibly Maurice Morgann, *An Essay on the Dramatic Character of Sir John Falstaff* (1777).

Selected Bibliography

Bonnie Kime Scott

Items listed contribute to an understanding of concepts of gender, modernism, a group of modernist authors, or theory related to these concerns. For bibliographies of authors included in the anthology, see Works Cited following the introductions to specific authors. With the exception of a few landmark works, essays contained in collections are not listed separately. Often a listed collection will yield several useful essays.

BOOKS

Abel, Elizabeth, ed. *Writing and Sexual Difference.* Chicago: U of Chicago P, 1982. First published as a special number of *Signs* 8.2(1981).

———, and Emily K. Abel, eds. *The Signs Reader: Women, Gender and Scholarship.* Chicago: U of Chicago P, 1983.

———, Marianne Hirsch, and Elizabeth Langland, eds. *The Voyage In: Fictions of Female Development.* Hanover, N.H.: UP of New England, 1983.

Aiken, Susan Hardy, Karen Anderson, Myra Dinnerstein, Judy Nolte Lensink, and Patricia MacCorquodale, eds. *Changing Our Minds: Feminist Transformations of Knowledge.* Albany: State U of New York P, 1988.

Anderson, Margaret, ed. *The Little Review Anthology.* New York: Horizon, 1953.

Appaignanesi, Lisa. *Femininity and the Creative Imagination: A Study of Henry James, Robert Musil and Marcel Proust.* New York: Barnes and Noble, 1973.

Ascher, Carol, Louise DeSalvo, and Sara Ruddick, eds. *Between Women: Biographers, Novelists, Critics, Teachers and Artists Write about Their Work on Women.* Boston: Beacon, 1984.

Auerbach, Nina. *Communities of Women.* Cambridge: Harvard UP, 1978.

Baker, Carlos Heard. *The Echoing Green: Romanticism, Modernism, and the Phenomena of Transference in Poetry.* Princeton: Princeton UP, 1984.

Baker, Denys Val. *Little Reviews: 1914–1943*. London: Allan and Unwin, 1943.

Baker, Huston A., Jr. *Modernism and the Harlem Renaissance*. Chicago: U of Chicago P, 1987.

Bakhtin, Mikhail. *The Dialogic Imagination: Four Essays*. Trans. Caryl Emerson and Michael Holquist. Austin: U of Texas P, 1981.

Beauman, Nicola. *A Very Good Profession: The Woman's Novel 1914–1934*. London: Virago, 1983.

Benstock, Shari, ed. *Feminist Issues in Literary Scholarship*. Bloomington: Indiana UP, 1987. First published as a special issue of *Tulsa Studies in Women's Literature*. 3.1–2(1984).

———. *Women of the Left Bank: Paris, 1900–1914*. Austin: U of Texas P, 1986.

Bergonzi, Bernard. *The Myth of Modernism and Twentieth Century Literature*. New York: St. Martin's P, 1986.

Bernikow, Louise. *Among Women*. New York: Harper and Row, 1980.

Bradbury, Malcolm and James MacFarlane, eds. *Modernism 1880–1930*. Sussex: Harvester and Atlantic Highlands, N.J.: Humanities P, 1978.

Broe, Mary Lynn, and Angela Ingram. *Women's Writing in Exile: Alien and Critical*. Chapel Hill: U of North Carolina P, 1989.

Brownstein, Rachel. *Becoming a Heroine: Reading about Women in Novels*. Harmondsworth: Penguin; New York: Viking P, 1982.

Butturff, Douglas, and Edmund L. Epstein, eds. *Women's Language and Style*. Akron, Ohio: L & S Books, 1978.

Chodorow, Nancy. *The Reproduction of Mothering: Psychoanalysis and the Sociology of Gender*. Berkeley: U of California P, 1978.

Christ, Carol P. *Diving Deep and Surfacing: Women Writers on Spiritual Quest*. Boston: Beacon, 1980.

———. *Victorian and Modern Poetics*. Chicago and London: U of Chicago P, 1984.

Christian, Barbara. *Black Feminist Criticism: Perspectives on Black Women Writers*. New York: Pergamon P; Berkeley: U of California P, 1985.

———. *Black Women Novelists: The Development of a Tradition, 1892–1976*. Westport, Conn.: Greenwood P, 1980.

Cixous, Hélène, and Catherine Clément. *The Newly Born Woman*. Trans. Betsy Wing. Minneapolis: U of Minneapolis P, 1986.

Cohan, Steven. *Violation and Repair in the English Novel: The Paradigm of Experience from Richardson to Woolf*. Detroit: Wayne State UP, 1986.

Cohn, Dorrit. *Transparent Minds*. Princeton: Princeton UP, 1978.

Connell, R. W. *Gender and Power: Society, the Person and Sexual Politics*. Stanford: Stanford UP, 1987.

Cooper, Helen, Adrienne Munich, and Susan Squier, eds. *Arms and the Woman: War, Gender and Literary Representation*. Chapel Hill: U of North Carolina P, 1989.

Cornillon, Susan Koppelman, ed. *Images of Women in Fiction: Feminist Perspectives*. Bowling Green, Ohio: Bowling Green U Popular P, 1972.

Crosland, Margaret. *Beyond the Lighthouse: English Women Novelists in the Twentieth Century*. London: Constable, 1981.

Culler, Jonathan. *On Deconstruction: Theory and Criticism after Structuralism*. Ithaca, N.Y.: Cornell UP, 1982.

———. *The Pursuit of Signs: Semiotics, Literature, Deconstruction*. Ithaca, N.Y.: Cornell UP, 1981.

Dasenbrock, Reed Way. *The Literary Vorticism of Ezra Pound*. Baltimore: Johns Hopkins UP, 1983.

Davidson, C. N., and E. M. Broner, eds. *The Lost Tradition: Mothers and Daughters in Literature*. London: Ungar, 1980.

Dearborn, Mary V. *Pocahontas's Daughters: Gender and Ethnicity in American Culture*. New York: Oxford UP, 1986.

De Beauvoir, Simone. *The Second Sex*. New York: Knopf, 1953.

Derrida, Jacques. *Writing and Difference*. Trans. Alan Bass. Chicago: U of Chicago P, 1978.

Dinnerstein, Dorothy. *The Mermaid and the Minotaur: Sexual Arrangements and the Human Malaise.* New York: Harper and Row, 1976.

Douglas, Ann. *The Feminization of American Culture.* New York: Knopf, 1977.

DuPlessis, Rachel Blau. *Writing beyond the Ending: Narrative Strategies of Twentieth-Century Women Writers.* Bloomington: Indiana UP, 1985.

Eco, Umberto. *Semiotics and the Philosophy of Language.* Bloomington: Indiana UP, 1984.

Eisenstein, Hester, and Alice Jardine. *The Future of Difference.* Boston: G. K. Hall, 1980.

Ellmann, Mary. *Thinking about Women.* New York: Harcourt Brace Jovanovich, 1968.

Elshtain, Jean. *Women and War.* New York: Basic Books, 1987.

Faderman, Lillian. *Surpassing the Love of Men: Romantic Friendship and Love between Women from the Renaissance to the Present.* New York: Morrow, 1981.

Faulkner, Peter. *Modernism.* New York: Methuen, 1977.

Fetterley, Judith. *The Resisting Reader: A Feminist Approach to American Fiction.* Bloomington: Indiana UP, 1978.

Fitch, Noel Riley. *Sylvia Beach and the Lost Generation.* New York: Norton, 1983; London: Souvenir Press, 1984.

Fleischmann, Fritz, ed. *American Novelists Revisited: Essays in Feminist Criticism.* Boston: G. K. Hall, 1982.

Foucault, Michel. *The Archaeology of Knowledge and The Discourse on Language.* Trans. A. M. Sheridan Smith. New York: Pantheon, 1972.

———. *The History of Sexuality.* Trans. Robert Hurley. New York: Pantheon, 1978.

Frazer, James. *The Golden Bough: A New Abridgment.* Ed. Theodore H. Gaster. New York: New American Library, 1959.

Freud, Sigmund. *Women and Analysis: Psychoanalytic Dialogue in Femininity.* New York: Grossman, 1974.

Fussell, Paul. *The Great War and Modern Memory.* New York: Oxford UP, 1975.

Gallop, Jane. *Feminism and Pyschoanalysis: The Daughter's Seduction.* London: Macmillan, 1982.

Garner, Shirley Nelson, Claire Kahane, And Madelon Sprengnether, eds. *The (M)other Tongue: Essays in Feminist Psychoanalytic Interpretation.* Ithaca, N.Y.: Cornell UP, 1985.

Gilbert, Sandra M., and Susan Gubar. *The Madwoman in the Attic.* New Haven: Yale UP, 1979.

———. *No Man's Land: The Place of the Woman Writer in the Twentieth Century.* Vol. 1. *The War of the Words.* New Haven: Yale UP, 1988.

———. *Shakespeare's Sisters: Feminist Essays on Women Poets.* Bloomington: Indiana UP, 1979.

Gilligan, Carol. *In a Different Voice.* Cambridge: Harvard UP, 1982.

Glasgow, Joanne, and Karla Jay, eds. *Radical Revisions: Lesbian Texts and Contexts.* New York: New York UP, forthcoming.

Gornick, Vivian, and Barbara K. Moran. *Women in Sexist Society.* New York: Basic Books, 1971.

Greer, Germaine. *The Female Eunuch.* London: McGibbon and Kee, 1970.

Griffin, Susan. *Woman and Nature: The Roaring inside Her.* New York: Harper and Row, 1978.

Hanscombe, Gillian E. *Writing for Their Lives: The Modernist Women, 1910–1940.* London: Women's Press, 1987.

Hardwick, Elizabeth. *Seduction and Betrayal: Women and Literature.* New York: Random House, 1974.

Harrison, Jane. *Prolegomena to the Study of Greek Religion.* Cambridge: Cambridge UP, 1908.

Heath, Stephen. *The Sexual Fix.* London: Macmillan, 1982.

Heilbrun, Carolyn G. *Reinventing Womanhood.* New York: Norton, 1979.

———. *Toward A Recognition of Androgyny: Aspects of Male and Female in Literature.* New York: Knopf; London: Gollancz, 1973.

Heilbrun, Carolyn G., and Margaret R. Higonnet, eds. *Representations of Women in Fiction.* Baltimore: Johns Hopkins UP, 1983.

Henley, Nancy, and Barry Thorne. *Language and Sex: Difference and Dominance.* Rewley, Mass.: Newbury House, 1975.

Hoffman, Frederick J., Charles Allen, and Carolyn F. Ulrich. *Little Magazines: A History and Bibliography.* Princeton: Princeton UP, 1947.

Hull, Gloria T. *Color, Sex and Poetry: Three Women Writers of the Harlem Renaissance.* Bloomington: Indiana UP, 1987.

Irigaray, Luce. *This Sex Which Is Not One.* Trans. Catherine Porter with Carolyn Burke. Ithaca, N.Y.: Cornell UP, 1985.

———. *Speculum of the Other Woman.* Trans. Gillian C. Gill. Ithaca, N.Y.: Cornell UP, 1985.

Jacobus, Mary. *Women Writing and Writing about Women.* London: Croom Helm, 1979.

Jameson, Frederic. *Fables of Aggression: Wyndham Lewis, the Modernist as Fascist.* Berkeley: U of California P, 1979.

Jardine, Alice. *Gynesis: Configurations of Woman and Modernity.* Ithaca, N.Y.: Cornell UP, 1985.

———, and Paul Smith, eds. *Men in Feminism.* New York: Methuen, 1987.

Jay, Karla. *The Amazon and the Page: Natalie Clifford Barney and Renée Vivien.* Bloomington: Indiana UP, 1988.

Johnson, Barbara. *The Critical Difference.* Baltimore: Johns Hopkins UP, 1980.

Juhasz, Suzanne. *Naked and Fiery Forms: Modern American Poetry by Women.* New York: Harper and Row, 1978.

Kaplan, Sydney Janet. *Feminist Consciousness in the Modern British Novel.* Urbana: U of Illinois P, 1975.

Keller, Evelyn Fox. *Reflections on Gender and Science.* New Haven: Yale UP, 1985.

Kenner, Hugh. *The Pound Era.* Berkeley: U of California P, 1971.

Kessler-Harris, Alice, and William McBrien, eds. *Faith of a (Woman) Writer.* New York: Greenwood P, 1988.

Kiberd, Declan. *Men and Feminism in Modern Literature.* New York: St. Martin's P, 1985.

Kiely, Robert. *Beyond Egotism: The Fiction of James Joyce, Virginia Woolf and D. H. Lawrence.* Cambridge: Harvard UP, 1980.

———, ed. *Modernism Reconsidered.* Cambridge: Harvard UP, 1983.

Kofman, Sarah. *The Enigma of Woman.* Trans. Catherine Porter. Ithaca, N.Y.: Cornell UP, 1985.

Kristeva, Julia. *Desire in Language: A Semiotic Approach to Literature and Art.* Ed. Leon Roudiez. New York: Columbia UP, 1980.

———. *Revolution in Poetic Language.* Trans. Margaret Waller. New York: Columbia UP, 1984.

Krutch, Joseph Wood. *The Modern Temper.* 1929. New York: Harcourt Brace Jovanovich, 1957.

Lacan, Jacques. *Feminine Sexuality: Jacques Lacan and the Ecole Freudienne.* Ed. Juliet Mitchell and Jacqueline Rose. Trans. Jacqueline Rose. New York: Norton and Pantheon, 1982.

———. *The Four Fundamental Concepts of Psychoanalysis.* Ed. Jacques-Alain Miller. Trans. Alan Sheridan. New York: Norton, 1978.

Lakoff, Robin Tolmach. *Language and Woman's Place.* New York: Harper and Row, 1975.

Lauter, Estella. *Women as Mythmakers: Poetry and Visual Arts by Twentieth-Century Women.* Bloomington: Indiana UP, 1984.

Lerner, Gerda. *The Majority Finds Its Past.* New York: Oxford UP, 1979.

Levenson, Michael H. *The Genealogy of Modernism: A Study of English Literary Doctrine 1908–1922.* New York: Cambridge UP, 1984.

Lévi-Strauss, Claude. *The Savage Mind.* London: Weidenfeld and Nicolson, 1972.

Lewis, Wyndham. *Men without Art.* 1934. Santa Barbara, Calif.: Black Sparrow P, 1987.

———. *Satire and Fiction.* London: Arthur P, 1930.

Little, Judy. *Comedy and the Woman Writer: Woolf, Spark and Feminism.* Lincoln: U of Nebraska P, 1983.
Locke, Alain. *The New Negro.* 1925. New York: Atheneum, 1968.
Lodge, David. *Modes of Modern Writing.* Ithaca, N.Y.: Cornell UP, 1977.
Lukács, Georg. "The Ideology of Modernism." *The Meaning of Contemporary Realism.* 1937. Trans. John and Necke Mander. London: Merlin, 1963.
Lyotard, Jean-Francois. *The Postmodern Condition: A Report on Knowledge.* Trans. Geoff Bennington and Brian Massumi. Minneapolis: U of Minnesota P, 1984.
Marcus, Jane. *Virginia Woolf and the Languages of Patriarchy.* Bloomington: Indiana UP, 1987.
Materer, Timothy. *Vortex: Pound, Eliot and Lewis.* Ithaca, N.Y.: Cornell UP, 1979.
Meese, Elizabeth A. *Crossing the Double-cross: The Practice of Feminist Criticism.* Chapel Hill: U of North Carolina P, 1986.
———, and Alice Parker. *The Difference Within: Feminism and Critical Theory.* Amsterdam: John Benjamins, 1988.
Meisel, Perry. *The Myth of the Modern: A Study of British Literature and Criticism after 1850.* New Haven: Yale UP, 1987.
Middlebrook, Diane W., and Marilyn Yalom, eds. *Coming to Light: American Women Poets in the Twentieth Century.* Ann Arbor: U of Michigan P, 1985.
Miles, Rosalind. *The Fiction of Sex: Themes and Functions of Sex Difference in the Modern Novel.* New York: Barnes and Noble, 1974.
Miller, Jane. *Women Writing about Men.* London: Virago, 1986.
Miller, Nancy K., ed. *The Poetics of Gender.* New York: Columbia UP, 1986.
Millett, Kate. *Sexual Politics.* New York: Avon, 1970.
Mitchell, Juliet. *Women, the Longest Revolution: On Feminism, Literature and Psychoanalysis.* New York: Pantheon, 1984.
Moers, Ellen. *Literary Women.* New York: Doubleday, 1976; London: Women's P, 1963.
Moi, Toril. *Sexual/Textual Poltics: Feminist Literary Theory.* London: Methuen, 1985.
Monnier, Adrienne. *The Very Rich Hours of Adrienne Monnier.* Ed. Richard McDougall. New York: Scribner, 1976.
Monteith, Moira. *Women's Writing: A Challenge to Theory.* Sussex: Harvester, 1986.
Moore, Harry Thornton. *The Age of the Modern and Other Literary Essays.* Carbondale: Southern Illinois UP, 1971.
Newton, Judith, and Deborah Rosenfelt, eds. *Feminist Criticism and Social Change: Sex, Class and Race in Literature and Culture.* New York: Methuen, 1985.
Ostriker, Alicia. *Stealing the Language: The Emergence of Women's Poetry in America.* Boston: Beacon, 1986.
———. *Writing like a Woman.* Ann Arbor: U of Michigan P, 1983.
Pearson, Carol, and Katherine Pope. *The Female Hero in American and British Literature.* New York: Bowker, 1981.
Perloff, Marjorie. *The Poetics of Indeterminacy: Rimbaud to Cage.* Princeton: Princeton UP, 1981.
Pratt, Annis. *Archetypal Patern in Women's Fiction.* Bloomington: Indiana UP, 1981.
Pryse, Marjorie, and Hortense Spillers, eds. *Conjuring: Black Women, Fiction, and Literary Tradition.* Bloomington: Indiana UP, 1985.
Quinones, Ricardo I. *Mapping Literary Modernism.* Princeton: Princeton UP, 1985.
Rich, Adrienne. *On Lies, Secrets and Silence: Selected Prose 1966–1978.* New York: Norton, 1979.
Riding, Laura, and Robert Graves. *A Survey of Modernist Poetry.* Garden City, N.Y.: Doubleday, Doran, 1928.
Roe, Sue, ed. *Women Reading Women's Writing.* Brighton: Harvester, 1987.
Rogers, Katherine M. *The Troublesome Helpmate: A History of Misogyny in Literature.* Seattle and London: U of Washington P, 1966.
Russ, Joanna. *How to Suppress Women's Writing.* London: Women's P, 1984.
Said, Edward W. *Orientalism.* 1978. New York: Random House, 1979.

Schwartz, Sanford. *The Matrix of Modernism: Pound, Eliot and Early Twentieth-Century Thought.* Princeton: Princeton UP, 1985.

Schwenger, Peter. *Phallic Critiques: Masculinity and 20th Century Literature.* London: Routledge and Kegan Paul, 1984.

Sedgwick, Eve Kosofsky. *Between Men: English Literature and Homosocial Desire.* New York: Columbia UP, 1985.

Sherman, Julia A., and Beck, Evelyn Torton, eds. *The Prism of Sex.* Madison: U of Wisconsin P, 1979.

Showalter, Elaine. *A Literature of Their Own.* Princeton: Princeton UP, 1977.

Spacks, Patricia M. *The Female Imagination.* New York: Avon, 1972.

Spender, Dale. *Man Made Language.* London: Routledge and Kegan Paul, 1980.

———, ed. *Time and Tide Wait for No Man.* London: Pandora P, 1984.

Spender, Stephen. *The Struggle of the Modern.* Berkeley: U of California P, 1963.

Spivak, Gayatri Chakravorty. *In Other Worlds: Essays in Cultural Politics.* New York: Routledge, 1988.

Squier, Susan Merrill, ed. *Women Writers and the City.* Knoxville: U of Tennessee P, 1984.

Stang, Sondra J., ed. *The Presence of Ford Madox Ford.* Philadelphia: U of Pennsylvania P, 1981.

Stead, C. K. *Pound, Yeats, Eliot and the Modernist Movement.* London: Macmillan, 1985.

Stubbs, Patricia. *Women and Fiction: Feminism and the Novel 1880–1920.* New York: Barnes and Noble, 1979.

Suleiman, Susan Rubin, ed. *The Female Body in Western Culture.* Cambridge: Harvard UP, 1986.

Sullivan, Alvin. *British Literary Magazines.* Westport, Conn.: Greenwood P, 1986.

Sultan, Stanley. *Eliot, Joyce and Company.* New York: Oxford UP, 1987.

Symons, Julian. *Makers of the New: The Revolution in Literature 1912–1939.* London: Deutsch, 1987.

Tindall, William York. *Forces in Modern British Literature, 1885–1956.* New York: Vintage, 1956.

Todd, Janet, ed. *Women Writers Talking.* New York: Holmes and Meier, 1983.

Torgovnick, Marianna. *The Visual Arts, Pictoralism, and the Novel: James, Lawrence, and Woolf.* Princeton: Princeton UP, 1985.

Vickery, John B. *The Literary Impact of the Golden Bough.* Princeton: Princeton UP, 1973.

Walker, Alice. *In Search of Our Mothers' Gardens.* New York: Harcourt, 1983.

Wandor, Michelene, ed. *On Gender and Writing.* Boston and London: Routledge and Kegan Paul, 1983.

Weston, Jessie. *From Ritual to Romance.* 1920. Garden City, N.Y.: Doubleday, 1957.

Whitely, Patrick J. *Knowledge and Experimental Realism in Conrad, Lawrence and Woolf.* Baton Rouge: Louisiana State UP, 1987.

Willis, Susan. *Specifying: Black Women Writing the American Experience.* Madison: U of Wisconsin P, 1987.

Wilson, Edmund. *Axel's Castle: A Study of the Imaginative Literature of 1870–1930.* New York: Scribner, 1931.

Woolf, Virginia. *Contemporary Writers.* New York: Harcourt Brace Jovanovich, 1976.

———. *A Room of One's Own.* 1929. New York: Harcourt Brace Jovanovich, 1957.

———. *Three Guineas.* 1938. New York: Harcourt Brace Jovanovich, 1966.

Yalom, Marilyn. *Maternity, Mortality and the Literature of Madness.* University Park: Pennsylvania State UP, 1985.

ARTICLES

Auerbach, Nin. "Artists and Mothers: A False Alliance." *Women and Literature* 9(Spring 1978):3–15.

Blanchard, Lydia. "Virginia Woolf and Her Critics: 'On the Discrimination of Feminisms.' " *Studies in the Novel* 17.1(Spring 1985):95–103.
Brownstein, Marilyn L. "Postmodern Language and the Perpetuation of Desire." *Twentieth Century Literature* 31.1(1986):1–24.
Buckley, W. K. "D. H. Lawrence's Answer to the 'Nightmare of History' in Joyce and Woolf." *Liberal and Fine Arts Review* 5.1(1985):43–54.
Burke, Carolyn. "Getting Spliced: Modernism and Sexual Difference." *American Quarterly* 39.1(1984):98–121.
Cixous, Hélène. "Castration or Decapitation?" *Signs* 7.1(Fall 1981):41–55.
———. "The Laugh of Medusa." *Signs* 1.4(Summer 1976):875–893.
Clark, Suzanne. "The Unwarranted Discourse: Sentimental Community, Modernist Women, and the Case of Millay." *Genre* 20(Summer 1987):132–152.
Cook, Blanche Wiesen. "Women Alone Stir My Imagination: Lesbians and the Cultural Tradition." *Signs* 4.4(Summer 1979):718–739.
Gardiner, Judith Kegan. "A Wake for Mother: The Maternal Deathbed in Women's Fiction." *Feminist Studies* 4(June 1978):146–165.
Gilbert, Sandra. "Costumes of the Mind: Transvestism as Metaphor in Modern Literature." *Critical Inquiry* 7.2(1980):391–417.
———. "Sexual Linguistics: Gender, Language, Sexuality. *NLH* 16.3(1985):515–543.
———. "Soldier's Heart: Literary Men, Literary Women, and the Great War." *Signs* 8.3(1983):422–450.
Gillespie, Diane. "Virginia Woolf and the 'Reign of Error.' " *Research Studies* 43(1975): 222–234.
Gubar, Susan. " 'The Blank Page' and the Issues of Female Creativity." *Critical Inquiry* 8(Winter 1981):243–263.
———. "Blessings in Disguise: Cross-Dressing as Re-Dressing for Female Modernists." *Massachusetts Review* 22.4:477–508.
———. Mother, Maiden and the Marriage of Death: Women Writers and Ancient Myth." *Women's Studies* 6(1979):301–315.
Jacobus, Mary. "Is There a Woman in This Text?" *NLH* 14.1(1982):117–141.
———. "Reading Woman (Reading)." *Reading Woman: Essays in Feminist Criticism*. New York: Columbia UP, 1986, 3–24.
Jehlen, Myra. "Archimedes and the Paradox of Feminist Criticism." *Signs* 6(1981):575–601.
Kofman, Sarah. "Freud's Suspension of the Mother." *Enclitic* 4.2(1980).
Kristeva, Julia. "Women's Time." Trans. Alice Jardine and Harry Blake. *Signs* 7(1981):13–35.
Miller, Nancy K. "Emphasis Added: Plots and Plausibilities in Women's Fiction." *PMLA* 96.1(1981):36–48.
Schor, Naomi. "Female Paranoia: The Case for Psychoanalytic Feminist Criticism." *Yale French Studies* 62(Fall 1981).
Scott, Joan. "Gender: A Useful Category of Historical Analysis." *American Historical Review* 91(1986):1053–1075.
Showalter, Elaine. "Critical Cross-Dressing: Male Feminists and the Woman of the Year." *Raritan* 3(October 1983).
Smith-Rosenberg, Carroll. "The Female World of Love and Ritual." *Signs* 1.1(1975):1–29.

SPECIAL NUMBERS OF JOURNALS

Contemporary Literature. Ecriture Feminine. 24(Summer 1983).
Modern Fiction Studies. 34.3(1988).
Modernist Studies: Literature and Culture 1920–1940. Special Supplement Women in the Literature and Culture of the Twenties and Thirties. 1.3(1974–1975).
Signs. Feminist Theory. 7.3(1982).

Tulsa Studies. Toward a Gendered Modernity. 8.1(1989).
Women's Studies. Ed. Sandra Gilbert and Susan Gubar. 7.1–2(1980).
Yale French Studies. Feminist Readings: French Texts/American Contexts. 62(1981).

ANTHOLOGIES

Cunard, Nancy, ed. *Negro: An Anthology.* London: Wishart, 1934.
Ellmann, Richard, and Charles Feidelson, eds. *The Modern Tradition.* New York: Oxford UP, 1965.
Faulkner, Peter, ed. *A Modernist Reader: Modernism in England 1910–1930.* London: B. T. Batsford, 1986.
Gilbert, Sandra M. and Susan Gubar, eds. *The Norton Anthology of Literature by Women: The Tradition in English.* New York: Norton, 1985.
Lodge, David, ed. *Twentieth Century Literary Criticism.* London: Longman, 1972.
Marks, Elaine, and Isabelle de Courtivron, eds. *New French Feminisms.* Amherst: U of Massachusetts P, 1980.
Reilly, Catherine. *Scars upon my Heart: Women's Poetry and Verse of the First World War.* London: Virago, 1981.
Showalter, Elaine. *Autobiographical Essays from the Twenties.* Old Westbury, N.Y.: Feminist P, 1978.
———. *The New Feminist Criticism.* New York: Pantheon, 1985.

BIBLIOGRAPHIES AND RESEARCH GUIDES

Davies, Alastair, ed. *An Annotated Critical Bibliography of Modernism.* Sussex: Harvester; Totowa, N.J.: Barnes and Noble, 1982.
Hinding, Andrea, Sheldon Bower Ames, and Clarke A. Chambers. *Women's History Sources: A Guide to Archives and Manuscript Collections in the United States.* 2 vols. New York: Bowker, 1979.
Kuda, Marie J., ed. *Women Loving Women: A Select Annotated Bibliography of Women Loving Women in Literature.* Chicago: Womanpress, 1975.
Myers, Carol Fairbanks. *Women in Literature: Criticism of the Seventies.* Metuchen, N.J.: Scarecrow P, 1976.
Schwartz, Narda Lacey. *Articles on Women Writers: A Bibliography.* 2 vols. Santa Barbara, Calif.: Clio Books, 1977.
White, Barbara Ann. *American Women Writers: An Annotated Bibliography of Criticism.* New York: Garland, 1977.
Williamson, Jane. *New Feminist Scholarship: A Guide to Bibliographies.* Old Westbury, N.Y.: Feminist P, 1979.
Women and Literature Collective. *Women and Literature: An Annotated Bibliography of Women Writers.* 3d ed. Cambridge, Mass.: Women and Literature Collective, 1976.

Contributors

Mary Lynn Broe is Noun Professor of Women's Studies and English at Grinnell College. She is author of *Protean Poetic: The Poetry of Sylvia Plath* (1980), co-editor (with Angela Ingram) of *Alien and Critical: Women Writers in Exile* (1989), and editor of *Silence and Power: Djuna Barnes: A Revaluation* (1990). She is presently researching and writing (with Frances McCullough) *Cold Comfort: A Biographical Portrait of Djuna Barnes.*

Marilyn L. Brownstein is Assistant Professor of English at the University of Georgia. She has published articles on Joyce, Woolf, Plato, and postmodernism and recently completed her first book, *Postmodern Strategies.*

Carolyn Burke is Research Associate in Humanities at the University of California, Santa Cruz. The author of many articles on the female modernists, as well as studies and translations of recent French feminist writing, she is working on a biography of Mina Loy.

Ronald Bush is Professor of Literature at the California Institute of Technology. He is author of *The Genesis of Ezra Pound's Cantos* (1976), *T. S. Eliot: A Study in Character and Style* (1983), and a number of articles on modernists and modernism. Most recently he edited *T. S. Eliot: The Modernist in History* (1989).

Thadious M. Davis is Professor of English at the University of North Carolina, Chapel Hill, and author of *Faulkner's "Negro": Art and the Southern Context* (1983). She has completed a literary biography of Nella Larsen and has published essays on nineteenth- and twentieth-century American women writers and on Afro-American and southern American literatures.

Marianne DeKoven is Associate Professor of English at Rutgers University. She has published articles on feminist theory, modernism, and women in the avant garde. She is author of *A Different Language: Gertrude Stein's Experimental Writing* (1983) and is finishing a book on gender in early modernist narrative.

Susan Stanford Friedman is Professor of English at the University of Wisconsin. She is author of *Psyche Reborn: The Emergence of H. D.* (1981) and *Penelope's Web: H. D.'s Fictions and the Engendering of Modernism* (forthcoming), co-author (with Linda Gams, Cindy Nesselson, and Nancy Gottlieb) of *A Woman's Guide to Therapy* (1979), and co-editor (with Rachel Blau DuPlessis) of *Signets: Reading H. D.* She has published articles on gender theory, women's poetry, autobiography, feminism and psychoanalysis, women's education, and feminist pedagogy.

Diane F. Gillespie is Professor of English at Washington State University. She is author of *The Sisters' Arts: The Writing and Painting of Virginia Woolf and Vanessa Bell* (1988) and editor (with Elizabeth Steele) of *Julia Duckworth Stephen: Stories for Children, Essays for Adults* (1987). She has published articles on Blake, Strindberg, Fry, Woolf, Sinclair, and Richardson. She is working on a book on early twentieth-century women playwrights.

Nancy K. Gish is Professor of English at the University of Southern Maine. She is author of *Hugh MacDiarmid: The Man and His Work* (1984), *Time in the Poetry of T. S. Eliot* (1981), and *The Waste Land: A Poem of Memory and Desire (1988).*

Clare Hanson is Lecturer in English at the College of St. Paul and St. Mary, Cheltenham, England. She is author of *Short Stories and Short Fictions, 1880–1980* (1985), co-author (with Andrew Gurr) of *Katherine Mansfield* (1981), and editor of *The Critical Writings of Katherine Mansfield* (1987) and *Re-reading the Short Story* (1988). She is working on a book on Virginia Woolf.

Suzette Henke is Professor of English at the State University of New York at Binghamton. She is author of *Joyce's Moraculous Sindbook: A Study of Ulysses* (1978) and *James Joyce and the Politics of Desire* (1990) and co-editor (with Elaine Unkeless) of *Women in Joyce.* She has published articles on Woolf, Lessing, Richardson, and Nin and is working on a book, *Women's Life-Writing.*

Coral Ann Howells is Lecturer in English at the University of Reading in England. She is author of *Love, Mystery and Misery: Feeling in Gothic Fiction* (1978) and *Private and Fictional Worlds: Canadian Women Novelists of the 1970s and 80s* (1987). She has written numerous articles on modern Canadian fiction and women's writing and is working on books on Jean Rhys and Margaret Atwood.

Jane Lilienfeld has taught at Assumption College, Boston University, and Clark University and now works as a freelance writer. She has published essays on Woolf, Atwood, Colette, Cather, Joyce, Hardy, mothers and daughters, and feminist theory. She is working on a book on alcoholism as narrative strategy in Joyce, Woolf, and Hardy.

Jane Marcus is Professor of English at City College and the Graduate Center of the City University of New York. She is author of *Virginia Woolf and the Languages of Patriarchy* (1987) and *Art and Anger: Reading like a Woman* (1988) and editor of *The Young Rebecca: Writings of Rebecca West, 1911–1917* (1982), *Suffrage and* *the Pankhursts* (1987), and three collections on Woolf, the most recent of which is *Virginia Woolf and Bloomsbury* (1987). She has also written numerous essays, prefaces, and afterwords.

Celeste M. Schenck is Ann Whitney Olin Fellow at Barnard College. She is author of *Mourning and Panegyric: The Poetics of Pastoral Ceremony* (1989) and *Corinna Sings: Women Poets and the Politics of Genre* (forthcoming) and co-editor of *Life/Lines: Theorizing Women's Autobiography*. She is co-founder of "Women Poets at Barnard," a series of readings and publications of new women poets, and general co-editor of Reading Women Writing, a series in feminist criticism published by Cornell University Press.

Bonnie Kime Scott is Professor of English at the University of Delaware. She is author of *Joyce and Feminism* (1984) and *James Joyce* (1987) in the Harvester Feminist Readings Series and editor of *New Alliances in Joyce Studies: "Whan It's Aped to Foul a Delfian"* (1988). She has published articles on women writers, feminist theory, and Irish literature.

Brenda R. Silver is Professor of English at Dartmouth College. She is author of *Virginia Woolf's Reading Notes* and numerous essays on Woolf, as well as articles on Forster, Le Carre, and other British novelists. She is currently editing a collection of essays on *Rape and Representation* and writing a book on feminist polemic.

Susan M. Squier is Associate Provost at the State University of New York at Stony Brook, where she is co-editor of *the minnesota review*. She is also co-editor (with Helen Cooper and Adrienne Munich) of *Arms and the Woman: War, Gender and Literary Representation* (1989), author of *Virginia Woolf and London: The Sexual Politics of the City* (1985), and editor of *Women Writers and the City* (1984). She has been working on a study of reproductive figures as cultural critique in contemporary fiction.

Cheryl A. Wall is Associate Professor of English at Rutgers University. She is editor of *Changing Our Own Words*, a volume of essays on criticism, theory, and writing by black women, and author of *Women of Letters in the Harlem Renaissance* (forthcoming). Her essays and reviews have appeared in *Phylon, Black American Literature Forum*, and *American Literature*.

Index

For the introductions, persons and subjects are indexed; for anthologized works, persons only.